BREADLINE BRITAIN IN THE 1990s

This book is dedicated to the memory of Hilary Holmes
who died on 8 May 1996

SUPPORTED BY

JR

JOSEPH
ROWNTREE
FOUNDATION

The **Joseph Rowntree Foundation** has supported this project as part of its programme of research and innovative development projects, which it hopes will be of value to policy makers and practitioners. The facts presented and views expressed in this report are, however, those of the authors and not necessarily those of the Foundation.

Breadline Britain in the 1990s

Edited by
DAVID GORDON
CHRISTINA PANTAZIS

Ashgate

Aldershot • Brookfield USA • Singapore • Sydney

Published by
Ashgate Publishing Limited
Gower House
Croft Road
Aldershot
Hants GU11 3HR
England

Ashgate Publishing Company
Old Post Road
Brookfield
Vermont 05036
USA

British Library Cataloguing in Publication Data
Breadline Britain in the 1990s. - (Studies in cash and
    care)
    1.Poverty - Great Britain 2.Poverty - Government policy -
    Great Britain 3.Basic needs - Great Britain 4.Poor - Great
    Britain
    I.Gordon, David II.Pantazis, Christina
    362.5'2'0941'09049

Library of Congress Catalog Card Number: 97-71291

ISBN 1 85972 479 5

Printed in Great Britain by Antony Rowe Ltd., Chippenham, Wiltshire

Contents

List of tables   *vii*
List of figures and CHAIDS   *xii*
List of contributors   *xviii*
Foreword   *xix*
Acknowledgements   *xxiii*

Introduction   1

Chapter 1   **Measuring poverty: Breadline Britain in the 1990s**   5
             David Gordon and Christina Pantazis

Chapter 2   **The poverty line: methodology and international
             comparisons**   49
             Peter Townsend

Chapter 3   **The public's perception of necessities and poverty**   71
             David Gordon and Christina Pantazis

Chapter 4   **Poverty and gender**   97
             Sarah Payne and Christina Pantazis

Chapter 5   Poverty and crime   115
             Christina Pantazis and David Gordon

Chapter 6   Poverty and health   135
             Christina Pantazis and David Gordon

Chapter 7   Poverty and mental health   159
             Sarah Payne

Chapter 8   Poverty, debt and benefits   177
             Christina Pantazis and David Gordon

Chapter 9   Poverty and local public services   193
             Glen Bramley

Chapter 10   Adapting the consensual definition of poverty   213
             Bjørn Halleröd, Jonathan Bradshaw
             and Hilary Holmes

Chapter 11   Conclusions and Summary   235
             David Gordon and Christina Pantazis

             Bibliography   243

             Appendix I: Technical appendix   269

             Appendix II: Annotated questionnaire   273

             Appendix III: Additional tables   295

List of tables

Table 1.1   Worthwhile great causes. Question "In your opinion, in this list which are the great causes which nowadays are worth the trouble of taking risks and making sacrifices for?"   6

Table 1.2   Reliability analysis on the deprivation questions from Breadline Britain in the 1990s that more than 50% of the population thinks are necessary and people should be able to afford   19

Table 1.3   Weekly income required to surmount multiple deprivation   26

Table 1.4   Question 16: "Do you think you could genuinely say you poor now, all the time, sometimes, or never?   31

Table 1.5   Poverty rates and transition out of poverty for families with children with poverty defined as an equivalised income below 50% of the median income for the population   33

Table 1.6   Question 17: "Looking back over your adult life, how often have there been times in your life when you think you have lived in poverty by the standards of the time?"   34

Table 1.7   Long term poverty/multiple deprivation   35

Table 1.8   Household expenditure on selected items for the top and bottom quintile groups of income and all households   37

Table 1.9   Alcoholic consumption level by sex and usual gross weekly household income   38

Table 1.10   Why do people live in need? By all respondents   39

Table 1.11   The public's view of why people live in need by deprivation group   40

Table 1.12   The public's view of why people live in need by present level of poverty   41

Table 1.13   The public's view of why people live in need by history of poverty   41

Table 1.14   The public's view of why people live in need by social class   42

Table 1.15   The public's view of why people live in need by political orientation   42

Table 1.16   The public's view of why people live in need by household type   43

Table 3.1   The perception of necessities: 1983 and 1990 compared   73

Table 4.1   Necessary consumption: Items and activities regarded as "Necessary, something that all adults should be able to afford"   104

Table 4.2   Multivariate logistical regression and univariate analysis of men's and women's perception of necessities   106

Table 4.3   Perceptions of necessities by sex: food items   107

Table 4.4   Perceptions of necessities by sex: clothing   108

Table 4.5   Perceptions of necessities by sex: consumer durables   109

Table 4.6   Perceptions of necessities by sex: leisure activities   110

Table 4.7   Perceptions of necessities by sex: social networks   111

Table 4.8   Perceptions of necessities by sex: child development   112

Table 4.9   Perceptions of necessities by sex: financial security   113

Table 5.1   Distribution of crime   119

Table 7.1   Percentage of respondents reporting mental health symptoms due to lack of money, by deprivation   163

Table 7.2   Percentages of each ethnic group reporting mental health symptoms as a result of money difficulties   167

Table 7.3   Percentage of those reporting mental health difficulties, as a result of lack of money, by category of employment status: unemployed, housewives and full-time employed   172

Table 7.4   Percentage of respondents experiencing mental health difficulties as a result of lack of money, by tenure group   174

Table 8.1   Respondent's own assessment of reasons for debt   180

Table 8.2   Incidence of debt for non-pensioner households   181

Table 8.3   Deprivation scores of those in debt and % of those in
               debt who are poor   184

Table 8.4   Experience of poverty and debt   185

Table 8.5   Poverty and income of households where one or more
               persons receive benefits - excluding households with
               pensioners   188

Table 8.6   Poverty and income of households where one or more
               persons receive benefits - excluding all households with
               pensioners   189

Table 8.7   Households receiving benefits that are 'poor' (%)   190

Table 9.1   Usage rates and standardised usage ratios by class,
               equivalent income and deprivation for 11 local services   196

Table 9.2   Supply, quality or cost constraints on usage by equivalent
               income and deprivation for 11 local services   200

Table 9.3   Influence of class, equivalent income and deprivation on
               usage of 11 local services in multivariate models   202

Table 9.4   Influence of expenditure and area type on usage   206

Table 9.5   Association of expenditure, standard spending assessment
               and sparsity on constraints and problems   208

Table 9.6   Proportion of respondents regarding selected local
               services as essential and desirable   210

Table 10.1   Proportion of the population regarding consumer items as
               necessary and proportion of the population that cannot
               afford them   220

Table 10.2   The population distributed in accordance with values on
               the MNI   221

Table 10.3   Distribution of the PDI and MNI in deciles. Mean value
               of PDI and MNI by decile and share of total deprivation
               in each decile   221

Table 10.4a   Overlap between PDI and MNI. Percent of population
and percent of 'poor' (in brackets)   222

Table 10.4b   Overlap between PDI and MNI. Percent of population
and percent of 'poor' (in brackets), excluding 'luxury'
items   223

Table 10.5   Self-evaluation of material standard and reported
difficulties in making ends meet   225

Table 10.6   Percentage of the population living in poverty by income
decile of net disposable income   229

Table 10.7   Percentage of the population living in poverty by income
decile of equivalent income   230

Table 10.8   Proportion of population in poverty according to PDIa
and NMIa   233

List of figures and CHAIDS

Figure 1.1   Homeless people in hostels, bed and breakfast, sleeping
              rough and concealed households   8

Figure 1.2   Modal deprivation by logarithm of income as a percentage
              of Supplementary Benefit scale rates   12

Figure 1.3   Total number proceeded against under the Wireless
              Telegraphy Acts (TV Licence) 1980-92   21

Figure 1.4   Convictions under the Wireless Telegraphy Acts as a
              percentage of all convictions 1981-92   21

Figure 1.5   Slope is hard to judge   23

Figure 1.6   Two well separated groups (the poor and the non-poor) with
              intermediate 'noise' points   25

Figure 1.7   Average net income of multiply deprived and less deprived
              households   31

Figure 2.1   The poor and the rich of different countries according to their income standardised in "international purchasing" dollars   58

Figure 2.2   GDP per person as a percentage of GDP per person in the US   59

Figure 3.1   Perception of necessities: 1983 and 1990 compared   75

Figure 3.2   Perception of necessities and deprivation   75

Figure 3.3   Perception of necessities and present level of poverty   77

Figure 3.4   Perception of necessities and history of poverty   77

Figure 3.5   Perception of necessities and education   79

Figure 3.6   Perception of necessities and social class   79

Figure 3.7   Perception of necessities and political orientation   80

Figure 3.8   Perception of necessities and sex   80

Figure 3.9   Percent considering that the government is doing too little to help the 'poor' by deprivation group   82

Figure 3.10   Percent considering that the government is doing too little to help the 'poor' by social class   82

Figure 3.11   Percent considering that the government is doing too little to help the 'poor' by present level of poverty   83

Figure 3.12   Percent considering that the government is doing too little to help the 'poor' by history of poverty   83

Figure 3.13   Percent considering that the government is doing too little to help the 'poor' by political orientation   85

Figure 3.14   Percent considering that the government is doing too little to help the 'poor' by household type   85

Figure 3.15   Percent supporting an increase in income tax to help alleviate poverty by deprivation group   87

Figure 3.16   Percent supporting an increase in income tax to help alleviate poverty by present level of poverty   87

Figure 3.17   Percent supporting an increase in income tax to help alleviate poverty by history of poverty   88

Figure 3.18   Percent supporting an increase in income tax to help alleviate poverty by social class   88

Figure 3.19   Percent supporting an increase in income tax to help alleviate poverty by political orientation   89

Figure 3.20   Percent supporting an increase in income tax to help alleviate poverty by household type   89

Figure 3.21   Incidence of deprivation by social class   91

Figure 3.22   Incidence of deprivation by household type   91

Figure 3.23   Incidence of deprivation by size of household.   92

Figure 3.24   Incidence of deprivation by household tenure   92

Figure 3.25   Incidence of deprivation by employment status of head of household   94

Figure 3.26   Incidence of deprivation by marital status   94

Figure 3.27   Incidence of deprivation by education level   95

Figure 3.28   Incidence of deprivation by political orientation   95

Figure 4.1   Present level of poverty by gender   100

Figure 4.2   Present level of poverty by gender and age group   100

Figure 4.3   History of poverty by gender   102

Figure 4.4   History of poverty by gender and age group   102

Figure 5.1   Indexed crime rate for combined 1984, 1988 and 1992 British Crime Surveys by ACORN neighbourhoods   117

Figure 5.2   Distribution of crime in the previous year and fear of crime   119

Figure 5.3   Percent experiencing crime and fear of crime by standard of living   121

Figure 5.4   Percent experiencing crime and fear of crime by social class   121

Figure 5.5   Percent experiencing crime by equivalised household income   123

Figure 5.6   Percent fearing crime by equivalised household income   123

CHAID 5.1   Experience of crime   125

CHAID 5.2   Fear of crime   126

Figure 5.7   Percent experiencing crime and fear of crime by history of poverty   128

Figure 5.8   Percent experiencing crime and fear of crime by type of household   128

Figure 5.9   Percent experiencing crime and fear of crime by standard of housing   130

Figure 5.10   Percent fearing crime by deprivation and victimisation   130

Figure 5.11   Percent of types of households fearing crime by deprivation and victimisation   132

Figure 5.12   Percent fearing crime by deprivation and victimisation   132

Figure 6.1   Percent with a long-standing illness by deprivation group   143

Figure 6.2   Percent in receipt of disability related benefit by deprivation group   143

Figure 6.3   Percent visiting their GP in the last year by deprivation group   144

Figure 6.4   Percent having hospital treatment in the last year by deprivation group   144

Figure 6.5   Percent on hospital waiting lists by deprivation group   145

Figure 6.6   Percent with health problems caused or made worse as a
                  result of housing situation by deprivation group   147

Figure 6.7   Percent with health problems caused or made worse as a
                  result of housing situation by standard of housing   147

CHAID 6.1   Experience of long-standing illness   149

Figure 6.8   Percent with a long-standing illness by history of poverty   151

Figure 6.9   Percent with a long-standing illness by debt   151

CHAID 6.2   Experience of disability   152

Figure 6.10   Percent with a disability by history of poverty   154

Figure 6.11   Percent with a disability by social class   154

Figure 6.12   Percent with a disability by Income Support   155

Figure 6.13   Percent with a disability by debt   155

Figure 6.14   Percent with a disability by household type   156

Figure 7.1   Percentage feeling isolated and depressed by present level
                  of poverty   165

Figure 7.2   Average mental health score by poverty   165

Figure 7.3   Percent feeling isolated and depressed by gender   169

Figure 7.4   Percent feeling isolated and depressed by gender and
                  deprivation group   169

Figure 7.5   Percent of parents feeling isolated and depressed by type of
                  household   171

Figure 7.6   Percent of parents feeling isolated and/or depressed by
                  deprivation group   171

Figure 7.7   Percent feeling isolated and depressed by standard of
                  housing   174

Figure 8.1   Loans for house purchases, consumer credit and other borrowing and savings as a percentage of total personal disposable income 1980-1991   179

Figure 8.2   Percent in debt and average number of debts by deprivation group   182

Figure 8.3   Percent in debt and average number of debts by poverty   182

Figure 8.4   Percent in debt and average number of debts by present level of poverty   183

Figure 8.5   Percent in debt and average number of debts by history of poverty   183

Figure 8.6   Percent with fuel debts by deprivation group   186

Figure 10.1   Relationship between equivalent household income and MNI and PDI   228

List of contributors

Dr David Gordon - School for Policy Studies, University of Bristol, 8 Woodland Road, Bristol BS8 1TN

Christina Pantazis - School for Policy Studies, University of Bristol, 8 Woodland Road, Bristol BS8 1TN

Professor Peter Townsend - School for Policy Studies, University of Bristol, 8 Woodland Road, Bristol BS8 1TN

Dr Sarah Payne - School for Policy Studies, University of Bristol, 8 Woodland Road, Bristol BS8 1TN

Professor Glen Bramley - School of Planning and Housing, Edinburgh College of Art, Heriot-Watt University, 79 Grassmarket, Edinburgh EH1 2HJ

Professor Jonathan Bradshaw - Department of Social Policy and Social Work, University of York, Heslington, York YO1 5DD

Dr Hilary Holmes - Department of Social Policy and Social Work, University of York, Heslington, York YO1 5DD

Dr Bjørn Halleröd - Department of Sociology, University of Umeå, S-901 87 Umeå, Sweden

Foreword

Joanna Mack and Stewart Lankly

In the last few years, the issue of poverty has been creeping off the political agenda. This is despite the uncomfortable truth that, for the poor, life has become an increasingly difficult struggle. Higher unemployment, widening wage differentials and cuts in benefit levels have meant that while the majority have seen their living standards rise, those at the bottom have seen them grow much more slowly and even in some cases fall.

In the past, this trend would not have been tolerated. For more than thirty years after the war, the political and social consensus was that all groups in society should share in growing wealth. Until the middle to late 1970's, although poverty persisted, the poorest groups in society at least kept pace with rising incomes.

Since then, successive Conservative Governments have adopted policies that have ensured that this is no longer the case. They have encouraged labour market changes which have contributed to the growth of low pay and abandoned the post-war commitment to full employment. In attempts to control public spending, the effectiveness of the social security safety net has been eroded; there are more loopholes and, for those who don't fall through, Income Support now guarantees a lower relative living standard.

Thinkers on the 'Right' have denied that this has resulted in an increase in poverty on the grounds that poverty is an absolute, not a relative, concept. Indeed, Cabinet Ministers have recently renewed claims that poverty does not exist in Britain, that it is confined to Third World countries.

Traditionally, the Labour Party has championed the cause of the poor. Indeed, when in power, Labour governments have implemented welfare reforms aimed at simultaneously reducing poverty and redistributing resources from the better-off to the poor. Today, however, Labour, while still regarding alleviating poverty as important, places it within the context of financial policies which allow for neither an increase in welfare spending nor higher taxes on the better-off. Faced with a different ideological climate and out of office for nearly two decades, 'new' Labour emphasises equality of opportunity rather than greater equality. Yet there seems little recognition that the unequal opportunities they wish to tackle stem from a deeply unequal society.

However, the issue of the fairness of the distribution of income and resources cannot be swept away. Poverty disfigures not only the lives and opportunities of those who suffer it but increasingly overspills into the lives of the majority. The widening gap between the rich and the poor is socially divisive, arguably leading to rising crime, lower educational standards and even a depressed economic performance. In addition, the growing job and income insecurity of recent years means that more people face the prospect of falling into severe financial problems than in the past; sometimes on a temporary but too often on a prolonged basis. Poverty will continue to plague governments of all political persuasions.

This book examines these issues, coherently and objectively. It provides new evidence on the measurement of poverty, on the relationship between poverty and living standards and on public attitudes towards both the nature of poverty and anti-poverty policy. It shows that the 'poor' face a living standard which the majority of people believe to be unacceptably low and that, contrary to the conventional view, there exists a public consensus that more should be done to tackle the problem.

The evidence outlined above is based on a more detailed analysis of the data provided by the surveys conducted in 1983 and 1990 by MORI for the two *Breadline Britain* television series which we made for London Weekend Television. These are the only special national surveys of poverty to be conducted since the Royal Commission on the Distribution of Income and Wealth reported in 1978.

In designing the surveys, we deployed a pioneering approach to the definition of poverty. We set out to define poverty in relation to the minimum living standards that the majority of people believe to be essential in Britain today. Survey respondents were asked which of a large bundle of items they thought "are necessary, which all adults (and children where appropriate) should be able to afford and which they should not have to do without". Respondents were also asked whether they had this item and if not, whether it was because they didn't want it or because they couldn't afford it. From these responses, the proportion of households living below this socially-determined minimum living standard, or 'consensual' poverty line, could be measured.

One of the important findings of the 1983 survey was that the public took a relative view of what constitutes poverty. Their list of necessities included items such as presents for friends/family once a year, holidays away from home for one week a year and a washing machine; these certainly didn't feature in the subsistence or absolute standards drawn up by either Booth or Rowntree some fifty years ago. The British people understand and accept the concept of relative deprivation; they endorsed the view that people are entitled to a living standard which reflects the standards of the time and place in which they live. This finding was confirmed in the second survey, in 1990, which found that items not considered necessities in 1983 were so considered seven years later; a phone and outings for children, for example. This shows that socially-defined minimum living standards clearly adjust to reflect changes in national prosperity even within a relatively short space of time.

Those of us who have worked with the Breadline Britain research sometimes refer to those living below this publicly determined minimum standard as being 'in poverty' and to those who suffer it as 'poor'. So did the respondents to our surveys. Others, including Ministers, are free to prefer more restrictive definitions of these terms, even at odds with common usage but it is sophistry to argue that they have thus resolved the policy issues at stake.

Comparisons between the two surveys reveal a number of findings which have pointed political implications. The first concerns the increasingly politically sensitive issue of redistribution. The Breadline Britain research shows that growth alone will not help the poorest to gain access to society at minimum acceptable levels. Socially-defined minimum standards rise as national prosperity rises and, without redistribution, the numbers living below that minimum at any given time will not be reduced.

When Peter Lilley, the Social Security Secretary, argues that the poor are no longer 'poor' because their average level of spending has risen and because they have items they didn't have 15 years ago, the question remains as to whether this increase has been in line with what would be required to meet the minimum standards of today. The Breadline Britain research shows that it is not. When new Labour talks of creating a fairer Britain coming into the next century but backs away from questions of redistribution, the same mistake is being made. To hold out hope of help to the poorest members of society - those the public accept live at unacceptably low levels - without being prepared to engage in a redistribution of resources from the better-off, is disingenuous.

The second finding of political significance is that there is a greater willingness among the general public to tackle poverty than is recognised by or evident among our political leaders. The proportion believing the Government is doing too little to help the poor rose dramatically: from 57% in 1983 to 70% in 1990. People are even prepared to countenance more - to use that increasingly taboo word - tax. A remarkable three out of four people across all social classes are prepared to pay 1p more in the £1 to help people afford the items they regard as necessities. The proportion who were prepared to pay more tax to help people afford the items they classed as necessities also rose between the two surveys. In 1983, only a third were prepared to pay as much as 5p in the £ to help the poor while, by 1990, there was an even split in views. This was true even of the much-courted middle class ABs and C1s who are increasingly perceived to have their pockets and purses firmly zipped up.

The changes between the surveys are striking but the consistency is perhaps politically even more significant. In both surveys there is a solid majority for political action to secure a more equal society. The strength of these feelings has grown as inequality has grown.

In practice, a straightforward increase in the basic rate of tax would not make much sense for many of the poor, taking away as much as might be given back. However, the importance of the Breadline Britain findings is not to do with the precise mechanisms of redistribution but to show that, in spite of political leadership that seems to have increasingly abandoned any idea of redistribution, the British public themselves recognise its importance for creating a fairer society.

On an academic level, the Breadline Britain surveys have contributed a new approach to measuring poverty. Back in 1983, the first survey had produced results consistent with other approaches to measuring poverty. In 1990, carrying out the second survey for the follow-up television series, we were concerned whether the methodology would prove robust through a period of rapid social change. Our preliminary examination of the results was as encouraging for the methodology as it was depressing for the picture it painted of the lives of the poor.

With the help of David Gordon of Bristol University, we carried out a series of statistical tests to see if there was a clearly separated group below minimum acceptable standards. As in 1983, we found consistent statistical evidence of a separation between those who could be seen to be in poverty from those that were not.

The results were shocking: 20% of households lived in poverty in 1990 (nearly 11 million people), a rise of nearly 50% over 1983, when 14% of households lived in poverty (7.5 million people). The figures were much publicised in 1991 at the time of the transmission of the "Breadline Britain in the 1990s" series and publication of the accompanying booklet. But the data deserved a much more thorough analysis. These were, and remain, the only major studies of British poverty during this period. A mass of detail, not just on material possessions but also on the wider quality of life and access to public services remained largely unstudied.

With the support of the Joseph Rowntree Foundation, whose funding has been crucial, we asked David Gordon to take over the data and oversee its analysis with other colleagues and experts. The research has therefore been conducted in a thoroughly academic setting with the proper resources for handling the complexities of two large data sets.

The results, published in this collection of papers, use the raw data in new and diverse ways to identify key trends and to examine and challenge the basic assumptions behind the methodology. New work has been done in critical areas such as the relationship between poverty and debt, health and crime and on the role that public services play in mitigating poverty. The methodology has been improved and strengthened (in particular, by Halleröd, Bradshaw and Holes), extending the consensual measure and confirming its reliability. These may constitute academic debates but, for millions in Britain today, they are far from academic. Their well-being and that of British society for generations to come, are crucially linked to the issues discussed in these chapters. It is long overdue that the question of poverty re-emerges as a central issue in British domestic policy.

Acknowledgements

The Breadline Britain in the 1990s Survey was funded by London Weekend Television (LWT) with additional funding from the Joseph Rowntree Foundation and was carried out by Marketing and Opinion Research International (MORI). It was conceived and designed by Joanna Mack and Stewart Lansley for Domino Films, with the help of Brian Gosschalk of MORI. Research for the six television programmes was by Harold Frayman with additional research by David Gordon and John Hills. We would also like to thank Clare Irving at MORI who has patiently answered all our questions. Kevin Wilkes at Numbers, Richard Jennings at CACI and Keith Hughes and Chris Johnson at Merlin and Co. and George Gooding and Ian Stewart at the University of Bristol, have all helped us with the data. We would like to thank Paddy Hillyard, David Bull, John Hills and Barbara Ballard for their helpful comments on the book as well as all our colleagues at the Statistical Monitoring Unit. Helen Anderson, Zaheda Anwar and Carrie Anderson did the editing, typing and formatting that made this book possible.

The Joseph Rowntree Foundation has supported this project as part of its programme of research and innovative development projects, which it hopes will be of value to policy makers and practitioners. The facts presented and the views expressed in this book are, however, those of the authors and not necessarily those of the Foundation

Studies in Cash and Care

Editors: Sally Baldwin and Jonathan Bradshaw

Cash benefits and care services together make a fundamental contribution to human welfare. After income derived from work, they are arguably the most important determinants of living standards. Indeed, many households are almost entirely dependent on benefits and services which are socially provided. Moreover, welfare benefits and services consume the lion's share of public expenditure. The operation, impact and interaction of benefits and services is thus an important focus of research on social policy.

Policy related work in this field tends to be disseminated to small specialist audiences in the form of mimeographed research reports or working papers and perhaps later published, more briefly, in journal articles. In consequence public debate about vital social issues is sadly ill-informed. This series is designed to fill this gap by making the details of important empirically-based research more widely available.

Introduction

Poverty can only be accurately measured by studying the living standards of people and families. Studies that concentrate mainly on income and expenditure (and not on living standards), such as the annual Family Expenditure Survey (FES), can provide good evidence about inequality but only limited evidence about poverty.

The two Breadline Britain surveys (1983 and 1990) are the only nationally representative surveys commissioned during the past 11 years that can be used to measure accurately the extent and nature of poverty in Britain. It is to the credit of London Weekend Television (LWT) and the Joseph Rowntree Foundation that they have funded the kind of detailed study of deprivation in Britain that the government and the academic research councils have not been prepared to finance.

Some of the results from the 1990 Breadline Britain study have been described in the 6 television programmes (first broadcast in 1991) and in a number of publications (Frayman, 1991; Gosschalk and Frayman, 1992). The major findings are now widely known (Frayman, 1991):

1 Between 1983 and 1990, the number of people who could objectively be described as living in poverty increased by almost 50%. In 1983, 14% of households (approximately 7.5 million people) were living in poverty and, by 1990, 20% of households (approximately 11 million people) were living in poverty.

2   Roughly 10 million people in Britain today cannot afford adequate housing: for example, their home is unheated, damp or the older children have to share bedrooms.

3   About 7 million go without essential clothing, such as a warm waterproof coat, because of lack of money.

4   There are approximately 2.5 million children who are forced to go without at least one of the things they need, like three meals a day, toys or out of school activities.

5   Around 5 million people are not properly fed by today's standards; they do not have enough fresh fruit and vegetables, or two meals a day, for example.

6   About 6.5 million people cannot afford one or more essential household goods, like a fridge, a telephone or carpets for living areas.

The purposes of this report are threefold. The first is to give more of the details behind these startling findings. The second is to look at some of the results from the survey that have not previously been analysed. The third is to examine the debates and criticisms surrounding the measurement of poverty and the Breadline Britain approach. We will also look further at the results of the survey that can throw light on some of the issues that are currently the topic of both academic and political debate.

A tremendous amount is written about poverty each year. The Social Science Citation Index records that at least 4000 academic articles on poverty or deprivation have been published since 1983. Intense debate usually surrounds all poverty studies, including the Breadline Britain studies. In this report, we have tried to examine the criticisms of the Breadline Britain approach rather than to ignore them.

Chapter 1 looks at the whole issue and debate surrounding the measurement of poverty and shows how the Breadline Britain survey can be used to produce scientific, 'objective' measurements of poverty.

Many commentators have criticised poverty studies in Britain for being 'parochial'. Chapter 2, by Professor Peter Townsend, looks at the methods used to study poverty around the world. He places the results of the Breadline Britain surveys in a wider context and argues for the construction of an international poverty line.

Chapter 3 deals with the findings from the 1990 survey on the public's attitudes to poverty and their perceptions of necessities. It also looks at which groups in society are likely to live in poverty.

Chapter 4, by Dr Sarah Payne and Christina Pantazis, examines the issues and debates surrounding poverty and gender. In particular, the differences and similarities of women and men in their perception and definition of poverty are explored.

Chapters 5, 6, 7 and 8 look at the results from the 1990 survey that throw light on current debates about poverty and crime, poverty and health, poverty and mental health and poverty and debt.

Poverty studies are often criticised for concentrating on the possessions and activities of individual families and households, rather than looking at the wider picture of the goods and services available to the community as a whole: "each individual's quality of life is affected by a whole range of public services, from sports centres to healthcare, from an emptied dustbin, to education" (Mack and Lansley, 1985). Chapter 9, by Professor Glen Bramley, examines the important issues around public services.

Chapter 10 by Dr Bjørn Halleröd, Professor Jonathan Bradshaw and Dr Hilary Holmes, develops the theoretical debate on the 'consensual' definition of poverty using a methodology that has been applied to a similar study in Sweden.

The Breadline Britain approach to measuring poverty

The 1983 Breadline Britain study pioneered what has been termed the 'consensual' or 'perceived deprivation' approach to measuring poverty. This methodology has since been widely adopted by other studies both in Britain and abroad (Mack and Lansley, 1985; Veit-Wilson, 1987; Walker, 1987).

The consensual or perceived deprivation approach sets out to determine whether there are some people whose standard of living is below the minimum acceptable to society. It defines 'poverty' from the viewpoint of the public's perception of minimum need:

> "This study tackles the questions 'how poor is too poor?' by identifying the minimum acceptable way of life for Britain in the 1980s. Those who have no choice but to fall below this minimum level can be said to be 'in poverty'. This concept is developed in terms of those who have an enforced lack of *socially perceived* necessities. This means that the 'necessities' of life are identified by public opinion and not by, on the one hand, the views of experts or, on the other hand, the norms of behaviour *per se*". (Mack and Lansley, 1985)

In order to determine the minimum standard of living, Market and Opinion Research International (MORI) interviewed a quota sample of 1174 adults aged 16+, in 1983, and 1831 adults in 1990 (see Appendix I and Mack and Lansley, 1985, pp. 287-290 for details).

In the 1990 survey, respondents were first asked the following questions about a list of 44 items designed to cover the range of possessions and activities that people might consider important (see Appendix II for details):

Q3　On these cards are a number of different items which relate to our standard of living. Please would you indicate by placing the cards in the appropriate box the living standards you feel all adults should have in Britain today. BOX A is for items which you think are necessary, which all adults should be able to afford and which they should not have to do without. BOX B is for items which may be desirable but are not necessary. Do you feel differently about any items if the adult is a pensioner?

Q4　And do you feel differently for any items in the case of families with children?

For the purpose of the study, an item was assumed to be a socially perceived necessity if more than 50% of respondents (after the sample had been weighted to represent the population) considered it to be a necessity.

Later in the questionnaire (Q11 and Q12), respondents were again asked about the 44 items to determine if they:

(A)　Have and couldn't do without (an item)
(B)　Have and could do without
(C)　Don't have and don't want
(D)　Don't have and can't afford
(E)　Not applicable/Don't know

Respondents (and their households) were assigned a deprivation index score each time they answered that they 'don't have and can't afford' an item that was considered to be a necessity by more than 50% of respondents (after weighting) in Q3 and Q4.

4

1 Measuring poverty: Breadline Britain in the 1990s

David Gordon and Christina Pantazis

Poverty and politics

During the 1980s the 'poverty debate' became much more politically sensitive than in the past. John Moore (who was then Secretary of State for Social Security) in his speech on 11.5.89 at St Stephen's Club claimed that poverty, as most people understood it, had been abolished and that critics of the government's policies were:

> "not concerned with the actual living standards of real people but with pursuing the political goal of equality ... We reject their claims about poverty in the UK, and we do so knowing that their motive is not compassion for the less well-off, it is an attempt to discredit our real economic achievement in protecting and improving the living standards of our people. Their purpose in calling 'poverty' what is in reality simply inequality, is so they can call western material capitalism a failure. We must expose this for what it is ... utterly false.

> — it is capitalism that has wiped out the stark want of Dickensian Britain.

5

- it is capitalism that has caused the steady improvements in living standards this century.
- and it is capitalism which is the only firm guarantee of still better living standards for our children and our grandchildren."

A senior Civil Servant, the Assistant Secretary for Policy on Family Benefits and Low Incomes at the Department of Health and Social Security (DHSS), had made the same point more succinctly when he gave evidence to the Select Committee on Social Services on 15.6.88. He stated "The word poor is one the government actually disputes."

Yet, despite the government's claim that poverty no longer exists, social attitude surveys have shown that the overwhelming majority of people in Britain believe that 'poverty' still persists. Even the 1989 British Social Attitudes survey, conducted at the height of the "Economic Miracle" found that 63% of people thought that "there is quite a lot of real poverty in Britain today" (Brook *et al*, 1992). The 1986 British Social Attitudes survey found that 87% of people thought that the government 'definitely should' or 'probably should spend more money to get rid of poverty'. In 1989, the European Union-wide Eurobarometer opinion survey found that British people thought the 'fight against poverty' ranked second only to 'world peace' in the list of great causes worth taking risks and making sacrifices for (Eurobarometer, November 1989). This view was widely held across the 12 member countries of the European Union, as shown in Table 1.1.

Table 1.1
Worthwhile great causes

Question: "In your opinion, in this list which are the great causes which nowadays are worth the trouble of taking risks and making sacrifices for?"

In order of preference	UK (%)	12 EC Countries (%)
World peace	71	75
The fight against poverty	57	57
Human rights	55	60
Protection of wildlife	48	57
Freedom of the individual	43	39
Defence of the country	41	30
The fight against racism	32	36
Sexual equality	25	25
My religious faith	18	19
The unification of Europe	9	18
The revolution	2	5
None of these	2	1
No reply	1	2

Some aspects of the increase in poverty in the 1990s have become very conspicuous. The 'problem' of homelessness is very visible; young people can be seen begging on the streets of virtually every major city in Britain. Sir George Young (then Housing minister) even noted that homeless beggars in London were "the sort of people you step on when you came out of the Opera" (*Guardian,* 29.6.91, p.2). Similarly, the Prime Minister (John Major) claimed that

> "the sight of beggars was an eyesore which could drive tourists and shoppers away from cities" and "it is an offensive thing to beg. It is unnecessary. So I think people should be very rigorous with it" (*Bristol Evening Post* 27.5.9, p.1-2)

A Department of Environment survey of 1,346 single homeless people in 1991 found that 21% of people sleeping rough said they had received no income in the previous week (Anderson, Kemp and Quilgars, 1993). The median income of those sleeping rough from all sources was only £38 per week, despite this only one fifth tried to beg. People who begged often encountered problems and begging was seen as an uncertain or precarious source of income (Anderson, Kemp and Quilgars, 1993).

The 'poverty' of the homeless people sleeping on the streets is shocking. An analysis of the coroner's court records in Inner London[1] indicated that the average age at death of people with 'no fixed abode' was only 47 (Keyes and Kennedy, 1992). This is lower than the average estimated life expectancy of people in any country in the world (not at war) with the exception of Gambia, Guinea, Guinea-Bissau, Mali, Niger and Sierra Leone (UN 1991, UNDP 1992).

The 1991 Census recorded the numbers of homeless people in hostels, bed and breakfast and sleeping rough on census night;[2] it also estimated the numbers of 'concealed' households. Figure 1.1 shows the rate of homelessness/housing need per 100 people (divided into quartiles) for each of the 366 local district authorities of England. A clear pattern is evident; there are high rates of homelessness in the Metropolitan districts and also in the more rural areas with little council housing, particularly in the South East (Gordon and Forrest, 1995).

Detailed analysis of the 1991 Census returns has shown that these homeless figures are just the 'tip of the iceberg'. There are between 200,000 and 500,000 additional people with no permanent home. They are largely young men (aged 18-36), mainly in the inner cities, who move frequently and stay with friends or relatives, probably sleeping on the sofa or in a spare bed. This phenomenon of 'hidden homelessness' was not found in the 1981 Census (Brown, 1993).

Figure 1.1
Homeless people in hostels, bed and breakfast, sleeping rough and concealed households

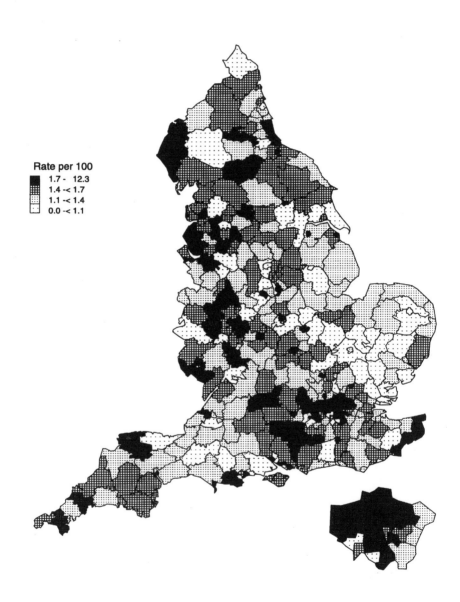

Rate per 100
- 1.7 - 12.3
- 1.4 -< 1.7
- 1.1 -< 1.4
- 0.0 -< 1.1

8

To understand the reasoning that allows the government to claim falsely that poverty does not exist, we must examine the debate surrounding the concept and measurement of poverty.

The concept of poverty

The concept of poverty has evolved over the past sixty years from an 'absolute' to a 'relative' conception. In the 1940s, the 'subsistence' idea was adopted by Beveridge (1942) as the basis for setting new benefit rates. Beveridge stated:

> "In considering the minimum income needed by persons of working age for subsistence during interruptions of earnings, it is sufficient to take into account food, clothing, fuel, light and household sundries, and rent, though some margin must be allowed for inefficiency in spending."

Around 6% of the total estimated requirement was allowed for this 'margin'. The 'subsistence' idea followed from the pioneering work of Rowntree in York, whose ideas on 'primary poverty' were based on the minimum needed for the 'maintenance of physical health' and 'physical efficiency':

> "A family living upon the scale allowed for must never spend a penny on railway fare or omnibus. They must never go into the country unless they walk. They must never purchase a half penny newspaper or spend a penny to buy a ticket for a popular concert. They must write no letters to absent children, for they cannot afford to pay the postage. They must never contribute anything to their church or chapel, or give any help to a neighbour which costs them money. They cannot save nor can they join a sick club or trade union, because they cannot pay the necessary subscriptions. The children must have no pocket money for dolls, marbles or sweets. The father must smoke no tobacco and drink no beer. The mother must never buy any pretty clothes for herself or her children, the character of the family wardrobe as for the family diet being governed by the regulation 'nothing must be bought but that which is absolutely necessary for the maintenance of physical health and what is bought must be of the plainest and most economical description." (Rowntree, 1922)

The subsistence approach to the definition of poverty is an 'absolute' concept of poverty; it is dominated by the individual's requirements for physiological efficiency. However, this is a very limited conception of human needs, especially when considering the roles men and women play in society. People are not just physical beings, they are social beings. They have obligations as workers, parents, neighbours, friends and citizens that they are expected to meet and which they themselves want to meet. Studies of people's behaviour after they have experienced a drastic cut in resources show that they sometimes act to fulfil their social obligations before they act to satisfy their physical wants. They require income to fulfil their various roles and participate in the social customs and associations to which they have become habituated and not only to satisfy their physical wants (Townsend and Gordon, 1989).

Poverty can be defined as where resources are so seriously below those commanded by the average individual or family that the 'poor' are, in effect, excluded from ordinary living patterns, customs and activities. As resources for any individual or family are diminished, there is a point at which there occurs a sudden withdrawal from participation in the customs and activities sanctioned by the culture. The point at which withdrawal escalates disproportionately to falling resources can be defined as the poverty line or threshold (Townsend, 1979 and 1993a).

This 'relative' concept of poverty is now widely accepted (Piachaud, 1987); even Rowntree used a less comprehensive concept of relative poverty in his second survey in York in 1936 (Veit-Wilson, 1986). The working papers of the Beveridge Committee show that they were well aware that their proposed benefit scales were insufficient to meet human social needs (Veit-Wilson, 1992).

In 1975, the Council of Europe adopted a relative definition of poverty as:

"individuals or families whose resources are so small as to exclude them from the minimum acceptable way of life of the Member State in which they live" (EEC, 1981)

and, on 19 December 1984, the European Commission extended the definition as:

"the poor shall be taken to mean persons, families and groups of persons whose resources (material, cultural and social) are so limited as to exclude them from the minimum acceptable way of life in the Member State in which they live". (EEC, 1985)

The Church of England's *Faith in the City* report also adopted a 'relative' definition of poverty that included notions of social exclusion, equity and justice. In the past, the British Government has strongly supported a 'relative' definition of poverty. In 1979, the Supplementary Benefit Commission stated:

"Poverty, in urban, industrial countries like Britain is a standard of living so low that it excludes and isolates people from the rest of the community. To keep out of poverty, they must have an income which enables them to participate in the life of the community. They must be able, for example, to keep themselves reasonably fed, and well enough dressed to maintain their self-respect and to attend interviews for jobs with confidence. Their homes must be reasonably warm; their children should not be shamed by the quality of their clothing; the family must be able to visit relatives, and give them something on their birthdays and at Christmas time; they must be able to read

10

newspapers, and retain their television set and their membership of trade unions and churches. And they must be able to live in a way which ensures, so far as possible, that public officials, doctors, teachers, landlords and others treat them with the courtesy due to every member of the community." (Supplementary Benefit Commission, 1979, p2).

Two senior economic advisers at the DHSS made the government's position very clear:

"it should be clear that EAO[3] is using a strong version of the 'relative' concept of poverty in its work on standards of living. We take the view that 'absolute' concepts of poverty are unrealistic and not very useful in the policy context". (Isherwood and Van Slooten, 1979)

Relative and absolute poverty

The only serious challenge to the concept of 'relative' poverty has come from Sen (1983). However, examination of the discussion between the two main protagonists (Professors Sen and Townsend)[4] reveals that much of the debate is semantic, revolving around their differing definitions of 'relative' and 'absolute'. For the purpose of scientifically measuring poverty the difference between 'absolute' and 'relative' poverty is a chimera. Indeed Sen (1985) concluded that:

"There is no conflict between the irreducible absolutist element in the notion of poverty ... and the 'thoroughgoing relativity' to which Peter Townsend refers."

The scientific 'objective' measurement of poverty

Although the 'relative' concept of poverty is now widely accepted, there is considerable debate about how to apply this theory to produce scientific measurements of poverty. It is not easy to measure 'poverty' directly (Atkinson, 1985a and 1985b; Lewis and Ulph, 1988) but it is possible to obtain measures of 'deprivation'. These two concepts are tightly linked and there is general agreement that the concept of deprivation covers the various conditions, independent of income, experienced by people who are 'poor', while the concept of poverty refers to the lack of income and other resources which makes those conditions inescapable or at least highly likely (Townsend, 1987).

Figure 1.2

Modal deprivation by logarithm of income as a percentage of Supplementary Benefit scale rates

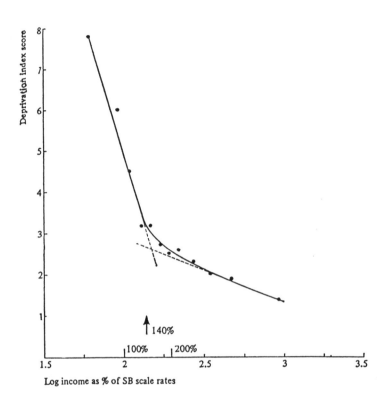

Log income as % of SB scale rates

Townsend (1979) devised 60 indicators of deprivation based on a detailed study of people's style of living and resources conducted in 2000 households between 1968-1969. These 60 indicators could be summed to create a single composite deprivation index score for each household. By plotting deprivation score against the log of income as a percentage of the Supplementary Benefit rates that existed then (Figure 1.2), Townsend determined, by eye, that a poverty threshold might exist at around 150% of the Supplementary Benefit standard. This result has since been confirmed by weighted regression analysis and canonical correlation analysis which placed the threshold at 160% of the Supplementary Benefit standard (Desai, 1986; Desai and Shah, 1988).

The Department of Social Security maintains that poverty cannot be 'objectively' measured although they have presented no analyses to substantiate this viewpoint. However, serious and detailed criticisms have been made by Professor Piachaud (1981, 1987) who argued that:

- The deprivation indicators used by Townsend (1979) did not allow for the identification of the effects of personal choice from those of constraint (i.e. those who could not afford an item and those who did not want an item).

- The goal of objective, scientific measurement of poverty was not attainable.

- The poverty threshold does not exist. He postulated that there may not be a marked change in deprivation below a certain level, only a continuum.

Piachaud's first criticism, relating to the separation of choice from constraint, was overcome by the 1983 and 1990 Breadline Britain studies which identified both those households/people who "don't have but don't want" and those who "don't have and can't afford" an item. However, it must be noted that the results of Townsend's (1979) study were relatively robust (Desai, 1986). The 'rich' rarely choose to live like the 'poor' and the choices the 'poor' can make are generally constrained.

Piachaud's second criticism is, of course, key. If the objective, scientific measurement of poverty is unattainable, then surveys such as the Breadline Britain studies are of only limited academic value. In addition, poverty could never be conquered since it could never be adequately measured and the requisite steps taken to alleviate it. Fortunately, the Department of Social Security and Piachaud are wrong. The scientific measurement of poverty is both possible and attainable.

The problem of 'experts'

The reasoning behind many claims that poverty cannot be measured 'objectively' is that, in order to measure deprivation, a selection of questions must first be drawn up by 'experts'. There is no 'objective' way of selecting these questions. They are just the experts' opinion of what is important. Even if a subset of these questions is also selected as important by the general population (the methodology of the Breadline Britain survey), this selection can be made only on the basis of the larger group of questions the experts first chose. There may be better questions for measuring poverty that were not chosen and, if they had, a different result might have been obtained.

There are two separate issues here that will be dealt with in turn:

- Can the answers to a selection of deprivation questions, chosen by experts, ever form the basis of the scientific, objective measurement of poverty?

- If a different set of questions were asked, would the results be the same, i.e. is the measurement of poverty reliable?

Scientific measurement

There are a number of widely held but incorrect beliefs about science, for example:

Science is objective.

Scientific knowledge is reliable knowledge because it is objectively proven knowledge.

Scientific theories are derived from observation of the facts or by objective experimentation.

Personal opinion and speculation play no part in science.

None of these statements is true: the idea that scientific theories are based on the study of objective facts is critically flawed. The 'inductive' idea of science, that correct theories will somehow 'bubble' to the surface once enough pure facts have been generated and sifted, is untenable. This inductive idea of science is attributed to the work of Francis Bacon and reached its apogee in the 1930s with the Logical Positivist School of Ayre (1936, 1955) and his co-workers. The work of Godel[5], Popper, Russell, Lakatos, Musgrave, Kuhn and many other modern philosophers and sociologists of science[6] has shown that scientific theories cannot be proven by inductive logic. Furthermore, all observations/measurements are theory-dependent. None can be independently objective. All measurement, whether it be the height of a person, the charge on an electron or the level of poverty, is dependent on the theory and not the converse. There can be no objectively true value to these measurements that are independent of the theories that are used to measure them.

Neither scientific theories nor scientific measurement are 'objectively true'. However, for a theory to be scientific, it must not only be logically internally consistent but also fulfil a number of strict criteria:

1   The theory must be falsifiable, e.g. it must be capable of being shown to be untrue. The existence of a Loving God and Freudian psychology are unfalsifiable theories and therefore unscientific.

2   The theory must be testable.

3   The theory must have predictive value.

4   The results of the theory must be reproducible. Other people using the same methods will reach the same results.

These criteria are known to philosophers as the Falsificationist View of science and are attributable to the work of Karl Popper (1968, 1972). They contain the idea of a logical asymmetry that a theory can never be proved only falsified. This work has been extended by Imre Lakatos (1974), who claimed that scientific research programmes must also:

5   Possess a degree of coherence that involves the mapping out of a definite programme for future research.

6   Lead to the discovery of novel phenomena, at least occasionally.

Modern sociology often fulfils the second of Lakatos' requirements but rarely the first. For the measurement of poverty to be scientifically 'objective', the theory on which the measurement is based must fulfil the criteria of Popper and Lakatos. The 'relative' theory of poverty can make this claim.

1   The relative theory of poverty can be falsified. If a survey finds that there are no people/households whose resources are so low that they are excluded from the ordinary living patterns, customs and activities of their culture, then no poverty exists. For example, Kibbutz societies would have no poverty and several Scandinavian countries have little poverty.

2   Surveys, such as the Breadline Britain studies, have provided tests of the relative poverty theory.

3   Numerous predictions are made by the relative poverty theory. For example, the 'poor' will experience a disproportionate 'fear of crime' (relative to their experience of crime) because of the greater consequences of crime for the 'poor' (see Chapter 5).

4   Several deprivation surveys have produced similar results, both in Britain and in other countries. Therefore, conclusions based on the relative poverty theory are reproducible.

5   Since Townsend's (1979) initial work, extensive research on relative poverty has been carried out by many researchers in several countries. This research has extended and developed the concepts and findings of the relative poverty model. (For example, see the studies referenced in Townsend and Gordon, 1989 and Grayson et al, 1992.)

6   A number of novel phenomena, predicted by the relative poverty theory, have been confirmed. The identification of poverty/deprivation as a major cause of ill health of equal or greater consequence than genetic, pathogenic and behavioural factors, has led to:

(i)   the recognition of the effects of stress on health, particularly cardiovascular disease (Marmot et al, 1987; Blaxter, 1990);

(ii)   the identification of some of the mechanisms by which poor housing conditions cause disease (Strachan, 1988); and

(iii) the use of deprivation indicators in conjunction with workload factors as the best method for health resource allocation (Carstairs, 1981; Jarman, 1983).

Indeed, Sir Donald Acheson, in his final report as the Chief Medical Officer, *On the State of the Public Health*, for 1990, said:

> "the issue is quite clear in health terms: that there is a link, has been a link and, I suspect, will continue to be a link between deprivation and ill health" and "analysis has shown that the clearest links with the excess burden of ill health are:
>
> - *low income;*
> - *unhealthy behaviour: and*
> - *poor housing and environmental amenities.*"

More generally, Jacobson (1993) has stated that:

> "Two out of three women around the world presently suffer from the most debilitating disease known to humanity. Common symptoms of this fast-spreading ailment include chronic anaemia, malnutrition and severe fatigue. Sufferers exhibit an increased susceptibility to infections of the respiratory tract. And premature death is a frequent outcome. In the absence of direct intervention, the disease is often communicated from mother to child with markedly higher transmission rates among females than males. Yet, while studies confirm the efficacy of numerous prevention and treatment strategies, to date few have been vigorously pursued."

The disease she is referring to is poverty. These insights are unlikely to have been made without the foundation of the 'relative' poverty theory.

Since the 'relative' poverty theory meets all the criteria of Popper and Lakatos, the measurement of poverty by deprivation studies is, by definition, scientific. The important question, then, is: are these measurements reliable?

Reliability

All measurement is subject to error which can take the form of either random variations or systematic bias (Stanley, 1971, lists many causes of bias). Random errors of measurement can never be completely eliminated. However, if the error is only small relative to the size of the phenomena being studied, then the measurement will be reliable. Reliable measurements are repeatable, they have a high degree of precision.

The theory of measurement error has been developed mainly by psychologists and educationalists and its origins can be traced to the work of Spearman (1904). The most widely used model is the Domain-Sampling Model, although many of the key equations can be derived from other models based on different assumptions (see Nunnally, 1981, Chapters 5-9, for detailed discussion). The Domain-Sampling Model assumes that there is an infinite number of questions (or, at least, a large number of questions) that could be asked about deprivation. If you had an infinite amount of time, patience and research grant, you could ask every person/household all of these questions and then you would know everything about their level of deprivation, i.e. you would know their 'true' deprivation score. The 32 questions used in the Breadline Britain in the 1990s study can be considered to be a subset of this larger group (domain) of all possible questions about deprivation.

Some questions will obviously be better at measuring deprivation than others; however, all of the questions that measure deprivation will have some common core. If they do not, they are not measuring deprivation by definition. Therefore, all the questions that measure deprivation should be intercorrelated such that the sum (or average) of all the correlations of one question, with all the others, will be the same for all questions (Nunnally, 1981). If this assumption is correct, then by measuring the average intercorrelation between the answers to the set of deprivation questions, it is possible to calculate both:

1   an estimate of the correlation between the set of questions and the 'true' scores that would be obtained if the infinite set of all possible deprivation questions had been asked; and

2   the average correlation between the set of questions asked (the deprivation index) and all other possible sets of deprivation questions (deprivation indices) of equal length (equal number of questions).

Both these correlations can be derived from Cronbach's Coefficient Alpha which, when transformed for use with dichotomous questions, is known as KR-20, short for Kurder-Richardson Formula 20 (Cronbach, 1951 and 1976; Cronbach *et al,* 1971; Kurder, 1970).

Cronbach's Coefficient Alpha is 0.8754 for the 32 questions used in the Breadline Britain in the 1990s study. This is the average correlation between these 32 questions and all the other possible sets of 32 questions that could be used to measure deprivation. The estimated correlation between the 32 Breadline Britain questions and the 'true' scores, from the infinite possible number of deprivation questions, is the square root of Coefficient Alpha, i.e. 0.9356.

Nunnally (1981) has argued that

> "in the early stages of research ... one saves time and energy by working with instruments that have modest reliability, for which purpose reliabilities of 0.70 or higher will suffice ... for basic research, it can be argued that increasing reliabilities much beyond 0.80 is often wasteful of time and funds, at that level correlations are attenuated very little by measurement error."

Therefore, the Alpha Coefficient score of 0.87 for the Breadline Britain questions indicates that they have a high degree of reliability and also that effectively similar results would have been obtained if any other reliable set of 32 deprivation questions had been asked instead.

Coefficient alpha can also be used to test the reliability of individual questions. Table 1.2 shows how the Alpha Coefficient would change if any single question was deleted from the deprivation index. There are only three questions (highlighted in bold) which would yield an increase in Alpha if they were removed and this increase would be in the fourth decimal place only.

However, it is important to examine the reasons why these three items are not reliable measurers of deprivation. The possession of a bath/shower and/or an indoor toilet not shared with another household has a long history of use as a deprivation measure. These questions have been asked repeatedly in the national Censuses, in order to identify the areas with poor housing conditions. These Census results then helped form the basis for the slum clearance programmes. These programmes have been so successful that the 1991 Census recorded that only 1.25% of households, containing only 0.8% of residents in households, still suffered from not having exclusive use of a bath/shower and/or an indoor toilet. Many of these households are likely to be student households in bedsit accommodation; and these student households are often not multiply deprived.

It is due to the triumph of the slum clearance and council house building programmes since the second World War that the possession of exclusive use of a bath/shower and/or an indoor toilet is no longer a good measure of deprivation. 'Poor people' now often have housing which includes these facilities.

Table 1.2

Reliability analysis on the deprivation questions from Breadline Britain in the 1990s that more than 50% of the population thinks are necessary and people should be able to afford

		Corrected Item-Total Correlation	Alpha if Item Deleted
1	A damp-free home	.3672	.8726
2	**An Inside Toilet (not shared with another household)**	**.0824**	**.8761**
3	Heating to warm living areas of the home if it's cold	.4031	.8720
4	Beds for everyone in the household	.2422	.8749
5	**Bath not shared with another household**	**.0512**	**.8763**
6	Enough money to keep your home in a decent state of	.5735	.8673
7	Fridge	.2100	.8752
8	A warm waterproof coat	.5072	.8696
9	Two meals a day (for adults)	.2648	.8746
10	Insurance of Contents of Dwelling	.5816	.8669
11	Fresh fruit and vegetables every day	.4853	.8698
12	Carpets in living rooms and bedrooms in the home	.2701	.8743
13	Meat or fish or vegetarian equivalent every other day	.3662	.8726
14	Celebrations on special occasions such as Christmas	.4306	.8713
15	Two pairs of all-weather shoes	.5600	.8680
16	Washing machine	.2578	.8746
17	Presents for friends or family once a year	.5227	.8689
18	Regular savings of £10 a month for "rainy days" or	.5002	.8723
19	A Hobby or Leisure Activities	.4703	.8701
20	New, not second-hand clothes	.4582	.8706
21	A roast joint or its vegetarian equivalent once a week	.4566	.8705
22	**Television**	**.1478**	**.8757**
23	Telephone	.3746	.8729
24	An annual week's holiday away, not with relatives	.5717	.8681
25	A "best outfit" for special occasions	.5460	.8680

Extra Questions for Families with Children

1	Three meals a day for children	.2875	.8745
2	Toys for children e.g. dolls or models	.3200	.8740
3	Separate bedrooms for every child over 10 of different sexes	.2540	.8747
4	Out of school activities, e.g. sports, orchestra, Scouts	.4718	.8703
5	Leisure equipment for children e.g. sports equipment or a bicycle	.4263	.8715
6	An outing for children once a week	.5012	.8694
7	Children's friends round for tea/snack once a fortnight	.4799	.8703

Coefficient Alpha for the 32 Questions = 0.8754

The possession of a television is a controversial indicator of deprivation; 51% of the Breadline Britain respondents thought that a television was a necessity in the 1983 study as did 58% in the 1990 study. In response to the 1983 study, S. Turner of Wolverhampton wrote to the *Sunday Times* (28.8.83):

> "Anyone who visits low-income families has experience of homes which are lacking in carpets, furniture, or decent clothing for children, but contain a large colour TV." (Mack and Lansley, 1985)

However, the importance of television to some 'poor' people was explained by Pamela in the 1983 study (Pamela was a lone parent with a nine month old child, living on Supplementary Benefit in an attic flat):

> "I watch TV from first thing in the morning till last thing at night, till the television goes off. I sit and watch it all day. I can't afford to do other things at all. The only thing I can do is sit and watch television. I can't go anywhere, I can't go out and enjoy myself or nothing. I should be able to take my daughter out somewhere. I would take her to the zoo and things like that. Places she's never been, or seen, and half the places I haven't seen in London myself. Things that I can't afford to do." (Mack and Lansley, 1985)

Given this importance of television, why is the possession of one not a reliable indicator of deprivation in the 1990 Breadline Britain Survey? Televisions are a consumer durable that have reached saturation point. The General Household Survey (GHS) shows that 98% of households have a television and this situation has persisted since the mid-1970s. Since some households have more than one television, there are probably more televisions than there are households in Britain. This saturation is evident from the second-hand prices of televisions. 21" colour televisions typically sell at auction for between £20 and £30 and black and white televisions for between £1 and £10. Televisions are not expensive, however, a television licence is.

The Breadline Britain Surveys have shown that poverty has increased during the 1980s (see Introduction). If these findings are correct, it would be expected that there would be a concomitant increase in the number of households that could not afford to buy a TV licence during the 1980s. Figure 1.3 shows the changes in the number of prosecutions for TV licence offences between 1980 and 1992. A massive four-fold increase in prosecutions has occurred. Part of this increase might be due to more effective policing of the Wireless Telegraphy Act or even to an increase in "wickedness" in the population, although there is little evidence for either (Wall and Bradshaw, 1987). However, at least some of this massive increase in prosecutions probably results from greater numbers of households being unable to afford a TV licence.

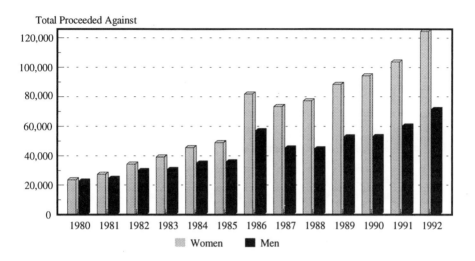

Figure 1.3
Total number proceeded against under the
Wireless Telegraphy Acts (TV Licence) 1980-92

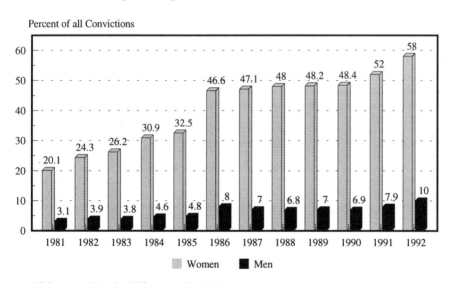

Figure 1.4
Convictions under the Wireless Telegraphy Acts as a
percentage of all convictions 1981-92

All Summary Motoring Offences are Excluded

21

In 1992, 58% of all convictions[7] of women for criminal offences were for Wireless Telegraphy Act offences (Figure 1.4). If the TV licence were abolished, female criminal convictions would fall by more than half. Between 1981 and 1992, criminal convictions for women increased by 42,000 (32%). However, Wireless Telegraphy convictions increased by 63,000 in the same period. If TV licence offences are excluded, then female criminal convictions fell during the 1980s. This is clearly a situation where poverty seems to be primarily responsible for a large part of the recorded increase in female crime during the 1980s.

The poverty threshold/line

Piachaud's final major criticism of the 'relative' theory of poverty relates to the problem of identifying the poverty threshold/line; he considered that a continuum may exist. Piachaud (1981) comments that:

"The combination of two factors - that there is a diversity in styles of living, and that poverty is relative: mean that you would *not*, in fact, expect to find any threshold between the 'poor' and the rest of society."

Townsend (1979) originally identified the poverty line/threshold at 150% of the Supplementary Benefit standard by observing the position of the break of slope on a graph of Deprivation Index plotted against the logarithm of income as a percentage of the Supplementary Benefit Scale that then existed (see Figure 1.2).

Regression analysis of Townsend's data showed that, statistically, the best position for the poverty line/threshold was at 160% of the Supplementary Benefit standard (Desai, 1986; Desai and Shah, 1988). Piachaud (1987) argued that the poverty line/threshold was a statistical artefact resulting from the transformation of the income data (the reciprocal of income equivalised by the Supplementary Benefit scale was used). Piachaud objected to the reciprocal transformation (1 ÷ Income) rather than to the equivalisation procedure used (the 1968 Supplementary Benefit scale). Even though, the 1968 Supplementary Benefit scale was based largely on political rather than scientific criteria.

There are three main problems with using these methods to determine the poverty line/threshold (Gordon and Townsend, 1990):

1   the size of changes in the slope of a graph is dependant on the transformations used for the axis (Figure 1.5, Kolata, 1984).

2   there is no universally agreed statistical definition of how large a change in slope is required to define the poverty 'threshold'; a number of different thresholds are possible.

3   the use of a single composite deprivation index results in information loss from the data.

22

Figure 1.5
Slope is hard to judge

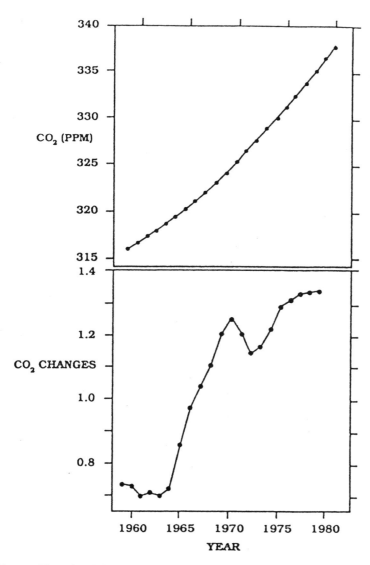

Note: The visual impression from the top panel is that the rate of change of atmospheric CO_2 is constant from 1967 to 1980. But in the bottom panel, where the yearly changes are graphed, it can be seen that there is a dip in the rate of change around 1970.

Discriminant analysis is one of the multivariate techniques that can be used to surmount these problems since it does not require a pre-defined poverty 'threshold'. Discriminant analysis allows the differences between two or more pre-defined groups to be studied with respect to several variables (Klecka, 1980). There are two required assumptions:

1   that two groups exist, a generally smaller 'multiply deprived' group ('poor') and a larger group that suffers from less deprivation ('non-poor').

2   that deprivation increases at a faster rate, as income falls, at lower income levels than at higher income levels.

However, there is agreement that both these assumptions are valid. Piachaud (1987) states "that there is genuine and severe poverty" (i.e. a group of people/households which can be defined as 'poor'); he also agrees that "In essence there is no dispute that deprivation increases as income falls, nor that, at low income levels, deprivation increases more rapidly as income falls than at higher income levels". Once these two key points are accepted the identification of a poverty line becomes a purely technical matter about which level of income best separates the two groups.

The level of income (or narrow band of income) at which the 'poor' and the 'not poor' groups (multiply deprived and less deprived) can best be separated is considered to be the poverty line/threshold. Obviously, there will never be perfect separation between these two groups since, even when a marked threshold exists, there will always be some overlap. For example, there are people with reasonable incomes who suffer from multiple deprivation owing to historic circumstances. They may only recently have got a job or paid off large debts. There are also people currently on low incomes who suffer little deprivation due to previously accumulated wealth. Other reasons for overlap turn on the comprehensiveness of the definition of the income variable; some people with a low cash income may also depend on subsidised meals or other benefits from an employer or be meeting some of their costs from savings. However, a good analysis will correctly classify the majority of cases (Gordon and Townsend, 1990).

The situation where two groups exist with a number of intermediate (noise) cases is a common problem to many subject areas. It is known statistically as 'chaining' and an example is shown in Figure 1.6 (Wishart, 1969; Everitt, 1993).

There are a large number of established statistical techniques that can be used to determine the best point of separation between such groups. These provide 'objective' means by which the poverty line/threshold can best be determined.

Figure 1.6
Two well separated groups (the poor and the non-poor)
with intermediate 'noise' points

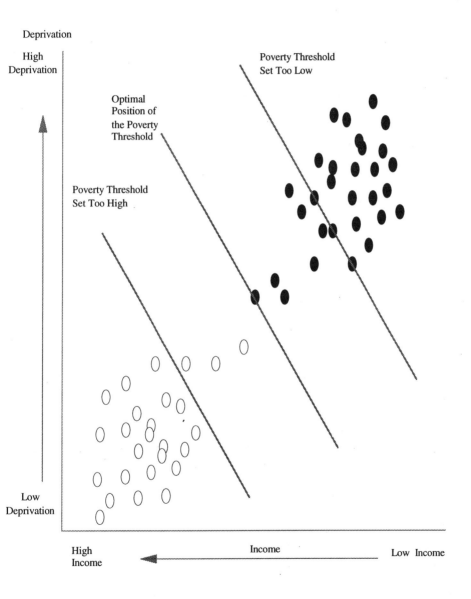

A simple but more 'subjective' way of measuring the poverty line/threshold is to ask people how much they would need to avoid poverty. The 1985-86 Booth Centenary Survey of Londoner's Living Standards asked "How many pounds a week do you think are necessary to keep a household such as yours out of poverty?" Interviewers were instructed to stress that income to be estimated must be total disposable income (i.e. income after taxes and deductions). From each individual estimate actual expenditure on housing per week was deducted (Townsend *et al*, 1987). A similar question was also asked in a related study carried out by MORI in Islington on behalf of the council (MORI, 1988). Table 1.3 shows the comparison between the Discriminant analysis poverty line and the self assessed weekly levels of income required to avoid poverty (Gordon and Townsend, 1989).

Table 1.3
Weekly income (in £s) required to surmount multiple deprivation
(Self-assessment and Discriminant analysis methods compared)

Household type	Self-assessment		Discriminant Analysis
	Greater London 1985-86	Islington 1987	Greater London 1985-86
Single person over 60	64	75	60
Couple under 60	104	107	75
Couple plus 2 children	109	132	110
Couple plus 3 children	118	121	125
Single parent plus 1 child	81	93	80

With the exception of the results for couples under 60, there is remarkably close agreement between these two methods. This demonstrates the possibility that by using statistical methods such as Discriminant analysis it may be possible 'objectively' to calculate a 'poverty line' for most household types that would correspond with the judgement of the majority of the population.

The American approach

There has been an official 'poverty line' in the United States of America (USA) since the mid 1960s, which is used by Federal Agencies to determine eligibility for benefits. In early 1992, the Committee on National Statistics of the National Academy of Sciences convened a panel of academic experts to conduct a 30 month study, requested by Congress, that includes an examination of the statistical issues involved in measuring and understanding poverty. The seriousness with which the

US Government treats the concept of poverty contrasts sharply with the attitude of the British Government which has consistently refused to identify any 'official' poverty thresholds.

In the USA, poverty thresholds are currently issued by the Bureau of the Census and were first developed in 1963/64 by Mollie Orshansky, an economist working for the Social Security Administration (Fisher, 1992). The poverty threshold is calculated for a family of any given size by multiplying the cost of the relevant 'economy food plan' by 3, for families of 3 or more, and by 3.7 for families of 2 people. The 'economy food plan' was developed by the Department of Agriculture for *"temporary or emergency use when funds were low"*. The multipliers of 3 and 3.7 are derived from the 1955 Household Food Consumption Survey, which showed that families of 3 or more typically spent a third of their after-tax income on food and families of 2 typically spent 27% of their after-tax income on food. The cost of the 'economy food plan' is adjusted by the Consumer Price Index (the American equivalent of the Retail Price Index).

The assumptions behind these poverty thresholds are: as income falls, all expenditure (food and non-food) is reduced proportionately until the amount spent on food is equal to the cost of the 'economy food plan'. At this point, non-food expenditure is considered to be minimal but adequate. These assumptions are obviously simplistic, however, Orshansky (1965) argued that, while they may not be sufficient "to state unequivocally how much is enough, it should be possible to assert with confidence how much, on average, is too little".

Although the American method for setting poverty lines is crude by modern standards, they at least have made an attempt to define 'objective' and meaningful poverty thresholds as a basis for benefit payments. By contrast, the British Income Support levels are based almost exclusively on political and historical criteria. For example, in the early 1980s, the basis for the uprating of State Retirement Pensions was changed from a link to average earnings to a link to the Retail Price Index. This change was largely political and not based on any assessment of the actual needs of pensioners, dependent on State Retirement Pensions.

Equivalisation

Equivalisation presents one of the major problems when determining the poverty line/threshold. Indeed, equivalisation is a major problem with all aspects of deprivation studies. It is self evident that the larger the household the more income will be needed to maintain the same standard of living. It is also clear that economies of scale exist within a household i.e. it does not cost a family of 4 twice as much as a family of 2 to maintain the same standard of living. However, it is not self-evident how much extra larger households need to have the same standard of living as smaller households.

There is general agreement that 'standard of living' like 'poverty' is only measurable 'relative' to society. McClements (1978) states:

"living standards describe the material well-being of the household or family unit as perceived by it and society as a whole, rather than personal happiness *per se.*"

Likewise, Jensen (1978) states:

"standard of living of a household is not an objectively defined function of its level of consumption, rather it is specified by the general consensus amongst members of the society about what the household's pattern of consumption is judged to represent in terms of material well-being."

Despite this agreement on definition, there is currently no methodology that allows the objective determination of equivalence scales in the same way that deprivation can be objectively measured. Many equivalence scales are unscientific because they are based on tautological reasoning.[8] The McClements' (1977) equivalence scale, used by the Department of Social Security for low income statistics, suffers from this problem (Muellbauer, 1979, 1980, Bardsley and McRae, 1982). Whiteford (1985) has argued that, while no objective equivalence scales have been derived, several proposed scales could be rejected on logical grounds. He stated:

"equivalence scales should be plausible, generally rising with the size of the household but showing economies of scale. A priori, it is implausible that a single individual requires only 49% of the income of a couple, as suggested by Podder, or that an individual requires 94% of the income of a couple, as suggested by Lazear and Michael. Similarly, the detailed basic equivalence scales derived by SWPS and ABS, using the ELES method, are implausible when they imply that the costs of a sole parent with two children are less than the costs of a sole parent with one child. What is a plausible estimate of the costs of a child is more difficult to determine. It can be suggested, however, that Seneca and Taussig's estimate that a child adds only 1% to the cost of a couple is implausible as is Habib and Tawil's estimate that a child adds 47%. Similarly, the pattern of additional costs implied by the detailed basic ELES equivalence scales is implausible - where the head works and the wife does not, the first child adds 11%, the second 6%, the third 16%, the fourth 3% and the fifth 17%. It is difficult to conceive of the reasons why this should be so."[9]

However, even after many proposed equivalence scales have been rejected on grounds of implausibility, numerous plausible scales remain (for example, Whiteford (1985), lists 59 scales, of which over half are plausible). This is problematic because the results obtained from a poverty study are sensitive to the equivalence scale used (Bradbury, 1989; Weir, 1992). Both the household composition of the 'poor' and the position of the poverty line can be influenced by equivalisation.

Therefore, in order accurately to determine the numbers of different sized households living in poverty, the likely position of the poverty line should be estimated before any equivalisation scales are applied.

The Breadline Britain approach

In the 1983 study, it was assumed that

> "poverty is a situation where such deprivation has a multiple impact on a household's way of life affecting several aspects of living thus, a family which just about manages but to do so does without an annual holiday, is deprived by today's standards; in our judgement, however, it is not in poverty. Deprivation has to have a more pervasive impact to become poverty."

Two criteria were identified for determining at what point multiple deprivation was likely to be causing poverty:

1 The poverty line should be drawn where the overwhelming majority of those who lacked necessities[10] have low incomes in the bottom half of the income range.

2 Their overall spending pattern should reflect financial difficulty rather than high spending on other goods.

By examining a large number of tables carefully, Mack and Lansley (1985) decided that: "A level of lack of one or two necessities is largely enforced though not overwhelmingly ... a level of lack of three or more necessities is, by contrast, overwhelmingly enforced".

The 'three or more necessities lacked' poverty line was later confirmed by regression analysis (Desai, 1986). Both the regression analyses and the examination of tables essentially do the same thing. They divide the surveyed households into two groups: the 'multiply deprived' and the 'less deprived', at the point which maximises the variation in income between the two groups and minimises the variations in income within the groups, i.e. the point where the overwhelming majority of the 'poor' group have low incomes and the overwhelming majority of the 'not poor' group have higher incomes.

A problem with the methods used in the 1983 study was that equivalisation was applied to allow a single analysis. As discussed in the previous section, equivalisation often distorts the data and make the results hard to interpret. Therefore, in the 1990 study, we attempted to identify the poverty threshold before equivalisation. The discriminant analysis procedure[11] of Townsend and Gordon (1989) was applied to all household types for which there was a sufficiently large sample size.[12] The optimum position for the poverty threshold was again found to be at the 'three or more necessities lacked' level.

Figure 1.7 shows the clear separation between the average incomes of the 'poor' and 'not poor' groups at the 'three or more necessities lacked' level by household type. The mean (average) incomes for each group are marked with a square and the bars represent the 95% confidence interval of the mean. The sample sizes for both groups, for each household type, are shown along the x axis. The 95% confidence intervals do not overlap for any household type except couples with one child. The overlap in this group is due to 3 households with very high incomes and deprivation scores of 3 or 4. These cases are, statistically, outliers and, if they are excluded, then the overlap disappears. However, as discussed previously, we would not expect perfect separation between the 'poor' and 'not poor' groups (these three households may only recently have achieved a high income) so we have not altered the data.

Figure 1.7 also illustrates the problem of equivalisation. There are clear differences in the average incomes of the 'poor' and 'not poor' groups for both retired and younger couples without children. However, there is a degree of overlap between the incomes of the 'poor' non-retired couples and the 'not poor' retired couples. The overlap is probably due to a number of causes; firstly, the income measure does not adequately take account of the wealth of retired households (their 'real' income has been underestimated), and, secondly, non-retired couples generally require a higher income than retired couples to maintain the same 'standard of living' because of the extra costs they incur when working. An equivalisation index that did not take account of the increased costs associated with working[13] would clearly yield biased results; which would underestimate the numbers of 'poor' non-retired couples and overestimate the numbers of 'poor' retired couples.

A good test of the reliability of the 'three or more necessities lacked' poverty line is to compare this 'objective' measure of poverty with people's opinion of whether they are genuinely 'poor'.

Table 1.4 shows that the group of households that answered that they are 'never poor' or 'don't know' have mean and median deprivation scores (number of lack of necessities) well above the poverty line (three plus). The households that consider they are 'poor all the time' have mean and median scores well below the objective poverty line. The 'sometimes' poor group has a mean score just above the poverty line, 63% of this group have a deprivation score of less than three. As would be expected, the 'sometimes poor' group contains many households who can objectively be measured to be on the margins of poverty or 'just poor'. It is clear that the objective categorisation of households into 'poor' and 'not poor' groups by the discriminant analysis method corresponds closely with people's own interpretation of their own circumstances. It should also be noted that 35% of respondents thought that their households were genuinely 'poor' now either 'all the time' or 'sometimes'.

Figure 1.7
Average net income of multiply deprived and less deprived households

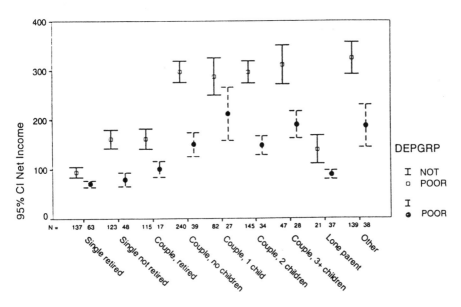

Type of household

Bars are 95% Confidence Intervals of the Mean

Table 1.4
Question 16: "Do you think you could genuinely say you are poor now, all the time, sometimes, or never?"

Are you genuinely poor? (n=1831)	Respondents (%)	Mean Deprivation Score	Median Deprivation Score
All the time	10	5.4	4
Sometimes	25	2.6	1
Never	64	0.6	0
Don't know	01	1.0	0

31

This emphasises the large number of people who have experienced at least a period of living in poverty recently. Only 1% of households had no view about whether they were genuinely 'poor' now: this again emphasises that 99% of respondents had some view about their own level of poverty.

Time and poverty

The division of the population into two groups, the 'poor' and 'not poor' is obviously an over-simplification which takes no account of the length of time spent living in poverty. Research in Europe and America has shown that, although at any one time a large number of households may experience poverty, for many this experience might be for only a relatively brief period.[14]

Table 1.5 shows that there are marked differences between European and North American countries in both the poverty rate and the likelihood of escaping from poverty. In Ireland, Luxembourg, The Netherlands and Sweden virtually no families with children lived continuously in poverty for the whole of a three-year period. In contrast, the majority of the poor in Canada and the United States remained in poverty for most of a three-year period. However, even in the United States, Bane and Ellwood (1986) found that about 60% of poverty spells lasted one or two years and only around 14% lasted eight or more years. It must be noted that these are single spells, some of which would have been followed rapidly by subsequent periods of poverty. Duncan et al (1993) have suggested that:

> "the static dichotomy of poor Vs not poor is very misleading and needs to be replaced by at least four dynamic categories of economic position - persistent poverty, transition poverty, the economically vulnerable and the financially secure."

Duncan et al (1993) also found, unsurprisingly, that transition rates out of poverty were higher the closer the households' incomes were to the poverty threshold. These studies of poverty dynamics lead to the prediction that those households who suffer from continuous or repeated spells of poverty are likely to be more deprived than households which suffer only from occasional or rare periods of poverty.

Table 1.5
Poverty rates and transition out of poverty for families with children with poverty defined as an equivalised income below 50% of the median income for the population (modified from Duncan *et al*, 1993)

Country	Poverty rate (% with income below 50% of median income of the whole population)	Transition out of poverty rate (% per year of the poor becoming non-poor)	Three year poverty rate (% of the population with incomes below 50% of median in all 3 years of a 3 year period)
Europe			
France	4.0	27.5	1.6
Germany (all)	7.8	25.6	1.5
German residents	6.7	26.9	1.4
Foreign residents	18.0	20.0	4.0
Ireland	11.0	25.2	N/A
Luxembourg	4.4	26.0	0.4
The Netherlands	2.7	44.4	0.4
Sweden	2.7	36.8	N/A
North America			
Canada	17.0	12.0	11.9
United States (all)	20.3	13.8	14.4
US white residents	15.3	17.0	9.5
US black residents	49.3	7.7	41.5

Table 1.6 shows that, in the Breadline Britain in the 1990s survey, there was a clear association between a respondent's history of poverty and their household's current level of deprivation. The majority of respondents who have lived in poverty 'often' or 'most of the time' can currently be objectively described as living in poverty i.e. they have both mean and median deprivation scores of three or more. It should be noted that 46% of respondents had lived in poverty at some time in the past and also that only 1% of respondents had no views about their history of poverty.

Table 1.6
Question 17: "Looking back over your adult life, how often have there been times in your life when you think you have lived in poverty by the standards of the time?"

Have you ever lived in poverty? (n=1831)	Respondents (%)	Mean Deprivation Score	Median Deprivation Score
Never	53	0.7	0
Rarely	15	1.4	0
Occasionally	19	2.3	1
Often	8	4.5	3
Most of the time	4	5.1	4
Don't know	1	2.0	0

In Table 1.7, the 'poor/multiply deprived' group has been further sub-divided by their history of poverty. The 'long term poor' group has been defined as households who have a deprivation score of three or more (objective poverty), consider that they are genuinely poor now 'all the time' (subjective poverty) and also have lived in poverty in the past either 'often' or 'most of the time'. Just over 4% of households are 'long term poor' and, as predicted, they have very high mean and median deprivation scores. However, the majority of the 'poor' group will probably not live in continuous poverty. For them, poverty is a transitory stage encountered due to temporarily adverse circumstances. The characteristics of this group are similar to those of the rest of the population and the composition of the 'poor' group will be discussed in detail in Chapter 3.

Table 1.7
Long term poverty/multiple deprivation

	Number of Households (%)	Mean Deprivation Score	Median Deprivation Score
Not poor	79.2	0.4	0
Poor	16.7	5.8	5.0
Long term poor	4.1	8.3	8.0

Common objections to poverty studies

There are a number of objections to poverty studies such as the Breadline Britain surveys, which are commonly voiced, particularly by those on the 'Right' of the political spectrum. These objections can be grouped into two main categories:

Anecdotal Denial This group of objections usually follows an argument such as "I know a family that can't afford three of the items in the Breadline Britain survey but they are not poor. Therefore, the Breadline Britain results cannot be correct." Objections of this type misunderstand the nature of scientific measurement. As previously discussed, we would not ever expect to be able to establish a poverty line that would correctly classify one hundred per cent of the population as 'poor' or 'not poor'. Inevitably, there will be some overlap and therefore there will be a small number of cases in which households lacking three or more items are incorrectly classified as 'poor'. These facts, however, do not negate the results which refer to the population as a whole and not to individual cases.

The Undeserving Poor This type of argument has a myriad of forms but generally assumes that "the households that lack three or more items are not really poor, they are lazy and shiftless and/or have chosen to waste their money on drink, cigarettes, drugs, gambling ....."[15] The main thrust of this argument is to show that the poor are poor only because of their own fecklessness and providing them with any extra resources would only encourage them in their reprehensible ways.

The attempt to divide the 'poor' into the 'deserving' (i.e. those who are poor through no fault of their own) and the 'undeserving' has a long history dating back at least to Elizabethan times. Indeed, it was concern about the 'residuum' (the Victorian name for the 'underclass') that resulted in the establishment of the social sciences in the 19th century. The residuum were the 'dangerous poor', the group of undeserving poor people who were 'criminally inclined and detached from the values of 'right-thinking society' (Stedman-Jones, 1984). The idea of a group of criminal, feckless poor people whose pathological culture and/or genes transmitted their poverty to their children, can be traced from the Victorian residuum through theories of pauperism, social problem groups and multiple problem families to the underclass arguments of today (Macnicol, 1987; Mazumdar, 1992). The problem of poverty was blamed on 'bad' genes before the Second World War and on 'bad' culture after the discrediting of the eugenics movement by the end of the War.[16] The underclass is currently claimed to suffer from a pathological 'culture of poverty/dependency' which causes their poverty (Bagguley and Mann, 1992).

These ideas are unsupported by any substantial body of evidence. Despite almost 150 years of scientific investigation, often by extremely partisan investigators, not a single study has ever found any large group[17] of people/households with any behaviours that could be ascribed to a culture or genetics of poverty. This failure does not result from lack of research or lack of resources. For example, the Transmitted Deprivation Programme of the 1970s lasted over 10 years, commissioned 23 empirical studies and cost over £3m at 1992 prices: the Pauper Pedigree Project of the Eugenics Society lasted over 20 years (1910-1933): the Social Survey of Merseyside Study lasted 5 years and the Problem Families Project started in 1947 and eventually petered out in the 1950s[18]. Neither these nor any other British study has ever found anything but a small number of individuals whose poverty could be ascribed to fecklessness or a 'culture/genetics of poverty/dependency'.

The 'culture of poverty/dependency' thesis requires that there is a significantly large, stable and relatively homogenous group of 'poor' people in order for a culture to develop that is different from the culture of the rest of society. The evidence we have on the prevalence and dynamics of poverty contradicts this thesis. As previously discussed (Table 1.6), 46% of respondents have experienced at least a brief spell of living in poverty at some time in their lives and 20% of households can 'objectively' be described as 'poor'. However, only 4% of households are currently 'poor' and also have a long history of poverty. The experience of poverty is a widespread but, for the large majority, relatively brief phenomenon. It is, therefore, unsurprising that there is little evidence that the 'poor' have a different culture from the rest of society. The ten year Transmitted Deprivation Programme concluded, from a comprehensive review of the literature, that "problem families do not constitute a group which is qualitatively different from families in the general population" (Rutter and Madge, 1976, p255) and, from the results of the 37 Transmitted Deprivation research projects, that "all the evidence suggests that cultural values are not important for the development and transmission of deprivation" (Brown and Madge, 1982, p226).

More recently Bagguley and Mann (1992) commented "what puzzles us is why both 'left' and 'right' academics find the concept of an emergent ... underclass so attractive when it has been so thoroughly destroyed by social scientific analysis."

Public attitudes to the poor

Despite the lack of evidence for the 'undeserving poor' thesis, there is still a fairly widespread view that the 'poor' spend a lot of their money on drink and cigarettes. No British deprivation study has attempted to measure the amount that multiply deprived households spend on alcohol. However, very detailed expenditure data are available from the annual Family Expenditure Survey (FES), which can be broken down by equivalised income.

Table 1.8 clearly shows that the households in the bottom 20% of the income range typically spend less per week on alcoholic drink and tobacco than all other households. This is unsurprising; the poorest households spend less on everything than all other households as they have less money to spend.

Table 1.8
Household expenditure on selected items for the top and bottom quintile groups of income and all households

Average weekly household expenditure (£)
(Figures in brackets are % of total expenditure)

Selected Expenditures	Lowest 20% (n=1484)	Highest 20% (n=1484)	All Households (n=7418)
Alcoholic drink	3.00 (3.2%)	20.94 (4.1%)	11.06 (4.1%)
Tobacco	3.51 (3.7%)	5.15 (1.0%)	5.38 (2.0%)
Food	22.85 (24.3%)	73.82 (14.3%)	47.66 (17.5%)
Housing (gross)	33.73 (35.8%)	91.45 (17.7%)	54.12 (19.9%)
Fuel, Light and Power	10.23 (10.6%)	16.28 (3.0%)	13.02 (4.8%)
Clothing and Footwear	5.22 (5.5%)	30.95 (6.0%)	16.39 (6.0%)
Motoring and Travel	6.98 (7.4%)	92.62 (17.9%)	42.86 (15.8%)
Total Expenditure	**94.22 (100%)**	**516.28 (100%)**	**271.83 (100%)**

Source: 1992 FES, Table 8

The General Household Survey (GHS) provides information on smoking and drinking patterns every two years. Table 1.9 from the 1990 GHS[19] shows that both men and women in households with gross weekly incomes of less than £100 drink less alcohol than the average household (Smyth and Browne, 1992).

Table 1.9
Alcoholic consumption level by sex and usual gross
weekly household income (%)
(1 unit is approximately a glass of wine/half a pint of beer/single measure of spirits)

Persons aged 16 and over   Great Britain: 1990

Units per week	£0.01-£100.00	Over £500.00	Total
Men	(n=655)	(n=1480)	(n=8097)
Non-drinker	14	3	6
Very Low (Under 1)	17	3	9
Low (1 to 10)	35	33	36
Moderate (11 to 21)	15	26	22
High (22 to 51+)	19	35	27
Women	(n=1378)	(n=1343)	(n=9424)
Non-drinker	20	6	12
Very Low (Under 1)	34	13	23
Low (1 to 7)	32	46	40
Moderate (8 to 14)	9	19	14
High (15 to 36+)	5	16	11

The lack of evidence for the 'culture of poverty' thesis would tend to indicate that it is based on prejudice rather than established fact. If this is correct, then you would predict that:

- Those who have the greatest knowledge of poverty (through direct or indirect personal experience) will be the least likely to believe that poverty results from fecklessness.

- If poverty increases, the numbers believing that poverty results from fecklessness will fall since more people will have direct or indirect knowledge of poverty.

Conversely, if the primary cause of poverty is due to laziness or lack of willpower of the 'poor', then you would expect the belief in the 'undeserving poor' thesis to increase with increased personal experience of poverty.

38

The 1983 and 1990 Breadline Britain Surveys asked respondents: "Why, in your opinion, are there people who live in need? Here are four opinions - which is the closest to yours?" A similar question had also been asked in a European Economic Community-wide survey in 1976 (EEC 1977) and these views are set out in the tables below.

Table 1.10
Why do people live in need? By all respondents (%)

	1976 EEC	1976 UK	1983 BBS (GB)	1990 BBS (GB)
Because they have been unlucky	16	10	13	10
Because of laziness and lack of willpower	25	43	22	20
Because there is much injustice in our society	26	16	32	40
It's an inevitable part of modern progress	14	17	25	19
None of these	6	4	5	3
Don't know	13	10	3	3

As the number of people living in poverty increased between 1976 and 1990, so the numbers of people who believed that the primary cause of poverty is 'laziness or lack of willpower' has fallen dramatically. In 1976, 43% of UK respondents considered that poverty was attributable to 'laziness or lack of willpower'. This was the highest figure of any EEC country. By 1990, only 20% of the British population still believed this. Conversely, the numbers of respondents considering that people live in need because 'there is much injustice in society' increased from 16% to 40% between 1976 and 1990. This shift in public attitudes is consistent with evidence that the primary causes of poverty are structural and not due to individual failings.

Tables 1.11, 1.12 and 1.13 show the response to Question 7 on the reasons why there are people who live in need, broken down by 'objective' and 'subjective' poverty. As expected, there appears to be a high correlation between a respondent's direct experience of poverty and their belief that the primary cause of poverty is injustice in society or misfortune rather than individual laziness or lack of willpower. This same pattern is found irrespective of whether objective (scientific) criteria or more subjective (individual perception) criteria are used to define poverty.

Table 1.11
The public's view of why people live in need by deprivation group (%)

Question 7: " Why, in your opinion, are there people who live in need?
Here are four opinions - which is closest to yours?"

	Deprivation Group		
	Less Deprived	Multiply Deprived	Long Term Poor
	(n=1450)	(n=306)	(n=75)
Because they have been unlucky	10	10	18
Because of laziness and lack of willpower	21	17	9
Because there is much injustice in our society	39	44	48
It's an inevitable part of modern progress	18	22	16
None of these	4	2	1
Don't know	9	5	9

In Table 1.11, 21% of the 'less deprived' group (objectively 'not poor') consider that people live in need because of laziness and lack of willpower, as do 22% of respondents who consider they could never describe themselves as 'genuinely poor' (Table 1.12) and 20% of respondents who have 'never lived in poverty' (Table 1.13). Conversely, only 9% of the 'long term poor' group, 10% of respondents who consider that they are 'genuinely poor all the time' and 11% of respondents who have lived 'most of the time' in poverty in the past, attribute the primary cause of poverty to laziness and lack of willpower. These findings are remarkably consistent considering the different sample sizes and compositions of these groups.

An equally consistent pattern emerges amongst those who consider the primary reason that people live in need is because 'there is much injustice in our society'. Thirty nine per cent of the 'less deprived' group, 36% of the 'never genuinely poor' group and 38% of the 'never lived in poverty' group, attribute living in need to injustice in society, compared with 48% of the 'long term poor', 50% of the poor 'all the time' and 50% of the poor 'most of the time' groups.

Tables 1.11, 1.12 and 1.13 also show that those respondents with the greatest direct experience of poverty are more likely to attribute the causes of living in need to bad luck than those with less experience of poverty. However, there is no clear trend with the attribution of living in need to an 'inevitable part of modern progress' although the middle groups ('multiply deprived', 'sometimes poor' and 'occasionally poor in the past') had similarly high levels of response to this question (i.e. 22%, 20% and 23% respectively). The reasons for this require further research.

Table 1.12
The public's view of why people live in need by present level of poverty (%)

Question 7: "Why, in your opinion, are there people who live in need?
Here are four opinions - which is closest to yours?"

	Are you genuinely poor?		
	Never	Sometimes	All the time
	(n=1166)	*(n=459)*	*(n=177)*
Because they have been unlucky	10	9	14
Because of laziness and lack of willpower	22	17	10
Because there is much injustice in our society	36	46	50
It's an inevitable part of modern progress	19	20	15
None of these	4	3	2
Don't know	9	6	10

Table 1.13
The public's view of why people live in need by history of poverty (%)

Question 7: "Why, in your opinion, are there people who live in need?
Here are four opinions - which is closest to yours?"

	Have you ever lived in poverty?				
	Never	Rarely	Occas-ionally	Often	Most of the time
	(n=977)	*(n=277)*	*(n=343)*	*(n=150)*	*(n=65)*
Because they have been unlucky	10	5	11	18	11
Because of laziness and lack of willpower	20	26	17	13	11
Because there is much injustice in our society	38	43	40	44	50
It's an inevitable part of modern progress	18	18	23	15	20
None of these	4	1	3	2	2
Don't know	10	7	6	8	6

The patterns found when the 'living in need' question is broken down by Head of Household social class (Table 1.14) are similar to those of the poverty questions but the trends are not as clear cut. This is as would be expected since, although experience of poverty is related to Head of Household social class (in general, the higher the social class, the less experience of poverty) this relationship is complex with numerous exceptions.

Table 1.14
The public's view of why people live in need by social class(%)

Question 7: "Why, in your opinion, are there people who live in need? Here are four opinions - which is closest to yours?"

	Social Class				
	AB (n=265)	C1 (n=476)	C2 (n=421)	D (n=346)	E (n=323)
Because they have been unlucky	10	8	10	10	14
Because of laziness and lack of willpower	24	18	20	20	18
Because there is much injustice in our society	39	40	37	43	43
It's an inevitable part of modern progress	15	24	20	16	16
None of these	4	4	3	3	2
Don't know	8	7	11	8	8

Table 1.15
The public's view of why people live in need by political orientation (%)

Question 7: "Why, in your opinion, are there people who live in need? Here are four opinions - which is closest to yours?"

	Political Orientation			
	Conservative (n=395)	Labour (n=435)	LibDems (n=122)	Green (n=61)
Because they have been unlucky	10	10	12	4
Because of laziness and lack of willpower	32	13	10	16
Because there is much injustice in our society	20	52	54	49
It's an inevitable part of modern progress	21	16	14	27
None of these	5	4	2	
Don't know	12	6	8	4

Table 1.16
The public's view of why people live in need by household type (%)

Question 7: "Why, in your opinion, are there people who live in need?
Here are four opinions - which is closest to yours?"

		Household Type			
	Retired	Lone Parents	Other Families with Children	Single People	Others no Children
	(n=439)	*(n=73)*	*(n=458)*	*(n=201)*	*(n=659)*
Because they have been unlucky	11	19	10	12	8
Because of laziness and lack of willpower	27	15	19	11	18
Because there is much injustice in our society	35	43	40	49	40
It's an inevitable part of modern progress	14	14	24	16	20
None of these	4	2	3	4	4
Don't know	9	6	6	9	10

Beliefs about the causes of poverty are clearly related to a respondent's political orientation (Table 1.15). Conservatives are two and a half times less likely than Labour, Liberal Democrat or Green supporters to believe that need is caused by injustice in society. Conversely, 32% of Conservatives believe that poverty is caused by 'laziness or lack of willpower' compared with 13%, 10% and 16% of Labour, Liberal Democrats and Greens, respectively. Greens are the most likely group to attribute living in need to an 'inevitable part of modern progress' (27%), followed by Conservatives (21%).

Household Type (Table 1.16) does not appear to be a major determinant of attitudes towards the causes of living in need, although single people (non-retired) are more likely than pensioners to believe in injustice in society and less likely than pensioners to believe in laziness and lack of willpower as causes.

Conclusion

The scientific 'objective' measurement of poverty is both possible and attainable. Deprivation studies, such as the Breadline Britain in the 1990s survey, provide objective and reliable criteria by which levels of poverty can be determined. These 'objective' measures generally correspond closely with the more 'subjective' individual's perceptions of their own levels of poverty. The relative concept of poverty provides the theoretical framework that permits this measurement.

Poverty increased during the 1980s and, by 1990, 20% of households could objectively be classified as 'poor'. Thirty-five per cent of respondents considered they were 'genuinely poor now' either 'all the time' (10%) or 'sometimes' (25%) (Table 1.4). Forty-six per cent of respondents have experienced at least a brief period of poverty at some time in the past (Table 1.6). Fortunately, for the overwhelming majority, their experience of 'living in poverty' is relatively brief. Only 4% of households, which can objectively be described as 'poor', also have a long history of living in poverty.

The public's attitudes to the causes of poverty have changed significantly during the 1980s. The number of people who consider that 'people live in need' because 'there is much injustice in society' more than doubled between 1976 and 1990 (from 16% in 1976 to 40% in 1990). Attitudes to the causes of poverty appear to be related to both direct and indirect experience of poverty.

Notes

---

1   Keyes and Kennedy (1992) examined all records of death between 1/9/1991 and 31/8/1992 notified to the coroners courts for Inner South London, Poplar, Westminster, St Pancras and Hammersmith. Additional information was obtained from the River Police.

2   The numbers of homeless people in Bed and Breakfast include a small number of people in a miscellaneous category, such as Lighthouse Keepers and people sleeping above fire stations.

3   The EAO was the Economic Adviser's Office at the Department of Health and Social Security

4   Sen (1983) has argued "there is ... an irreducible absolutist core in the idea of poverty. If there is starvation and hunger then, no matter what the relative picture looks like - there clearly is poverty." Examples of this absolutist core are the need "to meet nutritional requirements, to escape avoidable disease, to be sheltered, to be clothed, to be able to travel, to be educated ... to live without shame."

Townsend (1985) has responded that this absolutist core is itself relative to society. Nutritional requirements are dependent on the work roles of people at different points of history and in different cultures and foods available in local markets. Avoidable disease is dependant upon the level of medical technology. The idea of shelter is relative not just to climate but also to what society may use shelter for. Shelter includes notions of privacy, space to cook, work and play and highly cultured notions of warmth, humidity and segregation of particular members of the family as well as different functions of sleep, cooking, washing and excretion.

Much of the debate of absolute versus relative poverty revolves around the definitions of absolute and relative. Sen (1985) argued that "the characteristic feature of absoluteness is neither constancy over time nor invariance between societies nor concentration on food and nutrition. It is an approach to judging a person's deprivation in absolute terms (in the case of a poverty study, in terms of certain specified minimum absolute levels), rather than in purely relative terms vis a vis the levels enjoyed by others in society". This definition of absoluteness in non-constant terms is, from an operational point of view, effectively identical to the relative poverty concepts of Townsend and others.

5   Kurt Godel's (1931) Incompleteness Theorem demonstrated that any system of mathematics within which arithmetic can be developed is essentially incomplete. Even if an infinite number of axiomatic rules are shown to be true there would still remain 'true' arithmetic statements that could not be derived from these axiomatic rules. No mathematical system can ever be complete, unknowns will always remain (Nagel and Newman, 1958).

6   Much of the original work of these philosophers is difficult to understand. However, there are a number of simpler summaries of their ideas; for example Chambers (1978), *The Economist* (1981), Medawar (1984), Papineau (1987).

7   Excluding all summary motor offences i.e. parking tickets, etc.

8   Equivalent income is determined from equivalent consumption patterns, but in order to know what equivalent consumption is, equivalent income must first be known.

9   The equivalence scales mentioned are described in Podder (1971), Lazear and Michael (1980a, 1980b), ABS (1981), Seneca and Taussig (1971), Habib and Tawil (1974), SWPS (1981).

10   Lack of necessities refers to households that stated they did not have a necessity because they could not afford it and not to those households who lacked a necessity because they did not want it.

11   Discriminant analysis produces similar results to regression analysis and the examination of tables but involves much less effort in computing.

12   Household groups of one to four people, excluding lone parent households.

13   Such as the McClement's equivalisation index, used by the Department of Social Security.

14   Data on the length of time that households spend living in poverty is generally confined to arbitrary, income-based definitions of poverty: such as the numbers below 50% of median income. However, it is possible that deprivation-based poverty studies might show broadly similar results on the dynamics of poverty spells if such data were available.

15   A long list of different items can be inserted here, depending upon what it considered to be reprehensible to the prevailing 'middle class' morality of the time.

16   The eugenics movement was discredited both scientifically and politically by the late 1940s. Their arguments on differences in society resulting from the different genetic make-ups of groups did not stand up to the mathematics of the newly-emerging population genetics. The modern socio-biological attempts to revive eugenics arguments, likewise, do not stand up to close mathematical scrutiny (Gould, 1981; Kitcher, 1985; Maynard Smith and Warren, 1989). The revelations about the German Nazi concentration camps and the German mass-sterilisation programmes dealt eugenic theories a fatal political blow (Gould, 1985; Mazumdar, 1992). However the Bow Group of Conservative MPs is reported to have recently discussed the eugenic idea of breeding controls on the poor and criminal classes (*The Observer*, 28.11.93).

17   i.e. more than 1.5% of the population.

18   Key references for these studies are Brown and Madge (1982), Lidbetter (1933), Caradog-Jones (1934), Blacker (1937, 1952).

19   The 1990 GHS provides the most up to date data on drinking and smoking available at time of writing. Unfortunately, the published report did not contain information on smoking broken down by household income.

2 The poverty line: methodology and international comparisons

Peter Townsend

Introduction

Questions about the definition of poverty and the 'poor' have always governed attempts to establish scientific methodology for the study of these phenomena. Governments and international agencies have not been eager to finance genuinely independent and necessarily complex scientific work and, as a consequence, the vast literature on the subject is permeated with inconsistencies and contradictions. The science of poverty measurement is probably at the stage of pre-Newtonian physics.

Should the poverty line be arbitrary or objective?

If poverty **is** a measurable or observable phenomenon, then the specification of a 'poverty line', to distinguish the 'poor' from the 'non-poor', is not an arbitrary matter. There is bound to be disagreement about the criteria used to draw that line and any method agreed upon by the scientific community may in the future be replaced by successively more sophisticated and comprehensive measures. It is not enough to examine the spread of incomes and other resources in a population (such as wealth, property, employee welfare in kind and free or subsidised state and local services) and devise an arbitrary cut-off point at a low level of income. Even small variations can have a significant impact on the conclusions drawn. Thus, a poverty line drawn arbitrarily at 40%, instead of 50%, of mean household expenditure lowered the poverty rate for the United Kingdom (UK) more than it did on average in the EC (Eurostat, 1990, p23). See also Hagenaars *et al*, 1994.

As the authors of a detailed comparison of two EC member states concluded:

> "...different choices [in the construction of a measure] can change the conclusions drawn as to the relative extent of poverty in the two countries. Apparently innocuous differences in definitions can have major consequences. The degree of poverty in two countries such as France and the United Kingdom can be made to appear quite different depending on the choice of central tendency, on whether we count in terms of households or individuals, on the equivalence scale, and on the treatment of housing costs and housing benefit." (Atkinson *et al*, 1993)

The choice of 'equivalence scale' (Townsend and Gordon, 1992, pp. 8-14 and Whiteford, 1985) deserves particular attention. The arbitrary choice of poverty line has to be adjusted for different types and sizes of households. It is logically absurd to apply criteria for an adjustment between large and small families while at the same time denying the need for criteria to draw the line in the first place. Drawing the line for each major type of household is in fact an integral part of the scientific exercise.

A further problem arises when deciding on a necessary income level for different individuals or different income 'units' within the household. The demographic structure of households and society as a whole, the level and distribution of Gross National Product and the relationship between the levels of resources and levels of need (in **any** scientific sense in which that term is accepted) are continually changing. Therefore, any measure adopted must be able to be adjusted, or automatically adjust itself, in relation to these changes. Why should anyone take seriously the results of applying an arbitrary poverty line? Cannot governments dismiss the seriousness of any problem and the methodology of its measurement as so much conjecture?

Should the poverty line be absolute or relative?

Since 1945, the international agencies have tended to prefer 'absolute' poverty as a conceptual basis when comparing conditions in different countries. More accurately, they have preferred this concept to be applied to the poorer 'developing' countries. The term appears to have been adopted for two reasons. Firstly, it seemed to refer only to the basic necessities of life - especially the minimum nutrients for ordinary physical activity. Secondly, the basic necessities of life were supposed not to vary with time or place: but be fixed. As societies have developed rapidly in the last 50 years and living standards have diverged and become more complex, both reasons for using an 'absolute' criterion have come under scrutiny. How are the necessities of life to be defined? Necessities to do what? Survive until tomorrow? Do a job of work? Provide food, fuel, shelter and clothing for a growing family? Should citizens be able to fulfil their social obligations of marriage, family, friendship, employment and community?

There is another set of questions in relation to the concept that necessities are 'fixed' in time and location. Does the same list of operational necessities apply as appropriately to a 'modern' as to a 'traditional' society, or to a 'post-industrial' as to an 'industrial' society? The question applies as much to single countries at different times as to two or more countries at widely different stages of development. Why should a basket of marketable necessities selected, say in 1950, apply equally well in 1994 in the same country? If that basket of goods does not need to be changed after 40 or 50 years, does that imply that it was equally relevant to the conditions of 50 years, or even 150 years, previously? Is it equally relevant to the conditions of less-developed countries like India and China in 1994?

There are very real problems in using price indices to maintain a 'real' poverty line over time. In 1991, the World Bank defined a poverty line for 'poor' countries as $1 a day per person at 1985 prices. The trading and social upheavals of the late 1980s and early 1990s - internationalisation of the market, reduction of public sector subsidies and services, privatisation and the reduction of labour's share of national income - have all established at least the possibility of reconsidering the definition and weighting of basic necessities in many 'poor' countries in 1994.

The same points apply even more forcefully to the United States (US) poverty line. This is based on a low cost food plan derived from data from the 1955 Household Food Consumption Survey (see Chapter 1). Small changes have been made in methodology in the three decades since the measure was introduced but, in 1994, the poverty line is still defined in roughly the same way.[1] A major objection is that necessities are defined more in terms of consumables than, for example, activities and services. No investigation appears to have been made of the scope and proportion of legitimate necessities nor has the rationale for the selection of the minimum quantity of those necessities been adequately reviewed.

Another objection is that US society has changed radically since the 1960s and it is hard to justify the continued use of such an out-dated measure. The third objection must be that, since the 1960s, scientists and other professional observers have realised that an individual's membership of society and their relationships and obligations within that society play a large part in the specification of their necessities and no account is taken of this in the low cost food plan.

Does the poverty line recommended for the Third World provide the right international model?

One problem in studying the phenomenon of poverty is that assumptions that are made by many commentators about one country or region are inconsistent with those made about another country or region. Whilst this criticism is accepted readily enough when comparing, for example, the UK and India, commentators are less apologetic when asked to explain why different standards are not adopted for Scotland, Wales and Ireland when compared with England. These regions are felt to be located in a common economy and social order. However, it is important for a common set of scientific principles to be applied. The argument has to be examined in relation to a range of other countries. A common mistake is to define poverty differently for Eastern and Western Europe, North and South America and First and Third Worlds.

An illustration is provided by the World Bank, which has conceded a "loss of momentum during the 1980s" in reducing poverty and is developing a new strategy (World Bank, 1993a). "Poverty reduction is the benchmark against which our performance as a development institution must be judged", stated Lewis T. Preston, President of the World Bank (28 April 1993). But what is the benchmark? The 'poverty line' is defined, at 1985 prices, as "$31 per person per month or $1 per day at US purchasing power parity (PPP)" (World Bank, 1993a, p4; and see also World Bank, 1990, especially pp25-29). For 1990, this calculation produces an estimate of 1,133 million 'poor' in the developing world. "An extra $0.70 per day added to the poverty line implies a doubling of the number of people counted as being poor" (World Bank, 1993a, p4).

This revealing statistic shows how important it is to get the measure right initially. In their 1990 report, the World Bank had "argued the case for basing international comparisons" on this 'poverty line'. However, this measure differs from previous measures put forward by the Bank and is inconsistent with definitions of 'absolute poverty' and the 'poverty line' given in the same report. Thus, absolute poverty is "the position of an individual or household in relation to a poverty line the real value of which is fixed over time"; and the poverty line is "the standard of living (usually measured in terms of income or consumption) below which people are deemed to be poor" (World Bank, 1993a, p. vii).

It is clear that the living standard below which people are deemed to be 'poor' is, in practice, a fixed standard for which there is no country or regional variation and for which no criteria independent of *"$1 per day"* are given. For Latin America and the Caribbean, the World Bank actually adopted a different poverty line of $2 per day (World Bank, 1993a, p6). Earlier, the Bank had implied that its concept of poverty could be extended to the industrial countries. Poverty was defined as "the inability to attain a minimal standard of living", which in turn was defined by the expression: "Household incomes and expenditures per capita are adequate yardsticks" (World Bank, 1990, p25). However, income and expenditure measures do not capture dimensions of welfare such as access to public goods and services, clean drinking water and other 'common property' resources.

The authors of the Report do not attempt to produce a more consistent or 'objective' poverty line. All that appears to be necessary is to examine the drawbacks in relation to some norm - namely a 'consumption-based' poverty line.

This "can be thought of as comprising two elements: the expenditure necessary to buy a minimum standard of nutrition and other basic necessities and a further amount that varies from country to country, reflecting the cost of participating in the everyday life of society" (*ibid*, p26). The first is believed to be unproblematic. The cost of calorie intakes and other necessities can be calculated by "looking at the prices of the foods that make up the diets of the poor." The second "is far more subjective; in some countries indoor plumbing is a luxury, but in others it is a necessity"(*ibid*, pp26-27). This is a very odd statement. In what senses is the need for indoor plumbing, as distinct from the need for food, 'subjective'? And when is it a 'luxury' and when a 'necessity'? Does not the cost of food, as much as the cost of plumbing, reflect participation in the everyday life of society? If the latter is a 'luxury' in some societies does that mean that food never is?

In this account of the World Bank's procedures, I have tried to concentrate on the unexplained and unresearched elements in the specification. Indeed, at one point, the text suggests that country-specific poverty lines are plotted against per capita consumption "for thirty-four developing and industrial countries" but the figure on the same page shows only the plotted figures for the poorest 12 countries among them. For the 22 richer countries, country-specific poverty lines are not plotted. The Bank's poverty measurement cannot, therefore, remain acceptable in international practice.

Other international agencies compound the problem. The poverty line is defined by United Nations Development Programme (UNDP) as "that income level below which a minimum nutritionally adequate diet plus essential non-food requirements are not affordable" (UNDP, 1993 p225). The way in which such an "adequate diet and essential non-food requirements" are defined as appropriate for different countries and the criteria used to determine what is 'not affordable' are not investigated.

A report for the International Fund for Agricultural Development seems to introduce a measure of flexibility into a 'fixed' poverty line. It takes note of measures which originate nationally and which depend on more sophisticated investigation of changes in consumption as well as consumption prices. Thus their poverty line is:

"a commodity bundle tied to the minimum requirement (calories and protein for food, and some notional minimum for non-food items), and the determination of an appropriate set of prices to be applied to individual commodities to calculate the poverty expenditure and income." (Jazairy *et al*, 1992, p461)

Over the years, the International Labour Organisation (ILO) has contributed to a more 'structural' interpretation of poverty and its causes (International Institute for Labour Studies, 1993 but also see Franklin, 1967). In particular, its work on the structure of the labour market and access to that market balances the monetarist perspective of the IMF and World Bank. In the 1970s, the ILO began to explain poverty in terms of lack of community utilities or infrastructure - water, sanitation, health centres, primary schools and transport. The contribution to understanding poverty and its alleviation by means of the development of measures of collective or community need, as distinct from individual need, deserves renewed attention. Thus, it has been pointed out that the World Bank's 1990 report on poverty "represents a step away from neoliberalism and back toward the Bank's attitude of the 1960s: that the continuing existence of the poor in poor nations is the development problem. Indeed, the insistence [in the Bank's annual development reports] on remedying water and air pollution resembles nothing more strongly than 20-year-old strategies aimed at satisfying developing countries' basic needs." (Taylor, 1992, p57) The ILO's preoccupations of the 1970s are back in fashion (Townsend, 1993a).

Do the poverty lines in the 'rich' countries set the right example?

Any reference to the 'rich' countries illustrates the nature of the scientific problem. The US accepts a poverty line for its own territory based on assumptions far removed from those applied to the poorer countries. The line is based on the cheapest budget which can achieve adequate nutrition and conform in its overall distribution with the budgets of low-income families in the US. The specific amounts vary according to household size and composition and are adjusted each year in accordance with price changes (Committee on Ways and Means, 1992). In 1990, the poverty line varied from $6,652 for a person living alone to $26,848 for a household of nine or more members (US Department of Commerce, 1992, p11). Depending on size and type of household, therefore, the poverty line in the US varied from $3000 to over $6000 per person per annum (or between $8 and $18 a day).

This means that, at 'comparable purchasing standards', the US poor are allowed between 8 and 18 times as much income as the poor in countries like China, India and Mozambique. The likely scientific implication is not that the US poverty line must be lowered. On the contrary, available evidence suggests that Third World poverty lines should be raised substantially.

In Europe, the criteria applied are different from those in the US. In launching the Second European Poverty Programme (1985-1989), the Council of Ministers defined the 'poor' as "persons whose resources (material, cultural and social) are so limited as to exclude them from the minimum acceptable way of life in the Member State in which they live" (Commission of the European Communities (EEC, 1991, p2). This definition was reiterated subsequently in a report from the Statistical

Office of the European Communities (Eurostat, 1990). The concept of 'resources' had already been defined, in a previous Council decision, as "goods, cash income, plus services from public and private resources" (EEC, 1981, p8).

Sadly, criteria for giving effect to this definition were never used in the formulation of successive anti-poverty programmes. Instead, the number of those with less than 50%, and later 40%, of average disposable income in each member country was regarded as "a good indicator of the extent of poverty" (*ibid*, p2). The reasons for the adjective "good" were not specified. This indicator is a "relative income standard" - a term used to differentiate the standard, which is based on the choice of a point in the spread of income, from one which is based on criteria external to income (Townsend, 1979, especially pp. 247-248). The problem has been compounded in reports from sub-divisions of the EC and from other agencies[2].

In 1990, this standard would have provided a poverty line for a person living alone of approximately £3,500, or, at US rates, nearly $6000. For a family of four, the poverty line would have been about $17,000 per annum, compared with a figure of $13,359 for the US poverty line for the same family. Thus, although the US and Europe follow different procedures in measurement, in practice they both apply assumptions in constructing a poverty line radically more generous than those applied by international agencies to poor countries.

I doubt whether this form of discrimination can be allowed to persist. Once the poverty line is defined in a discriminatory fashion, there is a knock-on effect. The collected evidence becomes skewed. Theories are evolved to explain distorted evidence and policies are correspondingly evolved to suit that distorted evidence - but not reality. This happens because international agencies and others dodge the responsibility of defining the precise scope of human and social needs and because they do not specify criteria for estimating the collective and individual costs of meeting those needs minimally.

A definition is therefore required which stands the test of time and is genuinely international. The arbitrary selection of $1 per person per day as a poverty line conforms with an ideology which pre-supposes that economic growth is the principal strategy to overcome poverty (see World Bank, 1993a, p. ix) and suggests that the needs of poor countries are less than those of the rich countries. This carries racist imputations[3] which cannot be accepted in the 1990s and also results in entirely misplaced economic strategies.

What are the implications of defining a poverty line across countries and for defining a poverty line in one country through time?

There is a close link between specifying a common definition of poverty across countries and specifying a definition which will be appropriate for a country at different times. Societies change in crucial respects in successive decades - in terms of wealth, type of employment and forms of social and cultural institutions. However, there will be continuities as well as discontinuities. At successive stages in the history of different societies, social scientists have defined a poverty line which represents something very different from applying a price index to adjust for inflation and reconstitute the same poverty line in 'real' terms. Scholars have called attention, for example, to the **income elasticity of the poverty line** (Fisher, 1992b). There is evidence from different countries that minimum budgets devised by experts and low income measures based on public opinion tend to rise more closely in accordance with trends in GDP than with price increases. For example, "there is an impressive body of evidence that in the United States, both 'expert'-devised poverty/subsistence budgets and 'subjective' low-income measures rise in real terms when the real income of the population rises" (Fisher, 1992b, p23). The evidence cited includes answers to a routine Gallup Poll question, budget studies in New York city between 1903 and 1959, and a set of minimum subsistence budgets traced between 1905 and 1960.

Thus, a Gallup Poll question: "What is the smallest amount of money a family of four (husband, wife and two children) needs each week to get along in this community?" has been posed regularly in surveys over many years[4]. Fisher cites a series of review studies from the 1960s onwards which show, for spans of ten or more years, that the average amount specified by respondents rises between 0.6% and 0.85% for every 1.0% rise in the real average income of the population (Fisher, 1992b, pp. 23-26). The standards set by household budget experts have tended to follow the same pattern.

Can an international poverty line be developed?

In principle, there is a solution to the question raised in this paper. It is to identify forms of deprivation and multiple deprivation in relation to the whole range of material conditions and social activities and customs in all countries and to investigate what thresholds of income (and other resources for both individuals and community) can be shown to eliminate or greatly reduce such deprivation. That is a complex scientific assignment but the interrelationship of forms of nutritional, material, environmental, work-related and social deprivation is no more complex than the interrelationship of genes or sub-atomic particles. Once a scientific problem is comprehensively specified, means can be found to illuminate and then to resolve it.

There is overwhelming evidence of the rapid internationalisation of economic and social conditions. The international market is becoming the governing global institution. Multi-national corporations and international agencies have assumed much greater powers than ever before in determining world events. Groups of nation-states, like the EC, are increasingly acting in a concerted way to facilitate international capital flows and trade. The power of the nation-state is waning as a consequence. National boundaries are becoming less important, although one outcome of the regionalisation of some nation-states has been the expression of petty nationalism and ethnic rivalries. The cost of labour in the rich countries is being driven down towards the cheaper costs in poorer countries (Sen, 1993).

Despite annual and country variations, the level of overall unemployment in the rich countries has steadily increased since the 1960s. Among the rich countries, the US and the UK are not alone in experiencing widening inequality and growing poverty, in the 1980s and 1990s. Public facilities and services are declining, especially in countries turning towards market privatisation. There is a pressing need for more public housing. Protective labour, health and safety controls are being abandoned and no longer exercise much balancing influence. These circumstances are leading to Third World conditions and wages in First World countries. Ghetto conditions and mortality rates in some parts of the richest countries of the world are worse than those of most of the rural poor in Third World countries.

By 2050, the inequalities between rich and poor in each nation may have reached levels which are more striking than average differences today between rich and poor countries. This is illustrated in Figures 2.1 and 2.2.

Figure 2.1 shows the two forms of inequality - the huge difference between rich and poor countries when income is standardised in relation to the average income per person in the US and the already huge inequality in most countries between the average income of the richest 20% and that of the poorest 20%.

Figure 2.2 shows groups of countries categorised according to their income, again expressed as a percentage per person of the corresponding income per person in the US. The figure shows that, while there are sharp differences between the poorest countries and the richest countries, the poorest 20% in the 22 highest income countries have an average income only about the same as the average of that in the 43 'lower middle income' countries and only about twice that of the richest 20% in the 40 'low income' countries. The problems of poverty are evidently more widespread than generally assumed or, indeed, documented.

Figure 2.1

The poor and the rich of different countries according to their income standardised in "international purchasing" dollars

GDP per person as %of GDP per person in the US

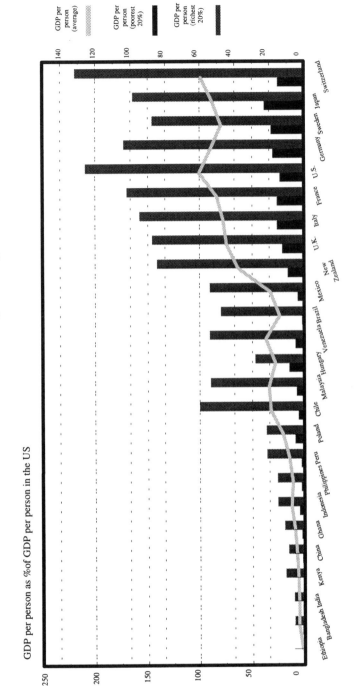

Source: World Bank, World Bank Development Report 1993, pp 296-297 and 319-321

Note: GDP per person for US = 100

58

Figure 2.2

GDP per person as a percentage of GDP per person in the US
- grouping low, middle income and high income countries

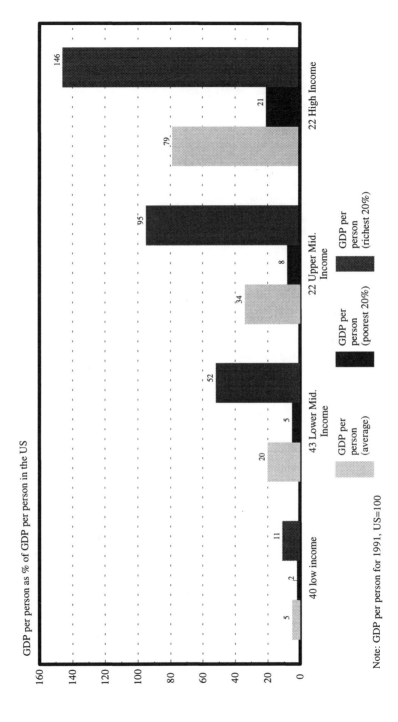

GDP per person as % of GDP per person in the US

Note: GDP per person for 1991, US=100

What are the alternative poverty lines for the UK?

The argument for an international poverty line sets the scene for the discussion of what might be an appropriate adaptation for rich countries like the UK and the US, as well as for the poorest countries of the world. As an example, I propose to review alternative standards which might be adapted for use in the UK. There are a number of interesting variations on offer.

The World Bank's 'global' standard

This is a "universal poverty line [which] is needed to permit cross-country comparison and aggregation" (World Bank, 1990, p27). Poverty is defined as "the inability to attain a minimal standard of living" (*ibid*, p26). Despite its acknowledgement of the difficulties in including, in any measure of poverty, the contribution to living standards of public goods and common-property resources, the World Bank settles for a standard which is 'consumption-based' and which, as discussed above, comprises "two elements: the expenditure necessary to buy a minimum standard of nutrition and other basic necessities and a further amount that varies from country to country, reflecting the cost of participating in the everyday life of society" (World Bank, 1990, p26).

The first of these elements is stated to be "relatively straightforward" because it could be calculated by "looking at the prices of the foods that make up the diets of the poor" (*ibid*, pp. 26-27). However, the second element is "far more subjective; in some countries indoor plumbing is a luxury, but in others it is a 'necessity'" (*ibid*, p27). For operational purposes, the second element was set aside and the first assessed as PPP (Purchasing Power Parity) - \$370 per person per year at 1985 prices for all the poorest developing countries.

Strengths. The standard is simple to comprehend and apply. It does not depend on the arduous and continuous collection and compilation of data about types as well as amounts of resources, changing patterns of necessities and changing construction of standards of living.

Weaknesses. It is not in fact a 'global' poverty line at all and is not assumed to be applicable to countries other than the poorest. On the Bank's own admission, an international poverty line which is more than 'consumption-based' should, ideally, be constructed. No cost is estimated for the second 'participatory' element of the definition. The logic of the Bank's own argument is not followed; the minimum value of the poverty line is underestimated and the number of poor in the world are therefore also underestimated.

The first element of the definition of the poverty line is neither rigorously investigated nor defended in respect of the type, number and amounts of necessities **other** than food. Equally importantly, variations in the sheer quantity of the diet required among populations with widely varying work and other activities, obligations and customs, as well as in the types of diet socially preferred or indeed available in local markets, and at what cost, are left unexplored. Again, the possibility that the second element of the definition might apply to the poorest countries and therefore demand scientific investigation and expert discussion, is also ignored. Although the Bank constructed a graph to show the rising real per capita value of 'country-specific' poverty lines in relation to average per capita consumption, the graph did not in fact fulfil this function. It merely showed an upper and a lower poverty line fixed by the Bank in dollars at 1985 prices for a small number of poor countries in relation to the average per capita consumption in those countries. The procedure offers no basis for UK adaptation.

European relative income standard

This is a standard which depends only on a criterion of low income rather than any independent condition or state of need. The choice of the standard seems to depend only on consideration of the distribution of income, and political as well as social values are plainly embodied in the choice. The most common indicator is 40%, or 50%, of the mean disposable household income, or expenditure, in a country. I have proposed the epithet 'European' mainly because, from the 1970s, European agencies and research institutes took the lead in using income cut-off points as means of identifying the numbers and composition of poor, in contrast to the different approaches to poverty line construction in both the US and, for the Third World, the World Bank and other international agencies.

In one UK study started at the end of the 1960s, the 'relative income standard' of poverty was distinguished from the state's standard and from the deprivation standard (Townsend, 1979, pp241-262). However, the UK's membership of the EC is leading to the absorption of national income measures into more conventional EC practice.

A variation on the relative income standard described above is the identification of income strata, such as decile groups or quintile groups, below average household income. This is the standard represented by the Households Below Average Income (HBAI) analyses carried out every two years (from 1994, annually) in the UK and published by the Department of Social Security (DSS). Other 'low-income' measures have been reviewed extensively in Canadian work (especially Wolfson and Evans, 1989; Canadian Council on Social Development, 1984).

Strengths. Most European states conduct income and expenditure surveys and maintain administrative information about income distribution. These data are easily available for analysis and can be compared in a standardised form. The results may vary from year to year, in proportion to population, and are therefore of more significance in relation to rates of economic growth, unemployment and employment and demographic change, than fixed divisions by decile or quintile group.

Weaknesses. The selection of a cut-off point low on the income scale is not related to any strict criteria of need or deprivation. The selection of cut-off point does in practice hold important implications for each country, which are only now beginning to be analysed and reported (as in Atkinson *et al*, 1993; Atkinson 1990b, and Atkinson, 1991). Different choices in the construction and operational application of the cut-off points can lead to surprisingly diverse results in the extent and composition of 'poverty' in different countries. The variation of the European relative income standard used by the UK, (the HBAI series) lacks the advantages and shares the disadvantages of the European standard. It also has a number of additional weaknesses - for example in the choice of median rather than mean in analysing information for each of the lower deciles, in obscuring year to year trends and making comparisons between certain substantial sub-categories of poor very difficult (see, in particular, Townsend and Gordon, 1992).

The State's standard of poverty

The minimum standards of benefit (or wage) sanctioned and institutionalised by the state, usually on test of means, have been treated in many studies as a 'social' standard of poverty. In some countries these are called social or national assistance, or income support, scales and in France the Revenue Minimum d'Insertion (RMI). Thus, by comparing household and individual income and expenditure derived from surveys with the minimum entitlements for comparable households and individuals, estimates can be produced of the numbers in the population with incomes of less than, the same as, or slightly above, these specific levels. This approach was pioneered in the 1960s and adopted for many different countries (see, for example, Townsend, 1979, Chapter 6; Oppenheim, 1993).

Strengths. Governments are obliged to concede that the standard of low income exists (because it is one which they have established through legislation and administrative follow-up) and it can be debated in terms of its 'adequacy'. While they may argue that families are sometimes expected to have small amounts of resources additional to benefit, they are nonetheless under pressure to rationalise the minimum levels of benefit. In that process, they must offer indirect, if not direct, criteria for the contribution the levels of benefit are supposed to make to the reduction of poverty.

Weaknesses. The standard institutionalised by the state may have little relationship to any scientific, or even social, criteria of need or deprivation. Moreover, there are difficulties in using the standard either to describe historical trends or to make comparisons between countries. Periods when the levels of benefit have been relatively generous and countries where the levels are relatively generous, produce disproportionately high rates of poverty, as the DSS in the UK has been quick to point out. The chequered history of the determination of benefit scales reveals some of the difficulties of interpreting these as a poverty 'standard' (Atkinson, 1990a; Veit-Wilson, 1989). As Atkinson concludes:

> "Britain has the dubious advantage that it has experimented extensively with a minimum income guarantee, and we have seen its shortcomings. The saying of Santayana that those who do not remember the past are condemned to repeat it, should perhaps be extended to include those who do not learn from the experience of their neighbours. A means-tested second tier is not the route for Europe to follow." (Atkinson *et al*, 1993, p15)

These depend on surveys of consumption. One influential example in the UK was produced following a series of research studies sponsored by the Joseph Rowntree Foundation (for example, Bradshaw, 1993a, and Bradshaw, 1993b). There are two standards, a 'low-cost' budget and a 'modest-but-adequate' budget. The 'low-cost' budget "includes items which more than two-thirds of the population regard as 'necessities' or which more than three-quarters of the population actually have. Only the cheapest items are included. It, therefore, represents a frugal level of living"[5] (Bradshaw, 1993a, p3). Authority for the detailed specifications was derived from "nutritionists, home economists and social scientists specialising in the domestic economy" and from a range of similar work completed in the US (from 1946), Sweden, the Netherlands, Norway, and Germany (*ibid*, pp3 and 6). This approach is intended to go beyond meagre definitions of either minimum subsistence or absolute poverty (*ibid*, p6) and draws on a range of previous work in the UK, including that on the 'cost' of children (Piachaud, 1979; Piachaud, 1984; and Oldfield and Yu, 1993).

The methodology corresponds with precedents set in a large number of countries. For example, in a review of alternative budget-based expenditure norms prepared for a panel on poverty measurement of the Committee on National Statistics of the US National Academy of Sciences, Watts distinguishes between three alternative budget standards - 'market basket', 'gross-up' and 'category' standards. The first covers necessities picked out from a wide range of consumer purchases. The second concentrates on minimum food costs and 'grosses up' the total budget from estimates of those costs. This approach closely resembles the procedure used over the years in the construction of the US poverty line, following Orshansky's recommendations (see Orshansky, 1965; and the historical review by Fisher, 1992b and 1992c). The third budget standard establishes a small number (usually 7-10) of spending categories - such as spending on food, housing, transportation, health care, child and other dependent care, clothing and clothing maintenance, and personal, e.g. dental care and haircuts. Watts concludes that the third standard offers the "most promising of the budget-based approaches" (Watts, 1993, p20; and see also Renwick and Bergmann, 1993).

Strengths. The strength of the methodology lies in its apparent practicality - using expenditure data and professional expertise about low-cost budgeting. This brings expert pressure to bear on Government policies. As the report concludes: "If the low-cost budget costs £36 per week more than the Income Support scales, then government can be asked to specify which budget items they believe that claimants should do without" (Bradshaw, 1993a, p31). The approach is also realistic - being dependent on country-specific information which requires a lot of effort to collect and keep up-to-date (Bradshaw, 1993a, p30). The fact that the standard is practical and specific makes it publicly and politically plausible.

Weaknesses. Among the problems of this methodology is the circularity of the reasoning. The transformation of actual amounts and patterns of household expenditure into 'desirable' or 'necessary' amounts and patterns of expenditure should use criteria which are scientifically independent of expenditure, otherwise the reasoning is tautological. It is important to investigate empirically 'needs' independent of budgetary resources and outlay. It is not the intensive scrutiny and elaborate analysis of household expenditure which will provide the answer to what level of income is required by different households in present day society. It is the investigation across the whole of society of activity conditions, customs, patterns and role obligations, on the part of interacting groups and communities as well as individuals and households, to find whether there is a high correlation between level of activity, deprivation and level of income. The social and material effects of a low level of income or expenditure have to be investigated not the composition or scope and balance of that income or expenditure.

The desirability of making reference to external criteria applies as much to the choice of equivalence scales as to the selected level on the income scale. The income 'needed' by different members of a household in relation to its (usually male) head cannot be derived from the existing amount and division between them of expenditure or income. Forms of discrimination which exist in contemporary society, related to gender, ethnicity, disability and age are implicit in the current or conventional disposition of either income or expenditure. Unless these forms of discrimination can be corrected by applying the independent criteria of need to the divisions of income and expenditure, they will be embodied as assumptions in the formulation of the 'household budget standards'. Some have suggested that the approach is paternalistic in its concern about consumption and the nature of that consumption (Atkinson, 1985a).

The methodology is also weighted too heavily towards the resources required to buy market commodities, rather than the resources required to satisfy collective needs for services and utilities and to fulfil social obligations - in parenthood, work-roles and citizenship, for example. In other words, the respects in which need is collective and in which resources therefore have to be collective too is not investigated.

Perceived deprivation

One alternative to budget standards is to find the level of income below which perceived deprivation multiplies. The pioneering 1983 Breadline Britain study presented a random sample of the national population with a list of 35 commodities, customs and activities to find which and how many of them were perceived as 'necessary' and also as 'affordable' (Mack and Lansley, 1985; Frayman 1991). The finding of the 1983 survey was that more than 7 million in the population, or 14% of Households, were in poverty in that they could not afford three or more of the necessities of life, as defined by a majority of the sample. This 'perceived deprivation' approach is sometimes described as a 'consensual' poverty line. However, 'consensual' is taken to mean different things (see Walker, 1987; Veit-Wilson, 1987; and Hallerod, 1993b). For example, it is sometimes taken to mean the average amount of income judged to be sufficient for a family of defined composition by a representative sample of the population. Little or no reference is made to the criteria that the sample might use, or have in mind, when making such estimates.

Strengths. The populace's perception of what is necessary and affordable provides an independent criterion in the construction of a poverty line. Rather than take the opinions of elite 'experts' or use officially approved sets of income and expenditure statistics, the opinions and attitudes of a cross-section of the population are explored. The evidence is direct and first-hand.

The realistic 'context' of the approach should also be recognised. Thus, opinions are sought about the priority that should be accorded to certain major social services and public utilities, as well as popular notions of 'poverty'. For example, compared with some other sources of evidence, considerable sections of the population referred to 'social injustice' as a cause of poverty rather than 'laziness and lack of willpower' (see Chapter 1). In short, answers to questions about the level of minimally adequate income acquire credibility if they are embedded in a variety of questions about social needs, conditions and development.

Weaknesses. The elucidation of opinion takes precedence over the elucidation of behaviour. Although this is understandable because of the limited resources (in this instance) available for research, it does mean that there can be no easy check on the extent to which people's views about need correspond with the behaviour which may be said to be revelatory of need. The 'consensual judgement of society' is a necessary but insufficient criterion upon which to build a complete picture of poverty.

Relative deprivation

This standard is built on the idea that in all societies there is a threshold of low income or resources marking a change in the capacity of human beings to meet the needs, material and social, enjoined by that society. Some such idea is the only one logically available to distinguish poverty from inequality. In descending a scale of income (or income combined with the value of other types of resources), instances of deprivation steadily increase. Below a certain level of income the forms and instances of deprivation are hypothesised to multiply disproportionately to the fall in income. Information is collected about both material and social needs - in the sense of role obligations, customs and activities[6].

Strengths. Investigation and analysis of the range as well as the type of human needs are comprehensive. By establishing what people do and do not do, at different levels of income, and what specific conditions they experience, generalisations can be developed about the priorities of human action, relationships and consumption and what can still be said to be 'normative' at the lowest threshold of income. If the broad assumption about the cohesion of society holds, then the identification of the level of income below which membership of that society and conformity with its customs, begins to collapse is a proper scientific objective. In nearly all countries, some such assumption, when poverty 'matters', is of course made - though attention is usually restricted to the borderlines of adequacy and inadequacy of food and other 'material' needs rather than including social needs.

This more comprehensive approach lends itself to cross-national and cross-cultural comparison much better than country-specific, or needs-specific, approaches. It also lends itself to the elucidation of the effects of discriminatory policies so that the needs, as distinct from the institutionalised living standards of men and women, disabled and elderly people, racial minorities and other groups may be brought to light.

Weaknesses. Scientific research is inevitably costly and time-consuming, given the deliberately comprehensive approach. This applies in particular to the selection (from that research) of indicators of deprivation, the assumptions which have to be made about the definition of 'society' to which the operational measure of poverty applies. This qualification also applies to the degree to which the society's internal cultures and groups are sufficiently cohesive or integrated to warrant both the establishment of what is 'normative' behaviour and what balance of types of resources which can be incorporated into a common measure of resources or income.

Conclusion

This elucidation of the extraordinary global variation in approach to the construction of a poverty line demonstrates the lack of scientific basis in cross-national as well as country-specific work and thereby shows the discriminatory features of definitions which have been put into operational practice.

The difficult task of arriving at an international formula for a poverty line has sharp implications for each country, compelling discussion of scientific criteria of deprivation and also 'adequate' resources or income. This will mean a radical change in current orthodoxies and is bound to prompt more appropriate research - not only into the deprivation and stultification of the role obligations and role potentialities of the poor but into the disproportionate seizure and domination of resources on the part of the rich. Most practical of all, it will afford more relevant criteria of the adequacy of minimum standards of income - as in a minimum wage or levels of social assistance, or income support.

The partial approaches towards an 'international' poverty line which have been made by the World Bank and other international agencies, placing undue emphasis on the idea of 'absolute' poverty, and by European agencies, placing undue emphasis on a 'relative' income standard, cannot be sustained. Each of these approaches distorts more than it helps - when related to international social relations and conditions. Again, the country-specific household or family budget standards developed in a variety of countries, including the US, Belgium, Germany and the UK, are insufficiently addressed to international market causes of 'country-specific' income inequality and poverty. The character of their methodology is nationally introspective. They also tend to be caught in the convolutions of circularity of reasoning. Patterns of expenditure are regenerated as patterns of need for income.

'Perceived' and 'relative' deprivation methodologies have brighter prospects for national and international use. They have complementary advantages as scientific instruments and as socially revelatory and practical standards for the investigation and reduction of poverty.

Glossary of principal definitions

World Bank

Absolute poverty is "the position of an individual or household in relation to a poverty line the real value of which is fixed over time." The poverty line is "the standard of living (usually measured in terms of income or consumption) below which people are deemed to be poor" (World Bank, 1993a, p. vii). This is interpreted as a 'consumption-based' poverty line (ibid, p26) comprising "two elements: the expenditure necessary to buy a minimum standard of nutrition and other basic necessities, and a further amount that varies from country to country, reflecting the cost of participating in the everyday life of society" (*ibid*, p26).

UNDP

The poverty line is defined by UNDP as "that income level below which a minimum nutritionally adequate diet plus essential non-food requirements are not affordable". (UNDP, 1993, p225).

European relative income standard

In launching the Second European Poverty Programme (1985-1989) the Council of Ministers defined the poor as "persons whose resources (material, cultural and social) are so limited as to exclude them from the minimum acceptable way of life in the Member State in which they live" (EEC 1991, p2).

The State's standard of poverty

This is simply the minimum levels of benefit (or wage) sanctioned and institutionalised by the state. It is generally means tested.

Household budget standard

There are two standards, a low-cost budget, and a modest-but-adequate budget. The low-cost budget "includes items which more than two-thirds of the population regard as 'necessities' or which more than three-quarters of the population actually have. Only the cheapest items are included. It, therefore, represents a frugal level of living" (Bradshaw, 1993a, p3).

Perceived deprivation

This is also often called the consensual approach to poverty, and is the method used in this study. Living in 'Poverty' is defined as falling below the minimum standard of living sanctioned by society due to the enforced lack of socially perceived necessities. The necessities of life are defined as those which more than 50% of the population thinks; "are necessary, and which all adults should be able to afford and which they should not have to do without" (see Appendix II).

Relative deprivation

"People are relatively deprived if they cannot obtain, at all or sufficiently, the conditions of life - that is, the diets, amenities, standards and services - which allow them to play the roles, participate in the relationships and follow the customary behaviour which is expected of them by virtue of their membership of society. If they lack or are denied resources to obtain access to these conditions of life and so fulfil membership of society they may be said to be in poverty." (Townsend, 1993a, p.36)

Notes

1   See the illuminating detailed history prepared by Fisher, 1992b and see also Fisher, 1992a; Fisher, 1992c and Ruggles, 1990.

2   For example, Eurostat, 1990, which differed in approach primarily by taking expenditure rather than income as the governing criterion in selecting 40% and 50% of the mean.

3   The great majority of all the populations of the 41 countries listed by the World Bank as the poorest are black; whereas the great majority of all the populations of the listed industrial nations, with the exception of Japan, are white.

4   A similar question has also been asked annually in Australia since 1945 by the Morgan Gallup Poll which asks; "In your opinion, what is the smallest amount a family of four -two parents and two children - need a week to keep in health and live decently - the smallest amount for all expenses including rent?" (Saunders and Bradbury, 1989).

5   The list of items was derived from the Breadline Britain in the 1990s survey.

6   See Townsend (1979) and Townsend (1993a) for an updating and discussion of alternative approaches. The relative deprivation model is close to the 'rights' approach identified by Atkinson (1985a), which he distinguishes from a budget standards approach and is also close to the renewed interest in the participative needs of 'citizenship' (see for example, Lister, 1991). Among empirical investigations and demonstrations of the existence of a threshold of multiple deprivation at a particular level of income are Desai and Shah, 1985; Desai, 1986; Desai and Shah, 1988; Hutton, 1989 and 1991; Chow, 1981; Bokor, 1984; De Vos and Hagenaars, 1988 and Townsend and Gordon, 1989.

3   The public's perception of necessities and poverty

David Gordon and Christina Pantazis

The public's perception of necessities

A primary purpose of the 1990 Breadline Britain survey was to establish what possessions and activities the public perceived as necessities (see Introduction and Appendix I for details of the methodology).

The 1983 Breadline Britain survey was the first to establish what 'standard of living' was considered unacceptable by society as a whole. Its central brief was:

> "The survey's first, and most important, aim is to try to discover whether there is a public consensus on what is an unacceptable standard of living for Britain in 1983 and, if there is a consensus, who, if anyone, falls below that standard. The idea underlying this is that a person is in 'poverty' when their standard of living falls below the minimum deemed necessary by current public opinion. This minimum may cover not only the basic essentials for survival (such as food) but also access, or otherwise, to participating in society and being able to play a social role."

A major achievement of the 1983 Breadline Britain study was that it established: "for the first time ever, that a majority of people see the necessities of life in Britain in the 1980s as covering a wide range of goods and activities, and that people judge a minimum standard of living on socially established criteria and not just the criteria of survival or subsistence."

The Breadline Britain approach defines poverty in terms of a standard of living unacceptable to the majority of the population. The validity of this approach rests on the assumption that there are not wide variations in the definition of necessities amongst the different groups in society. Otherwise, the definition of an unacceptable standard of living just becomes the opinion of one group against another. The 1983 Breadline Britain survey confirmed the validity of this assumption by showing that there existed a high degree of consensus amongst different groups in their perceptions of what are necessities:

> "The homogeneity of views shown by people both from very different personal circumstances and also holding very different political ideologies suggests that judgements are being made on the basis of a cohesive view of the kind of society we ought to live in. There is, it seems, a general cultural ethos about what is sufficient and proper."

The 1990 Breadline Britain survey developed and extended the methodology of the 1983 study. Respondents were asked about their attitudes to a greater range of possessions and activities (44 items in 1990 compared with 35 items in 1983) and new sections were added on the desirability of a range of public services. Table 3.1 compares the percentage of respondents who considered items to be necessities in 1990 and 1983. The relative theory of poverty predicts that, if a society gets richer, the number of people who perceive common possessions and activities as necessary will increase. Since the real income of average households increased between 1983 and 1990, we would expect that number of respondents considering items to be necessary would also have increased between 1983 and 1990.

Table 3.1 shows that this is true for 30 out of 33 items. There has clearly been a large shift in public attitudes between 1983 and 1990, with greater numbers in 1990, perceiving as necessities, a whole range of common possessions and activities. Respondents in 1990 only considered three items to be less important than they did in 1983:

1   A roast joint or its vegetarian equivalent once a week (-3%)
2   Two pairs of all-weather shoes (-4%)
3   An annual week's holiday away, not with relatives (-9%)

The question about a roast joint was modified in 1990 to include the vegetarian equivalent so that the 1983 and 1990 results are not strictly comparable. The differences on the results on the other two questions may reflect changes in attitude or may be statistical artefacts.

Table 3.1
The perception of necessities: 1983 and 1990 compared

Standard-of-living items in rank order	% claiming item as necessity	
	1990 *n=1,831*	1983 *n=1,174*
A damp-free home	98	96
Heating to warm living areas in the home if it's cold	97	96
An inside toilet (not shared with another household)	97	97
Bath, not shared with another household	95	94
Beds for everyone in the household	95	94
A decent state of decoration in the home	92	-
Fridge	92	77
Warm waterproof coat	91	87
Three meals a day for children	90	82
Two meals a day (for adults)	90	64
Insurance of contents of dwelling	88	-
Daily fresh fruit and vegetables	88	-
Toys for children e.g. dolls or models	84	71
Bedrooms for every child over 10 of different sexes	82	77
Carpets in living rooms and bedrooms	78	70
Meat/fish (or vegetarian equivalent) every other day	77	63
Two pairs all-weather shoes	74	78
Celebrations on special occasions	74	69
Washing machine	73	67
Presents for friends/family once a year	69	63
Child's participation in out-of-school activities	69	-
Regular savings of £10 a month for "rainy days"	68	-
Hobby or leisure activity	67	64
New, not second hand, clothes	65	64
Weekly roast/vegetarian equivalent	64	67
Leisure equipment for children e.g. sports equipment	61	57
A television	58	51
A telephone	56	43
An annual week's holiday away, not with relatives	54	63
A "best outfit" for special occasions	54	48
An outing for children once a week	53	40
Children's friends round for tea/snack fortnightly	52	37
A dressing gown	42	38
A night out fortnightly	42	36
Child's music/dance/sport lessons	39	-
Fares to visit friends 4 times a year	39	-
Friends/family for a meal monthly	37	32
A car	26	22
Pack of cigarettes every other day	18	14
Holidays abroad annually	17	-
Restaurant meal monthly	17	-
A video	13	-
A home computer	5	-
A dishwasher	4	-

Attitudinal scatter plots

Most people find it very difficult to identify quickly the key pattern in a data set when data are presented in the form of large tables, such as Table 3.1. Even 'experts' find 44-row tables, with several columns, hard to examine. Therefore, as an aid to interpretation, we have plotted the results from the most important contrasting groups as scatter plots (the full tabulated data are in Appendix III).

Figure 3.1 displays the data from Table 3.1. For each item in the table, the 1983 data are plotted on the x axis and the 1990 data on the y axis. If there had been no change in public attitudes between 1983 and 1990, then all the points would plot around a 45° straight line, from the Origin (0, 0) to 100, 100 (bottom left to top right). We would never expect all the points to fit exactly along a straight line as there will always be some deviations due to measurement error.

As can be seen clearly in Figure 3.1, all but three of the items are on the y axis side of the line (to the left and above the line), indicating that, in 1990, a higher percentage of respondents thought that all of these items were necessities. The seven labelled items

1	Two meals a day (for adults)
2	Children's friends round for tea/snack fortnightly
3	A fridge
4	Meat or fish or the vegetarian equivalent, every other day
5	A telephone
6	Toys for children, e.g. dolls or models
7	An outing for children once a week

are those which show the greatest change in public opinion (more than 12%). The two questions about food were modified versions of those used in the 1983 study so these results may not be strictly comparable. However, there appears to have been an unequivocal shift in public opinion between 1983 and 1990 on the necessity of the consumable durables, fridges and telephones, and on the importance of children's possessions and activities.

Figure 3.2 compares the perception of necessities of the 'multiply deprived' and 'less deprived' groups (objectively 'poor' and 'not poor'). If there was no agreement between 'multiply deprived' and 'less deprived' respondents about the necessity of different items, then we would expect to find a random scatter of points on the graph. However, all the items clearly cluster along the 45° line, indicating that there is no difference in the perception of what are necessities between the 'multiply deprived' and 'less deprived'. There are only two items where there is a greater than 12% difference in opinion between these two groups. Of the 'multiply deprived' group, 28% consider 'a packet of cigarettes every other day'[1], a necessity compared with only 15% of the 'less deprived' group. Conversely, 70% of the 'less deprived' group consider "a hobby or leisure activity" to be a necessity, compared with 57% of the 'multiply deprived' group.

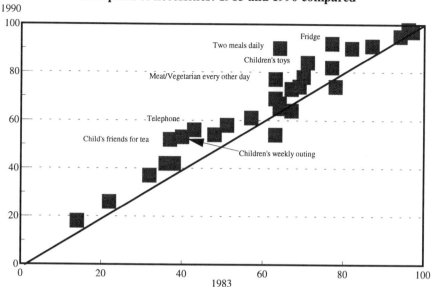

Figure 3.1
Perception of necessities: 1983 and 1990 compared

1990

Fridge

Two meals daily

Children's toys

Meat/Vegetarian every other day

Telephone

Child's friends for tea

Children's weekly outing

1983

Figure 3.2
Perception of necessities and deprivation

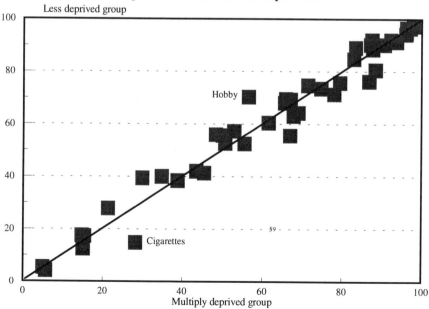

Less deprived group

Hobby

59

Cigarettes

Multiply deprived group

75

Both the 1983 and 1990 Breadline Britain surveys found that there was a higher incidence of smoking amongst 'multiply deprived' respondents than 'less deprived' respondents (45% and 20% respectively, in 1990). Cigarettes are highly addictive, both physically and psychologically. A physical addiction is, by definition, a physiological need. Therefore, it is unsurprising that a greater number of the 'multiply deprived' group considered cigarettes to be a necessity. Mack and Lansley (1985) found that the 'poor' often smoked to relieve the stresses and tensions associated with their circumstances:

"But there is also a sense in which their very deprivations **lead** to smoking or at least reinforce the habit and make it more difficult to give up ... It is our strong impression ... that smoking often provides the **one** release of tension people have from the constant worries that stem from circumstances that are often desperate and depressing."

Elaine, who struggled to bring up her three young children on the wages her husband brought home from the night shift at the local factory, explained in the 1983 Breadline Britain study:

"We don't go out, we don't drink; the only thing we do is smoke. Fair enough, it's an expensive habit but it's the only thing we do. All the money we have, it either goes on bills or food or clothes and, apart from smoking, we don't have anything. We're sort of non-existent outside, we **never** go anywhere. I'm in here seven nights a week. Four of those nights Roy's at work and we have had a lot of trouble round here. I've had threatened rape. I mean Roy works nights and I'm in this house on my own. It's terrible."

There is no evidence from either the 1983 or 1990 Breadline Britain studies that smoking either causes poverty or that giving up smoking would solve the financial problems of most of the 'poor'. Stopping smoking would, however, have a long term beneficial effect on the health of both 'poor' and 'non poor' smokers (see Chapter 6).

The greater perception of necessity of hobbies and leisure activities by the 'less deprived' group probably results from their having more leisure time and the additional financial resources to pursue such activities. The 1990 Breadline Britain study showed that 'less deprived' respondents made greater use of leisure services such as libraries, adult evening classes, museums and galleries and sports and swimming facilities (see Chapter 9 for details).

Figures 3.3 and 3.4 show the perception of necessities by respondents' 'subjective' opinions of their own levels of poverty and their history of poverty. Figure 3.3 shows the perceptions of necessities of those respondents considering that they are genuinely poor 'all the time now', plotted against those considering that they are 'never' genuinely poor now. Figure 3.4 shows the perception of necessities by respondents poor 'often' or 'most of the time' in the past, plotted against those who

Figure 3.3
Perception of necessities and present level of poverty

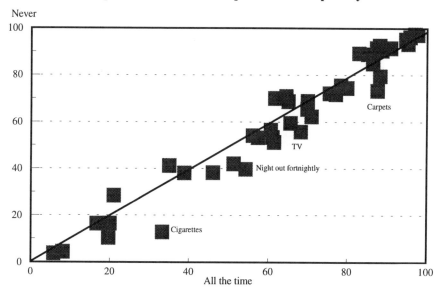

Figure 3.4
Perception of necessities and history of poverty

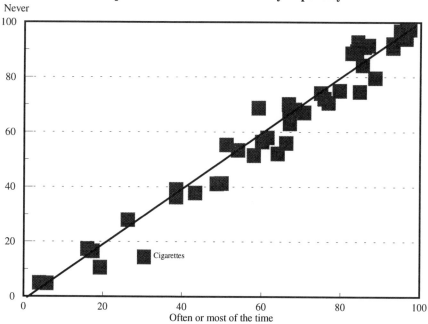

have 'never' been poor. The results are very similar to those of the 'multiply deprived' and 'less deprived' graph (Figure 3.2), again demonstrating the close agreement between the results obtained from both 'objective' and 'subjective' measurements of poverty.

Figure 3.3 shows that those respondents genuinely poor 'all the time' are more likely to consider four items to be necessities than those who are 'never' poor. The four items are:

1   A packet of cigarettes every other day (33% compared with 13%)
2   A night out fortnightly (59% compared with 40%)
3   Carpets for the living rooms and bedrooms (88% compared with 73%)
4   Television (68% compared with 56%)

Cigarettes and television have previously been discussed (see Chapter 1 for details about televisions). The greater perceived need for a *night out once a fortnight* by the poor 'all the time' group may reflect their desire to escape from the impoverished life that they lead. A floor covering of some kind is obviously an essential item, particularly for families with young children (you cannot put a baby down on rough floorboards). The differences in perception about the necessity of *carpets* may reflect the availability of alternative type of floor coverings (e.g. polished floorboards, cork tiles, rugs, etc.) to the 'never' poor group. Figure 3.4 shows that there is almost complete agreement about the necessities of life between respondents with different histories of poverty.

Figures 3.5 to 3.8 show the perception of necessities by education, social class, political orientation, and gender. Figure 3.5 indicates that ex-students (with degrees) are more prepared than those without educational qualifications to wear second-hand clothes, live without a washing machine or dressing gown and rarely sit down for a weekly roast. This may reflect differences in lifestyle, age, household structure and financial resources between these groups.

Figure 3.5 also shows that there are more points below the 45° line than above it, indicating that respondents with no educational qualifications, are more likely to consider many items to be necessities than respondents with degrees or equivalent qualifications. Figure 3.6 again shows that there is some divergence of opinion about the necessity of several items between social classes AB and E. However, it must be noted that, despite numerous differences over specific items, a high level of agreement still exists. The points in Figure 3.6 are not randomly dispersed but approximate to a 45° line, although with some scatter.

There is almost complete agreement on the necessities for items between Conservative and Labour supporters (Figure 3.7) and between men and women (Figure 3.8). This remarkable homogeneity of views across the political divide was also found in the 1983 Breadline Britain survey (Mack and Lansley, 1985). The main difference in the perception of necessities between men and women is that more women consider a *dressing gown* to be important. The importance placed on the necessity for a dressing gown is also strongly age-related.

78

Figure 3.5
Perception of necessities and education

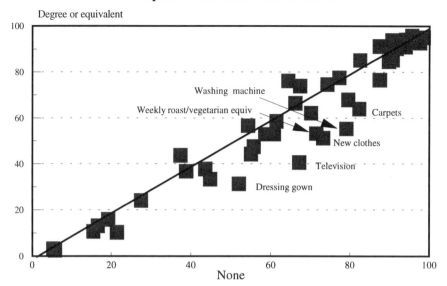

Degree or equivalent

Washing machine

Weekly roast/vegetarian equiv

Carpets

New clothes

Television

Dressing gown

None

Figure 3.6
Perception of necessities and social class

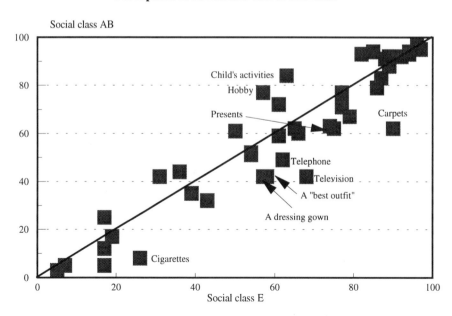

Social class AB

Child's activities

Hobby

Presents

Carpets

Telephone

Television

A "best outfit"

A dressing gown

Cigarettes

Social class E

Notes:Child's activities:Child's participation in
out-of-school activities; Presents: Presents for
friends or family once per year.

79

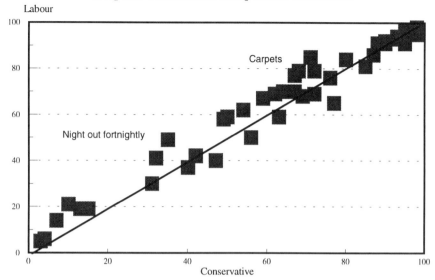

Figure 3.7
Perception of necessities and political orientation

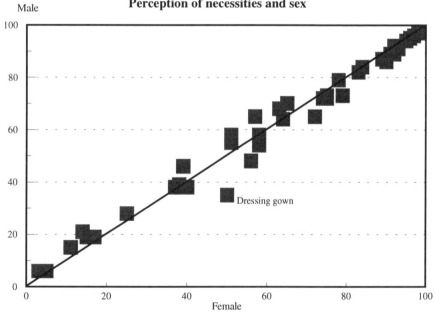

Figure 3.8
Perception of necessities and sex

Public perceptions of the government's response to poverty

The Breadline Britain survey asked respondents about their opinion on the government's response to the problems of poverty. In both the 1983 and 1990 study, the following question was asked:

Table 3.2
Question 16: "Still thinking about people who lack the things you have said are necessities for living in Britain today, do you think that the Government is doing too much, too little or about the right amount to help these people?"

	1983 (%) n=1174	1990 (%) n=1831
Too much	6	5
Too little	57	70
About the right amount	33	18
Don't know	4	7

Table 3.2 shows how public opinion has changed between 1983 and 1990. There has again been a remarkable shift in public opinion amongst those considering that the government is doing 'too little' to help. In 1983, 57% thought too little was being done but, by 1990, 70% of respondents thought this. There has been a concomitant decline in the percent of respondents that thought the government is doing 'about the right amount', with the numbers thinking that the government is doing 'too much' remaining relatively constant. This shift in public attitudes probably results from the greater visibility of the problems of deprivation as the numbers living in poverty have increased during the 1980s. Figures 3.9 to 3.12 show that the perception that the government is doing 'too little' is linearly related to respondents' experience of poverty.

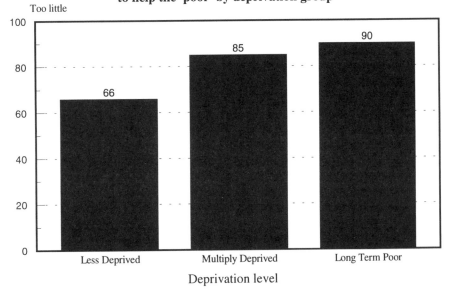

Figure 3.9
Percent considering that the government is doing too little
to help the 'poor' by deprivation group

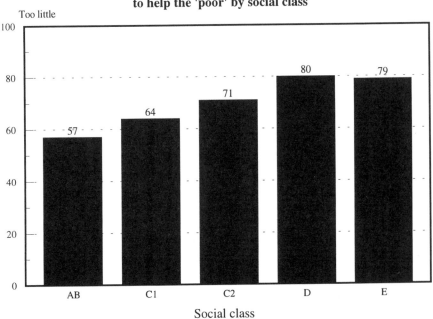

Figure 3.10
Percent considering that the government is doing too little
to help the 'poor' by social class

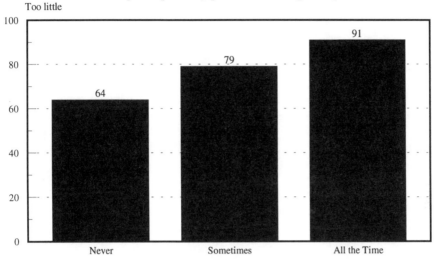

Figure 3.11
Percent considering that the government is doing too little
to help the 'poor' by present level of poverty

Q16 Are you genuinely poor?

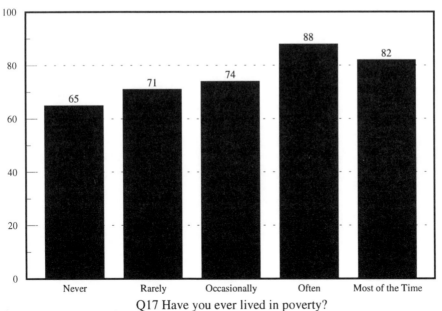

Figure 3.12
Percent considering that the government is doing too little
to help the 'poor' by history of poverty

Q17 Have you ever lived in poverty?

83

The greater the direct experience of living in poverty, the larger the numbers believing that too little is being done. This relationship holds true irrespective of whether poverty is measured 'objectively', by deprivation (Figure 3.9), 'subjectively', by respondents' opinion (Figures 3.11 and 3.12) or if a proxy for levels of poverty is used, such as social class (Figure 3.10). There is a remarkable consistency in the levels of opinion, irrespective of how poverty is measured. Approximately nine out of ten (90%) of the poorest groups consider that the government is doing 'too little' to help those in need.

Figures 3.13 and 3.14 show the percent of respondents who consider the government is doing 'too little' for those in need, by political orientation and household type. As would be expected, there are marked differences in opinion across the political divide. Only 34% of Conservative supporters think that the government is doing 'too little' compared with 90% of Labour supporters, 76% of Liberal Democrats and 86% of Greens. Conservative supporters are one of the few remaining groups in society that do not think that the government is doing 'too little' to help those in need. Figure 3.14 shows that the majority of all household types also consider that the government is doing 'too little'. Pensioner households are the least likely to hold this opinion (57%) and lone parents are the most likely (90%).

Criticism of government inaction on poverty carries little weight unless people are prepared to pay for the costs of change. Both the 1983 and 1990 Breadline Britain surveys asked respondents two questions to see how much they were willing to pay to help those living in need:

Q9a: "If the Government proposed to increase income tax by one penny (1p) in the pound to enable everyone to afford the items you have said are necessities, on balance would you support or oppose this policy?"

and

Q9b: "If the Government proposed to increase income tax by five pence (5p) in the pound to enable everyone to afford the items you have said are necessities, on balance would you support or oppose this policy?"

Both the increase in the real average household income between 1983 and 1990 and the increase in the numbers living in poverty would lead us to predict that more respondents would support income tax increases in 1990 than in 1983. Table 3.3 shows the change in public attitudes.

84

Figure 3.13
Percent considering that the government is doing too little
to help the 'poor' by political orientation

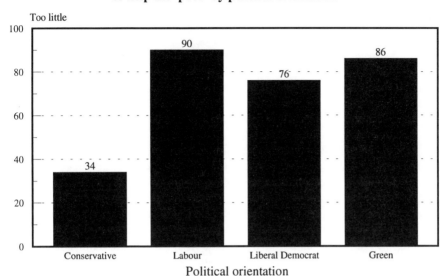

Too little

Political orientation

Figure 3.14
Percent considering that the government is doing too little
to help the 'poor' by household type

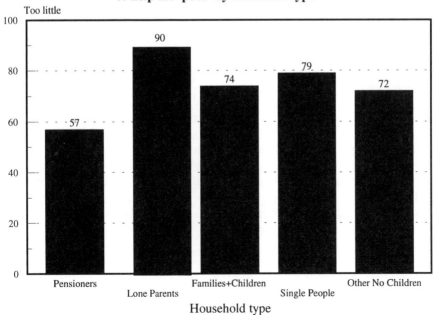

Too little

Household type

Table 3.3

Change in public opinion about income tax increases to help alleviate poverty between 1983 and 1990

	Opinion on a 1p in the £ income tax increase		Opinion on a 5p in the £ income tax increase	
	1983	*1990*	*1983*	*1990*
Support	74	75	34	43
Oppose	20	18	53	44
Don't know	6	7	13	13

In both 1983 and 1990, approximately three-quarters of respondents (74% in 1983 and 75% in 1990) supported a 1p in the £ income tax increase. There has been a significant shift in public attitudes amongst those supporting a 5p in the £ income tax increase. In 1990, almost as many respondents supported a 5p rise (43%) as opposed it (44%), whereas, in 1983, only 34% supported such a large income tax increase.

Figures 3.15 to 3.18 show the percent of respondents supporting income tax increases by their 'objective' level of deprivation, their 'subjective' level of poverty, their history of poverty and their social class. There again appears to be a clear linear pattern, irrespective of how poverty is measured. The 'poorest' groups are less likely to support a 1p in the £ income tax increase whereas the 'richest' groups are more likely to support such an increase (for example, 76% of the 'less deprived' group support a 1p increase compared with 70% of the 'long term poor' group). This may be due to the 'poorest' groups being the least able to afford a 1p in the £ income tax increase. However, no such clear trend is evident with the levels of support for a 5p in the £ income tax increase to help those in need. The level of support remains fairly constant across all levels of poverty, however measured. Support for such a large income tax rise appears unrelated to levels of poverty.

Figures 3.19 and 3.20 show support for income tax increases by political orientation and household type. As expected, there are clear differences in support across the political spectrum. Of Conservatives, 70% support a 1p increase compared with 91% of Greens. Greens, single people and those who have lived in poverty 'most of the time' in the past are the only groups where the majority supports a 5p in the £ income tax increase to help those in need. Despite these specific differences, there does appear to be a remarkable level of agreement across all divisions in society that the government should increase income tax by 1p in the £ to help alleviate poverty. Three-quarters of all voters and more than two-thirds of all sub-groups in society believe this.

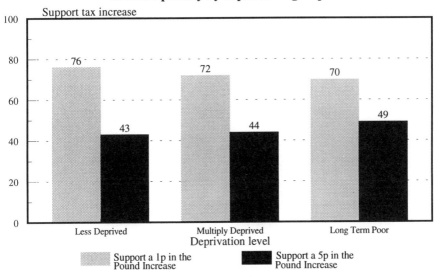

Figure 3.15
**Percent supporting an increase in income tax to help
alleviate poverty by deprivation group**

Figure 3.16
**Percent supporting an increase in income tax to help
alleviate poverty by present level of poverty**

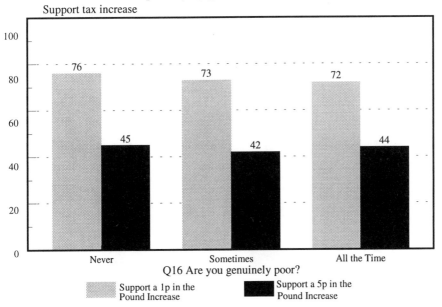

Figure 3.17
**Percent supporting an increase in income tax to help
alleviate poverty by history of poverty**

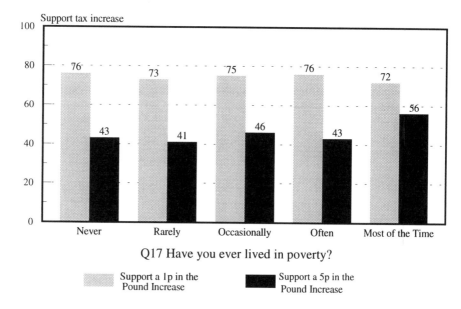

Q17 Have you ever lived in poverty?

Figure 3.18
**Percent supporting an increase in income tax to help
alleviate poverty by social class**

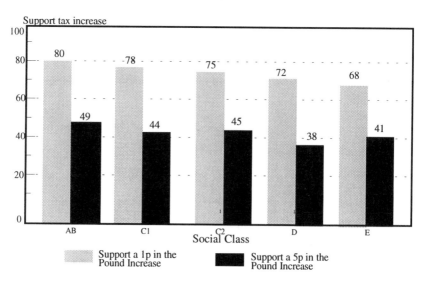

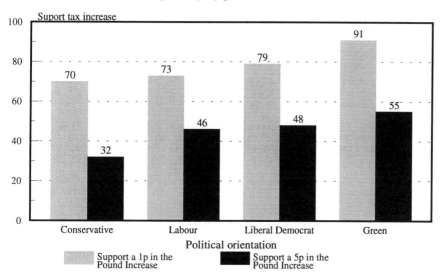

Figure 3.19
Percent supporting an increase in income tax to help alleviate poverty by political orientation

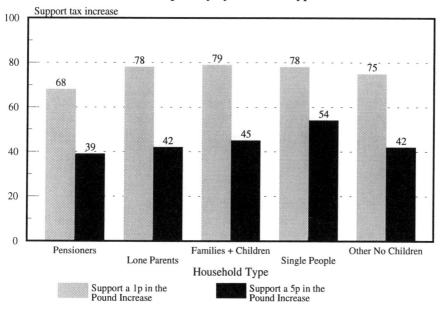

Figure 3.20
Percent supporting an increase in income tax to help alleviate poverty by household type

Who are the poor?

The groups in society most vulnerable to poverty have long been known: the unemployed, the sick and disabled, the elderly, lone parents and the low paid. The government's low income statistics (Households Below Average Income) were used to produce analyses for these groupings. They are, however, not mutually exclusive and can and do overlap, e.g. you can be both disabled and unemployed.

Figures 3.21 to 3.24 show the percent of respondents who are 'multiply deprived' (enforced lack of three or more socially perceived necessities) and can 'objectively' be described as 'poor', by social class, household type, number of people in the household and housing tenure. The figures also show the mean deprivation score[2] of each group. Figure 3.21 shows that there is a clear trend in the instance of poverty by social class. Only 1% of households in social classes A and B are 'objectively' poor, whereas the majority (54%) of social class E households are living in poverty (see Appendix I for social class definitions). A similar trend is also evident with the mean deprivation scores of these groups.

Figure 3.22 shows the instance of poverty by household type. Of lone parent households, 41% live in poverty compared with 14% of other households (mainly couples without children). A smaller proportion of lone parent households are 'objectively' poor than social class E households (41% compared with 54%), however, the higher mean deprivation score of lone parent households (4.6) indicates that, on average, they are more deprived than social class E households. The relatively low incidence of 'poor' pensioner households (21%) may be an underestimate caused by the limitations of the perceived deprivation approach to measuring poverty. Pensioners often have lower expectations than younger respondents.

Figure 3.23 shows that both single person and large households, with more than five people, have the highest incidence of poverty. Almost half (48%) of households of seven or more people are 'poor'. Similarly, Figure 3.24 shows that almost half (47%) of all households renting from local authorities are 'objectively' poor. A high incidence of poverty is also found in the private rented sector: 37% of housing association households are 'poor', as are 30% that rent privately. By contrast, the incidence of poverty is much lower in the owner occupied sector (8% for those owning outright and 10% for those households with a mortgage).

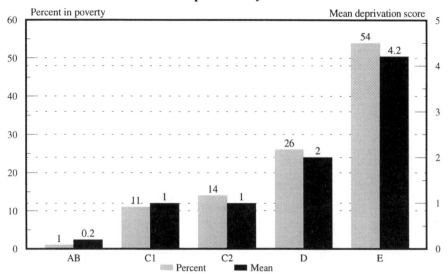

Figure 3.21
Incidence of deprivation by social class

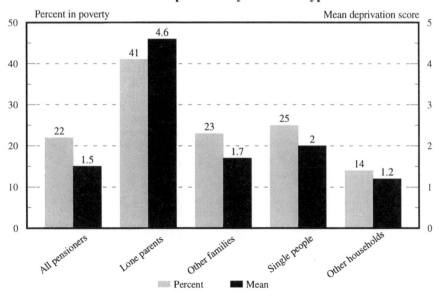

Figure 3.22
Incidence of deprivation by household type

Notes: Other families: all other families with children. Single people:
all non-retired single people without children.

Figure 3.23
Incidence of deprivation by size of household

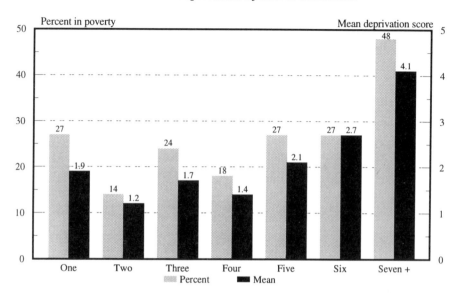

Figure 3.24
Incidence of deprivation by household tenure

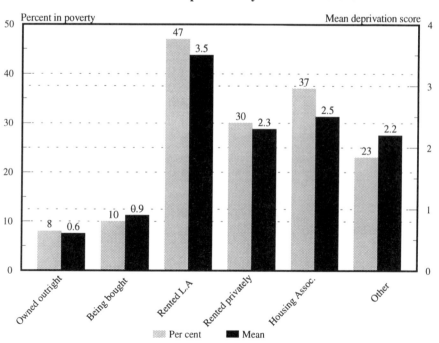

Figures 3.25 to 3.28 show the incidence of poverty by employment status of head of household, marital status, level of education and political orientation. Figure 3.25 shows the high incidence of poverty in unemployed households. Sixty per cent of households where the head is unemployed and seeking work are 'objectively' poor. These households, on average, cannot afford almost five socially perceived necessities (mean deprivation score 4.8). Similarly, 47% of households where the head is unemployed and not seeking work are living in poverty, as are 41% of households headed by housewives. There is a clear relationship between the number of hours worked by the head of household and the likelihood of poverty: the more hours worked, the less likely it is that the household is 'multiply deprived'. The lowest incidence of poverty are in those households where the head is in full time education (student households).

Figure 3.26 shows that 44% of divorced/separated respondents are living in poverty as are 28% of widowed respondents. Figure 3.27 shows that there is a clear relationship between education and incidence of poverty. The better the educational qualifications, the less likely the respondent is to be 'poor'. Finally, Figure 3.28 shows that Labour supporters are twice as likely to be 'poor' as Conservative supporters (21% compared with 10%). However, the highest incidence of poverty is found amongst the politically disaffected who 'won't say or don't know' their political persuasion. Twenty-eight percent of this group are 'objectively' poor.

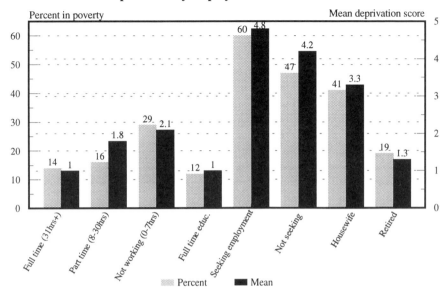

Figure 3.25
Incidence of deprivation by employment status of head of household

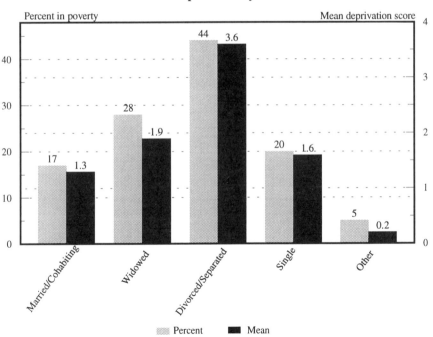

Figure 3.26
Incidence of deprivation by marital status

94

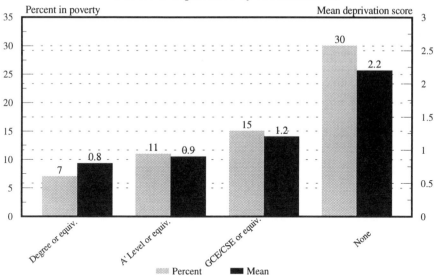

Figure 3.27
Incidence of deprivation by education level

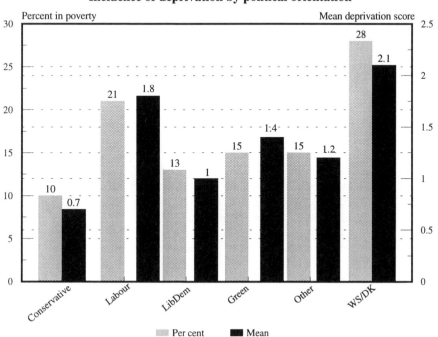

Figure 3.28
Incidence of deprivation by political orientation

Conclusion

1   There is a high degree of consensus, across all divisions in society, on the necessity of a range of common possessions and activities. Society as a whole clearly does have a view on what is necessary to have a decent standard of living.

2   70% of all respondents think that the government is doing 'too little' to help alleviate poverty.

3   75% (three-quarters) of all voters support a 1p in the £ income tax increase to help alleviate poverty. There is a high degree of consensus for this policy across the divisions in society: even 70% of Conservatives support such a tax increase.

4   The following households were 'objectively' living in poverty in 1990:
- 60% of households, where the head is unemployed and seeking work
- 48% of households, with seven or more people
- 47% of households, renting from local authorities
- 44% of respondents, who were divorced/separated
- 41% of lone parent households
- 37% of households renting from a housing association
- 30% of respondents with no educational qualifications.

Notes

---

1   Cigarettes were only considered to be a necessity by 18% of the whole sample and, therefore, were not used as an indicator of deprivation when constructing the deprivation index or classifying the sample into 'multiply deprived' or 'less deprived' groupings.

2   The deprivation score is the number of items a respondent lacks, because they 'can't afford them', that are considered to be necessities by more than 50% of the population.

4 Poverty and gender

Sarah Payne and Christina Pantazis

Introduction

Previous chapters have discussed the definition and measurement of poverty and deprivation. However, one dimension of poverty not yet fully addressed is the relevance of gender.

Whilst the term the 'feminisation of poverty' has at times been used to describe the part played by gender in poverty (Scott, 1984), such a term suggests that women's greater risk of poverty has been a recent development. However, it has been shown that British women constitute a roughly similar proportion of the 'poor' today as in 1900 (Lewis and Pichaud, 1992). Whereas, at the start of the century, 61% of adults in receipt of poor relief were women, in 1983, women formed 60% of those in receipt of supplementary benefit. Women's poverty has arguably become more visible as a result of a growth in female headed households. Recent research has highlighted the continued over-representation of women amongst those suffering poverty and women's greater vulnerability to the risk of poverty during their lives (Glendinning and Millar, 1992; Payne, 1991; Oppenheim, 1991).

Women's heightened vulnerability to poverty has a crucial effect on the question of how poverty is, and should be, measured. Firstly, this means quite simply being aware of the gender of those who are living in poverty or deprivation. Secondly, it requires a method which attempts to explore the life-long risk of exposure to

97

poverty, in addition to 'snap-shot' measures of the 'poor' at any one moment in time. Women's caring work and all that goes with it - periods out of the labour market, low paid work and insecure employment when they are economically active - results in an increased vulnerability to poverty (Millar, 1992). Thirdly, it requires a conceptualisation of poverty which goes beyond the measurement of household income and household consumption. Despite the fact that a number of studies have demonstrated the inadequacy of research which assumes an equal distribution of resources within households, poverty studies continue to focus on what Pahl (1989) has called the 'black box' of the household, without exploring both the actual way in which resources are shared within the household and the impact of this division on the experience of poverty.

This failure to open up the 'black box' has a number of consequences. Studies of household income, for example, fail to measure the contribution of household labour - largely carried out by women - in converting raw materials (food and cleaning materials, for example) into products or use values - food ready for consumption, a clean house, and so on. It is also important to consider the ways in which women may experience the same deprivation in a different way - for example, 'poor' housing or the lack of hot water will affect women more than men, where women are primarily responsible for domestic labour and childcare.

Some studies have attempted to overcome some of these difficulties. For example, Townsend *et al* (1987) used an increased weighting in the measurement of housing and environmental deprivation for respondents who were not in the labour market and who were more likely to spend longer periods in the home.

Research has also demonstrated the ways in which the distribution of household income is linked with the level of that income: where money is tight, women more often have the responsibility of managing the budget, whereas when income levels are higher it is more often men who control expenditure (Land, 1977; Wilson, 1987; Pahl, 1989; Payne, 1991). A recent report showed that the management of the household budget by women in 'poor' families exists in industrialised and underdeveloped countries alike (UNDP, 1995). Other studies have detailed the experiences of 'poor' women and particularly women who are mothers (Graham, 1987 and 1993; Charles and Kerr, 1987).

However, research has largely failed to explore the ways in which women and men may hold different perceptions about what constitutes a necessity and therefore what should be included in a consensual measure of poverty. One pioneering Swedish study has shown that there are differences in the way men and women view necessities (Nyman, 1996). This chapter uses material from the Breadline Britain survey to explore the issues relating to ways in which ideas about what constitutes an acceptable standard of living may differ for each sex.

Who are the poor? Gender and poverty in the Breadline Britain survey

The Breadline Britain survey tells us the distribution of resources between households. This means that we can count the number of 'poor' households in the study and, from that, estimate the number of 'poor' households in Britain in 1990. If we break this down by gender, the Breadline Britain survey shows that a higher proportion of women respondents lived in multiply deprived households. Of female respondents, 24% were 'poor', in contrast to only 17% of male respondents.

However, it would be misleading to assume from these figures that women are more at risk of poverty. Firstly, the questionnaire excluded information on the sex of household members other than the respondent. This means we have no information on the number of women or men within 'poor' households. Secondly, in this survey the respondents' answers were treated as representative of the household as a whole so we do not know the extent to which resources, and the experience of poverty, were shared amongst household members.

There are, nonetheless, some useful insights offered by the survey results regarding gender and poverty. In particular, the survey included a series of questions focusing on the respondents' own perceptions of their current poverty status and their history of poverty. Given that women are exposed to a greater risk of poverty over the course of a lifetime, we might expect that these questions, which relate to subjective and long-term experience of poverty, would be more revealing than those which reflect a snap-shot measure of poverty at the time of the survey.

Figure 4.1 shows that female respondents were slightly more likely than male respondents to see themselves as being 'poor', with 37% of women describing themselves as being 'poor' 'always' or 'sometimes', compared with a third of men (33%). Answers to this question varied considerably by age. Amongst those aged 16-24, over half (52%) of women compared with two fifths of men described themselves as feeling genuinely 'poor' 'all the time' or 'sometimes'. However, the picture is complex and in the 25-35, 45-54 and 55-64 age groups there were more men than women who considered themselves to be 'poor' (Figure 4.2). Amongst the oldest population (65+) women were twice as likely to consider themselves to be 'poor' either all the time or sometimes - two fifths of women (39%) compared with 19% of the men.

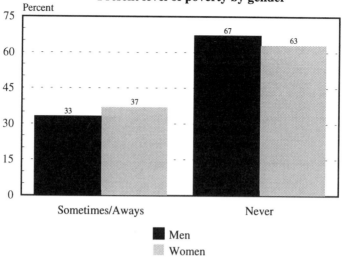

Figure 4.1
Present level of poverty by gender

Percent

- Men
- Women

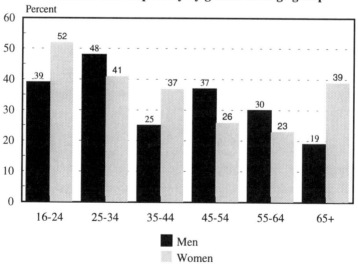

Figure 4.2
Present level of poverty by gender and age group

Percent

- Men
- Women

Question 17 asked respondents about their history of poverty:

"Looking back over your adult life, how often have there been times in your life when you think you have lived in poverty by the standards of the time?"

Figure 4.3 shows women are more likely than men to have been 'poor' in the past, with nearly half of all women having lived in poverty at some time during their life, compared with 42% of men. In every age group, more women had suffered poverty at some time during their lives in comparison with men. Figure 4.4 shows that the size of this difference between women and men did vary with age, with the most marked gap between women and men in the age group 25-34, where nearly half of the women (49%) compared with just over a third (37%) of the men had suffered poverty at some time. This may relate to the fact that this is the period in women's lives when they are likely to be responsible for bringing up children, either with a partner or alone - and that having responsibility for children is one of the major factors in women's vulnerability to poverty (Millar, 1992; Payne, 1991). Amongst older women the gap between the sexes is smaller, although even in the over 65 age group, 7% more women than men have suffered poverty at some time during their lives.

The meaning of these findings is complex - there is likely to be a cohort effect which, combined with different rates of mortality for each sex, means that there may be different sets of reasons for the findings for each age group. However, the responses given by women and men are supported by other studies which show women's lifelong risk of poverty to be higher than the risk for men (see Millar and Glendinning, 1992).

Levels of poverty amongst women vary according to their household type. In lone parent and single person households levels of poverty were higher for women than they were for men. More than half of female lone parents (55%) were living in poverty in 1990 and although the numbers of lone fathers in the study were small, the vast majority of men living in lone parent households (75%) were 'not poor'. This is unsurprising, and corresponds with other surveys which show that lone mothers are more at risk of poverty in comparison with lone fathers (Maclean, 1987), who are usually older and more likely to have become lone fathers as a result of widowhood rather than family breakdown.

In single person households, women were also slightly more likely than men to be 'poor'. Thirty percent of women in single person households were living in circumstances of multiple deprivation, compared with 24% of men. This difference is explained by the greater numbers of single older women compared with older men, since older women are more likely than men to be living in poverty, as a result of women's poorer or non-existent pensions and the inadequacy of basic state benefits for this age group (Walker, 1992; Groves, 1992). The Breadline Britain survey found that 28% of women aged over 65 were multiply deprived, compared with 17% of the male respondents.

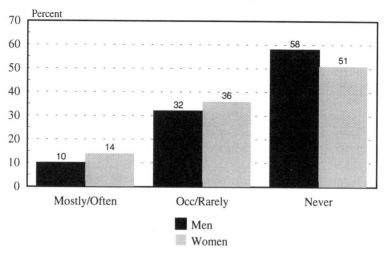

Figure 4.3
History of poverty by gender

Percent

Mostly/Often 10 14
Occ/Rarely 32 36
Never 58 51

■ Men
▨ Women

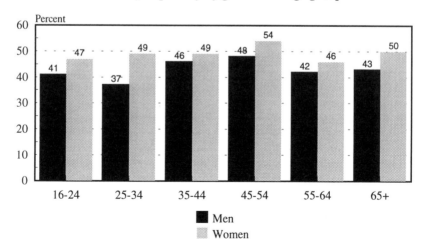

Figure 4.4
History of poverty by gender and age group

Percent

16-24 41 47
25-34 37 49
35-44 46 49
45-54 48 54
55-64 42 46
65+ 43 50

■ Men
▨ Women

102

Gender, health and deprivation

The important relationship between health and deprivation was also explored in the Breadline Britain survey. Although gender was not a statistically significant variable in influencing illness or disability (see Chapter 6), there are some important dynamics that warrant further exploration. In the Breadline Britain survey, the proportions of men and women suffering from a long term illness or disability were roughly equal: 20% of men and 18% of women. However, over a third of the women with ill-health lived in poverty (36%), compared with only a quarter of their male counterparts (24%).

To some extent, this greater proportion of poverty amongst women with a long-standing illness or disability, in comparison with men, is likely to be explained by the greater proportion of older women in the population - as older women are more at risk of both poverty and the experience of such illness or disability (Walker, 1992). However, the difference between women and men here is substantial - the proportion of disabled women who are 'poor' is considerably higher than the proportion of disabled men who are 'poor', and this needs further explanation. In particular, there may be a greater risk of poverty for disabled women - studies have shown that, amongst those of working age, men more often qualify for higher paid social security benefits, related to previous periods in employment, whilst women are more likely to qualify for the lower benefits (Lonsdale, 1990) and this may explain some of the difference.

Gender and the perception of needs

What we have seen so far is that a greater proportion of women respondents report having experienced poverty at some point during their lives, and a slightly greater proportion reported the on-going experience of poverty in the 1990s. However, to what extent might this reflect differences in the ways in which women and men perceive poverty? Chapter 3 looked at the public's perceptions of necessities and highlighted the similarities between women and men in terms of what was seen in 1990 as a necessity, with only one item - a dressing gown - being seen as a necessity by considerably more women than men (i.e. a 12% difference).

A similar analysis of the public's perceptions of necessity carried out on a large-scale study in Sweden found that men and women differed in their opinion of necessities in 13 out of a total of 42 items. Swedish women saw 4 of these items as necessities in comparison with men, whilst men saw a further 9 items as necessities more often than women (Nyman, 1996).

Table 4.1

Necessary consumption: Items and activities regarded as "Necessary, something that all adults should be able to afford"

Items/Activities	Women (%)	Men (%)	Key
Modern housing	86.9	81.8	*
Microwave	4.5	7.8	*
Modern clothes	17.8	12.9	*
Haircut once every three months	57.8	68.6	*
Automobile	43.0	51.6	**
Balcony/Garden	56.8	37.7	***
A 'best outfit' for special occasions	38.9	48.1	**
Save at least 500 SEK a month	25.6	33.2	**
Private insurance pension	25.4	19.0	*
Go out fortnightly	12.6	23.3	***
Cinema, theatre, concert once a month	10.6	15.2	*
Dishwasher	9.5	14.4	*
VCR	3.5	9.6	***

Note: Levels of significance: ***p<0.001, **p<0.01, *p<0.05. This table includes all men and women in the data set, n=793. Source: Nyman, C (1996)

In analysing these differences, Nyman points out that we cannot know the reasons behind the responses given. In particular, we do not know whether the respondent is thinking of the item for individual consumption, for collective or household consumption or, indeed, for the use of someone else altogether. For example, are women more likely to see 'modern clothes' as a necessity (as they did in the Swedish study) where they are thinking of the clothes worn by their children, rather than themselves? Do more men see a microwave as a necessity because they are "under the (possibly false) impression that is indispensable in modern cooking"? (Nyman, 1996, p100). We also do not know the extent to which respondents are 'trading off' answers - that is, seeing one item as less of a necessity in order to 'afford' another item - just as people make such decisions in their actual purchasing patterns. However, whilst we may be left with more questions than answers about why women and men in Sweden differ in terms of their perceptions of necessities, these differences are interesting in terms of what they might suggest about definitions of poverty for women and men, and also the value of consensus surveys.

In the following sections we have further explored the responses in the Breadline Britain Survey to this question on necessities by gender, taking into account the effects of other variables also thought to be significant. Logistic regression analysis was used to explore the independent effects of sex, deprivation, class, household type and age on the perception of necessities.

Logistic regression is a multivariate technique which enables the importance of an independent variable (for example, sex or age) to be assessed after allowing for the effects of other variables. For instance, sex and age are both related to whether a particular item is seen as a necessity, however, they are both related to each other (for example, there will be a higher proportion of women in some age groups). Logistic regression allows the assessment of whether sex has a correlation with a perception that an item is a necessity after allowing for these differences (effects) in the age of men and women.

Statistically significant (i.e. $p <= 0.05$) gender differences were found in relation to 18 out of 44 items in the Breadline Britain survey. The largest difference between men and women was in relation to whether a damp free home is seen as a necessity. The odds of women seeing this item as a necessity were twice that of men (an odds ratio of 2.16). However, given that nearly all respondents saw a damp-free home as a necessity, this difference is likely to have been exaggerated (i.e. unreliable). A warm, water-proof coat was also significant, but unreliable and both of these items have been excluded from Table 4.2 below which shows the results from the logistic regression analysis. The table shows that 6 out of the remaining 16 items were more likely to be seen as necessities by women and 10 items were more likely to be perceived as necessities by men.

There appear to be some strong patterns in the type of items which were more likely to be perceived as necessities by the different sexes. For instance, women had higher odds ratios regarding certain food items (for example, meat/fish/vegetarian equivalent every other day, fresh fruit and vegetables), clothing items (for example, a dressing gown), and various items relating to children (for example, children's friends round for tea once a fortnight and children's participation in out-of-school activities). Women also had higher odds ratios than men regarding presents for friends or family once a year (an odds ratio of 1.43). The biggest odds difference is in relation to a dressing gown, where the odds of women seeing this item as a necessity were almost twice as great as they were for men (an odds ratio of 1.93).

In contrast, the items more likely to perceived as necessities by men related to leisure (for example, a night out fortnightly, a weeks holiday away from home not with relatives, a monthly meal in a restaurant, annual holidays abroad), and certain items of clothing (for example, new, not second hand clothing, a 'best outfit' for special occasions). Leisure equipment for children and regular savings for retirement were also favoured by men. The biggest differences related to consumer durables (for example, a video and a dishwasher). Men were more than twice as likely as women to view a dishwasher as a necessity (an odds ratio of 0.44 to 1) and one and half times as likely to perceive a video as necessary (an odds ratio of 0.67 to 1). Men were also more than one and half times as likely as women to value an annual holiday abroad as a necessity (an odds ratio of 0.62 to 1). Table 4.2 also shows in the final two columns the results obtained from a univariate analysis of sex and perception of necessities. These are very close to the results from the multivariate logistic regression method, which suggests that these results are statistically robust.

105

Table 4.2
Multivariate logistical regression and univariate analysis of men's and women's perception of necessities

Item	Multivariate Logistic Regression		Univariate Analysis	
	odds ratios	*p level*	*odds ratios*	*95% Confidence Interval*
Q.2 Meat/fish/vegetarian equivalent every other day	1.41	.003	1.45	1.16-1.82
Q.4 A dressing gown	1.93	.000	1.88	1.55-2.27
Q.6 New, not second hand clothes	0.78	.013	0.77	0.64-0.95
Q.17 A night out fortnightly	0.77	.007	0.75	0.62-0.91
Q.20 A weekly holiday away from home, not with relatives	0.76	.005	0.75	0.62-0.91
Q.22 Presents for friends/family once a year	1.43	.001	1.42	1.16-1.74
Q.25 A 'best outfit' for special occasions	0.76	.005	0.74	0.61-0.89
Q.29 Leisure equipment for children	0.66	.000	0.67	0.55-0.81
Q.32 Kids' friends round for tea fortnightly	1.43	.000	1.40	1.16-1.69
Q.33 A dishwasher	0.44	.001	0.46	0.29-0.73
Q.34 A monthly meal in a restaurant	0.72	.012	0.72	0.56-0.91
Q.35 Regular savings (of £10 a month) for rainy days or retirement	0.77	.013	0.77	0.63-.094
Q.36 A video	0.67	.005	0.66	0.50-0.87
Q.38 Annual holidays abroad	0.62	.000	0.60	0.47-0.77
Q.41 Fresh fruit and vegetables daily	1.70	.001	1.65	1.23-2.21
Q.44 Kids' participation in out-of-school activities	1.34	.006	1.32	1.08-1.61

Note: *Age and social class were entered into the model as continuous variables. Effectively identical results were achieved when they were entered as categorical variables using the deviation method to produce contrasts.

The remainder of this chapter explores in more detail those 16 items shown in Table 4.2. In particular, we will examine the ways in which responses for men and women differed across different stages of the life course.

Food

Adequate food is seen as a necessity by the vast majority of respondents regardless of their gender. However, there are some interesting differences between women and men in different household types. Table 4.3 shows the percentage of women and men in different household types who thought various food items were necessities. The variations between men and women across different household types are small except for those in two or more adults and single person households. In the former type of households, women were much more likely than men to view daily fresh fruit and vegetables as necessities. Similarly, women in single person households were one and a half times as likely to perceive meat/fish/or vegetarian equivalent as a necessity, 91% as opposed to 64%.

Table 4.3
Perceptions of necessities by sex: Food items (%)

Do you feel that this item is a necessity?	Pensioners		Families with children		2+ Adults (inc. couples)		Single People	
	M	W	M	W	M	W	M	W
Meat/fish/vegetarian equivalent	82	83	73	79	78	81	64	91
Daily fresh fruit and vegetables	86	89	89	91	86	96	80	81

These differences may relate to young single women being more health conscious about their diets than young single men. There is little or no difference in the perception of the importance of food items between men and women in pensioner households and amongst families with children. Both men and women in families with children overwhelmingly consider that an adequate diet is a necessity. Research has shown that parents will often go without food in order to provide their children with an adequate diet. Additionally, Charles and Kerr (1987) found that women sometimes 'subordinate their own food preferences to those of their partners and children' and that women will often go without food when resources are tight. One of the respondents in the Breadline Britain survey described it in this way:

"Well, I do go without food once or twice a month, because I think of the children, for something to eat. Well, most of the time I have toast, or just bread and butter and a cup of tea, to feed the children." (Joyce, mother in two-parent household)

Housing

There was close agreement between women and men on the necessity of having adequate housing conditions. There were no significant and reliable differences between women and men in their answers to any of the housing items (e.g. a damp free home, heating to warm the living areas if it is cold, an inside toilet and bath/shower not shared with other households, beds for everyone in the household, a decent state of decoration in the home, bedrooms for every child over 10 of different sexes and carpets in living rooms and bedrooms).

Clothing

Table 4.4 shows that there were significant and reliable differences in the perceptions of women and men in regard to the necessity of a number of clothing items. More women than men thought a dressing gown was a necessity and this item emerged with the widest margin between the sexes, particularly amongst pensioner households. Seventy four percent of female pensioners, compared with 51% of male pensioners, considered a dressing gown as a necessity. However, men are significantly more likely to see new clothes and a best outfit as necessities. This does differ by household type - men are more likely than women to list these items as a necessity when they are pensioners, in families with children and in households with two or more adults. Single men, however, are less likely than women to see either new clothes or a best outfit as a necessity.

Table 4.4
Perceptions of necessities by sex: Clothing (%)

Do you feel that this item is a necessity?	Pensioners		Families with children		2+ Adults (inc. couples)		Single People	
	M	*W*	*M*	*W*	*M*	*W*	*M*	*W*
Dressing Gown	51	74	30	40	32	35	30	36
New, not second-hand clothes	76	63	69	60	66	66	66	71
Best outfit for special occasions	71	52	55	52	58	47	55	67

This may connect with the ways in which 'poor' households manage clothing costs. 'Poor' women, in particular, describe the ways in which they buy their own clothes from jumble sales and second-hand shops but will buy new clothes for children and men if possible:

> "I'll go to jumble sales for my clothes. I won't go to a catalogue for mine. But I'm not seeing me kid and me husband walk to town in second-hand clothes. I'll make do for myself but I won't make do for them." (Craig and Glendinning, 1990, cited Graham, 1992, pp219-220)

Consumer durables

There were very few differences between women and men in their likelihood of considering various consumer durables to be necessities of life. The only major difference was that slightly more men than women considered two luxury items - a video and a dishwasher - to be necessities (Table 4.5).

Table 4.5
Perceptions of necessities by sex: Consumer durables (%)

Do you feel that this item is a necessity?	Pensioners		Families with children		2+ Adults (inc. couples)		Single People	
	M	*W*	*M*	*W*	*M*	*W*	*M*	*W*
Dishwasher	6	3	5	3	4	1	9	4
Video	16	8	13	13	18	8	17	12

Although more men viewed a dishwasher and a video as a necessity, the difference between the sexes was least marked amongst those in families with children. The largest differences were found amongst single people and two adult households. Amongst older people, male pensioners were similarly more likely to view the video and the dishwasher as a necessity. Again, this finding reflects the findings of the Swedish study (Nyman, 1996) where men were more likely than women to see 'luxury items' as necessities.

Leisure

Women and men differ in terms of the amount of leisure time they have available, and what they choose to do with it. Having access to a private car increases opportunities for such leisure activities, as does the greater accessibility of public space for men. Women with children are more likely to have their leisure time interspersed during the day - often at times when other responsibilities are temporarily lifted, such as when the baby is asleep, or the child is at a playgroup. Women also have less access to private transport, are more reliant on public transport, and see themselves as less able to use public space. However, for both sexes leisure activities require money. These differences are reflected in the responses to questions in the Breadline Britain survey on leisure items as a necessity. There were four items where women and men differed in terms of whether the item was viewed as a necessity, and the difference was statistically significant. Table 4.6 shows the percentages of women and men viewing these items as a necessity, by household type.

Table 4.6
Perceptions of necessities by sex: Leisure activities (%)

	Pensioners		Families with children		2+ Adults (inc. couples)		Single People	
Do you feel that this item is a necessity?	*M*	*W*	*M*	*W*	*M*	*W*	*M*	*W*
Night out once a fortnight	41	35	43	41	47	35	55	59
Holiday away, one week a year not with relations	64	59	56	48	58	50	57	50
Monthly meal in restaurant	(24)	(19)	(17)	(13)	(19)	(19)	19	(13)
Holidays abroad once a year	(23)	(12)	(17)	(12)	(25)	(18)	19	16

All four items were more often listed as necessities by men. When further broken down by household type, two of the four - the holiday away from home, and a holiday abroad once a year - are more often seen by men as a necessity across all household types. However, single women were more likely than single men to see a night out once a fortnight as being a necessity and women in households containing two or more adults were equally likely as men to consider a monthly meal in a restaurant as a necessity.

Social networks and special occasions

There were some interesting differences in the perception of necessities for items which might be classified under the broad heading of maintaining social networks, with one item in particular, showing a significant difference between women and men. Table 4.7 below summarises these differences by household type.

Table 4.7
Perceptions of necessities by sex: Social networks

Do you feel that this item is a necessity?	Pensioners		Families with children		2+ Adults (inc. couples)		Single people	
	M	*W*	*M*	*W*	*M*	*W*	*M*	*W*
Yearly presents for friends and family	68	75	66	75	65	71	66	70

Women were more likely to see yearly presents for friends and family as a necessity, irrespective of household type. The widest gap is between women and men, in families with children, with 75% of women seeing such presents as a necessity, compared with just 66% of men in families.

This difference can be placed in the context of women's work in families in maintaining kinship and other networks - what has sometimes been described as the emotional housekeeping work women carry out. The issue of social networks and relations is undoubtedly complex and the responses here can only hint at some of the more interesting aspects of how this is gendered. However, a number of studies have shown that familial and community networks are a vital source of both social and practical support for 'poor' families (Craig and Glendinning, 1990). Lone mothers in particular talk of the help offered by families - both financial and other kinds of help, such as free childcare - as significant in their own survival (Graham, 1993; Glendinning and Millar, 1992).

Children's items

There were three items where the responses from women and men showed a statistically significant difference, and these items are shown in Table 4.8.

111

Table 4.8
Perceptions of necessities by sex: Child development

Do you feel that this item is a necessity?	Pensioners		Families with children		2+ Adults (inc. couples)		Single people	
	M	*W*	*M*	*W*	*M*	*W*	*M*	*W*
Leisure equipment for children	63	56	70	57	67	58	63	58
Fortnightly, child's friends for tea	57	64	41	49	49	60	52	61
Child's participation in out-of-school activities	65	76	71	67	67	78	62	74

One item - leisure equipment for children - was more often listed by men as a necessity across all household types, with the greatest gap between men and women amongst those living in families. These differences may be explained by men's own participation in leisure activities - which are more likely to be outside the home and to involve physical activity and equipment, compared with women's leisure activities (Social Trends, 1996) - and also the ways in which men's role in childcare is more frequently associated with children's sporting activities and leisure pursuits.

Women were more likely than men to view fortnightly children's friends for tea and children's participation in out-of-school activities as necessities. This difference holds true across all household types, except in families with children where men are more likely than women to see children's participation in out-of-school activities as a necessity.

Financial security

Finally, there were interesting differences in the ways in which each sex felt about issues of financial security, with one item - the need for regular savings - showing a significant difference between men's and women's responses. Table 4.9 below breaks these responses down by household type.

Table 4.9
Perceptions of necessities by sex: Financial security

Do you feel that this item is a necessity?	Pensioners		Families with children		2+ Adults (inc. couples)		Single people	
	M	*W*	*M*	*W*	*M*	*W*	*M*	*W*
Regular savings for retirement\rainy day	64	67	69	65	78	70	73	51

Men were significantly more likely than women to view savings for a rainy day (of around £10 a month) as a necessity, that everyone should be able to afford. However, when broken down by household type this greater tendency of men to view savings as a necessity is found amongst families with children, households with two or more adults and single people - with a particularly wide gap between single men and single women. Amongst pensioners, however, the difference is reversed, with slightly more female pensioners seeing savings for a rainy day as a necessity, compared with men. There are a number of ways these answers might be explored, albeit in a speculative way. Single women - with a younger age profile - may be less likely to consider savings as a necessity because they have been brought up within a society in which there remains an expectation of the male breadwinner - despite the fact that for many women reality does not match this 'ideal'. Similarly, amongst men the implicit notion of having the responsibility for family finances and for being the provider may affect the importance attached to the idea of savings to fall back on. Amongst older people, however, female pensioners may be more likely to view regular savings as a necessity as this may represent for many their only source of income other than the basic state minimum. Whilst the number of women with their own occupational pension has grown over the past few years, few of those women who are now over retirement age receive a pension in their own right. Most are dependent on either their husband's pension, where there is one, or on the basic state pension, together with any savings they may have made over their lives.

Conclusion

This chapter has explored the extent to which the Breadline Britain survey offers an insight into poverty and deprivation as gendered phenomena. In particular, responses to the questions in the Breadline Britain survey on the perception of necessities suggest that ideas about what constitutes poverty and deprivation may be different for men and women.

What emerges from this analysis is that there are some differences between each sex, in their ideas about necessities. Women more often viewed the following as necessities: meat, fish or a vegetarian equivalent every other day, daily fresh fruit and vegetables, having children's friends round to tea, and children being able to participate in out-of-school activities. However, the list of those items which men were more likely to view as necessities included the following: new clothes, a best outfit, a night out, a holiday away from home, a dishwasher and a video.

These differences begin to suggest that there may be differences in how women and men view poverty - what it means to be 'poor' and which items should be included in a deprivation index - and what the solutions to poverty may consist of. For some time there has been a feminist critique of traditional poverty analysis in that all too often it fails to lift the lid off the 'black box' of intra-household distribution of resources, and does not allow the researcher to view the different experiences of poverty and deprivation that are hidden behind closed doors. However, as the analysis here begins to suggest, there is also a need to critically re-evaluate these assumptions regarding consumption not only in terms of who does what, and who gets what, within the home, but also in terms of what each sex might view as being necessary.

5 Poverty and crime

Christina Pantazis and David Gordon

Introduction

Crime and fear of crime have emerged as major public and political issues in recent decades. This may, in part, be attributed to the enormous growth in recorded crime since the 1970s, where crimes recorded by the police have been averaging at approximately 5% per annum, reaching 5.4 million in 1992. However, this figure is widely acknowledged to be an under-estimate of the 'true' crime level. According to British Crime Survey (BCS) estimates, the 'true' level of crime is three times as high (Mayhew, Maung and Mirrless-Black, 1993). This growth in crime appears to have been matched by a growth in people's fear of crime, with surveys repeatedly showing crime having surpassed unemployment and health as an issue of major public concern (Jacobs and Worcester, 1991). Many commentators now conclude that fear of crime poses almost as large a threat to society as crime itself (Clemente and Kleinman, 1977).

Since the birth of the study of the victim, it has been acknowledged that victimisation is not a random event. Whilst early research focused on victim typologies to explain why individuals become victims (Von Hentig, 1948) more recent studies have explained how particular lifestyles and routine activities, shaped by structural socio-economic factors, determine patterns of victimisation (Hindelang, Gottfredson and Garofalo, 1978; Cohen and Felson, 1979). The proponents of these more recent theories argue that there is a direct link between an individual's routine daily activities and their exposure to high-risk victimisation.

Little consideration has been given to the impact of poverty on victimisation by these studies. Nevertheless, a consensus appears to exist between various government departments and some criminologists that 'poor' people experience more crime. A major basis for this belief appears to be the existence of relatively high levels of both victimisation and recorded crime in many poor areas, particularly in areas with large council estates (Ramsay, 1983; Hope, 1986; Hope and Shaw, 1988).

Recent Home Office research reinforces the link between crime and some 'poor' areas (Mayhew and Maung, 1992). Figure 5.1 shows the relative crime rates (national average=100) for burglary and robbery, for residents of different ACORN neighbourhood groups using the combined 1984, 1988 and 1992 BCS (CACI 1992). The Mixed inner metropolitan areas and the Less well off and Poorest council estates suffer from relatively high crime rates. These ACORN neighbourhoods are characterised by low income households. However, High status, non-family areas that are characterised by households with well above average incomes, also suffer from high crime rates. Agricultural areas and Older terraced housing which also typically contain many low income households have respectively very low and average burglary and robbery rates.

In recent decades, the high levels of crime experienced by many poor inner city council estates has received government attention. For instance, in 1979, the Department of the Environment sponsored the Priority Estates Project which aimed to reduce crime on poor and disadvantaged council estates through improved management (Foster and Hope, 1993).

Government departments have not been alone in believing that crime is disproportionately experienced by 'poor' people. Many criminologists also support this view, particularly those operating within the 'left realist' paradigm (Lea and Young, 1984). 'Left realist' criminologists argue that a realistic approach is needed to crime. Essentially this means focusing less on the crimes committed by the rich and powerful, and focusing more on the crimes by working class people. The theoretical rationale for this stance is two-fold. Firstly, it is argued that the crimes of the working class have a great impact on the 'poor'. Secondly, it is argued that the main target of working class crime is the working class itself (Lea and Young, 1984).

The 1990 Breadline Britain survey provides a unique opportunity to analyse in greater depth the relationship between poverty and victimisation and poverty and fear of crime. Victimisation risks and fear of crime will be explored in relation to deprivation, as well as to other indicators of poverty, such as income and social class. However, prior to this, will be a discussion of some of the problems involved in the measurement and definition of crime.

Figure 5.1
Indexed crime rate for combined 1984, 1988 and 1992
British Crime Surveys by ACORN neighbourhoods

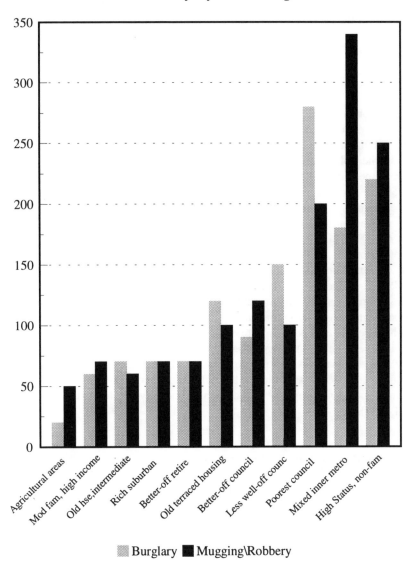

Problems of measurement and definition

The measurement of crime presents a major problem for criminologists. Many crimes are neither reported nor recorded, resulting in the police crime statistics underestimating the 'real' level of crime. Victimisation studies, or crime surveys, provide more reliable results and the Home Office has carried out the British Crime Survey (BCS) in England and Wales in 1982, 1984, 1988, 1992, 1994 and 1996, each measuring crime in the previous year (Hough and Mayhew, 1983; Hough and Mayhew, 1985; Mayhew, Elliot and Dowds, 1989; Mayhew, Maung and Mirrlees-Black, 1993).

There are obvious advantages to using crime surveys rather than recorded crime statistics. They provide a more accurate picture by assessing the crimes that police statistics fail to include. The 1992 BCS found that only 43% of crimes were reported to the police and that only 30% of crimes were recorded by the police. However, crime surveys do not uncover all crimes. Crimes are underestimated when people conceal crimes committed against them (for example, as in some rape cases where the offender is a friend or family member). Crime surveys will also have problems concerning response rate. For instance, although the BCS achieves a good response rate (77% in 1992), non-respondents may include a disproportionately high number of victims.

Most victimisation surveys count only certain types of crimes. For instance, the 1992 BCS acknowledges that it excludes crimes against organisations (e.g. fraud, shoplifting, fare evasion, commercial burglary and robbery). It also excludes 'victimless' crimes (e.g. drug and alcohol misuse, consensual sexual offences) or crimes where people may not be aware of having been victimised, as in fraud. Crime surveys also rely on a narrow concept of crime. Radical criminologists have demonstrated how crime is socially constructed to encompass the activities of the 'poor' but to exclude the activities of the rich and powerful, and this is reflected in the definition of crime adopted by traditional crime surveys (Sumner, 1976; Box, 1983 and 1987).

Findings from the Breadline Britain survey

Respondents of the Breadline Britain survey were asked whether, in the previous year, they or members of their household had experienced certain types of crime such as burglary, assault, mugging or robbery, or any other crime. Fourteen per cent of respondents said that they or members of their household had experienced crime. Figure 5.2 shows the distribution of crimes experienced by respondents or other household members in the previous year: 7.2% of households had been burgled, 2.5% had been mugged, 2.6% had been assaulted and 2.9% had been victims of other crimes.

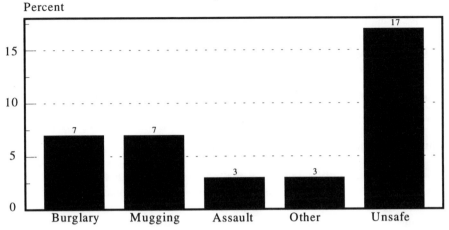

Figure 5.2
Distribution of crime in the previous year and fear of crime

In the Breadline Britain survey, fear of crime was assessed by asking respondents whether they or members of their household felt unsafe in their local neighbourhood. Seventeen percent of respondents said they feared crime. This is a relatively low result when compared the 1992 BCS figure of 32%. However, this difference may simply be the result of the wording of the questions. The BCS question asked respondents about feeling unsafe when walking alone at night, a question that would predictably give a much higher result, whereas the Breadline Britain survey question was much more specific.

Table 5.1 compares the percentage of crimes experienced in the Breadline Britain survey with the British Crime Survey, the General Household Survey, and recorded crime.

Table 5.1
Distribution of crime

Type of Crime	BBS 1990 (%) (n=1,831 households)	BCS 1992 (%) (n=10,059 people)	GHS 1991 (%) (n=9,555 households)	Recorded crime 1991 (% of households)
Burglary	7.2	6.8	4	3.1
Mugged/robbery*	2.5	1.5	-	0.2
Assaulted	2.9	3.4	-	0.4

Note: BCS definition of Mugged/robbery = Robbery and Theft from the person.

The Breadline Britain survey figures correspond closely with the findings of the 1992 BCS. Differences in the figures may result from the fact that the Breadline Britain survey is household-based whereas the BCS is individual-based and that, in the case of assault, different definitions were employed. The burglary rate estimated in the 1991 General Household Survey is much lower because, unlike the BCS, it excludes most attempted burglaries and all people who have moved in the past 12 months. However, when adjustments are made to the BCS data to allow for these differences, the burglary rate is effectively identical to that found in the GHS. As expected, recorded crime is significantly lower for all three offences.

Standard of living, social class and income

Criminologists often maintain that it is the 'poor' or the working class who suffer the most crime. They make little distinction between poverty and social class, often using the terms interchangeably (Lea and Young, 1984). This next section explores in greater depth the relationship between poverty and victimisation and poverty and fear of crime, using the variables of standard of living, social class and household income.

Standard of living

Figure 5.3 illustrates the association between crime, fear of crime and standard of living. The sample has been divided into three groups. The 'poor' group includes all those households living in multiple deprivation (i.e. lacking three or more necessities). The 'not poor' group includes all those households lacking at least two necessities, and the 'comfortable' group includes all other households (i.e. those which can afford all necessities). There is a complicated relationship between standard of living and victimisation but not between standard of living and fear of crime. The 'poor' and the 'comfortable' have roughly equal victimisation rates, 16% and 14% respectively, whilst those 'not poor' have the lowest levels of crime (12%). However, the 'poor' are almost three times as likely to fear crime than the 'comfortable'. Clearly, deprivation, although not closely linked to being a victim of crime, plays an enormous part in feeling unsafe.

Social class

Figure 5.4 illustrates a similarly complicated relationship between social class and victimisation. Victimisation is highest for Social Class E (17%) and lowest for Social Class C2 (11%). Social Class E also has the highest fear of crime (23%). Thus, these findings do not provide support for the claim that working class crime is intra-group.

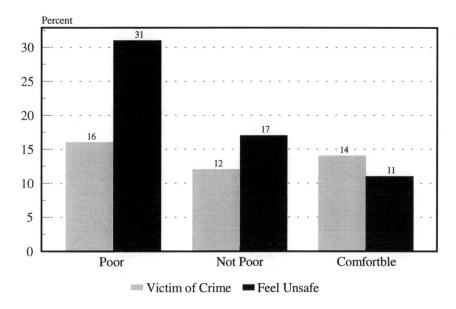

Figure 5.3
Percent experiencing crime and fear of crime by standard of living

Figure 5.4
Percent experiencing crime and fear of crime by social class

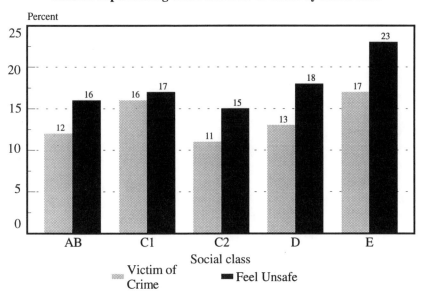

Equivalised income

A roughly U-shaped relationship exists between victimisation and equivalised income (Figure 5.5). Gross household income has been equivalised according to four widely used scales in order to take into account the differing size, composition, and characteristics of households. Minimum income is the actual raw income of the household, whereas Maximum income is simply household income divided by the size of the household (i.e. the income per person). In terms of Minimum income, the Poorest 20% and Richest 20% have roughly equal victimisation rates, 16% and 17% respectively. In terms of Maximum income, the poorest and richest have identical rates (16%). However, with regard to the other three scales the Richest 20% have consistently higher rates of victimisation than the Poorest 20%.

The relationship between fear of crime and household income is shown in Figure 5.6. There is a clear linear relationship between Minimum income and fear of crime. Whereas only 16% of the Richest 20% fear crime, 23% of the Poorest 20% do so. The results across all four types of equivalisation scales are remarkably consistent, showing that fear of crime is disproportionately experienced by the 'poor'.

These analyses, using the Breadline Britain survey, question the assumption that there is a simple positive relationship between poverty and victimisation. The findings show that, regardless of the measure of poverty used, the 'poor' are not necessarily more likely to become victims of crime than the rest of the population. In some instances, the 'better off' suffer by far the greatest levels of crime. However, the results regarding poverty and fear of crime are more conclusive: fear of crime disproportionately affects those living in poverty or on the margins of poverty.

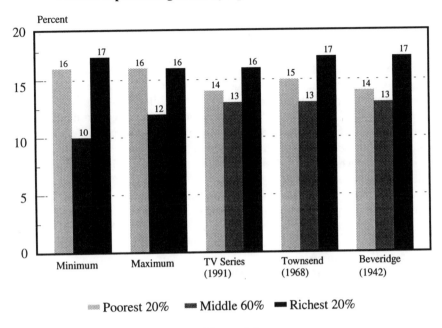

Figure 5.5
Percent experiencing crime by equivalised household income

Poorest 20%   Middle 60%   Richest 20%

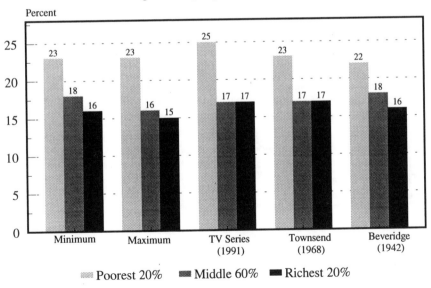

Figure 5.6
Percent fearing crime by equivalised household income

Poorest 20%   Middle 60%   Richest 20%

CHAID analysis

In order to assess which individuals were most likely to experience crime and fear crime, the Chi-Squared Automatic Interaction Detector method (CHAID) was used to explore the most significant variables affecting victimisation rates and fear of crime (see Appendix I for details). CHAID analysis allows both the combination of categories within variables and the sorting of variables to produce the most statistically significant results. CHAID also allows the identification of sub-groups with particularly high and low victimisation and fear of crime rates. CHAID 5.1 shows the most significant factors 'explaining' victimisation levels in the Breadline Britain survey. The boxes show the sample size of the sub-group and the percentage of the sample of households with victims of crime. The stems of the CHAID diagram indicate which are the most significant variables, with those of greater significance nearer the top.

Household type is the most significant factor affecting the likelihood of victimisation. The type that is most victimised is the single non-retired and large, adult only households. In this sub-group of 385 households, 85 households have been victims of crime (22%). This group can be further sub-divided into those who are in 'good' accommodation and those who are in 'poor' or 'adequate' accommodation. Of the 164 households in this latter group, 29% have been victims. This sub-group can again be sub-divided by their history of poverty. The likelihood of being a victim of crime is greatest (36%) for the sub-group who have 'never' or 'rarely' been poor in the past. Student and ex-student households might fit this description (see *The Guardian* 21/9/1993).

The CHAID analysis illustrates that poverty is not a determining factor in explaining victimisation. Type of household is the most statistically significant factor, followed by standard of housing and history of poverty. These factors are more significant than deprivation group, social class, household income, sex and age of the respondent in explaining victimisation risks.

CHAID 5.2 shows the most significant factors relating to fear of crime. In this case, deprivation is the most important factor for people fearing crime, affecting 30% of the multiply deprived. Furthermore, fear of crime increases when deprivation is compounded by a long history of poverty and a poor standard of housing. Of the multiply deprived, 36% who have experienced poverty in the past felt unsafe in their local neighbourhood and, of this group, 47% of those in poor housing fear crime. Age and sex are not as significant in explaining fear of crime.

The next section examines in more detail the relationship between victimisation, fear of crime and the factors found to be most significant in the CHAID analyses.

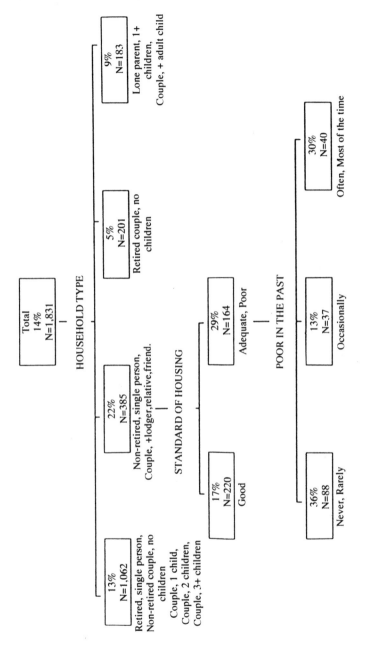

CHAID 5.1
Experience of crime

Total
14%
N=1,831

HOUSEHOLD TYPE

13%
N=1,062
Retired, single person,
Non-retired couple, no
children
Couple, 1 child,
Couple, 2 children,
Couple, 3+ children

22%
N=385
Non-retired, single person,
Couple, +lodger,relative,friend.

5%
N=201
Retired couple, no
children

9%
N=183
Lone parent, 1+
children,
Couple, + adult child

STANDARD OF HOUSING

17%
N=220
Good

29%
N=164
Adequate, Poor

POOR IN THE PAST

36%
N=88
Never, Rarely

13%
N=37
Occasionally

30%
N=40
Often, Most of the time

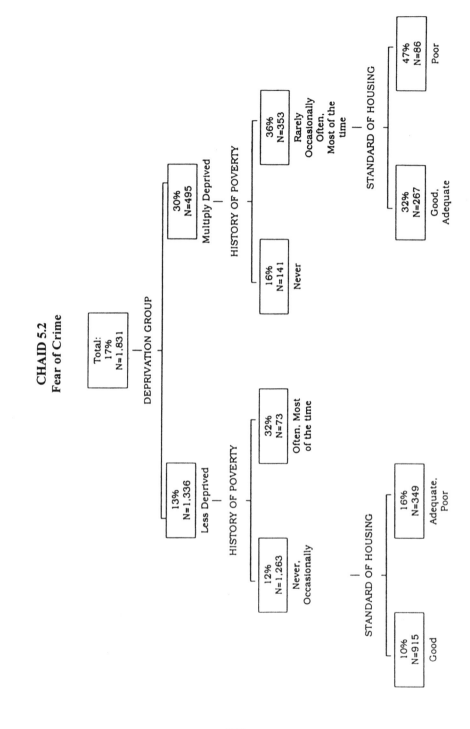

CHAID 5.2
Fear of Crime

Total: 17% N=1,831

DEPRIVATION GROUP

13% N=1,336 — Less Deprived

30% N=495 — Multiply Deprived

HISTORY OF POVERTY

12% N=1,263 — Never, Occasionally

32% N=73 — Often, Most of the time

16% N=141 — Never

36% N=353 — Rarely Occasionally, Often, Most of the time

STANDARD OF HOUSING

10% N=915 — Good

16% N=349 — Adequate, Poor

32% N=267 — Good, Adequate

47% N=86 — Poor

126

Factors affecting crime and fear of crime

History of poverty

Figure 5.7 shows the association between crime, fear of crime and a history of poverty. There is a linear relationship between fear of crime and a history of poverty. Thirty-three percent of those 'often' or 'mostly' poor fear crime, compared to only 11% of those 'never' poor in the past. Those who have been poor 'most of the time' also face the highest levels of victimisation (24%).

Household type

According to the CHAID analysis, household type is the most important factor explaining victimisation. Figure 5.8 illustrates the relationship between type of household, crime and fear of crime. The group experiencing the most crime is the single, non-retired. One quarter has experienced crime, yet its fear of crime is average (17%). Conversely, lone parents, who have the highest fear of crime (21%), have the second lowest victim rate (9%) and retired couples, who suffer the least crime (5%), have a fear of crime that is just marginally below the average for the whole sample. As these findings indicate, in many types of households, rates of fear do not correspond to actual risks of victimisation. The high levels of deprivation faced by many elderly or lone parent households, may help to explain why they have relatively high rates of fear.

Standard of housing

Figure 5.9 shows that both victimisation and fear of crime increase with deteriorating housing standards. Those in 'poor' housing have the highest levels of both victimisation and fear. They are almost twice as likely to experience crime and almost three times more likely to fear crime than those in 'good' housing. Those in 'poor' housing also have a distorted perception of crime, giving rise to a fear of crime which is almost double their actual victimisation rate. Again, factors closely connected to poverty play an important role in experiences of victimisation and fear of crime.

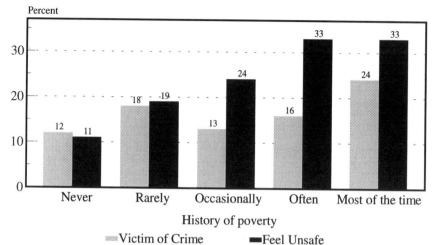

Figure 5.7
Percent experiencing crime and fear of crime by history of poverty

Note: % for Do not know: Experience of Crime = 13%
Feeling Unsafe = 19%

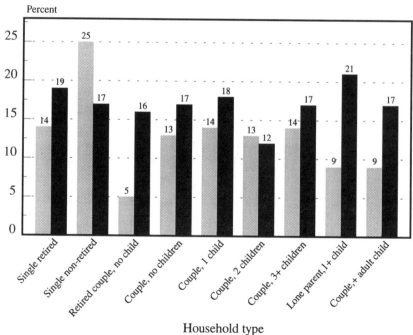

Figure 5.8
Percent experiencing crime and fear of crime by type of household

Poverty and fear of crime re-examined

The Breadline Britain survey confirmed the universal finding that rates of fear of crime and actual risks of victimisation do not correspond. Other than some analysis on income, there is very little research on the role of poverty in shaping these distortions (Maxfield, 1987). The Breadline Britain survey undertook an analysis of the impact of poverty on fear of crime, controlling for victimisation. Figure 5.10 compares the rates of fear for different combinations of factors. People living in poverty suffer the highest rates of fear regardless of victimisation; 48% of 'poor' victims also fear crime, compared to only 13% of the rest of the ('non-poor') victimised population.

The finding that poverty is closely associated to fear of crime, exists across different types of households. Figure 5.11 illustrates the relationship between household type and fear of crime, controlling for poverty and victimisation. 'Poor' pensioners experience the greatest fear regardless of whether or not they have experienced crime. Of 'poor' pensioners who have been victims, 62% fear crime. They are seven times more likely to fear crime than 'non-poor' pensioners who have been victims. Similarly, fear of crime is four times greater for 'poor' lone parents as it is for 'non-poor' lone parents; two times greater for other 'poor' families with children; twelve times greater for 'poor' single people; and three times higher for all other 'poor' households.

Figure 5.9
Percent experiencing crime and fear of crime by standard of housing

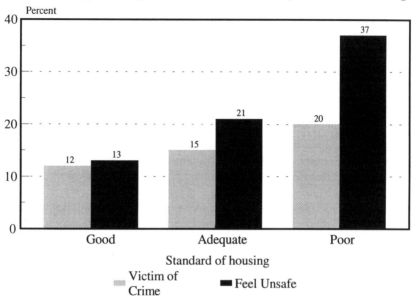

Figure 5.10
Percent fearing crime by deprivation and victimisation

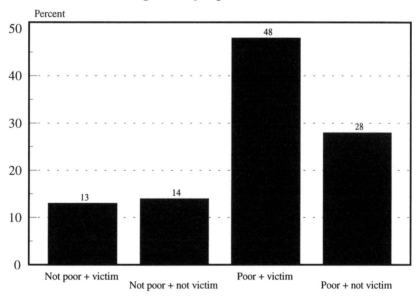

Fear of crime and lack of insurance

A considerable amount of research has been carried out on factors contributing to fear of crime (Garofalo, 1981; Box, Hale, and Andrews, 1988; Maxfield, 1987). These factors can be classified under six headings:

- vulnerability - physical and economic
- incivilities, especially in inner cities
- personal knowledge of crime and victimisation
- confidence in the police and the criminal justice system
- perceptions of personal risk
- seriousness of various offences

Vulnerable groups, such as the elderly, lone parents and the homeless, have the highest levels of fear of crime. They also have high deprivation levels. Kim, who appeared in the television series for Breadline Britain, spoke of the constant fear of living in London as a homeless teenager: "I mean it's bad, it's scary... because you do get some dodgy people" (Kim-2). Her friend Keisha made the comment: "a pervert walking past... it sometimes frightens you, going up and down the street." (Kim-4)

The physical characteristics of a neighbourhood or community may also contribute to fear of crime.

"Noisy neighbours and loud parties, graffiti, teenagers hanging around street corners, drunks and tramps on the streets, rubbish and litter lying around, boarded up houses and flats with broken windows"

can make a neighbourhood threatening and therefore exacerbate people's fear (Box, Hale and Andrews, 1988). The physical decay of a neighbourhood is also associated with poverty, particularly in inner cities.

Although fear of crime is often seen as irrational by many criminologists, the effects of crime, particularly property crime, will be greatest on low income households which cannot afford to replace lost possessions. In these circumstances, fear of crime cannot be considered to be irrational. Respondents to the Breadline Britain survey were asked if they had house contents insurance and, if they did not, whether this was because they could not afford it. Figure 5.12 shows that households with no insurance[1] suffer almost twice as much fear of crime as households with insurance, despite having only a 2% higher crime rate.

Eighty-five percent of the group with no insurance suffered from multiple deprivation. As Paula, who also appeared in the television series for Breadline Britain, made clear:

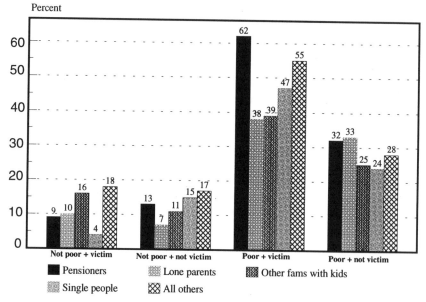

Figure 5.11
Percent of types of households fearing crime by deprivation and victimisation

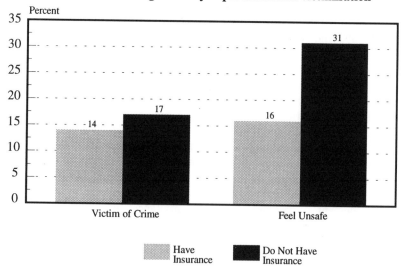

Figure 5.12
Percent fearing crime by deprivation and victimisation

*Excludes those who do not have insurance because they do not want it.

"We haven't got insurance simply for the fact that we can't afford it.... It's mainly for your personal possessions, if they break in, that's just gone... It's really pot luck, take your chance. You go out and you lock the doors, if they're broken when you come back there's nothing you can do about it."
(Paula 2)

Conclusion

The Breadline Britain survey found that poverty was more strongly related to fear of crime than actual victimisation. The CHAID analysis of victimisation demonstrated that single people and those living in large non-retired only households experience the highest risks of crime, particularly if they live in poor housing and have never experienced poverty. Thus, high levels of victimisation seem to be associated more with a lack of social cohesion in a community rather than with high levels of poverty. However, there is a definite link between poverty and fear of crime. Poor people suffer from a disproportionately high level of fear of crime regardless of whether or not they have been victimised. This fear is not irrational but results from the greater impact that crime has on 'poor' people.

Note

1   Those households without insurance because they do not want it have been excluded to prevent distortion in the analysis. This group's fear of crime is similar to that of the group that possesses insurance rather than the group that cannot afford insurance.

6 Poverty and health

Christina Pantazis and David Gordon

"If we care about the health of the poor we need to abolish their poverty."
(Tony Smith, Associate Editor, *British Medical Journal*, 18-25 August 1990)

Introduction

The recognition that poverty is a primary cause of ill health is again on the political agenda. As socio-economic inequalities have widened so have the differences in state of health. Tuberculosis, a disease with a strong association with poverty, is now on the increase. A recent report has shown that tuberculosis notification rates have risen in the United Kingdom and that this may be related to a rise in economic and social deprivation among a minority of the population (Spence *et al*, 1993).

The evidence proving a link between poverty and ill health is vast. Social class, as measured by the occupation of head of household, is often used to illustrate the relationship between poverty and health (Townsend and Davidson, 1988; Cartwright, 1992). Other measures such as income distribution (Wilkinson, 1992; Blaxter, 1990), car ownership and housing tenure (Goldblatt, 1990), educational level and deprivation (Benzeval *et al*, 1992) also highlight health inequalities.

The Black Report

The alarming findings concerning the persistence of health inequalities between social class groups provided the impetus for the setting up of *The Working Group on Inequalities in Health*. David Ennals, Secretary of State for the Social Services, stated on 27 March 1977:

> "The crude differences in mortality rates between the various social classes are worrying. To take the extreme example, in 1971 the death rate for adult men in social class V (unskilled workers) was nearly twice that of adult men in social class I (professional workers)...when you look at death rates for specific diseases the gap is even wider...the first step towards remedial action is to put together what is already known about the problem...it is a major challenge for the next ten or more years to try to narrow the gap in health standards between different social classes."

The Working Group had three tasks. Firstly, it was to review and analyse the data on social class differences in health. Secondly, it was to identify possible causes for the differences in health and suggest implications for public policy. Finally, it was to suggest further research.

The Group's Report concluded that health inequalities still persisted and had widened in some cases, despite the National Health Service. Using occupational class at the time of death, the Report showed that men and women in Social Class V had well over twice the chance of dying before retirement age than their counterparts in Class I. Class differences in mortality were "a constant feature of the entire human life-span" (Townsend and Davidson, 1988). The Report also found a similar class gradient with use of health services.

The Working Group concluded 'materialist' factors such as income, employment, education, housing, transport and specific work conditions were responsible for these health inequalities. Cultural and genetic explanations had some relevance, the latter being particularly important in early childhood. However, the overwhelming evidence was that social and economic factors were more important.

The Group recommended a broad approach by emphasising preventative, primary and community health care. It advocated a radical improvement in the material lives of the 'poorer' sections of society, particularly children and those with disabilities. Specifically, it recommended increasing child benefit and disablement allowance, introducing maternity grants and infant care allowances. It also suggested improved nurseries, ante-natal clinics, sheltered housing, and improvements relating to work conditions.

The Report received a hostile reception by the new, Conservative, Secretary of State, Patrick Jenkin and there was no publication by HMSO. The 260 duplicated copies of the Report were made available on the Friday before the August Bank Holiday. Commenting on the £2 billion a year required to meet the recommendations made by the Working Group, the Secretary of State claimed that it was:

> "unrealistic in present or any foreseeable economic circumstances, quite apart from any judgement that may be formed of the effectiveness of such expenditure in dealing with problems identified."

Margaret Whitehead's *The Health Divide* (1988) provided a review of studies on health inequalities since the 1980 Black Report. Whilst acknowledging improvements in health, particularly in life expectancy and infant mortality, Whitehead wrote:

> "Improvements in the health of the poor have failed to keep up with improvements enjoyed by the prosperous - a detail which is hidden when only overall health trends are quoted."

The review confirmed the findings of the Black Report and concluded that recent evidence further demonstrated that socio-economic factors were most important in explaining health inequalities between different social groups.

Alternative explanations of health inequalities

Alternative explanations of inequalities in health fall into three main groups: artefact explanations; theories of natural or social selection and lifestyle or cultural explanations.

Artefact explanations

A key finding of many studies on inequalities in health has been that, despite the overall decline in mortality rates since the Second World War, the differences in mortality rates between Social Class I, II and IV, V have increased (Hart, 1986; Davy-Smith *et al*, 1990). Health inequalities have widened despite the overall improvements in the health of the population (Townsend and Davidson, 1988; Whitehead, 1988). This finding has been challenged on the grounds that it may be a statistical artefact resulting from the changing relative sizes of Social Classes I, II and IV, V since the War (Illsley, 1986; Carr-Hill, 1990). Statistical problems arising from inaccuracies in the recording of occupation on Death Certificates have also made the finding questionable. However, no evidence has been advanced to show that changing class sizes explain widening mortality rates between social classes. Instead, these authors speculate on the importance of statistical artefact as an explanation of apparent health inequalities.

There is, however, evidence that mere 'artefact' cannot explain away health inequalities. Successive Census Reports show that poorer occupational classes have contracted in size less than is supposed. Furthermore, the OPCS Longitudinal Study provides evidence, free from statistical problems, that there is a clear gradient between classes in mortality rates. There is also a consistent pattern between poverty and health found in studies using other indicators of socio-economic circumstance, such as income, housing tenure, car ownership and education level.

Theories of natural or social selection

The 1980s saw a revival of the old nineteenth century 'social selection' explanation. According to this view, health inequalities are explained by a health selection process. It suggests that health status is a major factor for social mobility:

> "People in poor health would tend to move down the occupational scale and concentrate in the lower social classes, while people in good health would tend to move up into higher social classes." (Whitehead, 1988)

Illsley's 1955 study demonstrated a link between the height of women and social mobility. In his study, taller women tended to move up the social class scale at marriage, while shorter women tended to move down the scale. Taking height as an indicator of health before marriage, Illsley argued that a health selection process was operating at marriage and therefore contributing to class differentials in health. Illsley's 1986 Aberdeen study of first time mothers and the outcome of their pregnancies showed a gradient in prenatal mortality, birth weight of babies and health of mothers between occupational classes. Another study involving the construction of a probability model attempted to show how an increase in the rate of mobility increased with social class mortality differences (Stern, 1983).

Social mobility can account for some of the social class mortality and morbidity differences. The key question is how much of the difference can mobility explain? The National Child Development Study (NCDS) has been investigating the health of a cohort of 17,000 children born in 1958. Studies drawing on the NCDS data have shown that social mobility/selection can only account for a small proportion of the inequalities in health. Fogelman *et al* (1989) looked at the health of those who had remained in a stable social background. Mobility could not explain the differences in health between different socio-economic groups because no mobility had taken place. Power *et al* (1990) found that: "previous health and development, especially early in childhood, are not important in explaining class inequalities in health in young adults." In this study, large social class inequalities in health persisted at age 23 even after controlling for childhood ill health at ages 7, 11 and 16, as well as harmful behaviours such as smoking in adolescence.

138

Lifestyle or cultural explanations explain health inequalities in terms of an individual adopting a lifestyle, involving :

> "excessive consumption of harmful commodities, refined foods, tobacco, or by lack of exercise, or under-utilisation of preventative health care, vaccination, ante-natal surveillance or contraception." (Townsend and Davidson, 1988, p110)

Lifestyle or cultural explanations are 'victim-blaming' because an individual's health status is seen as their own responsibility.

Conservative Health Minister Edwina Currie did much to publicise the case for lifestyle explanations. She argued that ignorance explained the health inequalities between North and South, saying "The problem very often for people is just ignorance - failing to realise that they do have some control over their lives." Apparently, poverty could not explain health inequalities because "this nation spends £900 million a year on crisps; eating well can be done just as cheaply as eating badly."

Much of the research on health has focused on the lifestyle differences between social class groups. Lifestyle differences can partly explain health inequalities between social classes. Cigarette smoking is a good example. Studies that have established the class gradient for cigarette smoking all show that the percentage of smokers steadily increases from Social Class AB to Social Class E (OPCS, 1986). There is a similar class gradient for smoking-related diseases, such as coronary heart disease and lung cancer. This suggests that lifestyles play a part in explaining health inequalities. The crucial question regarding lifestyle explanations is the *extent* to which they do this.

Studies have shown that even after controlling for lifestyle factors, health inequalities persist. Marmot *et al* (1984) re-examined the 1967-69 Whitehall study of 17,530 civil servants which showed the importance of both smoking and employment grade in relation to coronary heart disease. There was a relationship between smoking and poor health in the highest grade. However, employees in lower grades were also susceptible to coronary heart disease, regardless of whether or not they were smokers.

Lifestyle explanations of health inequalities may have some limiting influence. Yet, such explanations are inadequate if they fail to account for the social and economic pressures that encourage lower social class groups to adopt certain lifestyles. Even Edwina Currie recognised this when she said that it was easy for her to make judgements about control over one's life. An explanation of health inequalities in terms of behaviour must therefore incorporate an understanding of how lifestyles are shaped by socio-economic pressures.

Results from the Breadline Britain survey

The Breadline Britain survey attempted to assess the relationship between poverty and health. The scope of this enquiry was two-fold. Firstly, it was to examine whether 'poor' people have disproportionately higher illness and disability rates than the rest of the population. Secondly, it was to examine whether they make more use of health services.

A definition of 'health'

'Health' is not a static concept. "It varies among different groups within a single society and between societies, as well as in any single society over time" (Morris, 1975). Definitions of health are therefore vast. At the end of the Second World War, the World Health Organisation (WHO) adopted a definition of health which included a social element as well as a concern with disease and the healing process. Its definition involved "a state of complete physical, mental and social well-being and not merely the absence of disease or infirmity" (WHO, 1948, p100). This 'social' model of health placed an emphasis on physical fitness, good diet, immunisation, and health education. There is now a consensus that health is a resource. "[Health is] a positive concept emphasising social and personal resources as well as physical capacities" (WHO, 1984).

The adoption of much wider definitions of health is in part due to the successes of medical science in reducing mortality rates. Social scientists have also influenced the social model by providing evidence for the link between health and social environment and therefore the role of socio-economic factors in the promotion of health and the causation of disease.

Measuring health

A systematic study of health requires indicators of health. There are many measures to choose from: mortality rates, prevalence or incidence of morbidity rates, sickness-absence rates and restricted activity rates. Indicators of health will therefore vary from country to country, as well as according to the objectives of the study. In industrialised nations, mortality rates are of less relevance because of the success in reducing premature death (Benzeval *et al*, 1992).

In recent years, there has been growing support for a 'subjective' measurement of health. Whether people feel themselves to be ill is an important dimension to health. Evidence demonstrates that self-assessment of health status is a good measure of health (Wannamethee and Sahper, 1991 and Mossey and Shapiro, 1982). The Breadline Britain survey added this 'subjective' element to the measurement of health.

In Q27a, respondents were asked:

"Do you or does anybody else in your household have any long-standing illness, disability or infirmity? By long-standing I mean anything that has troubled you over a period of time or that is likely to affect you over a period of time?"

Social class and health

Much of the literature on health and poverty has focused on health inequalities between social class groups. Historically, occupational classification has measured social class:

"Partly because it has been regarded as more potent than some alternatives, but partly because it has been regarded as the most convenient for statistical measurement and analysis. Occupation not simply designates type of work but tends also to show broadly how strenuous or unhealthy it is, what are the likely working conditions - for example whether it is indoors or outdoors and whether there is exposure to noise, dust or vibration - and what amenities and facilities are available, as well as level of remuneration and likely access to fringe benefits." (Townsend and Davidson 1988, pp39-40)

It was for these reasons that the Black Report Working Group chose to employ the Registrar General's occupation classification.

However, social class is not necessarily the best indicator of poverty. A deprivation index is a more precise measure of people's material circumstances. Results from the Breadline Britain survey show that deprivation exists even in the highest social class, 80% of the 'poor' are in social classes D and E, 1% are in social class AB (see Chapter 3). Previous poverty due to unemployment or time spent in education may account for this. The unequal distribution of income within families is another factor (see Chapter 4). Daly (1989) has shown that some women who do not work outside the home live in poverty because their (working) husbands fail to transfer sufficient income to them. However, if the Registrar General's classification of social class according to the occupation of the head of household is used, this type of deprivation remains hidden. In the following section, we examine the relationship between poverty and health in the Breadline Britain survey, using deprivation indices rather than social class.

Deprivation and health

The results of the Breadline Britain survey show the persistence of health inequalities. In 1990, 'poor' people still experience worse health than the rest of the population and they make more use of health services excluding preventative care.

The Breadline Britain survey reinforces the results of the study *The Health Status of Londoners: A comparative perspective* (Benzeval *et al*, 1992), that used a similar methodology (Townsend, 1987; Townsend *et al*, 1987). This study found that the 'multiply deprived' are almost ten times more likely to consider themselves as having poor health; twice as likely to have had an illness in the previous two weeks and more than three times as likely to have had a major health problem in the last year than the 'less deprived'.

Furthermore, other studies on the use of a full range of primary care services (preventative and curative), have shown that manual groups use General Practitioner services more than non-manual groups (OPCS, 1986).[1]

Figure 6.1 shows the relationship between deprivation and long-standing illness in the Breadline Britain survey. Of respondents living in poverty, 44% reported that they or somebody in their household was suffering a long-standing illness, compared with only 28% of 'less deprived' respondents.

Figure 6.2 illustrates inequalities with respect to disability. In Q27b, the questionnaire asked:

> "Are you/anybody else in your household registered as disabled or in receipt of a disability benefit such as attendance allowance or need physical aids such as a wheel chair?"

'Poor' households are more likely to contain persons with a disability. Of the 'multiply deprived' households, 17% reported that somebody was in receipt of disability related benefit, compared with only 9% of the 'less deprived' households. Respondents were also asked, in Q28a(b):

> "How many times have you (or other household member) consulted a Doctor for reasons other than pregnancy, contraception, screening or other preventative health care services in the last 12 months?"

Figure 6.3 shows the relationship between deprivation and frequency of visits to the doctor. Compared with the rest of the population, 'poor' households make more frequent visits to the doctor. Of the 'multiply deprived', 33% make between one and two visits to the doctor over a one year period, compared with only 26% of the 'less deprived'.

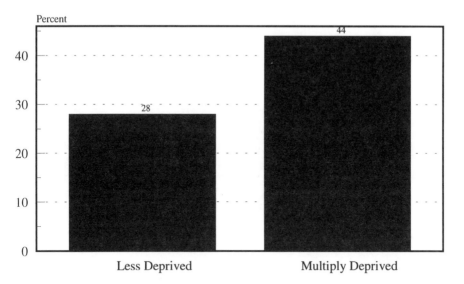

Figure 6.1
Percent with a long-standing illness by deprivation group

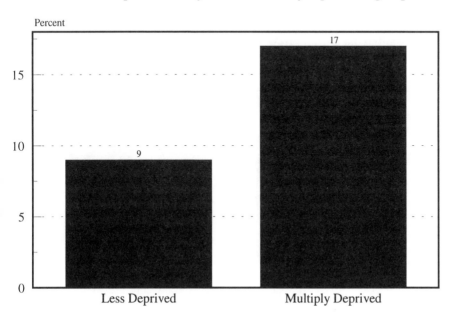

Figure 6.2
Percent in receipt of disability related benefit by deprivation group

Figure 6.3
Percent visiting their GP in the last year by deprivation group

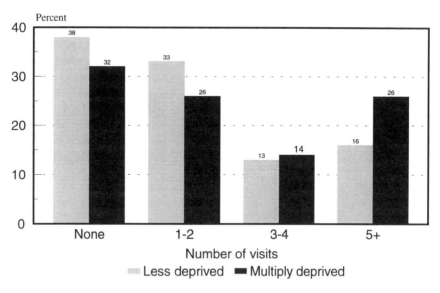

Note: Excludes visits to the doctor for pregnancy, contraception, screening or other
preventative health care.

Figure 6.4
Percent having hospital treatment in the last year by deprivation group

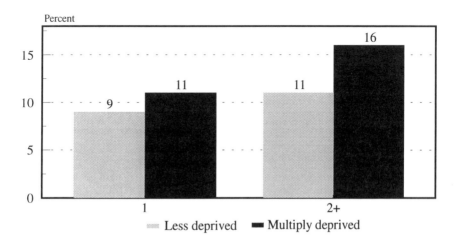

144

Figure 6.4 illustrates the relationship between deprivation and frequency of hospital treatment in the last year. The survey (Q29a & b) asked:

"How many times have you (or a member of your household) required hospital treatment for reasons other than pregnancy, screening or other preventative health care in the last 12 months?"

Poor households have more frequent hospital treatment with 16% having had two or more hospital treatments in the last year, compared with 11% of the rest of the population. In Q2, respondents were asked:

"Now, thinking about health related problems, I would like you to tell me whether each of the following applies to you personally or to anyone in your household now. a) Health problems caused or made worse by housing situation; b) On hospital waiting list for more than 6 months; c) On hospital waiting list for more than 12 months?"

Figure 6.5 demonstrates the relationship between deprivation and hospital waiting lists. 'Poor' households wait longer on hospital waiting lists despite having worse health. Compared with the rest of the population, the 'multiply deprived' are one and a half times more likely to be on hospital waiting lists for both more than six months and more than twelve months.

Figure 6.5
Percent on hospital waiting lists by deprivation group

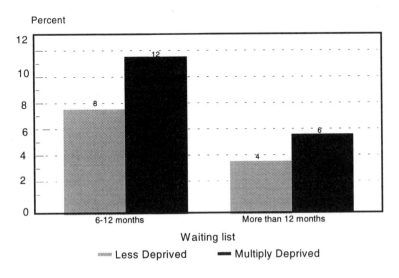

145

Standard of housing and health

Standard of housing has important implications for health. Blackburn (1990) explained the impact of housing on health:

> "The quality of our home environment has an important bearing on our quality of life. Most people spend at least half of their waking hours at home....Housing is, therefore, a major health resource." (p.77)

Certain housing situations can cause or aggravate health problems. Figure 6.6 shows the relationship between deprivation and health problems caused or made worse by housing situation. 'Poor' households are more likely to have health problems adversely affected by their housing situation. Of the 'multiply deprived', 19% feel that this is the case, compared with only 5% of the 'less deprived'.

'Poorer' households are clearly more likely to have health problems associated with their housing situation as they are more likely to live in housing conditions that are damp, over crowded, badly designed and generally in a bad state of repair. Poor people are also likely to spend proportionately more time at home. This applies particularly to women, if they are looking after children, and the unemployed.

In the Breadline Britain TV series, a mother living with her two small children on welfare benefits complained that her Bed and Breakfast accommodation had a whole door covered in asbestos and a ceiling infested with cockroaches. She explained:

> "My daughter has got asthma.... I was offered a flat but the doctor came round looked at the house and said that it was so bad that I couldn't take it because of my daughter's health. It would probably kill her. That's what the doctor said, and the council still didn't do anything about it. The doctor also told the council that I was suicidal, that I'd tried to commit suicide, but they still didn't help me." (Vox Pops - Mothers)

Figure 6.7 shows the relationship between standard of housing and health problems caused or worsened by housing situation. There is a clear relationship between households with health problems caused or worsened by housing situation and a deteriorating standard of housing. Only 4% of those living in 'good' accommodation claimed that their health problem was adversely affected by their housing situation compared with over one-third of those in 'poor' accommodation. Those in 'poor' accommodation are almost ten times more likely to have health problems connected with their housing situation than those in 'good' accommodation. Other studies have also shown that housing inequalities contribute to the relative inequalities in health (Townsend and Davidson, 1988; Whitehead, 1988).

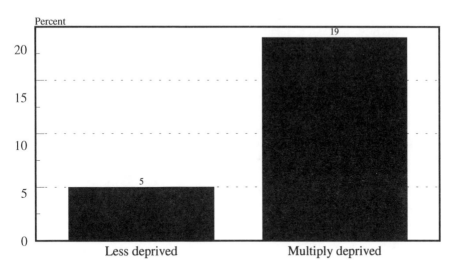

Figure 6.6
Percent with health problems caused or made worse as a result of housing situation by deprivation group

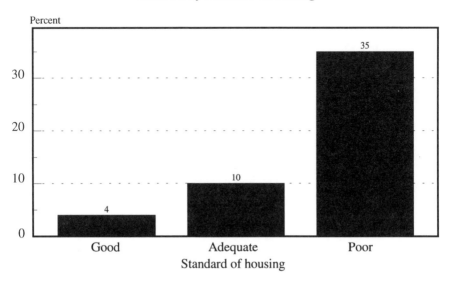

Figure 6.7
Percent with health problems caused or made worse as a result of housing situation by standard of housing

Inequalities and long-standing illness

The Breadline Britain survey established a clear link between deprivation and inequalities in health. CHAID analyses (see Appendix I) were undertaken in order to identify the most significant factors affecting long-standing illness and disability and particularly to assess the relative contribution of poverty and poverty-related factors. CHAID 6.1 shows that a total of 570 respondents either have a long-standing illness or live in a household where someone else does. This represents 31% of the whole sample which is a similar proportion to that found by the 1990 General Household Survey where 33% of men and 35% of women reported suffering from a long-standing illness.

As expected, age is the most important factor affecting long-standing illness[2]. However, for every age group, deprivation and poverty-related factors (previous poverty and debt) have the greatest contributory impact on health status. This suggests that when the effects of age are taken into account, health differentials are best explained by poverty and poverty-related factors.

The highest illness rate is experienced by those aged 54 and over. Of this sub-group of 649 households, 42% contain someone suffering from a long-standing illness. This sub-group can be further sub-divided by their history of poverty. Of those who have had either an 'occasional' or a substantial history of poverty, 57% have an illness. This sub-group can again be sub-divided by deprivation. Almost 70% of those aged 54+ who have been 'poor in the past' and are currently 'living in poverty' have a long-standing illness.

The second highest rate of illness is experienced by those aged between 45-54. Of this age group, 35% have a long-standing illness. Deprivation is the most important factor affecting this group's health status. This sub-group has an illness rate of 54%.

The lowest illness rate occurs in the age group 16-44. Those least likely to have a limiting long-standing illness are aged 16-44, have no debt problems and have 'never' or 'rarely' been poor in the past (15%).

CHAID 6.1
Experience of long-standing illness

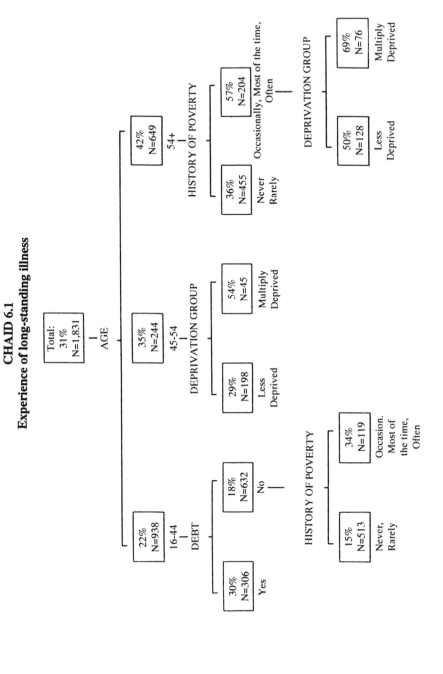

Factors affecting long-standing illness

Age

The CHAID analysis showed that age is the most important factor affecting long-standing illness. The Breadline Britain survey had a similar proportion of people with a long-standing illness as the 1990 General Household Survey. Differences in prevalence rates for illness between surveys are often due to differences in the wording of the illness questions. Forrest and Gordon (1993) argued that both the position and the wording of questions about illness will affect prevalence rates.

A history of poverty

Previous poverty is a major contributory factor affecting long-standing illness. Figure 6.8 shows that there is a clear linear relationship between a history of poverty and illness. Only 25% of households that have 'never' lived in poverty contain somebody with a long-standing illness, compared with 52% of those households that have been poor 'most of the time'.

Debt

Figure 6.9 shows the association between illness and debt. Indebted households are more likely to contain somebody suffering a long-standing illness. Of households in debt, there are 36% containing somebody with a illness, compared with only 30% of households not in debt.

Inequalities and disability

The Breadline Britain survey found that 187 households contained someone suffering from a disability (10%). CHAID 6.2 shows the most statistically significant factors affecting disability. As expected, age is the most important factor. The ageing process is responsible for impairments that cause many disabilities (Martin *et al,* 1988). After allowing for age, deprivation and other poverty-related factors (previous poverty, social class, Income Support, and debt) have the greatest impact on disability.

The disability rate is highest for those aged 45+, at 16%. This sub-group can be further sub-divided by deprivation. Of the multiply deprived, 28% have a disability. This sub-group can be again sub-divided by its history of poverty. Rather surprisingly, the 'occasionally' poor have highest disability rate (44%). The fact that the 'less deprived' in the age sub-group 45+ have a disability rate that is also higher than that of the whole sample (13%) indicates that disability occurs with age, independently of deprivation level - although, disability is twice as likely in situations of poverty.

Figure 6.8
Percent with a long-standing illness by history of poverty

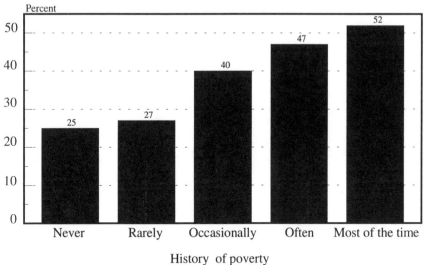

Percent

					52
50				47	
40			40		
30					
		27			
25					

Never   Rarely   Occasionally   Often   Most of the time

History of poverty

Figure 6.9
Percent with a long-standing illness by debt

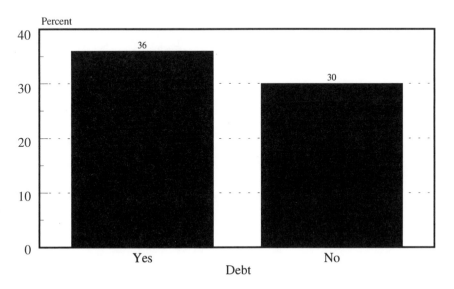

Percent

Yes   No
36   30

Debt

*Owe money to family/friends or money lenders.

151

CHAID 6.1
Experience of disability

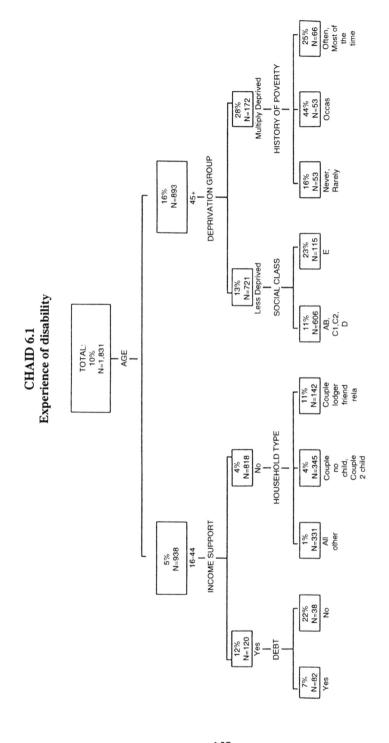

The lowest disability rate (5%) is experienced by those aged 16-44. This age sub-group can be sub-divided by receipt of Income Support. Of those on Income Support, 12% have a disability. This sub-group can again be sub-divided by debt. The disability rate is 22% for those not in debt compared with only 7% for those in debt. One explanation for this is that some people on Income Support can rely on friends and relatives for financial support. This financial support may be indicative of a social support network which acts to alleviate the effects of poverty.

Factors affecting disability

A history of poverty

A history of poverty is a significant contributory factor affecting disability. Figure 6.10 illustrates a near linear relationship between disability and history of poverty. Only 7% of households that have 'never' been poor contain somebody with a disability, compared with 19% of households that have 'often' been poor.

Social class

Figure 6.11 illustrates the relationship between disability and social class. The disability rate is 7% for Classes AB, C1 and C2. There is a three-fold increase (21%) in the disability rate for households in Social Class E.

Income support

Figure 6.12 illustrates the relationship between disability and Income Support. The disability rate for those households claiming Income Support is 17%, compared with only 9% for all other households.

Debt

Figure 6.13 shows that there is little relationship between disability and debt. Those households in debt have a marginally lower disability rate than those not in debt.

Household type

Figure 6.14 illustrates that there is a wide variation in the disability rates. Households with at least one retired person have the highest rate and households with children have the lowest. The average disability rate for all households with at least one retired person is 24%, whereas for households with children it is roughly 6%. However, within the former classification there are wide differences.

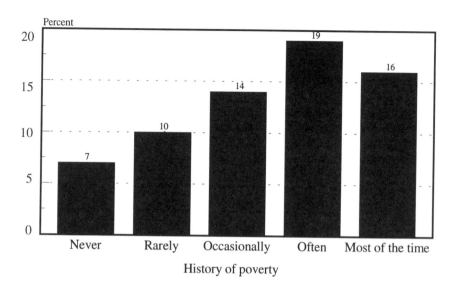

Figure 6.10
Percent with a disability by history of poverty

History of poverty

Figure 6.11
Percent with a disability by social class

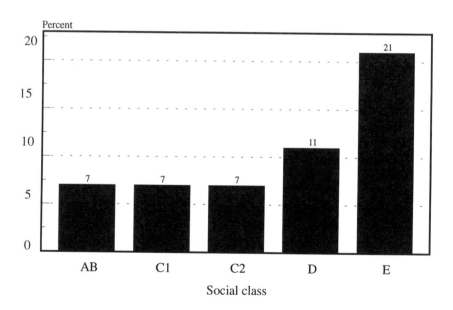

Social class

Figure 6.12
Percent with a disability by Income Support

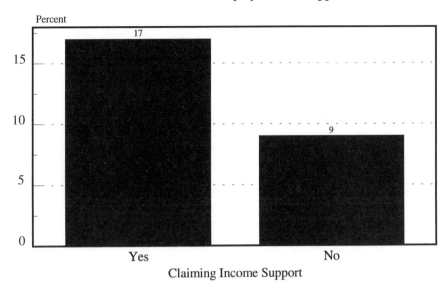

Figure 6.13
Percent with a disability by debt

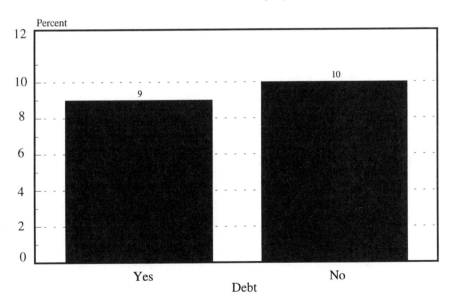

*Owes money to either family/friend or money lender.

155

Figure 6.14
Percent with a disability by household type

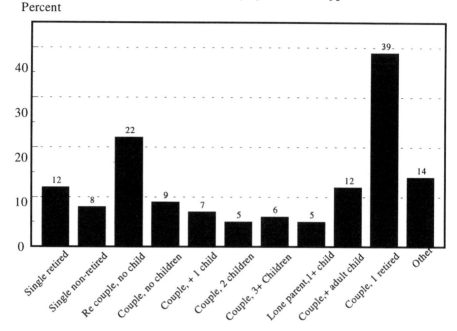

Conclusion

The 1990s have seen the re-emergence of health as a poverty issue. Socio-economic factors are replacing ideas of lifestyle and social mobility as determining influences on health status. Studies have shown that diseases of poverty, such as tuberculosis, are once again on the increase.

The Breadline Britain survey shows that, in 1990, 'poor' households were one and a half times more likely to contain somebody with a long-standing illness and twice as likely to contain somebody suffering a disability. Consequently, 'poor' households made more use of non-preventative health care. They were one and a half times as likely to visit their doctor on more than five occasions and had at least two hospital treatments over a one year period. Yet, they wait longer on hospital waiting lists. 'Poor' households are one and a half times more likely to be on hospital waiting lists of more than six months and of more than twelve months.

The CHAID analyses of illness and disability showed that, after age, poverty and poverty-related variables such as previous poverty, social class and reliance on Income Support were the most statistically significant influences on health. In most instances, deprivation was the primary cause of ill-health. The implications for health policy are clear. The cheapest and most effective way of improving the health of the population would be to reduce poverty.

Notes

1   There is plenty of evidence that members of Social Classes IV and V make less use of preventative services, e.g. Blaxter, 1984; Crombie, 1984; Nutbeam and Catford, 1987 and Fisher *et al,* 1983.

2   Note, we are assuming that the age of respondents and their partners fall in the same broad age bands.

7 Poverty and mental health

Sarah Payne

Introduction

This chapter concentrates on one specific aspect of the relationship between health and poverty: the impact on mental health of living in or on the margins of poverty. There is a substantial body of evidence which demonstrates the link between poverty and poor health in terms of both premature mortality and also morbidity. The experience of ill-health is greater amongst those who suffer from poverty and deprivation, whether this morbidity is measured by people's own perceptions or by objective measures of health status (Townsend *et al*, 1992). Studies have shown an association between poverty and poor mental health (Burgess *et al*, 1992; Jarman *et al*, 1992) and this is reflected in the responses to the 1990 Breadline Britain survey.

Poverty, deprivation and mental health

The evidence relating to the impact of poverty on mental health comes from a variety of sources. Some research has focused on people who have been treated for psychiatric illness and the extent to which these patients may come from lower occupational groups or live in 'poorer' areas (Burgess *et al*, 1992; Jarman *et al*, 1992).

159

Community studies have been based largely on random samples, designed to measure the prevalence of specific forms of mental distress in the population as a whole. Such studies explore the distribution of psychiatric symptoms alongside a range of socio-economic variables including education, employment, income and housing (e.g. Srole *et al*, 1963). In addition, attempts to explain the over-representation of different sub-groups with mental health problems (for example, the prominence of women and people from black and some ethnic minority groups amongst psychiatric patients) have also explored the higher rates of poverty and deprivation amongst such populations (Cox, 1986; Belle, 1988 and 1990; Payne, 1991).

Other research has highlighted links between specific aspects of deprivation, such as poor housing and unemployment and poor mental health (Brenner, 1973; Hammarstrom, 1994; Kammerling and O'Connor, 1994). However, there are relatively few studies that have focused directly on the link between poverty and mental well-being. Therefore, the 1990 Breadline Britain survey is particularly valuable in that it offers unusually rich data on poverty, deprivation and the respondents' mental health.

Studies that have suggested a link between poverty and poor mental health have been unable to prove the direction of causality. One explanation is the social causation model, which suggests that poverty causes poor mental health (Faris and Dunham, 1939), arguing that people who are 'poor' suffer a deterioration in their mental health as a result of the stress and burdens of living on a low income and the result of being denied the goods, services and social relations which are taken for granted by others. If this is the case, we would expect that long-term poverty and poverty without prospect of improvement to be the most damaging to mental health, whilst short-term poverty, particularly for those with a prospect of improvement, may be expected to have less effect.

The other direction in which causality might be interpreted suggests that people suffering mental health problems are more likely to become 'poor' because they are unable to hold onto paid employment or because periodic treatment as an in-patient interrupts and limits opportunities for both employment and housing. Some studies have suggested that people suffering with problems in mental health are more likely to be found in 'poorer' areas, not only because of the lower cost of living and, in particular, cheaper housing but also because, in more fragmented or disintegrated areas, such people are more able to fit in (Muijen and Brooking, 1989). This argument is based on the notion of 'drift' and was a significant aspect of social psychiatric research during the 1950s and 1960s (Gruenberg, 1961; Freeman, 1994). It focused primarily on people with the most severe or chronic mental health problems, in particular people diagnosed as being schizophrenic.

One of the problems with the 'drift' debate was that the focus was largely on the severely ill and was thus unable to explain the greater risk of poverty and deprivation amongst those suffering milder forms of disturbance. More recently, most commentators have accepted that explanations for individual mental health and social circumstances will probably comprise a mixture of different influences (Muijen and Brooking, 1989).

The evidence shows that there is an increased risk of poor mental health when an individual's life is stressful and beyond their control. One of the most important studies of women's depression (Brown and Harris, 1978 and 1989) found that depression was significantly more likely to occur in the face of untoward events or difficulties, including poor quality housing, overcrowding or a reduction in income. Later studies have supported these findings with higher rates of both treated and untreated mental ill-health found amongst those living in 'poorer' areas or suffering from housing difficulties and other forms of deprivation (Staples, 1992; Jarman et al, 1992; Manketlow, 1994).

The findings presented below draw on the 1990 Breadline Britain survey to explore ways in which the experience of poor mental health relates to poverty, housing condition, employment status, household type and neighbourhood circumstances. In addition, given the increased risk of treatment for mental health problems experienced by women and by people from some minority ethnic groups, the chapter explores the experience of mental health and poverty for these groups.

Measuring mental health problems

Problems arise in the measurement of mental ill-health because of the difficulty in determining what actually constitutes mental illness. A system of measurement should be able to distinguish between the different diagnostic categories used by the medical profession and also the ways in which concepts of depression, mental illness and distress are used by the general population. Treated mental illness is not an accurate objective measurement of the prevalence of mental illness in a population. It is only a reflection of the perceptions of mental illness of the individual, their friends and family and the extent to which this perception is shared by the medical profession, combined with the availability of psychiatric treatment. The vast proportion of psychiatric care is carried out in the community and, in general practice, over 90% of all mental health consultations are with GPs (Sheppard et al, 1966; Muijen and Brooking, 1989). There are also filters to more specialist care and different groups of the population pass through these filters more readily. For example, men are more likely to be referred to a consultant psychiatrist than women despite the fact that more women present with mental health problems (Goldberg and Huxley, 1980; Sheppard, 1991).

A number of studies have concentrated on a subjective measurement of health, accepting that self-perceptions are generally good measures of health status (Blaxter, 1990; Wannamethee and Shaper, 1991). It is particularly important that any measurement should reflect the individual's own perception of their state of well-being rather than an external assessment, given that such external assessment is not necessarily objective but is affected by bias (Littlewood and Lipsedge, 1988; Miles, 1988). It is significant that around two-thirds of those assessed in community surveys as suffering psychiatric symptoms are also being seen by the medical services for psychiatric treatment; around one third are not. This shows that, in mental health as in other health areas, there is an untreated group of the population who would not be included in a survey which recognised only those in treatment. The results of the 1990 Breadline Britain survey reflect how people themselves feel about their own mental health and, in particular, how far respondents feel that being 'poor' has affected their mental health.

In Q13b respondents were asked:

> "Have there been times in the past year when you've felt isolated and cut off from society because of lack of money?"

In addition, Q18 asked:

> "A number of people have told us they have different kinds of personal difficulties these days. Which if any of the items on this card have you worried about or have you experienced in the past month due to lack of money?"

The items listed included being depressed; worry about relations with friends or with one's family; being bored; feeling looked down on by other people; feeling a failure; feeling a lack of hope for the future and feelings of letting their family down. A score of one (equal weighting for each response) was assigned for each symptom mentioned in Q18 and noted by a respondent and this was summed to produce a 'mental health score'.

These questions are not based on a clinical schedule which has been subjected to validity testing, such as the General Health Questionnaire (GHQ) (Davenport *et al*, 1987) and the responses are not, therefore, open to the degree of significance testing or comparison with other surveys that such a schedule would have allowed. However, the responses do offer a much broader range of ideas about the nature of the link between mental well-being and poverty than is possible with a schedule which is based on clinically definable psychiatric illness. The 1990 Breadline Britain survey highlights the impact of living in deprived circumstances on the person's well being. These effects might not be measured as mental illness by a clinician but are nonetheless likely to affect daily interaction with others, feelings of confidence and enjoyment of life.

Poverty and mental health

The results from the 1990 Breadline Britain survey show that people who were 'poor' experienced worse mental health than the population as a whole. Those people in the survey who were 'multiply deprived' were more than four times as likely to report one or more symptoms of poor mental health compared with those who were not multiply deprived. Table 7.1 shows the difference in terms of the experience of a range of mental health difficulties due to a lack of money.

Table 7.1
Percentage of respondents reporting mental health symptoms
due to lack of money, by deprivation

Symptoms	Not multiply deprived *n=1450*	Multiply deprived *n=381*
Isolation	8.7	46.7
Depression	8.9	41.9
Worry about relations with friends	1.5	6.2
Worry about relations with family	2.5	11.7
Experienced/worry about being bored	8.2	29.3
Experienced/worry about people looking down on you	1.5	14.2
Experienced/worry about feeling a failure	2.6	17.3
Lack of hope for future	6.2	28.2
Letting down your family	4.7	19.5

The 'multiply deprived' respondents were more than five times as likely to feel isolated, four times more likely to be depressed and more than nine times as likely to feel looked down on. The 'multiply deprived' group were more likely than the 'less deprived' to report a problem due to a lack of money in all of the questions on mental well-being. These findings are consistent with results from other surveys which have demonstrated higher rates of depression amongst those living in poverty/deprivation (Brown and Harris, 1978; Belle, 1988).

Being 'poor' excludes people from the norms of society and inhibits social interaction in a range of ways; being unable to afford leisure activities outside the home, or feeling unable to invite friends into the home, due to lack of money to buy food or drinks or because the home itself is overcrowded or in bad repair. The effect of this is to increase the risk of social isolation and to decrease the person's ability to participate in society. This, in turn, may affect mental health and evidence suggests that, for most people, well-being is dependent on feeling part of a community or society and reduced opportunities for social activities are likely to lead to boredom and feelings of low self-esteem (Belle, 1988, Payne, 1991).

It is clear that people living in poverty are likely to suffer poorer mental health and an increased risk of clinically defined illness.

One respondent in the survey described how poverty had affected his mental well-being:

> "Sometimes I just crack up in here. I get so depressed. I mean, just drives you round the bend the money situation now like. You have to pay this, you have to pay that, and all that, and the government just don't realise. They have no idea as far as I'm concerned, they're not bothered, they don't care. It's stupid, it is." (John)

Subjective measures of poverty also appear to be related to poor mental health prospects. As Figure 7.1 shows, self-perceptions of poverty are also related to feelings of isolation and depression. Those who described themselves as 'always poor' were thirteen times as likely as the 'never poor' to report feeling isolated and twelve times as likely as the 'never poor' to report feeling depressed.

Not only does poverty or deprivation increase the risk of depression and isolation but prolonged poverty (where the experience of being 'poor' or deprived is long lasting) appears to have the worst effect. In the Breadline Britain survey, respondents were categorised as 'long-term poor' when they lacked three or more necessities (objective poverty), considered that they are 'genuinely poor' now 'all the time' (subjective poverty) and also have lived in poverty in the past either 'often' or 'most of the time' (see Chapter 1). Figure 7.2 shows that the average 'mental health score' of these respondents was nearly ten times that of those respondents who were 'not poor' and over twice that of respondents who were currently 'poor' but did not have a long history of continuous poverty.

Figure 7.1
Percentage feeling isolated and depressed by present level of poverty

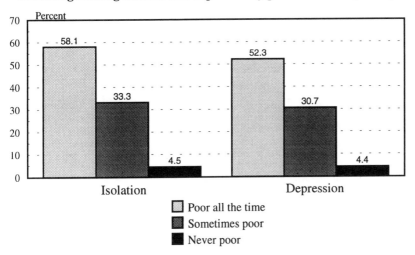

Figure 7.2
Average mental health score by poverty

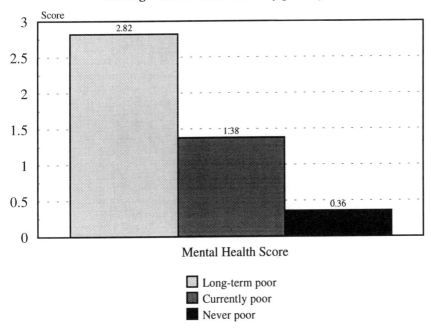

165

Poverty, ethnicity and mental health

A number of studies have examined the higher rates of treated mental illness amongst different minority ethnic groups. These studies have also demonstrated higher risks of poverty amongst people from minority ethnic groups (Thorogood, 1987; Littlewood and Lipsedge, 1988; Oppenheim, 1990).

Reasons for this over-representation include the effects of poverty on mental health, the impact of the experience of racism and discrimination on mental health and also the impact of racism and discrimination on the risk of being judged to be mentally ill and in need of psychiatric treatment (Littlewood and Lipsedge, 1988, Fernando, 1995).

Since the Breadline Britain survey was nationally representative, the number of respondents from minority ethnic groups was small. The proportion of the sample from minority ethnic groups was the same as the proportion of the population from minority ethnic groups as a whole. However, it is unlikely to be entirely representative of the minority ethnic population since many minority ethnic groups are concentrated in the inner city areas of the major conurbations and are not evenly distributed, geographically or otherwise.

However, the debate around mental health and ethnicity is a significant one and even indicative evidence, such as the Breadline Britain survey provides, is useful in assessing the likely impact of poverty and deprivation on mental well-being. The small number of respondents have been re-grouped into two simple categories: black and Asian respondents (N=54) and white UK and Irish respondents (N=1722). Though simplistic and obviously limited in that different minority groups have very different experiences of both mental health and deprivation (Fernando, 1995), the results do highlight some interesting differences which reflect other research findings and suggest that this is an important dimension of the distribution of mental well-being in the survey.

Overall, people from black and Asian groups were nearly twice as likely to report one or more symptoms of poor mental health as a consequence of financial difficulties, in comparison with the white UK and Irish population. As Table 7.2 shows, black and Asian respondents were more likely to be suffering from depression and isolation and were much more likely to be worrying about relationships with their families or about letting their families down or worrying about being looked down on. This is important in the context of the opportunities for positive experiences and for close relationships with others, which might act to decrease the risks of poor mental health as a result of poverty (Brown and Harris, 1978 and 1989). A number of studies have demonstrated the importance of families and other forms of social support for people from minority ethnic groups, as a means of countering a racist and discriminatory culture (Thorogood, 1987; Fernando, 1995).

Table 7.2
Percentages of each ethnic group reporting mental health
symptoms as a result of money difficulties

Symptoms	Black/Asian n=54	White UK/Irish n=1722
Isolation	25.0	16.5
Depression	25.1	15.6
Worry about relations with friends	5.4	2.4
Worry about relations with family	12.1	4.3
Experienced/worry about being bored	19.9	12.5
Experienced/worry about people looking down on you	13.0	4.0
Experienced/worry about feeling a failure	5.5	5.7
Lack of hope for future	20.8	10.7
Letting down your family	15.4	7.7

However, it is also interesting that the white UK/Irish respondents and the black/Asian respondents are equally likely to say that they do not feel a failure due to lack of money. Living in an area which is 'poor' or being part of a community where lack of money is commonplace may reduce such feelings of failure even where the individual may still feel depressed or isolated due to lack of money.

Gender, poverty and mental health

There is a greater likelihood that women will see themselves, or be seen by others, as suffering from poor mental health. Women are over-represented in figures for treated mental illness, whether this is as an in-patient in a psychiatric unit or as an out-patient (Ussher, 1991; Belle, 1990; Payne, 1995 and 1996). Women are also more likely to suffer poverty and deprivation and this appears to form at least part of the explanation of women's higher rates for psychiatric treatment (Belle, 1988 and 1990).

Particular groups of women are both more likely to suffer poverty and are more at risk of poor mental health, for example, lone mothers and older women living alone (Graham, 1993; Groves, 1992). This pattern was also found by the Breadline Britain survey.

A criticism of much poverty research is the way in which households are treated as a 'black box' in that resources are often assumed to be shared equally within the family or at least according to need (Glendinning and Millar, 1992; Pahl, 1989). Research into the division of resources within households clearly demonstrates that this assumption is false and that, where there is inequality in the distribution of resources it is often women who are most at risk of receiving too little. In 'poor' households, both women and men will restrict their own use or consumption of resources so that more is available for children and women will cut back on their own consumption so as to allow more for men (Daly, 1989; Payne, 1991).

Poverty may be experienced differently by women and men within households and this affects the stresses which in turn impact on mental health. When families are 'poor', women are more likely to carry the burden of managing the household's finances and making ends meet (Land, 1983; Daly, 1989). Equally, we cannot assume that resources are shared in more affluent households, where women may suffer deprivation in ways which are hidden from view (Pahl, 1989) and which may produce their own, particular, kinds of stress. Women outside the labour market, with no earned income of their own, are particularly vulnerable. Brown's recent work on women's depression describes the impact of poverty and increased risk of threatening 'events' on women's mental well-being:

> "what they had in common appeared to be a sense of imprisonment in a non-rewarding and deprived setting with the event itself underlining how little they could do about extracting themselves." (Brown, 1992)

In the Breadline Britain survey, women were more likely than men to describe themselves as suffering from mental health difficulties as a result of lack of money. In particular, more female respondents than male said that they had recently felt isolated or depressed due to a lack of money, as Figure 7.3 shows.

Since both poverty and gender have been shown to influence mental well-being it is necessary to explore the impact of poverty on the mental health of each sex. Figure 7.4 shows that 'poor' men and women were around four and a half times as likely to suffer from depression than 'non-poor' men and women. However, women were still more likely than men to suffer from depression after controlling for the effects of poverty. The impact of poverty in causing depression seems to be slightly greater for men than for women (e.g. 'poor' men are 4.7 times more likely to be depressed than 'non-poor' men, whereas 'poor' women are 4.4 times more likely to be depressed than 'non-poor' women).

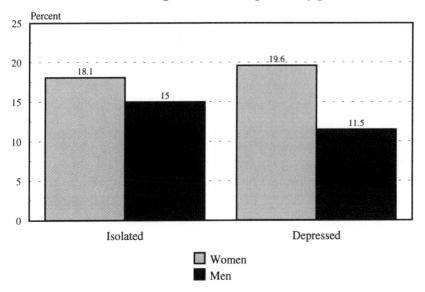

Figure 7.3
Percent feeling isolated and depressed by gender

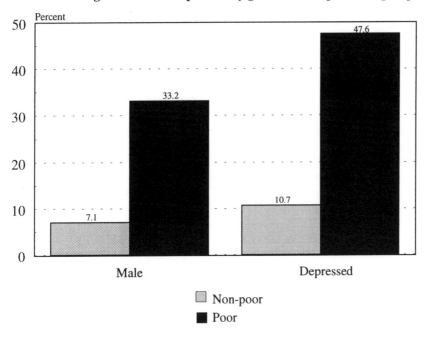

Figure 7.4
Percent feeling isolated and depressed by gender and deprivation group

Poverty, household type and mental health

One of the variables linked with poverty and health is household type. For example, parents of young children are particularly vulnerable to poverty, have poorer health and also feature prominently in figures for treated and untreated psychiatric illness (Oppenheim, 1990; Payne, 1991; Graham, 1993). However, mothers, rather than fathers, and lone mothers in particular, appear to be most vulnerable. The data on poor health amongst both cohabiting/married and lone mothers shows that, for all women with children, poor health is associated with indicators of poverty (Graham, 1991).

Figure 7.5 shows the responses to questions on isolation and depression as a result of lack of money by household type for families with children. Nearly half the lone parents in this study reported feelings of isolation as a result of lacking money, compared with less than a fifth of the parents in two-parent households. Similarly, over 40% of the lone parents reported feeling depressed due to a lack of money, compared with less than a fifth of the two-parent households. Is this due to the greater risk of poverty amongst lone parents or the greater risk of isolation and depression amongst people with sole responsibility for children who may, in consequence, have fewer opportunities for social activities? As one of the lone mothers in the survey said:

> "Since I've been in bed and breakfast our relationship has just gone down. It's - I think it's mainly me. I'll admit to that. It's just that he can go away, he can go to his - go to where he lives and he's - he goes out. But me, I've got Rickie with me 24 hours a day, most of the time. I don't get no time to myself. And with 'im there, I lash out - you lash out to people near to you - closest to you lash out on." (Alison)

Figure 7.6 looks at responses to the questions on depression and isolation by lone parents and parents in couple households who were also 'multiply deprived'. Isolation due to lack of money was reported by a much greater proportion of 'poor' lone parents (67.5%), compared with 'poor' couples with children (48.2%). Similarly, 'poor' lone parents were much more likely to report feelings of depression due to lack of money, compared with 'poor' couples with children.

Again, this reflects findings in other studies, which show that lone parents are particularly at risk of both poverty and poor mental health (Payne, 1991; Glendinning and Millar, 1992). Isolation is increased because lone parents are less able to afford the cost of social activities outside the home, are less likely to be able to afford the costs of childcare in order to go out and are less likely to be in paid employment which decreases isolation and increases self-esteem (Brown and Harris, 1989).

Figure 7.5
Percent of parents feeling isolated and depressed by type of household

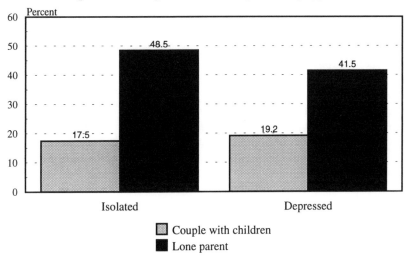

Figure 7.6
Percent of parents feeling isolated and/or depressed by deprivation group

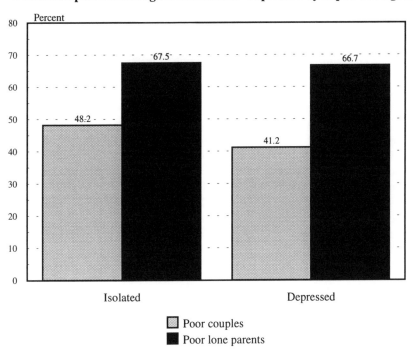

171

Employment status and mental health

The relationship between employment status and mental health has been explored frequently (Arber, 1987). For men, the focus has often been on the link between unemployment and poor mental health and, in particular, the extent to which suicide is greater amongst the unemployed (Platt, 1986). For women, especially for women with childcare responsibilities, it is the complexity of women's lives in the paid labour market combined with unpaid labour in the home that has been the focus (Arber et al, 1985). In particular, it is the combination of motherhood, domestic labour and paid employment which is significant in determining women's health and also their vulnerability to poverty (Graham, 1993).

In the survey, those respondents who were of working age but who were at that time out of the labour market were more likely than both the retired group and those currently in paid employment to report one or more mental health symptoms. One measure of this is the average 'mental health score' for different groups. The mean score for housewives was nearly twice that of people in full-time employment and nearly three times that of those in part-time employment. The average score for those respondents classified as unemployed but seeking work was higher still, being over three times the score for the full-time employed.

Table 7.3 shows mental health difficulties among the unemployed, housewives and the full-time employed.

Table 7.3
Percentage of those reporting mental health difficulties, as a result of lack of money, by category of employment status. unemployed, housewives and full-time employed

Symptoms	Unemployed n=174	Housewife n=104	Full-time employed n=988
Felt isolated	46.9	34.5	13.1
Depressed	39.3	31.3	13.0
Worry about relations with friends	6.1	2.2	2.6
Worry about relations with family	11.7	5.6	4.4
Worry about being bored	32.0	20.4	11.4
Worry about being looked down on	14.2	7.1	2.9
Worry about feeling a failure	15.5	9.0	5.1
Worry/lack of hope for future	26.4	17.6	9.5
Worry about letting down your family	23.1	11.3	6.9

The greatest risk to mental well-being is suffered by those who are unemployed. People in this group are 3.5 times as likely to say that they feel isolated compared with people in full-time employment - nearly half of those who are unemployed feel isolated due to lack of money. Nearly 40% of the unemployed describe themselves as depressed, three times as many as those in full-time employment and nearly a third of the unemployed describe themselves as bored, due to a lack of money. These results clearly suggest that unemployment has a major impact not only on income but also on people's mental well-being.

Rates of isolation and depression amongst housewives are over twice that for people in full-time employment. Whilst the status of housewife may conceal unemployment, studies have also shown that being a housewife is in itself stressful (see, for example, Radloff, 1977) and that the stress of domestic work is greater in circumstances of poverty and deprivation (Daly, 1989; Brannen and Wilson, 1989).

Housing and neighbourhood poverty and mental health

Housing and the local area conditions impact on levels of stress, in particular for those with primary responsibility for maintaining a pleasant home environment and for those who spend most hours in that environment. This mostly affects women but also people with limited mobility. A neighbourhood which is uninviting or which feels unsafe may act to limit a person's movements and an environment with few facilities for leisure activities similarly limits opportunities for social interaction, particularly for those on a low income who cannot afford transport to other areas.

Previous studies of the relationship between housing tenure and mental health have suggested that poorer mental health is experienced by those in both local authority and privately rented accommodation (OPCS, 1995). Whilst the type of tenure itself may be seen as an indicator for other forms of deprivation, there is also evidence that those living in the poorest quality housing, in any tenure group, experience the greatest threat to their mental well-being (see Payne, 1991). Studies have also highlighted the impact of a poor local environment on mental health (Hollingshead and Redlich, 1958; Faris and Dunham, 1939; Parry-Jones and Queloz, 1991). It remains true that the majority of those treated by the psychiatric services are to be found in poorer areas and the workload of both GPs and mental health teams in poorer areas of the community is greater (Muijen and Brooking, 1989; Hollander and Tobiansky, 1990; Freeman, 1994).

Answers to the mental health questions in the 1990 Breadline Britain survey support not only a link between poor mental health and housing tenure but also between poor mental health and the quality of housing and environment. Overall, the average 'mental health score' for all those who rented was higher than the average score for owner occupiers. The average score for respondents in local authority housing was 1.2, three times worse than the score of those who were owner occupiers (0.4). The average score of people in private rented accommodation was also high (0.9). Table 7.4 shows that local authority and housing association tenants report much higher levels of isolation, depression and other mental health difficulties than owner occupiers.

Table 7.4

Table 7.4
Percentage of respondents experiencing mental health difficulties
as result of lack of money, by tenure group

Symptoms	Owner occupied n=1208	Local Authority n=469	Private rented n=108
Felt isolated	9.7	33.5	22.1
Depressed	9.9	29.5	17.5
Worry about relations with friends	2.2	3.0	2.9
Worry about relations with family	2.9	6.3	8.0
Worry about being bored	7.0	24.4	22.4
Worry about being looked down on	1.7	8.5	8.7
Worry about feeling a failure	4.0	8.9	9.2
Worry/lack of hope for future	6.8	20.2	17.0
Worry about letting down your family	4.7	14.6	9.5

In addition to housing tenure, the quality of housing is also important. People living in housing which was in a poor state of repair were four times as likely to report isolation, depression and other worries compared with those people living in good quality housing. Figure 7.7 shows the proportion of respondents who felt isolated and depressed by standard of housing.

Figure 7.7
Percent feeling isolated and depressed by standard of housing

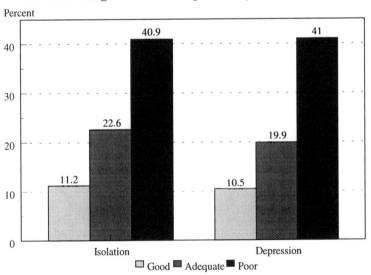

Similarly, people living in a 'poor' neighbourhood were also more likely to report mental health worries due to lack of money. There were three questions in the survey focusing on the neighbourhood in which people live. A quarter of those who felt that their local area was unpleasant or dirty reported that they felt isolated due to a lack of money, compared with 14.3% who did not perceive their neighbourhood in this way. The group living in a 'poor' area were also more likely to report the experience of depression (20.3% compared with 13.9%). Q1b extended this question to ask if "there is a lack of pleasant, open spaces within easy reach". Again, more of those living in an area without such amenities reported isolation and depression and also reported feeling bored. The third question, Q1c, asked about incivilities, if "there are houses boarded up/with broken windows nearby", again, those living in more derelict areas reported higher rates of isolation, depression and boredom.

The impact of a poor environment is wide ranging, affecting feelings of security and isolation:

> "High rates of vandalism, whether real or imagined, increase fear, isolation and alienation, and inhibit people from going out to meet others. Overcrowded housing reduces the ability to regulate the nature and frequency of social interaction and high rise flats contribute to difficulties in supervising children, restriction of social interaction and lack of territorial markers and defensible space." (Muijen and Brooking, 1989, p119)

The greatest impact on mental health is to be found amongst those living in the increasingly marginalised local authority housing, housing which is not only in poor condition but which is increasingly occupied by the poorest in our society: lone mothers on income support, people without paid work, the sick and disabled.

Conclusion

The material presented in this chapter suggests that there is a very real relationship between the experience of poverty and deprivation and the risk of poor mental health. Those respondents to the 1990 Breadline Britain survey who were living in poverty were more likely to report a range of problems reflecting mental well-being. Logistic regression analysis of depression, sex, ethnicity and deprivation status indicates that this increased vulnerability does not simply reflect the greater numbers of women or people from minority ethnic groups living in poverty. People living in poverty were more than 7 times as likely to suffer poor mental health than those who were not, whilst the impact of both gender and ethnicity was more muted. The Breadline Britain survey also shows that those who are in one of the groups most likely to be deprived - the unemployed and lone parents - reported high rates of difficulties and people whose living environment was 'poor' were also more likely to report problems. Poor mental health is a feature of poverty both as it is assessed objectively by the Breadline Britain index and also, subjectively, by the respondents' own assessment of their poverty status. Being 'poor', then, is likely to significantly affect mental health. The solution to this appalling additional burden on the 'poor' is not, however, a dose of psychiatry. The greatest risk factor is poverty and the solution to this problem comes from policies which are directed towards the eradication of poverty in the 1990s.

8 Poverty, debt and benefits

Christina Pantazis and David Gordon

Introduction

This chapter explores the relationship between both poverty and debt and poverty and state benefits. Personal debt is increasingly being seen as a problem. In 1988, the Citizens Advice Bureau reported half a million requests for help with debts. This figure has probably increased due to the effects of the recession. The 'poor' are particularly vulnerable to debt because their incomes are generally too low to cover even their basic needs.

There are a number of strategies that 'poor' households or individuals can adopt (Ford, 1991). Informal help from family or friends is a common resort. In the Breadline Britain survey, 20% of households had borrowed from friends or family. 'Poor' households were four times as likely to borrow money from friends or family than other households. Many of the people interviewed in the television series for Breadline Britain expressed their predicament. Richard, who lives on state benefits, explained the help he receives from his mother:

> "We only get through the week if we go down to my mother's and borrow some money off her, and she helps us out that way. Or she'll have Robert up at her house and we just have the little 'un here. So there's just me, my wife

and the little 'un here, while Robert is at his nannas and he gets fed over there. That helps us out a lot, having one less mouth to feed."

Alternatively, many 'poor' people simply go without. In the television series, many people talked about their daily dilemma of incurring debt or going without. Paula, her disabled husband and their two children, who live on state benefits, explained: "It's a case of ....like going into debt or going without. So most of the time we have to go without."

Finally, 'poor' households can borrow from credit agencies. The types of credit predominantly used by 'poor' households include the Social Fund loan system[1], mail order ('club catalogue') credit, 'tally men', money lenders and 'cheque-traders'. All these are used exclusively by those living in, or on the margins of, poverty (NCC Survey, 1980; Adler and Wozniak, 1981; Berthoud and Kempson, 1992).

Berthoud and Kempson (1992) found that, amongst low income borrowers, mail order was one of the two most frequently used forms of credit. Mail order provides the means to purchase clothes, shoes and household goods and pay for them over many weeks, thus effectively spreading the cost to small, manageable payments.

Traditionally, 'poor' households have also turned to money lenders for unsecured loans. In the Breadline Britain survey, 'poor' households were roughly ten times more likely to borrow from money lenders than all other households. In 1987, the Birmingham Settlement Money Advice Centre found that the average Annualised Percentage Rate (APR) for loans supplied by legally registered money lenders was 52%. Illegal money lenders are also an option for the 'poor'. A report on the Strathclyde region in Scotland (Bolchever *et al*, 1986) found that: "Illegal money lending...flourishes in areas suffering from a high level of poverty, where they prey on the most financially disadvantaged members of society." The same report claimed that 'loan sharks' operated openly, often outside benefit offices, post offices and pubs. In one case, an illegal money lender was found to have 62 benefit books in his possession with a face value of £23,000.

The 1980s and the growth of credit

Financial deregulation during the 1980s, combined with an increase in real incomes for the average household, led to an increase in both the supply and use of credit. Figure 8.1 shows that, by 1990, loans for house purchases, consumer credit and other personal borrowings represented more than 100% of the total personal disposal income of the population as a whole, e.g., in 1990, the population of Britain borrowed more money than it earned after taxes.

On the supply side, financial markets were deregulated and cash incentives offered to council tenants wishing to purchase their homes. For the first time, many 'poorer' households borrowed large sums of money via formal credit arrangements and many were drawn into home ownership. However, many of those taking advantage of looser credit regulations were not doing so out of choice.

178

Figure 8.1

Loans for house purchases, consumer credit and other borrowing and savings as a percentage of total personal disposable income 1980-1991

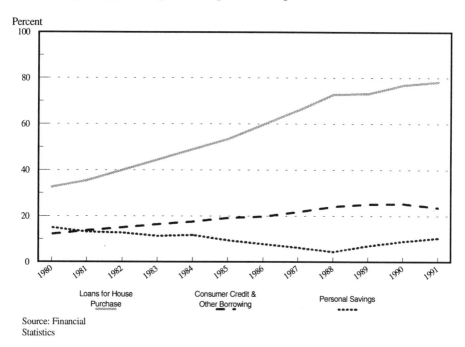

Source: Financial
Statistics

Public Attitudes Survey (PAS) for the Office of Fair Trading showed that, amongst low-income respondents, 'necessity' rather than 'convenience' was a more important reason to use credit. Overall, 36% of all respondents said they used credit out of necessity. However, for those on low weekly incomes of between £50 and £100, the number of respondents giving 'necessity' as a reason was 45%. For those unemployed for less than six months, it was 52% and for those unemployed for more than six months, 64%.

Whilst the use of credit by 'poorer' households relates to meeting day-to-day necessities, special occasions and celebrations place an additional burden on their financial budgets. Paula explained the financial problems she faces every Christmas:

> "For Christmas we had the catalogue for the children, because you can't really go out and get second hand toys for them, because obviously the kiddies are going to know they're not new. So we normally go into debt at Christmas. And then we get them and it takes us near enough twelve months to pay that off. So by the time Christmas is around again, you're just finishing off one and you're starting again for the next year. That's the only way we can do it."

179

The distribution of debt

Confusion can arise over use of the words 'credit' and 'debt' and they are often used interchangeably. Berthoud and Kempson (1992) make a clear distinction between the two. 'Credit' is the money people borrow and 'debt' is any commitments that are causing financial problems. Debt includes arrears on all types of household expenses, such as rent, mortgages and fuel debts, as well as consumer credit, such as hire purchase. There are many reasons why people might fall into debt. Berthoud and Kempson (1992), in their study of uses of personal credit and problems of debt, identified five causes of debt:

1   Poverty, i.e. debtors do not have the money to meet day-to-day expenditure.
2   A major change in personal circumstances which reduces income, or increases their spending needs unexpectedly. For example, redundancy, illness or lone-parenthood.
3   Over-commitment by debtors.
4   Money mis-management.
5   Delay or refusal to pay, e.g. the Poll Tax.

In the same study, respondents were asked to say why they felt they had fallen into debt (Table 8.1). This shows that over 50% of respondents blamed income-related factors for their debts and only 16% said they had either overlooked or withheld payments.

Table 8.1
Respondent's own assessment of reasons for debt

Reason given	%
Insufficient income	25
Reduced income	26
Changes in circumstances	7
Over-commitment	24
Unexpected bills	10
Overlooked payments	8
Withheld payments	8
Creditor action	7
Benefit problems	5

Source: Berthoud and Kempson (1992)

On average, 15% of households in this study had debt problems. However, these debt problems were not evenly distributed throughout the income groups. Only 3%

of households with incomes above £400 per week had debt repayment problems whereas 28% of households with incomes below £100 per week had such problems. Table 8.2 shows the incidence of debt for non-pensioner households, broken down by net weekly income.

Table 8.2
Incidence of debt for non-pensioner households

Net weekly income	Percentage with debts
Up to £100	28
£100-150	25
£150-200	15
£200-250	11
£250-300	11
£300-400	8
£400 or more	3
Average	15

Source: Berthoud and Kempson (1990)

Household type also influences the risk of debt; large families were found to have more debts than small families and over 40% of lone parent families had one or more problem debts. Berthoud and Kempson's (1992) study showed that some families are more likely to fall into debt than others. They identified three causative factors: age, children and level of income. When two of these factors were combined, there was a far higher risk of debt. This particularly affected young households and families on low incomes.

In the Breadline Britain survey, where a household said it was seriously behind with an expense, this was classified as a 'problem debt'[2]. The survey provided more evidence on the link between debt and poorer households. Figures 8.2 to 8.5 show the relationship between the incidence of debt and poverty. Figure 8.2 illustrates that more than half of 'poor' households have debts (56%). Compared with all other households, 'poor' households are four times as likely to have debts, and have, on average seven times the number of debts. Households defined as 'long-term poor'[3] have the greatest debt problems. Figure 8.3 shows that 72% of these households are indebted with an average of two debts.

These findings are reinforced when poverty is measured 'subjectively'. Figure 8.4 shows the link between debt and current poverty. Those defining themselves as genuinely 'poor all the time' are more than six times as likely to be in debt as those claiming 'never' to have experienced poverty. They have, on average, sixteen times the number of debts as those 'never' poor. Figure 8.5 demonstrates a clear linear relationship between the incidence of debt and the respondent's history of poverty. Households with a substantial history of poverty (i.e. 'often' or 'mostly' poor) are over four times as likely to have debts, as those households that have 'never' experienced poverty. They also have, on average, seven times the number of debts as those households that have 'never been poor'.

Figure 8.2
Percent in debt and average number of debts by deprivation group

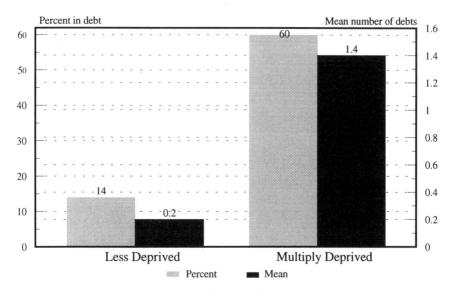

Figure 8.3
Percent in debt and average number of debts by poverty

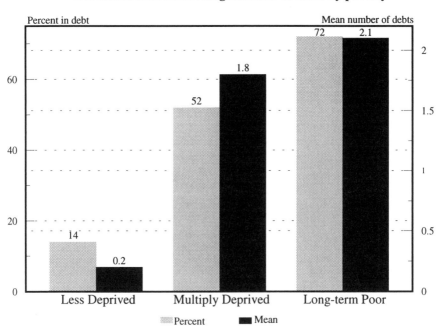

182

Figure 8.4
Percent in debt and average number of debts by present level of poverty

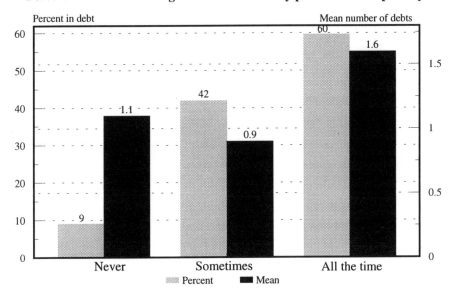

Figure 8.5
Percent in debt and average number of debts by history of poverty

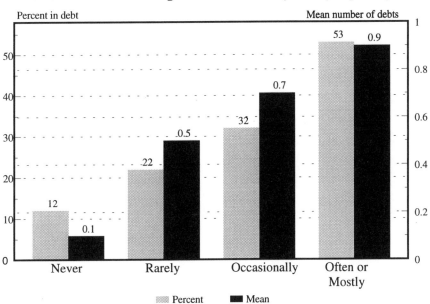

Table 8.3 shows the mean and median deprivation scores for households in debt for each service or credit commitment. The last column shows the percentage of households in debt that are 'poor'. The mean deprivation score for most items is over four, with rent, gas, electricity, hire purchase goods and other loans scoring over five. More than two-thirds of households with rent, gas and hire purchase debts are 'poor'. Households with hire purchase debts have the highest mean deprivation score (5.8). By contrast, the mean deprivation score of households with credit card debts is only 2.9 and only 37% of households with credit card debts are 'poor'. This reflects the relative inaccessibility of this form of credit to 'poorer' households.

By far the greatest number of households that are in debt are seriously behind with their Poll Tax payments. Households are more than twice as likely to suffer from Poll Tax debt than from any other form of debt. Despite this, the average deprivation score of those households with serious Poll Tax arrears is relatively low (4.1), compared with households with most other kinds of debt. This may be due to high Poll Tax bills placing financial strain even on households that are 'not poor' or to deliberate non-payment. The 1983 Breadline Britain survey found that only 4% of households had serious rates arrears whereas, in 1990, 14% of households had serious Poll Tax arrears. No other type of debt exhibits anything like this 3.5 times increase.

Apart from credit card and telephone debt, 'poor' households are the majority of households with all other forms of debt. Rather surprisingly, 61% of households with mortgage debts are 'poor'. However, the 1990 Breadline Britain survey interviews took place at the beginning of the recession and before the major collapse in house prices (see Appendix I).

Table 8.3

Deprivation scores of those in debt and % of those in debt who are 'poor'

Type of debt	Number of respondents in debt	Mean deprivation score	Median deprivation score	% of households in debt that are 'poor'
Rent	114	5.6	5	72
Gas	83	5.6	5	69
Electricity	124	5.1	4	64
Goods on HP	36	5.8	5	71
Mortgage	43	4.1	3	61
Poll Tax	253	4.1	3	54
Credit card	43	2.9	1	37
Mail order	61	5.0	4	64
Telephone	74	4.1	3	50
Other loans	32	5.4	3	56

Table 8.4 shows the percentage of 'poorer' households that are in debt. The Poll Tax presents the greatest difficulty for both 'poor' and 'non-poor' households. Thirty six percent of 'poor' households are seriously behind with Poll Tax payments, followed by rent arrears at 22%, electricity debts at 21% and telephone debts at 19%.

Fewer 'poor' households had credit card payment, mortgage repayment and hire purchase debts. As would be expected, those declaring themselves genuinely 'poor all the time' now experience slightly more problems with debt than those declaring themselves to be poor 'often' or 'most of the time' in the past. There is remarkable similarity in the results between those 'objectively' defined and those 'subjectively' defined as 'poor' again demonstrating that the results obtained from scientific 'objective' measurement of poverty correspond closely with people's own perceptions and understanding of poverty.

Table 8.4
Experience of poverty and debt

Type of debt	Poor (Multiply deprived)		Poor 'all the time' now		Poor 'often' or 'most of the time' in the past	
	Number	*%*	*Number*	*%*	*Number*	*%*
Rent	82	22	44	25	54	26
Gas	58	15	34	19	32	19
Electricity	79	21	49	27	46	21
Goods on HP	26	7	14	8	16	9
Mortgage	26	7	11	6	11	7
Poll Tax	137	36	60	34	67	34
Credit card	16	4	11	6	8	4
Catalogue	39	10	25	14	28	15
Telephone	37	19	27	15	18	11
Other loans	18	5	11	6	9	4

Deprivation and fuel debt

Fuel debt presents a particular problem for households. There are many reasons why households may get into debt with their gas and electricity bills. Apart from the general factors contributing to the likelihood of debt (see above), there are also specific reasons for fuel debt. A need for extra heating because of illness, old age or because there are young children in the household, or an unexpectedly high bill may lead to debt. Berthoud and Kempson (1992) showed that fuel debts are strongly associated with poverty. In their study the mean income of those seriously behind with payments was only £120 per week. There is a strong correlation between poverty and fuel debts, often because the root causes of fuel debt relate to multiple factors common to impoverished circumstances. 'Poor' households have specific problems with fuel debt:

- They spend a greater proportion of their total expenditure on fuel costs. In 1990, the poorest 20% of households spent 10.4% of their expenditure on fuel, compared with the richest 20%, who spent only 3.1% of their expenditure (FES 1990).
- Fuel costs have risen steadily since the 1970s. This has been due to both increases in the price of imported fuel and important changes in the

government's overall energy strategy. Consequently, fuel prices have risen dramatically compared with increases in the general retail price index (RPI) which is used to govern increases in social security benefits.

- A high proportion of poorer households live in rented accommodation, which may be more likely to be badly insulated, damp and more expensive to heat.

'Poor' households are likely to have problems in budgeting for large quarterly bills because, firstly, they are more likely to receive income on a weekly basis. Secondly, they are left with little or no surplus income to meet unexpectedly high bills. In these circumstances they have few options. Many 'go without' in order to save money. This may involve reducing their heating to levels which might be detrimental to health and also dangerous if alternative forms of lighting or heating, such as candles, are used. Others reduce the number of cooked meals or minimise the use of hot water in order to save money. Reducing other expenditure, such as food or clothing, in order to keep the home heated is another option. Finally, they can get into debt, with the attendant risk of disconnection.

In the 1990 Breadline Britain survey, almost 8% of respondents were seriously behind with paying their gas and electricity bills. Of those with fuel debts, 65% were 'poor'. The mean deprivation score for households with fuel debts is 5.2 (see Table 8.3). Figure 8.6 shows the percentage of the households that are in debt to fuel companies. 'Multiply deprived' households are more likely to have fuel debt, 24% compared with only 3% of 'less deprived' households.

Figure 8.6
Percent with fuel debts by deprivation group

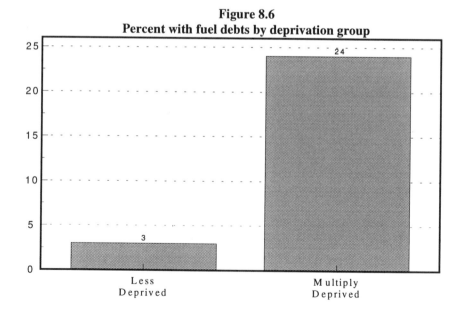

186

Various payment methods have been introduced for families in hardship or for families with a history of arrears. One of these is 'fuel direct', whereby customers in debt, who are also in receipt of state benefits, can have their gas or electricity payments deducted from their benefit cheque. However, for many households, the problems of debt still remain. Richard, living on income support, pays for his gas by 'fuel direct". He explained the consequences of this method of payment:

"Well it'll push us into more debt. And we'll have to cut down on different things. But there's nothing I can really possibly cut down anymore than what we're actually doing now, but...we'll have to. Instead of getting a full loaf we'll have to get half a loaf or something like that, it's the only way I can see. Instead of getting say a large loaf, we'll have to get a small loaf. Instead of getting five pounds of potatoes, we'll get three pounds or something like that."

For many families, fuel debt leads inevitably to disconnection. The evidence shows that a large proportion of those disconnected have below average incomes and are families with young children (Berthoud, 1981 and Rowlingson and Kempson, 1993). They are likely to be unable to pay rather than unwilling to pay. The plight of households who are without fuel is horrendous. Indeed they are being denied one of their basic needs. An MP once remarked that disconnection is "a barbaric punishment which is much more akin to Dickensian debtors' prison than to a twentieth century society" (John Cartwright MP, *Hansard* Vol 984).

Poverty and benefits

The purpose of this next section is to analyse the extent of poverty amongst households receiving state benefits. Excluding all households containing pensioners, there are 542 households (35%) where one or more persons receive state benefits.[4] Table 8.5 illustrates the proportion of households in receipt of benefits that live in poverty. It also shows their deprivation and income levels. A large proportion of households receiving benefits are 'poor' (41%), their respective mean and median deprivation scores are 3.2 and 2. The high levels of poverty faced by households receiving benefits is reflected in their low level of income. The average weekly income levels of households receiving benefits is also illustrated in Table 8.5. The actual average weekly income for households receiving benefits is only £139, compared to £277 for non-benefit households. Similarly, when income is equivalised to take into account household size, the weekly income for individuals is a mere £61.

Table 8.5
Poverty and income of households where one or more persons
receive benefits - excluding households with pensioners

% Poor	Mean deprivation score	Median deprivation score	Minimum mean weekly household income (£)	Maximum mean weekly household income (£)
41	3.2	2	139	61

Benefit claimants are not a homogenous group. Their deprivation and income levels vary according to the type of benefits they receive. Table 8.6 illustrates for each type of benefit the proportion of households living in poverty, deprivation and income levels. More than half of households on means-tested benefits, such as Unemployment Benefit, Income Support, Housing Benefit, and Family Credit, are 'poor'. This is a result of means-tested benefits being concentrated on the poorest. Thus, households in receipt of these benefits also face the highest levels of deprivation. These households have an average deprivation score of over 4 and a median deprivation score of at least 3.

Households receiving Family Credit experience the highest levels of poverty. Family Credit is paid to those in employment (or self employment) and who have at least one child. Almost 60% of households receiving Family Credit can be 'objectively' defined as 'poor' and they have respective mean and median deprivation scores of 4.4 and 3. These results highlight the high levels of poverty faced by many families with children. Those in receipt of Unemployment Benefit, Income Support or Housing Benefit also face high levels of poverty. Around 55-56% of these households live in poverty and they have an average deprivation score of at least 4.

Only around one third of households receiving benefits related to their health status are 'poor'. These households also have low deprivation scores. Recipients of Sickness Benefit, Invalidity Benefit and Attendance or Mobility Allowance have an average deprivation score of around 2 and a median deprivation score of 1. A total of 344 households receive Community Charge benefit. Although a large proportion of Community Charge benefit recipients are 'poor' (45%), their median deprivation score is only 2. This indicates that 'non-poor' households also receive help towards their Community Charge bills.

Table 8.6

Poverty and income of households where one or more persons receive benefits - excluding all households with pensioners

Type of Benefit	Number	% Poor	Mean deprivation score	Median deprivation score	Min mean household income (£/wk)	Max mean household income (£/wk)
Unemployment Benefit	108	56	4.0	4	121	52
Sickness Benefit	56	27	2.1	1	164	65
Invalidity Pension	100	27	2.0	1	151	69
Income Support	219	55	4.4	4	96	45
Family Credit	25	59	4.4	3	162	40
Housing Benefit	247	56	4.4	3	91	52
Community Charge	344	45	3.5	2	125	57
Attendance/Mobility Allowance	65	36	2.4	1	163	69

Inequalities in income exist between the different recipients of benefits. Minimum or actual average weekly household income is greatest for those receiving Sickness Benefit (£164) and Attendance/Mobility Allowance (£163), and lowest for those on Housing Benefit (£91) and Income Support (£96). Recipients of Sickness Benefit, Attendance Allowance and Family Credit have higher income levels because such payments are made in addition to other benefits or income. Sickness Benefit and Attendance Allowance are made to people who are already in receipt of other benefits, such as Income Support or Unemployment Benefit, whilst Family Credit is a payment for those people who are working 16 hours or more a week (and who have at least one child). As expected, when income is equivalised to take into account household size, the lowest weekly income is received by households in receipt of Family Credit (£40).

Many benefit households are likely to be in receipt of more than one benefit. It is therefore useful to examine the relationship between poverty and number of benefits. Table 8.7 demonstrates that there is an attendant rise in poverty as the number of benefits received by the household increases. Of households receiving one benefit, only 26% are 'poor' compared to 58% of households receiving three or more benefits.

Table 8.7
Households receiving benefits that are 'poor' (%)

Number of benefits	None n=997	One n=182	Two n=171	Three plus n=189
Percent 'poor'	11	26	39	58

Conclusion

In 1990, British households borrowed more money than they earned after tax. However, this historically high level of borrowing did not present a problem for the majority of households. Debt was largely a problem for a minority of 'poor' households. This situation may have changed owing to the intensification of the recession in the early 1990s and the collapse of house values that has resulted in many owner occupied households experiencing problems of negative equity.

There is also little evidence to suggest that the problems of fuel debt have improved. The recent imposition of VAT on fuel will almost inevitably increase the hardships already experienced by many 'poor' households.

A large proportion of British households in receipt of state benefits are living in poverty. Over 40% of households containing no pensioners that receive benefits are 'poor'. The proportion of people living in poverty increases as more benefits are received by a household. This indicates a failing of the benefit system to act as a safety-net and therefore to protect people from falling into poverty.

Notes

1   Social Fund loans are only available to those people receiving Income Support as long as they are not assessed as 'too poor' to repay the loan.

2   'Problem debt' is defined by Question 14 "Have there been times in the past year when you were seriously behind in paying for any of the following items" (see Appendix 2 for details).

3   Defined as those who are 'objectively' poor (i.e. lacked three or more necessities, who perceive themselves as currently living in poverty, and who have had a substantial history of poverty. The 'long-term poor' accounted for 75 households, representing 4% of the total sample.

4   As a result of the probable under-sampling of poor pensioners in the survey, pension households have been excluded from the analysis in order to avoid possible distortion of results.

9 Poverty and local public services

Glen Bramley

Introduction

This chapter considers the role played by local government in alleviating poverty through the provision of local public services. It is based mainly on the data collected in the 1990 Breadline Britain survey on a selection of specific services provided by local authorities but set in a comparative context provided by the author's research on the usage of local services.

Local government represents a substantial part of the overall welfare state in Britain and is particularly important in the provision of services in kind as opposed to cash benefits. Until recently, our knowledge of the distribution of such benefits in kind has been very patchy but recent surveys, including many carried out by MORI for individual authorities, have provided a fuller picture (Bramley *et al*, 1989, Bramley, 1990a and Bramley and Smart, 1993). The central question motivating these studies has been whether local public services are an effective mechanism of redistribution in favour of the 'poor' and disadvantaged or whether many of these services are in fact used more by the better off. Is the capture of welfare state services by middle class interests a particular feature of local government?

Examination of survey evidence about the use of and attitudes towards local government services also highlights a number of other issues. Comparison of usage patterns across services aids our understanding of the different nature of different services, in terms of how they are rationed and delivered and the differing role of demand and supply mechanisms. For example, Bramley and Le Grand (1992) emphasise the broad distinction between 'needs rationed' and 'demand led' services, while Bramley and Smart (1993) offer a more detailed eight-fold classification also taking account of pure public goods, compulsion, the packaging of services, charging and means tests. Another important feature of local government services is the significant degree of local discretion in spending and delivery, giving rise to considerable differences in what services are supplied and in what ways.

Comparisons across different local jurisdictions can reveal the extent to which local political and policy differences can impact on both the level and distribution of benefits. A third area of interest is the lessons which can be learned from relating usage of services to people's general preferences for, or valuations of, those same services. We can identify indirect, or external, benefits as well as direct user benefits and these are particularly important for some of the social care services.

In this collection, we are mainly addressing the issue of poverty. Thus the central question is about how much use the 'poor' make of local services. Does the provision of good quality public services at the local level, free or subsidised, enable households who are 'poor' in terms of income and command over private material consumption goods to at least gain access to a range of benefits in the fields of education, social and child care, recreation, transport and information? Are there still significant problems of access and quality which limit the effective use and benefit which 'poor' households can derive from such services? Are these problems more apparent among the poorest and most deprived households? Is access and use more limited in certain locations, due to the level of local authority expenditure and provision or to other characteristics of localities? Government grants are distributed to local authorities in a way which is intended to equalise for differences in local needs (Bramley, 1990b); does the evidence suggest that these grants are doing an adequate job? How important or essential are these local services?

These questions are tackled in this chapter by an analysis of two questions from the 1990 Breadline Britain survey. One of these questions (Q23) gave respondents a list of 11 selected local services and asked whether they used each service and if so whether it was adequate, or if they did not use it whether this was because the service was not relevant, unavailable/inadequate, or if they could not afford to use it (see Appendix II).

The other question (Q22) asked whether respondents considered each of these services essential or not. The 11 services were divided into groups according to whether they were relevant to all adults, to families with children under five or of school age, or chiefly relevant to pensioners or people with disabilities. The first approach to the analysis involves tabulating usage rates by household type against key indicators of socio-economic status, including class, income and deprivation, for the whole national sample. This enables us to see the general distributional pattern for different services, allowing crudely for the influence of demographic factors which are often the most important determinant of usage. The analysis can be refined by looking at the patterns of responses indicating service inadequacy and deterrence of usage.

The second approach is to use multivariate statistical models to predict usage as a function of a wide range of individual household attributes. This helps to sort out the relative role of different factors, including income and demographic factors as well as more specific attributes like car ownership, disability or ethnicity. Refinements here enable us to distinguish the determinants of effective demand, need and supply constraints.

Thirdly, we can address the question of how far people's location affects their chances of getting access to adequate local services. We do this in part by referring to the comparative evidence compiled in Bramley and Smart (1993) but also by incorporating in the statistical models a linkage between the Breadline Britain survey data for individual households and data on the neighbourhoods and local authorities where respondents lived, particularly data on spending levels.

Local authorities provide a wide range of services and the Breadline Britain survey is rather selective in the services it identifies. Nevertheless, those selected are reasonably representative of some of the more interesting services. Major services excluded are those which fall into the category of public goods, where usage cannot very meaningfully be attributed to individuals (e.g. law and order), services which are universal (e.g. refuse collection) or compulsory for particular groups (e.g. education from 5 to 16) and services which are intended to provide a uniform scale of benefits to eligible households (e.g. Housing Benefit, covered elsewhere in the survey). The services included are subject to significant local discretion in provision, provide private benefits to individual users and are subject to a mixture of demand side influences. Some are available to the population at large, while others are targeted on particular groups and rationed on the basis of some assessment of need. Unlike the Cheshire survey reported in Bramley et al (1989), this survey does not measure the volume of usage per household The same applies to the other MORI surveys reported in Bramley and Smart (1993) but, unlike those surveys, the usage question here provides richer information in terms of a range of responses referring to adequacy and affordability. Other parts of the survey also provide much richer information on some of the factors which might influence service usage, including income, deprivation and aspects of need.

Distributional profiles of different services

The first approach employed is to tabulate usage rates by household types against a number of measures of socio-economic (dis)advantage. Household type is important here because many local services are either specifically targeted on certain groups (e.g. the elderly) or are of greater relevance to households at certain stages in their lives. As with much of the welfare state, the most important redistributions effected by local services may be demographic (or horizontal) between different age groups and household types, rather than as between different income or class groups (vertical). Simple comparisons of usage rates by income, for example, may be misleading because of the confounding effects of demography. Cross-tabulating by household type provides a rough check on this; firstly, by enabling us to observe different socio-economic profiles within different demographic groups and, secondly, by enabling us to perform a general standardisation procedure. This entails calculating what the usage rate for each income, class or deprivation group would be if that group had the same demographic structure as the overall national population.

Table 9.1 summarises the results of this exercise for the 11 services identified in this survey. Three socio-economic measures are used: social (occupational) class; equivalent income (adjusted for household structure) and deprivation (see Chapter 1 and Appendix I).

Table 9.1

Usage rates and standardised usage ratios by class, equivalent income and deprivation for 11 local services

Service	Usage rate (%)	Usage ratio by class	Usage ratios equivalent income	Usage ratio by deprivation
Libraries	64	1.40	0.95	1.36
Sports & Swimming	55	1.34	1.39	1.19
Museums & galleries	39	2.03	1.60	1.56
Adult evening classes	22	1.88	1.29	1.52
Bus services	67	0.77	0.77	0.85
Child care	61	0.92	0.75	1.26
Play facilities	62	0.93	0.80	1.31
School meals	52	0.70	0.71	0.79
Home help	10.3	0.62	0.93	0.84
Meals on wheels	4.7	0.32	0.00	0.57
Special transport	9.6	0.29	0.06	0.94

Note: Usage ratios are the ratio between the usage rate for the most advantaged group and that for the least advantaged group, with four class groups, five income groups, and two deprivation groups. For the first group of services the relevant population is all households; for the second group households with children under five or at school; for the third group all elderly plus households with one or more disabled members.

Social class is particularly useful for comparisons with the other MORI surveys and may be a strong predictor for some services where middle class capture is a possibility. Equivalent income provides a single standard measure of current command over material resources. Deprivation is a particular focus of this study and captures a broader picture of disadvantage, reflecting past as well as present circumstances of households.

In each case we show, as a summary measure of the distributional profile, the ratio of usage by the top (most advantaged) group to usage by the bottom (least advantaged) group, after standardisation for household type. In commenting on these patterns, we draw out any particular features of the distribution across middle groups which may be obscured by these simple ratios. Comments are also offered on how these results compare with those derived from particular authorities in Bramley and Smart (1993). The table also shows the average usage rate for all relevant households. In this table usage includes those who used the service but classified it as inadequate, while the denominator comprises all relevant households including those answering 'don't know'.

The first group of services are open to all and essentially demand-led (Bramley and Le Grand, 1992). Apart from bus services, use of these services shows a pro-rich bias to varying degrees. This characteristic is rather typical of demand-led services. They represent normal economic goods, mainly in the leisure field, which 'better off' people tend to want to consume more of. Although they are free or subsidised, there are some costs involved in using them, including charges in some cases and the time and money costs of getting access to them.

The pro-rich pattern applies across the three measures of (dis)advantage used, although class is more important in some cases, those where cultural preference factors play more of a part. It is clear from the last column that the 'poor' make significantly less use of local public services in the leisure field, the difference being of the order of 20-50%. These services are not only failing to compensate for other deprivations but problems of access to them are on balance worsening the deprivation of some households. Another way of looking at these services, in particular, is that they represent examples of 'participating in the normal life of the community'. The evidence suggests that 'multiply deprived' households are less likely to participate in this 'normal life of the community'.

The patterns of use in Table 9.1 are broadly consistent with those found in particular local authority surveys. This is generally true for libraries and museums. The Breadline Britain national results for use of adult education evening classes suggest less of a bias to better off middle class usage than in any of the four local surveys reviewed in Bramley and Smart (1993) but the bias revealed in Table 9.1 is still quite marked. The middle class bias for sports and swimming is also less in the Breadline Britain survey than in some of the local surveys.

Buses provide the main mode of local public transport in most areas although the extent to which they receive subsidy varies. The finding that general bus services are used more by the less well off is consistent with the Cheshire survey, although there were some aspects of subsidised bus provision (e.g. home to school) that were shown in that survey to be pro-rich. It is not surprising that buses are used more by poorer households because such households are less likely to have the use of a car, let alone more than one car. Locational factors also play a part; bus services survive more in urban areas, where many poorer people are concentrated.

Buses may be regarded as a cheaper, slower, lower quality mode of transport, which better off people tend to choose to avoid if they can. However, bus services are important in many instances for giving people access to a range of other opportunities, services and facilities and their availability and affordability may be seen as crucial in enabling participation in the life of the community. Thus, from the usage evidence, bus services seem to be making some positive contribution to improving the position of the disadvantaged, although this is not very dramatic. 'Multiply deprived' households are only 15-20% more likely than other households to use buses. We should also take account of the evidence below on quality and supply constraints.

Children's services present a rather mixed picture. For both child care services (nurseries, playgroups) and child play facilities, the distribution is moderately pro-poor on income, closer to neutral on class and somewhat in favour of the 'less deprived' over the 'multiply deprived'. Examination of more detailed patterns reveals that, for these two services, usage peaks in one of the intermediate class (C2) or income (second highest quintile) groups, rather than sloping smoothly up or down the socio-economic scale. Various factors could account for this; in the case of child care, working mothers would tend to make more use of the service and have higher incomes. For smaller and lone parent families, deprivation is associated with lower usage, while for larger and complex families, deprivation is positively associated with usage.

School meals are much more consistent in showing a pro-poor bias on all three overall indicators. The detailed data shows more fluctuation within the intermediate groups, with some signs of peaks in take-up in the poorest group and in better off groups. This may be because of the role of free school meals targeted on the poorest group, with take-up among the rest being influenced by the relationship between income and charges and the incidence of working mothers. Cheshire data, which separated free and paid meals, confirmed that they had opposite distributions.

The final group of services considered here are social care and related services mainly intended for dependent elderly people and others with some form of disability. The original Cheshire usage study (Bramley *et al*, 1989), highlighted social care services for elderly and other clients as the main examples of strongly 'pro-poor' services. The more recent comparative work using MORI local surveys modified this conclusion slightly, by suggesting that the pro-poor character of these services could not be taken completely for granted. It depended in part on the rationing criteria used, given that these are broadly in the category of 'needs rationed services'.

The pro-poor character is more apparent if one looks at income, particularly total household income but also equivalent income, and is less apparent in terms of class or deprivation (see Table 9.1). The fact that home help and special transport are only slightly more likely to be used by the more deprived households is a rather surprising finding. This may imply that targeting is ineffective, or that the criteria used to allocate these services (heavily related to health/disability factors and household situation) are not in fact strongly correlated with poverty and multiple deprivation, especially within the retired group.

Supply constraints

We are able to shed more light on the patterns of usage of these local services by considering the incidence of constraints associated with the availability, quality and cost of services. The range of possible responses to the Breadline Britain service usage question includes three ways in which supply constraints can affect usage. Firstly, the service may be used but perceived as inadequate. Secondly, it may not be used because it is unavailable or inadequate in some way and, thirdly, it may not be used because the respondent cannot afford to use it. We bracket these three responses together to provide an index of supply constraint in the broad sense. In this way, the survey provides a unique additional source of evidence on the extent to which inadequacies of service provision arise across different services and impact on different groups.

We can also consider some additional services beyond the selected 11, including some important local public goods, by using responses to other questions in the survey. These deal with local environmental quality, open space, school resources (teacher availability, books, etc.), housing disrepair (due to landlord inaction or inability to afford) and crime (being a victim or feeling unsafe). Table 9.2 summarises these responses for high and low equivalent income groups and households below and above the key deprivation threshold (enforced lack of three or more socially perceived necessities).

The results for income are not very clear cut, at least when comparing the top and bottom groups. For quite a few services, the lowest income group report either a similar level of constraints or a lower level than the top group. However, examination of the figures across all five income quintiles shows in many cases a U-shaped pattern, with constraints falling as income rises up to the third or fourth quintile and then rising sharply for the top group(s). One explanation for this may be that the highest income groups are more concerned about the quality of provision. A second explanation, particularly for the needs-rationed services, may be that the rationing systems are effectively excluding the better off. It is certainly true that the greater incidence of constraints for the top income group is more pronounced for the social care services.

199

Table 9.2
Supply, quality or cost constraints on usage by equivalent income and deprivation for 11 local services

Service	Proportion of households constrained (%)			
	Equivalent Income		Deprived	
	Top	*Bottom*	*No*	*Yes*
Libraries	12	12	9	14
Sports & Swimming	20	18	20	15
Museums & galleries	25	19	17	21
Adult evening classes	9	16	9	20
Bus services	35	24	25	29
Child care	38	30	29	28
Play facilities	26	55	39	57
School meals	35	33	19	33
Home help	24	7	8	7
Meals on wheels	79	33	44	46
Special transport	83	38	55	52
Local area dirty etc.	20	39	22	42
Local open space	13	37	19	43
School resources	5	10		
Home disrepair	2	16	3	19
Crime victim/unsafe	29	30	22	39

Note: For the first eleven services, the percentage of relevant households using service but inadequate, not using because inadequate/unavailable, or can't afford, excluding don't knows; for remainder, percentage of all households reporting problems.

Nevertheless, there are some services where the low income households are more constrained: adult education and children's play facilities. Also, the additional set of services identified at the bottom of the table show a much stronger tendency for supply constraints or quality problems to be experienced more often by lowest income group. This is true for all of these cases except crime (see Chapter 5). The 'poor' seem to be more disadvantaged by their local public goods environment than by their access to individual services. This is strongly confirmed by the analysis in terms of deprivation. The 'poor' are much more likely to live in bad housing and in bad neighbourhoods.

Even for the individual user services in the upper part of the table, deprived households are more likely to report supply constraints in most cases, except sports and child care (need based rationing probably helps here). This suggests that the lower usage of leisure services by the deprived is not just a matter of tastes, preferences and relevance of services. For the rationed social care services, supply constraints are as likely to hit the multiply deprived as the rest of the population.

The differences between the services also provide interesting evidence on the relative adequacy of different kinds of local service provision. For example, the incidence of supply constraints is generally low for libraries and adult education. This is consistent with other evidence discussed in Bramley and Smart (1993), which suggested that the library service, in particular, was very highly developed and accessible. Services which seem to be much more frequently cited as inadequate include buses, child care, school meals and meals on wheels, and more especially children's play facilities and special transport.

Multivariate models

The next step in the analysis of usage is to undertake a multivariate statistical analysis to try to separate out the simultaneous influence of a large number of factors which may influence outcomes. We first do this using variables that represent the individual attributes of households using data from within the survey. Excluded at this stage are measures of the characteristics of areas, particularly the local authorities in which people live and the levels of service which they provide. Up to twenty individual attribute variables are included in the analysis, although the number is reduced for certain services as appropriate. Apart from class, income and deprivation, these include: demographic factors like age, sex, household types and number of children; economic activity factors like working full and part time and unemployment, including past and long term unemployment; housing tenure (council); health and disability; black and Asian ethnic groups; car ownership and receipt of benefits.

In reporting these results we concentrate on class, income and deprivation, partly to reduce the amount of detail, but we should remember that some of the other variables may capture some of the effects of poverty and deprivation. Table 9.3 draws out the key findings for the particular variables of greatest interest, using t-statistics from a logistic (logit) model to indicate the direction and statistical significance of the effects. The logistic model is appropriate to this situation where the variable to be explained takes the dichotomous (yes/no) form.

For the first four demand-led general services, the pattern is fairly consistent with the somewhat simpler analysis of Table 9.1. Higher social class exerts a positive influence on usage which is statistically significant in all cases except sports and swimming. Once allowance is made for all of the other influences, including class and deprivation, equivalent income does not have a strong or significant influence, although its direction is positive in most cases. Deprivation still has a consistently negative effect, although this is not statistically significant for libraries and sports. Most of the other significant influences for these services are demographic. In adult education particularly other income-related factors (car ownership, benefits) reinforce the pattern. Ethnicity is not generally very significant, but for libraries and adult education black respondents are more likely to use the services.

201

Table 9.3
Influence of class, equivalent income and deprivation on usage of 11 local services in multivariate models (t-statistics in logistics models including up to 20 individual household attributes)

Significance (t-statistic) Service	Class AB	Class C1	Equivalent Income	Deprivation
Libraries	3.54	3.06	-2.00	-1.23
Sports & Swimming	1.26	1.50	2.11	-1.49
Museums & Galleries	2.82	2.14	0.71	-1.76
Adult Evening Classes	1.36	2.93	1.25	-1.54
Bus services	-0.42	-0.05	-3.12	-1.54
Child care	-3.20	-1.67	0.92	-2.50
Play facilities	-1.72	-1.02	-0.19	-2.20
School Meals	1.49	0.11	-1.15	0.64
Home Help	1.77	1.13	-0.09	-1.13
Meals on wheels	0.26	0.22	0.59	0.01
Special transport	0.58	1.10	-0.92	-0.73

Note: t-statistics indicate the direction and significance of the effect of the particular variable on the probability of usage of each service, allowing for the simultaneous influence of all of the other variables included in the analysis; values greater than about 1.7 shown in bold indicate significance at the 10% level, and greater than 2.0 at the 5% level.

Broadly speaking, for demand-led services in the leisure field, our earlier conclusion that these services are used more by the higher socio-economic groups, and less by the most deprived, still stands.

As in the earlier analysis, bus services show a rather different pattern, with class having a negative influence although this is not statistically significance. Income has a significant negative effect on bus usage, even after allowing for the strong negative effect of car ownership (t=-7.31). Deprivation again has a negative effect, but this is of marginal statistical significance. So for this important service, some success is achieved in counteracting material disadvantage, but this is not very dramatic.

For child care and children's play facilities, usage is negatively associated with social class, while the income variable is again insignificant. But the most deprived households are still significantly less likely to use these services. For children's play there are also negative associations with receiving benefits and past unemployment. Lone parents are not significantly more likely to use these services either. Socio-economic variables as a group have a significant influence on constraints on usage. Since these are services where one would have hoped and expected that local government provision might materially help to compensate for other disadvantages, this finding is a source of concern. The evidence given above that these services may be particularly under-provided may be relevant here, and taken together these findings reinforce the arguments which have achieved national prominence recently for better pre-school provision.

The results for school meals suggest a more neutral pattern, in that none of the key variables are statistically significant and the deprivation effect may be weakly positive. Social class DE (semi/unskilled manual) and disability are positively related to usage. Socio-economic variables as a whole have only a limited effect on improving the usage model and an insignificant extra effect on the prediction of constraints.

The needs-based social care services are expected to be related to single elderly status and health/disability problems. This is true for home helps and special transport, but not apparently for meals on wheels. After allowing for these and other factors, there is still a tendency for there to be a positive relationship with high social class, which is rather surprising, although this is counterbalanced by a positive association with Class DE. The association with income is not significant. These are services which we would hope and expect would be particularly targeted on the most deprived, but this does not appear to be the case; for two of the services the direction of the effect is negative, although not statistically significant. Socio-economic variables as a group generally give a significant improvement to the model predictions, particularly of constraints on usage. These results rather confirm the findings of the author in some local surveys that these services are not consistently targeted on the least well off.

Overall, this multivariate modelling exercise confirms many of our earlier findings, while providing more detailed insights into some of the factors which affect usage of local government services. The picture is a disappointing one in terms of the hope that publicly provided local services might play a significant role in countering the material deprivations of the poorest households in Britain. It suggests that local government may still have some way to go in tailoring its service delivery practices to contribute effectively to anti-poverty strategies.

Local expenditure, needs and service usage

This technique can be extended to take account of the influence of factors which are associated with the area in which people live as well as attributes of individuals/households. This approach is sometimes known as 'multi-level modelling'. The evidence presented here is exploratory and concentrates on two issues where area-level effects are potentially important both for the incidence of deprivation and for policies to counter deprivation. These two issues are:

- the influence of local authority expenditure (on the services in question) on outcomes, in terms of usage or constraints on usage;

- the influence of type of neighbourhood, particularly 'deprived' areas, on outcomes, allowing for other individual influences.

In general, we would expect local authority expenditure on a particular service, say libraries, to have a positive relationship with the probability of using the service and a negative association with the experience of constraints on usage or problems with a service. This assumes that extra expenditure, at the margin, contributes to the quality, range, delivery and accessibility of a service in such a way that more usage is encouraged and constraints on usage are overcome. This need not necessarily apply, for example where the service is strictly rationed and the expenditure affects quality rather than quantity, or where the service is so well provided that the market is effectively saturated. Part of the motive for including local expenditure in the model is to see how this effect operates in different services.

A second motive is to see whether including this factor in the model alters the influence of any of the individual variables, such as income, class or deprivation. Are we to any degree confounding individual and area effects, who you are versus where you are? In general, standards of provision of local services are not uniform, and variations in expenditure are a major if not the only cause of such differences. There may be systematic associations between where different income/class/deprivation groups live and the supply/quality of local services, and if so this would mean that some confounding of the two effects is a real danger. In practice, in nearly all cases the inclusion of these extra area level variables does not seriously alter the effects of the income, class and deprivation variables from those shown in Table 9.3. Indeed, in the majority of cases the effect of the class/income/deprivation variables is slightly reinforced.

In order to interpret local expenditure effects, it is helpful to take account where possible of the government's official measure of local expenditure need, known as Standard Spending Assessment (SSA). This measure determines both the amount of grant received by each local authority and, to an increasing extent, the maximum level of spending permitted under so-called 'capping' rules (Audit Commission, 1993). If the SSA reflects the relative needs and costs of different areas in an appropriate way, then it is not expenditure per se but expenditure relative to SSA which should indicate the standard of service being provided. For example, if expenditure is 150% of SSA we would expect the service to be much better than if it were only 50%, and we would expect usage rates to reflect this. We could use this relative measure of expenditure, in some models, rather than raw per capita expenditure, but in many cases the services covered by SSAs are much broader or not precisely related to the services identified in the survey. In addition, it is often not possible to match actual expenditure precisely to the relevant SSA.

Of course the SSA may not be a particularly good measure of need. This is especially so for individual services now because, since 1990, SSA has been calculated for rather large combinations of services. Including the SSA (per capita) measure in the model as well as actual expenditure may provide some indication of the extent to which SSA is systematically not reflecting need in the right degree. For example, if usage was negatively associated with SSA and constraints were positively associated with SSA, we might tentatively conclude that SSA was not compensating sufficiently for variations in needs.

The way we incorporate local expenditure and SSA in the analysis is to link the households in the Breadline survey to a file of data on expenditure and SSA for the local authorities in which respondents live. The location of the sampling clusters (enumeration districts) used for the survey provides the link. The financial data refer to the financial year 1990/91. Expenditure is deflated for London area cost differences and divided by a relevant population (e.g. elderly, children). There are several practical limitations to these data which make them less than ideal. Firstly, standards of service may reflect spending in previous years. Secondly, SSAs are as already mentioned only calculated for groups of services, which are generally broader than the categories used in the Breadline survey. In some cases (e.g. children's' play), the expenditure data refer to a broader category (e.g. recreation) within which the particular service we are interested may only be a small part. Thirdly, we have to discard sample households in Wales and Scotland, because SSA and/or expenditure data are not available on a comparable basis. We are also unable to link part of the booster sample. Fourthly, for some services provision in non-metropolitan areas is made by a higher tier county authority.

Accessibility to services may be affected by the geographical characteristics of local areas. We try to take account of this by including one rather crude measure of population sparsity at the district level.

To test for the effect of neighbourhood characteristics we are able to make use of the ACORN classification of Enumeration Districts, which can also be linked to the sampling points (see Appendix I). Two of the ACORN types representing the most deprived types of area are tested, D (older terraced housing) and G (the most deprived council estates); dummy variables for these neighbourhoods are included in some of the regression models, as shown in Table 9.4.

Table 9.4
Influence of expenditure and area type on usage
(t-statistics in logistics models including up to 20 individual attributes)

Significance (t-statistic) Service	Expend- iture	SSA	Sparsity	Acorn Area Type D	G
Libraries	0.42	0.46	0.26	1.04	1.28
Sports & Swimming	1.51	-0.82	-0.03	0.09	-0.82
Museums & Galleries	0.70	3.44	-1.26	-3.12	-2.05
Adult Evening Classes	1.40	-0.57	0.60	-0.20	-0.61
Bus services	0.34	0.85	-2.53	-0.05	-1.59
Child care	1.94*	0.45	1.05	-0.40	-1.31
Play facilities	0.41	-1.22	-0.08	0.15	0.54
School Meals	0.82	0.24	1.59	-.68	-0.95
Home Help	1.25	0.66	0.14	-1.25	0.67
Meals on wheels	2.48*	-1.00	0.98	-0.10	0.87
Special transport	0.30	-1.12	1.14	-0.30	0.73

Note: Interpretation of t-statistics as in Table 9.3. Sparsity is district area divided by district population. ACORN classification: type D areas are 'older terraced housing', type G are council estates with the most serious social problems. Expenditure and SSA are divided by the relevant population. *In these cases two expenditure or SSA variables are both included, and the statistic shown is the larger of the two.

In fact, these variables are rarely significant once allowance is made for the individual/household variables. Only in the case of museums and (marginally) bus services does one or both of these variables show a significant negative effect on usage. In the models for constraints/problems, the type G areas (worst council estates) show significantly less constraints on school meals usage but more problems with the area being dirty etc. The lack of significant independent area effects apparent from this test suggests that the strong focus of some urban deprivation research and policy initiatives on small area initiatives and indicators may be somewhat misplaced.

Expenditure on libraries does not appear to have a very significant or consistent effect on the use of libraries, after allowing for individual variables (see Table 9.4). We argued above, partly based on other evidence, that the libraries service is highly developed, and it may be that this is a case of a service approaching saturation level. Other services where none of the financial effects seem to be very significant include children's play, school meals and special transport. However, for all of these to varying degrees the expenditure and SSA data are not closely related to the particular services covered in the survey question.

For sports and swimming, and childcare (nurseries) the relationships are slightly stronger although still not very significant. Here, expenditure is positively associated with usage, and negatively with constraints. In this case, the normal hypothesised relationship between spending on provision and take-up seems to apply. These two services come closest to the 'ideal' pattern: expenditure increases usage while reducing problems and constraints, and there are no indications of systematic inadequacies in SSA.

The results for museums are similar for expenditure, but different in other ways. SSA level has a strong positive association with usage, while sparsity has a negative association; this reflects the greater availability and role of museums in central cities. This service is the clearest case where neighbourhood type affects usage, with both ACORN types D and G having significantly lower usage of museums.

Adult education evening classes usage rises with expenditure, but so also does the reporting of constraints. Thus, expenditure may not be varying enough to meet need. SSA has a negative association with constraints, however, implying if anything an overcompensation. This paradoxical finding may well reflect the fact that the service is a small part of a much larger block for both expenditure and SSA purposes, but that the two financial variables are somewhat differently defined. Meals on wheels is a similar case.

For bus services the expenditure on subsidies seems to have little effect on usage, but there is a positive association between SSA and reported constraints. This suggests that SSA may be under-compensating for need in this case, one which has been very controversial in central-local relations in the past. Bus usage is significantly lower in sparse rural areas, an unsurprising finding, since this is where services are poorest. It is interesting to note a negative association with the most deprived council estates also.

Home help is the most important of the needs-based social care services targeted on elderly and disabled people, and it is one for which the data on provision are rather more extensive. Higher expenditure increases usage, but it is interesting to note that there is a significant positive association between expenditure and constraints. There is also a positive association between SSA and constraints. This suggests that neither SSAs (determined by central government) nor expenditure (determined by local government) are compensating fully for needs variations.

There is a similar pattern in the positive association of expenditure and SSA with the range of local environmental problems identified in Table 9.5. The positive association with SSA suggests that this official needs assessment under-compensates for these problems. However, as with children's' play the expenditure variables are also positively associated with these problems. The causality may be running in a different way here: localities with particularly poor local environments may demand more expenditure, but that expenditure is insufficient to overcome the environmental problems.

Table 9.5

Association of expenditure, standard spending assessment and
sparsity on constraints and problems (t-statistics in logistic models)

Significance (t statistics)

Service	2 variables		full model		
	Expend	SSA	Expend	SSA	Sparsity
Libraries	0.98	0.12	0.30	0.91	1.54
Sports & Swimming	-1.48	0.28	-0.22	0.13	1.69
Museums & Galleries	-1.41	-1.74	-0.96	0.31	2.06
Adult Evening Classes	1.45	-2.13	1.78	-0.64	0.08
Bus services	-1.05	2.96	-0.50	2.48	0.81
Child care	1.0*	-0.76	-1.69	-0.33	-2.02
Play facilities	1.50	0.68	0.76	1.08	0.53
School Meals	-0.88	0.84	0.18	-0.02	-0.39
Home Help	2.69	-2.05	2.53	-1.69	2.26
Meals on wheels	1.12	-1.58	1.59	-1.88	2.08
Special transport	-0.77	-0.83	-0.28	-0.91	1.03
Local area dirty etc.			1.81	1.58	-0.92
Local open space			2.01	-0.59	-0.80
School resources			0.29	2.21	-0.00
Home disrepair			0.54	1.65	-1.47
Crime victim/unsafe			1.80	2.67	-2.58

Note: Interpretation as in Table 9.4; first two columns show results for model with only these two variables included, while columns 3 and 4 show the effect of these variables in the full model.

Overall these patterns are a reflection of the fact that environmental problems, high spending and high SSAs are all associated with London and other central cities.

Finally, we can reflect on the extent to which constraints are a function of urban-rural location, by referring to the effect of the sparsity variable shown in the last column of Table 9.5. It appears that two kinds of services seem to leave rural dwellers with more problems of access to adequate services: facility-based leisure services like sports and museums, and domiciliary social care services like home helps. A number of reasons could lie behind these patterns. In the leisure case there is clearly a physical access and availability issue, since major facilities tend to be located in towns. In the case of the home help service, the reasons are less clear but may relate to different styles of rationing in rural local authorities. For child care (nursery) services and those services relating mainly to the local environment, shown at the bottom of the table, constraints or problems are generally less in the rural locations. Crime and security seems to be the type of local environmental problem which most sharply distinguishes rural and urban locations.

The evidence presented in this section is partly exploratory. It provides confirmation for some of the key findings on the use made of local services and constraints on usage experienced by different socio-economic groups. In particular, the tendency for deprived households to have their deprivation reinforced in terms of access to some of these local services is confirmed. Higher levels of local spending on services seems to increase usage in some but not all cases. The results also provide some indirect evidence that the official system of needs assessment underpinning the allocation of resources between local authorities (SSAs) may under-compensate for differences in needs in some cases and may not adequately reflect urban and rural situations. In this respect the evidence provides a pointer to a new way of looking at the adequacy of territorial needs indicators. Hitherto, such indicators and assessments have been derived mainly by analysing past patterns of expenditure. This study has explored in a limited way the possibility of examining this issue from the standpoint of outcomes, as suggested in Bramley (1990b).

How essential are local services?

So far in this chapter we have concentrated on the actual use of local public services, and on evidence of supply constraints which limit effective usage. The Breadline Britain survey also asked respondents to indicate which of the selected services they believed to be essential rather than just desirable. The responses to this question may be evaluated in two distinct but related contexts.

Firstly, in the context of the overall philosophy and approach of the Breadline Britain study, we can evaluate or rank these local public services alongside the range of private material consumption items in terms of how widespread is the belief that they are necessary or essential for an adequate life in Britain today. Such evidence is particularly important for an theory of needs founded on the concept of consensus, or widespread and hence stable political agreement.

Secondly, by relating views about the essential nature of services to the actual usage of those services, one can derive some indication of the extent to which these services are 'public goods' in the economic sense, in that they generate external benefits to non-users as well as private benefits to direct users. These indicators can be related to measures based on local spending preferences which try to capture the same phenomenon, as discussed in Bramley (1990a) and Bramley and Smart (1993, pp 62-84).

The responses to this question which are shown in Table 9.6 are rather striking. For most of the services identified, the proportion of respondents rating the services as essential is very high. For all bar two, the proportion is nearly 80% or more. Only museums and galleries fall below the criterion of a substantial majority regarding the service as essential and even here there is a small majority supporting this proposition. Even in the leisure oriented services of libraries and sports, the majorities for treating these as essential are very large. For bus services, children's services and services for elderly and disabled people the support is overwhelming.

Need based local public services for children, elderly and disabled people and the basic access provided by bus services are in the same league as the most essential of private consumption goods: meals, heating, basic housing amenities, waterproof clothing. Key leisure services like libraries and sports are not quite so universally supported but are still well up the league table, alongside things like meat/fish, all-weather shoes, carpets, toys, washing machines and enough separate bedrooms.

Table 9.6
Proportion of respondents regarding selected local services
as essential and desirable (%)

Service	Essential	Desirable
Libraries	79	20
Sports & Swimming	79	20
Museums & galleries	52	47
Adult evening classes	70	28
Bus services	96	2
Child care	90	9
Play facilities	92	7
School meals	87	11
Home help	95	2
Meals on wheels	93	4
Special transport	95	2

We can compare these findings with those of Bramley and Smart (1993, Table 7), who looked at the relationship between people who said in local surveys they wanted more spent on particular services and those who actually used those services. This evidence provides strong support for the proposition that needs based services targeted at groups like the elderly, disabled and children are widely supported by non-users. For example, in the case of social care of the elderly, non-users were nearly as likely (75%) as users to favour more spending and 88% of those favouring more spending were non-users. Similar ratios were found for social services for those with physical disabilities and children (non-users 54% as likely to want more spending and non-users accounting for 95% of those wanting more spending). In other words, these services are not just private goods but act in a significant way as public goods in the economic sense, with members of a wider public being willing to spend more through local taxes to secure provision.

This phenomenon applies more widely to many of the services provided by local authorities, although not always so strikingly as in the social care case. For example, such services as consumer advice, housing advice, countryside, youth clubs and further education and training score quite highly on these indicators. Even in the case of sport and leisure services, non-users are 69% as likely as users to favour more spending and a majority (55%) of those favouring more spending are non-users. Libraries and adult education score less highly, however.

Conclusion

The services provided by local government are diverse and the way they are targeted or rationed varies significantly, so we would not expect all to play an equal role in countering or alleviating poverty. Nevertheless, the findings reported in this chapter present a rather disappointing message on the distributional impact of local public services, particularly in relation to the poorest households. The results are based on an analysis of patterns of usage (and reasons for non-usage) of 11 selected services and some broader problems indirectly related to local services. We can compare relatively simple usage rates for different socio-economic groups, with crude demographic standardisation, with the results of more complex multivariate models, with and without the inclusion of area characteristics including service expenditure measures. These comparisons modify some of the detail but confirm the general shape of the results.

Demand-led services in the leisure field open to a broad spectrum of the population tend to be used more by the better off or the middle classes, and less by the 'multiply deprived' households. This conclusion applies to varying degrees to libraries, sports facilities, museums/galleries and adult education. The one general public service examined which shows a different pattern is bus services, which are used more by lower income households, particularly those without a car.

Services targeted on children present a more mixed picture, with less class bias but still a lower level of use by the most deprived. Underlying factors here may be a generally inadequate level of provision of nursery and play facilities and the influence of working mothers on access and take-up. School meals are neutral overall, with free meals boosting take-up among the poorest but charges possibly deterring usage among moderate income households.

Services targeted on the elderly and people with disabilities, including home help, meals on wheels and special transport, are distributed in a more pro-poor fashion than general demand-led services. We would expect this given the fact that these services are normally rationed on the basis of a needs assessment. Given this explicit rationing, it is surprising that our findings do not indicate a stronger degree of targeting. Once account is taken of the incidence of constraints (quality problems and deterred users) or the multivariate model results, it is necessary to qualify the overall conclusion somewhat. The most deprived are as likely to experience quality/access/cost problems as other households and are if anything less likely to use services holding other factors constant (although these relationships are not very significant statistically). There even seems to be some bias in favour of the higher social class households in the modelling results, especially for home help. This evidence suggests that further attention should be given to rationing processes, which may inadvertently disadvantage those who are most economically disadvantaged, perhaps by undue focus on health-related criteria or in other ways.

Although the available data are less than ideal, the modelling exercise using linked data on local expenditures suggests that in at least some cases higher expenditure can boost usage and reduce constraints on access. This and other evidence suggests that different local services are unevenly developed relative to underlying need; for example, libraries are highly developed in contrast with child care and play facilities or some social care services. In a number of cases evidence of constrained consumption relating positively to Standard Spending Assessment levels is consistent with a view that SSAs may under-compensate for differences in need between localities. Only rather limited support is found for the proposition that people living in the most deprived neighbourhoods are less likely to use local services than people with the same individual characteristics in other neighbourhoods. However, it is clear that the poor are much more likely to live in poor local environments and that local expenditure on environmental services is not sufficient to offset this effect.

In spite of these mixed findings on the redistributional role of local services, it is clear that there is widespread support for the provision of good quality local public services. Large majorities rate most of these services as essential, particularly the social care services but also some of the more general leisure and information services. This can be linked to evidence from some local surveys which suggest that many non-users are willing to pay more for better services, which implies that many of these services provide 'public' as well as 'private' benefits and that provision should continue to be regarded as a public responsibility.

10 Adapting the consensual definition of poverty

Bjørn Halleröd, Jonathan Bradshaw and Hilary Holmes

Introduction

The *consensual definition of poverty,* developed by Mack and Lansley (1985), represents one of the most important contributions to modern poverty research. The approach has several advantages compared to traditional 'expert definitions'. Firstly, a definition based on value judgements held by the population would probably reflect poverty as a social phenomenon in a more appropriate way. Secondly, there may be a better chance of getting broad public support for the definition. Thirdly, it is likely that poverty research based on a widely accepted definition will have a greater impact on political decisions and ultimately on social policy.

The purpose of this chapter is to develop this 'consensual definition of poverty'. The original Mack and Lansley approach will be compared with a new method developed by Halleröd (1994a and 1994b), using Swedish data but applied for the first time in an analysis of the data collected in the 1990 Breadline Britain Survey.

The original study was, to a large extent, a development and refinement of the theoretical and empirical work of Townsend (1979). Thus, the study was conducted in the tradition of direct measurement of poverty and Mack and Lansley defined poverty as 'enforced lack of socially perceived necessities' (1985, p39).

'Necessities' were restricted to a set of consumption items and people were regarded as 'poor' if they could not maintain a standard of consumption that was perceived as necessary by a majority of the population. Their empirical approach was based on two steps - identifying the necessities and identifying those who could not afford them (see Chapter 1).

The way Mack and Lansley defined, measured and finally identified those in poverty has been labelled 'the consensual poverty line'. Whilst the approach has had a vast impact on poverty research, the term 'consensual' is problematic and causes some confusion. The first attempt to develop a consensual poverty line was made by Goedhart, Halberstadt, Kapteyn and Van Praag (1977). They tried to establish an *economic* poverty line based on public opinion. Thus, the consensual poverty line was first used as a label for an indirect definition of poverty. The indirect approach has been further developed in several studies and is widely applied (see, for example, Van Praag *et al,* 1980; Haganaars, 1986; Saunders and Matheson, 1992). Another problem, to be addressed later, is that Mack and Lansley's definition does not reflect a state of consensus within the population. This can also be said of the indirect consensual poverty line (Saunders and Matheson, 1992, p47).

Critique of Mack and Lansley

The researchers have gone further than any of their predecessors in an effort to relate the definition of poverty to the view of public opinion and to reduce the impact of arbitrary decisions.

> ".....we have aimed to exclude our own personal value judgements by taking the consensual judgement of society at large about people's needs. We hope to have moved towards what Sen describes as 'an objective diagnosis of condition' based on 'an objective understanding of 'feelings'." (Mack and Lansley, 1985, p46)

There were nevertheless several arbitrary aspects and decisions remaining in their approach. These decisions are partly connected with the design of the survey and partly with the interpretation of the data.

Firstly, the way a study is designed will always have an important impact on the results. The results will therefore always reflect the researchers' interpretation of poverty. The core of the study was to identify necessities and those who went without them, using a list of 44 items selected by Mack and Lansley. They argued that the items 'on the one hand distinguished between the 'poor' and others, and on the other hand, to be of some significance to many people' (Mack and Lansley, 1985, p50). The argument is not that the goal was not achieved but that it was Mack and Lansley themselves who made the ultimate decision as to which items could be regarded as necessities. So, although the respondents decided which items on the list were necessary, they did not decide which items should be included on the list.

However, the reliability analysis demonstrated that, even if Mack and Lansley had chosen a completely different set of questions about necessities, the results they obtained would have been effectively identical (see Chapter 1).

Secondly, the term 'consensus' refers to a situation where everyone has the same opinion. A consensual definition of poverty should therefore refer to a definition that everybody accepts and that reflects *'the views of society as a whole'* (Mack and Lansley, 1985, p42). That is, however, not the case in Mack and Lansley's study. They decided that an item was a necessity if more than 50% of the population perceived it as such. Whilst it is seen as reasonable to let the majority decide what is necessary, 'majority' is not the same as 'consensus' and there are no theoretical reasons to take the level for 'necessities' as 50% rather than 30% or 70% or any other level. The decision is ultimately arbitrary.

The classification of consumer items into necessities and non-necessities is problematic if the consensual approach is interpreted as a ranking of preferences, as shown by the following example. Analysis of the 1990 Mack and Lansley data shows that, of the 44 items on the list, 32 items were identified as necessities by at least 50% of respondents. Let us imagine that a person X has an order of preferences identical to the standard preferences held by public opinion and also imagine that X wants to consume all the items on the list but can only afford 32 of them, namely those regarded as necessities by the majority of the population. X is a very rational human being so she or he does consume all the necessary items but nothing more. X will, if Mack and Lansley's approach is used, not be deprived at all and certainly not be 'poor' because she or he does not lack any of the necessities. The fact that she or he cannot afford anything else does not change that picture.

Let us then imagine Y who has quite a different order of preferences. Y also wants to have all the items on the list but the difference is that Y can afford all but three of them. Since Y's order of preferences is different from the majority of the population, these three are regarded as necessities and Y, in lacking them, is perceived to be 'poor' even though her or his actual consumption reflects choice and not constraint.

Although X and Y are unlikely to exist in the real world, they highlight an unresolved dilemma in Mack and Lansley's approach. The closer a person's order of preferences is to the aggregated preferences held by general public opinion, the more likely it is that she or he will try to consume in accordance with these aggregated preferences. The consequence of this, other things being equal, is that the closer a person's choices are to the average choice, the less likely that person is to be seen as deprived or 'poor'.

A third problem in this consensual definition of poverty is the important conclusion that there is a high degree of homogeneity in people's opinions of necessary consumption (see Chapter 3). Necessities were accounted as such by a majority of the population, independent of differences in demographic and social composition. However, these results do not imply that there are no differences in the extent to which different parts of society classified consumption as necessary. It only means that it is unusual that these differences change majority conditions. The point is best illustrated by a dressing gown! The 1990 Breadline Britain data shows, for example, that as only 42% of the population regard a dressing gown as necessary, it is not a necessity. However, older people classify a dressing gown as necessary to a much higher degree than younger people - 78% of female single people and 85% of female respondents in couples over 75 years of age considered a dressing gown as necessary. The proportion for both single people and childless couples under 20 years of age is zero. Mack and Lansley's approach would still lead to the conclusion that a dressing gown is not a necessity even though the difference between the age groups is so significant.   It is also significantly different by age and family composition.

The UK data show that there are statistically significant differences (at the 0.01 level) between age groups, men and women and different types of household on 19 of the 44 consumer items listed. These differences are hidden if Mack and Lansley's approach is used.

Finally, Mack and Lansley (1985, p39) did, as mentioned above, define poverty as 'enforced lack of socially perceived necessities'. They decided that people who could not afford three or more of the necessities were 'poor'. It could be argued that the poverty line should have been set at a score of one if a necessity is really a necessity. This raises the bigger and more general question of the need for a poverty line at all.

Poverty in an advanced society is not just a question of 'obvious want and squalor', it is also a question of being able to keep up with the ordinary lifestyle of that society.   This was the main point made by Townsend (Abel-Smith and Townsend, 1965; Townsend, 1970, 1979).   To relate poverty to ordinary lifestyle means that the centre of attention is moved from subsistence to social integration. Mack and Lansley's concept of poverty is more strict than Townsend's and poverty is still based on the notion of deviation from ordinary lifestyle and not just a matter of starvation and malnutrition. This is because 'socially perceived necessities', by definition, are related to the ordinary lifestyle of a society and it is this connection which makes Mack and Lansley's definition relative.

The question then is, how big should this deviation be before it is called poverty? Both Townsend (1979) and Mack and Lansley (1985) argued that poverty is the outcome of accumulated deprivation. Thus, deprivation is not the same as poverty. This is not to say that a small amount of deprivation is totally unproblematic for the deprived but the term 'ordinary lifestyle' refers to a mean value for the total population and the fact that most people tend to deviate to some degree from 'ordinary' is not a problem.   The implication is that enforced lack of socially perceived necessities must be concentrated on a relatively small part of the population before there can be talk of poverty. It is hard to argue that poverty equals an exclusion from ordinary lifestyle if this is not the case. Necessities are necessary because they are a normal part of daily life for most people. What defining poverty is all about is finding indicators which separate people suffering from multiple deprivation and hardship from people who live more or less ordinary but not necessarily totally unproblematic lives. How many problems and how much hardship must a person suffer before they are regarded as 'poor'?

It will be argued here that a poverty line serves a purpose if the definition of poverty is *indirect*, i.e. poverty is understood to be a lack of economic resources. The poverty line can be applied straightaway in these cases or can at least be used as guidance in social policy programmes but the value of the poverty line diminishes if the poverty is defined directly. This is especially the case when the deprivation index is restricted to a set of consumer items. To abolish poverty defined as 'lack of socially perceived necessities' would mean that the authorities would have to provide the 'poor' with these necessities. Such a policy implies 'planned consumption' and does not appear to be a realistic option. Furthermore, strict application of Mack and Lansley's poverty line would mean that a family lacking three necessities, for example *a garden, a roast meat joint or its equivalent once a week* and *a washing machine*, should have the right to be provided with these things. A family lacking just two necessities, for example *heating to warm living areas of the home if it's cold* and *indoor toilet*, should not have the same right because they are not below the poverty line. Direct observation of living conditions must be seen as indicators of poverty, not absolute evidence of poverty.

Mack and Lansley do not suggest that the 'poor' should be provided with the necessities they lack. They suggested instead a more common approach and proposed a guaranteed minimum income equivalent with 150% of the norm for social benefits. To use findings based on a direct definition of poverty to suggest income transfers directed to people at the lower end of the income distribution is, however, not enough. The aim of a direct definition is to identify people who are actually suffering hardship. There are, as mentioned above, several studies that have shown that the overlap between direct and indirect poverty is small (Heikkile, 1991; Hallerod, 1991, 1995; Van den Bosch, 1992; Muffels *et al*, 1992; Bradshaw *et al*, 1993; Nolan and Whelan 1995; Kangas and Ritakallio 1995). Thus, a guaranteed minimum income would only help a part, not necessarily the major part, of the population suffering the severest hardship. Direct definitions of poverty are mainly used because a straightforward relationship between economic resources and standards of living can be questioned. There are other components to the social fabric which affect people's living conditions and influence standards of living. To identify these components is one of the most important tasks for poverty research, a task that can only be solved by using direct definitions of poverty.

The proportional deprivation index

An alternative way to measure poverty is labelled the 'proportional deprivation index' (PDI). The PDI is based on the same basic assumptions as Mack and Lansley's original approach and poverty is still seen as a 'lack of social perceived necessities'. The aim of the PDI is to deal with shortcomings in their deprivation index and thereby strengthen the relationship between the preferences of consumption held by public opinion and a direct definition of poverty. It could be argued that the PDI is more theoretically appealing than the deprivation index (Majority Necessities Index) used by Mack and Lansley because it is less sensitive to the consumer items included in the list, does not make arbitrary classifications of necessary and non-necessary consumption, decreases the sensitivity to individual preferences and takes account of significant differences in preferences between demographic and social categories.

The PDI is not based on a classification of consumption of necessities and non-necessities. Instead of dividing consumption into two groups, each item is given a weight based on the proportion of the population that regards it as necessary. This approach makes it possible to include every item on the list in the deprivation index and gives each item a value based on the proportion of the population that sees it as necessary. The immediate advantage of this procedure is that we do not need an arbitrary classification of necessities. It can therefore be argued that the PDI gives a better reflection of preferences held by public opinion.

The MNI is sensitive to the items included on the list and this sensitivity increases when necessary consumption is defined. One list of consumer items may result in just a few items being defined as necessary while another may result in several. The number of consumer items defined as necessities will have an impact on the result. The PDI also depends on a choice of consumer items but the sensitivity is smaller because the choice will only affect the relative importance of each item, not the number of items on which the deprivation index is based.

Public opinion weighting has been further adjusted to reflect the differences between the various social and demographic groups. Thus, the PDI approach takes account of these differences by adjusting the weighting for each consumer item according to significant differences within the population. Account could be taken of the variation in the preferences of any number of different social or demographic groups but we have chosen three important characteristics - sex, age and family composition (whether they are single or couples with or without children).

Empirical analysis

The main purpose of the empirical analysis is to compare the outcomes of the PDI and the MNI regarding (a) the extent to which they are targeting the same part of the population and (b) whether the causes of poverty differ depending on the index used. The analysis can be seen as a validation for the robustness in Mack and Lansley's approach to direct consensual poverty definition. The reliability of the definition will increase if the differences between the indexes are small and decrease if the opposite is true.

Necessary consumption and lack of consumption

The list of consumer items, the proportion of the population regarding them as necessary and the proportion of the population that cannot afford them are presented in Table 10.1.

There are ten items in the list which 90% or more of the participants in the 1990 study regard as necessities:

- Two meals a day
- Heating to warm living areas of the home if it is cold
- Refrigerator
- Indoor toilet, not shared with another household
- Bath, not shared with another household
- Beds for everyone in the house
- Damp free home
- Warm waterproof coat
- Three meals a day for children
- Enough money to keep house decently decorated

There are 32 items that over 50% of the population regard as necessities including those mentioned above and these are the items on which the Majority Necessities Index (MNI) is based.

Table 10.1
Proportion of the population regarding consumer items as necessary and proportion of the population that cannot afford them (n=1831)

Consumer item	Necessary, should be able to afford (%)	Would like to have, can't afford (%)
Two meals a day	90	1
Meat/fish/vegetarian every other day	77	4
Heating to warm living areas of home if it is cold	97	3
A dressing gown	42	2
Two pairs all weather shoes	74	5
New, not second hand clothes	65	4
A television	58	1
A roast joint/vegetarian equiv. once a week	64	6
Carpets in living room and bedrooms	78	2
Telephone	56	7
Refrigerator	92	1
Indoor toilet, not shared with another household	97	0.1
Bath, not shared with another household	95	0.2
Beds for everyone in household	95	1
Damp-free home	98	2
A car	26	18
A night out once a fortnight	42	14
A packet of cigarettes every other day	18	5
A hobby or leisure activity	67	7
A holiday away one week a year, not with relatives	54	20
Celebrations on special occasions e.g. Christmas	74	4
Presents for family/friends once a year	69	5
Friends/family for meal once a month	37	10
A warm waterproof coat	91	4
A 'best outfit'	54	8
A washing machine	73	0.4
3 meals daily for children	90	0.4
Toys for children e.g. dolls, models	84	1
Leisure equipment for children e.g. bicycle	61	2
Own bedroom for all children 10+ of different sex	82	2
An outing for children once a week	53	4
Children's friends for tea/snack once a fortnight	52	3
A dishwasher	4	18
A meal in restaurant once a month	17	22
Regular savings (£10/month) for rainy day	68	30
A video	13	10
Enough money to keep house decently decorated	92	15
Holidays abroad once a year	17	32
Coach/train fares to visit family/friends 4 times a year	39	19
Insurance contents of dwelling	88	10
Fruit and vegetables every day	88	6
A home computer	5	16
Money to pay for special lessons e.g. music	39	6
Money to participate in out of school activities	69	3

Accumulated deprivation

The distribution of MNI is shown in Table 10.2. (Note that, for technical reasons, this analysis has had to be undertaken on the unweighted data file which means that the results will be slightly different from those elsewhere in this book which are based on the weighted data file.) Nearly half of the population do not lack any of the items regarded as necessities by the majority of the population. About 17% lack one necessity and about 8% lack two necessities. The remaining 28%[1] lack three or more necessities and can be regarded as suffering from accumulated deprivation or living in poverty.

Table 10.2
The population distributed in accordance
with values on the MNI (n=1831)

Score on the MNI	0	1	2	3	4	5	6	7	8+
Share of population	47.5	16.7	7.8	5.6	4.9	3.3	2.5	2.5	9.2

The Proportional Deprivation Index (PDI) depends on specific weights which have been given to each item. The score on the PDI is therefore the outcome of the number of items a person says he or she wants to have but cannot afford and the specific weight assigned to each item using the demographic variables outlined above (the weightings are summarised in Appendix I). The distribution of deprivation according to the PDI is shown in Table 10.3 and compared with MNI.

Table 10.3
Distribution of PDI and MNI in deciles. Mean value of PDI and MNI by decile
and share of total deprivation in each decile

Percentile	Mean PDI	Mean MNI	Percent PDI	Percent MNI
1	0	0	0	0
2	0	0	0	0
3	0	0	0	0
4	0	0	0.6	0
5	1.19	0	2.7	0
6	2.39	1	4.6	7.5
7	3.50	2	8.4	7.0
8	3.90	3	14.4	7.8
9	5.42	5.2	23.8	30.9
10	6.95	11.2	45.6	46.7

Given the way it is derived, PDI is distributed more widely in the population with PDI scores appearing in some of the lower decile groups. However, only a slightly lower proportion of PDI is concentrated in the top decile.

The overlap between MNI and PDI

The main purposes of poverty research are to define a poverty line and count the 'poor'. In this case the purpose is not to estimate the number of people classified as 'poor', but to see to what extent different definitions identify the same people as 'poor'. For this purpose three poverty lines based on the MNI are constructed - one based on a score of three or more on the deprivation index (labelled MNIa), one at a score of four or more (MNIb) and one set at a score of five or more (MNIc). According to these the poverty lines 28.1%, 22.2% and 17.4% respectively of the population are 'poor'. The poverty lines based on the PDI are fixed at levels that will create the same proportion of people in poverty and are accordingly labelled PDIa, PDIb and PDIc. Thus the same number of people are classified as 'poor' whichever index is used. The crucial question is whether these definitions are targeting the same groups of people.

Table 10.4a
Overlap between PDI and MNI.
Percent of population and percent of poor (in brackets)

	Poor according to at least one poverty line	Poor according to both MNI and PDI	Poor MNI only	Poor PDI only
PDIa & MNIa	29.8 (100)	26.5 (89.0)	1.6 (5.4)	1.6 (5.4)
PDIb & MNIb	24.0 (100)	20.6 (86.3)	1.6 (6.8)	1.6 (6.8)
PDIc & MNIc	18.3 (100)	16.5 (90.0)	0.9 (5.1)	0.9 (5.1)

The overlap between poverty defined via the MNI and PDI is, as can be seen in Table 10.4a, very substantial. Thirty percent of the survey sample falls under the first poverty lines and 89% of that group is 'poor' according to both definitions. Twenty four percent of the population are 'poor' according to the second set of poverty lines and over 86% are 'poor' according to both definitions. The third group contains over 18% of the population and the pattern is confirmed - the overlap is 90%.

The overall large overlap is to be expected since the underlying approach for both definitions is the same. Table 10.4a shows that although there may be substantial differences in the ranking of deprivation between the PDI and the MNI, most of those who fall below the PDI poverty lines also fall below the MNI lines. Nevertheless, between 14% and 10% of those defined as 'poor' by one definition are 'not poor' by the other and the results also indicate that the overlap is greatest at the most severe poverty definition (c).

One of the possible objections to the PDI index is that it incorporates some items that Mack and Lansley included in the 1990 study which were not poverty indicators but luxury items used to provide a spread of responses and not necessarily to measure deprivation. If these items are measuring deprivation, then including them in the PDI index will make it a less accurate measure, though if they are not considered to be necessities they will only have a small weighting. There are twelve such items:

- Dressing gown
- Monthly meal in a restaurant
- Car
- Video
- Night out once a fortnight
- Holidays abroad once per year
- Pack of cigarettes every other day
- Coach/train fares to visit others
- Ask others to a meal once a month
- Home computer
- Dishwasher
- Child's music/dance/sport lessons

Table 10.4b explores the overlap between the two measures with these twelve items excluded from the PDI measure. It can be seen that there are only very small changes in the proportion defined as 'poor' by at least one of the measures. The proportion defined as 'poor' according to both definitions increases for both a, b and c. So although PDI appears to be closer to MNI when the twelve items are excluded, because the difference is not very great we continue the analysis with all the items included in PDI.

Table 10.4b
Overlap between PDI and MNI
Percent of population and percent of poor
(in brackets), excluding 'luxury' items

	Poor according to at least one poverty line	Poor according to both MNI and PDI	Poor MNI only	Poor PDI only
PDIa & MNIa	28.5 (100)	27.6 (97.1)	0.4 (1.5)	0.4 (1.5)
PDIb & MNIb	22.8 (100)	21.7 (95.2)	0.5 (2.4)	0.5 (2.4)
PDIc & MNIc	18.1 (100)	16.7 (92.1)	0.7 (3.9)	0.7 (3.9)

Lack of social perceived necessities and other indicators of bad living conditions

One important finding by Mack and Lansley (1985) was that people with low material standards also tend to have other problems. This corresponds with Townsend's work in the late 1960s and is confirmed by the results of the 1990 Breadline Britain Survey (Gosschalk and Frayman 1992) (see Chapters 3, 6, and 7).

In Table 10.5, we compare the proportion of those having other problems with those who are PDI poor and MNI poor. The comparison is restricted here to a and b levels. In general, both measures give very similar proportions with other problems. Where there are differences it is usually the MNI measure which gives a higher proportion with other problems. Thus, more MNIb poor are short of money for food, isolated for lack of money, borrowing from family or friends, believe they are genuinely poor and so on. In contrast, more of the PDIb poor are unemployed, have houses in a poor state of repair and are receiving housing benefit.

Overall, the results show that lack of socially perceived necessities and other forms of deprivation are closely connected. Those suffering material hardship suffer from other problems to a much higher degree than those who live above the poverty lines. Labelling those as 'poor' who lack three or more items, considered as necessities by over 50% of the population, is justified by the self appraisal of those so identified but the PDI measure might be still better.

Table 10.5
Self-evaluation of material standard and reported difficulties in making ends meet

		PDIa poor %	PDIb poor %	MNIa poor %	MNIb poor %
Short of money for food	Yes	68.7	60.2	70.7	61.4
	No	21.6	16.0	20.9	15.9
Isolated for lack of money	Yes	64.5	56.1	66.0	58.6
	No	17.7	12.4	16.9	11.9
Borrow from friends/family	Yes	55.3	45.9	56.4	47.5
	No	18.2	13.6	17.5	13.0
Borrow from money lenders	Yes	58.7	56.0	60.0	56.0
	No	26.8	20.8	26.5	20.8
Genuinely poor	Always	68.9	60.4	70.3	61.3
	Sometimes	43.2	34.2	43.2	34.5
	Never	10.0	6.3	9.2	6.2
Ever lived in poverty	Never	12.9	8.5	12.3	9.1
	Rarely	22.2	19.5	24.1	18.8
	Occasionally	38.6	29.7	37.4	28.0
	Often	59.7	49.5	59.1	51.1
	Most of time	69.7	60.6	69.7	64.6
Been depressed in last month	Yes	19.7	14.5	19.4	14.9
	No	60.4	51.6	60.7	50.8
Worried about relationships with friends	Yes	27.5	21.6	27.3	21.7
	No	51.8	46.3	50.0	44.4
Worried about relationships with family	Yes	26.3	20.6	26.1	20.8
	No	60.4	49.1	59.4	49.1
Being bored	No	23.2	17.8	22.5	17.8
	Yes	53.5	44.9	55.8	45.5
Not having enough money	No	20.3	14.9	20.0	14.9
	Yes	68.2	59.6	68.5	60.3
Feeling looked down on	No	25.7	19.9	25.2	20.0
	Yes	68.8	59.6	72.5	60.6
Feeling a failure	No	25.3	20.0	25.1	19.8
	Yes	65.9	52.3	65.9	55.3
Lack of hope	No	22.8	17.9	23.0	17.8
	Yes	61.2	49.2	58.5	50.4
Letting down family	No	24.1	18.8	24.0	18.5
	Yes	62.0	50.5	60.5	54.0
None of these	No	50.8	41.0	50.6	41.3
	Yes	10.2	7.4	10.0	7.3
Problems at school	Yes	27.2	21.2	26.8	21.1
	No	34.2	28.4	34.9	29.8
State of repair	Good	16.4	11.1	16.0	12.7
	Average	37.0	30.5	37.0	28.6
	Poor	58.6	51.8	59.5	50.5
Victim of crime	Yes	38.0	30.3	38.3	30.1
	No	23.8	18.6	23.3	18.9
Respondent unemployed	Yes	34.9	33.7	38.4	31.4
	No	14.5	10.6	14.8	10.8
Spouse employed	Yes	42.2	40.0	44.4	37.8
	No	15.1	12.4	15.9	12.2
How long unemployed over last 10 years	Never	12.5	9.3	11.6	9.1
	Less 2 months	21.3	17.5	22.5	17.5
	2-6 months	24.3	16.5	26.1	16.5
	7-12 months	35.3	30.9	36.8	25.0
	12+ months	54.1	46.3	52.8	45.9

Table 10.5 (cont.)
Self-evaluation of material standard and reported difficulties in making ends meet

		PDIa poor %	PDIb poor %	MNIa poor %	MNIb poor %
Respondent has long-standing illness	No	26.0	20.7	25.9	20.9
	Yes	37.5	28.9	36.7	28.6
Other household member with long-standing illness/disability	No	26.4	20.5	26.3	20.6
	Yes	36.4	30.4	35.8	30.4
Registered disabled (respondent)	No	27.4	21.8	27.2	21.9
	Yes	39.8	29.7	39.8	29.7
Registered disabled (other household members)	No	27.4	21.6	27.2	21.5
	Yes	40.0	32.2	40.0	35.7
Not registered disabled	No	36.2	28.0	36.2	29.3
	Yes	27.0	21.4	26.8	21.3
Receiving unemployment benefits	Yes	58.9	50.3	56.8	48.6
	No	24.8	19.1	24.8	19.4
Receiving Sickness Benefit	Yes	45.9	36.1	43.6	34.6
	No	26.9	21.2	26.8	21.4
Receiving Invalidity Benefit	Yes	38.1	29.9	34.7	27.9
	No	27.4	21.6	27.4	21.9
Receiving Income Support	Yes	59.9	52.2	60.4	53.8
	NO	20.4	14.9	20.0	14.6
Receiving Family Credit	Yes	57.1	49.2	57.1	47.6
	No	27.2	21.3	27.0	21.5
Receiving Housing Benefit	Yes	59.7	48.8	58.8	50.2
	No	18.5	14.1	18.5	13.8
Receiving Poll-Tax Benefit	Yes	51.0	41.3	49.9	42.4
	No	18.6	14.3	18.8	14.0
Receiving Attendance Allowance	Yes	41.6	32.6	41.6	31.1
	No	26.7	21.1	26.4	21.4
Receiving State Pension	Yes	23.7	15.0	22.6	15.8
	No	29.5	24.3	29.5	24.2
Receiving Private Pension	Yes	24.0	16.2	22.8	15.0
Receiving Private Pension	No	29.2	28.6	29.2	24.0
Time spent on Income Support	< 3 months	48.6	45.7	45.7	40.0
	<6 months	42.9	38.1	42.9	42.9
	<12 months	61.8	58.2	61.8	54.5
	1+ year	68.3	58.1	68.7	60.4
	No	20.0	14.5	19.8	14.5
Have you ever had Income Support	In last year	45.3	41.3	48.0	41.3
	Last 5 years	33.3	29.5	32.6	28.7
	Over 5 years	22.8	12.7	22.8	15.2
	No never	16.6	11.3	16.4	11.2
Do you contribute to an occupational/private pension scheme	Yes	11.0	7.3	11.6	7.5
	No	21.7	16.9	21.5	17.3
	Don't know	16.7	16.7	25.0	16.7
How do you vote	Conservative	9.7	8.0	10.7	8.0
	Labour	29.2	22.3	28.0	23.1
	Liberal Dem	15.8	11.6	15.8	11.6
	Green	20.8	18.9	20.8	18.9
	Other	25.0	18.8	25.0	20.8
	None/DK	36.4	29.1	36.3	28.8

Deprivation and income

The reason for using direct measurement of poverty is the assumption that financial resources do not reflect a standard of living in an acceptable way. People have different abilities to transform equal amounts of money into equal living standards. People live under different circumstances and so need different amounts of money to gain the same standard. Although the connection between the two is important, both MNI and PDI are based on the assumption that lack of consumption is due to a shortage of economic resources. The problem is that 'shortage of economic resources' does not correlate perfectly with the size of income - people who, for one reason or another, have to spend a lot of money will soon run out of money even if they have a relatively high income. However, it is easier to run out of money if the income is small from the beginning. A correlation between income and deprivation should therefore be expected.

The income data used here is based on information collected at interview and it is not totally satisfactory. Respondents were asked to place their net weekly household income (after deduction of tax and national insurance) within a range of incomes provided. For the purposes of the analysis, we have assumed that their income falls in the middle of the range they identified.

Chart 1 shows the relationship between both MNI, PDI and equivalent net disposable income. Both MNI and PDI scores increase as income falls and there is clearly a threshold, at about £150 per week where decreasing income leads to an accelerated increase in deprivation. These results correspond with earlier findings - both Mack and Lansley (1985) and Townsend (1979) argued that deprivation accelerated at a certain income level and both estimated that income level to be approximately 150% of the level of UK Supplementary Benefit.

Figure 10.1
Relationship between equivalent household income and MNI and PDI

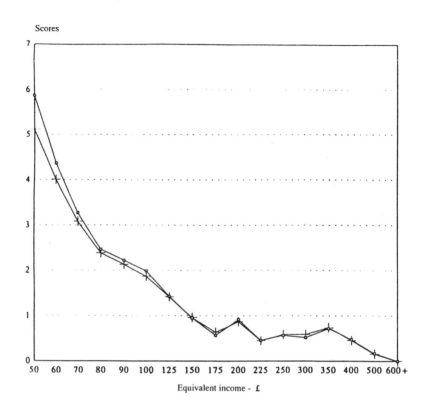

Scores

Equivalent income - £

Mean MNI scores
Mean PDI scores

In Table 10.6, the population has been divided into income deciles based on net disposable income and the percentage in each decile which falls under the poverty lines PDIa, PDIb, MNIa, and MNIb is shown. The table shows a strong relationship between income and poverty.

Table 10.6
Percentage of the population living in poverty
by income decile of net disposable income
(The percentage of poor in each decile is shown in brackets) (n=1119)

Decile	PD1a %	PD1b %	MNIa %	MNIb %
1 Lowest	56.3	47.7	57.8	(46.1
	(19.6)	(20.5)	(20.2)	(19.5)
2	54.4	44.1	54.4	47.8
	(20.2)	(20.1)	(20.2)	(21.5)
3	48.4	41.9	46.8	41.9
	(8.2)	(8.7)	(7.9)	(8.6)
4	41.7	32.1	39.9	34.5
	(19.1)	(18.1)	(18.3)	(19.1)
5	42.9	37.4	42.9	35.2
	(10.6)	(11.4)	(10.6)	(10.6)
6	31.2	23.7	30.1	23.7
	(7.9)	(7.4)	(7.6)	(7.3)
7	16.5	13.9	19.0	12.7
	(3.5)	(3.7)	(4.1)	(3.3)
8	12.8	10.3	14.5	11.1
	(4.1)	(4.0)	(4.6)	(4.3)
9	14.9	9.9	14.0	9.9
	(4.9)	(4.0)	(4.6)	(4.0)
10 Highest	5.6	4.8	5.6	4.8
	(1.9)	(2.0)	(1.9)	(2.1)

More than half of the population in the lowest decile falls below the poverty lines MNIa and PDIa and over half in the second decile. The pattern of the relationship between income and MNI and PDI is very similar; however it can also be seen that neither measure has all the poor concentrated in the bottom deciles. Indeed both (a) measures have about 7% of the poor in the upper two deciles.

The relationship between income and deprivation is complicated. Table 10.6 is based on the household's net disposable income and no adjustment has been made for household composition. This problem is usually tackled by the use of an equivalence scale which adjusts the household's income according to its composition. The purpose of an equivalence scale is to construct a formula which assigns the same level of 'well being' to households of different sizes with the same equivalent income. The equivalence scale used here is based on the concept that a single person needs 70% of the income of a couple to achieve the same living standard and a couple or single parent with children needs 50% more than a childless couple for each child. The effect that the application of this equivalence scale to income will have on the results can be seen in Table 10.7.

Table 10.7
Percentage of the population living in poverty
by income decile of equivalent income
(The percentage of poor in each decile is shown in brackets) (n=1119))

Decile	PD1a %	PD1b %	MN1a %	MNIb %
1 Lowest	71.0	61.8	73.3	63.4
	(25.3)	(27.2)	(26.2)	(27.4)
2	68.0	62.0	68.0	61.0
	(18.5)	(20.8)	(18.5)	(20.1)
3	51.9	42.5	48.1	41.5
	(15.0)	(15.1)	(13.9)	(14.5)
4	37.3	28.8	36.4	26.3
	(12.0)	(11.4)	(11.7)	(10.2)
5	28.8	20.5	27.4	23.3
	(5.7)	(5.0)	(5.4)	(5.6)
6	24.8	19.5	25.5	20.1
	(10.1)	(9.7)	(10.4)	(9.9)
7	24.3	13.1	22.4	15.9
	(7.1)	(4.7)	(6.5)	(5.6)
8	6.5	3.7	7.5	5.6
	(1.9)	(1.3)	(2.2)	(2.0)
9	9.1	7.4	10.9	7.0
	(3.0)	(3.0)	(3.8)	(3.0)
10 Highest	4.7	4.7	5.1	5.1
	(1.4)	(1.7)	(1.4)	(1.7)

The main difference between Tables 10.6 and 10.7 is that poverty is more concentrated in the lowest income deciles when equivalent income is used and the PDI measures give a slightly lower proportion of the bottom deciles being 'poor'. The proportion of the 'poor' in the top two deciles is reduced.

It is hard to justify that such a high percentage of the population in the two highest net disposable income deciles are 'poor'. This problem diminishes if the poverty lines are given less importance and the lack of socially perceived necessities are seen as indicators of poverty. The proportion of the population falling under the poverty lines can then be seen as being at risk of being 'poor'. This makes the interpretation of Tables 10.6 and 10.7 easier - people living in households with few economic resources have a high risk of being 'poor'. This risk decreases substantially as income increases and so the lack of socially perceived necessities is to a high degree the outcome of insufficient economic resources.

The fact that some people living in households in the upper end of the income strata fall under the poverty lines can be interpreted in two ways. Firstly, both the PDI and the MNI are, as has been pointed out earlier, sensitive to people's preferences. The priority that different people give to different consumer items and their expectations of possessing them does affect the results. Thus 'rich' people can fall under a poverty line because their preferences and expectations are odd in comparison to the rest of the population.

Secondly, the incomes used here are, as in most poverty studies, household incomes. The basic assumption behind this is that resources are equally shared within the household. This is not necessarily the case, or, to put it more strongly, it is certainly not the case in *all* households. The questions on which the PDI and MNI are based are answered by the respondent, not the household. It is possible for the respondent to be 'poor' even though she or he lives in a household with a high income simply because she/he does not have access to or influence over the money. The results used here could be the outcome of a 'poor' respondent living in a wealthy household.

Who is poor?

Even when poverty is defined directly, the prevalence of poverty is generally seen as an effect of lack of money and the poor are, as shown above, over represented in the lower end of the income distribution. Limited access to economic resources is therefore one of the main explanations for poverty. However, although the size of income is an important factor in making ends meet in a household's economy, it is not the only one and there are several other factors which influence the prevalence of poverty. It is obvious that long term low income causes bigger difficulties than short term low income and one problem is the lack of information about the duration of low income. Neither does income, as measured here, give any information about the households' assets. It will clearly make a large difference if a household owns a house and has money in the bank or if it is in debt and completely dependent on its weekly income. It is also important to acknowledge differences in the way households manage their income and expenditure. Differences in capabilities to transform money into consumption will lead to variance in living standard among households with equivalent incomes (Sen, 1988). Our data make it possible to analyse the impact of a number of variables, besides income, on the risk of falling under one of the poverty lines. The results are summarised in Table 10.8.

It has long been argued that there is an ongoing feminisation of poverty (Goldberg and Kremen, 1987). Women have a weaker position in the labour market. Also, there is the break down of the traditional two parent family and the increasing number of sole parents, usually women. Women also tend to be poorer in retirement. It can be seen that a higher proportion of women are 'poor' by both measures and by both measures they form a majority of the 'poor'.

Gender is of course related to household composition. The highest risk of being in poverty is being a lone parent family but the largest group in poverty are couples with children. The family type with the lowest chance of being in poverty and the lowest proportion of poor households are childless couples. The results are very similar for both MNI and PDI measures but PDI gives rather lower poverty rates for single people, lone parents and couples with children and rather higher rates for couples with no children. This finding, together with the results on gender above, may suggest that PDI is more sensitive to female evaluations of necessities. Another interesting result is the difference between men and women in the group couple with children. The risk that the household will be counted as 'poor' increases if the respondent is a women. This result was also found in Sweden (Halleröd, 1995) and clearly indicates differences between men and women in the conception of the households needs and how well they are meet. It also gives some initial support to the thesis of an unequal intra household distribution of recourses (Pahl, 1989).

The more children there are, the greater the chances of being 'poor' - families with three or more children have twice the chance of being 'poor' as families without children. Nevertheless, about three quarters of all families in poverty only have one or two children. The MNI measure gives slightly higher poverty rates for large families. The largest group of families with children in poverty are couples with three or more children.

About half of all those who are divorced are living in poverty. Another important variable is age. Poverty is traditionally connected with old age but relieving old people from poverty has been an important concern in most developed countries with a modern welfare state and there is probably no other area where welfare states have had so much success (Rowntree, 1942; Rowntree and Lavers, 1951; Vogel, 1987). Today, the highest chances of being in poverty are among the 20-35 age group (probably because these are child rearing years with only one breadwinner). They also form the largest proportion of the 'poor'. The second highest chance of being in poverty under both measures is the 35-45 age group, only then followed by the over 75's.

About two thirds of the unemployed are living in poverty and they form nearly a quarter of the 'poor'. The chances of poverty increase as social class status falls. Over half of social class E are in poverty and nearly half the 'poor' are concentrated in this class. Finally, there are clearly higher risks of poverty in some racial groups than others, with Afro-Caribbeans and the Irish having the highest poverty rates and Asians the lowest. However, over 90% of the 'poor' are white UK citizens.

Table 10.8
Proportion of population in poverty according to PDIa & MNIa

Category of Respondent	PDIa % poverty	PDIb % poor	MNIa % poverty	MNIa % poor
Man	24.8	41.8	23.7	40.2
Woman	31.4	58.2	32.0	59.8
All single, no child	31.0	17.8	32.3	18.7
All single with child	66.7	13.9	69.4	14.6
All couples, no child	16.8	12.4	15.0	11.1
All couples, no child	32.4	32.1	33.0	32.9
Other	23.1	23.8	21.8	22.6
Man, single, no child	30.4	10.7	29.7	10.3
Woman, single, no child	31.4	12.7	34.6	13.9
Man, single + child	50.0	1.0	50.0	1.0
Woman, single + child	68.0	17.3	71.0	17.9
Man, couple no child	15.3	8.4	12.5	6.8
Woman, couple no child	18.8	7.9	18.2	7.6
Man, couple + child	30.3	17.5	30.3	17.4
Woman, couple + child	34.2	24.6	35.2	25.2
0 child	23.0	54.0	22.2	52.4
1 child	33.7	12.8	33.2	12.7
2 children	35.2	17.2	36.8	18.1
3 or more children	48.5	16.1	50.3	16.8
Single,1 child	58.3	8.8	55.6	8.2
Single, 2 or more children	70.8	21.4	76.4	22.5
Couple, 1child	28.1	18.9	28.1	18.4
Couple, 2 children	26.1	22.7	27.1	23.0
Couple 3 or more children	46.2	28.2	46.9	27.9
Divorced	50.7	13.2	51.5	13.5
Not divorced	24.5	86.8	24.2	86.5
Age 16-20	22.1	5.2	22.1	5.7
Age 20-35	33.3	37.3	34.8	39.4
Age 35-45	30.4	18.8	30.7	19.1
Age 45-55	23.2	11.0	20.7	9.9
Age 55-65	25.0	11.4	22.0	10.1
Age 65-75	24.5	10.3	24.1	10.1
Age 75+	27.7	6.0	27.7	6.0
Social Class E	60.6	48.2	60.3	48.3
Social Class D	33.6	26.9	33.6	27.1
Social Class C2	17.0	14.9	17.0	15.0
Social Class C1	12.7	9.1	12.2	8.8
Social Class AB	2.7	1.0	2.2	0.8
Unemployed	66.1	22.6	65.0	22.4
Not unemployed	21.8	77.4	21.7	77.6
Afro-Caribbean/African	44.7	4.1	38.3	3.5
Asian	15.4	0.8	15.4	0.8
Irish	41.4	2.3	41.4	2.3
White UK	28.1	91.7	28.1	92.4
Other	17.6	1.2	14.7	1.0

Conclusion

The purpose of this chapter has been to extend the consensual measure of poverty developed by Mack and Lansley by first including the whole range of social indicators they used (not just those considered necessities by more than half the population) and, secondly, by taking account of the diversity of the judgements of what is a necessity by different groups in society. Thus a new Proportional Deprivation Index was developed which was a function of all items lacking, weighted by the proportion of that particular sex, age, family type considering them a necessity.

The results broadly confirm the robustness and reliability of the Mack and Lansley consensual measure. There is considerable overlap between the two measures - over three quarters are 'poor' by both measures and both measures relate very similarly to other indicators of hardship and income and both provide very similar estimates of the characteristics of the 'poor'.

Nevertheless, between 5% and 7% of the 'poor' are missed by one or other measure and there are quite strong theoretical reasons for using a consensual measure that does not use an arbitrary cut off point of 50% and does take account of the variety of judgements different types of people in society consider as necessities.

Note

1   Note that 28% of the unweighted sample lacked three or more necessities and can be defined as 'poor'. When the sample is weighted to reflect the British population this figure is reduced to 20.8%.

11 Conclusions and summary

David Gordon and Christina Pantazis

The Breadline Britain in the 1990s survey provides us with the only comprehensive view of the extent, nature and effects of poverty at the beginning of the decade. No other national survey has attempted to directly measure poverty at the beginning of the 1990s. It is an indictment on the state of British social science that there is no comparable academic work. Domino Films, London Weekend Television, the Joseph Rowntree Foundation and MORI must be thanked for filling in this important gap in our knowledge of British society.

The value of this knowledge can be judged in the light of the considerable importance placed on estimating the extent of deprivation/poverty from the 1991 Census, in order to form an equitable basis for distributing resources over the next decade to local government and health authorities.

The conclusions from the Breadline Britain surveys are clear and unambiguous; the number of people living in poverty rose during the 1980s from 14% of households (approximately 7.5 million people), in 1983, to 20% of households (approximately 11 million people), in 1990. This increase in poverty over the 1980s is a sharp reverse of the general historical trend of a progressive decline in the extent of poverty that occurred between the 1930's and 1970s.

The facts about poverty at the beginning of the 1990s are so stark that they bear repeating:

- Roughly 10 million people in Britain cannot afford adequate housing: for example, their home is unheated, damp or the older children have to share bedrooms.
- About 7 million go without essential clothing, such as a warm waterproof coat, because of lack of money.
- There are approximately 2.5 million children who are forced to go without at least one of the things they need, like three meals a day, toys or out of school activities.
- Around 5 million people are not properly fed by today's standards; they do not have enough fresh fruit and vegetables, or two meals a day, for example.
- About 6.5 million people cannot afford one or more essential household goods, like a fridge, a telephone or carpets for living areas.

Some groups were more likely than others to be living in need. The following households were 'objectively' living in poverty in 1990:

- 60% of households where the head is unemployed and seeking work
- 48% of households containing seven or more people
- 47% of households that rent from local authorities
- 44% of respondents who were divorced/separated
- 41% of lone parent households
- 37% of households renting from a housing association
- 30% of respondents with no educational qualifications

The Breadline Britain Surveys have not just revealed the facts about poverty but have also made possible a number of theoretical advances in the study of poverty. Chapter 1 showed that the approach adopted by the Breadline Britain surveys, the 'consensual' or 'perceived' direct measurement of poverty, produced reliable and valid scientific estimates on its extent. These estimates were also shown to be independent of the questions chosen by Mack and Lansley (see Chapters 1 and 10). Effectively identical results would have been obtained if any other reliable set of 32 deprivation questions had been asked.

This 'scientific' approach to measuring poverty has allowed a number of unexpected phenomena to be identified. For example, the fact that, in 1991, 52% of all female criminal convictions resulted from TV licence offences had previously remained hidden in the criminal statistics.

The belief that poverty is caused by laziness and lack of will power has been shown to relate directly to the respondents' likely experience of poverty. The public's attitude to the causes of poverty has changed significantly during the 1980s. The number of people who consider that 'people live in need' because 'there is much injustice in society' more than doubled between 1976 and 1990 (from 16% in 1976 to 40% in 1990). Attitudes to the causes of poverty appear to be related to both direct and indirect experience of poverty.

The Breadline Britain Survey provided some data on the dynamics of poverty. Of respondents, 46% have experienced at least a brief period of poverty at some time in the past (Chapter 1, Table 1.6). Fortunately, for the overwhelming majority, their experience of 'living in poverty' is relatively brief. Only 4% of households, which can objectively be described as 'poor', also have a long history of living in poverty.

Chapter 2, by Professor Peter Townsend, discussed the six major approaches that have been used in the developed world to measure poverty. None of these methods is without fault, however, as all assessments of poverty based solely on absolute or relative income criteria can be shown to be seriously flawed. The 'perceived' and 'relative' deprivation methodologies have brighter prospects for national and international use. They have complementary advantages as scientific instruments and as socially revelatory and practical standards for the investigation and reduction of poverty.

Chapter 3 highlights the high degree of consensus, across all divisions in society, on the necessity of a range of common possessions and activities. Society, as a whole, clearly does have a view on what is necessary for a decent standard of living. Other findings were that:

- 70% of all respondents think that the government is doing 'too little' to help alleviate poverty
- 75% of all voters support a 1p in the £ income tax increase to help alleviate poverty. There is a high degree of consensus for this policy across the divisions in society: even 70% of Conservatives support such a tax increase.

The 'relative' theory of poverty predicts that, as a society becomes wealthier, so its views on what constitutes an unacceptable 'standard of living' will change. This predicted change in attitudes was shown to have occurred between 1983 and 1990.

In Chapter 4 a greater proportion of women respondents reported that they had experienced poverty at some point during their lives, and a slightly greater proportion reported the on-going experience of poverty in 1990s. For example,

- Nearly 50% of women had lived in poverty at some time during their lives, compared with only 42% of men.
- Amongst the oldest population (65+), women were twice as likely to consider themselves 'poor' either all the time or sometimes - two fifths of women compared with only 19% of men.
- Women in lone parent and single person households were more likely to be living in circumstances of multiple deprivation. For example, 55% of female lone parents were living in poverty in 1990.
- In terms of perceptions of necessities, statistically significant gender differences were found in relation to 16 out of 44 items. There were some strong patterns in the type of items which were more likely to be perceived as necessities by the different sexes. Women were more likely to regard certain food items, clothing items and various items relating to children as

necessities, and men were more likely to view leisure items and consumer durables as necessities. These responses begin to suggest that there may be differences in how men and women view poverty.

Chapter 5 examined the controversial relationship between poverty and crime:

- In the 1990 Breadline Britain Survey, 14% of households had experienced crime in the previous year and 17% feared crime.
- Experience of crime was highest for single, non-retired and large, adult only households living in 'poor' or 'adequate' accommodation. Thirty-six percent of this group experienced crime, two and a half times the national average figure. Students and ex-student households might fit this description.
- The survey found no evidence to support the common-held belief that 'poor' households experience more crime. Victimisation seemed to be more closely connected to social cohesion rather than poverty.
- Poverty and poverty-related factors were closely connected with fear of crime. The highest rates of fear were experienced by those suffering from multiple deprivation, who were also living in 'poor' housing and who had been 'poor' most of their lives. Forty-seven percent of this group feared crime.
- In terms of household type, poor pensioners who had also been victims of crime, had a rate of fear of 62%. This was seven times higher than the rate of fear experienced by their counterparts who were not living in poverty.
- Lack of insurance seems to be a key reason why those living in circumstances of multiple deprivation fear crime. Respondents were twice as likely to fear crime if they lacked contents insurance because they could not afford it.

Chapter 6 looked at the now firmly established relationship between poverty and ill health. The key findings were:

- Multiply deprived respondents were one and half times as likely to report a long-standing illness and twice as likely to report a disability in their household.
- They were one and a half times as likely to visit their General Practitioner and have at least two hospital treatments over a one year period.
- Yet, multiply deprived households were one and a half times as likely to be on hospital waiting lists for both more than six months and more than twelve months.
- Housing is a key issue in the development of health. Multiply deprived respondents were three and a half times more likely to have health problems adversely affected by their housing situation. Poor people are more likely

to live in conditions that are damp, over-crowded, badly designed and generally in a bad state of repair.

- Age was the most statistically significant influence on illness and disability. However, for every age group, deprivation and poverty related factors (previous poverty, debt, social class, and income support) had the most important contribution to health status.

Chapter 7 analysed the relationship between poverty and mental health. People living in poverty were more than seven times more likely to suffer poor mental health than those who were not, whilst the impact of both gender and ethnicity were more marked.

- The 'poor' were more than five times as likely to feel isolated, four times more likely to be depressed and more than nine times as likely to feel looked down on.
- People from black and Asian groups were nearly twice as likely to report one or more symptoms of poor mental health as a consequence of financial difficulties, in comparison with the white UK and Irish population.
- Women were more likely than men to describe themselves as suffering from mental health difficulties as a result of lack of money.
- Women were more likely than men to suffer from depression after controlling for the effects of poverty. However, the impact of poverty in causing depression seems to be slightly greater for men than for women (e.g. 'poor' men are 4.7 times more likely to be depressed than non-poor men, whereas 'poor' women are 4.4 times more likely to be depressed than non-poor women).
- Nearly half the lone parents in this study reported feelings of isolation as a result of lacking money, compared with less than a fifth of the parents in two-parent households. Similarly, over 40% of the lone parents reported feeling depressed due to a lack of money, compared with less than a fifth of the two-parent households.

Chapter 8 looked at the inter-relationships between poverty, debt and state benefits. Apart from credit card and telephone debt, 'poor' households are the majority of households with all other forms of debt.

- The Poll Tax presented the greatest difficulty for both 'poor' and 'non-poor' households. Thirty six percent of 'poor' households are seriously behind with Poll Tax payments, followed by rent at 22%, electricity at 21% and telephone at 19%.
- In the 1990 Breadline Britain Survey, almost 8% of respondents were seriously behind with paying their gas and electricity bills. Of those with

fuel debts, 65% were 'poor'. Of the 'poor', 24% have fuel debts, compared to only 3% of the rest of households.

Recent debates surrounding welfare spending have focused on the curtailment of state benefits. However, the Breadline Britain survey shows that households receiving benefits already face high levels of poverty.

- Forty one percent of households receiving benefits have become 'poor', indicating that the benefit system fails to act as a safety-net.
- Those on means-tested benefits, such as Unemployment Benefit, Income Support, Housing Benefit, and Family Credit, are more likely to be 'poor'. More than half of these benefit claimants live in poverty.
- Households receiving Family Credit experience the highest levels of poverty. Almost 60% of these households live in poverty. They lack an average of 4.4 benefits, highlighting the high levels of poverty faced by households of families with children.
- Households receiving Housing Benefit or Income Support also face high levels of poverty. Around 55% of households receiving either Housing Benefit or Income Support live in poverty. They lack an average of 4.4 necessities.
- Many 'benefit' households are likely to be in receipt of more than one benefit. There is a concomitant rise in poverty with the increase in the number of benefits received. Fifty eight percent of households receiving three or more benefits live in poverty.

Chapter 9, by Professor Glen Bramley, examined the important role that Local Government Services can play in ameliorating the effects of poverty. The services provided by local government are diverse and the way they are targeted or rationed varies significantly, so we would not expect all to play an equal role in countering or alleviating poverty. Nevertheless, the findings reported in Chapter 9 present a rather disappointing message on the re-distributional impact of local public services, particularly in relation to poorest households.

Demand-led services in the leisure field, open to a broad spectrum of the population, tend to be used more by the better off or the middle classes and less by 'multiply deprived' households. This conclusion applies to varying degrees to libraries, sports facilities, museums/galleries and adult education. The one general public service examined which shows a different pattern is the public bus service, which is used more by lower income households, particularly those without a car.

Services targeted on children present a more mixed picture, with less class bias but still a lower level of use by the most deprived. Services targeted on the elderly and people with disabilities, including home help, meals on wheels and special transport, are distributed in a more 'pro-poor' fashion than general demand-led services. We would expect this, given the fact that these services are normally rationed on the basis of a needs assessment. Given this explicit rationing, it is surprising that our findings do not indicate a stronger degree of targeting. Once account is taken of the incidence of constraints (quality problems and deterred users), the most deprived are as likely to experience quality/access/cost problems as other households and are, if anything, less likely to use services. There even seems to be some bias in favour of the higher social class households, especially for home help. This evidence suggests that further attention should be given to rationing processes, which may inadvertently disadvantage those who are poorest, perhaps by undue focus on health-related criteria or in other ways.

Finally, in Chapter 10, Dr Bjørn Halleröd, Professor Jonathan Bradshaw and Dr Hilary Holmes examined possible developments of the consensual definition of poverty as formulated by Mack and Lansley (1985). The method was extended, firstly, by including the whole range of social indicators measured in the survey (not just those considered necessities by more than half the population) and, secondly, by taking account of the diversity of the judgements of what is a necessity by different groups in society. A new Proportional Deprivation Index was developed as a function of all items lacking, weighted by the proportion of that particular sex, age, family type considering them a necessity.

The results broadly confirm the robustness and reliability of the Mack and Lansley consensual measure. There is considerable overlap between the two measures - over three quarters are 'poor' by both measures and both measures relate very similarly to other indicators of hardship and income and both provide very similar estimates of the characteristics of the 'poor'. These findings confirm the reliability and attitudinal results discussed in Chapters 1 and 4.

Conclusion

The 1980s were characterised by increases in the wealth and standard of living of the majority but also by a rapid increase in the numbers of people forced to live in poverty. Britain has become an increasingly polarised nation, containing stark social and economic divisions. The growth of poverty is the root cause of many of the social ills that are of public concern. There is considerable unease in British society about the consequences of increasing deprivation and the lack of social justice that this implies. There are large majorities amongst all social groups that are both willing to pay increased taxes and want the government to be more active in reducing need. Many consider it obscene that, in one of the richest nations on earth, one in five is suffering from the effects of poverty and being progressively excluded from the normal activities of society.

Whilst poverty remains so widespread, Britain will never be a nation at ease with itself.

Bibliography

Abel-Smith, B. and Townsend, P. (1965) 'The Poor and the Poorest', Atkinson, A.B. (Ed.) (1973) *Wealth, Income and Inequality*, Penguin Books Ltd, Harmondsworth

Adler, M. and Wozniak, E. (1981) *The Origins and Consequences of Default*, Research report for the Scottish Law Commission, Scotland

Anderson, I., Kemp, P. and Quilgars, D. (1993) *Single Homeless People*, Department of Environment, HMSO, London

Arber, S. (1987) Social class, non-employment and chronic illness: continuing the inequalities in health debate. *British Medical Journal 294*: 1069-1073

Arber, S., Gilbert, N. and Dale, A. (1985) Paid employment and women's health: a benefit of source of role strain? *Sociology of Health and Illness 7*: 375-400

Atkinson, A.B. (1985a) *How Should we Measure Poverty? Some Conceptual Issues*. Discussion Paper No. 82, ESRC Programme on Taxation, Incentives and Distribution of Income, London School of Economics, London

Atkinson, A.B. (1985b) *On the Measurement of Poverty*. Discussion Paper No. 90, ESRC Programme on Taxation, Incentives and the Distribution of Income. London School of Economics, London

Atkinson, A.B. (1990a) *A National Minimum? A History of Ambiguity in the Determination of Benefit Scales in Britain*, Suntory-Toyota International Centre for Economics and Related Disciplines, WSP/47, London School of Economics, London

Atkinson, A.B. (1990b) *Comparing Poverty Rates Internationally: Lessons from Recent Studies in OECD Countries*, Suntory-Toyota International Centre for Economics and Related Disciplines, WSP/53, London School of Economics, London

Atkinson, A.B. (1991) *Poverty, Statistics, and Progress in Europe*, Suntory-Toyota International Centre for Economics and Related Disciplines, WSP/60, London School of Economics, London

Atkinson, A.B. (1993) *Beveridge, the National Minimum and its Future in a European Context*, Suntory-Toyota International Centre for Economics and Related Disciplines, WSP/85, London School of Economics, London

Atkinson, A.B., Gardiner K., Lechene V. and Sutherland H. (1993) *Comparing Poverty in France and the United Kingdom*, Suntory-Toyota International Centre for Economics and Related Disciplines, WSP/84, London School of Economics, London

Audit Commission (1993) *Passing the Bucks: the impact of standard spending assessments on economy, efficiency and effectiveness*. Vols 1 & 2, HMSO, London

Australian Bureau of Statistics (ABS) (1981) *Equivalence Scales: The Estimation of Equivalence Scales for Australia from the 1974/75 and 1975/76 Household Expenditure Surveys*, Australian Bureau of Statistics, Canberra.

Ayre, A.J. (1936) *Language, Truth and Logic,* Gollancz, London

Ayre, A.J. (1955) *The Foundation of Empirical Knowledge*, Macmillan, London

Bagguley, P. and Mann, K. (1992) Idle Thieving Bastards? Scholarly Representations of the Underclass. *Work, Employment & Society 6(1)*: 113-126

Bane, M.J. and Ellwood, D. (1986) Slipping into and out of Poverty: The Dynamics of Spells. *Journal of Human Resources 21(1)*: 1-23

Barclay, G.C., Drew, C., Hatton, R. and Abbot, C. (1993) Digest 2 Information on the Criminal Justice System in England and Wales. *Home Office Research and Statistics Department*, HMSO, London

Bardsley, P. and McRae, I. (1982) A Test of McClements' Method for the Estimation of Equivalence Scales. *Journal of Public Economics 17*: 119-122

Belle, D. (1988) Women's mental health research agenda: Poverty. *Women's Mental Health* occasional series, National Institute of Mental Health, Rockville

Belle, D. (1990) Poverty and Women's Mental Health. *American Psychologist 45*: 385-389

Benzeval, M., Judge, K. and Solomon, M. (1992) *The Health Status of Londoners: A comparative perspective*, King's Fund, London

Berthoud, R. (1981) *Fuel Debts and Hardship,* Policy Studies Institute, London

Berthoud, R. (1989) *Credit, Debt and Poverty*, Research Paper 1, Advisory Committee, HMSO, London

Berthoud, R. and Kempson, E. (1990) *Credit and Debt in Britain*, Policy Studies Institute, London

Berthoud, R. and Kempson, E. (1992) *Credit and Debt: The PSI Report*, Policy Studies Institute, London

Beveridge Report (1942) *Social Insurance and Allied Services,* Cmd 6404, HMSO, London

Birmingham Settlement and Community Energy Research (1993) Repayment systems for households in fuel debt. *Joseph Rowntree Foundation Social Policy Research Findings*, No 36

Blackburn, C. (1990) *Poverty and Health: Working with Families,* Open University Press, Milton Keynes

Blacker, C.P. (1937) *A Social Problem Group?* Oxford University Press, London

Blacker, C.P. (Ed.) (1952) *Problem Families: Five Enquiries,* Eugenics Society, London

Blaxter, M. (1984) Equity and Consultation Rates in General Practice. *British Medical Journal 288*: 1963-7

Blaxter, M. (1990) *Health and Lifestyle*. Tavistock, London

Boardman, B. and Houghton, T. (1991) *Poverty and Power,* Bristol Energy Centre, Bristol

Bokor, A. (1984) Deprivation; Dimensions and Indices, in *Stratification and Inequality*, (Andork, R. and Kolosi, T., Eds.), Institute for Social Sciences, Budapest

Bolchever, S., Stewart, S. and Clyde, G. (1986) Consumer Credit: Investigating the Loan Sharks. *Trading Standards Review, Issue One: Vol 98*: 18

Box, S. (1983) *Power, Crime and Mystification,* Routledge, London

Box, S. (1987) *Recession, Crime and Punishment*, Macmillan Education Ltd, London

Box, S., Hale, C. and Andrews, G. (1988) Explaining the Fear of Crime. *British Journal of Criminology 28(3)*: 240-357

Bradbury, B. (1989) Family Size Equivalence Scales and Survey Evaluations of Income and Well-Being. *Journal of Social Policy 18(3)*: 383-408

Bradshaw, J. (1993a) *Household Budgets and Living Standards*, Joseph Rowntree Foundation, York

Bradshaw, J. (1993b) *Budget Standards for the United Kingdom*, Avebury/Ashgate Publishing Ltd, Aldershot

Bramley, G. (1990a) The demand for local government services: survey evidence on usage, distribution and externalities. *Local Government Studies*, November/December: 35-61

Bramley, G. (1990b) *Equalization grants and local expenditure needs: the price of equality*. Avebury, Aldershot

Bramley, G. and Le Grand, J. (1992) *Who uses local services? Striving for equity*. The Belgrave Papers No. 4, Government Management Board, London & Luton: Local

Bramley, G. and Smart, G. (1993) *Who Benefits from Local Services? Comparative evidence from different local authorities*, Welfare State Programme Discussion Paper WSP/91, Suntory-Toyota International Centre for Economics and Related Disciplines, London School of Economics, London

Bramley, G., Le Grand, J. and Low, W. (1989) How far is the Poll Tax a "Community Charge"? The implications of service usage evidence. *Policy and Politics 17(3)*: 187-205

Brannen, J. and Wilson, G. (Eds) (1987) *Give and Take in Families: Studies in resource distribution,* Allen & Unwin, London

Bridgwood, A. and Savage, D. (Goddard, E., Ed.) (1991) *General Household Survey,* OPCS, HMSO, London

Brieman, L., Friedman, J.H., Olshen, R.A. and Stone, C. J. (1984) *Classification and Regression Trees*, Wadsworth, Belmont, CA

Brook, L., Hedges, S., Jowell, R., Lewis, J., Prior, G., Sebastian, G., Taylor, B. and Witherspoon, S. (1992) *British Social Attitudes Cumulative Sourcebook.* Gower, Bath

Brown, G. (1992) Life events and social support: possibilities for primary prevention, In *The Prevention of Depression and Anxiety: The role of the Primary Health Care Team.* (Jenkins, R.; Newton, J. and Young, R., Eds.) HMSO, London

Brown, G.W. and Harris, T.O. (1978) *The social origins of depression.* Tavistock, London

Brown, G.W. and Harris, T.O. (Eds) (1989) *Life events and illness.* Unwin Hyman, London

Brown, M. and Madge, N. (1982) *Despite the Welfare State: A Report on the SSRC/DHSS Programme of Research into Transmitted Deprivation,* SSRC/DHSS Studies in Deprivation and Disadvantage, Heinemann Educational Books, London

Brown, W. (1993) Hidden homeless who came to stay... *New Scientist 139(1891)*: 4

Burgess, P.M., Joyce, C.M., Pattison, P.E. and Finch, S.J. (1992): Social Indicators and the prediction of psychiatric inpatient service utilisation. *Social Psychiatry and Psychiatric Epidemiology 27*: 83-94

CACI (1992) *The ACORN User Guide,* CACI International Services, London

Campbell, D.A., Radford, J.M., John, M.C. and Burton, P. (1991) Unemployment rates: an alternative to the Jarman index. *British Medical Journal 303*: 750-755

Canadian Council on Social Development (1984) *Not Enough: The Meaning and Measurement of Poverty in Canada,* CCSD, Ottawa

Caradog Jones, D. (Ed.) (1934) *The Social Survey of Merseyside, Vol. III,* Hodder & Stoughton, London

Carr-Hill, R. (1990) The Measurement of Inequalities in Health: Lessons from the British Experience. *Social Science and Medicine 31*: 393-404

Carstairs, V. (1981) Multiple Deprivation and Health State. *Community Medicine 3*: 4-13

Cartwright, A. (1992) Social class differences in health and care in the year before death. *Journal of Epidemiology and Community Health 46*: 54-57

Central Statistical Office (CSO) (1990) *Family Spending: A Report on the 1990 Family Expenditure Survey,* HMSO, London

Chalmers, A.F. (1978) *What is this thing called Science?* The Open University Press, Milton Keynes

Charles, N. and Kerr, M. (1987) Just the way it is: Gender and age differences in family food consumption. In *Give and Take in Families: Studies in resource distribution* (Brannen, J. and Wilson, G. Eds) Allen & Unwin, London

Charlton, J *et al* (Ed.) (1993) Trends in Suicide Deaths, England & Wales. *Population Trends 69*, OPCS, London

Chow, N.W.S. (1981) *Poverty in an Affluent City: A Report on a Survey of Low Income Families,* Department of Social Work, Chinese University of Hong Kong

Clement, F. and Kleinman, M.B. (1977) The Fear of Crime in the United States. *Social Forces 56*: 519-53

Cohen, L. and Felson, M. (1979) Social change and crime rate trends: a routine activity approach, *American Sociological Review 44(4)*: 588-608

Committee on Ways and Means (1992) *1992 Green Book*, US Government Printing Office, Washington

Craig, G. and Glendinning, C. (1990) Parenting in Poverty. *Community Care 24(7)*: 24-25

Crombie, D.L. (1984) Social Class and Health Status: Inequality or Difference. *Journal of the Royal College of General Practitioners,* Occasional Paper

Cronbach, L.J. (1951) Coeffcient Alpha and the Internal Structure of Tests. *Psychometrika 16*: 297-334

Cronbach, L.J. (1976) *Research on Classrooms and Schools: Formulation of Questions, Design and Analysis.* Stanford University Evaluation Consortium, Stanford

Cronbach, L.J., Gleser, G.C., Nanda, H. and Rajaratnam, N. (1971) *The Dependability of Behavioural Measurements.* Wiley, New York

Currie, E. (1989) *Life Lines*, Sidgwick & Jackson Limited, London

Daly, M. (1989) *Women and Poverty*, ATTIC PRESS in conjunction with the Combat Poverty Agency, Dublin

Davenport, S., Goldberg, M. and Millar, T. (1987) Clinical diagnosis: How psychiatric disorders are missed during medical consultations. *The Lancet 330*: 439-441

Davey-Smith, G., Bartley, M. and Blane, D. (1990) The Black Report on Socio-economic Inequalities in Health 10 Years on. *British Medical Journal 301(1)*: 373-377

De Vos, K. and Hagenaars, A. (1988) *A Comparison Between the Poverty Concepts of Sen and Townsend*, Erasmus University, Rotterdam

Department of Health (1991) *On the state of the public health: the annual report of the Chief Medical Officer of the Department of Health for the year 1990*, HMSO, London

Department of Health and Social Security (DHSS) (1979) *The Definition and Measurement of Poverty*, HMSO, London

Der, G. and Bebbington, P. (1987) Depression in Inner London. *Social Psychiatry and Psychiatric Epidemiology 23*: 73-84

Desai, M. (1986) Drawing the Line: On Defining the Poverty Threshold, In *Excluding the Poor* (Golding, P. Ed.), Child Poverty Action Group, London

Desai, M. and Shah, A. (1985) *An Econometric Approach to the Measurement of Poverty*, Suntory-Toyota International Centre for Economics and Related Disciplines, WSP/2, London School of Economics, London

Desai, M. and Shah, A. (1988) An Economic Approach to the Measurement of Poverty. *Oxford Economic Papers 40*: 505-522

Dohrenwend, B.P. and Dohrenwend, B.S. (1974) Psychiatric disorders in urban settings. In *American Handbook of Psychiatry*, 2nd edn. Vol 2, (Caplan, G. Ed), Basic Books, New York

Dohrenwend, B.P., Dohrenwend, B.S., Gould, M.S., Link, B., Neugebauer, R. and Wunsch-Hitzig (1980) *Mental Illness in the United States: Epidemiological Estimates*, Praeger, New York

Downes, D. (1983) Law and Order: Theft of an Issue, *Fabian Society*, London

Duncan, G.J., Gustafsson, B., Hauser, R., Schmauss, G., Messinger, H., Muffels, R., Nolan, B. and Ray, J.C. (1993) Poverty Dynamics in Eight Countries. *Journal of Population Economics 6*: 215-234

EEC (1977) *The Perception of Poverty in Europe,* Commission of the European Communities, Brussels

EEC (1981) *Final Report from the Commission to the Council on the First Programme of Pilot Schemes and Studies to Combat Poverty,* Commission of the European Communities, Brussels

EEC (1985) *On Specific Community Action to Combat Poverty* (Council Decision of 19 December 1984), 85/8/EEC, Official Journal of the EEC, 2/24

EEC (1991) *Final Report on the Second European Poverty Programme 1985-1989,* Office for the Official Publications of the European Communities, Luxembourg

Eurobarometer (1989) Special on Racism and Xenophobia. *Eurobarometer,* November 1989, 1-5

Eurostat (1990) *Poverty in Figures: Europe in the Early 1980's,* Office for Official Publications of the European Communities, Luxembourg

Eurostat (1994) *Poverty Statistics in the late 1980s.*, Office for Official Publications of the European Communities, Luxembourg

Everitt, B.S. (1993) *Cluster Analysis,* 3rd edn., Edward Arnold (Hodder & Stoughton), London, Melbourne, Auckland and Halsted Press, New York and Toronto

Faris, R.E. and Dunham, H.W. (1939) *Mental disorders in urban areas.* University of Chicago Press, Chicago

Fernando, S. (Ed) (1995) *Mental Health in a Multi-ethnic society: A multi-disciplinary handbook* Routledge, London

Fisher, G.M. (1992a) Poverty Guidelines for 1992. *Social Security Bulletin 55,* No 1

Fisher, G.M. (1992b) *The Development of the Orshansky Poverty Thresholds and their Subsequent History as the Official US Poverty Measure, Office of the Assistant Secretary for Planning and Evaluation in the Department of Health and Human Services* (Unpublished paper)

Fisher, G.M. (1992c) The Development and History of the Poverty Thresholds. *Social Security Bulletin 55,* No 4

Fisher, M.J. *et al* (1983) Patterns of Attendance at Development Assessment Clinics. *Journal of the Royal College of General Practitioners (Scotland) 33(24):* 213-18

Fogelman, K., Fox, A. and Power, C. (1989) Class and tenure mobility, do they explain inequalities in health among adults in Britain? In *Health Inequalities in European Countries* (Fox, A.J. Ed.), Gower, London

Ford, J. (1991) *Consuming Credit: Debt and Poverty in the UK,* CPAG, London

Forrest, R. and Gordon, D. (1993) *People and Places. A 1991 Census Atlas of England.* SAUS, Bristol

Forrest, R. and Murie, A. (1990) *Moving the housing market : council estates, social change and privatization,* Avebury, Aldershot

Foster, J. and Hope, T (1993) *Housing, Community and Change: The Impact of the Priority Estates Project,* HMSO, London

Franklin, N.N. (1967) The Concept and Measurement of 'Minimum Living Standards'. *International Labour Review*

Frayman, H. (1991) *Breadline Britain -1990's: The Findings of the Television Series*, Domino Films and London Weekend Television, London

Freeman, H. (1994) Schizophrenia and City residence. *British Journal of Psychiatry 164*: 39-50

Garofalo, J. (1981) The fear of crime and its consequences, *Journal of Criminal Law and Criminology 72*: 839-857

Glendinning, C. and Millar, J. Eds (1992) *Women and Poverty in Britain: the 1990s* Harvester Wheatsheaf, Hemel Hempstead

Godel, K. (1931) Uber formal unnentscheidbare Satze der Principa Mathematica und verwandter Systeme I. (On Formally Undecidable Propositions of Prinicipa Mathematica and Related Systems) *Monatshefte fur Mathematik und Physik 38*: 173-198

Goedhart, Halberstadt, Kapteyn and van Praag (1977) The Poverty Line: Concept and Measurement, *Journal of Human Resources 12(4), Fall*: 503-20

Goldberg, G.S. and Kreman, E. (1987) The Feminization of Poverty: Only in America?, *Social Policy*, Spring: 3-14

Goldberg, D. and Huxley, P. (1980) *Mental Illness in the Community,* Tavistock, London

Goldblatt, P. (Ed) (1990) *1971-1981 Longitudinal Study: Mortality and Social Organisation*, HMSO, London

Gordon, D. and Forrest, R. (1994) *People and Places 2. Class and Economic Distinctions in England 1991.* SAUS, Bristol

Gordon, D. and Townsend, P. (1990) Measuring the Poverty Line. *Radical Statistics 47*: 5-12

Gosschalk, B. and Frayman, H. (1991) The Changing Nature of Deprivation in Britain - An Inner Cities Perspective. *Political and Social Issues in Urban Industrial Societies - Joint Session with WAPOR*

Gould, S.J. (1981) *The Mismeasure of Man,* W.W. Norton & Company, New York and London

Gould, S.J. (1985) Carrie Buck's Daughter, in *The Flamingo's Smile: Reflections in Natural History* (Gould, S.J. Ed.), Penguin, Suffolk

Graham, H. (1987) Being Poor: perceptions and coping strategies of lone mothers. In *Give and Take in Families: Studies in resource distribution* (Brannen, J. and Wilson, G. Eds) Allen & Unwin, London

Graham, H. (1992) Budgeting for Health: Mothers in low-income households. In *Women and Poverty in Britain: the 1990s.* (Glendinning, C. and Millar, J. Eds) Harvester Wheatsheaf, Hemel Hempstead

Graham, H. (1993) *Hardship and health in women's lives* Harvester Wheatsheaf, Hemel Hempstead

Grayson, L., Hobson, M. and Smith, B. (1992) *INLOGOV Informs on Poverty.* Vol 3, Issue 1, Institute of Local Government Studies, University of Birmingham, Birmingham

Groves, D. (1992) Occupational pension provision and women's poverty in old age. In *Women and Poverty in Britain: the 1990s.*(Glendinning, C. and Millar, J. Eds.) Harvester Wheatsheaf, Hemel Hempstead

Habib, J. and Tawil, Y. (1974) *Equivalence Scales for Family Size: Findings from Israeli Data,* The National Insurance Institute, Bureau of Research and Planning, Jerusalem

Hagenaars, Aldi J.M. (1986) *The perceptions of poverty*, Elsevier Science Publishers, BV, Amsterdam

Hagenaars, Aldi J.M., De Vos, K. and Zaidi, M.A. (1994) *Poverty Statistics in the Late 1980's*: Research based on Microdata, Luxembourg, Eurostat

Halleröd, B. (1991) *Den svenska fattigdomen: en studie av fattigdom och socialbidrgrafstagande*, Arkiv, Lund

Halleröd, B. (1993a) Surt sa raven: relativ deprivation, adaptiva preferenser och uppfattningar om nodvandig standard, Umeå Studies in Sociology

Halleröd, B. (1993b) *Poverty in Sweden: A New Approach to the Direct Measurement of Consensual Poverty*, Department of Sociology, University of Umeå and Social Policy Research Centre, University of New South Wales

Halleröd, B. (1994) *A New Approach to Direct Consensual Measurement of Poverty*. Discussion Paper No. 50, Social Policy Research Centre, University of New South Wales

Halleröd, B. (1994) *Poverty in Sweden: A New Approach to Direct Measurement of Consensual Poverty*. Umeå Studies in Sociology, No 106, University of Umeå

Halleröd, B (1995) The Truly Poor: Indirect and Direct Measurement of Consensual Poverty in Sweden, *Journal of European Social Policy 5(2)*: 111-29

Hammarstrom, A. (1994) Health Consequences of Youth Unemployment. *Public Health 108(6)*: 403-412

Hart, N. (1986) Inequalities in Health: the individual versus the environment. *Journal of the Royal Statistical Society A(149)*: 228-246

Heikkilä, M. (1991) Poverty and Accumulation of Welfare Deficit, In *Deprivation, Social Welfare and Expertise*, Juhani, L., (Ed.) Research Report No 7, National Agency for Welfare and Health, Helsinki

Hickey, S. (1988) Minutes of Evidence Taken Before the Social Services Committee, 15 June 1988. *Social Services Committee Fourth Report: Families on Low Income: Low Income Statistics*, HMSO, London

Hindelang, M., Gottfredson, M. and Garofalo, J. (1978) Victims of Personal Crime: An Empirical Foundation for a Theory of Personal Victimization, Ballinger, Cambridge, Massachusetts

Hollander, D. and Tobiansky, R. (1990) Crisis in Admission beds. *British Medical Journal 301*: 664

Hollingshead, A.B. and Redlich, F. (1958) *Social Class and Mental Illness*. John Wiley, New York

Home Office Standing Conference on Crime Prevention (December 1988), *Report of the Working Group on the Costs of Crime*, Home Office

Hope, T. (1986) Council Tenants and Crime. *Home Office Research Bulletin (21)*: 46-51

Hope, T. and Shaw, M. (Eds) (1988) *Communities and Crime Reduction*, HMSO: London

Hough, M. and Mayhew, P. (1983) *The British Crime Survey,* a HORPU Report, HMSO, London

Hough, M. and Mayhew, P. (1985) *Taking Account of Crime: Key Findings from the 1984 British Crime Survey,* a HORPU Report, HMSO, London

Hutton, S. (1989) Testing Townsend: Exploring Living Standards Using Secondary Data Analysis, In *The Quality of Life* (Baldwin, S., Godfrey, C. and Propper, C. Eds.), Routledge & Kegan Paul

Hutton, S. (1991) Measuring Living Standards Using Existing National Data Sets. *Journal of Social Policy 20,* No. 2

Illsley, R. (1955) Social Class selection and class differences in relation to stillbirths and infant deaths. *British Medical Journal 2*: 1520-1524

Illsley, R. (1986) Occupational Class, Selection and the Production in Inequalities in Health. *Quarterly Journal of Social Affairs 2(2)*: 151-65

International Institute for Labour Studies (1993) *The Framework of ILO Action Against Poverty,* IILS, Geneva

Isherwood, B.C. and Van Slooten, R. (1979) Current Programmes: Some DHSS Work on the Measurement of Poverty, in DHSS (1979) *The Definition and Measurement of Poverty,* 45-60

Jackson, B. (1985) *Youth Unemployment.* Croom Helm, London.

Jacobs, E. and Worcester, R. (1991) *Typically British? The Prudential MORI Survey.* Bloomsbury, London

Jacobson, J.L. (1993) Women's Health: The Price of Poverty. In *The Health of Women. A Global Perspective* (Koblinsky, M., Timyan, J. and Gay, J. Eds) Westview Press and The National Council for International Health, Boulder, San Francisco and Oxford

Jarman, B. (1983) Identification of Underprivileged Areas. *British Medical Journal 286*: 1705-1709

Jarman, B., Hirsch, S., White, P. and Driscoll, R. (1992) Predicting psychiatric admission rates. *British Medical Journal 304*: 1146-1151

Jazairy, I., Alamgir, M. and Panuccio, T. (1992) *The State of World Rural Poverty*, International Fund for Agricultural Development (IFAD), New York University Press, Rome and New York

Jensen, J. (1978) *Minimum Income Levels and Income Equivalence Scales*, Department of Social Welfare, Wellington

Kangas, O. and Ritakallio, V. (1995) *Different Methods - Different Results? Approaches to Multidimensional Poverty.* Paper presented at the ISA RC 19 conference, Pavi, Italy

Kass, G. (1980) An Exploratory Technique for Investigating Large Quantities of Categorical Data. *Applied Statistics (29)*: 119-127

Keyes, S. and Kennedy, M. (1992) *Sick to Death of Homelessness*, CRISIS, London

Kitcher, P. (1985) *Vaulting Ambition: Sociobiology and the Quest for Human Nature*, MIT Press, Cambridge, Massachusetts

Klecka, W.R. (1980) *Discriminant Analysis,* Sage Publications, Beverly Hills and London

Kolata, G. (1984) The Proper Display of Data. *Science 226*: 156-158

Kurder, F. (1970) Some Principles of Interest Measurement. *Educational and Psychological Measurement 30*: 205-226

Lakatos, I. (1974) Falsification and the Methodology of Scientific Research Programmes, In *Criticism and the Growth of Knowledge* (Lakatos, I. and Musgrave, A.E. Eds.) 91-196

Lakatos, I. and Musgrave, A.E. (Eds.) (1974) *Criticism and the Growth of Knowledge*, Cambridge University Press, Cambridge

Land, H. (1977) *Parity begins at home: Women's and men's work in the home and its effects on their paid employment.* Equal Opportunities Commission/ Social Science Research Council, London

Land, H. (1983) Poverty and gender: the distribution of resources within the family. In Brown, M.(Ed) *The Structure of Disadvantage,* Heinemann, London

Lazear, E.P. and Michael, R.T. (1980a) Family Size and the Distribution of Real Per Capita Income. *American Economic Review 70(1)*: 91-107

Lazear, E.P. and Michael, R.T. (1980b) Real Income Equivalence Among One-earner and Two-earner Families. *American Economic Review 70(2)*: 203-208

Lea, J. and Young, J. (1984) *What is to be Done About Law and Order?* Pluto Press, London

Lewis, G.W. and Ulph, D.T. (1988). Poverty, Inequality and Welfare. *The Economic Journal* 98 (Conference 1988): 117-131

Lewis, J. and Piachaud, D. (1992) Women and Poverty in the Twentieth Century In *Women and Poverty in Britain: the 1990s.*(Glendinning, C. and Millar, J. Eds) Harvester Wheatsheaf, Hemel Hempstead

Lidbetter, E.J. (1933) *Heredity and the Social Problem Group, Vol. 1*, Edward Arnold, London

Lister, R. (1991) Concepts of Poverty. *Social Studies Review, May*, 192-195.

Littlewood, R. and Lipsedge, M. (1988) Psychiatric Illness amongst Britain's Afro-Caribbeans. *British Medical Journal 296:* 950-951

Lobstein, T. (1991) *The Nutrition of Women on Low Incomes*, a paper by The Food Commission (October)

Lonsdale, S. (1990) *Women and Disability: The experience of physical disability among women* Macmillan, London

Lorant, J. (1981) *Poor and Powerless: Fuel problems and disconnections*, CPAG, London

Mack, J. and Lansley, S. (1985) *Poor Britain*, Allen and Unwin, London

Maclean, M. (1987) Households after divorce: the availability of resources and their impact on children. In *Give and Take in Families: Studies in resource distribution* (Brannen, J. and Wilson, G. Eds) Allen & Unwin, London

Macnicol, J. (1987) In Pursuit of the Underclass. *Journal of Social Policy 16(3)*: 293-318

Manketlow, R. (1994) *Paths to Hospitalisation: A sociological analysis.* Avebury, Aldershot

Manpower Services Commission (MSC) (1982) *Long-term Unemployment.* HMSO, London

Marmot, M.G., Shipley, M.J. and Rose, G. (1984) Inequalities in Death - Specific Explanations of a General Pattern? *The Lancet ii*: 1003-6

Martin, J., Meltzer, H. and Elliot, D. (1988) *OPCS surveys of disability in Great Britain Report 1: The prevalence of disability among adults*, HMSO, London

Maxfield, M. (1987a) *Explaining Fear of Crime: Evidence from the 1984 British Crime Survey*. HMSO, London

Maxfield, M. (1987b) *Incivilities and Fear of Crime in England and Wales, and the United States: A Comparative Analysis*. American Society of Criminology, Montreal

Mayhew, P., Elliot, D. and Dowds, D. (1989) *The 1988 British Crime Survey*, a HORPU Report, HMSO, London

Mayhew, P. and Maung, N.A. (1992) Surveying Crime: Findings from the 1992 British Crime Survey, *Home Office Research and Statistics Department Research Findings No 2*, 5pp

Mayhew, P., Maung, N.A. and Mirlees-Black, C. (1993) *The 1992 British Crime Survey*, a HOPRU Report, HMSO, London

Maynard Smith, J. and Warren, N. (1989) Models of Cultural and Genetic Change. First Published in *Evolution* (1982). Reprinted in Maynard Smith, J. (Ed.), *Did Darwin Get it Right? Essays on Games, Sex and Evolution*, Chapman and Hall, New York

Mazumdar, P.M.H. (1992) *Eugenics, Human Genetics and Human Failings*, Routledge, London and New York

McClements, L.D. (1977) Equivalence Scales for Children. *Journal of Public Economics 8*: 197-210

McClements, L.D. (1978) *The Economics of Social Security*, Heinemann, London

McCormick, A., Fleming, D. and Charlton, J. (1995) *Morbidity statistics from general practice: Fourth National Study, 1991-1992*. OPCS, London

McCormick, A., Rosenbaum, M. and Fleming, D. (1990) Socio-economic characteristics of people who consult their general practitioner. *Population Trends*, 59, 8-10.

Medwar, P. (1984) *The Limits of Science*, Oxford University Press, Oxford

Miles, A. (1988) *Women and mental illness*. Harvester Wheatsheaf, Hemel Hempstead

Millar, J. (1992) Lone Mothers and Poverty. In *Women and Poverty in Britain: the 1990s*. (Glendinning, C. and Millar, J. Eds) Harvester Wheatsheaf, Hemel Hempstead

Mirlees-Black, C., Mayhew, P., and Percy, A. (1996) *The 1996 British Crime Survey: England and Wales*, Home Office Research Bulletin, Issue 19/96, HMSO: London

Moore, J. (1989) *The End of the Line for Poverty*, Conservative Political Centre, London

MORI (1988), Gosschalk, B., Lancaster, H. and Townsend, P., *Service Provision and Living Standards in Islington,* Research Study conducted for the London Borough of Islington, MORI, 32 Old Queen Street, London

Morris, J.N. (1975) *Uses of Epidemiology*, 3rd edn., Churchill Livingstone, London

Morris, T (1957) *The Criminal Area,* Routledge and Kegan Paul, London

Mossey, J. and Shapiro, E. (1982) Self-rated health: predicator of mortality among the elderly, *American Journal of Public Health 72*: 800-808

Muellbauer, J. (1979) McClements on Equivalence Scales for Children. *Journal of Public Economics 12*: 221-231

Muellbauer, J. (1980) The Estimation of the Prais-Houthakker Model of Equivalence Scales. *Econometrica 48(1)*: 153-176

Muffels, R., Berghman, J. and Dirven, H.J. (1992) A Multi-Method Approach to Monitor the Evolution of Poverty, *Journal of European Social Policy 2(3)*: 193-213

Muijen, M. and Brooking, J. (1989) Mental Health. In While, A. (Ed) *Health in the Inner City*. Heinemann, London

Nagel, E. and Newman, J.R. (1958) *Godel's Proof.* Routledge & Kegan Paul Ltd, London

National Consumer Council (1980) *Consumers and Credit*, NCC, London

259

National Council for One-Parent Families (1978) *Fuel Debts and One-Parent Families*, London

Newnham, A. (1986) *Employment, Unemployment and Black people. Runnymeade Research Report.* Runnymeade Trust, London

Nolan, B. and Whelan, C.T. (1995) *Resources, Deprivation and Poverty.* Clarendon Press (Forthcoming)

Nunnally, J.C. (1981) *Psychometric Theory*, Tate McGraw-Hill Publishing Company Ltd, New Delhi

Nutbeam, D. and Catford, J. (1987) *Pulse of Wales Social Survey Supplement, Heartbeat Report No.7*, Heartbeat Wales, Cardiff

Nyman, C. (1996) Inside the black box: intra-household distribution of consumption in Sweden. In *Three Aspects of Consensual Poverty in Sweden - Work Deprivation, Attitudes towards the Welfare State and Household Consumptional Distribution.* (Bihagen, E., Nyman, C. and Strand, M., Eds.) Umeå University, Umeå, Sweden

Oldfield, N. and Yu, A.C.S. (1993) *The Cost of a Child: Living Standards for the 1990s*, Child Poverty Action Group, London

OPCS (1986) *The General Household Survey for 1984*, HMSO, London

OPCS (1995) OPCS Surveys of Psychiatric Morbidity in Great Britain Bulletin No 1: *The Prevalence of Psychiatric Morbidity among adults aged 16-64 living in private households in Great Britain.* OPCS, London

Oppenheim, C. (1991) *Poverty: The Facts.* Child Poverty Action Group, London

Oppenheim, C. (1993) *Poverty: The Facts* (revised and updated edition), Child Poverty Action Group, London

Orshansky, M. (1965) Counting the Poor: Another Look at the Poverty Profile. *Social Security Bulletin 28*, No.3

Pahl, J. (1989) *Money and Marriage.* Macmillan Education Ltd, London

Papineau, D. (1987) *For Science in the Social Sciences*, The Macmillian Press, Hong Kong

Parry-Jones, W.L.L. and Queloz, N. (Eds.) (1991) *Mental Health and Deviance in Inner Cities*. World Health Organisation, Geneva

Payne, S. (1991) *Women, Health and Poverty: An Introduction*. Harvester Wheatsheaf, Hemel Hempstead

Payne, S. (1995) The Rationing of psychiatric beds: changing trends in sex ratios in admission to psychiatric hospitals, *Health & Social Care in the Community* 3: 289-300

Payne, S. (1996) Psychiatric care in the community: does it fail young men? *Policy and Politics 24(2)*: 193-205

Piachaud, D. (1979) *The Cost of a Child*, Child Poverty Action Group, London

Piachaud, D. (1981) Peter Townsend and the Holy Grail. *New Society*, 10 September

Piachaud, D. (1984) *Round About Fifty Hours a Week: The Time Costs of Children*, Child Poverty Action Group, London

Piachaud, D. (1987) Problems in the Definition and Measurement of Poverty. *Journal of Social Policy 16(2)*: 125-146

Platt, S. (1986) Parasuicide and unemployment. *British Journal of Psychiatry 149*: 401-405

Podder, N. (1971) The Estimation of Equivalent Income Scales. *Australian Economic Papers*, December 1971

Popper, K.R. (1968) *The Logic of Scientific Discovery*, Hutchinson, London

Popper, K.R. (1972) *Objective Knowledge*, Oxford University Press, Oxford

Power, C., Manor, O., Fox, A.J. and Fogelman, K. (1990) Health in Childhood and Social Inequalities in Health in Young Adults. *Journal of the Royal Statistical Society 153(1)*: 17-28

Public Attitudes Surveys (PAS) (1987) *The Consumers Use of Credit*, PAS, London

Radloff, L. (1980) Risk factors for depression: what do we learn from them? In Guttentag, M. (Ed) *The mental health of women*. Academic Press, New York

Ramsay, M. (1983) City-Centre Crime. *Home Office Research Bulletin 16*: 5-8

Renwick, T.J. and Bergmann, B. (1993) A Budget-Based Definition of Poverty. *Journal of Human Resources 12(1)*: 1-24

Richardson, P. (1978) *Fuel Poverty*, Department of Social Administration and Social Work, University of York, York

Rowlingson, K. and Kempson, E. (1993) *Gas Debts and Disconnections.* PSI. London

Rowntree, B.S. (1922) *Poverty: a Study of Town Life.* Longmans, London

Rowntree, S. (1942) *Poverty and Progress*, Longmans, Green and Co., London

Rowntree, S. and Lavers, G.R. (1951) *Poverty and the Welfare State*, Longmans, Green and Co., London

Ruggles, P. (1990) *Drawing the Line: Alternative Measures and their Implications for Public Policy*, The Urban Institute Press, Washington DC

Rutter, M. and Madge, N. (1976) *Cycles of Disadvantage: A Review of Research*, Heinemann, London

Saunders, J. (1996) A comparative study of health inequalities and deprivation within Greenwich in the 80's and 90's. MSc dissertation (unpublished), School of Computing and Management Sciences, Sheffield Hallam University.

Saunders, P. and Bradbury, B. (1989) Some Australian Evidence on the Consensual Approach to Poverty Measurement. *Social Welfare Research Centre Discussion Papers No 14*, University of New South Wales, Kensington, New South Wales, Australia

Saunders, P. and Matheson, G. (1992) *Perceptions of poverty, income adequacy and living standards in Australia*, Reports and Proceedings No 99, Social Policy Research Centre, University of NSW, Sydney

Scott, H. (1984) *Working your way to the bottom : the feminization of poverty.* Pandora Press

Sen, A.K. (1983) Poor, Relatively Speaking. *Oxford Economic Papers 35*: 135-169

Sen, A.K. (1985) A Sociological Approach to the Measurement of Poverty: A Reply to Professor Peter Townsend, *Oxford Economic Papers 37*: 669-676

Sen, A.K. (1988) *The Standard of Living*. Cambridge University Press, Cambridge

Sen, A.K. (1993) The Economics of Life and Death, *Scientific American, 268(5)*: 40-47

Seneca, J.J. and Taussig, M.K. (1971) Family Equivalence Scales and Personal Income Tax Exemptions for Children, *Review of Economics and Statistics 53*: 253-262

Sheppard, M. (1991) General Practice, social work and mental health sections - the social control of women. *British Journal of Social Work 21*: 663-683

Sheppard, M., Cooper, B., Brown, A.C. and Kalton, G. (1966) *Psychiatric Illness in General practice*. Oxford University Press, London

Smith, G.E., Bartley, M. and Blane, D. (1990) The Black Report on socio-economic inequalities in health 10 years on. *British Medical Journal 301*: 373-377

Smith, S.J. (1983) Public Policy and the Effects of Crime in the Inner City: A British Example, *Urban Studies (20)*: 229-239

Smith, T. (1990) Poverty and Health in the 1990s. *British Medical Journal 301*: 349-350

Smith, T. (1995) Differences between general practices in hospital admission rates for self-inflicted injury and self-poisoning: influence of socio-economic factors. *British Journal of General Practice 45*: 458-462

Smyth, M. and Browne, F. (1992) *General Household Survey 1990*. Series GHS No 21, OPCS, HMSO, London

Social Trends (1996) HMSO, London

Social Welfare Policy Secretariat (SWPS) (1981) *Report on Poverty Measurement*, Australian Government Publishing Service, Canberra

Spearman, C. (1904) General Intelligence Objectively Determined and Measured, *American Journal of Psychology*, 15, 201-293

Spence, S., Hotchkiss, J., Williams, D. and Davies, D. (1993) Tuberculosis and Poverty, *British Medical Journal 307: 759-761*

Srole, L., Langner, T.S., Micheal, S.T., Opler, M.K. and Rennie, T.A.C. (1961) *Mental health in the metropolis: The Midtown Manhattan survey.* McGraw, New York

Stanley, J.C. (1971) Reliability, in *Educational Measurement* (Thorndike, R.L. Ed.), American Council on Education, Washington DC

Staples, B. (1992) *Morbidity survey of mental illness in Liverpool and South Sefton Health Districts.* Liverpool Health Authority, Liverpool

Stedman-Jones, G. (1984) *Outcast London*, Penguin, London

Stern, J. (1983) Social Mobility and Interpretation of Social Class Mortality Differentials. *Journal of Social Policy 12*(1): 27-49

Strachan, D.P. (1988) Damp Housing and Childhood Asthma: Validation of Reporting Symptoms. *British Medical Journal 297*: 1223-1226

Sumner, C. (1976) Marxism and deviance theory. In *Crime and Delinquency in Britain Vol 2*, Wiles, P. (Ed), Martin Robertson, London

Supplementary Benefit Commission (SBC) (1979) *Annual Report for 1978.* Cmnd 7725, HMSO, London

Taylor, L. (1992) The World Bank and the Environment: The World Development Report 1992, In UNCTAD, *International Monetary and Financial Issues for the 1990's,* Research Papers for the Group of 24, Vol II, United Nations, New York

The Economist (1981) The Nature of Knowledge. *Economist, December 26*: 99-105

Thorndike, R.L. (1971) *Educational Measurement*, American Council on Education, Washington DC

Thorogood, N. (1987) Race, Class and Gender: The politics of housework, In *Give and Take in Families: Studies in resource distribution* (Brannen, J. and Wilson, G. Eds) Allen & Unwin, London

Townsend, P. (1970) *The Concept of Poverty*, Heinemann, London

Townsend, P. (1979) *Poverty in the United Kingdom*, Allen Lane and Penguin Books, Harmondsworth, Middlesex and Berkeley, University of California Press

Townsend, P. (1985) A Sociological Approach to the Measurement of Poverty: A Rejoinder to Professor Amartya Sen. *Oxford Economic Papers 37*: 659-668

Townsend, P. (1987) Deprivation. *Journal of Social Policy 16(2)*: 125-146

Townsend, P. (1993a) *The International Analysis of Poverty*, Harvester Wheatsheaf, Milton Keynes

Townsend, P. (1993b) *The Repressive Nature and Extent of Poverty in the UK: Predisposing Cause of Crime*, Symposium on the Link Between Poverty and Crime, Proceedings of the 11th Annual Conference of the Howard League on "Poverty and Crime", 8-10 September 1993, Summary in *Criminal Justice 11, 4 (October)*, the magazine of the Howard League

Townsend, P. and Davidson, N. (1988) *Inequalities in Health: The Black Report*, 2nd edn., Penguin Books, London

Townsend, P. and Gordon, D. (1989) What is enough? New evidence on poverty in Greater London allowing the definition of a minimum benefit. *Memorandum of evidence to the House of Commons Social Services Select Committee on Minimum Income 579*: 45-73, HMSO, London

Townsend, P. and Gordon, D. (1992) *Unfinished Statistical Business on Low Incomes? A Review of New Proposals by the Department of Social Security for the Production of Public Information on Poverty*, No.3 in a series of reports from the Statistical Monitoring Unit, University of Bristol

Townsend, P., Corrigan, P. and Kowarzik, U. (1987) *Poverty and Labour in London*, Interim Report of the Centenary Survey, Low Pay Unit, London

Townsend, P., Davidson, N. and Whitehead, M. (1992) *The Black Report and The Health Divide*, 3rd edn. Penguin, Harmondsworth

United Nations (UN) (1991) *World Population Prospects 1990,* United Nations, Geneva

United Nations Development Programme (UNDP) (1992) *Human Development Report 1992*, Oxford University Press, New York and Oxford

United Nations Development Programme (UNDP) (1993) *Human Development Report 1993*, Oxford University Press, New York and Oxford

United Nations Development Programme (UNDP) (1995) *Human Development Report 1995,* Oxford University Press, New York and Oxford

United States Department of Commerce (1992) *Income, Poverty and Wealth in the United States: A Chart Book* (by Lamison-White L.), Current Population Reports, Consumer Income, series P-60, No 179

Ussher, J. (1991) *Women's Madness: Misogyny or mental illness?* Harvester Wheatsheaf, Hemel Hempstead

Van den Bosch, K. and Deleek, H. (1992) Poverty and Adequacy of Social Security in Europe: A Comparative Analysis, *Journal of European Social Policy 2(2)*: 107-20

Van Praag, B., Goedhart, T. and Kapteyn, A. (1980) The Poverty Line - A Pilot Survey in Europe, *The Review of Economics and Statistics*, 261-265

Veit-Wilson, J.H. (1986) Paradigms of Poverty: A Rehabilitation of B.S. Rowntree. *Journal of Social Policy 15(1)*: 69-99

Veit-Wilson, J.H. (1987) Consensual Approaches to Poverty Lines and Social Security. *Journal of Social Policy 16(2)*: 183-211

Veit-Wilson, J.H. (1989) Memorandum in House of Commons Social Services Committee, *Minimum Income*, House of Commons 579, HMSO, London

Veit-Wilson, J.H. (1992) Muddle or Mendacity? The Beveridge Committee and the Poverty Line. *Journal of Social Policy 21(3)*: 269-301

Vogel, J. (1987) *Ojamlikhet i Sverige*, Statistiska centralbyran, Rapport 51, Stockholm

Vogel, J. (1990) Inequality in Sweden: Trends and Current Situation, In *Generating Equality in the Welfare State: The Swedish Experience*, (Person, I. Ed.) Norwegian University Press, Oslo

Von Hentig, H. (1948) *The Criminal and his Victim*, Yale University Press, New Haven

Walker, A. (1992) The Poor Relation: Poverty among older women. In *Women and Poverty in Britain: the 1990s*. (Glendinning, C. and Millar, J. Eds) Harvester Wheatsheaf, Hemel Hempstead

Walker, R. (1987) Consensual Approaches to the Definition of Poverty: Towards an Alternative Methodology. *Journal of Social Policy 16(2)*: 213-226

Wall, D. and Bradshaw, J. (1987) The Television Licence: Prosecution and Poor Households. *Howard Journal 26(1)*: 47-56

Wannamethee, G. and Shaper, A.G. (1991) Self-assessment of Health Status and Mortality in Middle-Aged British Men, *International Journal of Epidemiology 20(1)*: 239-245

Watts, H.W. (1993) *A Review of Alternative Budget-Based Expenditure Norms*, prepared for the panel on poverty measurement of the US Committee on National Statistics, March, Washington DC

Weir, J. (1992) *Sensitivity Testing in HBAI: An Examination of the Results*, Department of Social Security Analytical Notes, No 1, London

Whiteford, P. (1981) The Concept of Poverty. *Social Security Journal*, published for the Australian Department of Social Security, Melbourne

Whiteford, P. (1985) *A Family's Needs: Equivalence Scales, Poverty and Social Security*. Research Paper No. 27, Development Division, Australian Department of Social Security

Whitehead, M. (1988) *Inequalities in Health: The Health Divide*, 2nd edn., Penguin Books, London

Whitfield, M. (1982) *The human cost of fuel disconnections*, Family Service Units, London

Wilkinson, R.G. (1992) Income distribution and life expectancy. *British Medical Journal 304*: 165-168

Wilson, G. (1987) Money: Patterns of responsibility and irresponsibility in marriage. In *Give and Take in Families: Studies in resource distribution* (Brannen, J. and Wilson, G. Eds) Allen & Unwin, London

Wishart, D. (1969) Mode Analysis, In *Numerical Taxonomy* (Cole, A.J. Ed.), Academic Press, New York

Wolfson, M.C. and Evans, J.M. (1989) *Statistics Canada's Low Income Cut-Offs: Methodological Concerns and Possibilities*, Research Paper Series, Statistics Canada, Analytical Studies Branch

World Bank (1990) *World Development Report 1990: Poverty*, World Bank, Washington DC

World Bank (1993a) *Implementing the World Bank's Strategy to Reduce Poverty: Progress and Challenges*, World Bank, Washington DC

World Bank (1993b) *World Development Report 1993: Investing in Health*, Oxford University Press for the World Bank, Washington DC

World Health Organization (WHO) (1948) *Official Records of the World Health Organization*, No 2: 100, WHO Interim Commission, United Nations, Geneva

World Health Organization (WHO) (1984) *Report of the Working Group on Concepts and Principles of Health Promotion*, 9-13 July 1984, World Health Organization, Copenhagen

Appendix I: Technical appendix

Survey methodology

This report is based on the Breadline Britain in the 1990s survey, conducted by MORI on behalf of LWT and Domino Films, with additional funding from the Joseph Rowntree Foundation. The six programmes of **Breadline Britain 1990s** were first broadcast on the ITV network in April and May 1991 and looked at poverty in Britain through the lives of eight people and families in Birmingham, Liverpool, Manchester, Teesside and London. Additional information has been included from the transcripts of the detailed interviews with these people and families.

Breadline Britain in the 1990s updates and extends the pioneering work carried out for LWT and Domino Films' **Breadline Britain** series which was first broadcast as four programmes in the summer of 1983. For the Breadline Britain in the 1990s survey, MORI interviewed a quota sample of 1319 adults aged 16+, face-to-face in their homes, between 14 and 25 July 1990. Additional fieldwork among households living in particularly deprived areas was carried out between 26 November and 9 December 1990, with 512 quota interviews conducted face-to-face in home. Quotas were based on sex, age and working status. Aggregated data was weighted by age, household type, tenure and ACORN housing type to be representative of the population of Great Britain (Frayman, 1991).

269

In order to ensure a large sample of people, living in deprived areas, over-sampling was targeted at ACORN areas known to contain poor households in particular at ACORN Group G areas, which are characterised as (CACI, 1992):

Group G: Council Estates - Category III
This Group comprises those council estates likely to have the most serious social problems, with exceptional levels of unemployment, overcrowding, large and single parent families and a widespread lack of private transport.

Such estates house large numbers of residents dependant upon the State for the provision of basic services.

ACORN Group G has four sub-categories:

G22: New Council Estates in Inner Cities
This Type includes modern local authority complexes, often in inner cities, housing homeless single people and single parent families in small flats, suitable neither for pensioners, nor for large families.

Much of the recent council housing in inner London falls into this category.

The Type is atypical of local authority housing by having many young single people and high proportions of people born in the West Indies.

The inner city location of this type of neighbourhood is reflected in the high levels of unemployment and unskilled workers. The decline of manufacturing jobs in the inner city results in dependence on public transport to reach clerical and semi-skilled jobs in service industries.

Half the people in the Type have household incomes of less than £10,000 and financial investments such as ownership of credit cards, wills and building insurance are roughly half the national average. Car ownership is also low.

G23: Overspill Estates, Higher Unemployment

This neighbourhood Type consists mostly of large local authority schemes on the outskirts of provincial English cities, designed in the form of medium-rise flats with walkways. Residents, re-housed from older communities in the inner city, find themselves distant from relatives and familiar shops and pubs and continue to be dependent upon buses.

These areas tend to have large numbers of residents who are unskilled and unemployed; consequently these are the areas where there are the most large and single parent families, the most overcrowding and the lowest levels of car ownership, within the English cities where they are found.

G24: Council Estates with some Overcrowding

Type 24 consists mostly of modern council estates in Scotland containing small houses and flats, unsuitable for the large families that live in them. The residents are frequently families with children of school age, there being relatively few single people or pensioners.

There is often a severe shortage of craft skills and unemployment tends to be high.

G25: Council Estates with Greatest Hardship

In this Type, much of the labour force is likely to be unemployed. A relatively high proportion of households live in circumstances of overcrowding and car ownership is very low.

Almost all of this type of area is found in West Central Scotland, Tayside and Merseyside.

Due to high unemployment and serious overcrowding, these estates provide some of the most intractable social problems in the UK.

Nearly 40% of the annual household income in this Type is likely to be below £5,000. Use of credit in the form of hire purchase is high, but participation in other financial investments is very low, especially in bank and building society accounts.

In 1991, just over 7% of the British population was estimated to be living in ACORN Group G areas (CACI, 1991).

CHAID CHi-Squared Automatic Interaction Detector Methodology

CHAID stands for CHi-Squared Automatic Interaction Detector. It is based on an algorithm developed by Kass in 1980. It has only recently become available as an add-in to the SPSS statistical package.

CHAID belongs to a family of techniques known as Classification Trees, which include AID (Automatic Interaction Detector) and CART (Classification And Regression Trees) techniques. These techniques can be used to perform discriminant analysis on categorical as opposed to continuous data.

The relative newness of these techniques means that little is known about them. However, CHAID has the advantage that it can produce intuitive, easy to understand, classification rules. It can also identify sub-groupings within the data that would be impossible to detect with conventional techniques.

271

In 1988, the US Committee on Applied and Theoretical Statistics' expert panel on Discriminant and Cluster Analysis considered that the status of Classification Trees was best summarised by the main developers (Breiman *et al*, 1984)

> Binary trees give an interesting and often illuminating way of looking at data in classification or regression problems. They should not be used to the exclusion of other methods. We do not claim they are always better. They do add a flexible nonparametric tool to the data analyst's arsenal.

SOCIAL CLASS DEFINITIONS

A   Professionals such as doctors, surgeons, solicitors or dentists; chartered people like architects; fully qualified people with a large degree of responsibility such as senior editors, senior civil servants, town clerks, senior business executives and managers, and high-ranking grades of the Services.

B   People with very responsible jobs such as university lecturers, matrons of hospitals, heads of local government departments; middle management in business; qualified scientists, bank managers and upper grades of the Services, police inspectors.

C1   All others doing non-manual jobs; nurses, technicians, pharmacists, salesmen, publicans, people in clerical positions and middle ranks of the Services, police sergeants.

C2   Skilled manual workers/craftsmen who have served apprenticeships; foremen, manual workers with special qualifications such as long-distance lorry drivers, security officers and lower grades of Services/police constables.

D   Semi-skilled and unskilled manual workers, including labourers and mates of occupations in the C2 grade and people serving apprenticeships; machine minders, farm labourers, bus and railway conductors, laboratory assistants, postmen, waiter/waitress, door-to door and van salesmen.

E   Those on lowest levels of subsistence including pensioners, casual workers, and others with minimum levels of income. (Source: Jacobs and Worcester, 1991)

Appendix II: Annotated questionnaire

Q1. Thinking about the area where you live, I would like you to tell me whether each of the following applies.

	Yes	No	DK
The local area is dirty and unpleasant	26	73	1
There is a lack of pleasant, open spaces within easy reach	23	76	1
There are houses boarded up/with broken windows nearby	16	83	1

Q2. Now, thinking about health related problems, I would like you to tell me whether each of the following applies to you personally or to anyone in your household now.

	Yes	No	DK
Health problems caused/made worse by housing situation	8	91	1
On hospital waiting list for > 6 months	9	90	1
On hospital waiting list for > 12 months	4	94	2

SHUFFLEBOARD SIDE 1 AND CREAM CARDS
EXCLUDE CARDS 27 TO 32 (ASTERISKED), WHICH RELATE TO
CHILDREN

Q3. On these cards are a number of different items which relate to our standard of living. Please would you indicate by placing the cards in the appropriate box the living standards you feel all adults should have in Britain today. BOX A is for items which you think are necessary, which all adults should be able to afford and which they should not have to do without. BOX B is for items which may be desirable but are not necessary. Do you feel differently about any items if the adult is a pensioner?

GIVE CARDS 27 TO 32 RELATING TO CHILDREN(*)

Q4. And do you feel differently for any items in the case of families with children?

		A Necessary	B Desirable	DK
1.	Two meals a day	90	10	*
2.	Meat or fish or vegetarian equivalent every other day	77	21	2
3.	Heating to warm living areas of the home if it's cold	97	2	1
4.	A dressing gown	42	56	2
5.	Two pairs of all weather shoes	74	25	1
6.	New, not second hand, clothes	65	34	1
7.	A television	58	41	1
8.	A roast joint or its vegetarian equivalent once a week	64	35	1
9.	Carpets in living rooms and bedrooms in the home	78	21	1
10.	Telephone	56	43	1
11.	Refrigerator	92	7	1
12.	Indoor toilet, not shared with another household	97	3	*
13.	Bath, not shared with another household	95	4	1
14.	Beds for everyone in the household	95	4	1
15.	Damp-free home	97	2	1
16.	A car	26	73	1
17.	A night out once a fortnight	42	57	1
18.	A packet of cigarettes every other day	18	79	3
19.	A hobby or leisure activity	67	32	1
20.	A holiday away from home for one week a year, not with relatives	54	45	1

21.	Celebrations on special occasions such as Christmas	74	25	1
22.	Presents for friends or family once a year	69	30	1
23.	Friends/family round for a meal once a month	37	61	2
24.	A warm waterproof coat	91	8	1
25.	A "best outfit" for special occasions	54	45	1
26.	A washing machine	73	26	1
27.	*3meals a day for children	90	8	2
28.	*Toys for children e.g. dolls or models	85	14	1
29.	*Leisure equipment for children e.g. sports equipment or a bicycle	61	38	1
30.	*Enough bedrooms for every child over 10 of different sex to have his/her own bedroom	82	16	2
31.	*An outing for children once a week	53	45	2
32.	*Children's friends round for tea/ a snack once a fortnight	46	2	

SHUFFLEBOARD SIDE 1 AND BLUE CARDS

EXCLUDE CARDS 43 AND 44 (ASTERISKED), WHICH RELATE TO CHILDREN

Q5 **On these cards are a number of different items which relate to our standard of living. Please would you indicate by placing the cards in the appropriate box the living standards you feel all adults should have in Britain today. BOX A is for items which you think are necessary, which all adults should be able to afford and which they should not have to do without. BOX B is for items which may be desirable but are not necessary.**

GIVE CARDS 43 AND 44 RELATING TO CHILDREN(*)

Q6 Now could you do the same, this time thinking of a family with children.

		A Necessary	B Desirable	DK
33.	A dishwasher	5	94	1
34.	A meal in a restaurant once a month	17	82	1
35.	Regular savings (of £10 a month) for 'rainy days' or retirement	67	31	2
36.	A video	13	85	2
37.	Enough money to keep your home in a decent state of decoration	92	7	1
38.	Holidays abroad once a year	17	81	2

275

39. Coach/train fares to visit family/friends in other parts of the country four times a year	39	59	2
40. Insurance of contents of dwelling	88	11	1
41. Fresh fruit and vegetables every day	88	11	1
42. A home computer	5	92	3
43. *Paying for special lessons such as music, dance or sport	59	2	
44. *Participation in out-of-school activities e.g. sports, orchestra/band, Scouts/Guides	69	29	2

SHOWCARD A

Q7 Why, in your opinion, are there people who live in need? Here are four opinions - which is the closest to yours?

Because they have been unlucky	10
Because of laziness and lack of willpower	20
Because there is much injustice in our society	40
It's an inevitable part of modern progress	19
None of these	3
Don't know	8

Q8 Still thinking about people who lack the things you have said are necessities for living in Britain today, do you think that the Government is doing too much, too little or about the right amount to help these people?

Too much	5
Too little	70
About the right amount	18
Don't know	7

Q9a   If the Government proposed to increase income tax by one penny (1p) in the pound to enable everyone to afford the items you have said are necessities, on balance would you support or oppose this policy?

Support	75	**GO TO Q9b**
Oppose	18	**GO TO Q10**
Don't know	7	**GO TO Q10**

Q9b   If the Government proposed to increase income tax by five pence (5p) in the pound to enable everyone to afford the items you have said are necessities, on balance would you support or oppose this policy? *(Number answering 1369)*

Support	43	(58)
Oppose	26	(35)
Don't know	6	(7)

Q10   Thinking about the items you have said are necessities, most people in Britain will be able to afford all of them. But some will lack one or more because they can't afford them. How many of these necessities would someone have to lack, because they can't afford them, before you would describe them as living in poverty by the standards of Britain today?

One	3	Six	5
Two	3	Seven	2
Three	5	Eight to Ten	16
Four	4	More than Ten	27
Five	6	Don't know	29

EXCLUDE CARDS 27 TO 32 (ASTERISKED), IF NO CHILDREN LIVING AT HOME

Q11 Now, could you please put the cream cards into these four boxes:

	A Have and couldn't do without	B Have and could do without	C Don't have but don't want	D Don't have and can't afford	NA DK
Two meals a day	81	13	4	1	1
Meat/fish/vegn equivalent every other day	64	26	5	3	2
Heating to warm living areas of the home if it's cold	91	5	*	3	1
A dressing gown	34	50	14	1	1
Two pairs of all weather shoes	70	20	5	4	1
New, not second hand clothes	58	31	5	4	2
A television	57	39	1	1	2
A roast joint or its vegetarian equivalent once a week	47	37	9	6	1
Carpets in living rooms and bedrooms in the home	76	20	1	2	1
Telephone	62	25	5	7	1
Refrigerator	91	6	1	1	1
Indoor toilet, not shared with another household	95	3	1	*	1
Bath, not shared with another household	94	4	1	*	1
Beds for everyone in the household	95	2	*	1	2
Damp-free home	91	3	2	2	2
A car	41	22	17	18	2
A night out once a fortnight	23	39	22	14	2
A packet of cigarettes every other day	19	17	56	5	3
A hobby or leisure activity	48	28	15	6	3
A holiday away from home for one week a year, not with relatives	31	34	13	20	2
Celebrations on special occasions such as Xmas	63	28	4	4	1
Presents for friends or family once a year	59	30	4	5	2
Friends/family round for a meal once a month	26	42	19	10	3
A warm waterproof coat	80	11	4	4	1
A "best outfit" for special occasions	46	39	5	8	2
A washing machine	71	16	6	4	3
*3 meals a day for children	25	3	1	*	71
*Toys for children e.g. dolls or models	21	7	*	1	71
*Leisure equipment for children e.g. sports equipment or a bicycle	15	11	1	2	71
*Enough bedrooms for every child over 10 of different sex to have his/her own bedroom	21	4	1	2	72
*An outing for children once a week	10	12	2	4	72
*Children's friends round for tea/a snack once a fortnight	7	14	5	2	72

SHUFFLEBOARD SIDE 2 AND BLUE CARDS

EXCLUDE CARDS 43 AND 44 (ASTERISKED), IF NO CHILDREN LIVING AT HOME

Q12   Now, could you please put the blue cards into these four boxes:

	A Have and couldn't do without	B Have and could do without	C Don't have but don't want	D Don't have and can't afford	N/A DK
A dishwasher	4	13	64	18	1
A meal in a restaurant once a month	8	35	33	22	2
Regular savings (of £10 a month) for ' rainy days' or retirement	45	15	6	30	4
A video	13	53	21	11	2
Enough money to keep your home in a decent state of decoration	75	6	2	15	2
Holidays abroad once a year	12	26	28	32	2
Coach/train fares to visit family/friends in other parts of the country four times a year	20	28	27	19	6
Insurance of contents of dwelling	78	5	4	10	3
Fresh fruit and vegetables every day	75	13	5	6	1
A home computer	3	20	58	16	3
*Paying for special lessons such as music, dance or sport	6	8	8	6	72
Participation in out-of-school activities e.g. sports, orchestra/band, Scouts/Guides	11	8	5	3	73

Q13a   A number of people have told us they have had to miss out on meals because of a lack of money. Have there been times during the past year when you did not have enough money to buy food you (and your family) needed?

Q13b   Have there been times in the past year when you've felt isolated and cut off from society because of lack of money ?

	Q13a Food	Q13b Isolated
Yes	11	17
No	88	81
Don't know	1	2

Q14   Have there been times during the past year when you were seriously behind in paying for any of the following items?

Rent	6
Gas	5
Electricity	7
Goods on hire purchase	2
Mortgage repayments	2
Community Charge/Poll Tax	14
Credit card payments	2
Mail order catalogue payments	3
Telephone	4
Other loans	2
None of these	77
No answer	*

Q15   And have there been times during the past year when you have had to borrow money from a) friends or family or b) money lenders, excluding banks or building societies, in order to pay for your day-to-day needs?

	Friends/family	*Moneylenders*
Yes	20	2
No	80	96
Don't know	*	2

Q16 **Do you think you could genuinely say you are poor now, all the time, sometimes, or never?**

All the time	10
Sometimes	25
Never	64
Don't know	1

SHOWCARD C

Q17 **Looking back over your adult life, how often have there been times in your life when you think you have lived in poverty by the standards of that time?**

Never	53
Rarely	15
Occasionally	19
Often	8
Most of the time	4
Don't know	1

SHOWCARD D

Q18 **A number of people have told us they have different kinds of personal difficulties these days. Which if any of the items on this card have you worried about or have you experienced in the past month due to lack of money?**

1	Being depressed	16
2	Relations with your friends	2
3	Relations with your family	4
4	Being bored	13
5	Not having enough money for day-to-day living	12
6	Feeling looked down upon by other people	4
7	Feeling a failure	6
8	Lack of hope for the future	11
9	Letting down your family	8
10	None of these	65
11	No answer	*

Q19   **(FOR THOSE WITH CHILDREN OF SCHOOL AGE ONLY) Here is a list of problems which some children of school age have experienced at school. Which, if any, of the following apply to your children?**

Child has missed classes because of teacher shortage	4
Child has shared school books in key subjects	4
Child has found difficulty in obtaining school books for homework	3
Other problems due to lack of resources at school:	3
None	1
	1
DK	5

Q20a   **Would you describe the state of repair of your home as good, adequate or poor?**

Good	62	
Adequate	29	
Poor	8	**GO TO Q20b**
Don't know	1	

Q20b   **If state of repair described as POOR: Why do you say that?**

Can't afford repairs	2
Landlord has failed to make repairs	4
Haven't got around to doing repairs	1
Other	1
Don't know	*

Q21   **Now, on the subject of crime, which, if any, of the following applies to you or other members of your household?**

Burgled in the last year	7
Mugged/robbed in the last year	2
Assaulted in the last year	3
Feel unsafe in local neighbourhood	17
Other	3
None of these	71
Don't know	*

Q22 I am going to read out a number of services which affect our standard of living which are usually provided or subsidised by local councils or other public bodies. Please could you tell me whether you think that these services are essential and should be available or whether they may be desirable but are not essential.

	Essential	Desirable	DK
ALL ADULTS			
Libraries	79	20	1
Public sports facilities e.g. swimming pools	79	20	1
Museums and galleries	52	47	1
Evening classes	70	28	2
Frequent and regular bus services	96	2	2
FAMILIES WITH CHILDREN UNDER 5			
Childcare facilities such as nurseries or playgroups	90	9	1
Play facilities for children to play safely nearby	92	7	1
FAMILIES WITH SCHOOL AGE CHILDREN			
Good quality school meals	87	11	2
PENSIONERS OR PEOPLE WITH DISABILITIES			
Access to home help	95	2	3
Access to meals on wheels	93	4	3
Special transport for those with mobility problems	95	2	3

Q23 Now, could you please tell me the category in which you would put the following items.

	Use - adequate	Use - in-adequate	Don't use - don't want/ not relevant	Don't use - unavail-able/ unsuit-able	Don't use - can't afford	Don't know
ALL ADULTS						
Libraries	56	8	33	2	*	1
Public sports facilities e.g. swimming pools	44	10	39	4	1	2
Museums and galleries	32	7	49	8	2	2
Evening classes	19	3	68	5	2	3
Frequent and regular bus services	46	21	27	4	*	2

FAMILIES WITH CHILDREN UNDER 5 (*Number answering 305*)

	Use - adequate	Use - in-adequate	Don't use - don't want/ not relevant	Don't use - unavail-able/ unsuit-able	Don't use - can't afford	Don't know
Childcare facilities such as nurseries or playgroups	7	3	4	2	*	1
	(42)	(18)	(24)	(8)	(1)	(7)
Play facilities for children to play safely nearby	6	5	3	2	*	1
	(35)	(27)	(16)	(15)	(*)	(7)

FAMILIES WITH SCHOOL AGE CHILDREN (*Number answering 447*)

	Use - adequate	Use - in-adequate	Don't use - don't want/ not relevant	Don't use - unavail-able/ unsuit-able	Don't use - can't afford	Don't know
Good quality school meals	10	3	4	1	*	6
	(39)	(12)	(19)	(5)	(*)	(25)

PENSIONERS OR PEOPLE WITH DISABILITIES (*Number answering 657*)

	Use - adequate	Use - in-adequate	Don't use - don't want/ not relevant	Don't use - unavail-able/ unsuit-able	Don't use - can't afford	Don't know
Access to home help	3	1	16	1	*	15
	(9)	(2)	(45)	(2)	(1)	(42)
Access to meals on wheels	1	*	19	1	0	15
	(3)	(1)	(52)	(2)	(0)	(42)
Special transport for those with mobility problems	3	1	16	1	0	15
	(8)	(2)	(46)	(3)	(0)	(41)

UNEMPLOYMENT

I'd now like to ask you some questions about unemployment. By unemployment, I mean either those registered as unemployed or those not entitled to benefit but available for and seeking work.

Q24 Are you/your spouse/partner unemployed at present? If yes, for how long?

	Respondent	Spouse/Partner
Yes, up to 3 months	3	1
Yes, 3 to 5 months	1	*
Yes, 6 to 11 months	1	1
Yes, 12 months or longer	7	3
No, not currently unemployed	55	39
Not applicable	33	56

Q25 Have you/your spouse/partner been unemployed in the last year?

	Respondent (1008)		Spouse/Partner (709)	
Yes	4	(7)	2	(6)
No	49	(89)	35	(90)
Not applicable	2	(4)	2	(4)

SHOWCARD I

Q26 Looking back over the last ten years, for how long have you been unemployed?

Never	43
Less than 2 months in total	4
2 to 6 months in total	7
7 to 12 months in total	3
Over 12 months in total	17
Not relevant	21
Don't know	5

Q27a   Do you or does anybody else in your household have any long-standing illness, disability or infirmity? By long-standing I mean anything that has troubled you over a period of time or that is likely to affect you over a period of time.

Yes, respondent	20
Yes, other household member/s	14
No	68
No answer	1

Q27b   Are you/anybody else in your household registered as disabled or in receipt of a disability benefit such as attendance allowance or need physical aids such as a wheel chair?

Yes, respondent	6
Yes, other household member/s	5
No	88
No answer	2

Q28a   How many times have you consulted a Doctor for reasons other than pregnancy, contraception, screening or other preventative health care services in the last 12 months?

None	27
1 to 2	31
3 to 4	14
5 to 7	9
8 to 10	2
11 to 15	6
16+	3
Don't know	1
Not applicable	3
No answer	4

Q28b How many times have other members of your household consulted a Doctor for reasons other than pregnancy, contraception, screening or other preventative health care services in the last 12 months?

None	18
1 to 2	18
3 to 4	9
5 to 7	8
8 to 10	4
11 to 15	5
16+	3
Don't know	4
Not applicable	28
No answer	3

Q29a How many times have you required hospital treatment for reasons other than pregnancy, screening or other preventative health care in the last 12 months? *(Number answering 1695)*

None	64	*(69)*
1	12	*(13)*
2	4	*(5)*
3	2	*(2)*
4 to 5	1	*(1)*
6 to 9	1	*(1)*
10+	2	*(2)*
Don't know	1	*(1)*
Not applicable	6	*(6)*

Q29b How many times have other members of your household required hospital treatment for reasons other than pregnancy, screening or other preventative health care in the last 12 months? *(Number answering 1732)*

None	44	*(46)*
1	11	*(11)*
2	4	*(4)*
3	2	*(2)*
4 to 5	1	*(2)*
6 to 9	1	*(1)*
10 plus	1	*(1)*
Don't know	2	*(2)*
Not applicable	29	*(31)*

Q30   How many people in this household at present receive: (READ OUT)

	None	One	Two	Three +	No answer
Unemployment benefit	91	6	1	*	2
Sickness benefit	94	3	*	0	3
Invalidity pension	91	6	*	*	3
Income support, the old supplementary benefit	85	12	1	*	2
Family credit, the old FIS	95	2	*	*	3
Housing benefit	82	14	2	*	2
Community charge/Poll Tax benefit	75	16	7	*	2
Attendance or mobility allowance (or other disability benefit)	92	4	*	0	4
A state retirement pension	74	16	8	*	2
An occupational or private pension	80	17	1	0	2

Q31   Do you or does your spouse/partner get Income Support, the old supplementary benefit, nowadays or not?   If yes, for how long have you/has he/she been getting it?

Yes, for up to 3 months	1	
Yes, for up to 6 months	1	
Yes, for up to 12 months	2	
Yes, for over a year	8	
No	87	**ASK Q32**
No answer	1	

Q32   Have you or your spouse <u>ever</u> received Income Support/Supplementary Benefit, except as a student, or not? *(Number answering 1589)*

Yes, in the last year	3	*(3)*
Yes, in the last 5 years	6	*(7)*
Yes, more than 5 years ago	4	*(5)*
No, never	73	*(84)*
No answer	1	*(1)*

IF IN WORK, ASK Q33, IF NOT GO TO Q34

Q33 **Do you contribute to an occupational/private pension scheme or not?**
(Number answering 967)

Yes	28	*(53)*
No	24	*(46)*
Don't know	1	*(1)*

SHOWCARD J

INCOME

Q 34 **Please could you indicate the letter from this card for the group in which you place the total household income <u>after deductions for tax and national insurance</u>. Does this figure include?**

All earnings from every source
Child Benefit (IF CHILDREN IN HOUSEHOLD)
Housing benefit
Community Charge/Poll Tax benefit
All Social Security benefits
Income of both husband/wife
Income of other members of the household (e.g. parents, adult son/daughter)
Income from investment and savings

Net Income/Take Home Pay (per week)	Number	Net Income/Take Home Pay (per week)	Number
Under £50	4	£200-£224	5
£50-59	4	£225-£249	4
£60-69	3	£250-£299	6
£70-79	4	£300-£349	4
£80-89	3	£350-£400	3
£90-99	3	£400-£499	3
£100-124	6	£500-£599	3
£125-£149	6	£600 plus	3
£150-£174	5	Don't know	15
£175-£199	5	Refused to say	11

(IF DON'T KNOW PER WEEK, ASK FOR NET INCOME PER YEAR)

IF HOUSEHOLD RECEIVES INCOME SUPPORT OR HOUSING BENEFIT (see Q30), ASK Qs35 & 36. OTHERS GO TO Q37

Q35a When you gave me your household income, did you include all contributions to the cost of the rent paid on your behalf in the figure you gave?

Yes	11	**ASK Q36**
No	6	**GO TO Q35b**
Not applicable	83	

Q35b How much income is your household receiving from Housing benefit?

IF HOUSEHOLD RECEIVES COMMUNITY CHARGE/POLL TAX BENEFIT (see Q30), ASK:

Q36a And did you include all contributions to the cost of your Community Charge/Poll Tax in the figure you gave?

Yes	9	**GO TO Q37**
No	9	**ASK Q36b**
Not applicable	82	

Q36b And how much income is your household receiving from Community Charge/Poll Tax benefit?

Q37 Generally speaking, do you think of yourself as Conservative, Labour, Liberal Democrat, Green or what?

Conservative	22
Labour	24
Liberal Democrat	7
Green	4
Other	2
None/Don't know/Refused to say	43

Q38 And finally, I've been asking you all these questions for one of the ITV television companies. They'd be very interested in talking directly to some of the people who have helped in the survey. They do not at this stage want to ask to film you, just to talk to you. Would you be prepared to be contacted by the television company?

Yes	35
No	56
No answer	9

DERIVED DEMOGRAPHICS

C1 AGE OF RESPONDENT

Age range	Male (878)		Female (953)	
16 to 19	4	*(8)*	4	*(8)*
20 to 24	4	*(8)*	4	*(8)*
25 to 34	9	*(19)*	10	*(20)*
35 to 44	7	*(16)*	8	*(16)*
45 to 54	7	*(14)*	7	*(13)*
55 to 59	4	*(8)*	3	*(6)*
60 to 64	4	*(8)*	4	*(7)*
65 to 69	3	*(7)*	4	*(8)*
70 to 74	3	*(6)*	3	*(5)*
75 to 79	2	*(4)*	3	*(5)*
80 plus	1	*(2)*	2	*(4)*

C2 HEAD OF HOUSEHOLD

Head of household	62
Not head of household	38

C3 OCCUPATION OF HEAD OF HOUSEHOLD

AB	14
C1	26
C2	23
D	19
E	18

C4   HOME OWNERSHIP DETAILS *(Number answering 1829)*

Owned outright	23
Being bought on mortgage	43
Rented from local authority	26
Rented from private landlord	5
Housing association	1
Other	2

C5   ACCOMMODATION DETAILS *(Number answering 1825)*

House/bungalow (entire property)	80
Flat/maisonette	19
Single room/bedsit	1
Other	*

C6   EMPLOYMENT STATUS

	Respondent (442)		Head of Household (1829)	
Full time (31+hours)	6	*(27)*	55	*(55)*
Part time (8 to 30 hours)	2	*(9)*	4	*(4)*
Not working (0 to 7 hours)	1	*(3)*	1	*(1)*
In full time education or training	1	*(4)*	2	*(2)*
Unemployed and seeking work	3	*(12)*	5	*(5)*
Unemployed but not seeking work	3	*(11)*	4	*(4)*
Housewife	3	*(12)*	6	*(6)*
Retired	5	*(22)*	23	*(23)*

C7   NUMBER IN HOUSEHOLD

	Frequency		*Frequency*
One	25	Five	6
Two	34	Six	1
Three	17	Seven Plus	1
Four	16		

C8 to C12 CHILDREN IN HOUSEHOLD

	None	One	Two	Three +
Aged 0 to 5	83	12	4	1
Aged 6 to 10	87	9	3	1
Aged 11 to 15	88	9	3	*
Aged 16 to 17	92	7	1	*
Aged 18+	91	8	1	*

C13   **TYPE OF HOUSEHOLD** (CODE MUST DESCRIBE <u>ALL</u> MEMBERS OF HOUSEHOLD FULLY, SINGLE CODE ONLY)

Single person, retired	14
Single person, not retired	11
Couple, no children, retired	10
Couple, no children, not retired	20
Couple, 1 child under 18	8
Couple, 2 children under 18	12
Couple, 3 children under 18	4
Couple, 4+ children under 18	1
Lone parent, 1 child under 16	2
Lone parent, 2 children under 16	2
Three adults (no children under 16):	
Couple plus adult child	5
Couple plus non-retired lodger, relative, friend	1
Couple plus retired person	1
Other	9

C14   **MARITAL STATUS** *(Number answering 1823)*

Married/cohabiting	59
Widowed	13
Divorced/separated	7
Single	21
Other	*

QA   Please could you tell me which of the categories on this card best describes your race or ethnic origin? *(Number answering 1806)*

Afro-Caribbean/African	2	*(2)*
Asian	1	*(1)*
Irish	1	*(1)*
White UK	93	*(94)*
Other	2	*(2)*

QB   What were the highest educational or professional qualifications you had when you left full time education?

QC   Since leaving full time education, have you gained any additional qualifications from full or part time study?   IF YES: Which ones? (CODE HIGHEST QUALIFICATIONS BELOW)

	QB (1747)		QC (1684)	
Government training scheme certificate	*	*(*)*	*	*(*)*
School certificate	7	*(7)*	*	*(*)*
CSE's	7	*(8)*	*	*(*)*
GCE O levels or equivalent	16	*(17)*	1	*(1)*
GCE A levels or equivalent	6	*(6)*	*	*(*)*
BTEC	*	*(*)*	1	*(1)*
ONC/OND	*	*(*)*	1	*(1)*
HNC/HND	*	*(*)*	1	*(2)*
City & Guilds	1	*(1)*	4	*(5)*
Membership of chartered institute	0	*(0)*	1	*(1)*
Other professional qualifications	2	*(2)*	6	*(6)*
Degree or higher	5	*(5)*	2	*(2)*
Still in full time education	0	*(0)*	0	*(0)*
Other	4	*(4)*	9	*(9)*
None	47	*(50)*	66	*(72)*

Appendix III: Additional tables

Table A.1
The perception of necessities: 1983 and 1990 compared

Standard-of-living items in rank order	% claiming item as necessity	
	1990	1983
A damp-free home	98	96
Heating to warm living areas in the home if it's cold	97	97
An inside toilet (not shared with another household)	97	96
Bath, not shared with another household	95	94
Beds for everyone in the household	95	94
A decent state of decoration in the home	92	-
Fridge	92	77
Warm waterproof coat	91	87
Three meals a day for children	90	82
Two meals a day (for adults)	90	64
Insurance of contents of dwelling	88	-
Daily fresh fruit and vegetables	88	-
Toys for children e.g. dolls or models	84	71
Bedrooms for every child over 10 of different sexes	82	77
Carpets in living rooms and bedrooms	78	70
Meat/fish (or vegetarian equivalent) every other day	77	63
Two pairs all-weather shoes	74	78
Celebrations on special occasions	74	69
Washing machine	73	67
Presents for friends or family once a year	69	63
Child's participation in out-of-school activities	69	-
Regular savings of £10 a month for "rainy days" or retirement	68	-
Hobby or leisure activity	67	64
New, not second hand, clothes	65	64
Weekly roast/vegetarian equivalent	64	67
Leisure equipment for children e.g. sports equipment	61	57
A television	58	51
A telephone	56	43
An annual week's holiday away, not with relatives	54	63
A "best outfit" for special occasions	54	48
An outing for children once a week	53	40
Children's friends round for tea/snack fortnightly	52	37
A dressing gown	42	38
A night out fortnightly	42	36
Child's music/dance/sport lessons	39	-
Fares to visit friends in other parts of the country 4 times a year	39	-
Friends/family for a meal monthly	37	32
A car	26	22
Pack of cigarettes every other day	18	14
Holidays abroad annually	17	-
Restaurant meal monthly	17	-
A video	13	-
A home computer	5	-
A dishwasher	4	-

Table A.2
Percent lacking item because they can't afford it: 1983 and 1990 compared

	% lacking each items	
	1990	1983
A damp-free home	2	7
Heating to warm living areas in the home if it's cold	3	5
An inside toilet (not shared with another household)	*	2
Bath, not shared with another household	*	2
Beds for everyone in the household	1	1
A decent state of decoration in the home	15	-
Fridge	1	2
Warm waterproof coat	4	7
Three meals a day for children	*	2
Two meals a day (for adults)	1	3
Insurance of contents of dwelling	10	-
Daily fresh fruit and vegetables	6	-
Toys for children e.g. dolls or models	1	2
Bedrooms for every child over 10 of different sexes	2	3
Carpets in living rooms and bedrooms	2	2
Meat/fish (or vegetarian equivalent) every other day	3	8
Two pairs all-weather shoes	4	9
Celebrations on special occasions	4	4
Washing machine	4	6
Presents for friends or family once a year	5	5
Child's participation in out-of-school activities	3	-
Regular savings of £10 a month for "rainy days" or retirement	30	-
Hobby or leisure activity	6	7
New, not second hand, clothes	4	6
Weekly roast/vegetarian equivalent	6	7
Leisure equipment for children e.g. sports equipment	2	6
A television	1	*
A telephone	7	11
An annual week's holiday away, not with relatives	20	21
A "best outfit" for special occasions	8	10
An outing for children once a week	4	9
Children's friends round for tea/snack fortnightly	2	5
A dressing gown	1	3
A night out fortnightly	14	17
Child's music/dance/sport lessons	6	-
Fares to visit friends in other parts of the country 4 times a year	19	-
Friends/family for a meal monthly	10	11
A car	18	22
Pack of cigarettes every other day	5	6
Holidays abroad annually	32	-
Restaurant meal monthly	22	-
A video	11	-
A home computer	16	-
A dishwasher	18	-

297

Table A.3
Deprivation and the perception of necessities

Standard-of-living items in rank order for the whole sample

	Less Deprived	Multiply Deprived
A damp-free home	97	98
Heating to warm living areas in the home if it's cold	97	97
An inside toilet (not shared with another household)	97	96
Bath, not shared with another household	95	96
Beds for everyone in the household	94	96
A decent state of decoration in the home	91	94
Fridge	92	92
Warm waterproof coat	92	88
Three meals a day for children	90	91
Two meals a day (for adults)	90	87
Insurance of contents of dwelling	89	88
Daily fresh fruit and vegetables	89	83
Toys for children e.g. dolls or models	85	83
Bedrooms for every child over 10 of different sexes	81	88
Carpets in living rooms and bedrooms	76	87
Meat/fish (or vegetarian equivalent) every other day	76	79
Two pairs all-weather shoes	74	75
Celebrations on special occasions	75	71
Washing machine	71	78
Presents for friends or family once a year	69	67
Child's participation in out-of-school activities	70	66
Regular savings of £10 a month for "rainy days" or retirement	68	66
Hobby or leisure activity	70	57
New, not second hand, clothes	64	69
Weekly roast/vegetarian equivalent	63	68
Leisure equipment for children e.g. sports equipment	60	62
A television	56	67
A telephone	57	53
An annual week's holiday away, not with relatives	56	50
A "best outfit" for special occasions	56	48
An outing for children once a week	52	55
Children's friends round for tea/snack fortnightly	53	51
A dressing gown	42	43
A night out fortnightly	41	45
Child's music/dance/sport lessons	40	35
Fares to visit friends in other parts of the country 4 times a year	38	39
Friends/family for a meal monthly	39	30
A car	28	21
Pack of cigarettes every other day	15	28
Holidays abroad annually	18	15
Restaurant meal monthly	17	15
A video	12	15
A home computer	5	5
A dishwasher	4	6

Table A.4
Present level of poverty and the perception of necessities
Q.16 'Do you think you could genuinely say you are poor now, all the time, sometimes, or never?'

Standard-of-living items in rank order for the whole sample	All the	Sometimes	Never
A damp-free home	97	98	98
Heating to warm living areas in the home if it's cold	96	98	96
An inside toilet (not shared with another household)	98	95	97
Bath, not shared with another household	95	95	95
Beds for everyone in the household	95	98	93
A decent state of decoration in the home	91	93	92
Fridge	88	92	93
Warm waterproof coat	87	92	92
Three meals a day for children	89	91	91
Two meals a day (for adults)	88	89	91
Insurance of contents of dwelling	85	89	89
Daily fresh fruit and vegetables	83	87	89
Toys for children e.g. dolls or models	86	83	85
Bedrooms for every child over 10 of different sexes	88	87	80
Carpets in living rooms and bedrooms	88	88	73
Meat/fish (or vegetarian equivalent) every other day	78	80	76
Two pairs all-weather shoes	75	78	72
Celebrations on special occasions	80	72	74
Washing machine	77	73	72
Presents for friends or family once a year	70	71	69
Child's participation in out-of-school activities	64	66	71
Regular savings of £10 a month for "rainy days" or retirement	65	66	69
Hobby or leisure activity	62	64	70
New, not second hand, clothes	70	63	65
Weekly roast/vegetarian equivalent	71	66	62
Leisure equipment for children e.g. sports equipment	66	63	59
A television	68	60	56
A telephone	61	54	57
An annual week's holiday away, not with relatives	56	55	54
A "best outfit" for special occasions	57	57	53
An outing for children once a week	61	55	51
Children's friends round for tea/snack fortnightly	61	46	53
A dressing gown	51	39	42
A night out fortnightly	54	45	40
Child's music/dance/sport lessons	35	36	41
Fares to visit friends in other parts of the country 4 times a year	46	36	38
Friends/family for a meal monthly	39	34	38
A car	21	23	28
Pack of cigarettes every other day	33	24	13
Holidays abroad annually	17	19	16
Restaurant meal monthly	20	17	17
A video	20	17	10
A home computer	8	7	4
A dishwasher	6	6	4

Table A.5 History of poverty and the perception of necessities

Q.17 'Looking back over your adult life, how often have there been times in your life when you think you have lived in poverty by the standards of that time?'

Standard-of-living items in rank order for the whole sample	Never (n=977)	Rarely (n=277)	Occasionally (n=343)	Often (n=150)	Most of the time (n=65)
A damp-free home	97	97	99	97	99
Heating to warm living areas in the home if it's cold	97	96	98	94	98
An inside toilet (not shared with another household)	97	95	96	96	97
Bath, not shared with another household	97	92	94	94	97
Beds for everyone in the household	94	94	96	97	96
A decent state of decoration in the home	92	89	93	94	92
Fridge	93	92	95	82	89
Warm waterproof coat	91	95	92	85	88
Three meals a day for children	91	92	87	93	94
Two meals a day (for adults)	92	88	88	88	84
Insurance of contents of dwelling	90	90	88	83	85
Daily fresh fruit and vegetables	89	88	89	85	77
Toys for children e.g. dolls or models	84	86	83	83	91
Bedrooms for every child over 10 of different sexes	80	84	84	86	95
Carpets in living rooms and bedrooms	75	79	85	84	86
Meat/fish (or vegetarian equivalent) every other day	75	77	79	80	78
Two pairs all-weather shoes	71	79	76	81	67
Celebrations on special occasions	74	76	72	72	83
Washing machine	72	72	74	75	78
Presents for friends or family once a year	67	74	69	70	72
Child's participation in out-of-school activities	68	73	70	69	61
Regular savings of £10 a month for "rainy days"	68	67	68	67	71
Hobby or leisure activity	69	74	64	58	61
New, not second hand, clothes	67	60	63	69	72
Weekly roast/vegetarian equivalent	63	64	65	64	74
Leisure equipment for children e.g. sports equipment	58	67	64	59	66
A television	56	53	61	61	77
A telephone	56	53	56	59	63
An annual week's holiday away, not with relatives	53	57	57	52	59
A "best outfit" for special occasions	55	56	53	47	60
An outing for children once a week	52	53	50	62	67
Children's friends round for tea/snack fortnightly	52	56	49	59	55
A dressing gown	41	41	42	43	62
A night out fortnightly	41	42	41	50	49
Child's music/dance/sport lessons	39	42	38	41	33
Fares to visit friends in other parts of the country	38	37	40	47	34
Friends/family for a meal monthly	36	46	33	37	43
A car	28	25	24	28	22
Pack of cigarettes every other day	14	16	19	28	36
Holidays abroad annually	17	20	16	17	18
Restaurant meal monthly	17	19	16	16	17
A video	11	16	14	18	22
A home computer	5	5	6	3	13
A dishwasher	5	3	5	4	4

Table A.6
Education and the perception of necessities

Standard-of-living items in rank order for the whole sample	Degree or equiv.	A'Level or equiv.	GCE/ CSE	None
A damp-free home	95	100	98	99
Heating to warm living areas in the home if it's cold	93	99	97	98
An inside toilet (not shared with another household)	96	97	98	96
Bath, not shared with another household	94	98	98	94
Beds for everyone in the household	94	96	96	95
A decent state of decoration in the home	91	89	90	94
Fridge	90	94	92	92
Warm waterproof coat	94	96	92	91
Three meals a day for children	85	87	92	91
Two meals a day (for adults)	85	90	91	90
Insurance of contents of dwelling	91	90	88	89
Daily fresh fruit and vegetables	91	92	86	88
Toys for children e.g. dolls or models	85	81	86	83
Bedrooms for every child over 10 of different sexes	77	76	79	88
Carpets in living rooms and bedrooms	64	77	82	82
Meat/fish (or vegetarian equivalent) every other day	78	84	77	77
Two pairs all-weather shoes	68	77	70	80
Celebrations on special occasions	75	65	77	74
Washing machine	55	59	76	79
Presents for friends or family once a year	62	70	72	70
Child's participation in out-of-school activities	74	80	67	67
Regular savings of £10 a month for "rainy days"	66	72	70	66
Hobby or leisure activity	76	74	67	64
New, not second hand, clothes	53	61	65	72
Weekly roast/vegetarian equivalent	51	51	60	73
Leisure equipment for children e.g. sports equipment	59	56	62	61
A television	41	33	56	67
A telephone	53	44	53	61
An annual week's holiday away, not with relatives	53	34	55	59
A "best outfit" for special occasions	47	52	59	56
An outing for children once a week	44	55	53	55
Children's friends round for tea/snack fortnightly	57	51	45	54
A dressing gown	31	28	39	52
A night out fortnightly	33	45	44	45
Child's music/dance/sport lessons	44	28	39	37
Fares to visit friends in other parts of the country	38	22	36	44
Friends/family for a meal monthly	37	36	35	39
A car	24	23	28	28
Pack of cigarettes every other day	10	15	16	21
Holidays abroad annually	13	11	19	17
Restaurant meal monthly	16	7	17	19
A video	11	8	12	16
A home computer	3	5	6	6
A dishwasher	3	5	5	5

Table A.7
Social class and the perception of necessities
Social Class (% classing item as necessity)

Standard-of-living items in rank order for sample	AB	C1	C2	D	E
A damp-free home	97	98	98	99	96
Heating to warm living areas in the home if it's cold	97	96	96	98	96
An inside toilet (not shared with another household)	95	98	96	95	97
Bath, not shared with another household	94	96	95	95	94
Beds for everyone in the household	93	95	95	96	94
A decent state of decoration in the home	92	89	93	95	92
Fridge	92	93	95	89	90
Warm waterproof coat	92	94	91	89	89
Three meals a day for children	88	91	90	92	89
Two meals a day (for adults)	91	89	90	90	88
Insurance of contents of dwelling	93	90	87	90	82
Daily fresh fruit and vegetables	94	90	87	85	85
Toys for children e.g. dolls or models	83	84	84	83	87
Bedrooms for every child over 10 of different sexes	79	80	82	84	86
Carpets in living rooms and bedrooms	62	74	80	85	90
Meat/fish (or vegetarian equivalent) every other day	77	78	79	71	77
Two pairs all-weather shoes	67	68	77	78	79
Celebrations on special occasions	71	73	76	73	77
Washing machine	63	69	77	80	74
Presents for friends or family once a year	62	66	71	70	75
Child's participation in out-of-school activities	84	72	67	61	63
Regular savings of £10 a month for "rainy days"	72	66	73	66	61
Hobby or leisure activity	77	70	68	66	57
New, not second hand, clothes	60	63	65	72	66
Weekly roast/vegetarian equivalent	62	59	68	66	65
Leisure equipment for children e.g. sports equipment	59	61	61	61	61
A television	42	52	61	65	68
A telephone	49	60	55	53	62
An annual week's holiday away, not with relatives	52	51	54	62	54
A "best outfit" for special occasions	42	55	56	59	58
An outing for children once a week	51	47	54	60	54
Children's friends round for tea/snack fortnightly	61	53	50	49	50
A dressing gown	42	34	41	42	57
A night out fortnightly	35	41	46	48	39
Child's music/dance/sport lessons	42	44	42	34	31
Fares to visit friends in other parts of the country	32	35	40	42	43
Friends/family for a meal monthly	44	36	39	34	36
A Car	25	28	32	28	17
Pack of cigarettes every other day	8	10	20	24	26
Holidays abroad annually	12	17	19	19	17
Restaurant meal monthly	17	13	19	18	19
A video	5	12	13	18	17
A home computer	5	3	7	4	7
A dishwasher	3	4	5	6	5

Age groups	(% classing item as necessity)					
Standard-of-living items in rank order	16-24	25-34	35-44	45-54	55-64	65+
A damp-free home	95	98	99	98	98	97
Heating to warm living areas in the home if it's cold	97	97	96	98	96	97
An inside toilet (not shared with another household)	96	97	98	97	98	95
Bath, not shared with another household	93	98	97	92	96	94
Beds for everyone in the household	95	98	96	93	95	91
A decent state of decoration in the home	91	90	92	91	94	93
Fridge	92	93	92	93	92	90
Warm waterproof coat	85	91	93	93	93	92
Three meals a day for children	93	89	90	90	89	91
Two meals a day (for adults)	95	86	86	85	91	93
Insurance of contents of dwelling	87	88	90	89	91	86
Daily fresh fruit and vegetables	87	86	87	90	89	88
Toys for children e.g. dolls or models	90	84	84	82	83	84
Bedrooms for every child over 10 of different sexes	77	76	86	84	89	83
Carpets in living rooms and bedrooms	82	79	76	75	75	82
Meat/fish (or vegetarian equivalent) every other day	70	76	74	84	74	81
Two pairs all-weather shoes	63	68	75	76	78	82
Celebrations on special occasions	77	71	80	71	67	76
Washing machine	68	73	77	76	75	68
Presents for friends or family once a year	72	69	65	67	64	74
Child's participation in out-of-school activities	64	66	71	74	73	67
Regular savings of £10 a month for "rainy days"	68	64	72	72	68	63
Hobby or leisure activity	67	63	73	65	75	64
New, not second hand, clothes	59	61	64	73	67	69
Weekly roast/vegetarian equivalent	55	51	68	71	71	70
Leisure equipment for children e.g. sports equipment	62	62	60	60	60	59
A television	53	48	57	51	64	72
A telephone	45	49	51	53	62	74
An annual week's holiday away, not with relatives	46	48	57	55	63	58
A "best outfit" for special occasions	54	49	55	54	55	60
An outing for children once a week	57	51	53	50	57	51
Children's friends round for tea/snack fortnightly	50	45	49	52	57	59
A dressing gown	24	32	34	42	53	65
A night out fortnightly	50	43	47	42	40	34
Child's music/dance/sport lessons	38	35	35	44	41	41
Fares to visit friends in other parts of the country	31	31	35	39	42	52
Friends/family for a meal monthly	35	30	37	33	45	44
A car	22	25	25	32	33	24
Pack of cigarettes every other day	20	14	20	19	19	15
Holidays abroad annually	23	17	11	14	22	16
Restaurant meal monthly	13	13	18	19	22	18
A video	17	13	10	13	14	12
A home computer	4	8	6	4	6	4
A dishwasher	4	3	6	4	6	4

Table A.9
Sex and the perception of necessities

Standard-of-living items in rank order for the whole sample	Male (n=878)	Female (n=953)
A damp-free home	97	98
Heating to warm living areas in the home if it's cold	96	97
An inside toilet (not shared with another household)	96	97
Bath, not shared with another household	95	96
Beds for everyone in the household	94	95
A decent state of decoration in the home	92	92
Fridge	91	93
Warm waterproof coat	90	92
Three meals a day for children	89	92
Two meals a day (for adults)	89	91
Insurance of contents of dwelling	87	89
Daily fresh fruit and vegetables	86	90
Toys for children e.g. dolls or models	84	84
Bedrooms for every child over 10 of different sexes	82	83
Carpets in living rooms and bedrooms	79	78
Meat/fish (or vegetarian equivalent) every other day	73	79
Two pairs all-weather shoes	72	75
Celebrations on special occasions	73	75
Washing machine	72	74
Presents for friends or family once a year	65	72
Child's participation in out-of-school activities	65	72
Regular savings of £10 a month for "rainy days" or retirement	70	65
Hobby or leisure activity	70	65
New, not second hand, clothes	68	63
Weekly roast/vegetarian equivalent	64	64
Leisure equipment for children e.g. sports equipment or bicycle	65	57
A television	58	58
A telephone	54	58
An annual week's holiday away, not with relatives	58	51
A "best outfit" for special occasions	58	51
An outing for children once a week	55	51
Children's friends round for tea/snack fortnightly	48	56
A dressing gown	35	50
A night out fortnightly	46	39
Child's music/dance/sport lessons	38	40
Fares to visit friends in other parts of the country 4 times a year	39	38
Friends/family for a meal monthly	38	37
A car	28	25
Pack of cigarettes every other day	19	17
Holidays abroad annually	21	14
Restaurant meal monthly	19	15
A video	15	11
A home computer	6	5
A dishwasher	6	3

Household type and the perception of necessities (% classing item as necessity)

Standard-of-living items in rank order for the sample as a whole	Pensioners All Groups (n=439)	Lone parent (n=73)	All with Children (n=458)	All others (n=659)	Single people (n=201)
A damp-free home	96	95	98	98	98
Heating to warm living areas in the home if it's cold	97	96	96	98	94
An inside toilet (not shared with another household)	95	98	97	97	97
Bath, not shared with another household	93	95	96	95	95
Beds for everyone in the household	90	100	96	96	94
A decent state of decoration in the home	92	92	91	92	93
Fridge	91	89	94	94	85
Warm waterproof coat	92	85	91	91	91
Three meals a day for children	91	83	90	92	86
Two meals a day (for adults)	93	82	89	90	86
Insurance of contents of dwelling	87	81	90	91	80
Daily fresh fruit and vegetables	88	92	88	90	80
Toys for children e.g. dolls or models	84	89	85	85	82
Bedrooms for every child over 10 of different sexes	85	80	79	84	79
Carpets in living rooms and bedrooms	80	90	79	76	79
Meat/fish (or vegetarian equivalent) every other day	80	71	75	77	72
Two pairs all-weather shoes	81	69	71	72	74
Celebrations on special occasions	75	73	80	71	69
Washing machine	69	72	82	73	58
Presents for friends or family once a year	71	68	72	66	66
Child's participation in out-of-school activities	69	70	69	70	63
Regular savings of £10 a month for "rainy days"	64	58	65	73	65
Hobby or leisure activity	65	58	65	71	69
New, not second hand, clothes	67	65	63	65	68
Weekly roast/vegetarian equivalent	67	63	59	65	66
Leisure equipment for children	58	59	63	62	60
A television	69	63	56	52	56
A telephone	73	36	50	53	52
An annual week's holiday away, not with relatives	60	41	51	54	54
A "best outfit" for special occasions	58	61	51	52	59
An outing for children once a week	55	59	48	54	57
Children's friends round for tea/snack fortnightly	60	65	41	53	54
A dressing gown	63	36	35	38	31
A night out fortnightly	37	47	38	44	57
Child's music/dance/sport lessons	39	38	39	40	35
Fares to visit friends in other parts of the country	51	30	29	37	40
Friends/family for a meal monthly	44	29	33	37	37
A car	25	11	31	30	14
Pack of cigarettes every other day	14	32	15	16	30
Holidays abroad annually	16	11	14	20	18
Restaurant meal monthly	21	19	14	16	19
A video	11	14	12	14	14
A home computer	3	6	8	5	3
A dishwasher	4	3	4	6	3

Table A.11
Political views and the perception of necessities
People identifying with (% classing item as necessity)

Standard-of-living items in rank order for sample as a whole	Con (n=395)	Lab (n=435)	Lib Dem (n=122)	Greens (n=61)
A damp-free home	98	98	97	98
Heating to warm living areas in the home if it's cold	95	97	96	100
An inside toilet (not shared with another household)	98	95	96	95
Bath, not shared with another household	97	95	95	94
Beds for everyone in the household	93	93	91	100
A decent state of decoration in the home	95	91	94	96
Fridge	93	94	88	93
Warm waterproof coat	88	91	97	97
Three meals a day for children	90	91	87	91
Two meals a day (for adults)	90	92	86	82
Insurance of contents of dwelling	89	91	91	78
Daily fresh fruit and vegetables	87	86	97	96
Toys for children e.g. dolls or models	85	81	82	98
Bedrooms for every child over 10 of different sexes	80	84	78	87
Carpets in living rooms and bedrooms	71	85	68	61
Meat/fish (or vegetarian equivalent) every other day	76	76	78	87
Two pairs all-weather shoes	67	77	68	84
Celebrations on special occasions	72	79	79	73
Washing machine	68	79	69	67
Presents for friends or family once a year	67	70	64	62
Child's participation in out-of-school activities	77	65	83	78
Regular savings of £10 a month for "rainy days"	69	68	79	60
Hobby or leisure activity	72	69	76	80
New, not second hand, clothes	62	69	59	45
Weekly roast/vegetarian equivalent	64	70	66	54
Leisure equipment for children	59	67	62	70
A television	54	62	46	47
A telephone	63	59	54	53
An annual week's holiday away, not with relatives	54	62	40	48
A "best outfit" for special occasions	49	58	47	47
An outing for children once a week	50	59	48	45
Children's friends round for tea/snack fortnightly	56	50	52	55
A dressing gown	42	42	42	25
A night out fortnightly	35	49	30	44
Child's music/dance/sport lessons	47	40	41	61
Fares to visit friends in other parts of the	32	41	34	43
Friends/family for a meal monthly	40	37	37	43
A car	31	30	25	26
Pack of cigarettes every other day	13	19	8	10
Holidays abroad annually	10	21	14	7
Restaurant meal monthly	15	19	12	9
A video	7	14	6	14
A home computer	4	6	3	3
A dishwasher	3	5	4	3

Table A.12
Political views and commitment to necessities

Q.9a "'If the Government proposed to increase income tax by one penny (1p) in the pound to enable everyone to afford the items you have said are necessities, on balance would you support or oppose this policy?"

	All (n=1,014)	Con	People identifying with (%) Lab	Lib Dem	Greens
Support	74	70	73	79	91
Oppose	21	26	20	17	5
Don't Know	5	4	7	4	4

Table A.13

Q.9b "If the Government proposed to increase income tax by five pence (5p) in the pound to enable everyone to afford the items you have said are necessities, on balance would you support or oppose this policy?"(question applies to those who agree with a penny increase in tax.

	All (n=746)	Con	People identifying with (%) Lab	Lib Dem	Greens
Support	56	45	64	61	61
Oppose	37	51	27	34	31
Don't Know	7	4	9	5	8

Table A.14
The relationship between the perception of necessities and possession of items

Standard-of-living items in rank order	% claiming	% of population
A damp-free home	98	94
Heating to warm living areas in the home if it's cold	97	96
An inside toilet (not shared with another household)	97	98
Bath, not shared with another household	95	97
Beds for everyone in the household	95	97
A decent state of decoration in the home	92	81
Fridge	92	98
Warm waterproof coat	91	91
Three meals a day for children	90	*74*
Two meals a day (for adults)	90	94
Insurance of contents of dwelling	88	83
Daily fresh fruit and vegetables	88	88
Toys for children e.g. dolls or models	84	*75*
Bedrooms for every child over 10 of different sexes	82	*65*
Carpets in living rooms and bedrooms	78	96
Meat/fish (or vegetarian equivalent) every other day	77	90
Two pairs all-weather shoes	74	90
Celebrations on special occasions	74	91
Washing machine	73	88
Presents for friends or family once a year	69	90
Child's participation in out-of-school activities	69	*50*
Regular savings of £10 a month for "rainy days" or retirement	68	60
Hobby or leisure activity	67	76
New, not second hand, clothes	65	89
Weekly roast/vegetarian equivalent	64	84
Leisure equipment for children e.g. sports equipment	61	*67*
A television	58	97
A telephone	56	87
An annual week's holiday away, not with relatives	54	65
A "best outfit" for special occasions	54	85
An outing for children once a week	53	*58*
Children's friends round for tea/snack fortnightly	52	*55*
A dressing gown	42	83
A night out fortnightly	42	62
Child's music/dance/sport lessons	39	*38*
Fares to visit friends in other parts of the country 4 times year	39	48
Friends/family for a meal monthly	37	67
A car	26	63
Pack of cigarettes every other day	18	37
Holidays abroad annually	17	38
Restaurant meal monthly	17	44
A video	13	66
A home computer	5	26
A dishwasher	4	17

Note: Figures in italics= Families with children only

308

Table A.15
The personal possession of items and the perception of necessities

Standard-of-living items in rank order for sample as a whole	Have/ could not do without	Have/ could do without	Don't have/ don't want	Don't have/ can't afford
A damp-free home	98	88	(97)	(89)
Heating to warm living areas in the home if it's cold	97	88	-	-
An inside toilet (not shared with another household)	97	92	-	-
Bath, not shared with another household	96	77	(52)	-
Beds for everyone in the household	97	(56)	-	-
A decent state of decoration in the home	94	75	(83)	90
Fridge	95	63	-	-
Warm waterproof coat	95	78	76	79
Three meals a day for children	95	62	-	-
Two meals a day (for adults)	95	67	59	74
Insurance of contents of dwelling	95	61	31	77
Daily fresh fruit and vegetables	94	74	48	79
Toys for children e.g. dolls or models	94	63	-	-
Bedrooms for every child over 10 of different sexes	89	49	(76)	(68)
Carpets in living rooms and bedrooms	88	48	(21)	(71)
Meat/fish (or vegetarian equivalent) every other day	88	58	26	77
Two pairs all-weather shoes	85	49	16	63
Celebrations on special occasions	84	61	37	48
Washing machine	85	44	28	54
Presents for friends or family once a year	82	51	24	56
Child's participation in out-of-school activities	82	66	59	62
Regular savings of £10 a month for "rainy days"	88	51	23	56
Hobby or leisure activity	84	61	39	47
New, not second hand, clothes	80	42	49	62
Weekly roast/vegetarian equivalent	88	45	25	48
Leisure equipment for children	80	48	(53)	(57)
A television	76	31	-	-
A telephone	70	34	15	38
An annual week's holiday away, not with relatives	79	49	28	47
A "best outfit" for special occasions	75	40	22	32
An outing for children once a week	73	38	(16)	44
Children's friends round for tea/snack fortnightly	72	41	12	(38)
A dressing gown	73	30	14	(44)
A night out fortnightly	68	41	18	44
Child's music/dance/sport lessons	66	35	27	33
Fares to visit friends in other parts of the country	69	34	22	39
Friends/family for a meal monthly	62	34	16	26
A car	47	18	6	12
Pack of cigarettes every other day	56	19	5	16
Holidays abroad annually	50	16	5	15
Restaurant meal monthly	60	18	7	13
A video	48	9	3	10
A home computer	21	8	3	8
A dishwasher	25	7	2	7

Anglo-American Securities Regulation

This important and innovative book examines the regulation of the earliest securities markets in England and the United States, from their origins in the 1690s until the 1850s. Stuart Banner argues that by the reign of Queen Anne a complex and moderately effective body of regulatory control was already extant, reflecting widespread English (and later American) attitudes toward securities speculation. He uses both traditional legal materials (including court opinions, statutes and legal treatises) as well as a broad range of non-legal sources (novels, broadsides, engravings) to examine contemporary images of stock markets and speculation practices, and he shows that securities regulation has a much longer ancestry than is often supposed. Insights from both legal and cultural history are utilized to explain how popular thought about the securities market was translated into regulation and, reciprocally, how that regulation influenced market structures and the activities of speculators.

This is a comprehensive treatment of a major theme in the development of corporate practice, of interest to all those with both academic and professional expertise in securities regulation.

STUART BANNER is Associate Professor of Law at Washington University, St Louis, Missouri. This is his first book.

Anglo-American
Securities Regulation

Cultural and Political Roots, 1690–1860

Stuart Banner

Washington University School of Law

CAMBRIDGE
UNIVERSITY PRESS

PUBLISHED BY THE PRESS SYNDICATE OF THE UNIVERSITY OF CAMBRIDGE
The Pitt Building, Trumpington Street, Cambridge CB2 1RP, United Kingdom

CAMBRIDGE UNIVERSITY PRESS
The Edinburgh Building, Cambridge CB2 2RU, United Kingdom
http://www.cup.cam.ac.uk
40 West 20th Street, New York, NY 10011–4211, USA
http://www.cup.org
10 Stamford Road, Oakleigh, Melbourne 3166, Australia

First published 1998

Printed in the United Kingdom at the University Press, Cambridge

Typeset in Plantin 10/12pt [CE]

A catalogue record for this book is available from the British Library

Library of Congress cataloguing in publication data

Banner, Stuart Alan, 1963–
Anglo-American securities regulation / Stuart Alan Banner.
    p.   cm.
Includes bibliographical references and index.
ISBN 0 521 62231 X (hb)
1. Securities – Great Britain – History.
2. Securities – United States – History.
I. Title.
K1114.B36   1998
346.42′092–dc21   97–27893   CIP

ISBN 0 521 62231 X hardback

For my father, who would have enjoyed it the most.

Philosopher: *And what kind of business is this about which I have often heard people talk but which I neither understand nor have ever made efforts to comprehend? And I have found no book that deals with the subject and makes apprehension easier.*

Shareholder: *I really must say that you are an ignorant person, friend Greybeard, if you know nothing of this enigmatic business which is at once the fairest and most deceitful in Europe, the noblest and the most infamous in the world, the finest and the most vulgar on earth. It is a quintessence of academic learning and a paragon of fraudulence; it is a touchstone for the intelligent and a tombstone for the audacious, a treasury of usefulness and a source of disaster . . .*

Joseph de la Vega, *Confusión de Confusiones* (1688), trans. Hermann Kellenbenz, in Martin S. Fridson, ed., *Extraordinary Popular Delusions and the Madness of Crowds & Confusión de Confusiones* (New York: John Wiley & Sons, 1996), 147.

Contents

Selected statutes and cases	*page* viii
Acknowledgments	xvi
Note on dates	xvii
Abbreviations	xviii
Introduction	1
1 English attitudes toward securities trading at its inception, 1690–1720	14
2 The South Sea Bubble and English law, 1720–1722	41
3 English securities regulation in the eighteenth century	88
4 The development of American attitudes toward securities trading, 1720–1792	122
5 American securities regulation, 1789–1800	161
6 American attitudes toward securities trading, 1792–1860	190
7 American securities regulation, 1800–1860	222
8 Self-regulation by the New York brokers, 1791–1860	250
Conclusion	281
Bibliography	290
Index	316

Selected statutes and cases

37 Hen. VIII c. 9 (1545)	22
5 & 6 Ed. VI c. 14 (1552)	15
13 Eliz. c. 8 (1571)	22
2 Jac. I c. 21 (1604)	20
8 & 9 Wm. III c. 32 (1697)	40, 223
6 Anne c. 16 (1708)	40
10 Anne c. 19 (1711)	40
6 Geo. I c. 18 (1720) (Bubble Act)	75–77
7 Geo. I stat. 2 (1721)	82
8 Geo. I c. 22 (1722)	82
7 Geo. II c. 8 (1734) (Barnard's Act)	105, 224
10 Geo. II c. 8 (1737)	105
14 Geo. II c. 37 (1741)	127
7 Geo. III c. 48 (1766)	109
6 Geo. IV c. 91 (1825) (Bubble Act repeal)	79
23 and 24 Vic. c. 28 (1860) (Barnard's Act repeal)	107
1 Stat. 65 (1789) (Treasury Act)	162–63
1 Stat. 138 (1790)	139
1 Stat. 191 (1791)	180, 232
1 Stat. 215 (1791)	163
1 Stat. 279 (1792)	163
12 Stat. 432 (1862)	227
30 Stat. 448 (1898)	170
38 Stat. 745 (1914)	170
40 Stat. 300 (1917)	171
79 Stat. 136 (1965)	171
15 U.S.C. § 78p	81, 111
31 U.S.C. § 329	164
Ala. Laws 1827–31, p. 3 (1828)	230
Conn. Laws, May Sess. 1818, c. X	188

Ill. Laws 1845, p. 4   227
Ind. Laws 1847, c. 42   227
Ind. Laws 1858–59, c. 17   230
Ky. Laws 1851, p. 271   227
Mass. Laws 1804, c. 125   229
Mass. Laws 1809, c. 65   229
Mass. Laws 1833, c. 187   229
Mass. Laws 1834, c. 161   228
Mass. Laws 1836, c. 279   174
Mass. Laws 1846, c. 45   229
Mass. Laws 1910, c. 171   174
Md. Laws 1841–42, c. 282   223–24, 227
Mich. Laws 1855, No. 109   229
Mich. Laws 1855, No. 128   243
Miss. Laws 1840, c. 1   226
N.C. Laws 1836–37, c. 11   229
N.H. Laws 1849, c. 860   229
N.Y. Laws, 15th Sess., c. 62 (1792) (stockjobbing act)   173
N.Y. Laws, 24th Sess., c. 116 (1801)   173
N.Y. Laws, 36th Sess., c. 70 (1813)   173
N.Y. Laws, 40th Sess., c. 275 (1817)   174
N.Y. Laws, 60th Sess., c. 235 (1837)   225–26
N.Y. Laws, 78th Sess., c. 155 (1855)   242
N.Y. Laws, 81st Sess., c. 134 (1858) (stockjobbing
    act repeal)   174
N.Y. Laws, 128th Sess., c. 241 (1905)   171
Pa. Laws 1812–17, c. 3902 (1814)   229
Pa. Laws 1824, c. 47   227, 229
Pa. Laws 1841, No. 140   223–24, 227
Tenn. Laws 1849–50, c. 72   229
Va. Laws 1834, c. 1   227
Va. Laws 1841–42, c. 3   227
Wis. Laws 1853, c. 68   230

Alexander v. *Macauley's Administrators*, 6 Md. 359 (1854)   244
Anonymous, 2 DeSaussure (2 S.C. Eq.) 333 (1806)   184
Arnold v. *Ruggles*, 1 R.I. 165 (1837)   187
Atkinson v. *Executors of Scott*, 1 Bay (1 S.C.) 307 (1793)   184
Bacon v. *Sanford*, 1 Root 164 (Conn. 1790)   237
Bank of Attica v. *Manufacturers' and Traders' Bank*, 20 N.Y. 501
    (1859)   233
Bank of Utica v. *Smalley*, 2 Cow. 770 (N.Y. Sup. Ct. 1824)   234

Bank of Washington v. *Arthur*, 3 Gratt. (44 Va.) 165 (1846)   186
Barrett v. *Hyde*, 73 Mass. 160 (1856)   178
Bates v. *N.Y. Ins. Co.*, 3 Johns. Cas. 238 (N.Y. Sup. Ct. 1802)   245
Batten v. *Whorewood*, Barn. C. 421, 27 Eng. Rep. 703 (Ch. 1740)   118
Bell v. *Mali*, 11 How. Pr. 254 (N.Y. Sup. Ct. 1855)   238, 242
Black v. *Zacharie & Co.*, 3 How. (44 U.S.) 483 (1845)   235
Blackwell v. *Nash*, 8 Mod. 105, 1 Str. 535, 88 Eng. Rep. 83 (K.B.
  1723), aff'd, 8 Mod. 106 (Ex. Ch. 1724)   112
Board of Commissioners of Tippecanoe Cty. v. *Reynolds*, 44 Ind.
  509 (1873)   243
Brachan v. *Griffin*, 3 Call. (3 Va.) 433 (1803)   182
Broadway Bank v. *McElrath*, 13 N.J. Eq. 24 (1860)   235
Brown v. *Holt*, 4 Taunt. 587, 128 Eng. Rep. 460 (C.P. 1812)   79
Buck v. *Buck*, 1 Camp. 547, 170 Eng. Rep. 1052 (N.P. 1808)   79
Bullock v. *Noke*, 1 Strange 579, 93 Eng. Rep. 712 (K.B. 1724)   113
Butler v. *M. Ins. Co.*, 14 Ala. 777 (1848)   244
Cannan v. *Bryce*, 3 Barn. & Ald. 179, 106 Eng. Rep. 628
  (K.B. 1819)   115
Case of Sutton's Hospital, 10 Co. Rep. 23a, 77 Eng. Rep. 960
  (K.B. 1615)   78
Cassard v. *Hinmann*, 14 How. Pr. 84 (N.Y. Super. 1856)   175, 183
Cazeaux v. *Mali*, 25 Barb. 578 (N.Y. App. Div. 1857)   241–43
Child v. *Morley*, 8 Term Rep. 610, 101 Eng. Rep. 1574 (K.B. 1800)   116
Chillas v. *Snyder*, 1 Phila. Rep. 289 (1852)   223
Clark v. *Tyson*, 1 Strange 504, 93 Eng. Rep. 663 (K.B. 1722)   113
Cleveland v. *Loder & Draper*, 7 Paige Ch. 557 (N.Y. Ch. 1839)   186
Cock v. *Goodfellow*, 10 Mod. 489, 88 Eng. Rep. 822 (Ch. 1722)   118
Coleman v. *Spencer*, 5 Blackf. 197 (Ind. 1839)   231
Colt v. *Woollaston*, 2 P. Wms. 154, 24 Eng. Rep. 679 (Ch. 1723)   117
Commercial Bank of Buffalo v. *Kortright*, 22 Wend. 348
  (N.Y. 1839)   234, 246
Conant, Ellis & Co. v. *Reed*, 1 Ohio St. 298 (1853)   235
Cowles v. *Cromwell*, 25 Barb. 413 (N.Y. App. Div. 1857)   245
Cross v. *Sackett*, 15 N.Y. Super. 617 (1858)   216, 241–42
Crossman v. *Penrose Ferry Bridge Co.*, 26 Pa. 69 (1856)   237
Crowell v. *Jackson*, 23 A. 426 (N.J. 1891)   243
Crump v. *United States Mining Co.*, 48 Va. 352 (1851)   237
Cud v. *Rutter*, 1 P. Wms. 570, 24 Eng. Rep. 521 (Ch. 1719)   114
Cunningham v. *Edgefield and Kentucky R.R. Co.*, 39 Tenn. 22 (1858)   237
Dauchy v. *Brown*, 24 Vt. 197 (1852)   245
Davis v. *Executors of Richardson*, 1 Bay (1 S.C.) 105 (1790)   189
Delaware and Atlantic R.R. Co. v. *Irick*, 23 N.J.L. 321 (1852)   245

Denton v. *Livingston*, 9 Johns. 96 (N.Y. Sup. Ct. 1812)   187
Dorvill v. *Aynesworth*, 1 Barn. K.B. 28, 94 Eng. Rep. 19
   (K.B. 1727)   113
Douglass & Mandeville v. *McAllister*, 3 Cranch (7 U.S.) 298 (1806)   189
Downing v. *Potts*, 23 N.J.L. 66 (1851)   245
Duke v. *Cahawba Navigation Co.*, 10 Ala. 82 (1846)   235
Dunn v. *Commercial Bank of Buffalo*, 11 Barb. 580 (N.Y. App. Div.
   1852)   235
Dutch v. *Warren*, 1 Strange 406, 93 Eng. Rep. 598 (K.B. 1720)   114
Dykers v. *Allen*, 7 Hill 497 (N.Y. 1844)   175, 246, 248
Eagleson v. *Shotwell*, 1 Johns. Ch. 536 (N.Y. Ch. 1815)   186
Eames v. *Wheeler*, 36 Mass. 442 (1837)   229
Ellison v. *Bignold*, 2 Jac. & W. 503, 37 Eng. Rep. 720 (Ch. 1821)   79
Everhart v. *West Chester and Philadelphia R.R. Co.*, 28 Pa. 339
   (1857)   245
Faikney v. *Reynous*, 4 Burr. 2069, 98 Eng. Rep. 79 (K.B. 1767)   115
Farmers and Mechanics Bank of Frederick Cty. v. *Wayman*,
   5 Gill 336 (Md. 1847)   244
Fisher v. *Essex Bank*, 71 Mass. 375 (1855)   231–32
Fiske v. *Carr*, 20 Me. 301 (1841)   231
Forrest v. *Elwes*, 4 Ves. Jun. 492, 31 Eng. Rep. 252 (Ch. 1799)   114
Frost v. *Clarkson & Clarkson*, 7 Cow. 24 (N.Y. Sup. Ct. 1827)   178
Gardener v. *Pullen & Phillips*, 2 Vern. 394, 23 Eng. Rep. 853
   (Ch. 1700)   114
Gerhard v. *Bates*, 2 El. & Bl. 476, 118 Eng. Rep. 845 (K.B. 1853)   242
Gibson v. *Fristoe*, 5 Call. (9 Va.) 62 (1797)   183
Gilchreest v. *Pollock*, 2 Yeates (7 Pa.) 18 (1795)   182
Graham v. *Bickham*, 4 Dall. (4 U.S.) 149 (1796)   130
Gram v. *Stebbins & Stebbins*, 6 Paige Ch. 124 (N.Y. Ch. 1836)   176
Grant v. *Mechanics' Bank of Philadelphia*, 15 Serg. & Rawle 140
   (Pa. 1827)   229
Greenhow's administratrix v. *Harris*, 20 Va. 472 (1820)   184
Groves v. *Graves*, 1 Wash. (1 Va.) 1 (1790)   130, 189
Hall v. *Cupper*, Skin. 391, 90 Eng. Rep. 174 (K.B. 1693)   112
Harrison v. *Hart*, 1 Comyns 393, 92 Eng. Rep. 1126 (K.B. 1727)   118
Harrison v. *Pryse*, Barn. C. 324, 27 Eng. Rep. 664 (Ch. 1740)   118
Helm v. *Swiggett*, 12 Ind. 194 (1859)   231
Hildyard v. *South-Sea Co.*, 2 P. Wms. 76, 24 Eng. Rep. 647
   (Ch. 1722)   118
Horton v. *Morgan*, 19 N.Y. 170 (1859)   243, 247
Howe v. *Starkweather*, 17 Mass. 240 (1821)   187
In re Empire City Bank, 6 Abb. Pr. 385 (N.Y. Sup. Ct. 1857)   245

In re Long Island R.R. Co., 19 Wend. 36 (N.Y. Sup. Ct. 1837)   245

Jacobs v. Crosley, 2 Barn. K.B. 156, 94 Eng. Rep. 418 (K.B. 1732)   113

James v. Woodruff, 2 Denio 574 (N.Y. 1845), aff'g 10 Paige Ch. 541
(N.Y. Ch. 1844)   245

Johnson v. East-India Co., Rep. Temp. Finch 430,
23 Eng. Rep. 234 (Ch. 1679)   118

Jones v. Brinley, 1 East 1, 102 Eng. Rep. 1 (K.B. 1800)   119

Josephs v. Pebrer, 3 B. & C. 639, 107 Eng. Rep. 870 (K.B. 1825)   79

Kortright v. Buffalo Commercial Bank, 20 Wend. 91 (N.Y. Sup. Ct.
1838)   234

Krause v. Setley, 2 Phila. Rep. 32 (1856)   223

Lancashire v. Killingworth, 13 Mod. 529, 88 Eng. Rep. 1498
(K.B. 1701)   112

Landreth Timber Co. v. Landreth, 471 U.S. 681 (1985)   7

Lane v. Morris, 8 Ga. 468 (1850)   245

Litchfield Bank v. Peck, 29 Conn. 384 (1860)   237

Livingston v. Swanwick, 2 Dall. (2 U.S.) 300 (C.C.D.Pa. 1793)   130

Lock v. Wright, 8 Mod. 40, 88 Eng. Rep. 30 (K.B. 1722)   113

Lowry v. Commercial & Farmers' Bank, 15 F. Cas. 1040
(C.C.D. Md. 1848)   228

Mabey v. Adams, 16 N.Y. Super. 346 (1858)   237

Mallory v. Leach, 35 Vt. 156 (1862)   243

Mann v. Currie, 2 Barb. 294 (N.Y. Sup. Ct. 1848)   245

Marlborough Mfg. Co. v. Smith, 2 Conn. 579 (1818)   231

Mead v. Mali, 15 How. Pr. 347 (N.Y. Super. 1857)   237, 243

Mechanics' Bank v. New-York and New Haven R.R. Co.,
13 N.Y. 599 (1856)   229, 236

Mechanics Bank of Alexandria v. Seton, 1 Pet. (26 U.S.) 299 (1828)   244

Merchants Bank v. Cook, 21 Mass. 405 (1826)   245

Metcalf v. Bruin, 12 East 400, 104 Eng. Rep. 156 (K.B. 1810)   79

Miller v. Illinois Central R.R. Co., 24 Barb. 312 (N.Y. App. Div.
1857)   245

Mitchell v. Broughton, 1 Ld. Raym. 674, 91 Eng. Rep. 1349
(K.B. 1701)   40

Moffat v. Winslow, 7 Paige Ch. 124 (N.Y. Ch. 1838)   240

Monk v. Graham, 8 Mod. 9, 88 Eng. Rep. 8 (C.P. 1721)   118

Mordant v. Small, 8 Mod. 218, 88 Eng. Rep. 156 (K.B. 1724)   113

Morgan v. Thames Bank, 14 Conn. 99 (1840)   245

Morris v. Langdale, 2 Bos. & Pul. 284, 126 Eng. Rep. 1284
(C.P. 1800)   120

Morse v. Swits, 19 How. Pr. 275 (N.Y. Sup. Ct. 1859)   242

Moses v. Macferlan, 2 Burr. 1005, 97 Eng. Rep. 676 (K.B. 1760)   114

Munn v. *Barnum*, 24 Barb. 283 (N.Y. App. Div. 1857)   244

Munn v. *East-India Co.*, Rep. Temp. Finch 298, 23 Eng. Rep. 163
(Ch. 1677)   118

Muskungum Valley Tpk. Co. v. *Ward*, 13 Ohio 120 (1844)   245

Nathan v. *Whitlock*, 9 Paige Ch. 152 (N.Y. Ch. 1841)   245

Nesmith v. *Washington Bank*, 23 Mass. 324 (1828)   225

New England Commercial Bank v. *Newport Steam Factory*,
6 R.I. 154 (1859)   245

Newbery v. *Garland*, 31 Barb. 121 (N.Y. App. Div. 1860)   242

Nightingal v. *Devisme*, 5 Burr. 2589, 98 Eng. Rep. 361 (K.B. 1770)   118

Northrop v. *Curtis*, 5 Conn. 246 (1824)   231

Northrop v. *Newton and Bridgeport Tpk. Co.*, 3 Conn. 544
(1821)   180, 231

Nourse v. *Prime, Ward and Sands*, 4 Johns. Ch. 490 (N.Y. Ch. 1820)   247

Nourse v. *Prime, Ward, and Sands*, 7 Johns. Ch. 69 (N.Y. Ch. 1823)   185

Noyes v. *Spaulding*, 27 Vt. 419 (1855)   182

Nugent v. *Cincinnati, Harrison & Indianapolis Straight Line R.R. Co.*,
2 Disn. 302 (Ohio Super. 1858)   239

Oxford Tpk. Co. v. *Bunnel*, 6 Conn. 552 (1827)   231

Palmer v. *Ridge Mining Co.*, 34 Pa. 288 (1859)   245

Peckham v. *Ketcham*, 10 Abb. Pr. 220 (N.Y. Super. 1860)   248

People v. *Devlin*, 17 Ill. 84 (1855)   245

Petrie v. *Hannay*, 3 Term Rep. 418, 100 Eng. Rep. 652 (K.B. 1789)   115

Philip v. *Kirkpatrick*, Add. (5 Va.) 124 (1793)   183

Pickering v. *Appleby*, 1 Comyns 354, 92 Eng. Rep. 1108 (K.B. 1721)   118

Pollock v. *National Bank*, 7 N.Y. 274 (1852)   245

Potter v. *Yale College*, 8 Conn. 51 (1830)   185

Powell v. *Hankey*, 2 P. Wms. 82, 24 Eng. Rep. 649 (Ch. 1722)   118

Pratt v. *Hutchinson*, 15 East 511, 104 Eng. Rep. 936 (K.B. 1813)   79

Presbyterian Congregation v. *Carlisle Bank*, 5 Pa. 345 (1847)   233

Quiner v. *Marblehead Social Ins. Co.*, 10 Mass. 475 (1813)   225

Reed v. *Ingraham*, 3 Dall. (3 U.S.) 505 (Pa. 1799)   234

Reves v. *Ernst & Young*, 494 U.S. 56 (1990)   7

Rex v. *Caywood*, 1 Strange 472, 93 Eng. Rep. 641 (K.B. 1722)   78

Rex v. *Dodd*, 9 East 516, 103 Eng. Rep. 670 (K.B. 1808)   78

Rex v. *Webb*, 14 East 406, 104 Eng. Rep. 658 (K.B. 1811)   79

Rianhard v. *Hovey*, 13 Ohio 300 (1844)   245

Ridgely v. *Riggs*, 4 Har. & J. (8 Md.) 358 (1818)   182

Rives v. *Montgomery South Plank-Road Co.*, 30 Ala. 92 (1857)   238

Roberts v. *Tremayne*, Cro. Jac. 507, 79 Eng. Rep. 433 (K.B.
1618)   22, 183

Rogers v. *Huntingdon Bank*, 12 Serg. & Rawle 77 (Pa. 1824)   229

Rogers v. *Wilson*, 1 Comyns 365, 92 Eng. Rep. 1114 (K.B. 1723)   82
Roosevelt v. *Brown*, 11 N.Y. 148 (1854)   245
Rose v. *Dickson*, 7 Johns. 196 (N.Y. Sup. Ct. 1810)   185
Sabin v. *Bank of Woodstock*, 21 Vt. 353 (1849)   231
Salem Mill-Dam Corp. v. *Ropes*, 26 Mass. 187 (1829)   239
Sanders v. *Kentish*, 8 Term Rep. 162, 101 Eng. Rep. 1323
    (K.B. 1799)   115
Sargent v. *Essex Marine Ry. Co.*, 26 Mass. 201 (1829)   232
Sargent v. *Franklin Ins. Co.*, 25 Mass. 90 (1829)   232
SEC v. *W.J. Howey Co.*, 328 U.S. 293 (1946)   7
Shales v. *Seignoret*, 1 Ld. Raym. 440, 91 Eng. Rep. 1192
    (K.B. 1699)   112
Shepherd v. *Hampton*, 3 Wheat. (16 U.S.) 200 (1818)   189
Shepherd v. *Johnson*, 2 East 211, 102 Eng. Rep. 349 (K.B.
    1802)   115, 189
Skipwith v. *Gibson and Jefferson*, 4 Hen. & M. (14 Va.) 490 (1810)   184
Smith v. *Nicholas*, 8 Leigh (35 Va.) 330 (1837)   186
Smith v. *Westall*, 1 Ld. Raym. 316, 91 Eng. Rep. 1106 (K.B. 1697)   40
Spencer v. *Spencer*, 11 Paige Ch. 299 (N.Y. Ch. 1844)   244
Stamford Bank v. *Ferris*, 17 Conn. 258 (1845)   245
Staples v. *Gould*, 9 N.Y. 520 (1854), aff'g 7 N.Y. Super. 411 (1852)   176
State v. *Jefferson Tpk. Co.*, 22 Tenn. 305 (1842)   238
Stebbins v. *Leowulf*, 57 Mass. 137 (1849)   177
Stebbins v. *Phenix Fire Ins. Co.*, 3 Paige Ch. 350 (N.Y. Ch. 1832)   234
Steers v. *Lashley*, 6 Term Rep. 61, 101 Eng. Rep. 435 (K.B. 1794)   115
Stent v. *Bailis*, 2 P. Wms. 217, 24 Eng. Rep. 705 (Ch. 1724)   113
Steptoe's administrators v. *Harvey's executors*, 7 Leigh (34 Va.) 501
    (1836)   186
Stribbling v. *Bank of the Valley*, 5 Rand. (26 Va.) 132 (1827)   185
Tate v. *Wellings*, 3 Term Rep. 531, 100 Eng. Rep. 716 (K.B. 1790)   117
Thompson v. *Alger*, 53 Mass. 428 (1847)   178
Thomson v. *Harcourt*, 1 Brown 193, 1 Eng. Rep. 508 (H.L. 1722)   86–87
Thornton v. *Moulton*, 1 Strange 533, 93 Eng. Rep. 682 (K.B. 1723)   113
Trenchard v. *Wanley*, 2 P. Wms. 166, 24 Eng. Rep. 685 (Ch. 1723)   118
Trevor v. *Perkins*, 5 Wharton (55 Pa.) 243 (1839)   188
Union Bank of Georgetown v. *Laird*, 2 Wheat. (15 U.S.) 390
    (1817)   231, 235
United States v. *Vaughan*, 3 Binn. 392 (Pa. 1811)   232
Vaupell v. *Woodward*, 2 Sandf. Ch. 156 (N.Y. Ch. 1844)   177
Vicksburg, Shreveport & Texas R.R. v. *McKean*, 63 La. 638 (1857)   237
Waldo v. *Chicago, St. Paul, and Fond du Lac R.R. Co.*,
    14 Wis. 625 (1861)   237

Walker v. *Mobile and Ohio R.R. Co.*, 34 Miss. 245 (1857)   239
Ward v. *Van Duzer*, 2 N.Y. Super. 162 (1829)   176
Warren v. *Consett*, 8 Mod. 107, 88 Eng. Rep. 84 (K.B. 1723)   113
Welles v. *Cowles*, 2 Conn. 567 (1818)   188
Wells v. *Jewett*, 11 How. Pr. 242 (N.Y. Sup. Ct. 1855)   241, 243
West Philadelphia Canal Co. v. *Innes*, 3 Whart. 198 (Pa. 1837)   245
Whitackre v. *Whitackre*, Sel. Cas. T. King 13, 25 Eng. Rep. 195
    (Ch. 1725)   118
Wigg v. *Executors of Garden*, 1 Bay (1 S.C.) 357 (1794)   189
Wilkinson v. *Meyer*, 8 Mod. 173, 88 Eng. Rep. 127 (K.B. 1722)   112
Wilmington and Philadelphia Tph. Co. v. *Bush*, 1 Harr.
    (1 Del.) 44 (1832)   228
Wivell v. *Stapleton*, 8 Mod. 68, 88 Eng. Rep. 54 (H.L. 1723)   113
Yates v. *Alden*, 41 Barb. 172 (N.Y. App. Div. 1863)   239

Acknowledgments

I would like to thank the many colleagues who offered useful suggestions, particularly Dan Keating, Pauline Kim, David Konig, Ronald Mann, Curtis Milhaupt, Bob Thompson, and Peter Wiedenbeck. For research assistance, I would like to thank Steven Wheeler at the New York Stock Exchange, the staffs at the New-York Historical Society and the New York Public Library, and Mark Kloempken, Peggy McDermott, Charles Morriss, Linda Ritter, and Shawn Van Asdale at Washington University.

A different version of chapter 8 appeared as "The Origin of the New York Stock Exchange, 1791–1860," *Journal of Legal Studies*, 27 (1998).

Note on dates

Dates before the 1752 calendar reform have been modified to read as if the year began on January 1, to better convey sequences of events to modern readers. The month that contemporaries called February 1719, for instance, is here called February 1720.

Abbreviations

NYHS	New-York Historical Society
NYPL	New York Public Library
NYSE	New York Stock Exchange

Introduction

This book is about the regulation of the earliest securities markets in England and the United States. Because that regulation was the product of widespread attitudes toward securities markets, the book necessarily discusses those attitudes as well. And because popular attitudes toward securities trading depended heavily (although not entirely) on what the market was like at any given time, the book is as much about the institution being regulated as it is about the regulation itself.

I

The subject is one that has been, with a few minor exceptions, largely overlooked. Accounts of securities regulation in the United States tend to begin with the Securities Act of 1933, or at best with the state "blue sky" laws of the preceding two decades. When the seventeenth, eighteenth, and nineteenth centuries receive any attention, they are usually brushed aside with the poorly informed assumption that securities markets were subject to no law at all. As one account of the nineteenth-century market puts it, "speculators were bound by no rules beyond the natural ones of the market."[1] Or in the words of one widely-used American securities law treatise, "[s]ecurities regulation in this country began around the turn of the century."[2] The assumption should seem dubious to anyone familiar with Anglo-American legal history, and this book will demonstrate its falsity. During the period covered by this book, English and American securities markets were intensively regulated – in some respects, more intensively than they are regulated today.

The notion that securities markets were unregulated before this century is partially due to the lack of attention the subject has received, but it is also in large part indicative of a fundamental misconception of

---

[1] John Steele Gordon, *The Scarlet Woman of Wall Street* (New York: Weidenfeld & Nicolson, 1988), xviii.
[2] Louis Loss and Joel Seligman, *Fundamentals of Securities Regulation*, 3rd edn (Boston: Little, Brown, 1995), 9.

the nature of legal development. That misconception, usually assumed pre-rationally rather than elaborated explicitly, is that new institutions or new technologies are born naked into the world; that they emerge into a legal vacuum, where they remain untouched by law until the legal system responds with regulation. It would make sense, given this assumption, to suppose that securities markets could have existed in England and the United States for centuries before the managers of the legal system got around to devising a legal framework for them. Securities markets, one might think, were never large enough during this period, and only rarely controversial enough, to be considered a "problem" deserving the legal system's attention.

One goal of this book is to provide an extended example to demonstrate the error of this view of legal development. No institution in the Anglo-American world is born unregulated, because no institution, no matter how new, is so new that judges and legislators cannot instantly place it in the same conceptual category as more familiar institutions.[3] As we will see more clearly in chapters 1 through 3, securities were a form of property new to late seventeenth-century England. The market that grew up in London to trade them was an institution the likes of which had never been encountered by the English legal system. But securities were in some ways similar to older forms of property; the securities market was in some ways reminiscent of older markets; and once these categorizations had been made the managers of the English legal system had well-established legal principles governing older property and older markets to draw upon. Nothing needed explicitly to be done to regulate the new market; like any new institution, it could easily be assimilated to older categories and rules. This pattern is typical of Anglo-American legal change. We can see a similar process taking place today, with new technologies like computer software and new institutions like the Internet often analogized for regulatory purposes to older technologies like books and older institutions like public parks. Securities markets are a familiar institution today, but they were often perceived as strange and threatening when they first began. By taking a close look at how they were regulated at the start, I hope to be able to clarify the manner in which Anglo-American legal change relates to institutional and technological change.

A second goal of the book is to add to our understanding of the

---

[3] By "institutions" I mean, following Douglass North, "the humanly devised constraints that shape human interaction." Douglass C. North, *Institutions, Institutional Change and Economic Performance* (Cambridge: Cambridge University Press, 1990), 3. A securities market, for instance, is an institution – it embodies a collection of written and unwritten restraints on participants' behavior that enables participants to do something they would otherwise have great trouble doing.

process of legal change itself. Students of the process have tended to divide into two camps, one emphasizing the ways in which new law is generated within the professional community of lawyers, the other emphasizing the effects of non-legal developments – changes in economic circumstances, in political thought, and so on – on the law. The origin and development of securities regulation provide an excellent case study, because they incorporate aspects of both. Legal change was sometimes transparently the result of external forces, but it was also sometimes clearly generated by an internal process of reasoning by analogy from older legal rules and categories. This book accordingly takes both an "external" and an "internal" view of its subject; that is, it discusses the political and economic trends that influenced the development of securities law on the one hand, and the changes in legal doctrine confronted by lawyers and speculators on the other.

The evidence presented in this book, I will argue in the concluding chapter, illustrates the relationship between the two types of change. I will briefly state the conclusion here: Where legal change was produced by an autonomous process of legal reasoning, that reasoning was predicated upon analogies to decisions reached by earlier generations of government officials, decisions which were themselves the products of external developments when they were made, and regarding which the relevant political and economic pressures had not changed in the interim. As we will see in chapters 3 and 5, for example, the law of usury was adapted to the new securities market through an internal reasoning process accessible only to lawyers, but the pertinent aspect of the law of usury had itself embodied a compromise of a tension in economic thought reached centuries earlier.

One thus cannot understand why securities markets were regulated the way they were without situating them in the broader culture, not just of the time but of earlier times as well. How people in England regulated speculation in government debt in the early eighteenth century, for instance, was strongly influenced by what they thought about speculation in government debt at the time, but that thought in turn was strongly influenced by what they thought about grain speculation in the sixteenth century. How people in the United States regulated transactions in the shares of business enterprises in the middle of the nineteenth century, to take another example, often followed from their ideas about corporations at the time, but those ideas in turn were in large part drawn from what people in early eighteenth-century England thought about speculation in the public debt. Regulation has cultural roots in two overlapping but analytically distinct senses; it draws upon both the culture of its own time and the culture of the past. The evidence presented in this book will, I hope, be ample proof of both.

The book's third goal is to demonstrate that most of the ways of thinking about and regulating securities markets characteristic of the twentieth century were present in England and the United States long before securities markets were important economic institutions. The familiar modern rift between Wall Street and Main Street – between a community of securities professionals pursuing its private interest while certain that it is meanwhile essential to the public welfare, and a wider political community suspicious of both the practices and the power of the securities industry – is as old as securities trading.[4] The common current beliefs that securities transactions involve more deception than transactions in other kinds of property, that stock speculators immorally profit from events harmful to the nation as a whole, that stock speculation is tantamount to gambling, that money invested in the market is diverted from more productive pursuits[5] – all date back to the late seventeenth and early eighteenth centuries. Most of today's regulatory techniques, including prohibitions of certain types of transactions, mandatory disclosure rules, minimum holding periods, and rules forbidding deception and price manipulation, were tried or at least suggested in the eighteenth and early nineteenth centuries. The market and the government were both much smaller, but a good part of the landscape would be familiar to a twentieth-century lawyer.

This conclusion has two consequences. First, it casts some doubt on the common assumption that the regulation of the early twentieth century was prompted solely by contemporary events. Popular attitudes toward the market in the late nineteenth and early twentieth centuries, to the contrary, inherited and built upon a centuries-old tradition of Anglo-American thought. The growth of the market and the conduct of speculators around the turn of the century may have triggered our current scheme of regulation, but behind that trigger lay hundreds of years of preparation.

Second, awareness of the previous centuries of thought about securities markets opens up all sorts of questions that have long been hidden from view. Our securities regulation in the late twentieth century rests in large part on the answers judges, legislators, lawyers, and traders provided to a host of questions in the seventeenth, eighteenth, and

---

[4] On that split, see Mark J. Roe, *Strong Managers, Weak Owners: The Political Roots of American Corporate Finance* (Princeton: Princeton University Press, 1994).

[5] See, e.g., Molly Ivins, "Budget Deal More About People Than Numbers," *Charleston Gazette*, Dec. 8, 1995, 6A; Roy Fish, Letter to the Editor, *Houston Chronicle*, Sept. 26, 1995, 19; Tom Petruno, "Any Way You Look at It, Investing in Stock Market is a Gamble," *Dallas Morning News*, Oct. 8, 1995, 14H.

nineteenth centuries, but we have lost sight not just of the choices they made but of the fact that the choices even had to be made. Should securities trading be allowed? Does the risk involved make it a form of illegal gambling? Does a high rate of return make the investment illegal usury? Should trading be banned, on the ground that excessive speculation harms the public? Are futures contracts enforceable? What if the seller does not actually own the stock he is purporting to sell? If the price drops between the contract date and the date delivery is due, can the buyer rescind on the theory that the stock was not truly worth the purchase price? May the parties settle a futures contract by netting the difference between the prices on the contract date and the delivery date, or must they physically transfer the stock? Should a small number of brokers be permitted to form a cartel – a stock exchange – and trade only among themselves? Today most of these questions seem so basic that we forget they once had to be answered, but the answers were far from obvious when the questions first arose.

My own background and training – I am an American law professor – may go a long way toward explaining some of the book's emphases. The book's first three chapters track English developments from the seventeenth century only through the early nineteenth century; that is, only insofar as English events and English thought had a strong influence on patterns of thought and behavior in the United States. The rest of the book, chapters 4 through 8, covers the United States, from the beginnings of organized American securities trading in the early 1790s through the middle of the nineteenth century. As a result, the book nearly tells a single chronological story running from approximately 1690 to approximately 1860, but the location of that story jumps from England to the United States (and jumps a bit backwards chronologically) between chapters 3 and 4. Readers primarily interested in England will notice the absence of any extended discussion of English events after roughly 1800. Throughout, the book focuses primarily on law, and treats other aspects of life only to the extent that they are useful in explaining how and why the law developed. This is only one of a handful of conceivable modes for writing legal history, and for some purposes it may not be the most fruitful, but it seemed the most useful for answering the questions of how and why English and American people chose to regulate early securities markets in the ways that they did.[6]

The beginning of the time period covered by this book, the 1690s, requires little explanation. That was the decade when England saw its

---

[6] See Louis E. Wolcher, "The Many Meanings of 'Wherefore' in Legal History," *Washington Law Review* 68 (1993): 598–607.

first substantial securities trading, and its first securities regulation. The book's ending, approximately 1860, is less dictated by the subject, but there are three good reasons for stopping there. First, one of my objectives is to demonstrate that all the primary forms of twentieth-century popular thought about securities markets were already wide-spread in England and the United States well before securities markets were important economic institutions. The American Civil War serves as a useful stopping point, because the American market grew so substantially during and after the war.[7] Second, the two paradigmatic eighteenth-century regulatory measures – Sir John Barnard's Act in England (discussed in chapter 3) and New York's stockjobbing act (discussed in chapter 5) – were repealed in 1860 and 1858 respectively. Beginning in the late 1850s and early 1860s, a common class of securities transactions was given recognition by the legal system for the first time since the market was in its infancy. The middle of the nineteenth century saw the rejection of the main products of eighteenth-century legal thought concerning securities markets, and is thus a convenient place to end. Finally, the mid-nineteenth century is the last logical stopping point before the enactment of the federal securities statutes in the 1930s, but the period from the 1860s to the 1930s, which in the United States included two intense bursts of regulatory activity, deserves a book to itself. To attempt to include that material here would have resulted in a book approximately twice the length of this one. Although 1860 in some respects is an arbitrary cutoff point, for these reasons it seemed less arbitrary than any other. As a result, this book does not tell a story from beginning to end, nor does it describe a neat transition from one state of affairs to another. It starts at the beginning, but it leaves off somewhere in the middle, because the story it tells has no clear end.

The subject of this book and the sources it incorporates cut across conventional disciplinary boundaries. I hope it will attract readers from a few different walks of life. I have accordingly tried to minimize the amount of technical legal and financial detail in the book. Where such detail was essential to an accurate picture of events, I have tried to provide explanations as brief as possible, so as not to bore specialists. There were many points at which such decisions had to be made. These were among the most difficult judgment calls involved in writing the book.

The book's interdisciplinary nature also prompts two apologies. The first is the standard one. I am by no means an expert in securities law,

---

[7] Richard Franklin Bensel, *Yankee Leviathan: The Origins of Central State Authority in America, 1859–1877* (Cambridge: Cambridge University Press, 1990), 249.

finance, English or American history, or English or American literature. I have tried to learn enough of each, but I ask the indulgence of specialists, who are likely to find only partial coverage of the relevant portions of their fields. My second apology is occasioned by the inconsistent conventions of the different disciplines. Law professors and lawyers, accustomed to scholarship presenting normative conclusions, may be disappointed that I offer none. I do not argue that the law of any particular time was good or bad, nor do I take sides in the debates I describe. I do not claim that the past offers any lessons as to what our securities law should or should not be like today, because it does not: Both the market and the state were so much smaller and so qualitatively different that it would be absurd to base current policy on anything that happened during the period covered by this book. Economists, accustomed to discounting what people *say* about markets and focusing on what people actually *do* in markets, may be frustrated by the attention I pay to the arguments for and against securities trading. Throughout, I devote more attention to what people thought about the market than to whether they were right, simply because their thought, right or wrong, was what drove them to regulate the market the way they did, and that is what I am trying to explain. Specialists in literature, finally, accustomed to close readings of individual texts, may be unhappy with the rapid accumulation of snippets of large numbers of texts. Where I use poems or plays as evidence, however, I am not primarily interested in the poems or plays in themselves; I am interested in them as evidence of widespread thought when they were written, and they can serve that purpose best when they are piled up in groups.

Throughout this book I will be speaking of the market in and the regulation of "securities." Lawyers will recognize that as a technical term the word is ambiguous around the edges,[8] but I intend only its modern colloquial sense, which includes two types of financial assets – shares of government debt and shares of business corporations. The first type, which was much more common than the second in the eighteenth century, usually entitled the holder to a periodic payment from the government, normally expressed as a percentage of the face value of the instrument. Today these are usually called "bonds," but during the period covered by this book they were generally called "stock." The second type, which probably became more common than the first around the middle of the nineteenth century, usually entitled the holder to a periodic dividend from the corporation, to some voting power in the affairs of the corporation, and to a share of the corporation's assets after

---

[8] See, e.g., *Reves* v. *Ernst & Young*, 494 U.S. 56 (1990); *Landreth Timber Co.* v. *Landreth*, 471 U.S. 681 (1985); *SEC* v. *W. J. Howey Co.*, 328 U.S. 293 (1946).

the claims of creditors had been satisfied. During the period covered by this book, the shares of corporations were also generally called "stock," as they are today. The people whose thought I describe would thus have been likely to use the word "stock" where I use "securities," particularly in the seventeenth and eighteenth centuries, but I use "securities" as the umbrella term to avoid confusing modern readers. The category of "securities regulation" is likewise a slight anachronism, as there was no such category of legal thought in England or the United States at the time, but the term's familiarity to lawyers today makes it a useful shorthand way of referring to all the rules of law with a direct effect on the securities market.

II

The book's attempt to link the development of law with the wider culture in which that law was situated raises three groups of methodological questions that will be familiar to historians, but may not be to other readers.

First, throughout the book, I infer from the available evidence that particular ways of thinking were "widespread," or "common," or "popular." There were no public opinion polls during the period covered by this book, of course, nor were many of the issues discussed in the book ever put up to an explicit vote. Estimates of the pervasiveness of thought are thus necessarily open to question. For any given period, I have tried to find every published expression of opinion relative to securities markets, but of course the points of view that were published may not be representative of the points of view that were generally held, the surviving evidence may not be representative of the spectrum of opinion that existed at the time, and the evidence I have been able to discover may not be representative of the evidence currently in existence. This potential for sampling error is inherent in the attempt to write any sort of cultural history beyond accounts of the thought of individual people. The best one can do is to make educated guesses, based on a sense of the arguments people at the time would have considered plausible and on a feeling for the relative frequency with which particular arguments are made. Guidelines like these only help a tiny bit, but they at least convert blind guesses into reasonable hypotheses worth further testing. In chapter 2, for example, I assert that many English people in the early eighteenth century understood the securities market as a zero-sum game, and that they therefore assumed that for every winner in the market there had to be a loser. My direct evidence for this claim is slim; it consists of only a few people who actually said so. But this understanding of the market fits in well with the belief that the domestic economy as a whole was a zero-sum game, a belief that Joyce Appleby has found present in seventeenth-century England and J. E. Crowley has observed in the eighteenth-century North American colonies.[9] And while I have found only a few people making this argument, I have found none making the contrary argument. The claim that many people held this belief has not, strictly speaking, been proven, but it has been shown to be more probable than not on the basis of the evidence uncovered so far. It can then serve as the basis for the gathering of new evidence, which will strengthen or weaken it.

The question of representativeness is particularly difficult because of the subject matter of this book. The volume of published criticism of securities trading, I quickly discovered, tended to swell every time the market declined, which raises the question of whether it is important to distinguish between short-run sour grapes and more permanent dissatisfaction with the market, and if so, how that might be done. I decided not to attempt to distinguish the two categories, because both contributed to legislative proposals, enacted statutes, and the outcomes of judicial decisions. Sour grapes or not, new regulation tended to come immediately after price declines. The two sorts of criticism were thus equally relevant to understanding legal developments. The volume of published support for the market, meanwhile, proved to be a function of the likelihood of regulation; that is, when regulation seemed imminent, people who ordinarily published nothing about securities trading would rush to defend the market in print. (This relationship became even more apparent in the early twentieth century, when the prospect of state and then federal regulation launched a flotilla of published defenses of trading.) The volume of published evidence is thus a poor indicator of public interest in and acceptance of securities trading. A better indicator is the size of the market at any given time, measured either in money or in investors. People vote with their pocketbooks, in effect, much more often than they set their opinions down on paper.

An additional difficulty concerning the representativeness of published opinions stems from the fact that one's interest in the stock market, in both the past and the present, is pretty clearly dependent upon one's wealth. That is not to say that people without money to invest lack opinions about the market. Some of those opinions, usually strongly negative, will be discussed in this book. But such evidence is

---

[9] Joyce Oldham Appleby, *Economic Thought and Ideology in Seventeenth-Century England* (Princeton: Princeton University Press, 1978), 158–64; J. E. Crowley, *This Sheba, Self: The Conceptualization of Economic Life in Eighteenth-Century America* (Baltimore: Johns Hopkins University Press, 1974), 86–88.

normally much more difficult to come by than the opinions of the propertied. Most of the evidence cited in this book, on both sides of any question, was produced by people who were wealthy enough to invest in the market if they wanted to, who had associates who invested in the market, and who spent time thinking about whether the market's growth was desirable. My references to "widespread thought" and the like should be taken with this in mind. The word "popular," in particular, may carry for some readers a uniquely working-class connotation that is inapplicable in this context.

The second group of methodological questions is more fundamental. Even apart from the question of the representativeness of evidence, what does it mean to say that a particular mode of thought was "widespread" or "widely held"? What percentage of a population has to believe something before that belief can be said to be "popular"? Words like these obviously conceal a great deal of uncertainty as to how many people held the belief. The best definition one can give is "more than a trivial number." If one considers the United States today, for instance, I think all would agree that many people believe the stock market to be equivalent to a casino. That is a belief, one senses, that is widely held, even if one cannot specify how many people hold it. When I use similar language with reference to periods in the past, I mean to suggest a similar notion. Because the concept does not imply any given percentage of the population, much less a majority, two incompatible beliefs can both be widely held. That is, the belief that the stock market is a casino, and the belief that the stock market is not a casino, can be (and probably are) both widely held, by different groups of people, or sometimes even by the same people.

This sort of vocabulary can be maddeningly imprecise, but it is at least an improvement over the sort of history where one reads that during a particular period "people thought X," or that the period was "an age of X." Even if one cannot know how many people thought what, one can at least acknowledge that at all periods inconsistent beliefs are simultaneously present.

A third set of methodological questions concerns the particular types of evidence cited in this book, which include polemical pamphlets, fictional sources (including poems, plays, novels, and songs), and court opinions. How valuable are such sources in getting a sense of public attitudes? Are some more trustworthy than others?

Each type of source has strong points and weak points. Pamphlets are often reliable indicators of the writer or speaker's own personal views, because the conventions of the medium, unlike others (especially court opinions), permit him to state his honest opinions. As Lawrence

Friedman has suggested, however, pamphlets are "notoriously unreliable as measures of actual feeling among a diverse population."[10] Pamphlets are often written by zealots, or by deliberately provocative writers, who are writing precisely because they wish to state an unpopular opinion. The English and early American tradition of writing pamphlets anonymously or under a pseudonym further complicates the question, because one never knows whether these devices were chosen because the author feared that his views would be unpopular. If so, then the existence of the pamphlet is actually weak evidence of its own unrepresentativeness. These difficulties can never be surmounted, but they can be minimized by two strategies. First, one can take account of sheer numbers; if one or two pamphlets state a proposition, it should be taken with a grain of salt, but if many pamphlets over a long period of time state the same proposition, it is more likely to have commanded the assent of many people. From a single author, the idea that stock speculators are unusually deceitful might be the opinion of a crackpot, but when scores of authors distributed over a century say so, one can be more confident that one is seeing a widely shared belief. Second, one can use the pamphlets not for what they say directly but for their unstated assumptions. A large variety of pamphlets published in 1720 and 1721, for instance, expressed different opinions about the South Sea Bubble, but every author tacitly assumed that readers were familiar with the details of the story, including the fact that stock in business enterprises had been bought and sold in unprecedentedly large amounts. The pamphlets, taken together, thus support the assertion made in chapter 2 that the Bubble focused public attention on the still relatively new securities market.

The use of fictional sources like novels, plays, poetry, and songs raises problems of its own.[11] Themes are sometimes common in such sources because they are common in life. In the popular songs of the last forty years, for example, heterosexual love between young people is by far the dominant topic, probably appearing with a frequency in excess of all other subjects combined. A future historian of the period would be correct in deducing the topic's importance to a large number of people. Popular songs might in fact be the best evidence to use for that purpose; they might be superior, for instance, to books by psychologists or other self-professed experts on the subject. On the other hand, themes are

---

[10] Lawrence M. Friedman, *A History of American Law*, 2nd edn (New York: Simon & Schuster, 1985), 95.

[11] This paragraph owes a great deal to John Boswell, *The Kindness of Strangers: The Abandonment of Children in Western Europe from Late Antiquity to the Renaissance* (New York: Pantheon, 1988), 3–22.

often common in fictional sources precisely because they are unusual in real life, and thus provide more entertaining material for the audience. The historian of recent popular culture unfamiliar with the concept of "love" as it was understood in the late twentieth-century United States would be likely to conclude, upon studying the lyrics of the most popular songs, that for most people love involved oscillating between two states, one of complete bliss and the other of the darkest despair. The result would be a misleading picture, because it would be based upon only those aspects of love that make for the most dramatic songs. To choose another example, the future historian might reasonably conclude, from a study of the films of the 1970s and 1980s, that many American houses of the period were either haunted or inhabited by psychotic killers. Again, the problem of representativeness arises because of the audience's preference for the dramatic.

The only way to minimize this difficulty is to compare common fictional themes with the themes appearing in non-fictional sources of the period. In chapter 6, for instance, I will show that much mid-nineteenth-century American fiction contained derogatory references to the stock market. Were these references representative of anti-market sentiment among readers, or were they dramatic devices, like haunted houses? I will suggest that the former is more probable, on the ground that contemporary non-fictional sources included similar anti-market arguments in contexts where a dramatic function seems unlikely. As with the pamphlets, the claim cannot be "proven" in a strict sense of the word. All one can do is show it to be more probable than any of the alternatives.

The interpretation of court opinions, finally, requires an awareness of all the constraints on expression faced by Anglo-American judges.[12] During the time period covered by this book, like today, the informal norms of the profession limited the judges to resolving the disputes before them by using preexisting rules of law. It was considered improper by nearly all judges and lawyers for judges to state their personal opinions on the issues in controversy, to let personal opinions influence decisions, or explicitly to invent new law. Most of the opinions discussed in this book, as a result, have a flatness and a matter-of-factness that cannot be taken as representing the judges' own views. Toward the end of the eighteenth century and the beginning of the nineteenth, opinions tended to become longer, and occasional eruptions of personality became a little more frequent. Particularly in the United

---

[12] See G. Edward White, "The Appellate Opinion as Historical Source Material," in G. Edward White, *Patterns of American Legal Thought* (Indianapolis: Bobbs-Merrill, 1978), 74–95.

States, one finds early nineteenth-century judges a bit more willing to express approval or disapproval of social developments, and slightly more prone to providing explicit policy justifications for their decisions. I have emphasized such passages, despite their rareness, for the insight they provide into the judges' thinking, perhaps at the risk of leaving non-lawyers with a misimpression of the overall composition of the opinions. Because I am primarily interested in understanding why the law developed as it did, such explanatory comments on the part of judges assume particular importance.

1 English attitudes toward securities trading at its inception, 1690–1720

Two institutional developments in late seventeenth-century England – the beginning of the permanent national debt and the rapid spread of the corporate form of enterprise – caused the volume of English securities transactions to become large enough to give rise to an organized securities market. This new market in turn led almost immediately to other institutional innovations. It took little time for practitioners of a brand new occupation – securities trading, or "stock-jobbing" as it was often called – to invent and routinize new kinds of transactions. By 1720, the year of the South Sea Bubble, the market and its participants were established London institutions.

All institutional change occurs in a preexisting climate of thought, which influences not only the course of institutional change but the way that change is perceived by contemporaries. To begin to understand contemporary attitudes toward the new securities market, therefore, the first part of this chapter will examine earlier English attitudes toward speculation generally. Section II will provide an account of the new market, with an emphasis on those features contemporaries found most striking. In section III, we will then be able to make sense of the various calls for, and opposition to, regulation of the securities market in its earliest years.

I

Long before the invention of securities trading, English attitudes toward speculation were marked by a deep ambivalence, vestiges of which still remain in American thought today. On the one hand, the forms of speculation available in early modern England tended to be either illegal or heavily regulated. On the other hand, they were quite commonly practiced, apparently because they were widely perceived to serve a useful function. The result was an uneasy tension: The practice of buying to resell at a higher price was the subject of official and popular rhetorical disapproval, but was simultaneously the subject of

14

tacit support among the countless people willing to transact with speculators.

Speculating in food, for instance, had for centuries been unlawful under three related common law headings, all of which became statutory offenses as well in the mid-sixteenth century.[1] One who purchased from a producer outside of a market, and then resold in the market, or who persuaded a producer to forbear from bringing his goods to the market, was guilty of forestalling. One who purchased food in a market, and then resold it in the same market or one nearby, was guilty of regrating. One who purchased food before the harvest for the purpose of reselling was guilty of engrossing.[2] The common element to all three offenses was purchase and resale without transporting food from one area to another; a middleman who reallocated food over time rather than space was not conceived to be performing a useful function.[3] These prohibitions were widely understood to be for the benefit of the consumer; without them, "the prices of victuals and other merchandize shall be inhaunced, to the grievance of the subject; for the more hands they passe through, the dearer they grow, for every one thirsteth after gaine."[4] Speculation in food was understood to be particularly "oppressive to the poorer Sort," who might thereby find it "out of their Power to supply themselves with a Commodity, without an unreasonable Expence."[5] If such practices were to be allowed, "a Rich Man might Ingross a whole Commodity, and sell it at what Price he thought Fit," a notion "of such dangerous Consequence, that the bare Ingrossing of a whole Commodity with the Intent to sell it at an unreasonable Price, is an Offence indictable at the Common Law, whether any Part thereof be sold by the Ingrosser, or not."[6] Thus speculation in food, one of the few assets in which large-scale speculation was possible in early modern England, was proscribed by the official rhetoric of the legal system, a system ostensibly devoted to suppressing "Practices, which tend to make the commodities of the Realm more dear."[7]

---

[1] 5 & 6 Ed. VI c. 14, §§ 1–3 (1552).

[2] W. S. Holdsworth, *A History of English Law* (Boston: Little, Brown, 1922–38), IV, 375.

[3] Norman Scott Brien Gras, *The Evolution of the English Corn Market From the Twelfth to the Eighteenth Century* (Cambridge, MA: Harvard University Press, 1915), 201.

[4] Donald Grove Barnes, *A History of the English Corn Laws From 1660–1846* (New York: Crofts, 1930), 2; Edward Coke, *The Third Part of the Institutes of the Laws of England* (1644) (London: E. and R. Brooke, 1797), 195.

[5] William Hawkins, *A Treatise of the Pleas of the Crown* (London: J. Walthoe, 1716), I, 234.

[6] Thomas Wood, *An Institute of the Laws of England*, 3rd edn (London: Richard Sare, 1724), 434; Hawkins, *A Treatise*, I, 235.

[7] Edmund Wingate, *The Body of the Common Law of England*, 2nd edn (London: H. Twygford and Roger Wingate, 1655), 28.

Popular discourse was equally disapproving of grain speculators, in ways that would foreshadow later popular disapproval of stockjobbers.[8] Grain speculators, as in one characteristic accusation, intentionally profited from the misfortunes of others, by hoarding food so as to drive up the price:

> Of corne and vytayle they stuff theyr howses full
> Therby to ingender nede, and paynfull penury
> Unto the pore, that they may wyn therby.
> So of all vytayle these wretches get plentye
> To sell it derer, whan some great darth shalbe.[9]

"[B]y this meanes," another critic of the practice explained, "these hellishe ingratours, and forestallers make corne and all thinges else deere, all times of the yeere."[10] Even in times of famine, contemporaries charged, speculators "desire to make the famine greater . . . how doe they sweat in braine and body, to hoord up corne to their neighbours hinderance?"[11]

Such an unnatural way of making a profit gave rise to some equally unnatural consequences. Speculation created the possibility of strange transactions, in which commodities which did not yet exist were sold by those who did not yet possess them, to people who would never consume them:

> And some saye the woule
> is bought ere it do growe,
> And the corne long before
> it come in the mowe.[12]

Speculation caused men to be deceitful, as they discovered they could profit from spreading misinformation about market conditions. "There is no Vermine in the Land" like an engrosser, one early seventeenth-century writer complained. "He slaunders both Heaven and Earth with pretended Dearths, when there's no cause of scarcitie."[13] Worst of all, because food speculators profited most during times of shortage, their preferences were the mirror-image of what they should be. Like "the

---

[8] Burton Milligan, "Sixteenth- and Seventeenth-Century Satire Against Grain Engrossers," *Studies in Philology* 37 (1940): 585–97.

[9] Alexander Barclay, *The Ship of Fools* (1509), ed. T. H. Jamieson (Edinburgh: W. Paterson, 1874), II, 167.

[10] Phillip Stubbes, *The Anatomie of Abuses* (1583), ed. Frederick J. Furnivall (London: New Shakspeare Society, 1882), II, 46.

[11] John Boys, *The Workes of John Boys* (London: William Ashley, 1622), 737.

[12] Robert Crowley, "Of Forestallars," *One and Thyrtye Epigrammes* (1550), in J. M. Cowper, ed., *The Select Works of Robert Crowley* (London: Trubner, 1872), 33.

[13] Thomas Overbury, "An Ingrosser of Corne" (1615), in W. J. Paylor, ed., *The Overburian Characters* (New York: AMS Press, 1936), 65.

Devill and his brokers," a speculator hoped for events contrary to the public good:

> He prayes for raine in harvest, night and day,
> To rot and to consume the graine and hay.
> . . .
> But if a plenty come, this ravening thiefe
> Torments & sometimes hangs himselfe with griefe.[14]

The law's prohibition of food speculation thus rested on a solid base of popular disapproval. Speculation raised prices, harmed the poor, and exacerbated shortages, but opposition ran even deeper than that. Speculation indirectly gave rise to deceit, and more subtly undermined the common good, by creating a class of people whose goals – bad weather, famine, and starvation – gave them every incentive toward evil.

And yet, as with the narcotics market in the late twentieth-century United States, official and popular disapproval of food speculation in early modern England is only half the story. Throughout the period, despite heavy government enforcement both nationally and locally, speculators found countless customers willing to buy and sell.[15] Food speculators may have been unpopular, but there was a market for their services.[16]

Such was certainly the view of the government, which in the sixteenth and seventeenth centuries received a constant stream of reports of "the greedy and insatiable covetous desires and appetites of the breeders, broggers, engrossers, graziers, victualers, and forestallers," a group widely perceived to be "minding only their own lucre without respect of the commonwealth."[17] In 1550, for example, Edward VI reported having received "divers and sundry complaints of enhancing of the prices of victuals necessary for man's sustenance, and in especial of corn, grain, butter, and cheese" on the part of certain speculators, who were "purposing of their perverse minds to make great dearth and scarcity, more than necessity requireth, of corn, grain, beeves, muttons,

---

[14] Thomas Adams, *The White Devil, or the Hypocrite Uncased* (London: Ralph Mab, 1613), 46; John Taylor, "The Water-Cormorant," in *Works of John Taylor the Water-Poet Comprised in the Folio Edition of 1630* (New York: B. Franklin, 1967), 494.

[15] Holdsworth, *History of English Law*, IV, 377–78; Dorothy Davis, *A History of Shopping* (London: Routledge, 1966), 6; I. S. Leadam, ed., *Select Cases Before the King's Council in the Star Chamber* (London: B. Quaritch, 1911) (Publications of the Selden Society, vol. 25), II, xxi–xxxviii.

[16] Alan Everitt, "The Marketing of Agricultural Produce," in Joan Thirsk, ed., *The Agrarian History of England and Wales* (London: Cambridge University Press, 1967), IV, 543–63.

[17] Paul L. Hughes and James F. Larkin, eds., *Tudor Royal Proclamations* (New Haven: Yale University Press, 1964), I, 526. "Brogger" was an early variant of "broker."

veals, porks, butter, cheese, and other victuals."[18] A few decades later, Elizabeth I learned "by report out of sundry counties" that "rich farmers and engrossers do pretend to raise the prices by color of the unseasonableness of the summer." This sort of news – tales of "the wicked and unsatiable greediness of sundry bad-disposed persons who, preferring their own private gain above the public good . . . forestall, regrate, and engross all manner of grain and so raise high prices thereby"[19] – came pouring in, year after year.[20]

Contemporaries shared the view that food speculation was common. "Laws are eluded," one minister sermonized, "the Kings edicts not regarded, the Magistrates endevors frustrated, and the hopes of the poore disappointed."[21] Another complained that speculators were so numerous that they bid up the prices paid by consumers: "ther is many of theim, that neither hath nor wyll have corne, whyche make corne most dere."[22] As one seventeenth-century balladeer summarized:

> Ingrossing is growne such a trade,
> that the poore have great cause to be sad.[23]

Food speculation in sixteenth- and seventeenth-century England was thus widely criticized and widely practiced at the same time. There was not yet a body of economic thought justifying speculation (that would come in the eighteenth century),[24] so we have little or no surviving evidence of any contemporary defense of the practice. But many contemporaries were, in effect, voting with their pocketbooks. A middleman, even one brokering a commodity with a demand as insensitive to price changes as the demand for food, cannot survive unless he is providing some kind of benefit to buyers or sellers. Farmers must have welcomed the opportunity for early sales; they were paid sooner, they were spared the time and expense of moving food to the market, and they were able to transfer the risk of the marketplace to an intermediary.[25] Whenever a

---

[18] Hughes and Larkin, eds., *Tudor Royal Proclamations*, I, 505. "Beeves" was the plural of "beef."

[19] Ibid., III, 165; II, 194.

[20] Ibid., I, 99, 172, 181, 188, 190, 221, 269, 318, 343, 521; II, 165, 170, 216; III, 276, 414, 532.

[21] Charles Fitz-Geffrie, *The Curse of the Corne-horders* (1631), 2, cited in Milligan, "Sixteenth- and Seventeenth-Century Satire," 589.

[22] Thomas Lever, "A Sermon Preached at Pauls Crosse" (1550), in Thomas Lever, *Sermons*, ed. Edward Arber (London: A. Murray, 1871), 128.

[23] Martin Parker, "Knavery in All Trades" (1632), in Hyder E. Rollins, ed., *A Pepysian Garland: Black-Letter Broadside Ballads of the Years 1595–1639* (Cambridge: Cambridge University Press, 1922), 412.

[24] E. P. Thompson, *Customs in Common* (New York: New Press, 1993), 200–07.

[25] Ray Bert Westerfield, *Middlemen in English Business Particularly Between 1660 and 1760* (New Haven: Yale University Press, 1915), 144–45.

farmer sold to a speculator rather than to a consumer, these benefits had to have exceeded any reduction in the price the farmer received, or else he would have sold directly to the consumer. (Although what look like consensual transactions from afar can look more like exploitation closer up. As William Harrison explained in 1577, "[a]t Michaelmas-time poor men must make money of their grain that they may pay their rents. So long, then, as the poor man hath to sell, rich men will bring out none but rather buy up that which the poor bring."[26]) Consumers, despite the higher prices so often complained of, may sometimes have gained as well, from the ability of speculators to even out fluctuations in supply over a harvest cycle or from a good crop to a bad one; consumers may have benefitted from the opportunity to buy food at times and places other than those of established markets; they may have saved time and expense in finding commodities they preferred; or, if a speculator could bring food to the consumer more easily than the producer could have, consumers may have saved on the transportation cost built into the price. The higher prices often charged by speculators would have been limited by whatever ability purchasers had to buy directly from the farmer. Speculators could not have flourished to the extent they apparently did without providing some service to someone. As with drug dealers today, their success is evidence of a quiet but widespread pattern of preferences lurking beneath the surface of official and popular written culture.

Food speculation was thus the subject of two inconsistent but internally coherent patterns of thought. To the legal system, committed to the centuries-old ideal of a closed market,[27] speculation produced aberrant prices and modes of transacting, and gave rise to deceit and dissension. To its practitioners and many of their customers, living a newer open-market ideal that would not find theoretical justification for another century, speculation would have been at worst harmless, and at best a way of making a market, by providing a food supply at times and places where one would otherwise be lacking.

It bears remembering, because we will see this tension again in connection with the securities market, that neither of these competing conceptions of speculation was in any sense more "correct" than the other. The latter is closer to our dominant mode of thought today, but only because we are closer to it in time. Unless we are to reject the repeated observations of contemporaries, grain hoarders *did* sometimes tell lies to turn a profit, they *did* sometimes exacerbate shortages, and

---

[26] William Harrison, *The Description of England* (1577), ed. Georges Edelen (Ithaca: Cornell University Press, 1968), 248.

[27] P. S. Atiyah, *The Rise and Fall of Freedom of Contract* (Oxford: Clarendon Press, 1979), 128–29.

they *did* often make food more expensive to its eventual consumer; there was nothing irrational about the odium in which they were held.[28] Whichever way one thought about speculation, some people would be winners and some would be losers. Ambivalence toward food speculation was not a result of backwardness; it was instead the result of a genuine tension between two competing visions of a well-functioning food market, one focusing on the gains from trade, the other on the reallocation of resources from producers and consumers to middlemen.

In the period just before the development of securities markets, this ambivalence existed with respect to other forms of speculation as well. There had long been a small number of licensed brokers, who were primarily intermediaries between merchants, often for the purpose of facilitating international trade; they would buy from importers for domestic resale, and buy from domestic producers for resale to exporters.[29] By the early seventeenth century, however, it became apparent that many people were "terming and naming themselves brokers, whereas in truth they are not." These "upstart brokers" or "counterfeit brokers" were unlicensed, and were intermediaries not between merchants but between members of the public. They were "men of manual occupation and handicraftmen," who had left their occupations to "set up a trade of buying and selling and taking to pawn all kind of worn apparel . . . houshold-stuff and goods, of what kind soever the same be of, finding thereby that the same is a more idle and easier kind of trade" than manual labor. In the government's view, these were "friperers [i.e., sellers of frippery, or old clothing], and no brokers, nor exercising of any honest and lawful trade," yet they had "grown of late to many hundreds within the city of London," and threatened "to increase to far greater multitudes."[30]

Brokering of this sort was another form of speculation; it consisted of buying items for the sole purpose of reselling them at a higher price, without any significant transport to justify the profit. We can again detect two contrasting patterns of thought at work, corresponding to two divergent understandings of the economy. The rhetoric of the legal system condemned the new brokers for adding no value to the commun-

---

[28] Cf. John Walter, "Grain Riots and Popular Attitudes to the Law: Maldon and the Crisis of 1629," in John Brewer and John Styles, eds., *An Ungovernable People: The English and Their Law in the Seventeenth and Eighteenth Centuries* (New Brunswick: Rutgers University Press, 1980), 49.

[29] See Gerard Malynes, *Consuetudo, vel Lex Mercatoria, or The Antient Law-Merchant* (London: Adam Islip, 1636), 143; Charles Gross, ed., *Select Cases Concerning the Law Merchant* (London: B. Quaritch, 1908) (Publications of the Selden Society, vol. 23), I, xxxiv.

[30] 2 Jac. I c. 21 (1604).

ity; they were "idle," they had no "honest" trade, they did nothing but shuffle used goods from one household to another. But beneath the rhetoric, people were increasingly finding it worthwhile to buy from and sell to brokers. The theoretical justification for the brokers' existence – the notion that they facilitated the movement of items to their highest-valued uses – would not be developed for more than a century. Yet practice preceded theory; speculation in clothing and household goods received wide tacit support at a time when it was subject to equally wide disapproval.

A similar tension existed in the legal thought concerning the purest form of speculation available in early modern England, speculation in money. There was, of course, a long tradition of thought condemning usury as unnatural, running back at least to Aristotle and the Old Testament.[31] That tradition was still vivid enough at the close of the sixteenth century for Shakespeare to assume that his audience would understand "[a] breed for barren metal" as a reference to interest.[32] At the same time, however, it was widely recognized that "no State or common-wealth can or ever did stand without it."[33] In many circumstances, loans could be indispensable.

For this reason, the general proscription of usury had, by the seventeenth century, become riddled with exceptions, which coincided with the most useful applications of credit. By the eleventh century at the latest, canon law recognized that investment in a *societas*, or partnership, a common form of trading enterprise in the middle ages, was not usury, so long as the investor bore some risk of losing his investment.[34] Such remained the rule even after jurisdiction over usury cases was transferred from ecclesiastical to secular courts in the sixteenth century.[35] "A man unskilfull in trading," one English trea-

---

[31] Richard McKeon, ed., *The Basic Works of Aristotle* (New York: Random House, 1941), 1141 (*Politics* I, 10) ("of all modes of getting wealth this is the most unnatural"); Leviticus 25:36–37; Deuteronomy 23:19–20.

[32] William Shakespeare, *The Merchant of Venice*, I.iii.131 (1596–97), ed. Kenneth Myrick (New York: New American Library, 1987), 57. See generally Norman Jones, *God and the Moneylenders: Usury and Law in Early Modern England* (Oxford: Basil Blackwell, 1989).

[33] Robert Filmer, *A Discourse Whether it may be Lawful to take Use for Money* (London: W. Crook, 1678), preface. For a close study of medieval ambivalence toward money-lenders, stemming from this more general ambivalence toward usury, see Joseph Shatzmiller, *Shylock Reconsidered: Jews, Moneylending, and Medieval Society* (Berkeley: University of California Press, 1990).

[34] John T. Noonan, Jr., *The Scholastic Analysis of Usury* (Cambridge, MA: Harvard University Press, 1957), 133–53; James A. Brundage, *Medieval Canon Law* (London: Longman, 1995), 78.

[35] See Richard H. Helmholz, *Roman Canon Law in Reformation England* (Cambridge: Cambridge University Press, 1990), 116.

tise-writer put it, "hath a stock of money, which he delivereth to a merchant or tradesman to imploy; receiveth part of the gaine, and beareth part of the hazard proportionably. This is no usurie, but partnership."[36] "[I]f the interest and principal are both in hazard," agreed the King's Bench in 1618, "it is not then usury."[37] The exception for investments where principal was at risk was essential to the financing of shipping ventures, which often required mortgaging the ship at high interest rates to raise money for food and other supplies necessary for a long voyage.[38]

Money lent could be at risk in other types of useful investment, and the law of usury quickly included exceptions for these as well. By the late middle ages, canon law already exempted credit sales of speculative commodities, in order to permit purchasers to promise to pay a sum higher than a good's current value, if there was real doubt as to what the good's value would be at the time of payment.[39] This exception also survived the transfer of jurisdiction to English secular courts. In the early seventeenth century, an English writer clarified the doctrine: "To sell wares for time [i.e., on credit], and in respect of time to sell dearer," would ordinarily be viewed as a disguised loan for interest, and thus the transaction as a whole would be subject to the law of usury. But the sale "may be free from usurie . . . in respect of the rising of the commoditie so sold, if by the ordinarie course of seasons, it will be worth more at the day of paiment of the money, then it was at the time of sale."[40] A similar exemption from the usury laws applied to the international currency exchange necessary to finance trade.[41]

Finally, after some waffling in the fifteenth and sixteenth centuries, usury was redefined to include only interest over a certain statutory rate.[42] Even these statutes, which gradually reduced the rate from 10 percent in 1571 to 5 percent by 1714, did not bind the Crown, so they were no impediment to public borrowing.[43] In short, where credit was most useful, the law of usury gave way. In the contrast between general disapproval and particular acceptance, we can again see two divergent attitudes toward speculation.

[36] Roger Fenton, *A Treatise of Usurie* (London: William Aspley, 1611), 19.
[37] *Roberts v. Tremayne*, Cro. Jac. 507, 508, 79 Eng. Rep. 433, 434 (K.B. 1618). See A. W. B. Simpson, *A History of the Common Law of Contract* (Oxford: Clarendon Press, 1975), 517–18.
[38] See Malynes, *Consuetudo*, 122; Hawkins, *Treatise of the Pleas*, I, 247.
[39] Noonan, *Scholastic Analysis*, 90–92.   [40] Fenton, *Treatise of Usurie*, 20.
[41] James Steven Rogers, *The Early History of the Law of Bills and Notes* (Cambridge: Cambridge University Press, 1995), 70–74.
[42] 37 Hen. VIII c. 9 (1545); 13 Eliz. c. 8 (1571).
[43] P. G. M. Dickson, *The Financial Revolution in England* (London: Macmillan, 1967), 39.

Speculation, in whatever form it took, was simultaneously useful and dangerous; it served some valuable functions, but it often caused harm to the vulnerable. Speculation was both productive and wasteful; it satisfied an evident demand, but its practitioners added no value to the community. These tensions, aspects of which still linger today, characterized English legal thought in the centuries leading up to the 1690s, a decade that would see rapid institutional change.

II

The idea of a permanent government debt, divided into pieces small enough to be regularly bought and sold, was already an old one by the time it reached England. Venice had a secondary market for government debt securities as early as the fourteenth century. The mid-sixteenth century saw the development of a publicly-traded government debt in Holland.[44] The idea travelled to England near the end of the seventeenth century, possibly with the Dutch advisors to William III. In 1693, in the midst of an expensive war with France, the English government issued its first long-term annuities.[45] England would borrow money from the public on similar terms a few more times during the decade. In 1694, the government created the Bank of England, a corporation which also borrowed money from the public in the form of long-term tradeable securities. From then on, the English government would be financed largely through long-term public loans, in units small enough to permit an active secondary market.[46]

The idea of dividing a business into shares, to permit the accumulation of a larger capital than that which could be possessed by an individual, was likewise an old one. Medieval shipping partnerships took this form.[47] The first English businesses to be formally denominated "joint-stock companies" were the foreign trading enterprises, the first of which may have been the Russia Company, formed in 1553, in which

---

[44] James D. Tracy, *A Financial Revolution in the Habsburg Netherlands: Renten and Renteniers in the County of Holland, 1515–1565* (Berkeley: University of California Press, 1985), XI, 108–38. For a contemporary description of securities trading in late seventeenth-century Amsterdam, see Joseph de la Vega, *Confusión de Confusiones* (1688), trans. Hermann Kellenbenz, in Martin S. Fridson, ed., *Extraordinary Popular Delusions and the Madness of Crowds & Confusión de Confusiones* (New York: John Wiley & Sons, 1996).

[45] J. R. Jones, *Country and Court: England, 1658–1714* (Cambridge: Cambridge University Press, 1979), 65. On English government borrowing in the preceding decades, see C. D. Chandaman, *The English Public Revenue 1660–1688* (Oxford: Clarendon Press, 1975), 285–300.

[46] Dickson, *Financial Revolution*, 39–57.

[47] M. M. Postan, *Medieval Trade and Finance* (London: Cambridge University Press, 1973), 86–91.

shareholders subscribed £6,000 in shares worth £25 each.[48] The transferability of shares in these early corporations was apparently not taken for granted.[49] A 1657 advertisement for subscriptions to the East India Company, for example, announced that shareholders would have the opportunity to cash in their shares for whatever profits had been earned at the end of seven years, and then every three years thereafter, a privilege which seems to presuppose the difficulty or impossibility of terminating the investment in a secondary market.[50] Six years later, the Company of the Royal Adventurers into Africa found it necessary to include in its charter an explicit grant of power to its members "to grant and assign over to any person or persons whatsoever any of their stock or stocks and the proceed and profit thereof."[51] In any event, by the 1690s, the transferability of shares was commonplace, and the number of joint-stock companies had skyrocketed. By the end of 1695, at least 150 corporations had their shares publicly traded, and trading had centralized in a group of London coffee houses lining "Exchange Alley."[52] These corporations included the foreign trade companies, as well as a host of enterprises engaged in manufacturing, insurance, mining, and banking.[53] Exchange Alley was also the focal point of transactions in the public debt. (Both kinds of instruments traded – shares of businesses and shares of the public debt – were generally called "stock." It would not be until the nineteenth century that the word "stock" would cease to encompass the public debt.)

These seemingly modest institutional changes had enormous social and intellectual consequences. As the secondary market in government debt and shares of businesses grew, the portion of the nation's total wealth consisting of land and other tangible things gradually declined, replaced more and more by mobile pieces of paper, representations of intangible fractions of a future stream of income. Within a generation, contemporaries came to realize that an entirely new form of property had come into existence.[54] The owners of this new property formed a

---

48 John P. Davis, *Corporations* (New York: G. P. Putnam's Sons, 1905), II, 114–56; William Robert Scott, *The Constitution and Finance of English, Scottish, and Irish Joint-Stock Companies to 1720* (Cambridge: Cambridge University Press, 1912), I, 17–20.

49 K. G. Davies, "Joint-Stock Investment in the Later Seventeenth Century," *Economic History Review* 4 (1952): 294; but see George Cawston and A. H. Keane, *The Early Chartered Companies* (London: E. Arnold, 1896), 12–13.

50 *All Corporations, and Particular Persons, that are willing to become Adventurers to East-India* . . . ([London]: East India Co., 1657).

51 Cecil T. Carr, ed., *Select Charters of Trading Companies, A.D. 1530–1707* (London: B. Quaritch, 1913) (Publications of the Selden Society, vol. 28), 180.

52 Larry Neal, *The Rise of Financial Capitalism: International Capital Markets in the Age of Reason* (Cambridge: Cambridge University Press, 1990), 46.

53 Scott, *Constitution and Finance*, I, 326–45.

54 Lawrence E. Klein, "Property and Politeness in the Early Eighteenth-Century Whig

correspondingly new political class which threatened to upset the traditional hierarchy of power. This "momentous intellectual event," in Pocock's words, was thus a major cause of the rise "of an ideology and a perception of history which depicted political society and social personality as founded upon commerce."[55] In short, the development of an established securities market was a crucial step in the eighteenth-century transformation of English and American political thought. The market itself would eventually feel the effects of these changes, as we will see in subsequent chapters.

The new securities market had more immediate effects as well. People quickly discovered that profits could be made, independent of the eventual success or failure of any given enterprise, simply by exploiting short-term fluctuations in the prices of shares. A "great many *Stocks* have arisen since this War with *France*," an observer of the new market noted in 1694,

for Trade being obstructed at Sea, few that had Money were willing it should lie idle, and a great many that wanted Employments studied how to dispose of their Money, that they might be able to command it whensoever they had occasion, which they found they could more easily do in *Joint-Stock*, than in laying out the same in Lands, Houses, or Commodities, these being more easily shifted from Hand to Hand: This put them upon Contrivances, whereby some were encouraged to Buy, others to Sell, and this is it that is called *Stock-Jobbing*.[56]

In Thomas Shadwell's 1693 play *The Volunteers, or the Stock-Jobbers*, a participant in the new market explains that he does not care whether the fanciful enterprises in which he invests ever actually conduct any business. "[B]etween us," he confides, "Its no matter whether it turns to use or not; the main end, verily, is to turn the Penny in the way of Stock-Jobbing, that's all."[57]

The word "stock-jobbing" quickly entered the popular vocabulary, where it took on multiple shades of meaning. "Stock-jobbing" was sometimes merely a synonym for buying and selling stock, with no judgment intimated as to the value of that activity. It was sometimes a pejorative way of describing the same pursuit. It sometimes referred specifically to buying or selling stock in a deceitful manner. It sometimes

---

Moralists," in John Brewer and Susan Staves, eds., *Early Modern Conceptions of Property* (London: Routledge, 1995), 222.

[55] J. G. A. Pocock, *Virtue, Commerce, and History: Essays on Political Thought and History, Chiefly in the Eighteenth Century* (Cambridge: Cambridge University Press, 1985), 108–09; see also J. G. A. Pocock, "*The Machiavellian Moment* Revisited: A Study in History and Ideology," *Journal of Modern History* 53 (1981): 64.

[56] John Houghton, *A Collection, for Improvement of Husbandry and Trade* (London: Randall Taylor, 1692–1703), No. 98, June 15, 1694, 1.

[57] Thomas Shadwell, *The Volunteers, or, the Stock-Jobbers* (London: James Knapton, 1693), 24.

meant dealing in stock through methods more complex than simple buying or selling (these methods will be described shortly). As time went on, the word tended to be used more often as a means of expressing disapproval. By the middle of the eighteenth century, a reference to "stock-jobbing" or "stock-jobbers" would almost invariably be contained within an argument critical of the practice.

This new activity of "stock-jobbing" gave rise to two new occupations. By 1694, there were already stockbrokers, who took a commission in exchange for buying or selling a principal's stock.

The manner of managing the Trade is this; the Monied Man goes among the *Brokers* (which are chiefly upon the *Exchange*, and at *Jonathan's* Coffee House, sometime at *Garaway's*, and at some other Coffee Houses) and asks how *Stocks* go? and upon Information, bids the Broker buy or sell so many Shares of such and such Stocks if he can, at such and such Prizes: Then he tries what he can do among those that have Stock, or power to sell them; and if he can, he makes a Bargain.[58]

A similar report a few years later suggested that trading had become continuous enough that investors no longer needed to instruct brokers as to their desired price; one could simply have the broker buy or sell "at the Price currant on the Exchange."[59]

The same coffeehouses were also the workplaces of a community of "stock-jobbers" – professional speculators, who made a living buying and selling stock for their own account, often while acting as a broker at the same time.[60] "Sometimes," the commercial newspaper editor John Houghton explained, "the Dealers in *Stock* sell to one, and buy of another different Shares of the same *Stock* for different prices, and so make Advantages."[61] By early 1692, a member of the House of Commons was lamenting that "[t]he trade of stockjobbing is now become the sole business of many persons, which has ruined great numbers of tradesmen and others."[62] Shadwell's 1693 play included a character satirically said to be "of the honest Vocation of Stock-jobbing."[63] A 1697 broadside complained that "great Quantities" of stock "are daily Bought and Sold by Brokers, Stock-jobbers, and

---

[58] Houghton, *Collection for Improvement*, No. 99, June 22, 1694, 1.

[59] Edward Hatton, *The Merchant's Magazine: or, Trades-Man's Treasury*, 3rd edn (London: Chr. Coningsby, 1699), 212.

[60] E. Victor Morgan and W. A. Thomas, *The Stock Exchange: Its History and Functions*, 2nd edn (London: Elek, 1969), 21.

[61] Houghton, *Collection for Improvement*, No. 102, July 13, 1694, 1.

[62] Henry Horwitz, ed., *The Parliamentary Diary of Narcissus Luttrell* (Oxford: Clarendon Press, 1972), 147.

[63] Shadwell, *Volunteers*, 10.

Others."[64] The same year, Daniel Defoe noticed "a New Trade, which we call by a new Name, *Stock-Jobbing*."[65] By 1700, brokers and stock-jobbers were so thickly clustered in Exchange Alley that pedestrians claimed they were unable to get through.[66] The following year, Defoe castigated "that new *Mistery* or *Machine* of Trade we call *Stock-Jobbing*," and argued that "the Villainy of Stock-Jobbers" was ruining the English economy.[67]

These new professional securities traders formed the first English institutional market for new issues, the existence of which enabled the English government and the promoters of joint-stock companies to seek new investment repeatedly.[68] As John Houghton explained in 1694, anyone with a plan for making money could take advantage of this new market:

The plain, honest Proceeding whereof is this, When some one has thought of an Art or Invention, or discover'd some Mine, or knows, or thinks of some New (or New manner of) way of Trade, whereby he thinks a considerable gain may be gotten, and yet this cannot well, or not so well as otherwise be carried on by a private Purse, or if it could, the Hazard of it is too great: He then imparts it to some Friend or Friends, who commonly consider or enquire of the Learned, Whether 'twill stand good in Law; and if so, they contrive some Articles for its constitution, whereof to give the first Inventer a Summ of Money for his Invention and charge, or some certain number of the Shares, or both, is certainly, and with good reason one of the principal Articles.[69]

The existence of a permanent market rapidly increased the number of outstanding securities, which in turn fortified the market by making professional traders more numerous. This spiral of expansion caused Exchange Alley to be a familiar institution by the end of the decade. Within a short time, tables of stock prices and advertisements for investments became staples of the press.[70] The very first number of John Houghton's *Collection*, dated March 30, 1692, included prices for "actions" (an early synonym for shares, taken from French) in eight enterprises, including "India," "Guinea," and "H. Bay."[71] This table

64 *A Proposal for Putting some Stop to the* Extravagant Humour *of* Stock-jobbing (s.l.: s.n., 1697), 1.

65 Daniel Defoe, *An Essay upon Projects* (London: T. Cockerill, 1697), 29.

66 *Upon Reading the Humble Petition of the Inhabitants and Shopkeepers in and about* Exchange-Alley . . . (London: Samuel Roycroft, 1700).

67 Daniel Defoe, *The Villainy of Stock-Jobbers Detected* (London: s.n., 1701), 4.

68 See Douglass C. North and Barry R. Weingast, "Constitutions and Commitment: The Evolution of Institutions Governing Public Choice in Seventeenth-Century England," *Journal of Economic History* 49 (1989): 824–28.

69 Houghton, *Collection for Improvement*, No. 98, June 15, 1694, 1.

70 Karin Newman, *Financial Marketing and Communications* (Eastbourne: Holt, Rinehart and Winston, 1984), 49–52, 174–75.

71 Houghton, *Collection for Improvement*, No. 1, March 30, 1692.

continued as a regular feature in Houghton's eleven-year run. By the early eighteenth century, much longer tables of this sort were common.[72]

Brokers and jobbers soon realized that stock, because it fluctuates in value and is imperishable, could be the subject of transactions well beyond simple buying and selling. By 1694, traders were already using a standard form contract for a "refuse" of shares, or what would much later be termed a "call" – the option to purchase shares at a given price at a given time in the future.[73] (Current terminology emphasizes the right to buy ("call") the shares; seventeenth-century terminology emphasized the right to decline ("refuse") the shares.) The value of these refuses, it was widely understood, was that they enabled a purchaser, at a small cost, to benefit from a rise in prices, while limiting his loss from a fall, because in the event of a fall he could simply decline to exercise the option.

[F]or a small hazard he can have his chance for a very great Gain, and he will certainly know the utmost his loss can be . . . so in plain *English*, one gives Three Guinea's for all the profits if they should rise, the other for Three Guinea's runs the hazard of all the loss if they should fall.[74]

Market participants were also familiar with "puts," which still go by that name today – the option to sell shares at a given price at a given time in the future. This sort of option also served, at a small cost, to reduce the risk inherent in price fluctuations, by setting a floor below which the loss would be borne by someone else. "By this means," Houghton advised, "many are incouraged to come into new Stocks, the success whereof is very uncertain."[75] Traders would also "buy Shares and sell them again for time"; that is, agree simply to buy or sell shares at a given future time at a given price.[76] This type of transaction would soon be called a "time bargain."

Once puts, refuses, and time bargains were common, it did not take long to discover that one did not need to transfer any stock, or indeed to own any stock, in order to speculate in the market. If A thinks the price of East India Company stock will decline, for example, and B thinks it will rise, A and B can enter into a time bargain, in which A agrees to sell a given number of shares to B at their current price, on a given date in the future. When the transfer date comes, if A was right, there is no need

---

[72] Neal, *Rise of Financial Capitalism*, 18. See, e.g., John Freke, *The Prices of the Several Stocks, Annuities, and other Publick Securities &c. with the Course of Exchange* ([London]: John Freke, 1714).

[73] Houghton, *Collection for Improvement*, No. 100, June 29, 1694, 1.

[74] Ibid., No. 99, June 22, 1694, 1.   [75] Ibid., No. 101, July 6, 1694, 1.

[76] Ibid., No. 102, July 13, 1694, 1.

for him to purchase shares in the market and transfer them to B; B can simply pay A the difference between the old price and the new price. If B was right, A can pay the difference to B. Neither A nor B ever needs to own any shares to participate in this sort of transaction. Neither even needs to be wealthy enough to buy any shares, because the most either could lose from the transaction is the difference in share prices between the two dates. By the early eighteenth century, observers were noticing that "a very beneficial Trade was daily driven with imaginary Stocks, and many Thousands bought and sold, to great Advantage, by those who were not worth a Groat."[77]

With these new kinds of transactions came expanded methods of deceit, new opportunities for profiting at the expense of others. The initial sale of stock in a new company, which as yet had no earnings to distribute, provided a means of hoodwinking the gullible with no parallel in other markets. By 1697, Daniel Defoe was already weary of

too many, fair pretences of fine Discoveries, new Inventions, Engines, and I know not what, which being advanc'd in Notion, and talk'd up to great things to be perform'd when such and such Sums of Money shall be advanc'd, and such and such Engines are made, have rais'd the Fancies of Credulous People to such height, that meerly on the Shadow of Expectation . . . People have been betray'd to part with their Money for Shares in a *New-Nothing*; and when the Inventors have carri'd on the Jest till they have Sold all their own Interest, they leave the Cloud to vanish of itself, and the poor Purchasers to Quarrel with one another.[78]

Defoe had an axe to grind: He had lost his entire £200 investment in a company that promised to use a newly invented "diving engine" to salvage treasure from shipwrecks.[79] But he was only one voice in a chorus. "[T]he spirit of Scheming and Projecting reigns in a such a degree," an anonymous writer claimed, that the word "project" itself had come to denote "something too designing, chimerical, and ridiculous" to warrant investment.[80] A commission appointed by the government to inquire into the situation agreed. "[T]he pernicious art of stock-jobbing," it concluded in 1696, had "perverted the end and design of companies . . . to the private profit of the first projectors," who sold worthless stock to "ignorant men, drawn in by the reputation, falsely raised and artfully spread, concerning the thriving state of their stock."[81]

[77] *The New Way of Selling Places at Court, in a Letter from a Small Courtier to a Great Stock-Jobber* (London: John Morphew, 1712), 4.
[78] Defoe, *An Essay upon Projects*, 11–12.
[79] Christine Macleod, "The 1690s Patents Boom: Invention or Stock-Jobbing?," *Economic History Review* 34 (1986): 563.
[80] *An Essay Towards Restoring of Publick Credit* (London: J. Roberts, 1721), 4.
[81] *Journals of the House of Commons*, 11:595 (Nov. 25, 1696).

The secondary market, in which traders bought and sold shares among themselves, also provided increased opportunities for bilking others. Unlike other things that can be acquired in a market, securities cannot be consumed by the purchaser; they tend instead to be bought for eventual resale to someone else. The price of a security, therefore, unlike the price of other items, depends largely on how market participants will value it in the future. For this reason, stockjobbers soon discovered, the price of stock was much more easily manipulated than the price of anything previously known. As early as 1694, John Houghton noticed that "in small Stocks 'tis possible to have Shares rise or fall by the Contrivances of a few Men in Confederacy."[82] One of these "Contrivances," as Defoe had noted, was the spreading of false information about the likely success of a corporation: "So have I seen Shares in Joint-Stocks, Patents, Engines, and Undertakings, blown up by the air of great Words."[83]

Food speculators had been spreading misinformation for centuries, but the room for profiting from such lies had to have been limited by the narrow range of possible fluctuation in the demand for food. Food, unlike stock, is consumed by its purchasers and endures for a relatively short time. (Indeed, the fear that hoarded grain would rot before it could be sold was a recurring theme in the anti-speculative literature of the sixteenth and seventeenth centuries.[84]) Regardless of popular beliefs as to future food prices, the demand for food could not have sunk below what was needed for sustenance, and could not have risen above the limit set by the length of time the food could remain in storage. With stock, however, speculators faced no limits on the effect that price misinformation could have on demand. By spreading false news as to the value of a stock, speculators discovered that they could shift demand for the stock dramatically in either direction. Although lying was nothing new, the stock market opened up unprecedented opportunities to gain from it.

Another "Contrivance," with even more striking consequences, was the "corner," in which a group of traders would secretly agree to simultaneously purchase as many "refuses," or options to buy stock in the future, as they could. Many of the sellers of refuses would typically not own any stock themselves; these sellers were hoping that the stock price would decline, and that the purchasers of refuses would therefore

---

[82] Houghton, *Collection for Improvement*, No. 101, July 6, 1694, 1.
[83] Defoe, *An Essay upon Projects*, 12–13.
[84] See, e.g., Thomas Nashe, "Christs Teares over Jerusalem" (1593), in Ronald B. McKerrow, ed., *Works of Thomas Nashe* (London: A. H. Bullen, 1910) II, 158; Taylor, "The Water-Cormorant," 494; Overbury, *Overburian Characters*, 65.

not exercise their option to purchase at the higher option price. In the event the price rose, and the purchasers exercised their options, the sellers of refuses were expecting to be able to buy stock in the market when the time came for delivery to the purchasers. But if the confederates in the corner could purchase more shares and refuses for shares than the number of shares actually in existence (which was possible if enough refuses were sold by people who did not own any shares), and the price rose, the sellers of refuses would find, when they tried to buy shares in the market for delivery to the confederates, that the confederates already owned all the shares. To satisfy their obligations, sellers of refuses would have to buy shares from the very people to whom they would be delivering the shares. And because the confederates owned all the shares, they could exact extraordinarily high prices for selling them. As early as 1694, John Houghton observed:

the great *Mystery* of all is, That some Rich Men will join together, and give money for REFUSE, or by Friendship, or some other way, strive to secure all the Shares in a Stock, and also to give Guinea's for Refuse of as many Shares more as Folk will sell, that have no Stock: and a great many such there are, that believe the Stock will not rise so high as the then Price, and Guinea's receiv'd or they shall buy before it does so rise, which they are mistaken in; and then such takers of Guinea's for Refuse as have no Stock, must buy of the other that have, so many Shares as they have taken Guinea's for the Refuse of, at such Rates as they or their Friends will sell for; tho' Ten or Twenty Times the former Price.[85]

Grain engrossers had tried to corner the food market for centuries, but stock speculators quickly realized that the new stock market had suddenly made cornering much easier and much more profitable.

By creating new ways of obtaining other people's money, the new securities market facilitated government borrowing and private investment to an unprecedented degree, but at the same time it engendered strange new kinds of transactions which permitted the unscrupulous an unprecedented opportunity to exploit some old techniques of deception. It would not be long before there developed a lively public debate about the market, and particularly about the activities of stockjobbers.

III

In 1694, when anything resembling an established market had existed for only a couple of years, John Houghton already assumed that his readers would "come pre-possessed against Trading in Stocks." He prefaced his description of the market with the concession that "[s]ome abuses may probably have been committed by Traders therein," but

---

[85] Houghton, *Collection for Improvement*, No. 102, July 13, 1694, 1.

begged his readers nevertheless to be open-minded: "must we presently thereupon run down all with a full cry that so deal therein?" It is "a great hardship on such Gentlemen," Houghton concluded, "to undergo the Censures of Mankind, who inveigh against all Traders and Trading in Stock, tho' at the same time they know little or nothing of it."[86]

Opposition to securities trading developed quickly. The leading early critic, at least in print, was Daniel Defoe, ordinarily not one to criticize a method of expanding commerce, who within a decade of the market's birth viewed "this destructive *Hydra*; this new *Corporation of Hell, Stock-Jobbing*," as a menace to English trade.[87] But even in the earliest years, when investment in government debt and corporate stock was an activity largely limited to the wealthy,[88] suspicion of the new market appears to have run deeply in contemporary consciousness, among people with no personal experience of it and unlikely to be much concerned with trade. One man hanged at Tyburn in 1717 argued from the gallows that he was guilty only of "out-witting the Directors of the Bank of England by a sort of Collusive Practice, and that Body Corporate has play'd the same Game in their Turn."[89] Two years later, Defoe reported that "[t]he General Cry against Stock-Jobbing has been such, and people have been so long, and so justly Complaining of it as a publick Nuisance," that the government should take some action.[90] London merchants complained to Parliament of the "many notorious Abuses committed by Stock-jobbers."[91] Among writers in the market's early years, stockjobbing had many more critics than defenders, across the political spectrum.[92]

The early criticism of stockjobbing introduced four themes that would become much more well developed in the 1720s. One persistent element of the early criticism was the deceit understood to permeate the market, a market "manag'd with the greatest Intriegue, Artifice, and Trick," where one encountered "the Frauds and Tricks of *Stock-Jobbers*."[93] It was a market "made up of such strange Members, subtil, politick and designing Men, that all pretend the Good of the Re-publick

---

[86] Ibid., No. 97, June 8, 1694, 1.

[87] Thomas Keith Meier, *Defoe and the Defense of Commerce* (Victoria: University of Victoria, 1987); Defoe, *Villainy*, 9.

[88] Peter Earle, *The Making of the English Middle Class: Business, Society, and Family Life in London, 1660–1730* (Berkeley: University of California Press, 1989), 146–51.

[89] Quoted in Peter Linebaugh, *The London Hanged: Crime and Civil Society in the Eighteenth Century* (Cambridge: Cambridge University Press, 1992), 19.

[90] Daniel Defoe, *The Anatomy of Exchange-Alley: or, A System of Stock-Jobbing* (London: E. Smith, 1719), 1.

[91] *Journals of the House of Commons*, 15:502 (Jan. 17, 1708).

[92] J. G. A. Pocock, *The Machiavellian Moment: Florentine Political Thought and the Atlantic Republican Tradition* (Princeton: Princeton University Press, 1975), 448.

[93] Defoe, *An Essay upon Projects*, 29, 13.

only, when that of the Re-private is chiefly intended."[94] It was a market unlike any other, where prices were determined "without any regard to the Intrinsick worth of the Stock"; insiders instead "rais'd and lower'd the Prices of Stocks as they pleas'd," to whatever level "might best serve their Private Interest."[95] Indeed, Defoe asked:

Is not the whole Doctrine of Stock-Jobbing a Science of Fraud? And are not all the Dealers, meer Original Thieves and Pick-Pockets? Nay, do they not own it themselves? Have not I heard [two stock-jobbers] a thousand times say they know their Employment was a Branch of Highway Robbing, and only differ'd in two things, *First in Degree (viz.)* that it was ten Thousand times worse, more remorseless, more void of Humanity, done without Necessity, and committed upon Fathers, Brothers, Widows, Orphans, and intimate Friends; in all which Cases, Highwaymen, generally touch'd with Remorse, and affected with Principles of Humanity and Generosity, stop short and choose to prey upon Strangers only. *Secondly in Danger (viz.)* that these rob securely; the other with the utmost Risque that the Highwaymen run, at the Hazard of their Lives, being sure to be hang'd first or last, whereas these Rob only at the Hazard of their Reputation which is generally lost before they begin, and of their Souls, which Trifle is not worth the mentioning.

Stockjobbing was "a compleat System of Knavery," in which money was made by "Coining false news" and then "preying upon the Weakness of those, whose Imaginations they have wrought upon." "Letters have been ordered," charged Defoe,

to be written from the *East-Indies*, with an Account of the Loss of Ships which have been arriv'd there, and the Arrival of Ships lost; of War with the *Great Mogul*, when they have been in perfect Tranquility, and of Peace with the *Great Mogul*, when he has come down against the Factory of *Bengale* with One Hundred Thousand Men.

All these false rumors were "for the Raising and Falling of the Stock."[96]

This image of the market, as a place where values were manipulated by spreading false news from abroad, soon permeated English culture. In Susanna Centlivre's 1718 play *A Bold Stroke for a Wife*, performed repeatedly in England all through the eighteenth century, a stockjobber spreads a rumor that a certain siege has been raised. None of the permanent residents of Exchange Alley believes it. But when a Dutch merchant arrives, the stockjobbers pounce; they lure him into buying stock by telling him of the raising of the siege. Once the transaction has

---

[94] *Angliae Tutamen: or, The Safety of England* (London: s.n., 1695), 10.

[95] Defoe, *Villainy*, 5; Defoe, *An Essay upon Projects*, 30; *Considerations Against Repealing that Part of an Act of Parliament, Which Restrains the Number of Exchange-Brokers to One Hundred* (London: s.n., 1705), 1.

[96] Defoe, *Anatomy*, 8, 3–4, 13.

been closed, a stockjobber chortles, as an aside, "Ha, ha, ha! I have snapped the Dutchman."[97]

If prices bore no relationship to intrinsic value, then it followed that "Stock-jobbing, properly speaking, is only another word for Gaming."[98] An investor could never know how the insiders would be rigging the market, so from his perspective "Stock-jobbing is Play; a Box and Dice may be less dangerous, [but] the Nature of them are alike, a Hazard."[99] As the familiar forms of gambling were illegal, so too should be its newest manifestation.

A second theme in the early criticism, and again one that would develop more fully in the 1720s, was the multifaceted political threat posed by the stockjobbers. This sort of criticism did not rest upon the presence of deceit; it would have applied to even an entirely honest market. The mere existence of a public debt, it was argued, created internal division, because it required taxing land and trade in order to pay the interest due to the holders of the debt.[100] Speculation in the public debt even divided the speculators themselves into two antagonistic classes – those betting on a rise in value and those betting on a fall. The first group would profit from the government's stability, while the second would benefit from the fear of disorder. No good could come of this opposed set of incentives. "What safety can we have at home," asked Defoe, "while our Peace is at the Mercy of such Men, and 'tis in their Power to *Jobb* the Nation into Feuds among our selves, and to declare a new sort of Civil War among us when they please?"[101] A holder of government securities might have personal reasons to favor an aggressive military policy, "for War is his Harvest," in the sense that he might profit from an increase in government borrowing.[102] Even more frightening was the danger posed by those speculating on a fall in the value of the public securities, whose potential profit from a national calamity made them likely to be "Abettors of Treason, assistant to Rebellion and Invasion."[103]

In fact, according to Defoe, this sort of speculators' treason had already occurred in an indirect form in connection with the war against France, when the fear of invasion had increased the perceived risk that

[97] Susanna Centlivre, *A Bold Stroke for a Wife* (1718), ed. Thalia Stathas (Lincoln: University of Nebraska Press, 1968), xiii–xv (for the play's production history), 54–60 (for the scene), 59 (for the quotation).

[98] Daniel Defoe, *The Gamester: A Benefit-Ticket for All that Are Concern'd in the Lotteries* (London: J. Roberts, 1719), 12.

[99] Defoe, *Anatomy*, 43.   [100] Dickson, *Financial Revolution*, 24–32.

[101] Defoe, *Villainy*, 21.

[102] W. Wagstaffe, *The State and Condition of Our Taxes Considered: or a Proposal for a Tax Upon Funds*, 2nd edn (London: John Morphew, 1714), 36.

[103] Defoe, *Anatomy*, 23 (erroneously printed as page 15).

the government would be unable to pay its debts, which had caused the value of the public securities to fall. Professional traders, Defoe reasoned, were the ones who had bid down the value of the government debt, and thus the ones responsible for weakening the public credit in a crisis. "[W]ho were the Men," he asked rhetorically,

who in the late Hurry of an expected Invasion, sunk the Price of Stocks 14 to 15 *per Cent*? . . . Will they tell us that running upon the *Bank*, and lowering the Stocks, was no Treason? We know, that literally speaking, those things are no Treason: But is it not a plain constructive Treason in the Consequences of it? Is not a wilful running down the publick Credit, at a Time when the Nation is threaten'd with an Invasion from Abroad, and Rebellion at Home? Is this not adding to the Terror of the People? Is not this disabling the Government, discouraging the King's Friends, and a visible Encouragement of the King's enemies? Is not all that is taken from the Credit of the Publick, on such an Occasion, added to the Credit of the Invasion?[104]

The damage allegedly caused by these speculators had been a real one, because a decline in the value of the extant public debt made it more expensive, and thus more difficult, for the government to raise money by issuing new debt. (To modern readers, having fallen out of the habit of holding market participants personally accountable for market movements, this is likely to seem as much a case of blaming the messenger as earlier criticism of grain speculators for causing price increases.) In the context of the wider eighteenth-century debate over whether an increasingly commercial culture would result in a declining sense of civic obligation,[105] Defoe emphasized the apparent willingness of the stockjobbers to seek personal gain at the national expense. "[I]s not all this then," he wondered, "a Species of Treason and Rebellion?"[106]

The stockjobbers' political threat did not stop there. Their power to manipulate the value of the public debt gave them an insidious lever with which to influence public policy, and thus established Exchange Alley as a locus of political power rivaling the government. The result was a classic case of corruption in the eighteenth-century sense – public policy made for the benefit of private interests. Again, Defoe was irate:

Is this an Advantage fit to be put in the Hand of a Subject? Are the King's Affairs to go up and down as they [i.e., the stockjobbers] please, and the Credit of his Majesty's Councils rise and fall as these Men shall please to value them? This would be making them Kings, and making the King Subject to the Caprice of their private Interest.

---

[104] Defoe, *Anatomy*, 28.
[105] See Linda Colley, *Britons: Forging the New Nation 1707–1837* (New Haven: Yale University Press, 1992), 71–72.
[106] Defoe, *Anatomy*, 34.

Such a system "would make all the Kings of *Britain* Pensioners to *Exchange-Alley*."[107] The problem could grow even worse if members of Parliament were themselves holders of public debt, because the taxes voted by Parliament would then be paid indirectly into the members' pockets. "[W]e find we are swingingly Tax'd," Defoe observed, "and they tell us 'tis done by the Parliament; but we never understood they had any of the Mony themselves."[108]

The new securities market threatened more than the stability of the government; it also threatened the stability of the social order. This was the third theme of the early criticism, one that also did not rest upon the existence of deceit. By 1701, enough "Bankrupts and Beggars" had taken up stockjobbing, Defoe warned, that "we can now reckon up a black List of 57 Persons, who within this ten years past have rais'd themselves to vast Estates, most of them from mechanick, and some of them from broken and desperate Fortunes."[109] This kind of class reversal was unsettling; complaints about it would mushroom in the early eighteenth century, as the volume of securities trading grew. But, even in the early years, it was observed, great sums of money were being made by people who evidently did not deserve them. Just as bad, many of the newly rich were Jewish. Exchange Alley, Defoe lamented, "throngs with Jews, Jobbers and Brokers, their Names are needless, their Characters dirty as their Employment."[110]

Fourth, and finally, critics emphasized the danger that securities trading, a pursuit understood to add nothing to the national wealth, posed to productive commerce. One writer complained in 1697 that stockjobbing tended "to the Discouragement of the Trade of this Kingdom," because it diverted "the Stock [i.e., the assets] and Time of the Traders, whose Heads and Tongues being busied how to Outwit and Circumvent one another, are not at leisure to mind and follow their proper Trades and Callings."[111] Another critic attributed "the Ruine of our Trade" to the greater profits available in the securities market; as a result, he argued, England had "become inconsiderable Abroad, and a Nation of Stock-Jobbers at Home."[112] In Defoe's view, "*Jobbing* their Stocks about, raising and sinking them at the Pleasure of Parties and private Interests, is more prejudicial to Trade" than companies could compensate for by the value they added to the economy.[113]

---

[107] Ibid., 59–60.
[108] Daniel Defoe, *The Free-Holders Plea Against Stock-Jobbing Elections of Parliament Men* (London: s.n., 1701), 11.
[109] Defoe, *Villainy*, 26.   [110] Defoe, *Anatomy*, 41.   [111] *A Proposal*, 1.
[112] Wagstaffe, *State and Condition of Our Taxes*, 17–18.   [113] Defoe, *Villainy*, 17.

In the face of this kind of opposition, the new market found few defenders in print. John Houghton argued that the greater number of traders were being criticized for the bad acts of a few. "I know many worthy Persons of great Honour and Probity," he testified, "who deal in Stocks, that do abominate the least unjust Action, and would not for the World have an ill gotten Penny among the rest of their Estates."[114] Even Defoe had to admit that, despite the abuses he catalogued, stock offerings in new enterprises "are doubtless in general of publick Advantage, as they tend to Improvement of Trade, and Employment of the Poor, and the Circulation and Increase of the publick Stock of the Kingdom."[115] Another critic was careful to separate the financing of new ventures from the transfer of shares in existing enterprises. "Nothing thrives, where ever they admit Stock-Jobbing," he explained; "it has spoil'd more good and really useful Designs than all the ill Accidents that have attended them besides."[116]

It was the anonymous author of a 1697 broadside, published in an effort to keep Parliament from prohibiting options and time bargains, who offered – apparently for the first time in a form recoverable today – three more sophisticated defenses of the value of securities trading. First, the market allowed participants to mitigate losses resulting from short-term fluctuations in their need for money. To "pay Bills of Exchange, and for other pressing Occasions," he observed, many people "have been forced to Sell Bank-Stock, and Shares in other Stocks." The new kinds of transactions developed by stockjobbers permitted these emergency sellers to "save themselves from too great Loss," by making "Agreements to receive back the said Stocks and Notes on certain Terms, whereby they know their certain Loss." Second, options and time bargains served as a form of insurance for merchants who sold goods on credit, and were due to receive securities as payment. By purchasing puts, or by agreeing to sell those securities for a given price at a future date, such merchants were assured "that they should not lose above a certain Rate." This sort of insurance was important to the general mercantile economy because without it, "many Contracts" would never be entered into. Third, the existence of a market for options and futures limited the supply of the underlying securities available for purchase at any given time, because many potential sellers "have kept their Bank-Notes and Bank-stocks, and other Stocks, to deliver according to their Agreements, which otherwise they would have sold." The result was to increase the overall value of outstanding securities, which was good for everyone, particularly the government, who was the

---

[114] Houghton, *Collection for Improvement*, No. 97, June 8, 1694, 1.
[115] Defoe, *An Essay upon Projects*, 10–11.   [116] *Angliae Tutamen*, 19.

chief borrower.[117] (This last argument might be more persuasive to modern ears if put the other way around: The opportunity to buy securities in complex ways as well as simple ones increased the demand for securities, which drove up the price.) These were all arguments that would be elaborated in more detail in years to come.

But as was the case with earlier forms of speculation, the explicit published defense of securities trading was misleadingly minimal. The market's persistence and growth into the early eighteenth century was evidence of tacit support among a growing sector of the population, those willing to transact with the brokers and jobbers of Exchange Alley. By early in the eighteenth century, stock in large enterprises like the Bank of England was generally understood to be a prudent investment for the wealthy.[118] Within a few decades of the market's existence, investing in securities was a practice that had trickled well down the social scale, to include all elements of propertied English society.[119] By 1720 (an unusual year, as will become clear in the next chapter), it was a common observation of satirists that securities trading was popular among everyone with enough money to participate:

> Our *Courtiers, Merchants, Mob* and *Citizens*
> Run to *'Change-Alley*, without Wit or Sence:
> And there, like Men possest and frantic,
> Subscribe and Buy, at Rates Romantic.[120]

While published criticism of the market was almost certainly just the tip of an iceberg of popular suspicion, published support was likewise a weak indicator of widespread participation. Both views appear to have run deep.

Opposition to the early securities market led to repeated calls for regulation. One anonymous 1697 writer proposed four techniques of curtailing "the *extravagant* and *unaccountable Methods* of Brokers, Stock-jobbers, and Others": (1) a transfer tax on securities sales; (2) a requirement "[t]hat no *Stock* bought shall be sold again, until it be first Transferred" to the purchaser; (3) a prohibition of sales without transfer of possession and payment; and (4) a requirement "[t]hat no *Stock* be sold till the Owner have had it a certain space of Time."[121] All four

---

[117] *Reasons Humbly Offered, Against a Clause in the Bill for Regulating Brokers* (s.l.: s.n., 1697), 1.

[118] D. W. Jones, *War and Economy in the Age of William III and Marlborough* (Oxford: Basil Blackwell, 1988), 286.

[119] Paul Langford, *A Polite and Commercial People: England 1727–1783* (Oxford: Oxford University Press, 1989), 642.

[120] Elias Brockett, *The Yea and Nay Stock-Jobbers, or the 'Change-Alley Quakers Anatomiz'd* (London: J. Roberts, 1720), 6.

[121] *A Proposal*, 1.

recommendations, and particularly the first and fourth, involved slowing the velocity with which securities changed hands. The second and third sought to put a stop to fictitious time bargains and options contracts, in which the parties owned no stock, but intended to settle differences between the prices in the present and the future.

Four years later, Defoe proposed a similar package of reforms, including a transfer tax and a requirement that securities sold actually be transferred to the purchaser. He recommended another method of slowing the rate of stock turnover, by requiring transfers to be entered on the books of the corporation.[122] Defoe recognized, however, that the government's growing dependence on the credit market posed an obstacle to regulation, a barrier evident to the stockjobbers themselves:

[O]ne of the top of the Function the other Day, when I casually told him, That if they went on, they wou'd make it absolutely necessary to the Legislature, to suppress them, return'd, That he believ'd it was as absolutely necessary to the Legislature, to suppress them, as ever it could be; But how will they do it? 'Tis impossible, said he, but if the Government takes Credit, their Funds should come to Market; and while there is a Market we will buy and sell; there is no effectual way in the World, says he, to suppress us but this, *viz.* That the Government should first pay all the publick Debts, redeem all the Funds, and dissolve all the Charters, *viz. Bank, South-Sea,* and *East-India,* and buy nothing upon Trust, and then, says he, they need not hang the Stock-Jobbers, for they will be apt to hang themselves.[123]

The government itself, like public opinion, was of two minds. As the securities market grew larger and more established, the multiplication of perceived abuses created a powerful argument for regulation. Yet the same expansion and institutionalization of the market made it more and more necessary to the operation of the government.

The result was a temporary compromise. After considering and shelving bills in 1694 and 1696,[124] Parliament enacted its first securities statute in 1697, one which by its own terms was due to expire three years later. The statute, "An act to restrain the number and ill practice of brokers and stock jobbers," was neither as restrictive as critics of the market had advocated nor as mild as the market's defenders would have liked. It limited the number of brokers to 100, and required that they be licensed by the lord mayor of London. (The lord mayor would adopt quotas allocating up to twelve of these positions to aliens and up to twelve to Jews.[125]) Brokers were forbidden from trading for their own account. Their fees were capped at one half of one percent of the value

---

[122] Defoe, *Villainy,* 23.   [123] Defoe, *Anatomy,* 2.
[124] *Journals of the House of Commons,* 11:116, 123, 128, 132 (March 3, 10, 15, and 20, 1694); 11:535, 541, 541 (March 27, April 1, and April 2, 1696).
[125] Dickson, *Financial Revolution,* 516.

of the securities they bought or sold. As for the more complex futures transactions that were particular objects of suspicion, the statute took a middle ground. It allowed them to continue, but deprived them of much of their value, by requiring that the period between the contract date and the transfer date be three days or less.[126] The statute was later extended to 1708, at which point it expired.[127] During the statute's brief life, the three-day limit on options and time bargains was interpreted narrowly by the courts, which upheld contracts permitting a duration longer than three days, so long as the purchaser actually made his request for the shares within the three-day period.[128]

In 1708, when the statute expired, Parliament authorized the city of London to license brokers and charge a fee for doing so, but the new statute placed no limit on the number of brokers, and appears to have been intended primarily as a means of raising revenue for the city rather than curbing securities trading.[129] In 1711, after failing to pass a bill that would have revived the 1697 statute,[130] Parliament reimposed a ceiling on the fees brokers could charge.[131] These would be the only statutory limits on securities trading for many years to come.

By 1720, the institutional innovations of the 1690s were a familiar part of the English financial world. An established community of jobbers and brokers provided a market for the public debt and for shares in commercial enterprises. This new market, like older and more familiar speculative markets, was simultaneously useful and dangerous, because the same mechanisms that permitted the mobility of capital permitted new kinds of deception. Attitudes toward the market in its early years, both among the public and within the legal system, thus exhibited the same ambivalence as that which characterized older attitudes toward older speculative markets.

The dramatic rise and fall of the securities market in 1720 focused public attention on the market to an unprecedented degree. Criticism of the market, expressed in a blurred and sporadic manner in its early years, increased both in precision and quantity. It was in 1720 and 1721 that popular attitudes toward stock speculation took their modern form. That is the subject of the next chapter.

---

[126] 8 & 9 Wm. III c. 32 (1697).   [127] 11 & 12 Wm. III c. 13 (1700).

[128] *Smith* v. *Westall*, 1 Ld. Raym. 316, 91 Eng. Rep. 1106 (K. B. 1697); *Mitchell* v. *Broughton*, 1 Ld. Raym. 674, 91 Eng. Rep. 1349 (K. B. 1701).

[129] 6 Anne c. 16 (1708).

[130] *Journals of the House of Commons*, 16:618, 627, 628, 637, 657, 679, 682 (April 28, May 4, 5, 7, 10, 26, and 31, 1711).

[131] 10 Anne c. 19, § 121 (1711).

2 The South Sea Bubble and English law, 1720–1722

The eightfold rise in the value of shares in the South Sea Company during the first half of 1720 put the securities market in the public spotlight. As speculation in South Sea stock carried in its wake speculation in all sorts of smaller enterprises, the market for the first time drew investment from all strata of the propertied public, from all quarters of England and beyond. With expanding public participation came a far greater degree of public scrutiny, and published criticism, than the market had received in its first three decades. When South Sea stock, in the second half of 1720, fell by nearly as much as it had risen, dragging the smaller enterprises with it, that criticism grew even more intense.

This sequence of events, the first stock market crash in English history, has been known ever since as the South Sea Bubble. In the profusion of literature criticizing the market during and after the Bubble, opposition to the market crystallized into a few clearly defined arguments against securities trading. When securities markets began operating in the United States in the late eighteenth century, many of these arguments would reappear in American culture, and would stay there, with only minor changes, over the next two centuries. The Bubble would also bring forth a variety of proposals for regulation, some of which were adopted, but most of which were not. Many of these regulatory proposals would also be replicated later in the United States. To understand the origin of modern regulation of securities trading, therefore, we need to take a close look at the Bubble and its aftermath.

Section I of this chapter will describe the rise and fall of the market in 1720, with emphasis on the enormous increase in public attention to securities trading. Section II will detail the characteristic types of criticism of the market and the lessons contemporaries drew from the experience. Section III will consider the response of the legal system during and immediately after the Bubble.

41

I

The South Sea Company was chartered in 1711, and granted the exclusive right to trade with the Spanish colonies in South America.[1] The Company never turned a profit from trade in its first decade; the income it earned came instead from the government, as interest on the Company's enormous holdings of the national debt. The Company was formed by issuing stock to holders of £9 million of government debt in exchange for their public securities, resulting in an enterprise whose only assets were a trade monopoly of uncertain value and a big slice of the national debt. By statute, the Company received a guaranteed 6 percent annual interest payment on its debt holdings – in effect, a government annuity. In 1715, the Company was permitted to increase its capital to just over £10 million, which amounted to approximately half of the entire capital of all joint-stock enterprises in the country at the time.

Not long after, the same idea was carried further in France. In 1712, the Mississippi Company had been granted the exclusive right to trade with the French possessions in North America. The Mississippi Company never made money from trade. But in 1717, a controlling interest in the Mississippi Company was acquired by John Law, a Scottish financier with the ear of the French government. Law refinanced his enterprise – renamed the Company of the West – largely in the same manner in which the South Sea Company had been financed, by accepting French government debt in exchange for newly issued shares. In 1719, the Company of the West grew even more. It absorbed the other French overseas trading monopolies (and was renamed the Company of the Indies), it acquired from the French government the exclusive right to coin money, and then ultimately reached an agreement with the French government by which the entire French national debt would be converted into shares of the Company of the Indies. With each step, the Company of the Indies issued new stock, and was able to sell the stock at increasingly high premiums through 1719 and early 1720.

By late 1719, capital was pouring into Paris from all over Europe. Some of the profits earned by investors in the Paris market began

[1] This account of the South Sea Company's first decade is drawn primarily from the best work on the subject, John Carswell, *The South Sea Bubble*, rev. edn (Dover: Alan Sutton, 1993), and to a lesser extent from Dickson, *Financial Revolution*, 90–156, and Scott, *Constitution and Finance*, III, 288–360. Price data are from Neal, *Rise of Financial Capitalism*, 234–35. On the relationship of events in France and England (and other European countries as well), see Eric Stephen Schubert, "The Ties That Bound: Market Behavior in Foreign Exchange in Western Europe During the Eighteenth Century" (University of Illinois Ph.D. dissertation 1986), 121–60.

trickling into England, and began a small boom in the stocks in London. The managers of the South Sea Company had been watching events in France closely, and were eager to embark on the same venture. The English government was equally eager to consolidate the national debt. In early 1720, as the French market neared its peak, the English government and the South Sea Company agreed to a scheme similar to the one pursued in France: The South Sea Company would issue £31 million in new stock, in exchange for that amount of government debt. The broad outlines of the plan were approved by Parliament in February 1720; that month, South Sea stock rose from 130 to 173.

As the South Sea Bill, with the details of the scheme, worked its way through Parliament (assisted by gifts of shares to Members), the market broke in Paris; shares in the Company of the Indies began to drop. But South Sea shares continued to rise. The Bill passed the House of Commons in March; at the end of the month, South Sea stock had risen to 310. The Bill passed the House of Lords in early April; by the end of April, South Sea stock was at 342. Its value had doubled in the space of two months, and nearly tripled in the last six months. Other stock prices began to rise as well. Advertisements for investments in new projects began to multiply. The sight of so much money being made caused an explosion of interest in stock trading. This was a "Stock-jobbing Age," one contemporary concluded.[2] But the biggest enterprise of all, and the one whose stock price was rising the fastest, was the South Sea Company. As a result, observed an anonymous writer, "all the whole Nation attends the *South Sea*."[3]

The rise in South Sea stock accelerated through the spring, to 595 at the end of May, and 950 at the end of June. Smaller stocks kept pace. It seemed like everyone with any money to spend was spending it on stocks:

> from all Corners of the Nation,
> The Wise, Fools, Cits, and Folk of Fashion,
> Repair promiscuous to the *Alley*,
> To lose or gain more Money daily.[4]

---

[2] W. R. Chetwood, *The Stock-Jobbers: or, the* Humours *of Exchange-Alley* (London: J. Roberts, 1720), dedication.

[3] *The South Sea Ballad, Set by a Lady* (London: s.n., 1720).

[4] C. C——m, *A Familiar Epistle to Mr. Mitchell* (London: T. Jauncy, 1720), 4. "Cits," short for "citizens," was a mildly derogatory name for ordinary townspeople, or what would later come to be called the middle class – tradesmen, shopkeepers, and so on. "Cits" were residents of towns who were *not* "Folk of Fashion"; the two categories, taken together, encompassed all townspeople except those too poor to invest in the stock market.

The booming market attracted people from all walks of life to Exchange Alley:

> Here Stars and Garters do appear
> Among our Lords, the Rabble,
> To buy and sell, to see and hear
> The *Jews* and *Gentiles* squabble.[5]

No matter where one went, the securities market was foremost on everyone's mind. "If you Resort to any publick Office, or place of Business," one writer complained, "the whole Enquiry is, *How are the Stocks?* if you are at a *Coffee-House*, the only Conversation turns on the *Stocks* . . . if you Repair to a *Tavern*, the edifying subject (especially to a Philosopher) is the *South-Sea Company*."[6] In short:

> All the Town is so eager their Fort[u]ne to try,
> That no body can the Temptation deny.[7]

This widespread passion for stock trading continued through the summer of 1720, as South Sea stock slowly began dropping, to 850 by the end of July and 810 at the end of August.[8]

The crash came in September; South Sea stock fell from 810 to 310, dragging with it the price of shares in other enterprises. East India Company stock, for instance, had doubled in the spring of 1720, but in September dropped below the point from which it had started. The price of shares in the more speculative projects that had been floated throughout the spring and summer fell close to zero.[9] The market continued to decline for most of the rest of the year. Paper riches that had been made in the first half of 1720 were wiped out in the second half. Investors lucky enough to sell at the peak escaped with fortunes, while those unlucky enough to buy at the peak lost all they had.[10] By November, one Londoner reported, "[t]his town is in a very shattered condition, eleven out of the twelve Judges are dipped in South Sea:

---

[5] Edward Ward, *A Looking-Glass for England: or, the Success of Stock-Jobbing Explain'd* (Bristol: S. Farley, 1720).

[6] *Exchange-Alley: or, The* Stock-Jobber *Turn'd* Gentleman; *with the Humours of our Modern Projectors* (London: T. Bickerton, 1720), preface.

[7] *South Sea Ballad.*

[8] For a summary of the scholarship as to whether the South Sea Bubble was a true bubble in the technical sense of the word, i.e., whether the rise in the price of South Sea stock was due to the self-fulfilling expectations of purchasers rather than their rational assessment of the stock's intrinsic value, see Robert P. Flood and Peter M. Garber, *Speculative Bubbles, Speculative Attacks, and Policy Switching* (Cambridge, MA: MIT Press, 1994), 3–4, 31–33, 36–50.

[9] Many of these are listed, with appropriate satirical verses, in *The Bubblers Mirrour: or England's Folly* (London: Bowles & Carver, 1720).

[10] W. A. Speck, *Stability and Strife: England, 1714–1760* (Cambridge, MA: Harvard University Press, 1979), 198.

Bishops, Deans and Doctors, in short everybody that had money. Some of the Quality are quite broke."[11] The decline was helped along by the directors of the South Sea Company, who took the opportunity to unload large amounts of stock held by the Company itself (pledged as security to buy additional stock) in the hope of buying it back later at a lower price. The directors further exacerbated the crash by releasing insiders and the politically connected from commitments they had made to subscribe to stock at prices that were now well above the market price.

The fall focused even more attention on the market, and especially on the South Sea Company. "The Affairs of the *South-Sea* Company," a contemporary observed toward the end of 1720, "have of late made a great Noise in the Town, and many Pens, more Tongues, [are] daily employ'd in the most bitter Invectives, against the Company in general, and the *Directors* in particular."[12] Just as all classes of propertied society had participated in the gain, all shared in the loss:

> The covetous Infatuation
> Was smittle out o'er a' the Nation,
> Clergy, and Lawyers, and Physicians,
> Mechanics, Merchants, and Musicians;
> Baith Sexes of a' Sorts and Sizes
> Drap'd ilk Design and job'd for Prizes.[13]

The slump rippled through the country, felt as a sudden contraction in the availability of money even by those who had stayed out of the securities market.[14] (This effect was most likely much weaker, on the other hand, than the effect of a similar stock market crash would be today, because the market was much smaller, and links between the securities market and the general economy were still relatively weak.[15])

---

[11] Quoted in Joan Johnson, *Princely Chandos: James Brydges 1674–1744* (Gloucester: A. Sutton, 1984), 61.

[12] "Timothy Telltruth," *Matter of Fact; or, The Arraignment and Tryal of the Di——rs of the S——S– Company* (London: John Applebee, 1720), 1.

[13] Allan Ramsay, "The Rise and Fall of Stocks, 1720" (1721), in Allan Ramsay, *Poems* (Edinburgh: Allan Ramsay, 1721), 265. Ramsay wrote this poem, and the others quoted in this chapter, in Scottish dialect.

[14] Neil McKendrick, John Brewer, and J. H. Plumb, *The Birth of a Consumer Society: The Commercialization of Eighteenth-Century England* (Bloomington: Indiana University Press, 1982), 212.

[15] Julian Hoppit, *Risk and Failure in English Business 1700–1800* (Cambridge: Cambridge University Press, 1987), 132–33 (demonstrating that English bankruptcy figures show no response to any national crisis, including the Bubble, in the first half of the eighteenth century); Moshe Buchinsky and Ben Polak, "The Emergence of a National Capital Market in England, 1710–1880," *Journal of Economic History* 53 (1993): 17–18.

Looking back on the events of 1720, observers saw a nation that had lost its reason in the pursuit of profit:

> No wonder, they were caught by *South-Sea* Schemes,
> Who ne'er enjoyed a Guinea, but in Dreams;
> No wonder, they their Third Subscriptions sold,
> For Millions of imaginary Gold.[16]

The prospect of easy money, of getting something for nothing, had, as many contemporaries saw it, lured the nation into an irrational frenzy of securities trading.

> Sair have we pelted been with Stocks,
> Casting our Credit at the Cocks.
> Lang guilty of the highest Treason
> Against the Government of Reason;
> We madly, at our ain Expences,
> Stock-job'd away our Cash and Senses.[17]

Stories of individual tragedy abounded, tragedy in the classic sense of disaster brought upon oneself by aiming too high. "I was yesterday in the *Alley*," the widely read "Cato" recounted in late 1720:

there I was shewn an unhappy Man (*amongst many others*) with this Account of him; He had a good Estate in the Country, which brought him in a plentiful Income of *Fifteen hundred Pounds a Year*, but this did not satisfy him; he wanted to be worth a Million, and his Wife to be a Dutchess; it cut the Hearts both of him and her to behold *little prim Prick'd-ear'd Citizens* wallowing in Luxury, and boasting their *Hundred Thousands*, while they themselves, who were People of Breeding, and had never stood behind Compters, were forced to sit down with their original Fortune, which only afforded them ENOUGH: He therefore turn'd his whole Estate into Money, and brought his whole Money into the *Alley*; and behold the Effect! Two Months ago he had *Forty five thousand Pounds*, but it's now all gone, and *Ten thousand Pounds* into the Bargain; and all the miserable Man has left is, *a Wife and Seven Children*.[18]

A songwriter summed up the country's mood at the end of 1720, playing upon the double meaning of the word "Stocks."

> Farewell your Woods your Houses Lands your Pastures
>   And your Flocks.
> For now you have nought but your Selves in ye Stocks.[19]

---

[16] John Gay, *A Panegyrical Epistle to Mr. Thomas Snow* (London: Bernard Lintot, 1721), 2. "Third Subscriptions" is a reference to one of the issues of new stock in the South Sea Company. Gay had been a South Sea stockholder during the crash. William Henry Irving, *John Gay: Favorite of the Wits* (Durham: Duke University Press, 1940), 186.

[17] Ramsay, "The Rise and Fall," *Poems*, 264.

[18] Thomas Gordon and John Trenchard, *A Collection of All the Political Letters in the London Journal, to December 17, Inclusive, 1720* (London: J. Roberts, 1721), 11–12.

[19] Thomas D'Urfey, *The Hubble Bubbles* (London: J. Roberts, 1720).

If contemporaries could take any satisfaction from the events of 1720, it was that stockjobbers suffered as much as anyone else. Even "ruin'd fools are highly pleased," explained one anonymous poet, "[t]o see the Knaves that bit 'em squees'd."[20] It was no doubt consoling, after the fall of South Sea stock, to read of a bankrupt stockjobber contemplating suicide:

> On the Shore of a low ebbing Sea,
> A sighing young Jobber was seen
> Staring wishfully at an old Tree
> Which grew on the Neighbouring Green;
> There's a Tree that can finish the Strife
> And Disorder that wars in my Breast,
> What need one be pain'd with his Life,
> When a Halter can purchase him rest?[21]

In the end, it was agreed, the Bubble had been an extraordinary event, one that would be remembered for some time:

> Let the immortal Annals of old Fame,
> No more her antique Works with Wonder name;
> . . .
> But the sole Wonder of the World shall be,
> The modern Project of the *Southern Sea*.[22]

One side of Hogarth's 1721 print *The South Sea Scheme* is dominated by an enormous monument, whose inscription reads: "This monument was erected in memory of the destruction of this city by the South Sea in 1720."[23]

An event this momentous was one from which lessons had to be drawn. While the price of South Sea stock was still falling, contemporaries began searching for ways of dealing with the consequences. One aspect of this search was backward looking; throughout late 1720 and 1721, Parliament and the nation took part in a lively debate over what, if anything, should be done to punish the directors of the South Sea Company, to restructure the Company's finances, and to redress the claims of those who had been ruined. This debate and its outcome have

---

[20] *The Bubblers Medley, or a Sketch of the Times: Being Europes Memorial for the Year 1720* (London: Carrington Bowley, 1720).

[21] Allan Ramsay, "The Satyr's Comick Project for Recovering a Young Bankrupt Stockjobber" (1721), *Poems*, 274. In 1721, readers would have recognized the "low ebbing Sea" in the first line as a reference to the fall of the South Sea Company.

[22] J. B., *A Poem Occasion'd by the Rise and Fall of* South-Sea *Stock* (London: Samuel Chapman, 1720), 25–26.

[23] David Dabydeen, *Hogarth, Walpole and Commercial Britain* (London: Hansib, 1987), 20, figure 2.

been amply described elsewhere,[24] and will not be considered here. The other kind of lesson to be drawn from the Bubble was forward looking. What might be done to prevent such an event from happening again? Was it the fault of securities traders? Should the market be regulated? Should it be banned? Questions like these focused public attention on the securities market to an unprecedented degree, and led to the formation of a body of thought critical of the market.

II

"[T]he method of improving Money in the publick Funds," one satirist noted while South Sea stock was still on the rise, "hath as an Emphasis of Contempt been term'd *Stock-jobbing*."[25] After the fall, that contempt grew even greater. Stockjobbers had become *"manifest Enemies to God and Man, no Man can call them his Neighbours; they are Rogues of Prey, they are Stock-Jobbers, they are a Conspiracy of Stock-Jobbers: A Name which carries along with it such a detestable deadly Image, that it exceeds all humane Invention to aggravate it."*[26] Other writers had more sympathy for the traders, but located the cause of the Bubble in the existence of the market itself. The year after the Bubble saw an outpouring of this sort of anti-securities literature, much of it quite bitter.[27]

Criticism of the market and the stockjobbers took four main lines of argument. All had been present in rudimentary form in pre-Bubble English thought, but all became more detailed in 1720 and 1721. These four types of criticism would become long-running motifs in English and American culture. Securities markets and securities traders were criticized for (a) giving rise to deceit, particularly by permitting new forms of predatory behavior; (b) constituting a non-productive sphere of the economy, and diverting resources from more productive pursuits; (c) creating a subtle political threat to the nation's wellbeing; and (d) undermining the social order, in a few different ways. These modes of thought obviously overlap, and can often be found intermingled in the views of a given individual, but it will be

[24] Carswell, *South Sea Bubble*, 172–234; Dickson, *Financial Revolution*, 157–98.

[25] Elizaphan Shemajah, *A Letter to the Patriots of Change-Alley* (London: J. Roberts, 1720), 4.

[26] Gordon and Trenchard, *Collection*, 32. For a parody of this overdrawn portrait, see "Telltruth," *Matter of Fact*, 9.

[27] For an overview, see Thaddeus Seymour, "Literature and the South Sea Bubble" (University of North Carolina Ph.D. dissertation 1955). Some of this literature is also discussed in Paul Harrison, "The More Things Change the More They Stay the Same: Analysis of the Past 200 Years of Stock Market Evolution" (Duke University Ph.D. dissertation 1994), 62–108.

useful to consider them separately, because some would survive, to reappear in the United States at the century's end, with greater strength than others.

Some of these complaints are unlikely to sound persuasive to modern readers, particularly those most familiar with modern securities markets. Where I suspect this to be the case, I will briefly attempt to convey why contemporaries might have held such views. It bears remembering throughout, however, that the law governing an institution is often the product of widely held beliefs concerning that institution, whether or not those beliefs prove "correct" (a word that lacks meaning in some of the contexts that follow) in the long run. For this reason, we will be concerned more with *what* was believed, and *why* it was believed, than with whether the believers were right. It bears emphasizing as well that this chapter is concerned only with elaborating the structure of *anti-market* thought that grew out of the South Sea Bubble. These views were certainly not held by everyone. In chapter 3, when we examine eighteenth-century regulation of the market, we will have occasion to inquire into how widely the thought considered here permeated English culture.

Deceit

Many contemporaries saw the securities market as a breeding ground for deceit, a place where "Brother cheats Brother, And Knaves and Fools trick one another."[28] The unique incentives faced by securities traders, it was argued, created a subculture where lying was the norm. In one poem, the emblematic "Genius of Exchange-Alley" explains:

> Cunning in Perfection reigns,
> In that fam'd Alley I frequent,
> Where Brokers, Jobbers, Jews and Saints,
> Each Day new tricking Arts invent.[29]

It was bad enough that this localized ethos existed: What made it so dangerous was the possibility that it might spread beyond the market into the wider culture. For some, that process was already underway. The Bubble – attributed to "a Set of crafty Men having undertaken to delude the World into an Opinion, that they can, by a little *hocus pocus* Management, make a single Unit become a good Ten" – had caused the

---

[28] Brockett, *Yea and Nay*, 7.
[29] Edward Ward, "Between the Genius of Billingsgate, and the Genius of Exchange-Alley," in Edward Ward, *The Poetical Entertainer: Or, Tales, Satyrs, Dialogues, and Intrigues, &c. Serious and Comical* (London: J. Morphew, 1721).

immorality of Exchange Alley to spill over the market's boundaries.[30] As the Bubble drew the nation's wealth into the market, new investors were lured into the market's ways:

> When *Stocks* ran high, and Wit's Productions fell,
> Wit grew a Stock, which *Wits* began to Sell.
> These taught the *Cits* their Birth-right was to Cheat,
> That Fortune could l[e]gitimate Deceit.[31]

This vision of the market rested on empirical observations growing out of the events of 1720. It became a commonplace that stock prices fluctuated wildly with news from abroad.

> The Stocks serene so Whispers discompose,
> And make them die mysterious as they rose.
> If Rumours fly, imported from afar,
> Of faithless Tyrants, or a rising War,
> Then strange Convulsions they begin to feel.
> Embroil'd by Fame, from high to low they reel.[32]

In the pivotal scene of the 1720 play *Exchange-Alley*, traders are depicted buying and selling stock in the "Flying Ships" company, an evidently absurd enterprise that would have instantly reminded contemporaries of some of the stranger projects floated earlier that year. As the scene begins, the stock price is 100. But as news arrives that the Russian czar (a threat to the success of the company's flying ships) is dying, the price skyrockets, in a flurry of trading back and forth among a small number of people. (The characters "Bite" and "Mississippi" are stockjobbers; to "bite" someone was Exchange-Alley slang meaning to make money at someone's expense, while "Mississippi" is a reference to the Mississippi Company.)

BITE. Flying Ships, Gentlemen.
1ST BROKER. At what Rate?
BITE. One Hundred and Fifty *per Cent.* – Don't ye hear the News?
1ST BROKER. You shall have it.
MISSISSIPPI. Flying Ships, Flying Ships –
2ND BROKER. Your Price?
MISSISSIPPI. One Hundred and Seventy-five *per Cent.*
2ND BROKER. I'll give it.
1ST BROKER. Flying Ships – Two Hundred *per Cent.* who Buys?

---

30 *A Letter to a Conscientious Man: Concerning the Use and Abuse of* Riches, *and the Right and Wrong Ways of Acquiring Them: Shewing that Stock-Jobbing is an Unfair Way of Dealing; and Particularly Demonstrating the Fallaciousness of the South-Sea Scheme* (London: W. Boreham, 1720), 14–15.

31 William Bond, *An Epistle to his Royal Highness the Prince of Wales* (London: E. Curll, 1720), 3.

32 John Fowler, *The Last Guinea* (London: T. Jauncy, 1720), 13.

2ND BROKER. I do.
MISSISSIPPI. Who'll buy Flying Ship's Stock?
3RD BROKER. I will, at what Rate?
MISSISSIPPI. Three Hundred *per Cent.*
3RD BROKER. There's earnest for Ten Thousand Pounds Stock – (*giving Money.*)

Moments later, however, news arrives that the czar is in fact at sea with a thousand warships. Worse, an account is given of "a great and terrible Whale, that swallows up whole Fleets of Ships at Sea." Stock in the Flying Ships company is now unloaded at any price. Mississippi is able to buy back the stock he just sold, at the new low prices.

1ST BROKER. Flying Ships – who Buys? –
2ND BROKER. Flying Ships – Ships Flying –
3RD BROKER. Flying Ships, Insur'd from the Whale.
4TH BROKER. Flying Ships – will no Body buy? –
5TH BROKER. Flying Ships.
. . .
6TH BROKER. A Bargain – Flying Ships.
MISSISSIPPI. Your lowest Price? –
6TH BROKER. Two Hundred and Fifty *per Cent.*
MISSISSIPPI. Will you accept of One Hundred and Fifty?
6TH BROKER. Yes, Sir.
MISSISSIPPI. Will you take One Hundred?
6TH BROKER. The Stock is yours at One Hundred.
MISSISSIPPI. I'll give about Fifty.
6TH BROKER. A Bargain.
MISSISSIPPI. No, I won't give beyond Twenty.
6TH BROKER. You have it at that Rate.

As soon as Mississippi has repurchased the Flying Ships stock, more news comes: The great whale has been slain. The future looks brighter for the Flying Ships company. Mississippi is back in the market.

MISSISSIPPI. Flying Ships, Ships at Sea –
1ST BROKER. What d'ye ask? –
MISSISSIPPI. One Hundred *per Cent.* – The Danger's over.
1ST BROKER. You shall have it.
. . .
MISSISSIPPI. Flying Ships – who give Two Hundred?
1ST, 2ND, 3RD, and 4TH BROKERS. We all do –
MISSISSIPPI. The Stock is yours, Gentlemen . . . we've done Business sufficient for to Day – I've got about Twenty Thousand Pounds – A good Days work.

Prices thus swung up or down, depending on the moment's news.

Equally common was the observation that traders, knowing that stock prices behaved this way, often manipulated the news for their own gain.

The audience at *Exchange-Alley* was clearly to infer that Mississippi was the one responsible for the three news reports; the play concludes with the line "Thus Those are Wealthy who but dare to Cheat."[33] Other writers were more explicit about traders' propensity to lie about foreign news. As one anonymous post-Bubble poet described the scene:

> In close Cabal there the old Gamesters sit,
> And study Means raw Country Heirs to cheat;
> Whisper strange Treaties in each other's Ear,
> But Whisper so as all Mankind may hear;
> Tell what new Conquests by our Fleets are made,
> And how in Course, that must advance our Trade;
> What, sell at such a Rising Time as this?
> It must Two Thousand be, it cannot miss.
> The gaping Culls, with strict Attention wait,
> And swallow in a Trice the gilded Bait:
> The Land's sold off with ev'ry Stick and Tree,
> And the old Mannor's drowned in the Sea.[34]

"These irregular and deceitful Methods of growing Rich," Thomas Gordon concluded, "have been (sometimes) maintain'd and carry'd on, partly by spreading false Reports concerning the publick Affairs, either Foreign or Domestick, in such a Manner, as may influence the Buyers and Sellers of Stock."[35]

In the years after the Bubble, the securities market was thus condemned as a den of liars, a place where deceit was so lucrative that it became a way of life. From a distance of nearly three centuries, it is difficult to gauge the accuracy of these observations. On one hand, the picture drawn by the market's critics was surely exaggerated; a market could hardly exist unless most participants think they can trust their fellows most of the time. On the other hand, the stereotype of the devious stockjobber, profiting from spreading misinformation calculated to influence securities prices, could not have become such a fixture without some grounding in reality. There must have been occasions where traders actually did make money by disseminating false news.[36] How often this occurred seems impossible to measure.

---

[33] *Exchange-Alley*, 25–26, 27–29, 29–30, 40.   [34] J. B., *Poem*, 14.

[35] Thomas Gordon, *An Essay on the Practice of Stock-Jobbing* (London: J. Peele, 1724), 3.

[36] In a celebrated trial nearly a century later, while England was at war with France, some prominent people were convicted of having spread false rumors of the death of Napoleon, for the purpose of boosting the value of English government securities. William Brodie Gurney, *The Trial of Charles Random de Berenger, Sir Thomas Cochrane, Commonly Called Lord Cochrane, The Hon. Andrew Cochrane Johnstone, Richard Gathorne Butt, Ralph Sandom, Alexander McRae, John Peter Holloway, and Henry Lyle, for a Conspiracy* (London: J. Butterworth, 1814). See also *Rex v. De Berenger*, 3 M. & S. 67, 105 Eng. Rep. 536 (K.B. 1814).

The price fluctuations characteristic of the securities market, combined with the invention of options and time bargains, meant that for every person who made money in the market there was often another, and sometimes many, who lost money. When prices rose, the holders of stock were winners, but traders with commitments to sell stock in the future were losers. When prices fell, the opposite was true. This lesson was brought home even to casual observers of the market in the second half of 1720, when the general decline in stock prices caused many to lose fortunes, but worked to the advantage of the much smaller number of more sophisticated traders holding rights to sell stock at older, higher prices.

This was a state of affairs with no parallel in older markets. Critics charged that the very structure of the securities market encouraged predatory behavior among participants. One post-Bubble cartoonist accused traders of being willing to

> Ruine your Country for your own By-Ends,
> Cozen your Neighbours, and delude your Friends.
> . . .
> Impov'rish thousands by some *Publick Fraud*,
> And worship *Intrest* as your only God.[37]

Other writers after the Bubble said the same. According to William Bond, stockjobbers could not prosper without providing for the ruin of countless others:

> Each makes Tribes fall, to make him singly great.
> How many Families, nay, Towns undone,
> To make one *Monster*'s Fortune over-grown![38]

In the years after the Bubble, securities trading was thus conceived of by many as a zero-sum game, an arena in which there could be no winners without losers. Every attempt to make money by stockjobbing was, by definition, an attempt to make someone else lose money. As Thomas Gordon explained "the Practice of Stock-jobbing," it consisted of trying "to gratify the immoderate and insatiable Desires of some covetous and ambitious Persons, at the Expence of lessening the Substance, and procuring the irreparable Loss and Calamity of others."[39]

The diffusion of this understanding of the market was facilitated by a widespread belief that market insiders were able to control securities prices. This belief also attained currency in the second half of 1720, amid countless accusations that the price trajectory of South Sea stock had been engineered, in both directions, either by the directors of the

---

[37] *Lucipher's New Row-Barge* ([London]: s.n., 1721).
[38] Bond, *Epistle to the Prince of Wales*, 8.   [39] Gordon, *An Essay*, 2.

South Sea Company or by a conspiracy of stockjobbers. Such was the view of the committee of the House of Lords appointed to investigate the matter, which concluded that nearly everything the South Sea directors had done during the previous year had been for this purpose. The directors had declared a midsummer dividend: This "was calculated to put an Imaginary Value on the said Stock, and was one of the Causes of the unhappy Turn of Affairs." Some of the directors had personally purchased "refuses," or call options, at prices higher than the current market price: Again, this "was a fraudulent Artifice to raise the Price of Stock, far above the Value they knew it could bear." The directors had issued new stock (which sold out quickly) at high prices: This "was fraudulently Calculated to answer the Ends of Particular Persons," and "was a notorious Cheat on the Publick." While the stock price was declining, the directors had declared more dividends: These "were vile Artifices us'd by the Directors, to delude his Majesty's good Subjects, by possessing them with false Notions of the Value of the Stock, and in Consequence thereof, to encourage them to Buy at excessive Rates."[40] The Lords' assumption throughout was that the price of South Sea stock was easily manipulable by the directors. That assumption was evidently shared by many. "It is notoriously known," a contemporary charged, "that the false Insinuations and vile Practices of the late Directors, was designedly to impose upon innocent and credulous Persons, whereby Multitudes were drawn in to Purchase their Stock and Subscriptions at those high Rates."[41] "[W]hen they had rais'd the Notional Value of their Stock to the utmost Height," argued another, "they revers'd their Scheme, and bought for small Premiums the Liberty to put the Stock on the Gamesters for distant Time at Prices equally Exorbitant."[42]

Others attributed the same facility to stockjobbers. "[I]t's in the Power of a sett of Jobbers," one writer explained, "to raise or sink Stock as they please." When the Jobbers hold refuses, or the option to buy stock in the future at its current price, "then is their time to advance Stocks, and when they are come to a certain height, demand the Stock." Once they have done so, the Jobbers then sell puts, or the option to sell the stock in the future at its new higher price. "[T]hen it's their Business to go sinking the Stock, and when they see their time, demand the

---

[40] *Proceedings of the House of Lords in Relation to the Late Directors of the South-Sea Company* (London: Zachariah Stokey, 1721), 9–10.

[41] *The Case of the Purchasers of the First and Second Subscriptions to the* South-Sea *Company* ([London]: s.n., 1721).

[42] *Further Reasons Offer'd, and Fresh Occasions Given for Making Void and Annulling* Fraudulent *and* Usurious Contracts (London: s.n., 1721), 3.

Money for the Stock."[43] Again, stock prices are understood to be the product of manipulation by insiders, not the result of the interplay of supply and demand in the wider market.

With prices manipulable by insiders, and with the market structured so as to encourage predatory behavior, the moral was clear: The ordinary person should under no circumstances venture his money in Exchange Alley, because he would most likely be fleeced by the Alley's permanent residents. The most well-known (and in my view the best) of the satirical poems concerning the Bubble, Jonathan Swift's "Upon the South Sea Project," took this as its lesson.

> One fool may from another win,
> And then get off with money stored;
> But if a sharper once comes in,
> He throws at all, and sweeps the board.
> As fishes on each other prey
> The great ones swallowing up the small;
> So fares it in the Southern Sea;
> But, whale directors eat up all.
> . . .
> Each poor subscriber to the Sea,
> Sinks down at once, and there he lies;
> Directors fall as well as they,
> Their fall is but a trick to rise.[44]

The fall of the South Sea Company had so great an influence on attitudes toward the market that marine imagery was consistently used to describe this relationship between market insiders and investors. The directors and the stockjobbers were fishermen, waiting in the Alley for the investor-fish to come along:

> Come all who would by *Fishing* Gain,
> Venture like *Gamesters* on the Main,
> What e'er you loose *Projecters* Get,
> For you're the *Gudgeons* in the Net.[45]

Or the market was a treacherous waterway, where the market insiders were sandbars, waiting for the investor-boats to run aground:

> [N]eighbouring Alleys swell with sweating Shoals
> Of cheating Sharpers mix'd with cheated Fools.[46]

Or insiders were pirates, lying in wait for passing investor-ships:

[43] James Milner, *A Visit to the* South-Sea *Company and the Bank* (London: J. Roberts, 1720), 22–23.

[44] Jonathan Swift, "Upon the South Sea Project" (1721), in Pat Rogers, ed., *Jonathan Swift: The Complete Poems* (New Haven: Yale University Press, 1983), 209–10.

[45] D'Urfey, *Hubble Bubbles.* A "gudgeon" is a kind of fish.   [46] J. B., *Poem*, 25.

> To prove successful Pirates on the Main,
> Else all our deep Designs will prove in vain;
> False Colours we'll assume to vail our Crime,
> And pass for honest Traders on the Brime.[47]

Whatever the metaphor, the securities market was understood as a forum for predatory behavior, where insiders with the ability to manipulate prices could turn a profit only by taking money away from innocent investors.

The accuracy of these charges is, again, hard to assess. Some of the sillier-sounding projects launched in 1720 while the market was on the rise were almost certainly fraudulent from the outset. Stock in the company organized "for the immediate, expeditious and cleanly manner of emptying necessary houses throughout England,"[48] for instance, apparently sold well in the first half of the year, as did stock in an enterprise devoted to the "Bleaching of Hair,"[49] although in the absence of any evidence that either of these corporations ever conducted any business, it is hard to imagine that they were anything other than vehicles for obtaining money from investors.[50] In smaller companies like these, a group of speculators able to afford a significant percentage of the shares would probably have been able to influence the stock price in a desired direction by concerted buying or selling. Outside investors had no systematic means of obtaining information about the financial state of a corporation, and thus the movement of the stock price was one of the few available signals of the enterprise's health.[51] How often this sort of manipulation actually occurred is another question, but the fact that contemporaries thought it happened frequently suggests that it happened at least occasionally. In an enterprise as large as the South Sea Company, on the other hand, and one in which stock ownership was as widely dispersed, it seems less likely that a group of insiders, whether professional speculators or South Sea directors, would be able to manipulate the stock price to any significant extent by concerted buying

---

[47] Alexander Pennecuik, *An Ancient Prophecy Concerning Stock-Jobbing, and the Conduct of the Directors of the South-Sea-Company* (Edinburgh: John Mosman, 1721). For a similar reference to "the *Land-Pirates* of *Exchange-Alley*," see *A Vindication of E[usta]ce B[ud]g[el]l, Esq* (London: W. Boreham, 1720), 5–6.

[48] Scott, *Constitution and Finance*, III, 447.   [49] *The Bubblers Mirrour*.

[50] The most famous of the bubble companies of 1720 – "A Company for Carrying On an Undertaking of Great Advantage, but Nobody to Know What It Is" – is almost surely apocryphal, and may well have been an invention of William Cobbett, in *Parliamentary History of England* (London: T. C. Hansard, 1806–20), VII, 662 n.*.

[51] For empirical support for this proposition, see Philip Mirowski, "What Do Markets Do? Efficiency Tests of the 18th-Century London Stock Market," *Explorations in Economic History* 24 (1987): 125. On the eighteenth-century market's efficiency generally, see Philip Mirowski, "The Rise (and Retreat) of a Market: English Joint Stock Shares in the Eighteenth Century," *Journal of Economic History* 41 (1981): 559.

or selling, unless South Sea stock was so thinly traded that the small fraction of shares controlled by the group accounted for a significant percentage of the shares traded.

The "fraudulent" practices identified by the House of Lords – declaring dividends, buying options, and issuing stock at a high but market-clearing price – would be thought by most modern theorists to be unlikely to have much of an influence on the stock price, although modern theory tends to proceed from assumptions concerning information costs and transaction costs that are probably unrealistic as applied to the early eighteenth century.[52] The cost of information may be crucial here, because without any other organized method of obtaining accurate information about the intrinsic value of a share of stock, a corporation's decision to declare a dividend almost certainly played a much larger role as a signaling device than a similar decision would play today.[53] The fact that the South Sea directors bought call options before they declared dividends suggests they anticipated that the dividends would cause the stock price to rise. Even under eighteenth-century conditions, on the other hand, it seems less plausible to fault the directors for their other "vile Artifices." In setting prices for new issues, for example, the directors were more likely riding a preexisting wave of public opinion than they were causing the wave in the first place. Still, until we know more about how stock market participants made investment decisions when stock markets were new, we cannot dismiss the possibility that the price of a new issue of stock was understood by some investors as a signal from insiders as to the intrinsic value of the shares already in existence.

The conception of the market as a zero-sum game, as a forum where there could be no winners without losers, would likewise be contrary to the views of most current theorists, who can by now draw on the experience of hundreds of years of expanding and contracting markets, and who can draw upon a background of economic theory that understands *all* markets as positive-sum institutions. This background of thought was already available in early eighteenth-century England, but was probably less widespread than the older contrary view, that domestic markets added nothing to the national wealth, but were merely

---

[52] See (respectively) Merton H. Miller and Franco Modigliani, "Dividend Policy, Growth, and the Valuation of Shares," *Journal of Business* 34 (1961): 411; Richard A. Posner, *Economic Analysis of Law*, 4th edn (Boston: Little, Brown, 1992), 445; Franco Modigliani and Merton H. Miller, "The Cost of Capital, Corporation Finance and the Theory of Investment," *American Economic Review* 48 (1958): 261.

[53] Jonathan Barron Baskin, "The Development of Corporate Financial Markets in Britain and the United States, 1600–1914: Overcoming Asymmetric Information," *Business History Review* 62 (1988): 199.

fora for shuffling goods from one person to another.[54] "'[T]is not what
is consumed among our selves . . . that is beneficial to us," one early
critic of the market explained, "but the sending abroad vast Quantities
of" English manufactures.[55] The securities market, as one such domestic market, would have fallen within this general presumption.

Non-productivity

The morality of the market was called into question in a more general
sense as well, by accusations that securities trading was a non-productive
pursuit, one that added nothing to the national wealth, but merely
diverted time and effort from other, more worthwhile activities. This
conception sometimes took the form of solicitude for individuals, who,
it was feared, would lose their hard-earned savings chasing profits that
could never exist. "[T]he artificial and prodigious Rise of the *South-Sea*
Stock," argued the Duke of Wharton in early 1720, in an unsuccessful
effort to prevent the House of Lords from authorizing the South Sea
Company to increase its capital, "was a dangerous Bait, which might
decoy many unwary People to their Ruin, and allure them, by a false
Prospect of Gain, to part with what they had got by their Labour and
Industry, to purchase imaginary Riches."[56] Or as Elias Brockett more
memorably put it while South Sea stock was still rising, investors were:

> Deluded with fallacious Dreams,
> Of Golden Mines in S**** S** Schemes:
> Or growing wealthy without trouble
> By some more advantageous *Bubble*.[57]

More often, however, the concern with non-productivity was on a
larger scale; it was not just that individuals might lose their money, but
that the country as a whole would be the loser, because people who
might be producing something were instead merely shuffling money and
paper around. "[T]he Business of the Stocks and Gaming have often-
times been compared,"[58] an anonymous critic of the South Sea
Company wrote, and that was true in two distinct ways. Securities
trading was conceptualized as gambling, not just in the obvious sense
that risk was involved (which led to the conclusion that stockjobbing
was equally immoral), but also in the sense that both pursuits reallo-

---

[54] Appleby, *Economic Thought*, 158–64.   [55] *Angliae Tutamen*, 8.

[56] *The History and Proceedings of the House of Lords, from the Restoration in 1660, to the
Present Time* (London: Ebenezer Timberland, 1742), III, 125.

[57] Brockett, *Yea and Nay*, 6.

[58] *The South-Sea Scheme Detected; and the Management Thereof Enquir'd into*, 2nd edn
(London: W. Boreham, 1720), 21–22.

cated resources among participants without adding to the participants' cumulative wealth. When one character in the play *Exchange-Alley* tells a broker, "Sir, I am a Gamester," the broker (named "Cheat-all") responds: "Your Business and ours is the same." Moments later, Cheat-all explains that the similarity arises from the fact that overall gain is impossible:

> Some rise, and some fall,
> The Devil and all,
> All Fools here their Fortunes may try,
> The Prospect is gain,
> They ne'er can attain,
> Like Gamesters at Hazard and Dy.[59]

Analogies between the securities market and gambling abounded in the year after the Bubble.[60]

Meanwhile, the hard work that built up Britain's economy – particularly trade and agriculture – was being discarded, in favor of this new non-productive way of life:

> But now th' old-fashion'd Ways are laid aside,
> And Men Post-haste to Wealth and Honour ride.
> Who to the Waves would ev'r instrust his Store,
> Or weltring lie in his own reeking Gore?
> Who flatter Courtiers? Who at Bar would plead?
> Torture a Text, or sow the Teeming Seed?
> When one small Venture in the *South-Sea* Stocks,
> Exceeds the wealthiest Farmer's choicest Flocks[?][61]

Merchants had diverted their resources from trade to investment; as a result, "the Regular Course of Business has been interrupted, and Avarice took the place of Industry."[62] But who could blame them? Why should they "think of Long Voyages, great Risques, and small Profits, whilst their Heads are turn'd round with vast Expectations from this most accursed and pernicious trade of *Stock-Jobbing*?"[63] Sprawled across the right foreground of Hogarth's *South Sea Scheme* lies the body of a woman, representing "trade," either sleeping or dead.[64]

While trade slumbered because of the securities market, it was argued, so did other productive pursuits. "The *Whim* of the *Stocks* in this Kingdom is of late so far cultivated and improv'd," one Londoner complained, "that one might reasonably conclude, the numerous In-

---

[59] *Exchange-Alley*, 22, 26.
[60] See, e.g., *The Bubblers Mirrour*; "Telltruth," *Matter of Fact*, 17.   [61] J. B., *Poem*, 11.
[62] Erasmus Philips, *An Appeal to Common Sense: Or, Some Considerations Offer'd to Restore Publick Credit* (London: T. Warner, 1720), 19.
[63] "Telltruth," *Matter of Fact*, 16.   [64] Dabydeen, *Hogarth*, 29, 53 (figure 14).

habitants of this great Metropolis, had for the most part deserted their Stations, Businesses, and Occupations; and given up all Pretensions to Industry, in pursuit of an *imaginary Profit*."[65] Even ministers and physicians had abandoned their posts (although that was not all bad):

> From factious Noise the Pulpit did refrain,
> And Priests preach'd Gospel out of Love to Gain:
> Physicians tainted with the Time's Disease,
> The People died, without the Cost of Fees.[66]

In early 1720, while Parliament was debating whether to permit the South Sea Company to increase its capital, the bill's opponents alleged that it only "countenanced the pernicious Practice of Stock-jobbing, which diverted the Genius of the People from Trade and Industry."[67] It was reported at the Hague that English "trade has completely slowed down, that more than one hundred ships moored along the river Thames are for sale, and that owners of capital prefer to speculate on shares than to work at their normal business."[68] By the following year, after the market had soared and crashed, this way of thinking had become common. "This Nation cannot, nor ever did thrive, but by Industry and Trading," the argument went, *both of which are much at a stand for the present*, by the ingenuous and publick-spirited Management of Stock-Jobbers."[69] The market had its winners and losers, but the net effect was that of "hindring the necessary Growth and Increase of Trade and Commerce."[70]

An argument that the market was unproductive, that it added nothing to the national wealth, ran up against an empirical observation that became quite striking in the summer of 1720: As shares in the South Sea Company and other enterprises grew more valuable, it appeared as if the country was growing richer. The most ordinary people had become wealthy overnight:

> So oddly Rich, so madly Great,
>   Since BUBBLES came in Fash'on:
> Successful *Rakes* exert their Pride,
>   And count their Airy Millions,
> Whilst homely *Drabs* in Coaches ride,
>   Brought up to Town on *Fillions*.[71]

---

[65] *Exchange-Alley*, preface.

[66] Leonard Welsted, *Epistles, Odes, &c. Written on Several Subjects* (London: J. Walthoe, 1724), 76.

[67] *History and Proceedings of the House of Lords*, III, 125.

[68] Quoted in Antoin E. Murphy, *Richard Cantillon: Entrepreneur and Economist* (Oxford: Clarendon Press, 1986), 170.

[69] Gordon and Trenchard, *Collection*, 12–13.   [70] Gordon, *An Essay*, 6.

[71] Ward, *A Looking-Glass*.

How could such wealth be generated by a market in which nothing was produced and nothing tangible was sold? The market's critics had an answer. The apparent expansion of 1720 was merely "Expence and Luxury, without real Wealth"; it represented an increase in the amount of nominal money in circulation, but not in the overall amount of property in the country.[72] The underlying real economy, critics charged, would inevitably bring the paper economy back to earth.

> Five Hundred Millions, *Notes* and *Bonds*,
>   Our *Stocks* are worth in Value,
> But neither lie in Goods nor Lands,
>   Or Money, let me tell ye.
> Yet, though our Foreign Trade is lost,
>   Of Mighty Wealth we Vapour,
> When all the Riches that we Boast
>   Consist in Scrips of Paper.[73]

A securities market created only the illusion of wealth, without contributing any real wealth to the country. Each increment of money invested in the market rather than in trade, and each hour spent in Exchange Alley rather than at a more traditional occupation, thus represented that much more of a reduction in England's standard of living.

Twentieth-century readers are likely to find that this non-productivity argument omits the ways in which a securities market actually does contribute to the national wealth, by facilitating the movement of capital between the people who have it and the people who want it. (Here again, modern readers have the benefit of a backdrop of theory finding value added by *all* markets, and they are accordingly likely to give securities markets the benefit of this presumption.) Twentieth-century readers might also point out that money invested in stocks does not necessarily mean that less money is available for trade, because the enterprise whose stock is being bought is itself likely to be conducting trade of some sort, which will increase in proportion to the amount of capital invested in the enterprise. Current theorists would most likely conclude that an economy in which no one is engaged in securities trading will be poorer than one in which some are, but that the desirability of trading has an upper limit – if the entire population were engaged full-time in securities trading, the nation would be poorer still. There is thus some optimal amount of money and time to be invested in a securities market, somewhere between zero and 100 percent. The amounts so invested at any given time may, in the view of some

---

[72] Gordon and Trenchard, *Collection*, 12.   [73] Ward, *A Looking-Glass*.

observers, be above the optimum; current criticism of the securities industry for "taking too many of our business school graduates" and similar sins proceeds along these lines. This sort of critique is a more refined version of the non-productivity argument popular around the time of the Bubble, but the essential point is the same – that the nation's overall productivity is suffering because too many resources are being put into the securities market. Thus if one asks whether early eighteenth-century critics of the market were correct that its *existence* harmed the economy, the twentieth-century answer is likely to be no, but if the question is whether they were right to argue that the market was absorbing too much of the country's labor and capital, the answer is no clearer with reference to the market in 1720 than it is with reference to the market today. Since 1720, we have developed a body of theory justifying the market's existence, but not necessarily the market's size at any given time.

Politics

When Gordon and Trenchard defined *"Stock-Jobbers"* as "A sort of Vermin that are bred and nourish'd in the Corruption of the State," they drew upon a third line of criticism of the market – its tendency to divide the public into factions, each with the incentive to advance its own interests at the expense of those of the nation as a whole.[74] This political threat was especially dangerous regarding the public debt, because it caused division over public policy depending on whether one hoped for a rise or a fall in the value of government securities, but the prospect of "clandestine Clubs, and secret Cabals, to invent diverse Schemes, and various Projects, promoting the unequal Advantage and Interest of separate Parties" loomed wherever stock of any kind was bought and sold.[75] The misdeeds that came to light after the fall of the South Sea stock – the Company's bribery of members of Parliament with stock, in exchange for statutes allowing the Company to increase its size – only intensified the perceived connection between the securities market and political corruption, because here was the clearest possible case of government diverted to the advantage of the few, and all for the purpose of making a profit from securities.

At its extreme, this line of thinking went, the political division created by the market caused the formation of a faction whose interests ran counter to those of the nation itself. Such was the theme of one of the more striking post-Bubble cartoons, *Britannia Stript by a S. Sea Director.*

---

[74] Gordon and Trenchard, *Collection*, 39.   [75] Gordon, *An Essay*, 3.

The conventional female figure of Britannia, representing the nation, is shown being offered a small bag (presumably of money) by a director of the South Sea Company. The director holds out the bag in his left hand; his right hand, meanwhile, is picking Britannia's pocket. Britannia says "Will you ne'er have done fleeceing me," to which the director responds "It is all for y^r Good." In the background is a ship, suggesting that Britannia's wealth is being taken elsewhere. Beneath the image is an explanation of what is happening:

> See how a crafty vile *Projector* picks
> BRITANNIA's purse, by *South Sea* shams & tricks;
> Drains her of Wealth till he has made her mourn,
> And humbly Cheats her with a *false Return*;
> Takes much, leaves little for her own Support,
> Gives her fair Words, but all he says comes short;
> Conveys her Riches to a distant Shore,
> And daily courts the silly Dame for more.[76]

In another cartoon of the same year, South Sea Company insiders are called "vile *Traytors*"; one of them is depicted being rowed to Hell by a crew of demons.[77] "[M]ercenary Stock-jobbers" owed no loyalty to the nation or the government; they were willing to take "every convenient Opportunity of embroiling the peaceful State of publick Affairs whensoever it serves their private Interest, or gratifies their covetous Desires."[78]

This sort of criticism is a subset of a larger mode of eighteenth-century thought on both sides of the Atlantic that has been much explored by historians in recent decades, often under the rubric of "republicanism."[79] It rested on a core of empirical truth. The English public debt had skyrocketed within the memory of people alive at the time of the Bubble, from near zero in 1691 to more than £50 million by 1720, because of recurring wars with France.[80] All those public securities had financed an unprecedented expansion in the size of the government, and especially in the Treasury.[81] Many government insi-

---

[76] *Britannia Stript by a S. Sea Director* ([London]: s.n., 1721).

[77] *Lucipher's New Row-Barge.*   [78] Gordon, *An Essay*, 9.

[79] On the place of public credit within this sort of political thought, see Julian Hoppit, "Attitudes to Credit in Britain, 1680–1790," *The Historical Journal* 33 (1990): 309–11. See generally Caroline Robbins, *The Eighteenth Century Commonwealthman* (Cambridge, MA: Harvard University Press, 1959); Isaac Kramnick, *Bolingbroke and His Circle* (Cambridge, MA: Harvard University Press, 1968); Pocock, *Machiavellian Moment*; H. T. Dickinson, *Liberty and Property: Political Ideology in Eighteenth-Century Britain* (New York: Holmes and Meier, 1977).

[80] John Brewer, *The Sinews of Power: War, Money and the English State, 1688–1783* (New York: Alfred A. Knopf, 1989), 114.

[81] J. H. Plumb, *The Growth of Political Stability in England, 1675–1725* (London: Macmillan, 1967), 112.

ders – from members of Parliament to ministers to the King's German mistresses – were shareholders in the South Sea Company.[82] From these observations, the critics drew some troubling conclusions. As the government grew larger, and as it came to have more and more funds at its disposal, opportunities for patronage grew. This new bureaucratic state, as the critics saw it, was self-perpetuating: As more and more people depended on the bureaucracy's existence for their livelihood, they developed a vested interest in keeping the bureaucracy alive, by issuing more and more debt to finance ever more extensive military projects.[83] And a similarly vicious circle was driving the stockjobbers: As they invested more deeply in government securities, they developed a greater interest in keeping that profitable relationship going, by encouraging the government to incur expenditures of increasing magnitude (often through an aggressive military policy), which would require more borrowing in the future.[84] The result was public policy made with a view, not to the overall public good, but to the benefit of a faction – the people involved in this new fiscal-military state.[85] Meanwhile, the members of that faction – the new "monied men" – were siphoning off the nation's wealth from its traditional holders, the owners of land, who paid into the Treasury the taxes that the government eventually paid back out to stockjobbers as interest payments on the public debt.[86]

This whole enterprise was funded by securities trading, especially in the public debt and in nominally private enterprises so closely connected with the government as the South Sea Company and the Bank of England. Within a system of political thought that abhorred factions – that understood interest groups as dangers to be avoided because of their tendency to divert policy away from the public good – the political danger posed by the mere existence of a securities market was unmistakable. Stockjobbers would inevitably pursue their own private gain rather than the public benefit; in this pursuit they would inevitably press the government for policies that would advance stock prices; and such policies (war, for instance) might have nothing at all to do with what an objective assessment of the nation's benefit would dictate.

Modern readers, accustomed to a bureaucratic state financed by borrowing, and comfortable in a tacit political theory finding nothing

---

[82] Ron Harris, "The Bubble Act: Its Passage and Its Effects on Business Organization," *Journal of Economic History* 54 (1994): 616.

[83] Pocock, *Machiavellian Moment*, 425.   [84] Brewer, *Sinews of Power*, 206–07.

[85] The phrase is Brewer's, 206, but the concept will be familiar to those who recall the "military-industrial complex" – another subgroup favoring a belligerent foreign policy for reasons of personal profit.

[86] D. C. Coleman, *The Economy of England 1450–1750* (London: Oxford University Press, 1977), 194–95.

wrong with the clash of rival interest groups, are no doubt unlikely to find this line of argument persuasive. That we no longer perceive any such political danger in securities trading, however, is evidence more of how our own political thought has changed over the years than of the unreasonableness of the post-Bubble critics.

Social structure

Of all the criticisms of the market generated by the South Sea Bubble, perhaps the most common concerned the market's effect on the social structure of England. Securities trading upset accustomed patterns of social life, it was argued, in a few different ways.

To begin with, observers of the market often noted that Exchange Alley drew investors from all walks of life, and thus became one of the rare physical spaces in early eighteenth-century England in which people of widely different social ranks intermingled as if they were equals.

> Here Lords and Porters undistinguish'd walk,
> And Skips with quondam Masters freely talk.
> In *Babel* ne'er more different Tongues were heard,
> Nor e'er more Nations in one Place appear'd.
> . . .
> All Sects and all Religions here agree,
> And all Distinctions mingle in this Sea.[87]

A set of South Sea Bubble playing cards printed in 1721, each bearing a cartoon and an appropriate verse, included a five of hearts depicting a chaotic scene full of people of various sorts buying and selling stock, above the lines:

> Here Stars and Garters, Jews and Gentiles, Crowd,
> The Saint, the Rake, the Humble and the Proud.[88]

As the verses suggest, not only were rich and poor rubbing shoulders in Exchange Alley, but members of normally unconnected religious groups were also in close contact. The 1720 play *South-Sea* included this exchange:

PLOW. A Stock-jobber! Pray, Sir, what Religion may he be of?

SCRAPE. Religion! why, they don't mind Religion in *Change-Alley*. But *Turks*, *Jews*, *Atheists*, and *Infidels*, mingle there as if they were a-kin to one another.[89]

---

[87] J. B., *Poem*, 12–13. The "Sea" in the last quoted line is, of course, a reference to the South Sea Company.

[88] [South Sea Bubble playing cards] ([London]: Carrington Bowles, 1721).

[89] W. R. Chetwood, *South-Sea; or, the Biters Bit* (London: J. Roberts, 1720), 16.

All became equal in the pursuit of money. The securities market washed away social distinctions, political affiliations, religious denominations, and national boundaries. It was a place where

> The Turk, and the Jew,
> And Priests not a few,
> The Country, the Town, and the C[our]t;
> Here Ladies and Peers,
> And some without Ears,
> To Cheat, and be Cheated resort.[90]

The market encompassed

> *Jew* and *Gentile, Saint* and *Sinner,*
> *Tory* and *Whig, Monsieur* and *Mynheer.*[91]

Exchange Alley was a great leveller. Many of the new "monied men" were from established families, but some were not, and some were from groups traditionally excluded from power.[92] It made no difference who you were or whom you knew before you entered: The market rewarded those who picked their investments shrewdly and ruined those who did not. Success or failure did not correlate with social rank or connections. It was easily measured in pounds gained or lost, and could not be concealed by one's origins.

And that, judging from the proliferation of complaints published in 1720 and 1721, was profoundly disturbing to many. People of no apparent skill or intelligence were striking it rich:

> [W]ithout thought these dawted Petts of Fate
> Have jobb'd themsells into sae high a State,
> By pure Instinct sae leal the Mark have hit,
> Without the use of either Fear or Wit.[93]

The most ordinary Englishmen were suddenly claiming eligibility for a social status that would have been out of reach before 1720. In the pack of South Sea Bubble playing cards, the three of hearts reads:

> An Upstart to the Herald's Office flys,
> Grown Rich in Stock, a Coat of Arms he Buys.

The cartoon above the poem portrays an official telling the Upstart that he "must give me your Pedigree." The Upstart answers: "Why S[r] as for my father & mother I never saw them."[94]

As the market rose in 1720, and investors of humble origin grew

---

[90] *Exchange-Alley*, 26.   [91] Brockett, *Yea and Nay*, 6.

[92] Brewer, *Sinews of Power*, 209.

[93] Allan Ramsay, *A Poem on the South-Sea* (London: T. Jauncy, 1720), 15–16.

[94] [South Sea Bubble playing cards].

richer, the effect could be unsettling for those accustomed to receiving deference.

> A Race of Men, who t'other Day
>> Lay Crush'd beneath Disasters,
> Are now by *Stock* brought into Play,
>> And made our Lords and Masters.[95]

To those missing out on the boom and watching their material and social superiority erode, even more galling was the tendency of the newly rich to mimic the trappings of the traditional elite.

> [R]ead some *Panegyricks* read some *Odes*,
> You'd think these *Nation-Robbers* had been Gods;
> Peruse some Verse on their Triumphant Carrs,
> Some mighty *Stock-Jobber* wou'd pass for *Mars*:
> There these high pompous Words *Magnificence,*
> *Bounty, & caetera* – would by their Sense
> Make you mistake a *Broker* for a *Prince*.[96]

While the market rose in the first half of 1720, it was criticized for allowing a new class of holders of paper wealth to rub shoulders with older propertied elites.

And when the market fell in the second half of the year, dragging many of the older elites down with it, this sort of criticism mounted.

> Some Lords and Lairds sell'd Riggs and Castles,
> And play'd them aff with tricky Rascals,
> Wha now with Routh of Riches vapour,
> While their late Honours live on Paper.[97]

The social reversal occasioned by securities trading was now complete. The lowly and devious had risen, while the mighty and well-bred had fallen:

> Say how, and by what means, a *Lord*,
> On sudden, turns not worth a T–d,
> While, from a Dunghill to a Coach,
> A *Rascal* rises in a Touch.[98]

Familiar hierarchies had been turned upside down:

> On haughty *Clerks* did humble *Nobles* wait,
> And *Brokers* rul'd, like Ministers of State.[99]

The London social scene was summed up in the 1720 play *The Broken*

---

[95] Ward, *A Looking-Glass.*   [96] Bond, *Epistle to the Prince of Wales*, 9.
[97] Ramsay, "The Rise and Fall," *Poems*, 266.   [98] C——M, *A Familiar Epistle*, 5.
[99] Welsted, *Epistles*, 76.

Stock-Jobbers. The play opens with a prologue "By a GAINER" in the market, an ex-shopkeeper who can now join the nobility:

> In all I Traded, *Stocks* and *Bubbles* too,
> My Wealth, by Shadows, and by Substance grew.
>   . . .
> What's to be done? A *Country House of Note*,
> And from the *Herald's Court* a borrowed *Coat*;
> Some *Idle Thousands* I'll my Girl's afford,
> *Titles* run low now, – each shall have a Lord.
>   Thus I from dirty Shop, and Counter free,
> Will mimick what, I scorn, the first Degree.

The play closes with an epilogue "By a LOOSER" – a mirror-image character, whose life has taken the exact opposite trajectory:

> With a fair flowing Fortune in my Hand,
> A clear *Estate*, a *Borrough* at Command.
> What mov'd me from my Country Seat to range!
> And take a Lodging near the damn'd *Exchange*:
>   . . .
> And now reduc'd, which Way must I contrive
> To beg or borrow! – any Means to live?[100]

The South Sea Bubble was widely perceived at the time to be as great a social reversal as a financial shock. In retrospect, of course, we can see the Bubble as one of the early stages of the long-term commercialization of social and political life. All one could know in the 1720s, however, was that something troubling and unprecedented was going on.

Contemporary criticism of the market's effect on England's social structure dripped with a degree of snobbery possible only among a class of people desperately afraid that it was losing its accustomed position. "[T]here is a very great difference," insisted the anonymous author of a 1720 pamphlet,

between a *South-Sea Gentleman* at Best, and a *Man* of an *Ancient Family*, tho' they both equally enjoy the good things of this Life. Our Ancient Families could not be rais'd without some Merit and Industry to entitle them to Respect; but these [i.e., the newly rich] are rais'd meerly by the *Whim* and Madness of the People, without any Merit or Pretence to Industry. There is certainly greater Honour due to a Person, who by his laborious Endeavours has acquir'd a Fortune, in an honest and laudable Calling, than to one that only runs into *Change-Alley*, and Bawls out *South-Sea Stock*.[101]

Trenchard and Gordon claimed to take a mischievous pleasure in

---

[100] *The Broken Stock-Jobbers: Or, Work for the Bailiffs* (London: T. Jauncy, 1720), prologue, epilogue.
[101] *The South-Sea Scheme Detected*, 18.

deflating the pretensions of "these over-grown rich Men" by publicly reminding them of their former stations. "There is a certain Tallow-Chandler," their pseudonymous "Cato" recalled,

who is deep in Stocks, and is grown a great Man by Virtue of his Gettings; but the poor Man is only Rich, he has not One other Endowment about him . . . I observed this same *Upstart* sitting lately at a Coffee-House in the Midst of a great Circle of People, who were worshipping him because he was Richer than they: I knew the great Revolution of the Man's Fortune, and his great little Worth, and so going up to him, Mr. *Swellwell*, says I, *I want Half a Dozen Pound of Farthing Candles; I know there are some good ones at your Shop* . . . He told me (after some resentful Wriggles in his Seat) that his Name was *Smellwell*; but that he kept no Shop. *Codso*, says I, Mr. *Smellwell*, *I ask you a Thousand Pardons; I had quite forgot: I have heard indeed that you have pull'd off your Frock, and put on your Chariot.*[102]

Whether or not this scene actually happened, it easily could have – the flustered chandler trying to invent a new identity, the sniping intellectual trying to knock the chandler back into place – and that alone is a powerful testament to the securities market's effect on social life.

Some of the newly rich were Jewish, and that circumstance played into an ancient strain of anti-Semitism to produce another reason to dislike securities trading – it permitted Jews to become too wealthy and too powerful. References to Jews abound in the post-Bubble literature critical of the market. One songwriter pointedly addressed his criticism to "Ye Circum, and Uncircumcis'd."[103] Another satirist derided the traders of Exchange Alley as a

> . . . crafty jobbing Crew,
> Who oft sell Stock, when they have none,
> And, with the *Christian*, blend the *Jew*.[104]

One 1721 cartoon presented the stereotypical image of a Jew, with the hooked nose and the hunched back, and urged readers to:

> Behold his mighty sword, his Back, his Nose.
> All are joynt Emblems of the *Nations Foes*.[105]

Reversals in social status must have been all the more disquieting because they appeared to benefit a traditionally suspect group of people.

Equally disturbing to contemporaries was the market's disruption of traditional gender roles. Women had been buying securities from the beginning – of the original subscribers to stock in the Bank of England, for example, 11.9 percent were women, who bought 5.9 percent of the

---

[102] Gordon and Trenchard, *Collection*, 3–4.   [103] D'Urfey, *Hubble Bubbles*.
[104] Ward, "Between the Genius of Billingsgate."
[105] *A Late Member* ([London]: s.n., 1721).

shares, and these percentages increased in the eighteenth century.[106]
But as securities trading grew more popular in 1720, "*Women of the
Town* are become Dealers in the *Stocks*";[107] women of all classes began
to frequent Exchange Alley to buy and sell stock for themselves:

> Our greatest Ladies hither come,
>   And ply in Chariots daily,
> Oft pawn their Jewels for a Sum,
>   And venter't in the Alley.
> Young *Harlot's* too from *Drury-Lane*,
>   Approach the *Change* in Coaches,
> To *Fool Away* the Gold they gain
>   By their *Obscene Debauches*.[108]

This new role for women was often satirized, in verses that suggest some
discomfort with the independence that securities trading could bring.[109]
If women could control their own wealth, sexual power might follow:
One author described a "wither'd Maid" who:

> Now Travels thro' the winding Alleys free,
> Rejoicing in the new-gain'd Liberty;
> Whilst with the glitt'ring Store, she seeks to Bribe
> Some needy Fop to warm her frozen Side.[110]

The idea that independent wealth, gained in the stock market, would
permit women to exercise new-found power over men was evidently in
the mind of the anonymous designer of the South Sea Bubble playing
cards. The jack of clubs depicts:

> Ancient Maids, that ne'er Defil'd the Smock,
> Boast of their great Success in South Sea Stock;
> Says one, when Poor, tho' Young, no Man would Sue me
> But now I'm Rich, Six Irish Captains Woo me.

On the queen of clubs:

> A Brisk Young Gentleman Attacks an Old
> Rich Fusty Beldam for her South-Sea Gold.
> She pleads her Age. He vows she's Young and Healthy
> And Swears no Woman can be Old that's Wealthy.

And, more ominously, on the jack of hearts:

---

[106] Dickson, *Financial Revolution*, 256, 298.   [107] *Exchange-Alley*, preface.
[108] Ward, *A Looking-Glass*.
[109] Catherine Ingrassia, "The Pleasure of Business and the Business of Pleasure: Gender,
    Credit, and the South Sea Bubble," *Studies in Eighteenth-Century Culture* 24 (1995):
    191–210, especially 200–05.
[110] J. B., *Poem*, 22.

> A South Sea Lady having much improv'd
> Her Fortune proudly flighted him the Lov'd.

The market's decline was actually a positive development in this light, because it caused a corresponding decline in the sexual power women could wield, and accordingly brought matters back into their traditional balance. This development was lampooned, with some appropriately risqué language, on the eight of spades:

> A Broker went to let a Lady know
> That South Sea Stock was falling very low;
> Says she, then what I gain in my good Calling
> By rising things, I find I loose by falling.[111]

The market's openness to anyone with money to invest enabled women to participate as equals, and thus, in the eyes of some contemporaries, reversed the conventional power relationships between the sexes.

The market's perceived threat to conventional gender roles was more often the subject of amusement than alarm, but the joke proceeded from the same connection between securities trading and women's independence. Nicholas Amhurst complained that his wife had made so much money in the stock market that she no longer cared for his company:

> Nay LAURA (which afflicts me most)
> So many Years my constant Toast,
> So warmly and so truly lov'd,
> False to our mutual Vows has prov'd;
> Her Fortune chang'd, she changes too,
> (Rich Maids alass! are seldom true!)
> Spurns at my low, *plebeian* Fires,
> And to an Equipage aspires.[112]

The Stock-Jobbing Ladies, a song probably published in 1720, suggested facetiously (in C major) that as long as women were preoccupied with securities trading, they would no longer be as available to men as sexual partners:

> *Ombre* and *Basset* laid aside,
>   new Games employ the Fair:
> and *Brokers* all those Hours divide,
>   which Lovers us'd to Share.
>   . . .
> With *Jews* and *Gentiles*, undismay'd,
>   Young, tender Virgins mix;

[111] [South Sea Bubble playing cards].
[112] Nicholas Amhurst, *An Epistle (With a Petition in it) to Sir John Blount, Bart., One of the Directors of the South-Sea Company* (London: R. Francklin, 1720), 9–10.

> Of Whiskers, nor of Beards afraid,
> Nor all their couzening Tricks.

> Bright Jewels, polish'd once to deck
> The fair one's rising breast,
> Or Sparkle round her Ivory Neck,
> Lye pawn'd in Iron Chest.

> The genuine Passions of the Mind
> How Avarice controuls!
> Even Love does now no longer find
> A place in Female Souls.[113]

The song can hardly have been intended to have been taken seriously, but the fact that the joke could be made suggests the effect the securities market was perceived to be having on conventional gender roles.

Lessons

The South Sea Bubble thus turned the relatively new securities market into a well-known cultural institution, one that provided critics a wide variety of ammunition for attacks.[114] Some, like Jonathan Swift, blamed the market's insiders, and urged drastic punishment:

> Directors thrown into the sea
> Recover strength and vigor there,
> But may be tamed another way,
> Suspended for a while in air.[115]

"Monsters as they are," asked Cato in reference to stockjobbers, "what would you do with them? The Answer is short and at hand, *Hang them*."[116] If taking other people's money on the highway was a capital crime, after all, why not taking other people's money in Exchange Alley?

> For sure if *Tyburn* had a just Supply,
> More *Stock-Jobbers*, than *Highway-Men*, would die.[117]

Others placed the blame not on the stockjobbers themselves, but on the market in general, which served as a metaphor for a world in decline.[118]

---

[113] *The Stock-Jobbing Ladies* (s.l.: s.n., 1720). Ombre and basset were card games.

[114] See David Barton, "Pro-Fund Wit: Jonathan Swift and the Scriblerians" (New York University Ph.D. dissertation 1994), 176–230.

[115] Swift, "Upon the South Sea Project," 213.

[116] Gordon and Trenchard, *Collection*, 32.

[117] *The Broken Stock-Jobbers*, epilogue. See also *Lucipher's New Row-Barge*.

[118] See Sandra Sherman, "The Poetics of Trade: Finance and Fictionality in the Early Eighteenth Century" (University of Pennsylvania Ph.D. dissertation 1993), 46.

> Fools lost when the *Directors* won;
> But now the *Poor Directors* loose,
> And where the *S. Sea Stock* will run
> *Old Nick*, the first *Projector knows.*[119]

On this view, the Bubble served as a warning that England had better mend its ways.

> Ye Fools in Great-Britain, repent in your Folly
> Bewailing the Loss of your Money and Lands,
> Unto your Vexation, 'tis fled from the Nation,
> And Blockheads and Ninnies have got it in hand.[120]

Although the misbehavior of securities traders had "brought upon this . . . Nation all our present dreadful and intolerable Calamities," more would be needed than simply punishing the particular people involved. "[T]here can be no Cure for our dying Country, unless there be an entire Change wrought in the Minds of Men."[121] The fault lay with human greed in general:

> Oh! foolish, mad, degen'rate Race,
> So fond of *Ruin*, Wedded to Disgrace![122]

And while reform would have to be fundamental, it would also have to come quickly. As one writer recalled, the Biblical pharaoh had once been in an analogous situation; England might do well to remember what happened to him:

> [I]f I mistake not, I've read that his Host,
>   And himself in the *Red Sea* were utterly lost:
> He thought to get Riches, and why should not we,
>   Remember the *Red*, when we cross the *South Sea?*[123]

Where one laid the blame for the Bubble was important, because it dictated the kind of reform that would be necessary for the future. If a small number of dishonest stockjobbers was at fault, then they could be punished, and perhaps the market should be regulated so as to make it more difficult for similar dishonesty to prevail in the future. But if the market itself was to blame – if securities trading was inherently bad,

---

[119] *The Bubblers Medley*, 2.
[120] *The Bublers Medley, or the D-v-l will have his own* (s.l.: s.n., 1720).
[121] Thomas Coningsby, *The Naked and Undisguis'd Truth, Plainly and Faithfully Told: What was the Unhappy Rise, Which were the Fatal Causes, And Who the Wicked Authors, of Great Britain's and Ireland's Present Dreadful (and Before Unheard of) Calamities* (London: J. Moore, 1721), 9.
[122] Francis Tolson, *A Poem on His Majesty's Passing the South-Sea Bill* (London: John Morphew, 1720), 6.
[123] *The South Sea Ballad.*

regardless of who the particular traders were at any given time – then a more drastic solution was necessary.

In the face of this sort of criticism, few were bold enough in 1720 and 1721 to defend the market in print. Some were careful to point out that opprobrium should be reserved for the dishonest, and that ordinarily there was nothing disreputable about buying or selling stock. "[A] serious Man may laudably purchase such Stock," one writer took pains to explain, "with Intention to share in the fair Profits which may be gained by it; or if he finds a better Opportunity of employing his Money, may as reputably sell it again."[124] Others defensively pointed out that there was no law against buying or selling stock, and accordingly no reason to condemn those who did so. "If to sell Stock, and buy Stock," a contemporary argued, "be a capital Crime, or any Crime at all, they ha[v]e a great many sharers in their Guilt, and the Losers as well as the Gainers, are equally Criminal."[125] Defenders of the market were quick to note that many of the critics had been willing participants while the market was on the rise, and had developed their moral sensitivity only after they had lost their money. "[I]f the Caprice of the People puts a higher value on a Share in these Funds than the Projector ever design'd," one observed, "the fault was their own, and the loss must fall on the most Credulous."[126] "As for the Inability of some to make good their Contracts," lectured another, they "themselves ought to have thought of that before they contracted."[127] Daniel Defoe, who could not be expected to sit this debate out, took a similar position. Some of the losses suffered during 1720, he conceded, had been caused by the fraudulent conduct of corporate promoters. "[Y]et a great Number of" the losses, he concluded,

must be attributed to the Misconduct of those upon whom they have fallen. Some arising either from an insatiable Desire of gaining Treasures not thought of by our Ancestors, and thereby have neglected those Opportunities which would have secured Happiness and Plenty to themselves and their Families, while others by purchasing vastly beyond what their Abilities could make good, are plunged into irretrievable Ruin.[128]

If the supposed victims of the Bubble were not victims at all, if they brought their own misfortune on themselves, that also had consequences for the future, because it suggested that the market should

---

[124] *A Letter to a Conscientious Man*, 12–13.   [125] "Telltruth," *Matter of Fact*, 33.

[126] *Mr.* Law's *Character Vindicated in the Management of the Stocks in France, with the True Reasons for their Sinking* (London: T. Warner, 1721), 23.

[127] J. Way, *The Case of Contracts for the Third & Fourth Subscriptions to the* South-Sea Company, Consider'd (London: J. Roberts, 1720), 11.

[128] Daniel Defoe, *The South-Sea Scheme Examin'd; and the Reasonableness Thereof Demonstrated* (London: J. Roberts, 1720), 8–9.

continue to operate much as it had in the past. Investors, presumably a bit wiser than before, would moderate their expectations, and the events of 1720 would not be seen again.

Popular attitudes toward the securities market thus crystallized in 1720 and 1721. As chapters 3 and 4 will demonstrate, these attitudes remained fixed in English culture for the rest of the century, and then crossed the Atlantic when the United States developed a securities market of its own at the century's end. These attitudes also created demands for regulation designed to limit or suppress the practice of stockjobbing. The efforts made during and immediately after the Bubble, and the regulation they produced, will be discussed in the remainder of this chapter. The regulation attempted and attained through the rest of the century will be addressed in chapter 3.

III

The first legal change occasioned by the Bubble took place while stock prices were still rising. The boom of early 1720 caused shares to be advertised in all sorts of new projects, the promoters of many of which had never received corporate charters. The House of Commons formed a committee in February to draft legislation on the matter. The resulting statute was enacted in June. Its title – "An act for better securing certain powers and privileges intended to be granted by his Majesty by two charters for assurance of ships and merchandizes at sea, and for lending money upon bottomry; and for restraining several extravagant and unwarrantable practices therein mentioned" – gave little indication of its contents.[129] Years later, the statute would come to be called the Bubble Act.

The bulk of the statute comprised the articles of incorporation of two new marine insurance companies. But in section 18, the subject matter of the statute changed abruptly, as if Parliament had combined two separate statutes into one. (In fact, section 18 begins with a preamble, the first to appear in the Act since before section 1, which further suggests that two statutes on different subjects had been merged.) Parliament found it "notorious, that several undertakings or projects" had recently been "publickly contrived and practiced" throughout

---

[129] 6 Geo. I c. 18 (1720). Writers since Blackstone have erroneously suggested that the Bubble Act was enacted "after the infamous south sea project had beggared half the nation." William Blackstone, *Commentaries on the Laws of England*, 9th edn (London: W. Strahan, 1783), IV, 117. See, e.g., F. W. Maitland, "Trust and Corporation," in F. W. Maitland, *Selected Essays*, ed. H. D. Hazeltine, G. Lapsley, and P. H. Winfield (Cambridge: Cambridge University Press, 1936), 208. The Act went through Parliament, and went into effect, while stock prices were still on the rise.

England, by people who "under false pretences of publick good, do presume, according to their own devices and schemes, to open books for publick subscriptions, and draw in many unwary persons to subscribe therein towards raising great sums of money." Many of these projectors have "presumed to act as if they were corporate bodies, and have pretended to make their shares in stocks transferrable or assignable, without any legal authority, either by act of parliament, or by any charter from the crown for so doing." For the purpose of "suppressing such mischievous and dangerous undertakings and attempts," Parliament prohibited the sale of stock in unchartered enterprises and in enterprises exceeding the scope of their charters. "[T]he acting or presuming to act as a corporate body or bodies," the statute read, "the raising or pretending to raise transferrable stock or stocks, the transferring or pretending to transfer or assign any share or shares in such stock or stocks, without legal authority, either by act of parliament, or by any charter from the crown . . . shall . . . be deemed to be illegal and void."[130]

The Act went onto provide four mechanisms of enforcement. The sale of stock in an unchartered enterprise was "deemed to be a publick nuisance," thereby subjecting the promoter "to such fines, penalties, and punishments, whereunto persons convicted for common and publick nuisances are, by any of the laws and statutes of this realm, subject and liable." Violators of the statute were additionally made subject to the penalties applicable to a *praemunire*, a species of non-capital criminal offense; such penalties typically included imprisonment and the forfeiture of property to the crown.[131] Any "merchant or trader" suffering a loss as a result of a violation of the act was provided with a cause of action for treble damages.[132] Brokers who bought or sold shares of unchartered enterprises would lose their licenses and forfeit £500 to the government, one half of which would be available to the informant who revealed the broker's conduct.[133]

At the time, the Bubble Act was widely understood to have been enacted for the benefit of the South Sea Company, as a means of driving a large swath of alternative investment vehicles from the market, thus channeling more capital into South Sea shares.[134] The language of the statute and the events of 1720 support this interpretation. Three sections of the Bubble Act specifically exempted the South Sea Company from its provisions, but the Act mentioned no other previously chartered enterprise by name, with the exception of a single

---

[130] 6 Geo. I c. 18, § 18.

[131] Ibid., § 19. On the *praemunire*, see Blackstone, *Commentaries*, IV, 103–17.

[132] 6 Geo. I c.18, § 20.   [133] Ibid., § 21.   [134] Dickson, *Financial Revolution*, 148.

reference to the East India Company.[135] The South Sea directors took an active role in following the progress of the Act through Parliament, and probably in making the Company's views known to members, many of whom were, in any event, South Sea shareholders, and thus already likely to have a sympathetic view of the Company's interests.[136] Shortly after the Bubble Act took effect, the Treasury proceeded against four enterprises exceeding the scope of their charters whose stocks had risen quickly in the preceding months. The South Sea Company appears to have had a hand in instigating these proceedings.[137]

The possible alternative explanations of the Bubble Act are less persuasive. If the Act was genuinely intended to prevent the fraudulent sale of shares in new enterprises, it was woefully inadequate to that end. It required no proof of soundness before a new company could receive a charter, and, once an enterprise was chartered, the Act contained no provisions protecting the purchasers of shares. There was nothing about a corporate charter that made the promoters any less likely to be bilking the public. Prohibiting the sale of shares of stock in unincorporated enterprises would thus have been an extraordinarily roundabout way of suppressing fraud. As we will see below, all sorts of regulatory proposals circulated in 1720 and 1721 that would have been much more effective, which suggests that, even when the market was still as new as it was in the early eighteenth century, it would not have been difficult to draft a statute that went after fraud more directly.

The recent influence of public choice theory has prompted another explanation of the Bubble Act – that it was for the benefit of the government itself, as a means of preserving the revenue stream from the granting of corporate charters.[138] No contemporary evidence has been found to support this view. Payments for corporate charters amounted, by 1720, to only a tiny fraction of the government's overall revenue, and there is no evidence that charters contributed on any significant scale to the personal income of anyone associated with the government.[139]

Whatever the Bubble Act's purpose, the Act failed to achieve it. It did

---

[135] 6 Geo. I c. 18, §§ 24, 26, 27. The reference to the East India Company is in section 26.

[136] Harris, "The Bubble Act," 615–17.

[137] Such is the view of Dickson and Carswell, the closest students of the subject, although the evidence on this point is uncertain. Dickson, *Financial Revolution*, 149–50 & 150 n.1; Carswell, *South Sea Bubble*, 141 & n.*. For the contrary view, see L. C. B. Gower, "A South Sea Heresy?," *Law Quarterly Review* 68 (1952): 214.

[138] Margaret Patterson and David Reiffen, "The Effect of the Bubble Act on the Market for Joint Stock Shares," *Journal of Economic History* 50 (1990): 163; Henry N. Butler, "General Incorporation in Nineteenth Century England: Interaction of Common Law and Legislative Processes," *International Review of Law and Economics* 6 (1986): 172–73.

[139] Harris, "The Bubble Act," 620–21.

not prop up the price of South Sea stock by diverting capital from other enterprises; it did nothing to prevent investment in the South Sea Company's main competitors for capital, the other large English corporations, and in fact the stock of all these enterprises began to fall within a few months after the Act took effect. The Act did not dampen the speculative trading or the fraudulent promotions of the first half of 1720; those ends were achieved only by the crash of stock prices in the second half of the year. The Act did not increase the government's revenue from granting corporate charters; the number of bills to incorporate new enterprises did not rise after 1720.[140] It is not even clear that the Bubble Act changed the law in any meaningful way. The creation of a corporation with transferable shares of stock was probably understood, even before the Act, to require the government's license; a few decades later, Blackstone suggested that the common law imposed such a requirement, without any reference to the Act.[141] The Act thus appears to have provided only remedies for violations of a preexisting rule, and at most to have clarified a previously nebulous area of law.[142]

Indeed, the Bubble Act appears to have had a negligible effect on securities trading and on eighteenth-century corporate finance generally.[143] In the entire century there was only one reported case involving the Act. In 1722, Francis Caywood was prosecuted for selling shares in an unchartered venture to trade in the North Sea. He was fined £5 and sentenced to imprisonment during the King's pleasure.[144] Despite the apparent prevalence of unchartered joint-stock companies, the next reported case did not take place until 1808.[145] In that case, Rex v. Dodd, the King's Bench refused to enforce the Act, in part because of the "lapse of so many years since any similar prosecution was instituted," but left open the possibility of enforcement in the future.[146] After a brief

---

[140] Ibid., 621.

[141] Blackstone, *Commentaries*, I, 472. See also *Case of Sutton's Hospital*, 10 Co. Rep. 23a, 29b, 77 Eng. Rep. 960 (K. B. 1615). See Samuel Williston, "History of the Law of Business Corporations Before 1800," *Harvard Law Review* 2 (1888): 114.

[142] The content of the common law in this regard became an important disputed issue once the Bubble Act was repealed in 1825. After a series of inconsistent decisions, the courts determined that the formation of a joint-stock company without the government's permission was not a violation of the common law. These cases are discussed in Bishop Carleton Hunt, *The Development of the Business Corporation in England 1800–1867* (Cambridge, MA: Harvard University Press, 1936), 41–44.

[143] See generally Ron Harris, "Industrialization Without Free Incorporation: The Legal Framework of Business Organization in England, 1720–1844" (Columbia University Ph.D. dissertation 1994).

[144] *Rex v. Caywood*, 1 Strange 472, 93 Eng. Rep. 641 (K.B. 1722).

[145] Armand Budington Dubois, *The English Business Company after the Bubble Act 1720–1800* (New York: Commonwealth Fund, 1938), 10–11, 39.

[146] *Rex v. Dodd*, 9 East 516, 103 Eng. Rep. 670 (K.B. 1808).

flurry of litigation over its coverage,[147] the Bubble Act was repealed in 1825, in the midst, ironically, of the greatest stock market rise and fall since the Bubble.[148]

The Bubble Act, formulated and enacted while the market was on the rise, thus most likely had the curbing of speculative securities trading as neither its purpose nor its effect. When the market fell, on the other hand, many proposed various sorts of regulation aimed directly at curbing the perceived excesses of the market.

One proposal was to revive the 1697 statute which had limited options and time bargains by voiding those where the transfer date was more than three days after the contract date. The statute "was an Act so plainly founded upon *Reason* and *Justice*," in the view of one writer, "that it is *very surprizing* it should have been suffered to expire" in 1708.[149] Another exclaimed: "Happy had it been for this Nation had it never expired!"[150] Revival of the old statute was particularly appealing to those who believed that the South Sea insiders had caused the stock price to rise and fall by their own trading, because, had the statute been in place in 1720, the directors would have been limited in their ability to buy "refuses" on the way up or "puts" on the way down. "This vile Practice of Bargains for Time to *Put* and *Refuse* Stock, &c., was one of the chief *Artifices* used by the *late South-Sea Directors* and their *Agents* for imposing on the Credulous, and obtaining their fraudulent Purposes," explained one such critic. The problem "may easily be remedied, and the ill Consequences prevented, to the Quiet of very many Families," he concluded, by reenacting a statute "to the Effect of the [Act] passed in 1697."[151] Another "most humbly hoped, That such a *Clause* may yet be added to some *Bill*, since the Occasion is infinitely greater than it was in that Reign."[152]

Other proposals were more drastic. Some suggested prohibiting altogether the more esoteric techniques of buying and selling securities,

---

[147] See *Buck* v. *Buck*, 1 Camp. 547, 170 Eng. Rep. 1052 (N.P. 1808); *Metcalf* v. *Bruin*, 12 East 400, 104 Eng. Rep. 156 (K.B. 1810); *Rex* v. *Webb*, 14 East 406, 104 Eng. Rep. 658 (K.B. 1811); *Brown* v. *Holt*, 4 Taunt. 587, 128 Eng. Rep. 460 (C.P. 1812); *Pratt* v. *Hutchinson*, 15 East 511, 104 Eng. Rep. 936 (K.B. 1813); *Ellison* v. *Bignold*, 2 Jac. & W. 503, 37 Eng. Rep. 720 (Ch. 1821); *Josephs* v. *Pebrer*, 3 B. & C. 639, 107 Eng. Rep. 870 (K.B. 1825).

[148] 6 Geo. IV c. 91 (1825). See C. A. Cooke, *Corporation, Trust and Company* (Cambridge, MA: Harvard University Press, 1951), 95–109.

[149] *Reasons for Making Void and Annulling Those Fraudulent and Usurious Contracts Into Which Multitudes of Unhappy Persons have been Drawn . . .* (London: J. Roberts, 1721), 3.

[150] *Some Considerations with Respect to the Bill for Preventing the Infamous Practice of Stock-Jobbing* ([London]: s.n., 1721), 1.

[151] *Further Reasons Offer'd*, 6.

[152] *A Short, But True Account, &c.* ([London]: s.n., 1721), 1.

and restricting market participants to the transactions characteristic of simpler markets. "[L]et there be no such Thing as a Contract for time," the author of one pamphlet proposed, "and that no Bargain, without ready Money paid down, and a Transfer of Stock for the same shall be good. Let us now see, how we shall hereafter Buy and Sell. Why? By no other Means than giving Value for Value."[153] Such a rule, its proponents argued, would drive from the market those stockjobbers who attempted to manipulate prices, because prices would become unmanipulable when traders were restricted to simple purchases and sales. "Now if nothing is sold but what is paid for," explained one such analyst, "all their Tricks must end, and the true Intrinsick Value of our Stocks needs no Tricks, their own Weight will carry them up, when no formed designs, by giving out small Sums for time, can be carried on to depress them."[154] Some wished to go even farther, and to ban options and time bargains retroactively, so as to void "the great Numbers of Time-Contracts for *South-Sea*, and other Stocks, at the most exorbitant high Prices, which will now daily be growing due: VERY MANY OF WHICH, ARE BY THE ENSNARING AND FRAUDULENT WAY OF PUT AND REFUSAL." There was no doubt a large degree of self-interest behind the calls for the retroactive invalidation of contracts – one suspects that many of the proponents of such measures had made commitments in happier times to buy stock at prices that now seemed ludicrously high – but part of the motivation for such proposals may have been genuine concern for the "great Numbers of honest, tho' incautious and deluded Persons of both Sexes" who stood to lose large amounts of money.[155]

The Bubble drew forth a variety of other ideas about how to use regulation to counteract the evils of the market. Erasmus Philips, after noting that the passion for stock trading had diverted capital from more productive pursuits, suggested that the government re-divert that capital back to trade by subsidizing exports: "this might be a Temptation for 'em to . . . ingage heartily in their old Callings, to the Re-establishment of Commerce."[156] An Irish author proposed requiring a three-month holding period before resale as a means of preventing price manipulation, evidently on the theory that it is much more difficult to take advantage of short-run price movements if one cannot sell stock soon

---

[153] T. Goodall, *Every One's Interest in the South-Sea Examined; and by Rules of Justice and Equity Settled* (London: T. Bickerton, 1721), 19–20.
[154] Milner, *A Visit*, 23.
[155] *An Humble Remonstrance to the Lords and Commons of Great Britain* ([London]: s.n., 1721), 1.
[156] Philips, *An Appeal*, 19.

after purchasing it.[157] (Two centuries later in the United States, the same insight would give rise to section 16(b) of the Securities Exchange Act of 1934, which effectively discourages insiders from selling stock within six months of buying it.)[158] An anonymous pamphleteer proposed statutory price ceilings for stock, to prevent the sharp increases that had preceded the crash. The same author suggested that the government should police the soundness of the enterprises in which shares were sold, by imprisoning and confiscating the estate of "every *Projector* of a *Bubble*, which cannot fairly demonstrate a *Real Prospect* of *Benefit* beyond buying and selling of Shares."[159] None of these ideas came close to being implemented.

Both before and after the crash, Parliament considered legislation on the subject of stockjobbing. In May 1720, during the debates on the bill that eventually became the Bubble Act, a member of the House of Commons proposed that a clause "be added to the Bill, for restraining Stock-Jobbing." The House of Commons rejected the proposed amendment.[160]

In December, when stock prices had declined to their pre-Bubble levels and the idea of curbing stock trading was more likely to be favorably received, Parliament took up the issue again. The House of Commons formed itself into "a grand Committee" to consider "the present State of the publick Credit of the Kingdom." After a member persuaded the committee that "the present Calamity was mainly owing to the vile Arts of Stock-Jobbers," the committee resolved that "nothing can tend more to the Establishment of publick Credit, than preventing the infamous Practice of Stock-Jobbing," and ordered the drafting of an appropriate bill.[161] Desire within Parliament for such a bill could only have grown stronger when, a few days later, the House of Commons received a petition from the city of Worcester complaining that "Trade, of all Sorts is at the lowest ebb" because of "that pernicious and destestable Practice of Stock-jobbing," and asking that Parliament do something about it.[162]

A "Bill for the better establishment of publick Credit, by preventing, for the future, the infamous Practice of Stock-jobbing" was introduced in the House of Commons in February 1721.[163] After passing the Commons, it was sent to the House of Lords in April, where it

[157] *A Strange Collection of May-Be's* (Dublin: John Harding, 1721), 1.
[158] 15 U.S.C. § 78p(b).   [159] *The South-Sea Scheme Detected*, 21, 27, 20–21.
[160] *Journals of the House of Commons*, 19:367 (May 27, 1720).
[161] *The History and Proceedings of the House of Commons from the Restoration to the Present Time* (London: Richard Chandler, 1742), 6:225–26.
[162] *Journals of the House of Commons*, 19:393 (Dec. 23, 1720).
[163] *Journals of the House of Commons*, 19:418 (Feb. 8, 1721).

languished through the spring and summer.[164] In July the Lords sent the bill to a committee, which apparently never took any action, as the bill never came back to the full House.[165] Parliament did enact a weaker statute in 1721, one which governed only securities contracts already entered into but not yet performed, because of the perceived need "for preventing a multiplicity of vexatious and doubtful suits in law or equity concerning the same." These transactions were regulated in two new ways. First, contracts not yet performed or settled by September 29, 1721, were declared void unless they were registered on the books of the corporation by November 1.[166] The concept of requiring the registration of options and time bargains would return later in the century, in proposals to regulate the market prospectively. Second, all unperformed contracts for the sale of stock were declared void with respect to any amount of stock in which the seller "was not, at the time of such contract or within six days after, actually possessed of, or entitled" to.[167] The concept of requiring sellers actually to own the stock they purported to sell would also return to Parliament in the context of prospective regulation. With the exception of a 1722 statute punishing by death the crime of forging or counterfeiting the power to transfer shares of stock,[168] it would be a decade before Parliament would take up the issue again.[169]

Meanwhile, many legal commentators argued that no legislation was necessary, because the more complex agreements entered into by stock-jobbers were already unenforceable under existing law. These commentators advanced two groups of theories: First, that options and time bargains were by their nature unenforceable, regardless of the price; and second, that such agreements were unenforceable where, as was true of South Sea stock, a price change between the contract date and the transfer date made the agreement look unfair in retrospect.

The first of these theories rested on the speculative nature of such transactions. Money made in this manner was tantamount to "Moneys

---

[164] *Journals of the House of Lords*, 21:493, 535, 537, 578 (April 3, June 7, and July 24, 1721).

[165] *Journals of the House of Lords*, 21:579 (July 25, 1721).

[166] 7 Geo. I stat. 2, § 8 (1721). The one reported case interpreting this provision was *Rogers* v. *Wilson*, 1 Comyns 365, 92 Eng. Rep. 1114 (K.B. 1723).

[167] 7 Geo. I stat. 2, § 9.

[168] 8 Geo. I c. 22, § 1 (1722). This time period saw many other property crimes become capital offenses for the first time. Douglas Hay, "Property, Authority and the Criminal Law," in Douglas Hay *et al.*, *Albion's Fatal Tree: Crime and Society in Eighteenth-Century England* (New York: Pantheon, 1975), 17–24.

[169] In 1731, Parliament considered but did not pass a bill that would have revived the old (1697–1708) limit on the number of brokers. See *Case of the Licens'd Brokers, Upon the Bill Depending in Parliament* (s.l.: s.n., 1731).

won at *Play*, or by *Betting*," argued one writer; "certainly such Bargains ought to be set aside" under the law pertaining to gambling.[170] Some of these transactions, moreover, were "down right Usury."[171] If, in a rising market, the purchaser agreed to pay a price in the future higher than the stock's current price, solely on account of the time lapse between the contract date and the transfer date, "this Method of selling stock was unquestionably a Way or Device of indirectly taking *Usury*" whenever the seller's profit in the interim exceeded the lawful rate of interest.[172] "I have seen *Extravagant Usury*," testified another critic of time bargains, "Fashionable among Gentlemen" investing in securities.[173] Defenders of the market could respond only by arguing that the statutes regulating gambling and usury did not contain "one Word of Bargains for Stock or Subscriptions, or any thing that can be said directly to affect those Bargains."[174] No reported eighteenth-century English case has been found in which anyone attempted to have a stock purchase contract set aside on either of these two grounds. (The related issue of the validity under the law of usury of *loans* of stock will be considered in the next chapter.)

It is understandable in light of the events of 1720 that the second argument for unenforceability, premised on the price change between the contract date and the transfer date, was pressed more forcefully by the post-Bubble commentators. In what may with some justification be called the first English securities regulation treatise – Sir David Dalrymple's *Time Bargains Tryed by the Rules of Equity and Principles of the Civil Law* (1720) – Dalrymple reported: "The present great Question in all Companies is, what will become of TIME BARGAINS? Will they be good or not?" Dalrymple avoided what he saw as the difficult issue that would be presented "if this Point were to be try'd at Common Law," because the lengthy discussion that would be necessary "would swell my little Volume to a Bulk too great for the Use of those Gentlemen, for whom I principally design it." He resolved instead to consider the issue "according to the Laws of Nature and Nations, and the universal Rules of Equity."[175] Dalrymple found that "Writers upon the Law of Nature and Nations are of Opinion" that lopsided contracts are voidable to the

[170] *Reasons for Making Void*, 1–2.
[171] David Dalrymple, *Time Bargains Tryed by the Rules of Equity and Principles of the Civil Law* (London: Eliz. Morphew, 1720), 33.
[172] *Reasons for Making Void*, 2.
[173] *A Reply to a Modest Paper, Call'd, Reasons for Making Void* Fraudulent *and* Usurious Contracts, *Proved to Be, &c.* ([London]: s.n., 1721), 1.
[174] *An Answer to the Reasons for Making Void and Annulling Fraudulent and Usurious Contracts, &c.* ([London]: s.n., 1721), 3.
[175] Dalrymple, *Time Bargains*, 4–5.

extent of their unfairness; that is, "if the Buyer pays more than the Value" of the goods received, "the Seller is obliged, either to refund the Superplus, or to take back his Goods, and restore the whole Price received."[176] Dalrymple recognized that commodities have no intrinsic or natural value, and that value embodies nothing but "The General Opinion of the World about the thing sold," because "every thing is worth as much as the People of the Country where it is sold generally give at that time for such things." The mere fact that the market price for an item such as stock is unusually high, therefore, would give a purchaser no ground for relief from the obligation to pay; in such a case, the market has determined the value of the stock, and the purchaser has, by definition, received equivalent value for his money. In Grotius, however, Dalrymple found support for the proposition that if a man is "led into a bargain by any Error about the value of the thing he bought," he may avoid his obligation. If that was true of a single person, Dalrymple reasoned, it should also be true of "a whole People," because "a whole People may be deceived as well as one Man." The conclusion Dalrymple drew was that "If a whole People are in an Error, and believe a thing of more Value than it intrinsically is, no one of these People are obliged to fulfill the Bargains they made while they were led into them by this Error."[177] This was a conclusion that stood in considerable tension with Dalrymple's earlier premise that value resided nowhere but in the popular consensus, but if that tension troubled Dalrymple he showed no signs of it.

Dalrymple then proceeded to apply this reasoning to the case of a purchaser who incurred an obligation to buy South Sea stock while the market was at its peak, where the obligation came due after the crash. He assumed the set of facts least favorable to the buyer, in which "the Directors and Managers have been guilty of no Sinister Means or Methods to raise the Price of their Stock above its real Value (which I should be glad it were possible to believe)." He further assumed that "the Stock was Bought from a Man who was no ways concern'd in the Management, and knew nothing about the Value of it." Even in such a case, Dalrymple concluded, "The Buyer, by the Law of Nature, is free from his Bargain in as far as the Price exceeds the real Value of the Thing bought." This was because the buyer "was in an Error when he promised so much for it: He imagined that the Company, that is, the Directors had a Scheme of Trade in their View, which would make great Returns Yearly." Because the directors "never had such a Thought," the buyer's promise was founded in part on a mistake, and to that extent he

---

[176] Ibid., 6–7.   [177] Ibid., 9–10.

could be relieved from his promise. Dalrymple analogized the situation to one in which "there was a latent Defect in the Thing Sold, which if the Buyer had known, he would never have promised so much for it." Because the law of nature provided a remedy for the buyer in the latter case, Dalrymple explained, it should likewise relieve those who overpaid for South Sea stock.[178]

If such bargains even with honest sellers were unenforceable under these principles, it followed *a fortiori* that purchases directly from the South Sea Company were unenforceable. Such insiders, in Dalrymple's view, "ought to know the Value of the Stock they have under their Care as well as any Artist ought to know that sort of Work he deals in." If representatives of the South Sea Company "knew that what they sold was not worth half of what they got for it, they surely were great Cheats, and Guilty of the most heinous Fraud." In such cases, concluded Dalrymple, natural law required more than just releasing investors from their obligations; it obliged the insiders to "make up any Loss they have sustain'd by making such unreasonable Bargains."[179]

Most commentators agreed that a contract for the sale of stock at a price later proven to have been unduly high would not be enforceable in a court of equity. "[I]t is very plain," argued one, "that selling Stock above [its] Intrinsic [value] is the same kind of cheat as passing bad Money, for the Fraud in both Cases is the same, viz. The making them current for more than they are worth under Cover of a false fictitious Stamp."[180] Such contracts would be unenforceable, it was argued, even by a seller who was merely another market participant who had done nothing wrong and may well have been cheated himself. One writer provided some analogous hypothetical cases:

A buys Plate, believing it Standard, and pays for it as such: And afterwards Contracts to sell the Plate to *B* for 1000 l. to be delivered at a future Time: And the last Buyer gives his Bond to pay the 1000 l. But before the Day, it is discovered, that the Plate is mixed with Dross, and not of half the Value of Standard.

Will a Court of Equity relieve the last Buyer against his Bond or Contract, for the Fraud; although the Seller knew nothing of the Mixture with Dross, but was himself cheated, having bought and paid for the Plate as Standard?

Doubtless it will relieve.

A buys a Jewel as and for a Diamond, and pays 700 l. for it as such: And afterwards, believing it still to be a Diamond, Contracts to sell it as and for a Diamond for 1000 l. to be paid at a future Time. The last Buyer gives his Bond or Covenant to pay the Money; but before the Day, it is discovered that the

---

[178] Ibid., 11–12.   [179] Ibid., 13.
[180] *The Pangs of Credit* (London: J. Roberts, 1722), 44.

Jewel is a Counterfeit; a meer *Bristol* Stone, and not a Diamond.

Will a Court of Equity relieve the last Buyer against the Contract and Bond, though *A* the first Buyer was himself cheated?

Doubtless it will relieve.[181]

If such contracts could not be enforced in equity, the argument went, neither should obligations to buy stock at prices now revealed to have been far too high. The sellers may have been innocent victims as well, but to hold the buyer to the bargain would be to adopt as the law a "new invented Maxim of fair Dealing" authorizing the seller "TO CHEAT BECAUSE HE WAS CHEATED."[182]

The House of Lords resolved the question in *Thomson v. Harcourt* (1722), a case arising out of a transaction entered into "[d]uring the time of the wicked execution of the South-Sea scheme, and of the general infatuation thereby occasioned."[183] At the market's peak, Thomson had contracted to sell South Sea stock to Harcourt at a price of 920. By the time the bargain came due, the stock had fallen to approximately one quarter of its former value. Harcourt argued that the "Agreement is very unreasonable, [and] therefore ought not to be favour'd in a Court of Equity." Under "the Civil or *Roman* Laws," he explained, "all such exorbitant Contracts, were null and void, as carrying in themselves an Evidence of Fraud."[184] Thomson responded that "[n]o Contract is unreasonable, where the thing contracted for is sold at the usual or common Price." The very purpose of contracts, Thomson suggested, was that they insulated buyers and sellers from market fluctuations: "if Contracts were to be set aside only because the thing contracted for is fallen in Price or Value, there must be an end of all Contracts or Agreements, and consequently of Trade and Commerce." The rule proposed by Harcourt and by the legal commentators would have ramifications far beyond the securities market. "[N]o man will contract to sell any thing," predicted Thomson, "if such Contract be not to be perform'd, if the Price of the thing contracted for should happen to fall after the making and before the time for Performance thereof."[185]

The Court of Exchequer agreed with Thomson. "I can see no Pretence for calling it an unreasonable Bargain," held one of the judges,

---

[181] *Queries, Whether the* South Sea *Contracts for Time, and Now Depending Unperformed, Ought to be Annulled or Not?* ([London]: s.n., 1721), 1.

[182] *A Reply*, 1.

[183] *Thomson v. Harcourt*, 1 Brown 193, 1 Eng. Rep. 508 (H.L. 1722).

[184] Henry Thomson, *A Report of a Case Argued and Adjudged in the Court of Exchequer, and Affirm'd in the House of Lords, Relating to a Contract about* South-Sea *Stock* (London: J. Roberts, 1724), 4.

[185] Ibid., 5.

"unless it be unreasonable to sell things at the Market Price."[186] Another professed his inability to ascertain the intrinsic "Price or Value of this Stock, whether it was sold too dear or too cheap; for if we should enter into an examination of that matter, we should be out at high Sea, and not know where we are."[187] The court thus required Harcourt to pay the contract price of 920. The House of Lords affirmed the decree.[188] (In accordance with the 1721 statute, Harcourt was required to pay for only the number of shares actually held by Thomson on the date of the contract, which was smaller than the number Harcourt had agreed to buy.)

In the immediate aftermath of the Bubble, despite a profusion of regulatory proposals, and despite Parliament's consideration of some of them, almost nothing was done. Parliament and the courts declined repeated opportunities to curb securities trading. As a result, transactions of all sorts, including the options and time bargains most frequently complained of, continued to be unimpeded by the legislature and enforced by the courts. Many judges and members of Parliament, like many propertied Englishmen generally, had their own assets invested in the market, a circumstance which no doubt played a part in the government's reluctance to intervene. It is also plausible to suppose that the mass of published thought critical of the market did not tell the whole story. As had been the case with speculation in earlier markets, a large percentage of the propertied population were in effect voting with their pocketbooks, by investing in a market that seemed useful and even safe much of the time. The securities market thus emerged from its first crisis relatively unregulated.

[186] Ibid., 7.   [187] Ibid., 10.   [188] 1 Eng. Rep. at 513.

3 English securities regulation in the eighteenth century

The attitudes toward the market engendered by the Bubble remained latent in English culture in the decades that followed. They would reemerge during every market downturn for the rest of the eighteenth century, even as participation in the market continued to grow and securities trading grew more familiar. Section I will describe this bifurcated pattern of thought. Section II will examine a similar pattern in Parliament: Whenever stock prices endured a period of sustained decline, Parliament would again consider legislation designed to limit the perceived excesses of stockjobbers. Although the only statute to come out of this process was Sir John Barnard's Act, passed in 1734 and surviving with limited actual effect for over a century, more drastic measures were regularly proposed. Yet the market's increasing familiarity and respectability, its very ordinariness, over the course of the century prevented any of these later proposals from becoming law. In Barnard's Act, and in some of the bills never passed by Parliament, we can see the early models for the American securities regulation of the following century. Finally, section III will examine the ways in which the courts facilitated the development of the securities market in the eighteenth century. In the courts as well, decisions made in England in the eighteenth century would heavily influence decisions to be made later in the United States.

I

In 1780, Christopher Anstey noticed that an old word – "speculation" – had taken on a new meaning.

> If right I ween, in Times of yore,
> This harmless Term express'd no more
> Than ocular, or mental View,
> Or Thoughts that from the same accrue.

By the later part of the eighteenth century, however, a word once associated with contemplation had acquired connotations that were nearly the opposite.

> Whate'er the wretched basely dare
> From Pride, Ambition, or Despair,
> Fraud, Luxury, or Dissipation,
> Assumes the Name of – SPECULATION.

Speculation was once the pursuit of philosophers; now it was an activity conducted by a very different sort of person.

> The swindling Jew, the gambling Peer,
> The ruin'd Squire turn'd Auctioneer,
> The Pimp, the Quack, the broken Banker,
> Unknowing where to cast their Anchor,
> Their Fortune's shatter'd Fragments rally,
> And fix their stations in the Alley.

These were men who

> give each base Negotiation
> The well-bred Term of – SPECULATION.[1]

But while the word's connotations were new, the activity it described was not, and neither was Anstey's antipathy toward it. Securities trading persisted all through the eighteenth century. The market was never again the focus of as much public criticism as it received in the early 1720s, but the modes of anti-market thought that crystallized in the aftermath of the Bubble remained, to reemerge whenever stock prices underwent a sustained period of decline. During or shortly after each of these prolonged downturns – in 1733–34, 1746–48, 1753–56, and 1758–62 – critics trotted out the old arguments against stockjobbing.[2] These themes would be repeated well into the nineteenth century.

The idea that stockjobbers were unusually deceitful, for instance, was a staple of anti-market thought throughout the century. The pseudonymous "Gideonite" (a vaguely anti-Semitic synonym for "stockjobber," current in the 1740s, taken from the surname of Samson Gideon, one of the wealthiest securities traders of the mid-eighteenth century) suggested that

> we may prove Stock-jobbers from our Youth,

---

[1] Christopher Anstey, *Speculation; or, a Defence of Mankind* (London: Christopher Anstey, 1780), 5, 6, 6–7, 18. The *Oxford English Dictionary*'s earliest citation of "speculation" in the financial sense is a 1774 letter of Horace Walpole, who referred to "what is called *speculation*," a phrase likewise suggesting the word's novelty in this sense.

[2] Information about stock prices is from Philip Mirowski, *The Birth of the Business Cycle* (New York: Garland, 1985), 235–38, 243, 247–48.

> Provided that we seldom speak the Truth;
> For Truth with them as incoherent seems,
> As Honesty with crafty Courtiers Schemes.[3]

In the 1750s, Samuel Johnson defined "stockjobber" as a "low wretch who gets money by buying and selling shares in the funds."[4] The first popular guide to stock trading, Thomas Mortimer's *Every Man His Own Broker* (1761), was devoted largely to warning investors not to believe anything a professional trader said, "for which reason," Mortimer concluded, "I intreat those who have not yet entered the Alley, never to frequent it on a jobbing account."[5] The securities market continued for some time to be perceived, at least by non-participants, as a producer of "lies habitual and incessant."[6] In the early nineteenth century, as the corporate form became more prevalent, even insiders continued to observe that the number of fraudulent projects issuing shares showed no signs of abating.[7]

The image of the market as a place where stockjobbers profited only from fleecing the unsophisticated likewise remained strong. Stockjobbers were men "constantly racking their Invention, in making an ill Use of every Piece of true News, and for Want thereof, coining, counterfeiting false News, purely to impose on the ignorant Part of Mankind."[8] In the aftermath of an extended price decline in the late 1750s and early 1760s, one close observer of markets asked why stock prices are "every day fluctuating without any visible cause?" He explained that "[t]he real cause" was stockjobbers' ability to manipulate prices.

The method in which this practice is carried on is as follows. A man who has not perhaps 1000£ in the world subscribes for 100,000£, which is to be delivered at several fixed times and in certain portions. He therefore hopes to get these several portions sold out to great advantage by the rising of the stocks

---

[3] *The Art of Stock-jobbing: A Poem, In Imitation of Horace's* Art of Poetry, *by a Gideonite* (London: R. Baldwin, 1746), 14. On Samson Gideon, see Dickson, *Financial Revolution*, 222 and n.4.

[4] E. L. McAdam, Jr., and George Milne, eds., *Johnson's Dictionary: A Modern Selection* (1755) (New York: Pantheon, 1963), 401.

[5] Thomas Mortimer, *Every Man His Own Broker: Or, A Guide to Exchange-Alley*, 3rd edn (London: S. Hooper, 1761), 23–63; the excerpt quoted is at 63. Mortimer's book was so popular that it was published in fourteen editions between 1761 and 1807.

[6] Samuel Egerton Brydges, *Human Fate* (Great Totham: Charles Clark, 1846), 4.

[7] *Observations on Public Institutions, Monopolies, Joint Stock Companies, and Deeds of Trust* (London: J.M. Richardson, 1807), 6; Anthony Romney, *Three Letters, on the Speculative Schemes of the Present Times* (Edinburgh: Bell & Bradfute, 1825), 3; *The Real Del Monte Mining Concerns Unmasked, and a Few Facts on Stock Jobbing Schemes* (London: Cochrane and M'Crone, 1833), 3; *Ruminations on Railways, No. I, Railway Speculation* (London: J. Weale, 1845), 5; *The Railway Investment Guide*, 2nd edn (London: G. Mann, 1845), 3.

[8] *Truth: A Letter to the Gentlemen of* Exchange Alley (London: T. Cooper, 1733), 11.

before they fall due. But as any thing he is worth would go if the stocks should fall, he uses all means to make them rise. He spreads reports at Change Alley that victories are gained, that peace is to be concluded, etca. On the other hand they who want to purchase a stock, and want that it should fall, propogate such reports as will sink the stocks as low as possible, such as that war will continue, that new subscriptions are thought on, etca. It is owing to this that in time of war our newspapers are so filled with invasions and schemes that never were thought of.

This critic of the stock market was Adam Smith, then lecturing on jurisprudence at Glasgow University, who concluded that there was nothing the government could do to prevent such abuses.[9] Smith was hardly alone in understanding the market as rigged by insiders; such was a widespread conception of the market through the eighteenth century, and it was supported by occasional well-publicized examples.[10] Stock-jobbers were people who

> without remorse, would martyr
> Half mankind for half a quarter;
> All who, preying on the nation,
> Call their rapine speculation.[11]

When investment guides and exposés of the market (the line between them is often not clear) began appearing in the late eighteenth and early nineteenth centuries, they were saturated with this view.[12] If prices could be manipulated by stockjobbers, and if the income of stockjobbers consisted of money extracted from investors, the lesson was clear:

> If to the Stock Exchange you speed,
>   To try with bulls and bears your luck,
> 'Tis odds, you soon from gold are freed,
>   And waddle forth a limping duck.[13]

All through the eighteenth and early nineteenth centuries, English

---

9 Adam Smith, *Lectures on Jurisprudence* (1766, probably delivered 1763–64), ed. R. L. Meek, D. D. Raphael, and P. G. Stein (Oxford: Clarendon Press, 1978), 536–38.

10 For a discussion, see H. V. Bowen, "'The Pests of Human Society': Stockbrokers, Jobbers and Speculators in Mid-Eighteenth-Century Britain," *History* 78 (1993): 41–44.

11 Henry Luttrell, *Crockford-House* (London: J. Murray, 1827), 80.

12 Mortimer, *Every Man*, 36–37; *Tricks of the Stock-Exchange Exposed*, 2nd edn ([London]: C. Chapple, 1814), 3–8; *The System of Stock-Jobbing Explained* (London: C. Chapple, 1816), 19–27; *The Art of Stock Jobbing Explained*, 7th edn (London: W. Clarke, 1819), 11–13; J. Lancaster, *The Bank – The Stock Exchange – The Bankers – The Bankers' Clearing House – The Minister, and the Public: An Exposé* (London: E. Wilson, 1821), 2; *A New Guide to the Public Funds; or, Every Man His Own Stockbroker* (London: Woodward, 1825), 4; Cobbett, *Paper Against Gold*, 127–30; Francis Playford, *Practical Hints for Investing Money*, 5th edn (London: Virtue Brothers & Co., 1865).

13 Samuel William Henry Ireland, *Stultifera Navis; or, The Modern Ship of Fools* (London: William Miller, 1807), 54.

critics repeated another of the themes common in the early eighteenth century – that securities trading was a non-productive enterprise, and harmed the nation by diverting labor and capital from more productive pursuits. The market, a scene of "unwarrantable Gaming, and imaginary Contracts," added nothing to the nation's real wealth.[14] The "Gideonite" asked, with reference to a stockjobber:

> Isn't such a Man much fitter for the Plough?
> Some Good at least he there may hap to do.[15]

In the 1748 play *A Winter Evening's Conversation*, published toward the end of a long decline in stock prices, one stockjobber complains to another of the prospect of government regulation of the market, which "will at last render it impossible for any Man to get an Estate, but by the slow and dull way of *Economy*, or the laborious or uncertain Ways of *Trade* and *Commerce*."[16] Malachy Postlethwayt's immense mid-eighteenth-century commercial dictionary explained that "STOCK-JOBBING has been, and still continues to be, detrimental to the commerce of this nation," because "traffic in the stocks of companies, so engrosses the thoughts of the proprietors, that the national commerce often suffers, for want of that money being employed in a free trade." Even "industrious and skilful traders" engaging in productive commerce were deprived of credit, "for the monies of the opulent being locked up in these channels of domestic bubbling." As a result, Postlethwayt concluded, "instead of increasing in skilful traders, we swarm in stockholders and stock-jobbers, brokers and usurers," a group of people who "can never increase, but must daily lessen the commerce of the nation, which must daily lessen it's real and substantial wealth."[17] Because of securities trading, an early treatise-writer agreed, "[t]he attention that might, and ought, otherwise . . . be directed to useful purposes, in fulfilling the great duties of life, is thus diverted into barren, unfruitful, and polluted channels."[18]

The idea that stockjobbing, particularly in government debt, would lead to political corruption also continued to receive expression throughout the century.[19] "The Publick Funds," one member of Parlia-

---

[14] *An Answer to a Pamphlet on* Publick Credit (London: T. Cooper, 1733), 15.

[15] *The Art of Stock-jobbing*, 41.

[16] *A Winter Evening's Conversation* (London: G. Smith, 1748), 13.

[17] Malachy Postlethwayt, *The Universal Dictionary of Trade and Commerce* (London: J. & P. Knapton, 1755), II, 764–65.

[18] J. I. Burn, *A Brief Treatise, or Summary of the Law Relative to Stock-Jobbing* (London: T. Boosey, 1803), 2.

[19] For a summary of mid-eighteenth-century English thought concerning the political consequences of the public debt, see Herbert E. Sloan, *Principle and Interest: Thomas Jefferson and the Problem of Debt* (New York: Oxford University Press, 1995), 88–108.

ment observed, "divide the Nation into two Ranks of Men, of which one are Creditors and the other Debtors."[20] This division, complained another, had a dangerous effect on national policymaking. "It is in the interest of the stockholders," he argued, "to involve the nation in war, because they get by it. It is in the interest of the landed men and merchants, to submit to any insult rather than engage in war, since they must bear the whole burden of it."[21] Satirical treatments of the market continued to depict stockjobbers, and even government officials, as men willing to shift their national allegiances to make money.[22]

Finally, the market's effect on the nation's social structure, perhaps the most often noted result of the burst of trading in 1720, remained a subject of interest for the rest of the century.[23] The market was still the only place in the country where one could find instant class reversals, as fortunes could be won or lost much faster in Exchange Alley than anywhere else.

> Stock-jobbing is the most bewitching Thing,
> 'Twill from a Beggar raise you to a King.
> Two good Estates Sir *Thomas* now has lost,
> By coining News, which now he feels t' his Cost.[24]

Foreigners and Jews were still among the most successful speculators, and that continued to bring out old strains of anti-Semitism and xenophobia.[25]

The structure of anti-market thought that emerged from the Bubble thus remained fixed in English culture for some time afterwards. In 1733, Alexander Pope (who had been a big loser in the market himself) saw securities trading as a symbol of the new commercial spirit into which England was degrading.

> Statesman and Patriot ply alike the stocks,
> Peeress and Butler share alike the Box,
> And Judges job, and Bishops bite the town,
> And mighty Dukes pack cards for half a crown.
> See Britain sunk in lucre's sordid charms,
> And France reveng'd of ANNE's and EDWARD's arms![26]

---

[20] John Barnard, *Reasons for the More Speedy Lessening the National Debt* (London: J. Roberts, 1737), 22–23.

[21] *An Inquiry Into the Original and Consequences of the Publick Debt* (London: s.n., 1753), 16.

[22] *The Art of Stock-jobbing*, 16; *A Winter Evening's Conversation*, 25–26.

[23] Hoppit, *Risk and Failure*, 136.   [24] *The Art of Stock-jobbing*, 46.

[25] *A Winter Evening's Conversation*, passim; *The System of Stock-Jobbing Explained*, 46.

[26] Alexander Pope, "Epistle to Allen Lord Bathurst" (1733), in Herbert Davis, ed., *Pope: Poetical Works* (London: Oxford University Press, 1966), 306. On Pope's personal losses, see Barton, "Pro-Fund Wit," 217.

At the end of the century, so did the lesser-known playwright Frederick Reynolds.

> Fine subject ours – rare times! when Speculation
> Engrosses every subject in the nation;
> To help the State, – Jews, Gentiles, all are willing,
> And for the Omnium, venture their last shilling;
> Nay, some subscribe their thousands to the Loan,
> Without a single sixpence of their own.[27]

All through the eighteenth century and most of the nineteenth, writers could assume that "Jobbing is equally Notorious" as robbery, that "nothing surely is more common than to hear of 'Stock Exchange or Stock-jobbing swindles,'" or that public opinion concerning professional securities traders was "not of a very flattering character."[28]

And yet, very quietly, public participation in the market continued to grow.[29] Approximately 40,000 people owned shares of the national debt at the time of the Bubble. By the 1750s, despite all the rhetoric condemning stockjobbing, that number had grown to around 60,000. By 1815, it was probably over half a million.[30] Participation in the market for shares in joint-stock companies was expanding at the same time, and would grow even faster in the early nineteenth century.[31] This diffusion of securities must have softened public attitudes toward securities trading.[32] The publication of popular guides to the stock market, beginning in the mid-eighteenth century and then increasing in

---

[27] Frederick Reynolds, *Speculation; A Comedy, in Five Acts* (London: T. N. Longman, 1795), 77.

[28] *The Art of Stock-jobbing*, ix; Playford, *Practical Hints*, 69; *Fenn's Compendium of the English and Foreign Funds*, 5th edn (London: Effingham Wilson, 1855), 108.

[29] Phyllis Deane, "Capital Formation in Britain Before the Railway Age," in François Cruzet, ed., *Capital Formation in the Industrial Revolution* (London: Methuen, 1972), 100.

[30] Dickson, *Financial Revolution*, 273, 285–86 & n.1. These figures are estimates, based on the size of the public debt at various times and the relationship of the public debt's size to the number of accounts as of the early eighteenth century. They are, to my knowledge, the best estimates available; if the numbers are imprecise, they at least give a sense of the order of magnitude of the growth in the number of public creditors.

[31] For the eighteenth century, see Harris, "Industrialization," 98–141; George Herberton Evans, Jr., *British Corporation Finance 1775–1850: A Study of Preference Shares* (Baltimore: Johns Hopkins Press, 1936), 1–38. The diffusion of shares in joint stock companies did not immediately lead to an expansion in organized securities trading; that would come only in the early nineteenth century. See Mirowski, "Rise (and Retreat)," 559. For the early nineteenth century, see *Remarks on Joint-Stock Companies* (London: J. Murray, 1825), 1; Arthur D. Gayer, W.W. Rostow, and Anna Jacobson Schwartz, *The Growth and Fluctuation of the British Economy 1790–1850* (Oxford: Clarendon Press, 1953), I, 412–54; Frank Griffith Dawson, *The First Latin American Debt Crisis: The City of London and the 1822–25 Loan Bubble* (New Haven: Yale University Press, 1990), 98–107.

[32] Brewer, *Sinews of Power*, 210; Langford, *Polite and Commercial People*, 642.

volume toward the end of the century, suggests both an increase in the public interest and a heightened degree of respectability associated with investment in the market (even if the guides did often take pains to warn readers about the tricks of insiders).[33] In the second half of the century, the brokers themselves began to brush up their public image by organizing as a "Stock Exchange" in order to regulate their own conduct and exclude the less reputable.[34] By the middle of the nineteenth century, near the end of his life, Charles Dickens could complain that the younger generation saw nothing more respectable, and no activity so well correlated with social status, as participation in the stock market.

As is well known to the wise in their generation, traffic in Shares is the one thing to have to do with in this world. Have no antecedents, no established character, no cultivation, no ideas, no manners; have Shares. Have Shares enough to be on Boards of Direction in capital letters, oscillate on mysterious business between London and Paris, and be great. Where does he come from? Shares. Where is he going to? Shares. What are his tastes? Shares. Has he any principles? Shares. What squeezes him into Parliament? Shares. Perhaps he never himself achieved success in anything, never originated anything, never produced anything! Sufficient answer to all: Shares.[35]

One could hardly ask for a more concise account of the way the market had penetrated the consciousness of those who could afford to invest in it.

As securities trading became more familiar, new ideas about the market began to surface, ideas which would eventually become commonplace. As early as 1736, one observer noticed something interesting about how investors seemed to calculate the value of their securities – "'tis remarkable, that the Expectation of any Scheme hath, for the generality, greater Influence on the Stocks than its Accomplishment" –

---

[33] In addition to the guides already cited, see George Clerke, *The Dealers in Stock's Assistant* (London: Edward Symon, 1725); Benjamin Webb, *Tables for Buying and Selling Stocks* (London: Benjamin Webb, 1759); *An Essay on the Present State of the Public Funds* (London: s.n., 1778); *A Pocket Companion for the Purchasers of Stock in Any of the Public Funds* (London: Dan. Browne, 1790); William Fairman, *The Stocks Examined and Compared* (London: J. Johnson, 1795) (republished in seven new editions in the late eighteenth and early nineteenth centuries); Thomas Fortune, *An Epitome of the Stocks and Publick Funds*, 2nd edn (London: T. Boosey, 1796) (republished in sixteen editions in the late eighteenth and early nineteenth centuries); Charles Hales, *The Bank Mirror; or, a Guide to the Funds* (London: J. Adlard, 1796); Bernard Cohen, *Compendium of Finance* (London: W. Phillips, 1822); *American Securities: Practical Hints on the Tests of Stability and Profit* (London: M. Nephews, 1860).

[34] Morgan and Thomas, *Stock Exchange*, 68–69; S. R. Cope, "The Stock-Brokers Find a Home: How the Stock Exchange Came to Be Established in Sweetings Alley in 1773," *Guildhall Studies in London History* 2 (1977): 213.

[35] Charles Dickens, *Our Mutual Friend* (1865) (New York: Modern Library, 1992), 110.

that is, the price of a share in an enterprise depended not on past events but on the popular estimation of what would happen in the future.[36] By the 1760s, Blackstone already recognized that the rate of return demanded by an investor for temporarily giving up possession of his money "depends on two circumstances; the inconvenience of parting with it for the present, and the hazard of losing it entirely." Current theorists would substitute a term like "risk-free rate of return" for the first of these circumstances, and "risk premium" for the second, but their understanding of how to calculate the required rate of return differs little from that of Blackstone, who explained that the rate is

in a compound *ratio*, formed out of the inconvenience, and the hazard . . . Thus, if the quantity of specie in a nation be such, that the general inconvenience of lending for a year is computed to amount to *three per cent*: a man that has money by him will perhaps lend it upon good personal security at *five per cent*, allowing two for the hazard run; he will lend it upon landed security or mortgage at *four per cent*, the hazard being proportionably less; but he will lend it to the state, on the maintenance of which all his property depends, at *three per cent*, the hazard being none at all.[37]

By the 1770s, Adam Smith was noticing what would much later come to be considered a serious difficulty in policing the behavior of the directors of publicly traded companies.[38] "The directors of such companies," he predicted, "being the managers rather of other people's money than of their own, it cannot well be expected, that they should watch over it with the same anxious vigilance with which the partners in a private copartnery frequently watch over their own." Smith's conclusion was that "[n]egligence and profusion, therefore, must always prevail, more or less, in the management of the affairs of such a company," and thus that publicly traded corporations would never be able to compete successfully against partnerships. He proved his point with an example: the "knavery and extravagance" of the directors of the South Sea Company, which he attributed to the fact that the Company comprised "an immense capital divided among an immense number of proprietors" – an invitation to "folly, negligence, and profusion."[39]

---

[36] J. S., *A Dialogue Between a Gentleman and a Broker* (London, T. Cooper, 1736), 18; cf. Richard Brealey and Stewart Myers, *Principles of Corporate Finance*, 2nd edn (New York: McGraw-Hill, 1984), 45–46.

[37] Blackstone, *Commentaries*, II, 456–57; cf. Brealey and Myers, *Principles of Corporate Finance*, 128–30.

[38] Cf. Adolf A. Berle, Jr., and Gardiner C. Means, *The Modern Corporation and Private Property* (New York: Commerce Clearing House, 1932). See James P. Henderson, "Agency or Alienation? Smith, Mill, and Marx on the Joint-Stock Company," *History of Political Economy* 18 (1986): 129.

[39] Adam Smith, *An Inquiry into the Nature and Causes of the Wealth of Nations*, ed. R. H. Campbell and A. S. Skinner (Oxford: Clarendon Press, 1976), 741, 744–45. Smith did

In the middle of the eighteenth century, writers for the first time began to make a theoretical case for the value of stockjobbing. The market's mere existence, it was argued, contributed to the national wealth, but the market could not exist without the stockjobbers or without their most speculative transactions. One opponent of regulation put forth a five-step justification of stockjobbing:

I It seems to be necessary, for the Support and Circulation of Publick Credit, that there should be a constant open Market, for the Sale and Purchase of the Funds, where every Person may have his Business transacted, for the Time, and in the Manner that suits him best, with Ease, Readiness, and Dispatch.

II By the Means of this Dealing for Time, in great Measure, is that constant open Market kept, which is found to be so convenient and necessary.

III There are not sufficient Ready-Money Transactions in the Funds, enough in Quantity and Quality, without Time Bargains, to keep, or induce a sufficient Number of Brokers, or others, constantly to assemble for the Purpose of buying and selling.

IV Entirely destroy the Practice of Jobbing, and the Market is lost.

V And it is humbly conceived, the Loss of this Market will be a greater Injury, Damage, and Inconvenience to the Proprietors of the Funds, and also to the Government, when they are in want of Money, than they have ever yet suffered, or can possibly suffer by the Practice of Jobbing.[40]

As time went on, this sort of argument became more common. The market was no longer a zero-sum game: "the general rule is here suspended, that what one wins another must lose – and for this reason; additional capital, has been, as it were, created and diffused, *from nothing*."[41] There was now even a case to be made for the existence of a class of professional stockjobbers. The lawyer Henry Keyser explained in 1850 that jobbers added value to the market by reducing the difficulty of making transactions. "Were it not for this intermediary class," he pointed out,

the public would experience great delay and inconvenience in their sales or purchase of stock. For instance, *A* wishing to sell, say £3250 worth of stock, would have to wait until his broker could meet with a party desirous to purchase that precise amount: this disadvantage is entirely obviated by the readiness of the jobber to buy or sell.[42]

not add this part to *The Wealth of Nations* until the third edition, published in 1784, but he appears to have written it by 1774. Gary M. Anderson and Robert D. Tollison, "Adam Smith's Analysis of Joint-Stock Companies," *Journal of Political Economy* 90 (1982): 1240.

[40] *Reasons Humbly Offered to the Members of the Honourable House of Commons, Against a Bill Now Depending* (s.l.: s.n., [1756?]).

[41] *The Railway Investment Guide*, 5.

[42] Henry Keyser, *The Law Relating to Transactions on the Stock Exchange* (London: L.H. Butterworth, 1850), 23.

In one of the mid-century investment guides, a broker agreed that "without the mediation of the Jobber . . . business which now – to the great convenience of the public – only occupies a few minutes, might very possibly require many days, or even weeks, for its transaction."[43]

But if securities trading was becoming familiar, and if stockjobbers were beginning to be perceived as useful and even necessary, the South Sea Bubble still lingered in memory as a lesson in how easily a useful institution could spin out of control. For over a century, whenever a writer wished to argue in favor of regulation or to criticize perceived abuses, he had only to recall "the Phrenzy of the Realm" and the "widespreading Mischief" of 1720.[44] "[L]ook back to the Year 1720," one writer suggested as a means of urging Parliament to suppress stockjobbing: "Remember the Infatuation of the People at that Time."[45] The year was one which "ought to be had in perpetual remembrance," argued the former South Sea clerk Adam Anderson in the 1760s, "as it may serve for a perpetual memento to the legislators and ministers of our own nation, never to leave it in the power of any, hereafter, to hoodwink mankind into so shameful and baneful an imposition on the credulity of the people."[46] In the early nineteenth century, accounts of the Bubble were "Intended as a Warning to the Present Age," and "As a Beacon to the Unwary Against Modern Schemes Equally Visionary and Nefarious."[47] Investors a century later hardly needed to be told of the Bubble itself – the event "still enjoys an enduring notoriety," explained one writer in 1825, and was still "well known" and "infamous" as of 1850 – but the story needed to be told and retold to remind investors of how "close indeed is the parallel" between 1720 and the present.[48] The nineteenth-century account of the Bubble that was probably the most widely read drew as its moral "a tendency to over-speculation" that would inevitably recur in "times of great commercial prosperity," unless investors could learn from their past mistakes.[49]

In the century after the Bubble, English attitudes toward securities trading followed two contradictory paths. Securities trading was dan-

---

[43] Playford, *Practical Hints*, 10.   [44] Welsted, *Epistles, Odes, &c.*, 75.

[45] *Truth*, 10.

[46] Adam Anderson, *An Historical and Chronological Deduction of the Origin of Commerce* (1762) (London: J. White, 1801), III, 91.

[47] *An Account of the* South Sea Scheme; *and a Number of Other Bubbles; Which Were Encouraged by Public Infatuation in the Year 1720* ([London]: J. Cawthorne, 1806), title page; *The South Sea Bubble, and the Numerous Fraudulent Projects to Which it Gave Rise in 1720* (London: T. Boys, 1825), title page.

[48] *Remarks on Joint Stock Companies*, 6; Keyser, *The Law*, 10.

[49] Charles Mackay, *Extraordinary Popular Delusions and the Madness of Crowds* (1841) (New York: Crown Trade Paperbacks, 1980), 88 (the original 1841 title was *Memoirs of Extraordinary Popular Delusions*).

gerous, for all the reasons identified by the post-Bubble critics – it bred deceit and predatory behavior, it diverted resources from more productive activities, and it threatened the political and social stability of the country. This mode of thought tended to swell whenever stock prices fell. At the same time, however, securities trading was useful – it allowed the government (and, as time went on, more and more private entrepreneurs) to borrow money with a minimum of difficulty, and it provided a safe investment for an ever-increasing percentage of the population. This way of thinking is less easily documented, but if it spread along with participation in the market, its growth appears to have been fairly constant throughout the century. This split in English thought was closely patterned on the earlier split in attitudes toward earlier speculative markets discussed in chapter 1. As with earlier forms of speculation, practice proceeded in advance of theory; the practice of securities trading received tacit practical support from hundreds of thousands of willing investors long before it received any significant explicit theoretical justification.[50]

II

This tension in popular thought toward securities trading was reflected in the ways in which Parliament regulated and attempted to regulate the securities market during the eighty years between the immediate aftermath of the Bubble and the end of the eighteenth century. During the first serious market downturn after the Bubble, Parliament finally passed a statute intended to limit the more speculative methods of stockjobbing. This statute, however, limped through the century with almost no practical effect, and the practices it was intended to suppress remained commonplace. With each market downturn thereafter, Parliament considered new legislation to strengthen this paper limitation, but none of these bills was passed. The sum of Parliament's efforts thus replicated the split in popular thought, with strict regulation on paper and stricter limits regularly threatened, but in practice almost no statutory intervention in the market for the rest of the century.

Soon after the failure of the 1721 bill to prohibit stockjobbing, Thomas Gordon suggested that the evils commonly associated with securities trading could be eliminated at a single stroke, by a statute

---

[50] There is a parallel here to the history of European science, where in many instances theoretical development has likewise lagged behind practical advances. Kuhn concludes that "the scientists who turned to technology for their problems succeeded in merely validating and explaining, not in improving, techniques developed earlier and without the aid of science." Thomas Kuhn, *The Essential Tension: Selected Studies in Scientific Tradition and Change* (Chicago: University of Chicago Press, 1977), 144.

"declaring all fictitious Contracts hereafter Illegal and Void, which shall not be immediately comply'd with." As a means of enforcing such a ban, Gordon proposed "inflicting a proper Punishment on all Persons assuming a false Power, and pretending to sell and buy Stock for themselves, or others, who have neither Money to Purchase, nor Stock to Deliver." This sort of law, Gordon predicted, would put an end to "the unhappy Schemes, and unsuccessful Projects of Stock-jobbers,"[51] because if one could only sell stock one actually possessed, and if the seller were required actually to transfer the stock to the buyer, many of the more complex methods of stockjobbing could no longer exist. Puts could only be bought, or refuses sold, by people who currently held stock, which would deprive these contracts of much of their speculative value. Time bargains could be entered into only where the seller was a current stockholder, which would prevent nominal sellers from profiting from price declines by agreeing to future sales of stock they did not yet own. Traders could no longer recover on differences between actual and predicted prices, but would have to exchange stock for money on the settling day. Corners would no longer be feasible. The securities market would consist only of the types of transactions conventional in other markets. Stockjobbing would be considerably less lucrative.

In 1733, during the first sharp drop in stock prices after the Bubble, Parliament again considered a bill "to prevent the infamous Practice of Stock-jobbing."[52] The bill included provisions similar to Gordon's suggestions; it would have banned time bargains, prohibited parties from entering into contracts to sell stock or transfer money they did not currently possess, and required parties to a stock purchase doctrine actually to transfer the stock subject to the contract, rather than settling with a cash payment based on price differentials. The debate on the bill in the House of Commons in April revealed the existence of two sharply divergent views of the securities market.

Opponents of the ban on time bargains argued that these transactions served a valuable purpose wholly apart from speculation. "It often happens," reported one member of the House of Commons,

that a Gentleman, who foresees that he shall have Use for his Money in three or four Months Time, is well satisfied with the Price his Stock then bears; he cannot then sell out his Stock for ready Money, because he does not know what to do with his Money in the mean Time: But as the Law now stands, he may sell it out at that Price, or perhaps at an advanced Price, to be delivered only when he knows he shall have Occasion for the Money; this he acquaints his Broker of, and the Broker may probably find him out a Man who likes the then current Price, and expects Money to be thrown into his Hands in three or four Months,

---

[51] Gordon, *Essay*, 18–19.   [52] *Journals of the House of Commons*, 22:10.

which he resolves to employ in that Fund: In this Case the Buying and Selling for Time is convenient for both.[53]

Supporters of the ban on time bargains were led in the House of Commons by Sir John Barnard, a wine merchant who began his Parliamentary career soon after the Bubble, and who consistently represented the interests of smaller London merchants in opposition to the securities market and all that it stood for.[54] Barnard responded with an entirely different vision of the market, according to which time bargains served no function beyond that of facilitating gambling. In the hypothetical case just considered, Barnard alleged, neither the buyer nor the seller would be willing to enter into a time bargain

unless he knows, or thinks he knows, some Secret relating to that Stock which other People are not aware of; for if he that is to sell expects no Variation in the Value of his Property, why should he sell 'till he has Occasion for his Money? But granting that he is so much satisfied with the then current Price, that he absolutely resolves to sell at that very Time, may he not sell for ready Money, and lodge his Money in the Bank 'till he has Occasion for it, since no Man can pretend but that his Money is as secure when lodged in the Bank, as it can be in any of our Publick Funds? And as to the Buyer, I am sure no wise Man will venture to purchase Stock 'till he has the Money at Command; unless he does it in Expectation that the Stock will rise, which is downright Gaming, and what is intended by this Bill to be prevented.

Opponents of the ban on time bargains also argued that the bill imposed a hardship on stockholders that was not borne by the holders of any other class of property. "As the Law now stands," one member pointed out,

a Gentleman may sell his Estate, a Merchant or Tradesman may sell his Goods, every Man may dispose of his Property by a Bargain for Time, or in whatever Manner he pleases: But by this Bill the Creditors of the Publick, those who have put their Trust in the Publick Faith, are to be laid under a particular Restraint.

Again, Barnard had a response on behalf of the bill's supporters: Permitting merchants to sell property in futures transactions promoted trade, but time bargains in securities were "a great Discouragement to Trade" because they were "the Ruin of all private Credit." The inability to enter into time bargains would be no "Hardship upon any fair Purchaser or Seller," and indeed would "make the Value of every Man's Property in the Publick Funds more certain and invariable."[55]

The remaining provisions of the bill also faced vigorous opposition in

---

[53] *History and Proceedings of the House of Commons*, 7:376–77.
[54] Ian R. Christie, *British "Non-Elite" MPs 1715–1820* (Oxford: Clarendon Press, 1995), 45–46, 195.
[55] *History and Proceedings of the House of Commons*, 7:383, 376, 382.

the House of Commons. One member argued that the portion of the bill requiring buyers and sellers actually to possess the stock or money they promised to transfer would be so "extremely inconvenient to all the Proprietors or Dealers in any of our Publick Securities" that the bill "ought to be called a Bill for the destroying of Publick Credit." The portion of the bill "to prevent Men's coming to an amicable Composition of any Differences," another opponent charged, would have the effect of preventing litigants from using cash payments to settle lawsuits over stock contracts, because any such settlement would violate the literal terms of the statute. This outcome "will be such a Discouragement, that no Man, I believe, will chuse to become a Purchaser of our Funds."[56] These arguments against regulating the market presumed the market's utility, and accordingly reckoned as a cost any additional disincentive to investment resulting from regulation.

Barnard's response to these criticisms was premised on a very different view of the market. As Barnard and the supporters of the bill understood it, the market was "a Lottery, or rather a Gaming-House, publickly set up in the Middle of the City, by which the Heads of our Merchants and Tradesmen are turned from getting a Livelihood or an Estate, by the honest Means of Industry and Frugality." Indeed, the market was not just a lottery, "but a Lottery of the very worst Sort; because it is always in the Power of the principal Managers to bestow the Benefit-Tickets as they have a mind." The existence of securities might sometimes be useful, but the unlimited *transferability* of securities was "an Evil that ought to be remedied." On this view, the disincentives to investment caused by the proposed regulation were not a cost at all, but were in fact intended by the bill; investment for the purposes of speculation was precisely the sort of investment the bill was designed to discourage. In the end, Robert Walpole predicted, the bill would have the effect of causing "the Price of all publick Stocks [to] become more certain and fixed, which will, I am sure make them more valuable to all honest Purchasers."[57]

Public opinion, insofar as it can be gauged, was split along the same lines. Opponents of the bill emphasized how inefficient the market would be without the stockjobbers, and how that inefficiency would translate into higher borrowing costs for the government. "Why are People contented with 3 *per Cent.* in the *Funds*," one opponent of regulation asked,

when they can make 4 *per Cent.* on *Land* Security, but because they can change their *Property* without Difficulty, and at a small Expence? But should a Restraint

---

[56] Ibid., 378–79, 377.   [57] Ibid., 381, 380, 388.

be laid on this *free Commerce*, how would the Case be altered? The *Seller* (be his Necessity never so urgent) must then wait, till by Accident a *Buyer* is thrown in his Way, who will take care to have a cheap *Bargain*, when, for want of a *Market*, it will be no easy Matter to fix a *Price*. This will soon make the Possessor weary of so precarious an *Estate*, and unwilling to engage in any new *Loan*, when the Emergencies of the *State* may require his Assistance.

The market would grow even thinner with a prohibition of options and time bargains, because then securities trading would be limited to men "of large Fortunes and superior Power." And there was nothing so mysterious about puts and refuses; they were just a form of insuring one's interest in the stock one owned, "as properly *Insurances* of our *Interest* in them, as any other *Policies of Insurance* are of *Ships* and *Merchandize*."[58]

Supporters of the bill began with a very different understanding of the market. "Consider the vile Arts . . . made use of to blow up Stock above its real intrinsick Value," one such writer urged, "Mens Properties in the several Companies need not such base Arts to make them mark[e]table."[59] The "new-fangled Mushroom Commerce called *Bulling* and *Bearing*," argued another, was hardly beneficial to the government when it sought to borrow money; to the contrary, stockjobbing had a "Tendency to disturb the Minds of the People, and consequently in some measure to stob the very Vitals of Publick Credit, and is this a Practice to be defended?"[60] And if puts and refuses were "to be called an Insurance, it was a very odd sort of one," in that purchasers of these options often owned no stock themselves, so they held no interest that could be insured; "by that Method a Man was to insure not only his own Property in the Publick Funds, but in some Manner the whole Publick Funds of *England*."[61]

The bill squeaked through the House of Commons on a 55–49 vote, and was sent to the House of Lords.[62] The Lords received petitions from both opponents and supporters of the bill – the opponents were "several Proprietors of *South Sea* Stock, and other Public Securities," while the supporters were "divers Merchants and Traders," who feared that they were extending credit to "Persons in the Way of Trade, who are clandestinely, and unknown to their Creditors, risking their Fortunes in the wicked Practice of Stock-jobbing." In June, the Lords added a group of amendments to the bill, passed it, and sent it back to the

[58] *Some Considerations on Publick Credit and the Nature of its Circulation in the Funds Occasioned by a Bill Now Depending in Parliament, Concerning Stock-jobbing* (London: J. Brotherton, 1733), 10, 17, 14.

[59] *Truth*, 11. [60] *An Answer*, 10. "Stob" was a variant of "stab."

[61] *History and Proceedings of the House of Lords*, 4:249.

[62] *History and Proceedings of the House of Commons*, 7:393.

House of Commons.[63] The House of Commons deferred consideration of the Lords' amendments.[64]

The bill was superseded the following January, when, as the market continued its sharp decline, the House of Commons began to consider a second bill very similar to the first.[65] This new bill was approved by the House of Commons in early March 1734.[66] In the House of Lords, arguments for and against the bill proceeded from the same split in views of the market that had characterized the House of Commons the year before. Opponents of the bill argued that "tho' Stock-jobbing was an Inconvenience, yet considering how much it contributed to the ready Circulation of Money, and to the supporting the Credit of our Funds, it was therefore to be tolerated." This view emphasized the value of "the ready Access that People had at all Times to their Money, and that this ready Access was chiefly owing to the Practice of Stock-Jobbing," because stockjobbers ensured that "every Man was always sure of finding a Purchaser for his Stock whenever he had a Mind to sell." Regulating the market would only make matters worse than they now stood, as "it was certain, that every sort of Property was of the less Value, the more Conditions and Restrictions it was subjected to." Supporters of the bill had a vision of the market that bore no resemblance to this picture. "[T]here really was no Difference between Stock-jobbing and gaming," they urged, "or if there was any, it consisted in this, that the former was much more fatal in its Consequences, and much more destructive." On this view of the market, "the Credit of our Funds did not depend on the gaming or Stock-jobbing in them, but rather suffered by it." Stock-jobbers added no value to the market, because "the Readiness of finding a Purchaser for any Thing, depended upon the People's being certain as to the Value, as to the Right, and as to the Method of conveying the Thing to be sold"; it did not depend upon the presence of speculating middlemen. In short, "it was to be hoped the publick Credit of this Nation depended upon a much more stable Foundation than that of Stock-jobbing."[67]

The bill received the assent of the House of Lords, and became law in April.[68] The resulting statute – entitled "An act to prevent the infamous practice of stock-jobbing," but known since as Sir John Barnard's Act – included a sunset provision causing it to expire at the end of three

[63] *Journals of the House of Lords*, 24:259, 284, 303, 305.
[64] *Journals of the House of Commons*, 22:201.   [65] Ibid., 212.
[66] *History and Proceedings of the House of Commons*, 8:137.
[67] *History and Proceedings of the House of Lords*, 4:245, 246–47, 247–49.
[68] *Journals of the House of Lords*, 24:400, 426.

years.[69] In 1737, when the expiration date was imminent, Parliament made the statute perpetual.[70]

Barnard's Act prospectively suppressed the more speculative methods of securities trading in three ways. First, it banned options of all kinds, by voiding all contracts involving payment "for liberty to putt upon, or to deliver, receive, accept or refuse any publick or joint stock . . . and all contracts in the nature of putts and refusals, relating to the then present or future price or value of any such stock or securities." This ban was enforced (apart from simply denying parties the ability to sue on such contracts in court) by granting the purchaser of an option the right to recover his money from the seller within six months of the transaction, and by imposing a £500 fine on parties entering into such contracts, half of which would go to a party who in good faith either brought suit to recover the money he had paid or returned the money he had received. Second, Barnard's Act prohibited parties from settling contracts by paying price differentials, and required them instead actually to deliver the stock contracted for. This requirement was enforced with a £100 fine, half of which would go to the party suing the violator. Parliament was careful to respond to the objection that a delivery requirement would have the effect of preventing parties from suing to recover expectation damages in the event of a breach of a contract to purchase stock; the statute expressly excepted such a situation from its coverage. Third, Barnard's Act declared void all contracts for the sale of stock which the seller was not actually possessed of or entitled to at the time the contract was entered into. This ban was enforced (again, apart from simply denying parties the ability to sue on such contracts in court) with a £500 fine on any person who agreed to sell stock he did not currently own, half of which would go to the person bringing suit, and a £100 fine on any broker negotiating such a contract. The statute also required brokers to keep a register of all transactions in which the broker was involved.[71]

With Barnard's Act, Parliament had finally, after four decades of intermittent consideration, taken action to suppress stockjobbing. On its face, the statute made it impossible to gamble on a price decline, because to do so required the speculator either to purchase puts or to contract to sell stock he did not yet own, both of which were now illegal. For a parallel reason, the Act made it impossible, in theory, even to gamble on a price rise, except by simply purchasing the stock and holding it. After 1734, had Barnard's Act had its intended effect, only the most limited techniques of trading should have been left available.

[69] 7 Geo. II c. 8, § 12 (1734).   [70] 10 Geo. II c. 8 (1737).
[71] 7 Geo. II c. 8, §§ 1, 4–9 (1734).

The transactions ostensibly prohibited by Barnard's Act, however, apparently remained common. A decade after the law's enactment, "*Puts*" and "*Refusals*" were still "Terms in Vogue" among traders.[72] In 1761, Thomas Mortimer reported that "[b]rokers and others, buy and sell for themselves, without having any interest in the funds they sell, or any cash to pay for what they buy, nay even without any design to transfer, or accept, the funds they sell or buy for time," despite the fact that "[t]he business thus transacted, has been declared illegal."[73] Similar descriptions of the market abounded. "Although this practice is not sanctioned by law," one critic explained, referring to the settlement of contracts by the payment of price differentials, "yet it is carried on to a great extent."[74] One early nineteenth-century guide to the market estimated that the volume of "time-speculations" exceeded the volume of cash transactions by a factor of ten.[75] "Barnard's Act," concluded another, "has been utterly and singularly powerless in its effect."[76] "That this Act has utterly failed to effect its object is well known," complained a nineteenth-century lawyer, "for it is alike anomalous as notorious that a numerous and highly-respectable body of men earn their livelihood by the daily and hourly violation of the clauses of the statute."[77] Adam Smith drew the lesson that economic activity of any sort could never be stifled by governments: "In the same manner all the laws against gaming never hinder it . . . It is quite the same in stockjobbing."[78]

Without the ability to enforce their contracts in court, the only circumstance inducing stockjobbers to perform their obligations was the need to maintain a good reputation among their fellows. "As neither party can be compelled by law to complete bargains of this kind," explained one observer, "their sense of *honour*, and the disgrace and loss of future credit, which attend a breach of contract, are the principles by which the business is supported."[79] One of the first functions of the newly-formed Stock Exchange was to publicize the names of those who had defaulted on such otherwise unenforceable contracts; the names of defaulters were "exhibited in the hall of the Stock Exchange, where they dare not appear afterwards."[80] This technique worked well much of the time; as a great deal of recent research has shown, a commercial community can get by without the assistance of the official legal system, so long as its members expect to transact with one another in the

---

[72] *The Art of Stock-jobbing*, 17.   [73] Mortimer, *Every Man*, 31.
[74] George G. Carey, *Every Man His Own Stock-broker* (London: J. Johnston, 1821), 63.
[75] *The Art of Stock Jobbing Explained*, 87.
[76] John Francis, *Chronicles and Characters of the Stock Exchange* (Boston: W. Crosby and H. P. Nichols, 1850), 27.
[77] Keyser, *The Law Relating*, 152.   [78] Smith, *Lectures on Jurisprudence*, 538.
[79] *The System of Stock-Jobbing Explained*, 15.   [80] Carey, *Every Man*, 63.

future.[81] But Barnard's Act left stockjobbers without protection against speculators who were not long-term participants in the market, who could avoid their losses by, in effect, "pleading the act against Jobbing."[82] As a result, it was argued, "the effect of the statute is, not to prevent respectable men from speculating, but to make rogues refuse to pay their losses."[83] After over a century of such ineffectiveness, Barnard's Act was finally repealed in 1860.[84]

In March 1746, during another decline in stock prices, Sir John Barnard introduced "a Bill more effectually to prevent the infamous Practice of Stock-jobbing."[85] Notwithstanding the "wholsome Provisions" of his previous statute, the bill's preamble recited, "many evil-disposed Persons, out of Regard to their own private Interest, have contrived several Ways to lower the Prices of Publick Funds." The bill accordingly proposed to make it a crime to "conspire and combine together, to do any Act or Thing, with the Design and View of lowering the Price or Prices of any Publick or Joint Stocks." As all of the other techniques of doing so had been outlawed in 1734 or were proposed to be outlawed by other parts of the bill, this provision was most likely intended to prohibit the dissemination of false information calculated to reduce the price of stock. The bill would further have made it illegal to sell any stock "to be delivered at a future Time" for any price "under the then current Market-Price." This kind of sale was still lawful after Barnard's Act, so long as the seller owned the stock he was selling. The proposal proceeded from the common post-Bubble assumption, still widespread enough to be held by Barnard and his allies in Parliament, that stockjobbers could manipulate market prices by entering into forward contracts with prices set in the desired direction. As discussed in chapter 2, this assumption may have been correct; we do not know enough about the kind of information available to eighteenth-century investors to know whether forward prices had value as signals from insiders as to future price movements. The bill also proposed to ban the sale of securities held as collateral for a loan, unless the securities were declining in value (and the lender presumably feared that they would soon drop to a level insufficient to secure the loan), or unless the borrower defaulted on the loan and the lender needed to sell the securities to be reimbursed. Again, this proposal would have closed an

---

[81] See, e.g., Stewart Macaulay, "Non-Contractual Relations in Business: A Preliminary Study," *American Sociological Review* 28 (1963): 55; "Symposium: Law, Private Governance and Continuing Relationships," *Wisconsin Law Review* 1985 (1985): 461; David Charny, "Nonlegal Sanctions in Commercial Relationships," *Harvard Law Review* 104 (1990): 373.

[82] *The Art of Stock Jobbing Explained*, 56 n.*.   [83] Francis, *Chronicles*, 27.

[84] 23 & 24 Vic. c. 28 (1860).   [85] *Journals of the House of Commons*, 25:88.

avenue of short-selling left open by the literal terms of Barnard's Act, which permitted the sale of any stock of which the seller was "actually possessed," including stock that had been taken as collateral for a loan. The bill attempted to cut off another method of profiting from price declines; it would have prohibited people who held stock for the account of someone else (a category including brokers and trustees) from selling the stock "with Design to repurchase and replace the same." Any gain from such a sale and repurchase would go to the stock's true owner; any loss would be borne by the person doing the trading. Finally, Barnard's 1746 bill would have made it illegal to sell stock "on the Condition of the happening, or not happening, any future Contingency."[86] It is not clear how often speculators reached agreements like this, but from the fact that Barnard sought to prohibit them we can infer that some existed. A contract to sell stock only in the event it reached a certain price would be a device enabling traders to simulate an option without violating the literal terms of the 1734 ban on options, so this may be the "Contingency" that Barnard had in mind.

This bill never even came to a vote in the House of Commons, which suggests that members viewed stockjobbing as less of a menace in 1746 than they had in the 1720s and 1730s. None of the bill's provisions ever became law in the eighteenth century, although the first – the apparent attempt to prohibit the circulation of false information – did not need to, as will be discussed below in section III.

Barnard was back again with another stockjobbing bill in 1756, during the next sustained market downturn.[87] The bill would have required all time bargains to be registered with the government, and would have imposed a tax on those of the longest duration. Both of these measures were evidently intended primarily to make time bargains less attractive, as registration would not have subjected parties to any government supervision beyond the collection of the tax, and the tax could not have been large enough to provide the government with a significant amount of revenue without making time bargains prohibitively expensive. Both proposals drew immediate opposition. The registration requirement, it was pointed out, would only cause the behavior of market participants to grow even more predatory. Even if "the strictest Caution" were used, "some Persons, having great Command both of Money and Stock, will find Means to get Intelligence of the Registers to be made pursuant to this Act, and, by reason of this Foreknowledge, will be enabled to fleece the Proprietors wanting to buy or sell." In this manner, it was argued, the bill would only increase the

---

[86] British Sessional Papers, House of Commons, Bills, Vol. I, No. 27.
[87] Journals of the House of Commons, 27:546.

power of the wealthiest traders, who, "having terrified a great Number of Persons from frequenting the Market for Stocks, will have all the Game to themselves."[88] Opposition to Barnard's proposed tax on time bargains was grounded in the growing view that domestic markets – and particularly capital markets – contributed to the national wealth. "Not only the apparent Value," lectured one of Barnard's critics, "but the Being and Existence of Publick Credit, depend on a free and uninterrupted Circulation thereof; and what Cause soever shall check or interrupt the Circulation, more or less will depreciate the Value of Publick Credit."[89] Another argued, along the same lines, that "free and ready" transactions in public debt securities "will be found not to depreciate, but to support publick Credit, and not to raise, but lower the Rate of Interest to the Government, and not to the Uneasiness, but to the greater Satisfaction of the Proprietors."[90] The House of Commons voted by a three to one margin not to have Barnard's bill even printed.[91]

Parliament did enact a statute in 1766 that related tangentially to securities trading, "An act for regulating the proceedings of certain publick companies and corporations carrying on trade or dealings with joint stocks." The preamble recited that "of late years a most unfair and mischievous practice has been introduced," that of "temporary conveyances" of shares in order to obtain voting power "immediately before the time of declaring a dividend, of chusing directors, or of deciding any other important question." Parliament's solution was not to limit the transferability of shares, but rather to restrict their voting power. The statute prohibited shareholders from voting their stock until they "shall have have been possessed of such stock six calendar months."[92]

Occasional corporate charters throughout the century also enabled Parliament to restrict securities trading in various ways. Charters sometimes specified precisely how stock was to be transferred from one person to another.[93] Sometimes they limited the ability of shareholders to sell stock. The initial subscribers to the Northumberland Fishery Society, for instance, could not sell their shares for three years.[94] Such restrictions were common in eighteenth-century charters, and were apparently intended to prevent the bubbles of earlier in the century, by ensuring that the promoters of an enterprise could not sell out until the enterprise had a record of performance for potential investors to evaluate.[95] These types of charter provisions amounted to piecemeal

---

[88] *Reasons Against Passing into an Act, At this Time, Any Further Bill Relating to Stock-Jobbing* (s.l.: s.n., 1756), 1.

[89] *Considerations on a Bill Now Depending in Parliament* (s.l.: s.n., 1756), 1.

[90] *Reasons Against*, 2.   [91] *Journals of the House of Commons*, 27:596.

[92] 7 Geo. III c. 48, § 1 (1766).   [93] 26 Geo. III c. 106, §§ 11–12 (1786).

[94] 29 Geo. III c. 25 (1789).   [95] DuBois, *English Business Company*, 109–10.

regulation of the securities market, each provision applicable only to shares in an individual enterprise. Because Parliament chartered few business corporations in the eighteenth century, however, provisions like these did not have a broad reach.

During the early 1770s, a period of wide fluctuations around a trend of declining stock prices, Parliament considered its two final regulatory proposals of the eighteenth century. A bill in 1771 would have beefed up Barnard's Act by dramatically increasing the penalties to which brokers would be subject.[96] The bill would have imposed an additional £500 fine (beyond the £500 already provided for in Barnard's Act) on anyone contracting to sell stock he did not currently own, plus an additional £1,000 fine (beyond the £100 imposed by Barnard's Act) on any broker making such a contract.[97] The bill never made it out of the House of Commons.

Two years later, the House of Commons passed an elaborate bill that revived Barnard's 1756 plan for the registration of time bargains. The 1773 bill would have created a Publick Register Office, for the registry of all time bargains. Brokers and principals would have been required to register all contracts for time bargains within two days after they were made; principals who failed to do so would have been fined £1,000; brokers would have lost their licenses. The registry would have been open to public inspection. Any person would have been permitted to enforce Barnard's Act, by taking a copy of the contract in question to the relevant transfer office and inquiring whether the seller was possessed of the stock he was purporting to sell at the time of the contract. The clerk in the transfer office was required, upon payment of five shillings from the would-be enforcer, to certify an answer in writing. The enforcer could then use this answer to bring suit against the seller for violating Barnard's Act.[98] (Barnard's Act, it will be recalled, gave half of the seller's fine to whoever brought suit against the seller.) This bill would most likely have given Barnard's Act real teeth. The Act was rarely enforced, because the only people likely to know that an illegal time bargain existed were precisely those who had voluntarily entered into one. The 1773 bill would have, for the first time, given outsiders to the transaction an incentive to learn of contracts for the future sale of currently unowned stock and to sue violators of Barnard's Act. (One hundred and sixty years later in the United States, a similar enforcement mechanism would be created in section 16(a) of the Securities Exchange Act of 1934, which requires insiders to register their trades in order to

[96] *Journals of the House of Commons*, 33:349.
[97] British Sessional Papers, House of Commons, Bills, Vol. VI, No. 189.
[98] British Sessional Papers, House of Commons, Bills, Vol. VII, No. 240.

give third parties an opportunity to learn of illegal transactions and bring suit to undo them.[99]) The result, assuming the bounty for informants was large enough, would probably have been a quick upswing in enforcement actions, and a corresponding decline in the number of time bargains. The bill was rejected, however, by the House of Lords.[100] Parliament did not return to the issue of stockjobbing for the rest of the century.

With respect to the securities market in the eighty years after the Bubble, Parliament was representative of the nation. Stockjobbing was morally, politically, and socially dangerous; Parliament passed a statute (Barnard's Act) designed to strike at its heart. But stockjobbing was simultaneously useful and even productive; Parliament let the statute lie dormant on the books, and regularly declined, after much discussion, to breathe life into it by adding stronger mechanisms of enforcement. The result was the same tension that had characterized the English legal system's response to earlier forms of speculation – lots of rhetoric, but not much action. And, as with earlier speculative markets, that tension permitted the quiet expansion of the securities market in the eighteenth and early nineteenth centuries.

III

Eighteenth-century English appellate courts did not manifest the same tension in thought toward securities trading. Judges tended to give as much latitude as possible to the securities market, by enforcing even the more speculative transactions and narrowly construing would-be statutory limits on trading, while helping the market develop by giving redress for those abuses which fit into the traditional categories of judge-made law. This too was securities regulation, although in a form greatly constrained by the traditional role of the English judge. Case by case, the courts incrementally facilitated the growth of the market.

From the beginning, the courts were willing to enforce contracts to buy and sell securities to the same extent as contracts to buy or sell any other item. In view of the attention given recently to whether executory contracts were enforceable and expectation damages available by the early eighteenth century,[101] it bears emphasizing at the outset that the

---

[99] 15 U.S.C. § 78p(a).
[100] *Journals of the House of Lords*, 33:672, 676, 687.
[101] James Oldham, *The Mansfield Manuscripts and the Growth of English Law in the Eighteenth Century* (Chapel Hill: University of North Carolina Press, 1992), 213–44; Atiyah, *The Rise and Fall*, 194–216; Morton J. Horwitz, *The Transformation of American Law, 1780–1860* (Cambridge, MA: Harvard University Press, 1977), 160–88; J. H. Baker, "Book Review," *Modern Law Review* 43 (1980): 467; A. W. B.

reported cases involving securities suggest a positive answer to both questions. Either time bargains or ordinary agreements to buy stock could be executory contracts – the time bargains because both the payment of money and the transfer of stock would take place on a date in the future, and the ordinary agreements because stock was often transferable only on the books of the corporation, and the books were often open only intermittently, and were thus likely not be open when the contract was entered into.[102] The earliest of these cases was *Hall v. Cupper* (1693), in which the King's Bench enforced against the seller a contract according to which the parties agreed to a future sale of East India stock, at the buyer's option.[103] In *Lancashire v. Killingworth* (1701), the King's Bench would have enforced against the buyer a similar contract at the seller's option, had the seller adequately pleaded his tender of the stock.[104]

The many post-Bubble cases all apparently involved sellers, after the crash, trying to hold buyers to agreements made at pre-crash prices. In *Blackwell v. Nash* (1723), the parties had entered into a contract in 1720 while the market was still on the rise, according to which the plaintiff would transfer a specified amount of South Sea stock to the defendant on a particular date in the future, on which date the defendant would pay a certain sum of money to the plaintiff. When the plaintiff brought an action of debt on the agreement, "[t]he question was, whether these were *mutual convenants*, or only a *condition precedent?*" – that is, whether the plaintiff's failure to transfer the stock to the defendant would bar him from recovering his loss. The King's Bench held that the plaintiff's attempt to transfer the stock was sufficient to allow him to recover.[105] The court enforced a similar contract in *Wilkinson v. Meyer* (1722).[106]

In the remaining reported cases from the period, executory contracts for the sale of stock were not enforced, but in each case the lack of enforcement rested on a basis that had nothing to do with the fact that

Simpson, "The Horwitz Thesis and the History of Contracts," *University of Chicago Law Review* 46 (1979): 542–61.

[102] Dickson, *Financial Revolution*, 462–63.

[103] *Hall v. Cupper*, Skin. 391, 90 Eng. Rep. 174 (K.B. 1693).

[104] *Lancashire v. Killingworth*, 13 Mod. 529, 88 Eng. Rep. 1498 (K.B. 1701). In *Shales v. Seignoret*, 1 Ld. Raym. 440, 91 Eng. Rep. 1192 (K.B. 1699), the court held that a plaintiff-seller could not enforce an executory contract where he had never transferred the stock to the defendant-buyer, because "without transfer to the defendant, the defendant is not bound to pay the money, for the money was to be paid upon the transfer; and therefore no transfer, no money." The court went on, however, to suggest that had the seller made an adequate tender of the stock, he would have been able to recover, a suggestion difficult to reconcile with the excerpt quoted.

[105] *Blackwell v. Nash*, 8 Mod. 105, 1 Str. 535, 88 Eng. Rep. 83 (K.B. 1723), aff'd, 8 Mod. 106 (Ex. Ch. 1724).

[106] *Wilkinson v. Meyer*, 8 Mod. 173, 88 Eng. Rep. 127 (K.B. 1722).

an executory contract was involved. *Stent* v. *Bailis* (1724) concerned a contract in stock in the Lustring Company, one of the four enterprises against which the government proceeded shortly after the enactment of the Bubble Act for exceeding their charters. The government's action fell between the contract date and the expected transfer date, to the surprise of both buyer and seller, neither of whom were insiders. The Court of Chancery relieved the buyer of the obligation to pay for stock in a company that effectively had ceased to exist, on the ground that "[i]t is against natural justice, that any one should pay for a bargain which he cannot have; there ought to be *quid pro quo*, but in this case, the defendant has sold the plaintiff a *bubble* or *moonshine*."[107] Although the contract was not enforced, that was not because of its executory nature. Similarly, a group of cases from the early 1720s involved sellers trying to recover on executory contracts with which the buyers failed to comply. In each of the cases, the only issue in dispute was simply whether the seller had made an adequate tender of the stock. In all, the tender was held to be inadequate. The result was that the contract was not enforced in any of the cases, but the non-enforcement had nothing to do with the executory nature of the contract.[108] The reported cases involving stock thus suggest that executory contracts were understood to be enforceable in the early eighteenth century. This conclusion is reinforced by the 1721 statute requiring the retrospective registration of unperformed time bargains and the various later proposals for similar prospective registration schemes, which likewise seem to presume their enforceability.

Options were typically not executory contracts in the sense in which that term is normally used. The buyer of an option ordinarily paid *today* for the right to buy or sell stock in the future. Time bargains were sometimes not executory either, because the purchaser sometimes paid the seller on the contract date rather than the delivery date. In the three early reported cases where the buyer had already paid for the right to receive stock in the future, expectation damages or their equivalent were held to be available. In *Dutch* v. *Warren* (1720), the plaintiff had paid

---

[107] *Stent* v. *Bailis*, 2 P. Wms. 217, 24 Eng. Rep. 705, 706 (Ch. 1724).

[108] *Lock* v. *Wright*, 8 Mod. 40, 88 Eng. Rep. 30 (K.B. 1722); *Clark* v. *Tyson*, 1 Strange 504, 93 Eng. Rep. 663 (K.B. 1722); *Wivell* v. *Stapleton*, 8 Mod. 68, 72, 88 Eng. Rep. 54, 57 (H.L. 1723); *Thornton* v. *Moulton*, 1 Strange 533, 93 Eng. Rep. 682 (K.B. 1723); *Warren* v. *Consett*, 8 Mod. 107, 88 Eng. Rep. 84 (K.B. 1723); *Bullock* v. *Noke*, 1 Strange 579, 93 Eng. 712 (K.B. 1724); *Mordant* v. *Small*, 8 Mod. 218, 88 Eng. Rep. 156 (K.B. 1724). See also *Dorvill* v. *Aynesworth*, 1 Barn. K.B. 28, 94 Eng. Rep. 19 (K.B. 1727), where an executory contract for the sale of South Sea stock would have been enforced but for a pleading error on the part of the plaintiff, and *Jacobs* v. *Crosley*, 2 Barn. K.B. 156, 94 Eng. Rep. 418 (K.B. 1732), where the adequacy of the tender was "a matter proper to be farther considered of."

money to the defendant in exchange for the defendant's promise to transfer stock at a future date, but the defendant had failed to make the transfer. The King's Bench held that the plaintiff could properly bring an action for money had and received. In a declining market, the plaintiff was allowed to recover "not for the whole money paid," and not the specific shares of stock the defendant failed to transfer, but rather the plaintiff's expectation damages – "the damages in not transferring the stock at that time, which was a loss to the plaintiff, and an advantage to the defendant."[109] In *Cud* v. *Rutter* (1719), the Court of Chancery refused a buyer's request for specific performance of the seller's promise to convey shares of stock, on the ground that the buyer had an adequate remedy at law in the form of a suit for damages for his loss in not receiving the stock.[110] The third case, and the only one to award specific performance rather than expectation damages, was from two decades earlier. In *Gardener* v. *Pullen & Phillips* (1700), the Court of Chancery awarded specific performance of a promise to transfer stock which had "much risen" since the date the defendant should have transferred it.[111] This is a small bit of evidence, but it suggests an understanding, at least where stock was involved, that the measure of damages should be what the plaintiff could have expected to gain from the transaction. In a declining market, as in *Dutch*, the plaintiff would recover the value of the stock as of the transfer date (in order to make the wrongdoing defendant rather than the plaintiff bear the ensuing loss); in a rising market, as in *Gardener*, the plaintiff would recover the value of the stock as of the time of trial, either in money or as the stock itself (in order to let the plaintiff rather than the wrongdoing defendant have the advantage of the gain). This tendency to give the plaintiff the benefit of his expectation from the transaction solidified by the end of the century. Where the stock in question had gone down in price between the date it should have been transferred and the date of trial, the damage award would be pegged to the stock's price on the transfer date,[112] but where

---

[109] *Dutch* v. *Warren*, 1 Strange 406, 93 Eng. Rep. 598 (K.B. 1720). Horwitz is right that "the case obviously does not establish the modern rule" that expectation damages are generally available in both rising and falling markets, Horwitz, *The Transformation*, 163 (for support see Mansfield's discussion of *Dutch* in *Moses* v. *Macferlan*, 2 Burr. 1005, 1011–12, 97 Eng. Rep. 676 (K.B. 1760)), but the case does stand as a single example of the award of expectation damages. With respect at least to the stock cases, the most accurate thing one can say is that there were not enough to establish the existence of *any* rule. In most of the cases cited in this chapter, the measure of damages was not an issue discussed by the court, and was probably, as Simpson, "The Horwitz Thesis," suggests, an issue for the jury.

[110] *Cud* v. *Rutter*, 1 P. Wms. 570, 571, 24 Eng. Rep. 521 (Ch. 1719).

[111] *Gardener* v. *Pullen & Phillips*, 2 Vern. 394, 23 Eng. Rep. 853 (Ch. 1700).

[112] *Forrest* v. *Elwes*, 4 Ves. Jun. 492, 31 Eng. Rep. 252 (Ch. 1799).

the stock had risen in price, "the plaintiff can only be indemnified by giving him the price of it at the time of trial."[113]

The English courts thus offered redress for stockjobbers in the early part of the century, even when their public reputation was at its lowest, and even when they were seeking the enforcement of their newest and most complicated transactions. Barnard's Act prevented securities traders from seeking this sort of relief after 1734 with respect to most types of contracts. Because the effect of Barnard's Act was to take a large class of securities transactions out of the official court system, there were few reported cases interpreting the Act, and those that existed concerned the question of whether a particular type of transaction was covered by the Act.[114] In most of these cases, the courts interpreted the Act narrowly, which further limited its impact on the market, and thus facilitated the market's continued existence throughout the rest of the century. In *Faikney* v. *Reynous* (1767) and *Petrie* v. *Hannay* (1789), the King's Bench held that Barnard's Act did not prohibit agreements to reimburse a broker or a fellow investor for trading losses, even where the person being reimbursed had incurred his losses in transactions made illegal by the statute.[115] These holdings enabled brokers to engage in any of the transactions prohibited by Barnard's Act without fear that their principals would use the Act as a shield when the time came to settle, and thus contributed to the normal functioning of the market despite the Act. In *Sanders* v. *Kentish* (1799), the court held that the Act did not prohibit agreements by which A loaned stock to B for B to sell, in exchange for B's promise to put an equal number of shares of stock back in A's possession on a future date.[116] The case involved facts provoking "great indignation at the conduct of the defendant Kentish," a broker who tried to use Barnard's Act to swindle Sanders, a clergyman, by borrowing Sanders' stock, selling it, and then refusing to return either the stock or the cash to Sanders on the ground that Barnard's Act made the whole transaction illegal. "[I]f the defendant's objection were to prevail," suggested Lord

---

[113] *Shepherd* v. *Johnson*, 2 East 211, 102 Eng. Rep. 349 (K.B. 1802).

[114] Such was also the primary concern of the commentary on Barnard's Act. See *The Law of Stock Jobbing, As Contained in Sir John Barnard's Act, and the Cases Decided Thereon* (London: E. Wilson, 1835).

[115] *Faikney* v. *Reynous*, 4 Burr. 2069, 98 Eng. Rep. 79 (K.B. 1767); *Petrie* v. *Hannay*, 3 Term Rep. 418, 100 Eng. Rep. 652 (K.B. 1789). These cases were slightly limited by *Steers* v. *Lashley*, 6 Term Rep. 61, 101 Eng. Rep. 435 (K.B. 1794), which invalidated under Barnard's Act an arrangement identical in substance but structured differently, in which the payment went directly to pay the differences rather than reimbursing the broker for the broker's payment of the differences. They would be overruled in *Cannan* v. *Bryce*, 3 Barn. & Ald. 179, 106 Eng. Rep. 628 (K.B. 1819).

[116] *Sanders* v. *Kentish*, 8 Term Rep. 162, 101 Eng. Rep. 1323 (K.B. 1799).

Kenyon, "the title of the Act ought to be altered; and it should run thus: 'An Act to Encourage the Wickedness of Stock-Jobbers, and to give them the Exclusive Privilege of Cheating the Rest of Mankind.'"[117] The outcome allowed speculators to continue using one method of short-selling left open after Barnard's Act, in which a trader gambling on a price decline would borrow stock on a promise to replace it in the future or take it as collateral for a loan, sell the stock, and then replace it by repurchasing it in the future at, he hoped, a lower price. Finally, in *Child v. Morley* (1800), the King's Bench decided that Barnard's Act did not prevent a broker from contracting on behalf of his principal for the sale of stock which the broker did not actually possess, even if the broker never disclosed the principal's name to the purchaser, so long as the principal actually possessed the stock at the time the contract was entered into.[118] *Child* had the effect of ratifying the surface legality of the ordinary course of trading, in which brokers bought and sold while possessing little or no stock, on behalf of undisclosed principals who played no role in the transactions beyond reimbursing the broker for losses or collecting gains, and in which there was rarely any occasion to inquire into whether the principal actually possessed any of the stock the broker was selling. All told, the handful of cases involving Barnard's Act construed it narrowly enough to prevent it from having much of an effect.[119] Contemporaries complained that "Gamesters by studying the act evaded it"; to the extent that is true, the courts facilitated their evasion.[120]

Another potential statutory limitation on securities trading involved the law of usury, but here too the courts assisted in the market's development by narrowly construing a suggested obstacle to trading. It was not uncommon for stock to be loaned from one person to another, with the understanding that the stock or its equivalent in money, including any dividends that had been paid on the stock while out on loan, would be returned to the lender after the expiration of a certain period of time. If the stock's value substantially increased while on loan, or if during that time a significant dividend had been paid, the lender could realize a profit from the loan – the functional equivalent of an interest rate – higher than the maximum allowed by statute for loans of money. Were such loans of stock therefore illegal? In *Tate v. Wellings* (1790), the King's Bench rejected the argument that they were. A "mere

---

[117] 101 Eng. Rep. at 1325.
[118] *Child v. Morley*, 8 Term Rep. 610, 101 Eng. Rep. 1574 (K.B. 1800).
[119] Keyser, *The Law Relating*, 152.
[120] Quoted in S. R. Cope, "The Stock Exchange Revisited: A New Look at the Market in Securities in London in the Eighteenth Century," *Economica* 45 (1978): 9.

loan of stock is not usurious," Lord Kenyon concluded, "nor the payment of the dividends in the mean time, though they exceed the legal rate of interest." The court drew upon a strand of legal thought that dated back to medieval canon law (and which was discussed briefly in chapter 1), according to which a high return on an investment could not be condemned as usury so long as the money invested had been at risk. Because the stock's price could have declined while on loan as easily as it rose, the transaction was not usurious. The court recognized the possibility that a loan of stock could be "merely colourable, and intended as a loan of money," in order to serve as "a mere cloak for usury." In such a case, the court observed, a return to the lender higher than the statutory maximum would violate the law. In *Tate*, however, a jury had found that no such subterfuge was intended, and the loan was therefore permissible.[121] Again, a possible statutory check on the securities market had been construed narrowly enough by the courts to permit the more complex forms of trading to continue.[122]

Where perceived abuses fell within traditional common law categories, however, the courts were willing to be far more active in policing the securities market. From at least the early seventeenth century, English courts had awarded relief, under the heading of fraud, to buyers deceived by sellers as to the nature of the item they had purchased.[123] The doctrine was applied to securities transactions shortly after the Bubble. In the summer of 1720, at the peak of public interest in investing in new enterprises, the promoters of a scheme for extracting oil from radishes sold shares to the public with the representation that it was "a most advantageous project without any hazard." The Court of Chancery held that the promoters, by "giving them *moonshine* instead of any *thing real*," as they had promised, had committed fraud. "If this were fraud against any private or single person," the court observed, "a court of equity would relieve; *a fortiori*, where it is a fraud against great numbers, against multitudes, where the mischief is more extensive, and many families thereby ruined."[124] By the end of the eighteenth century, it was common ground among English lawyers that fraud applied to sales of securities in the same way that it applied to sales of any other item. Whether a sale could be voided because *both* buyer and seller were victims of false information spread by a third party was a difficult issue

---

[121] *Tate* v. *Wellings*, 3 Term Rep. 531, 100 Eng. Rep. 716 (K.B. 1790).

[122] The usury issue is discussed in detail in George Cochrane, *Opinions on Loans of Government Stock; Respectfully Addressed to the Landed, Commercial, and Professional World* (London: Smith, Elder and Co., 1847).

[123] A. W. B. Simpson, *A History of the Common Law of Contract* (Oxford: Clarendon Press, 1975), 535–36.

[124] *Colt* v. *Woollaston*, 2 P. Wms. 154, 156, 24 Eng. Rep. 679, 680 (Ch. 1723).

on which divergent opinions were entertained, and would be in the United States as well, but there appears to have been no question that a buyer who was the direct victim of false information spread by the seller could get his money back.[125]

Securities were more likely than most items to be bought and sold by agents rather than actual owners, which meant that transactions frequently raised agency-related legal issues. Here too the courts policed the securities market as if it were any other market. Courts did not hesitate to set aside transactions entered into by the administrator of an estate who sold the estate's stock as if it were his own,[126] or by a trustee who in effect sold his beneficiary's stock to himself;[127] or to make whole a stockholder whose stock was sold by her agent without her authorization,[128] or whose stock was erroneously credited to another stockholder on the books of the corporation;[129] or to require a pledgee to account for the money he received from the sale of pledged stock.[130] These cases were not conceptualized as belonging to a category called "securities law," but they did not need to be. Familiar bodies of law – the law of trusts, the law of wills, the law governing principal and agent – were available to be used. The relatively new institution of securities trading was easily assimilated into the older legal categories whenever a securities transaction became the subject of litigation.[131] Although stock was, as Mansfield put it, "a new species of property, arisen within the compass of a few years" (and thus it could not be the subject of an action for money had and received, since it was not money), it was a form of property all the same, and could be governed by the same judge-made law applicable to other types of property.[132]

Eighteenth-century English courts thus facilitated the establishment

---

[125] Burn, *A Brief Treatise*, 72–74.
[126] *Munn* v. *East-India Co.*, Rep. Temp. Finch 298, 23 Eng. Rep. 163 (Ch. 1677); *Johnson* v. *East-India Co.*, Rep. Temp. Finch 430, 23 Eng. Rep. 234 (Ch. 1679).
[127] *Whitackre* v. *Whitackre*, Sel. Cas. T. King 13, 25 Eng. Rep. 195 (Ch. 1725).
[128] *Monk* v. *Graham*, 8 Mod. 9, 88 Eng. Rep. 8 (C.P. 1721); *Hildyard* v. *South-Sea Co.*, 2 P. Wms. 76, 24 Eng. Rep. 647 (Ch. 1722).
[129] *Harrison* v. *Pryse*, Barn. C. 324, 27 Eng. Rep. 664 (Ch. 1740); when the erroneously credited stockholder learned of the mistake, "he was struck with a great deal of Confusion, and died the Day after."
[130] *Harrison* v. *Hart*, 1 Comyns 393, 92 Eng. Rep. 1126 (K.B. 1727).
[131] See *Cock* v. *Goodfellow*, 10 Mod. 489, 88 Eng. Rep. 822 (Ch. 1722) (bankruptcy); *Powell* v. *Hankey*, 2 P. Wms. 82, 24 Eng. Rep. 649 (Ch. 1722) (coverture); *Trenchard* v. *Wanley*, 2 P. Wms. 166, 24 Eng. Rep. 685 (Ch. 1723) (trusts); *Batten* v. *Whorewood*, Barn. C. 421, 27 Eng. Rep. 703 (Ch. 1740) (wills). For some uncertainty as to whether contracts for the sale of stock were subject to the Statute of Frauds, a statute then less than fifty years old, see *Pickering* v. *Appleby*, 1 Comyns 354, 92 Eng. Rep. 1108 (K.B. 1721).
[132] *Nightingal* v. *Devisme*, 5 Burr. 2589, 98 Eng. Rep. 361 (K.B. 1770). Cf. Blackstone, *Commentaries*, I, 328. For later confirmation of the view that stock was a new kind of

of the securities market by tending to enforce contracts, even the most speculative contracts, as written; by narrowly construing potential statutory limits on trading; and by policing misbehavior falling under familiar legal headings. This pattern of decisions was the product of a handful of characteristics of the English judicial system in the eighteenth century, including (1) its general tendency to permit whatever behavior had not been expressly prohibited by statute or common law, (2) the capacity of the common law to absorb new institutions and new types of behavior into older legal categories, and (3) the terse manner in which judicial decisions were generally reported, which prevented the judges' own views of disputed matters of policy from becoming widely known. These characteristics had nothing directly to do with securities trading or with economic matters. It is likely that *any* new institution or pattern of behavior, economic or otherwise, planted in England in the eighteenth century, would have received the same treatment in the courts. The outcomes of all these cases thus cannot be understood to mean that the English legal system as a whole was particularly conducive to the development of a securities market, except in the most obvious sense that a legal system highly protective of property rights will be a comfortable home for any institution devoted to transferring property from one person to another. Nor can all these decisions necessarily be taken as representative of the judges' personal opinions of securities trading or of stockjobbers.

On the other hand, eighteenth- and nineteenth-century English judges often invested their capital in government securities. That the judges considered the public debt a prudent investment may be inferred from the frequency with which they provided in their wills for the purchase of government securities with their residuary personal estates, as a means of supporting their widows and children. Judges less often invested in shares of business enterprises, but such investments were not uncommon; the limited available evidence suggests that judges owned shares of railroads, canals, turnpikes, insurance companies, and even the South Sea Company.[133] To most of the judges deciding cases involving securities, the market was a familiar institution and one in which they held a small stake. The judges thus stood to gain from a course of decisions facilitating the market's growth. One can never be certain of the unstated motives of appellate judges, but here one can at least say

---

property, different from money, see *Jones* v. *Brinley*, 1 East 1, 102 Eng. Rep. 1 (K.B. 1800).

[133] Daniel Duman, *The Judicial Bench in England 1727–1875: The Reshaping of a Professional Elite* (London: Royal Historical Society, 1982), 135–39.

that the judges' personal interests and the cumulative effect of their decisions on the development of the market were in alignment.

In the one reported case in which a judge permitted himself to express his own view of the matter, Lord Eldon (who left £96,000 in government securities in his will) admitted in 1800 that his impression had been "that a jobber or dealer in the funds was always to be considered as a culpable person."[134] This impression had been "removed from my mind" by one of his colleagues, who showed Eldon "the necessity of such persons for the accommodation of the market."[135] The market was good; its permanent inhabitants were not, but were a necessary evil, because the market could not exist without them. There, in a nutshell, was the conventional wisdom at the end of the eighteenth century.

To the eighteenth-century English legal system, stock was indeed "a new species of property," and this was true in two senses. Stock was *property*; it was thus conventionally understood to be governed by the various doctrines regulating the interaction of people with respect to other kinds of property. In this sense, the new institution of organized securities trading required no explicit response from the legal system. The law, like a gas, was capable of expanding to fill all available space. A new institution could easily be assimilated into the older legal categories simply by analogizing the institution's attributes to those of the most homologous institutions already in existence. And those analogies would have been so self-evident to English lawyers and judges that they would not have seemed analogies at all. The law had never before encountered time bargains for the sale of stock, for instance, but lawyers hardly needed to make any explicit analogies between time bargains and more familiar kinds of transactions, or between stock and more familiar kinds of property. A time bargain self-evidently fell within the established legal category of agreements for the sale of an item, and stock self-evidently fell within the established legal category of property. Once those classifications had been subconsciously made, the rest was easy, because the legal system already included well-worn rules for regulating the sales of property.

But stock was also a *new* species of property, one with certain attributes not possessed by the older species, particularly its amenability to speculative transactions. In this sense, the new institution demanded, in the view of many, an explicit response from the legal system, directed at suppressing precisely those characteristics that differentiated securities from other kinds of property. Given the conventional division of

[134] On Eldon's will, see ibid., 135 & n.86.
[135] *Morris* v. *Langdale*, 2 Bos. & Pul. 284, 288, 126 Eng. Rep. 1284, 1286 (C.P. 1800).

labor in the common law system between Parliament (the maker of new law) and the courts (the finders of old law), the location of this response had to be Parliament. The stockjobbing debates in Parliament over the course of the eighteenth century are best understood as the manifestations of a deeper disagreement over a simple question: Was stock sufficiently like older kinds of property to be governed by the same law, or was it sufficiently different from older kinds of property to require new law specific to itself? In the early part of the century, when the securities market was still relatively new and unfamiliar, stock seemed more different. But as the market aged, and as more and more people began investing in it, the emphasis in Mansfield's phrase gradually changed; stock became less of a *new* species of property, and more of a new species of *property*. As that happened, new law treating securities differently from other sorts of property became more difficult to obtain.

4   The development of American attitudes toward securities trading, 1720–1792

Shares of government debt and of business enterprises were not traded in North America on a significant scale until the later part of the eighteenth century, nearly a century after the development of organized securities trading in England. Long before they copied these English institutional arrangements, however, Americans inherited English ideas that would bear upon securities trading. These ideas and the processes by which they were transmitted to North America are discussed in section I of this chapter. Section II will describe the American securities market from its beginnings in the 1770s through the crash of 1792, with an emphasis on the experiences which shaped American attitudes toward securities trading. The resulting pattern of thought, copied from English sources and then modified in light of more recent local experience, will be analyzed in section III.

I

England's North American colonies were largely populated by emigrants from England, of course, who brought with them English attitudes toward speculation and toward securities markets. Communication between England and the colonies, moreover, was frequent enough in the eighteenth century to permit the colonies to share in contemporary trends in English thought, including the thought generated by the effects of the South Sea Bubble, and to permit the wealthiest Americans to invest in English securities. For these reasons, when the American economy became large enough to permit the development of securities trading, that practice was born into a world of preexisting thought.

Colonial attitudes toward speculation exhibited the same ambivalence as in England.[1] Soon after the founding of Virginia, for example, the

[1] David Thomas Konig, *Law and Society in Puritan Massachusetts* (Chapel Hill: University of North Carolina Press, 1979), 74.

colonial Assembly deplored "the excessive and exorbitant ingrossing of commodities brought into this country," and accordingly mandated that "such as buy may buy only for their particular use, and if they can spare any of the same, then not to sell any of the same goods at any dearer rate to their neighbours for more than they paid at the first penny." Two years later the Assembly ordered "the statutes and lawes of England agaynst forestallers, and engrossers, to be made known and executed in this colony." Yet after another decade the Assembly reversed its course; the Assembly repealed its previous statutes, and provided instead "[t]hat ffree trade be allowed to all the inhabitants of the collony to buy and sell at their best advantage."[2] The contrast was the product of the same competing visions of a well-functioning economy as were contemporaneously present in England.[3] At roughly the same time, the General Court at Plymouth was hearing "greate abuse complayned of by buying and regratinge goods and commodities wch come in boates & vessels to be sould in divers places." The Court accordingly banned residents from buying any items such that "the price may be enhaunced by selling them againe in the same towne or markett (except he [that] buy by whole sale to retayle the same againe at reasonable gaine)."[4] Early in the eighteenth century the Maryland Assembly found speculation in commodities so "mischievous and prejudicial to the Inhabitants of this Province" that it attempted to prohibit the purchase of "any Goods or Merchandizes whatsoever, or Servants, to the Intent to sell the same again within the space of six Months."[5] Later in the century, when war drove up food prices, Americans again tried to suppress speculation.[6] But speculation continued all the same. One early nineteenth-century commentator, looking back on the preceding century, observed that although forestalling, engrossing, and regrating had always been common law crimes in North America, "notorious violations have often been complained of, but scarcely in any instances prosecuted." He

---

[2] William Waller Hening, ed., *The Statutes at Large; Being a Collection of all the Laws of Virginia*, 2nd edn (New York: R. & W. & G. Bartow, 1823), I, 150–51, 172, 296 (the statutes are from 1630, 1632, and 1645).

[3] Edmund Morgan, *American Slavery, American Freedom: The Ordeal of Colonial Virginia* (New York: Norton, 1975), 113–14; Wesley Frank Craven, *The Southern Colonies in the Seventeenth Century 1607–1689* (Baton Rouge: Louisiana State University Press, 1949), 237–38.

[4] David Pulsifer, ed., *Plymouth Colony Records* 11:29 (Boston: W. White, 1861) (the record is from 1638).

[5] *The Laws of the Province of Maryland* (1718), ed. John D. Cushing (Wilmington: Michael Glazier, 1978), 36.

[6] See, e.g., *A Meeting of the Inhabitants of this Town, Being Formerly Called to Consider of Prudent and Effectual Measures, for Putting a Stop to Forestalling Extortion . . .* (Lancaster: Francis Bailey, 1779).

attributed this lack of enforcement to "the easy and indulgent temper and character of the people generally, who have ever been disposed to suffer themselves to be cheated and imposed upon in these ways, by these kinds of offenders, in hundreds of instances, complaining generally, but never prosecuting."[7] Americans, like the English, were simultaneously practitioners and critics of speculation.

The same tension may be found in the seventeenth-century Massachusetts prosecution and conviction of Robert Keayne for making an excessive profit from reselling commodities imported from England. Keayne did not deny having engaged in the transactions for which he was charged; he instead denied that there was anything wrong with speculation. "Was it such a heinous sin," he asked, "to sell 2 or 3 dozen of great gold buttons for 2s. 10d. per dozen that cost 2s. 2d. ready money in London[?] . . . Was the selling of 6d. nails for 8d. per lb. and 8d. nails for 10d. per lb. such a crying and oppressing sin?" Keayne emphasized that his prices were "not for taking but only asking," and that his supposed victims had thus freely agreed to them. Keayne and his prosecutors represented the opposing views of speculation composing what Bailyn has called the "delicate balance of tensions in the life of the pious merchant."[8]

Eighteenth-century Americans also inherited the prevailing English conception of the economy, according to which the national wealth was increased only by production and by selling goods abroad, not by internal trade.[9] The merchants who bought and sold in domestic markets were thus understood to contribute nothing to the public good. "[I]f the same Goods are bought by *Ten Persons* one after another," a resident of Massachusetts argued,

each of those *Ten Persons* aims at *Gain* in passing thro' his hands . . . yet the *Province* or *Publick* is not enrich'd *one Farthing* by their Labour. If they had been employ'd in *Husbandry* or *Handycraft-Business*; there would probably have been some produce of their labour for the Publick Good . . . but their meer *handing of Goods one to another*, no more increases any Wealth in the Province, than Persons *at a Fire* increase the *Water in a Pail*, by passing it thro' *Twenty* or *Forty* hands.[10]

---

[7] Nathan Dane, *A General Abridgment and Digest of American Law* (Boston: Cummings, Hilliard & Co., 1823–29), VII, 39.

[8] *The Apologia of Robert Keayne* (1653), ed. Bernard Bailyn (New York: Harper & Row, 1965), 52, xi. See E. A. J. Johnson, *American Economic Thought in the Seventeenth Century* (New York: Russell & Russell, 1961), 88–90, 123–27.

[9] Crowley, *This Sheba*, 86–88.

[10] *The Present Melancholy Circumstances of the Province Consider'd, and Methods for Redress Humbly Proposed* (Boston: B. Gray and J. Edwards, 1719), 6–7.

Internal commerce was conceptualized as a zero-sum game, as in England at the same time. For every person gaining from a domestic transaction, someone else had to be the loser. "[M]erchants . . . as well as usurers or money-jobbers . . . may all *very possibly* grow rich," suggested one Pennsylvanian, but for that to happen "the rest of the community are oppressed and kept poor."[11] In America as in England, securities trading – an activity undertaken largely in an internal market – would fall within this more general presumption of non-productivity.

The concern with non-productivity also played a large role in colonial Americans' condemnation of gambling, another activity often practiced yet often criticized.[12] Gambling was "a Waste of precious Time, which might be employ'd to much better Purpose."[13] In this sense gambling was much like internal trade. "[W]hat possible advantage can accrue to a Country from the Practice of Gaming?" asked William Stith.

What useful Art is promoted? What Manufactures are carried on? Or what Addition is there made by it to the publick Stock and Wealth of a People? None certainly. For the Whole of Gaming is only to shift the Property and Specie, which hath been acquired to a Country and brought in by the honest Labourer's Industry, from one Hand to another.[14]

The risk inherent in securities trading caused it to resemble gambling, which made it easy for late eighteenth-century Americans to transpose this criticism of gambling to the new securities market, which in turn reinforced the preexisting view that the securities market, like any other domestic market, added nothing to the national wealth. This was another respect in which American thought tracked English thought.

A final aspect of colonial economic thought that would shape American attitudes toward securities was an awareness of a sharp divide between the interests of debtors and creditors.[15] Creditors were people, one contemporary charged, who would "swallow up the Estates of their poor Neighbours . . . for failure of paying Debt and Interest."[16] They were "a detestable Company of Extortioners," complained a Providence

[11] John Webbe, *A Discourse Concerning Paper Money* (Philadelphia: Bradford, 1743), 7.

[12] T.H. Breen, "Horses and Gentlemen: The Cultural Significance of Gambling among the Gentry of Virginia," *William and Mary Quarterly* 34 (1977): 239; Rhys Isaac, *The Transformation of Virginia 1740–1790* (Chapel Hill: University of North Carolina Press, 1982), 98–104.

[13] D. Fowle and Z. Fowle, *A Letter to a Gentleman on the Sin and Danger of Playing at Cards and Other Games* ([Boston]: s.n., 1755), 3.

[14] William Stith, *The Sinfulness and Pernicious Nature of Gaming* (Williamsburg: William Hunter, 1752), 13.

[15] Peter J. Coleman, *Debtors and Creditors in America* (Madison: State Historical Society of Wisconsin, 1974), 6–15.

[16] *Some Considerations Upon the Several Sorts of Banks* (Boston: T. Fleet and T. Crump, 1716), 15.

cooper, "who would burn your Houses, for the Convenience of roasting their Eggs at the Flame." But even the cooper recognized that "no Society of Men can live together without an Intercourse of Dealing, and of Consequence there must be both *Debtor* and *Creditor*."[17] This sense of an inevitable opposition between the two groups would play a large role in the opposition to the issuance of long-term public debt securities in the new United States, just as it had a century earlier in England.

Colonial Americans thus shared in the strands of English thought that underlay English attitudes toward securities trading well before the existence of securities trading in North America. When the South Sea Bubble burst in 1720, Americans interpreted the event much the same way as it was interpreted in England; it was widely understood as proof of the danger posed by stockjobbing.[18] "[W]here one hath Gained by this Evil Trade," remarked a resident of Massachusetts in early 1721, "many poor Families have been ruined."[19] As in England the word "bubble" itself became a general pejorative term.[20] The writings of Trenchard and Gordon casting the Bubble in ominous political terms were widely circulated as pamphlets and reprinted in the newspapers of every colony, which ensured that literate Americans could not overlook this line of criticism.[21]

Colonists applied the Bubble's lessons to what seemed like the most analogous American circumstance, the issuance (or anticipated issuance) of paper currency by colonial governments. In Massachusetts, the government's emission of bills of credit was described by a critic as "the Second Part of [i.e., the sequel to] South-Sea Stock."[22] When the colony in 1740 planned to create a land bank that would issue paper notes, to be financed by the sale of shares to the public, opponents successfully petitioned Parliament to prevent the plan from going forward by extending the Bubble Act to the colonies.[23] The resulting statute – "An act for restraining and preventing several unwarrantable schemes and undertakings in his Majesty's colonies and plantations in

[17] T.R., *A Letter to the Common People of the Colony of Rhode Island* (Providence: William Goddard, 1763), 2, 4.

[18] Gary B. Nash, *The Urban Crucible: Social Change, Political Consciousness, and the Origins of the American Revolution* (Cambridge, MA: Harvard University Press, 1979), 164.

[19] John Higginson, *The Second Part of South-Sea Stock* (Boston: D. Henchman, 1721), 1.

[20] See, e.g., James Flagg, *A Strange Account of the Rising and Breaking of a Great Bubble* (Boston: s.n., 1767) (concerning a disputed land grant). McAdam, Jr., and Milne, eds., *Johnson's Dictionary*, 107 (defining "to bubble" as "[t]o cheat").

[21] Bernard Bailyn, *The Ideological Origins of the American Revolution* (Cambridge, MA: Harvard University Press, 1967), 36.

[22] Higginson, *Second Part*, 1.

[23] Joseph Albert Ernst, *Money and Politics in America, 1755–1775* (Chapel Hill: University of North Carolina Press, 1973), 33–35; Edwin Merrick Dodd, *American Business Corporations until 1860* (Cambridge, MA: Harvard University Press, 1954), 366–67.

America" – permitted the land banks already in existence in other colonies to wind up their operations, but prohibited the creation of any similar unchartered joint-stock companies in the future.[24] The extension of the Bubble Act was controversial and long remembered; John Adams would claim in 1775 that it "raised a greater ferment in this province, than the Stamp Act."[25] Even after the war, Paine continued to invoke the events of 1720 as a means of highlighting the dangers of paper currency, which he described as "both the bubble and the iniquity of the day."[26] Americans experienced the Bubble vicariously, both as an actual event and as a cultural icon representing the dangers of speculative finance.

Some residents of the colonies experienced the English securities market first hand, as investors in government debt or in the shares of English enterprises. Thomas Hutchinson, the last royal governor of Massachusetts, had most of his capital invested in shares of the East India Company, and it seems reasonable to suppose that a similar pattern of investment could be found among other wealthy Americans with close connections to England.[27] Maryland invested the proceeds of its tobacco export tax in Bank of England stock.[28] Below the wealthiest stratum of the population, however, investment in English securities appears to have been unusual.[29] The distance between North America and England, and the persistent shortage of liquidity in the colonies, prevented the ownership of English securities from diffusing as far down through the American population in the eighteenth century as was the case in England.

Until the second half of the eighteenth century, there was little possibility to own American securities. No colonial government borrowed money by issuing bonds; because wealth tended to be so illiquid, government was financed primarily by issuing unbacked paper currency to pay for government expenses, currency which was then taken back in

---

[24] 14 Geo. II c. 37 (1741). On land banks and their prevalence in other colonies, see Edwin J. Perkins, *The Economy of Colonial America*, 2nd edn (New York: Columbia University Press, 1988), 172–73.

[25] Quoted in John J. McCusker and Russell R. Menard, *The Economy of British America, 1607–1789* (Chapel Hill: University of North Carolina Press, 1985), 337.

[26] Quoted in Eric Foner, *Tom Paine and Revolutionary America* (New York: Oxford University Press, 1976), 197.

[27] Bernard Bailyn, *The Ordeal of Thomas Hutchinson* (Cambridge, MA: Harvard University Press, 1974), 259.

[28] Jacob M. Price, "The Maryland Bank Stock Case: British–American Financial and Political Relations Before and After the American Revolution," in Aubrey C. Land, Lois Green Carr, and Edward C. Papenfuse, eds., *Law, Society, and Politics in Early Maryland* (Baltimore: Johns Hopkins University Press, 1977), 5.

[29] Robert Sobel, *The Big Board: A History of the New York Stock Market* (New York: Free Press, 1965), 15.

for taxes.[30] Very few business enterprises raised capital by issuing stock. Only six business corporations were chartered by colonial governments during the entire colonial period.[31] When one adds the handful of American enterprises chartered by the English government and the unchartered joint-stock companies in existence despite the extension of the Bubble Act to the colonies,[32] the likelihood of owning shares in an American enterprise before the late eighteenth century was still minimal.[33] Credit was still largely decentralized; in an economy in which enterprises tended to be small enough to borrow capital directly from lenders in face-to-face transactions, there was little need to buy and sell stock.[34]

Before the second half of the century, widespread investment in small shares of an enterprise was a phenomenon largely limited to the shipping industry, where large amounts of capital were necessary to finance individual vessels. As had long been the case in England, colonial ships tended to be owned by large numbers of investors forming partnerships. Investors were drawn from a wide segment of the population. Almost one-third of the adult men in early eighteenth-century Boston, for instance, owned at least one share of a ship.[35] In England, where shares in ships were similarly dispersed among the population, shares were freely transferable and were frequently bought and sold in major port cities; similar trading most likely occurred on a smaller scale in American ports as well.[36] These partnership shares differed in a technical legal sense from shares in a corporation, but closely resembled corporate shares in their transferability and their representation of fractional ownership of a commercial enterprise.

In the later part of the century, as the American economy grew larger and more liquid, Americans began to copy what were by then the familiar English institutions of shares in government debt and in domestic enterprises. Massachusetts in 1751 became the first colony to

---

[30] E. James Ferguson, *The Power of the Purse: A History of American Public Finance, 1776–1790* (Chapel Hill: University of North Carolina Press, 1961), 7–10.

[31] Simeon E. Baldwin, "American Business Corporations Before 1789," in *Annual Report of the American Historical Association for the Year 1902* (Washington: Government Printing Office, 1902), I, 257.

[32] Shaw Livermore, *Early American Land Companies* (New York: The Commonwealth Fund, 1939), 215–16, 229–30.

[33] See Alice Hanson Jones, *Wealth of a Nation to Be: The American Colonies on the Eve of the Revolution* (New York: Columbia University Press, 1980), 127–34.

[34] Edwin J. Perkins, *American Public Finance and Financial Services 1700–1815* (Columbus: Ohio State University Press, 1994), 56–75.

[35] Bernard Bailyn and Lotte Bailyn, *Massachusetts Shipping 1697–1714* (Cambridge, MA: Harvard University Press, 1959), 31, 35, 56.

[36] Ralph Davis, *The Rise of The English Shipping Industry in the Seventeenth and Eighteenth Centuries* (London: Macmillan, 1962), 100–04.

borrow money by issuing transferable bonds, made "payable with Lawful Interest in Six Months to the Lender or Bearer," which were sold for specie to members of the colony's mercantile community.[37] This method of financing proved successful, and continued through the 1770s. Connecticut, New Hampshire, Rhode Island, and North Carolina did the same soon after.[38] The unprecedented expense of the Revolution caused the Continental Congress to issue its first debt securities in 1776. The national government, soon joined by all the state governments, continued to borrow from the public in this fashion all through the war. Public securities also provided a useful medium, at times the only one available to governments at the limits of solvency, for paying soldiers and military contractors.[39] By the end of war, large amounts of state and national debt securities were in circulation.

The amount of corporate stock in circulation also rose dramatically during the same period, although not to the same extent as public debt. The states and the national government chartered thirty new business corporations in the 1780s, or five times as many as had been chartered during the entire colonial period.[40] These included some substantial enterprises, such as the Bank of North America, created by the Continental Congress in 1781, and the Bank of New York, chartered by New York in 1784, as well as many canals and a few manufacturing and insurance companies.[41] Shares in these enterprises were widely held. A study of probated estates in a rural county in Massachusetts found that in the 1780s securities of all types began to constitute a significant percentage of the estates' financial assets, including shares in a variety of bridges, turnpikes, banks, insurance companies, and manufacturing companies, as well as shares in the public debt of the national govern-

---

[37] *The Acts and Resolves, Public and Private, of the Province of the Massachusetts Bay* (Boston: Wright & Potter, 1907), XIV, 561; Ferguson, *Power of the Purse*, 10.

[38] Perkins, *American Public Finance*, 205–06; Leslie V. Brock, *The Currency of the American Colonies 1700–1764: A Study in Colonial Finance and Imperial Relations* (New York: Arno Press, 1975), 434.

[39] William G. Anderson, *The Price of Liberty: The Public Debt of the American Revolution* (Charlottesville: University Press of Virginia, 1983), 26.

[40] Joseph Stancliffe Davis, *Essays in the Earlier History of American Corporations* (Cambridge, MA: Harvard University Press, 1917), II, 22. For arguments that this sudden increase in the rate of corporate chartering can be attributed to changes in American popular thought occasioned by the Revolution, see Gordon S. Wood, *The Radicalism of the American Revolution* (New York: Vintage Books, 1993), 318–22; Pauline Maier, "The Revolutionary Origins of the American Corporation," *William and Mary Quarterly* 50 (1993): 51. Colonial governments may simply have been uncertain of their authority to create corporations; if so, that uncertainty was removed by the Revolution. Davis, *Essays*, I, 7–29.

[41] Robert A. East, *Business Enterprise in the American Revolutionary Era* (New York: Columbia University Press, 1938), 287, 294.

ment and the New England states.[42] It is likely that securities were even more widespread in more urban areas.

The ballooning amount of securities in circulation in the 1780s enabled Americans to mimic another English institution: By the later years of the decade, there was a group of people in the leading commercial cities of New York, Philadelphia, and Boston trying to make a living as brokers and jobbers, often in local coffee houses. In 1787, for example, Isaac Franks advertised himself in Philadelphia as a "stock and exchange broker."[43] The New York merchant Andrew Craigie boasted to a colleague in 1788 that "[t]he public Debt affords the best field in the world for speculation."[44] Newspaper quotations of securities prices began to appear as early as 1786, and began to be regularly printed in 1789.[45] These early brokers and speculators were generalists – they also bought and sold currency, land, insurance, and commodities – operating within circles of merchants who were growing accustomed to buying and selling securities on a regular basis.[46] The early American speculators consciously copied English techniques. The Philadelphia trader Edward Fox, for example, suggested to Craigie in 1789:

> that a sum of Continental Debt . . . might be sold to be *delivered* in any given time: that is to fix the price at present, and agree upon a mode of fixing it at the end of the Time, – and then without transferring, or delivering any Certificate to *pay* or receive the difference of price. This is the Common practice in England – and is what is there called "*Stock Jobing*."[47]

Options, time bargains, and the settlement of contracts by the payment of price differentials quickly became conventional.[48] "Much of this business," the Congressman William Maclay lamented in 1790, "is done in the Change Alley Way."[49]

---

[42] Winifred B. Rothenberg, "The Emergence of a Capital Market in Rural Massachusetts, 1730–1838," in Ronald Hoffman, John J. McCusker, Russell R. Menard, and Peter J. Albert, eds., *The Economy of Early America: The Revolutionary Period, 1763–1790* (Charlottesville: University Press of Virginia, 1988), 135–36.

[43] Edwin Wolf 2nd and Maxwell Whiteman, *The History of the Jews of Philadelphia from Colonial Times to the Age of Jackson* (Philadelphia: Jewish Publication Society of America, 1957), 168.

[44] Craigie to Daniel Parker, May 1788, quoted in Davis, *Essays*, I, 188.

[45] Davis, *Essays*, I, 197–98.   [46] McCusker and Menard, *The Economy*, 347.

[47] Fox to Craigie, Nov. 30, 1789, quoted in Davis, *Essays*, I, 196.

[48] Examples can be found in *Groves* v. *Graves*, 1 Wash. (1 Va.) 1 (1790) (concerning a 1787 time bargain entered into in Virginia), in *Livingston* v. *Swanwick*, 2 Dall. (2 U.S.) 300 (C.C.D.Pa. 1793) (an action on the case to recover the price differential on a 1791 time bargain entered into in New York), and in *Graham* v. *Bickham*, 4 Dall. (4 U.S.) 149 (1796) (an action on the case to recover the price differential on a 1792 time bargain in Philadelphia). One of the plaintiffs in the second case was Brockholst Livingston, the future Justice of the US Supreme Court.

[49] Linda Grant De Pauw *et al.*, eds., *Documentary History of the First Federal Congress of the United States of America* (Baltimore: Johns Hopkins University Press, 1972–), IX, 324.

By the 1780s, when shares of corporate stock and public debt became familiar institutions in the United States, Americans had long known what to think about them, because they had inherited nearly a century of English thought on the subject, and had participated in that thought both in England and in North America. Speculators took little time in mimicking English practices. For this reason, most of the characteristic eighteenth-century English arguments for and against securities trading would be quick to arrive in the United States.

II

American attitudes toward securities trading would also be shaped by three local experiences during the market's first two decades. The first of these was the Revolution, which gave rise to a rash of speculation, including speculation in securities, that seemed to many to be clearly contrary to the national interest. The second was the course of unorganized securities trading in the years after the war, which caused the outstanding public debt to become concentrated in the hands of a relatively small number of northern merchants, and created the regional and occupational divides with respect to securities trading that would persist for some time thereafter. The third was the sequence of events in the years 1790–92, which encompassed (a) a boom in securities trading after the new federal government committed to assume the states' debts and then (b) a dramatic crash in stock prices in early 1792. These experiences and the opinions of the market they engendered would influence American securities regulation in succeeding decades.

The onset of war in the mid 1770s created shortages of food and other items needed by the military, which caused prices to fluctuate and opened up new opportunities for speculators. As these opportunities grew, so did the volume of public criticism of speculation. "The complaints in the country are chiefly levelled against the merchants, in the maritime towns," a Boston minister reported in 1777. "[T]hey have taken advantage of the times and laid extravagant prices on almost every article, which the necessities of the people have compelled them to purchase."[50] Public anger over speculation in Pennsylvania led to the detention in 1779 of "divers persons of suspicious characters . . . who are charged with forestalling and engrossing,"[51] and to threats to the safety of merchants suspected of charging unduly high prices.[52] George

---

[50] Jonathan French, *A Practical Discourse Against Extortion* (Boston: T. & J. Fleet, 1777), 17.

[51] *Whereas It Has Been Represented to This Board . . .* (Philadelphia: John Dunlap, 1779).

[52] East, *Business Enterprise*, 200.

Washington complained that "Speculation, Peculation, Engrossing, forestalling with all their concomitants, afford too many melancholy proofs of the decay of public virtue."[53] Many contemporaries agreed.[54]

Wartime speculation was equally common in government debt. The rapid infusion of public debt securities into the American economy during the war gave rise to a flurry of securities trading, the first in American history. Public criticism of this form of speculation was no less intense. It drew upon what was nearly a century-old English tradition of pointing out the political danger posed by wartime speculation in government debt, which gave investors a set of preferences contrary to the public good. "[I]t is now consistent with the views of Speculators, various tribes of money makers, and stock jobbers of all denominations," Washington wrote to George Mason in 1779, "to continue the War for their own private emolument, without considering that their avarice, and thirst for gain must plunge every thing (including themselves) in one common Ruin."[55] The pseudonymous "Lucius" argued in a Philadelphia newspaper that Robert Morris, the wartime Superintendent of Finance, was "so engaged in those deep speculations, that have been made in loan office certificates," that for his own gain he would have "the United States be thrown into convulsions, and, as far as you can effect it, their credit ruined."[56] The clash of personal and national interests caused by securities trading, a theme prominent in the writings of Defoe, Trenchard and Gordon, and the other critics of the early English securities market, had crossed the Atlantic.

Morris responded to this sort of criticism of speculators with an argument that had also been heard before in England. "[I]t is not in human Prudence to counteract their Operations by Laws," he began, "whereas when left alone they invariably counteract each other." More important, however, was the benefit provided by an active securities market, for which speculators were a necessary ingredient. "[E]ven if it were possible to prevent Speculation," Morris concluded,

it is precisely the Thing which ought not to be prevented; because he who wants Money to commence, pursue or extend his Business, is more benefited by selling Stock of any Kind (even at a considerable Discount) than he could be by

---

[53] Washington to James Warren, March 31, 1779, John C. Fitzpatrick, ed., *The Writings of George Washington* (Washington: Government Printing Office, 1931–41), XIV, 312.

[54] Janet A. Reisman, "Money, Credit, and Federalist Political Economy," in Richard Beeman, Stephen Botein, and Edward C. Carter II, eds., *Beyond Confederation: Origins of the Constitution and American National Identity* (Chapel Hill: University of North Carolina Press, 1987), 131.

[55] Washington to George Mason, March 27, 1779, Fitzpatrick, ed., *Writings of George Washington*, XIV, 300.

[56] John Catanzariti *et al.*, eds., *The Papers of Robert Morris 1781–1784* (Pittsburgh: University of Pittsburgh Press, 1973–), VII, 561.

the Rise of it at a future Period; Every Man being able to judge better of his own Business and Situation, than the Government can for him.[57]

The primary argument of the Parliamentary opponents of regulation – that the utility of the market to the ordinary merchant far exceeded any damage that could be caused by speculators – had also resurfaced in North America. The American market was, by that point, scarcely more than five years old.

After the war ended all the various public debt securities were still in circulation, generally trading at a substantial discount from face value, reflecting investors' lack of confidence that the debts of which they were a part would ever be repaid. The original holders of these depreciated securities – including many war veterans who had received them instead of a salary, and who urgently needed money – gradually sold them over the course of the 1780s to speculators willing to gamble on the future stability and solvency of the national and state governments. The largest speculators were northern merchants, concentrated in small circles in New York and Philadelphia. As of 1786, for instance, a group of eight or nine New York merchants owned more than 15 percent of the combined South Carolina, North Carolina, and Virginia state debts.[58] By the end of the decade, a large fraction of the nation's outstanding public debt securities was in the hands of a relatively small number of wealthy northerners.[59]

Because of this migration of securities during the 1780s, the decade's debates over appropriate national financial policy and its effect on securities trading were marked by regional and occupational divides even sharper than those which had characterized the earlier similar debates in England. Before the 1780s, stock had been a symbol of cooperation;[60] civil society had been analogized to "a trading company, possessed of a common stock, into which every one hath given his proportion,"[61] and government argued to imply "a surrender of something into a common stock, constituting a common property, and to be used for the mutual good of all the proprietors."[62] But by the middle of

---

[57] "Report on Public Credit" (July 29, 1782), in Catanzariti *et al.*, eds., *Papers of Robert Morris*, VI, 70.

[58] Cathy Matson, "Public Vices, Private Benefit: William Duer and His Circle, 1776–1792," in William Pencak and Conrad Edick Wright, eds., *New York and the Rise of American Capitalism* (New York: New-York Historical Society, 1989), 96.

[59] Whitney Bates, "Northern Speculators and Southern State Debts: 1790," *William and Mary Quarterly* 19 (1962): 42–48.

[60] David Thomas Konig, "Jurisprudence and Social Policy in the New Republic," in David Thomas Konig, ed., *Devising Liberty: Preserving and Creating Freedom in the New American Republic* (Stanford: Stanford University Press, 1995), 205–06.

[61] Levi Hart, *Liberty Described and Recommended* (Hartford: Eben. Watson, 1775), 11.

[62] Thomas Paine, "A Serious Address to the People of Pennsylvania on the Present

the decade, it became apparent that stock was the subject of a set of the most divisive questions facing the new nation. How should the out-standing public debt be repaid? To its current holders (largely northern speculators) or to its original holders (a more sympathetic group of people, spread across the country, including many veterans)? At its market value (which was substantially below what it was originally worth) or its face value (which would enable speculators who had bought well below face value to realize astronomical rates of return)? When Madison, in the tenth *Federalist*, depicted a nation inevitably divided into a "landed interest, a manufacturing interest, a mercantile interest, [and] a monied interest," all of which were "actuated by different sentiments and views," he was not just drawing upon a tradition of English political theory,[63] he was describing a current American controversy.[64]

The side of this debate taken by the speculators hardly needs explaining today. Paying the face value of a debt, to its current holder, is of course (and was at the time) the normal practice, and the one most likely to encourage lenders to be willing to lend again in the future. The other side of the debate requires some reconstruction. The "grand question," as Pelatiah Webster described it in 1785, was "Whether they will pay these public monies to the soldiers and other virtuous citizens, who are the original creditors; or, Whether they will pay these same monies to a parcel of stock-jobbers and speculators." Service during the war, and financial assistance to the government when it was most in need, produced strong normative claims to a share of the public wealth. Snapping up securities at a discount by exploiting "the poor soldiers, who in their penury and distress sold their certificates at 2/6 in the pound," or one-eighth of face value, did not.[65] This distinction between original and secondary holders would be remembered for years. In 1792, for instance, a correspondent to the *National Gazette* proposed inscribing a series of pictures on certificates of the new national debt – "1. The *bloody arm* of a soldier. 2. The *wooden leg* of a soldier. 3. A *soldier's heart* pierced with a bayonet" – to remind speculators of those who had been "grossly defrauded and injured by our government."[66]

Situation of Their Affairs" (1778), in Philip S. Foner, ed., *The Complete Writings of Thomas Paine* (New York: Citadel Press, 1945), II, 295.

[63] James Madison, *The Federalist* No. 10 (1787), in Michael Kammen, ed., *The Origins of the American Constitution: A Documentary History* (New York: Penguin, 1986), 147.

[64] Cathy D. Matson and Peter S. Onuf, *A Union of Interests: Political and Economic Thought in Revolutionary America* (Lawrence: University Press of Kansas, 1990), 155.

[65] Pelatiah Webster, *Seventh Essay on Free Trade and Finance* (Philadelphia: Eleazer Oswald, 1785), 11–12, 6.

[66] *[Philadelphia] National Gazette*, May 7, 1792, 3.

On this view, repaying the debt at face value only made matters worse. Speculators who bought 6 percent bonds at one-eighth of their face value, for instance, would realize an effective return of 48 percent on the interest payments alone, and even more if the debt were paid off at face value. The money that would make up these enormous gains would have to be raised by taxing the general population, which was made up in large part of the very same impoverished war veterans. Webster concluded that debt securities should be redeemed at market value; that is:

at that price or exchange at which they generally pass at the time of redemption, EXCEPTING ONLY such securities as are in the hands of the original holder, and have never been alienated. Such securities are evidence of full consideration paid, and of course of a full debt due to such holder: But securities in the hands of a purchaser cannot be such evidence.[67]

Distinguishing between original and secondary holders – paying face value to the first group but current market value to the second – would have the effect of treating all holders consistently, in the sense that all would receive from the government the approximate amount they expected to receive when they acquired the securities.[68]

This divide in public opinion manifested itself at the Constitutional Convention, in the debate over what eventually became the first clause of Article VI, which provided that the pre-Constitution national debt "*shall* be as valid against the United States under this Constitution, as under the Confederation."[69] George Mason objected to the word "shall," on the ground that it would require the new government to redeem the old debt at face value, which would provide a windfall to certain speculators. "The use of the term *shall*," Mason argued,

will beget speculations and increase the pestilent practice of stock-jobbing. There was a great distinction between original creditors & those who purchased fraudulently of the ignorant and distressed. He did not mean to include those who have bought Stock in open market. He was sensible of the difficulty of drawing the line in this case, but He did not wish to preclude the attempt.

Mason's objection drew a response from Elbridge Gerry, who first

[67] Webster, *Seventh Essay*, 29.

[68] Participants in both sides of the debate ignored a technical problem that would likely have required modifying any plan to redeem the debt at market value. If the market value was to be as of the time of redemption or the time of acquisition, and if market participants had advance notice of the legislation establishing that rule (as they almost certainly would have), the market value of the relevant securities should be bid up to infinity. The problem could have been solved by using the market value as of a given date in the past, or, less satisfactorily given the political climate, capping redemption at face value.

[69] US Const., art. VI (emphasis added).

observed that "as the public had received the value of the literal amount [i.e., the face value of the securities], they ought to pay that value to some body." Gerry then went on to defend the practice of securities trading, with the argument that had become the conventional wisdom in England by that time. "As to Stock-jobbers," he explained to Mason, there was "no reason for the censures thrown on them. They keep up the value of the paper. Without them there would be no market." Gerry's view prevailed; the word "shall" remained.[70]

Securities prices began to rise when the states ratified the Constitution. The rise grew especially pronounced in late 1789, after Alexander Hamilton was appointed Secretary of the Treasury and he began drafting the Report on Public Credit, as speculators anticipated the main points of Hamilton's program.[71] They were most likely assisted in this regard by information furnished by Assistant Secretary William Duer, himself a leading New York speculator, including during the seven months he served as Assistant Secretary.[72] Speculators repeatedly asked Hamilton and Duer for investment advice, in the hope of profiting from the early receipt of inside information.[73] In November 1789, for instance, when Hamilton had been Secretary for two months, Henry Lee had some questions for him. "From your situation," Lee began,

you must be able to form with some certainty an opinion concerning the domestic debt. Will it speedily rise, will the interest accruing command specie or any thing nearly as valuable, what will become of the indents already issued?

These querys are asked for my private information, perhaps they may be improper, I do not think them so or I would not propound them – of this you will decide & act accordingly.[74]

Hamilton was uncertain as to whether there was anything legally

---

[70] *Notes of Debates in the Federal Convention of 1787 Reported by James Madison* (New York: Norton, 1987), 528, 529. The extent to which involvement in the securities market influenced the views of delegates at the Constitutional Convention has, of course, been the subject of debate at least since the publication of Charles A. Beard, *An Economic Interpretation of the Constitution of the United States* (1913) (New York: Free Press, 1986). My point here and in the following pages has no bearing on that debate. I am not seeking to explain the delegates' votes; my point is only that the speculation of the 1770s and 1780s, understood in light of the earlier English experience, gave rise to two opposing views of the market by the late 1780s, and that evidence of those opposing views can be found in many places, including at the Constitutional Convention.

[71] Stanley Elkins and Eric McKitrick, *The Age of Federalism: The Early American Republic, 1788–1800* (New York: Oxford University Press, 1993), 138–39.

[72] Robert F. Jones, *"The King of the Alley": William Duer, Politician, Entrepreneur, and Speculator, 1768–1799* (Philadelphia: American Philosophical Society, 1992), 128–31.

[73] Broadus Mitchell, *Alexander Hamilton: The National Adventure, 1788–1804* (New York: Macmillan, 1962), 159–63.

[74] Henry Lee to Hamilton, Nov. 16, 1789, Harold C. Syrett *et al.*, eds., *The Papers of Alexander Hamilton* (New York: Columbia University Press, 1961–81), v, 517.

improper about answering Lee's questions, but he recognized the political liabilities that would result, and he accordingly refused to provide Lee with any information.[75] Duer, however, was apparently less circumspect. "During the whole Time I have been Engaged in Operations of the Public Debt," he boasted to Hamilton more than a year after he left the Treasury, "I can with Truth Aver that I have Scrupulously adhered to the most rigid Principles of Candor." Duer was referring to the past year, when he had spent much of his time speculating in government securities, but his statement probably applied equally well to his tenure as Assistant Secretary. "I have Endeavored to make any Knowledge I possest on this Subject, a Common Stock," Duer continued. "By my advice and Example, Numbers in this City have by Embark'g in the Funds, supported the Public Credit, and advanced their own Fortunes."[76] An example of Duer's apparent willingness to help his friends may be found in a letter he received in late 1789, while Assistant Secretary, with reference to the Amsterdam banker Théophile Cazenove:

he is to settle himself in america, & I believe to make some speculations in your funds. I am sure, knowing your obliging temper, you'll give him good informations about his speculations; & I'll be much obliged to you to do it & to introduce him to your acquaintances.[77]

Duer was not the only source of inside information as to future financial policy. His successor as Assistant Secretary, Tench Coxe, was equally prone to helping his friends with timely advice.[78] Duer's fellow New York speculator Andrew Craigie repeatedly touted his own access to government officials. "I know no way of making safe speculations," he explained to a colleague, "but by being associated with people who from their Official situation know all the present & can aid with future arrangements either for or against the funds." In a letter soliciting business from a Dutch firm, Craigie announced his intention "to cultivate & improve such officials [sic] connections as shall give me the best opportunity for acquiring information & forming just opinions respecting the finances & Politics of the U. States." The national capital was still in New York, which enabled speculators to mingle with executive officials and members of Congress – Craigie, for instance, lived in a boarding house with several members of Congress – and this close contact facilitated the movement of information likely to affect

[75] Hamilton to Lee, Dec. 1, 1789, Syrett *et al., Papers of Alexander Hamilton*, VI, 1.
[76] Duer to Hamilton, Aug. 16, 1791, Syrett *et al., Papers of Alexander Hamilton*, XXVI, 618.
[77] Brissot de Warville to Duer, Nov. 27, 1789, Duer papers, Reel 3, NYHS.
[78] Jacob E. Cooke, *Tench Coxe and the Early Republic* (Chapel Hill: University of North Carolina Press, 1978), 176–77.

stock prices. That flow of information caused prices to rise in late 1789, and stimulated a flurry of trading; Edward Fox reported from Philadelphia in December that "the Rage of the Day is the purchase of Stock."[79] In anticipation of the Treasury's next move, according to Hamilton, securities prices rose by 33 percent between January and November 1789, and by another 50 percent between November 1789 and January 1790.[80] New York had already become the leading city for securities trading, in part because of speculators' proximity to government officials, and in part because New York was already eclipsing Boston and Philadelphia as the nation's commercial capital.[81] "The Reason why our Market is so thin, and no sellers upon it, is very plain," complained Edward Fox in Philadelphia to Andrew Craigie in New York. "[S]peculators . . . find New York the best Market, and therefore have forwarded every thing there. No man will sell here because he knows more money is to be had in Your City."[82] The close relationship between investors and government officials, however, would provide powerful arguments against securities trading in subsequent years.

Hamilton's Report on Public Credit was published in January 1790. It included everything holders of securities had been hoping for – a plan for a funded national debt on the English model, a proposal to pay current holders of national debt securities at face value, a proposal to have the national government assume the debts of the states, and a suggestion that Congress create a national bank.[83] The Report sparked greater demand for public securities, both state and federal, which now seemed even more likely to be redeemed in full. A week after it was issued, Robert Livingston observed that in New York "money continues as scarce as ever & that no property or credit can raise a shilling. This is principally owing to the rise of our funds & the spirit of stock Jobing which has invaded all ranks of people."[84] The Report also confirmed the fears of many that the new national government, by imitating English techniques of public finance, would inevitably succumb to the same kind of corruption and internal division that had so often been argued to follow from securities trading in England.[85] Echoes of the post-Bubble

---

[79] Craigie to Daniel Parker, May 1788, Craigie to Van Staphorsts, June 1789, Fox to Craigie, Dec. 7, 1789, quoted in Davis, *Essays*, I, 188.

[80] Alexander Hamilton, "Report on Public Credit," *Annals of Congress*, II, 2042 (1790).

[81] McCusker and Menard, *The Economy*, 189.

[82] Fox to Craigie, Dec. 7, 1789, quoted in Davis, *Essays*, I, 200.

[83] *Annals of Congress*, II, 2043–44, 2046–49, 2050, 2072.

[84] Quoted in George Dangerfield, *Chancellor Robert R. Livingston of New York 1746–1813* (New York: Harcourt, Brace, 1960), 247.

[85] Drew McCoy, *The Elusive Republic: Political Economy in Jeffersonian America* (Chapel Hill: University of North Carolina Press, 1980), 152–61; Lance Banning, "Political

criticism of Trenchard and Gordon would grow louder in the next few years. Even Hamilton was worried about the effects his program would have on speculative activity, not just due to the political opposition speculation was likely to bring forth, but because the rapid price swings historically associated with speculation were not, in his view, conducive to economic growth.[86] The solution was careful regulation of the market. "There is," concluded Hamilton, "at the present juncture, a certain fermentation of mind, a certain activity of speculation and enterprise which, if properly directed, may be made subservient to useful purposes; but which, if left entirely to itself, may be attended with pernicious effects."[87]

Congress debated the funding and assumption plan through the spring of 1790, and enacted the measures into law in early August.[88] Northern speculators promptly headed out to remote areas in search of state debt held by people who had not heard the news. In August William Duer (who had resigned as Hamilton's assistant in order to devote himself full time to speculating) received a letter from an associate who had travelled to the south only to find the area "so thronged with Speculators . . . that Certificates can rarely be had" at bargain prices. Duer's associate resolved to go to an area that "has not hitherto been explored by the Speculators and it is so much a Wilderness that I hope to find but few competitors. It borders on South Carolina and probably Certificates of their State may offer – if they do I will strike."[89] Once again, the transfer of securities from their original holders to a small group of northern speculators armed with superior information, and wealthy enough to tie up assets while awaiting better prices, looked too much like exploitation, and would cause the practice of securities trading to be viewed with disfavor by many in the years to come. The public image of the practice was further tarnished by the fact that many members of Congress had themselves purchased public securities, the value of which would increase because of the enactment of Hamilton's program. "The Unexampled Success" of these investments, muttered William Maclay, "has obliterated every Mark of reproach . . . and from henceforth we may consider Speculation As a

Economy and the Creation of the Federal Republic," in David Thomas Konig, ed., *Devising Liberty*, 44.

[86] John R. Nelson, Jr., *Liberty and Property: Political Economy and Policymaking in the New Nation, 1789–1812* (Baltimore: Johns Hopkins University Press, 1987), 38–39.

[87] Alexander Hamilton, "Report on Manufactures" (1791), in Alexander Hamilton, *Papers on Public Credit, Commerce and Finance*, ed. Samuel McKee, Jr. (New York: Columbia University Press, 1934), 233.

[88] 1 Stat. 138 (1790).

[89] Unidentified correspondent to Duer, Aug. 21, 1790, Duer papers, Reel 2, NYHS.

congressional Employment."[90] This conflation of public policy and private gain – "corruption" in the eighteenth-century sense of the word[91] – would often be cited in subsequent years as an argument against securities trading.

The assumption of the state debts and the commitment to create a funded national debt were the final steps necessary to permit organized securities trading in the United States. Within a short time, a bewildering variety of state and national securities, the values of many of which depended upon the fluctuating fortunes of state governments, were replaced by three simple issues of new securities, all backed by the credit of the United States government. Estimating the value of public debt securities now required much less time and much less knowledge than had formerly been the case, and investing in public securities entailed much less risk than it had before. These developments enabled more people to participate in the market. To accommodate this increased public participation, traders began to organize. The buying and selling of securities had formerly been conducted in a scattered fashion, in *ad hoc* transactions conducted in the street and in coffee houses. Soon after the consolidation of the public debt became a certainty, merchants in the leading commercial cities established regular daily public auctions. In New York, for instance, by July 1791 brokers and jobbers were conducting two auctions daily.[92] As demand for the new government securities increased, prices began to rise.[93]

Public interest in securities trading further accelerated in the summer of 1791 when, as a preliminary step in organizing the Bank of the United States, the government began selling off the rights to purchase shares in the Bank. These rights, called "scrip" or "script" – short for "subscription" – were extraordinarily popular. They were sold to the public in early July at $25 each; by late July they were trading at double their initial value, and by early August they had reached nearly $300 in New York and slightly more than $300 in Philadelphia.[94] In Philadelphia, Jefferson was stunned at "the rapidity with which the subscriptions

---

[90] De Pauw *et al.*, eds., *Documentary History of the First Federal Congress*, IX:324.

[91] On the concept of "corruption" in the eighteenth century, see Isaac Kramnick, "Corruption in Eighteenth-Century English and American Political Discourse," in Richard K. Matthews, ed., *Virtue, Corruption, and Self-Interest: Political Values in the Eighteenth Century* (Bethlehem: Lehigh University Press, 1994), 55–75; John M. Murrin, "Escaping Perfidious Albion: Federalism, Fear of Aristocracy, and the Democratization of Corruption in Postrevolutionary America," in ibid., 103–47.

[92] Walter Werner and Steven T. Smith, *Wall Street* (New York: Columbia University Press, 1991), 21.

[93] See, e.g., unidentified correspondent to Duer, April 11, 1791, Duer papers, Reel 2, NYHS.

[94] Davis, *Essays*, I, 202–03.

to the bank were filled. As yet the delirium of speculation is too strong to admit sober reflection."[95] From New York, Madison reported in early July that "Bank-Shares have risen as much in the Market here as at Philadelphia," and in early August that "Stock & script continue to be the sole domestic subjects of conversation."[96] In Boston, "the Script mania was at as great a height" as anywhere else.[97] Even when prices dipped in mid August, Benjamin Rush explained to his wife, "You hear of nothing but *script* and of all the *numbers* between 50 and 300 at every corner. Merchants, grocers, shopkeepers, sea captains, and even prentice boys have embarked in the business."[98] Members of Congress were also well represented among the owners of scrip; of the initial subscribers, thirty were members of Congress, which was more than a third of the whole membership at the time, and more than half of the number who had voted in favor of establishing the Bank.[99] These thirty men, like the other initial subscribers, multiplied their investments by a factor of twelve within a month. The close links between public policy and private profit would, as before, prove too close for the comfort of many, who would cite "bank-jobbing" as yet another instance of the corrosiveness inherent in the practice of securities trading.

Through the rest of 1791 and early 1792, participation in the market continued to grow. "SPECULATION now employs the heads and hearts of all the monied characters in the state," complained a resident of New York.[100] A Virginia woman seeking a husband in Richmond attributed her lack of success to the fact that "the gentlemen's minds are I believe occupied chiefly with speculating in paper money certificates &c. which they find more profitable than wives."[101] Her story was corroborated by Henry Lee, who described his journey between Philadelphia and Alexandria as "one continuous scene of stock gambling; agriculture commerce & even the fair sex relinquished, to make way for unremitted exertion in this favorite pursuit."[102] The "appetite for gambling," as

[95] Jefferson to Edmund Pendleton, July 24, 1791, Julian P. Boyd et al., eds., *The Papers of Thomas Jefferson* (Princeton: Princeton University Press, 1950–), XX, 670.

[96] Madison to Jefferson, July 10 and Aug. 4, 1791, William T. Hutchinson *et al.*, eds., *The Papers of James Madison* (Chicago: University of Chicago Press, 1962–), XIV, 43, 65.

[97] George W. Corner, ed., *The Autobiography of Benjamin Rush* (Princeton: Princeton University Press, 1948), 206.

[98] Aug. 12, 1791, L.H. Butterfield, ed., *Letters of Benjamin Rush* (Philadelphia: American Philosophical Society, 1951), I, 603.

[99] Bray Hammond, *Banks and Politics in America* (Princeton: Princeton University Press, 1957), 123.

[100] *The Glass; or, Speculation: A Poem* (New York: s.n., 1791), 2.

[101] Quoted in Suzanne Lebsock, *The Free Women of Petersburg: Status and Culture in a Southern Town, 1784–1860* (New York: Norton, 1984), 19.

[102] Henry Lee to Madison, Aug. 24, 1791, Hutchinson *et al.*, eds., *Papers of James Madison*, XIV, 73.

Jefferson put it, extended even to shares in business enterprises.[103] Apprentices in Philadelphia were deserting their posts, one employer despaired, because they had "been infected with the Turnpike Rage. Everything is now turned into Speculation."[104] Newspaper headlines described a "SCRIPOMANIA" sweeping the country.[105] A Connecticut newspaper asked:

> What Magic this among the people,
> That swells a Maypole to a steeple?
> Touch'd by the wand of speculation,
> A frenzy runs through all the nation.[106]

"There happens to be a rage in the present day, for acquiring property by accident," observed the Boston lawyer James Sullivan. "[T]oo many are ready to lay aside their ordinary business, to pursue *chance* as the only goddess worthy of human adoration."[107] There was almost certainly a great deal of exaggeration in all these remarks – most investors had neither abandoned their regular jobs nor invested a significant percentage of their assets in government securities.[108] But if the public interest in the new market was not deep, it was far wider than it had ever been before.

As the market grew thicker and better organized, speculators were able to copy English techniques even more closely. "Many thousand shares were bought and sold," Benjamin Rush reported in August 1791, "to be delivered and paid for at a future day by persons who had neither Script, nor money."[109] Surviving records of market participants suggest that Rush was correct; one finds many instances of time bargains entered on the books, but many fewer instances of stock actually being transferred.[110] Rumors abounded of efforts to corner the market in scrip. "Very serious attempts have been making for several days past," charged a correspondent to New York's *Daily Advertiser* in August 1791,

[103] Jefferson to Monroe, July 10, 1791, Boyd *et al.*, eds., *Papers of Thomas Jefferson*, XX, 298.

[104] Quoted in Charles I. Landis, "History of the Philadelphia and Lancaster Turnpike: The First Long Turnpike in the United States," *Pennyslvania Magazine of History and Biography* 42 (1918): 133.

[105] *[New York] Daily Advertiser*, Aug. 15, 1791, 2; *[Philadelphia] General Advertiser*, Aug. 12, 1791, 3.

[106] *[New Haven] Connecticut Journal*, Aug. 17, 1791, 2.

[107] James Sullivan, *The Path to Riches* (Boston: I. Thomas and E. T. Andrews, 1792), iii.

[108] Thomas M. Doerflinger, *A Vigorous Spirit of Enterprise: Merchants and Economic Development in Revolutionary Philadelphia* (Chapel Hill: University of North Carolina Press, 1986), 314.

[109] Corner, ed., *Autobiography of Benjamin Rush*, 206.

[110] See, e.g., Constable-Pierrepont papers, Vol. XL, at 6, 8 (Aug. 1791), NYPL; Alexander Macomb to William Duer, Jan. 1, 1792, Duer papers, Reel 3, NYHS.

"to purchase all the Script in this city and Philadelphia." The correspondent cautioned readers not to sell scrip unwittingly to participants in the corner.[111] The following month, according to one New York merchant, it was "universally said & believed" that "a cursed scheme of depression" in bank shares had been "planned & executed" under the leadership of "our friend Brockholst."[112] (That early American stockjobber was Brockholst Livingston, who would later become one of the more obscure Justices ever to serve on the United States Supreme Court.[113]) American speculators were even able to invent a method of making money with no parallel in England. Because there were securities markets in each of the major commercial cities, speculators discovered that there could be profits in arbitraging between prices in multiple cities – that is, taking advantage of price differences between cities by simultaneously buying a stock in one city and selling it in another. In early 1792, for example, Standish Forde in Philadelphia wrote to Peter Anspach in New York to discuss entering "into a joint sale & purchase between here and New York."[114] By the winter of 1791–92, three express stagecoaches were running daily between New York and Philadelphia to convey stock price information between the two cities.[115] Prices in New York and Philadelphia were moving in tandem by early 1792, which suggests that this sort of arbitrage was occurring with some regularity.[116]

Prices kept rising, and public participation in the market kept growing, but observers of the market worried that the boom could not last. "It has risen like a rocket," one newspaper warned, and "like a rocket it will burst with a crack – then down drops the rocket-stick. What goes up must come down – so take care of your pate brother Jonathan."[117] Another urged readers to get out before it was too late:

> For soon or late, so truth advises,
> Things must assume their proper sizes –
> And sure as death all mortals trips
> Thousands will rue the name of SCRIPS.[118]

Others saw in the boom of 1791 an ominous precedent – "I mean that scheme remembered in England for two generations past, and known by

---

[111] [New York] Daily Advertiser, Aug. 8, 1791, 3.
[112] Robert Troup to Hamilton, Sept. 12, 1791, Syrett et al., eds., Papers of Alexander Hamilton, XXVI, 622.
[113] David P. Currie, "The Most Insignificant Justice: A Preliminary Inquiry," University of Chicago Law Review 50 (1983): 470.
[114] Forde to Anspach, Feb. 25, 1792, Anspach papers, NYHS.
[115] Corner, ed., Autobiography of Benjamin Rush, 217.   [116] Davis, Essays, I, 286.
[117] [New York] Daily Advertiser, Aug. 15, 1791, 2.
[118] [New Haven] Connecticut Journal, Aug. 17, 1791, 2.

the name of the South-Sea Bubble" – and foretold a similar result.[119] John Adams predicted that these "mad speculations . . . will probably be cured by a few bankruptcies which may daily be expected, I had almost said, desired."[120]

Prices began falling in early March 1792, and then dropped dramatically when William Duer, still the nation's leading speculator, proved unable to pay his promissory notes.[121] Duer's failure set off a chain reaction of bankruptcies among his creditors, who included not just other New York speculators but "shopkeepers, Widows, orphans – Butchers, Carmen, Gardners, market women, & even the noted Bawd Mrs Macarty – many of them if they are unpaid are ruined."[122] Duer and some of the other leading New York speculators wound up in debtors' prison. All over the country, the value of securities plummeted. "The crash has been tremendous," reported Jefferson from Philadelphia.

The dead loss at New York has been equal to the value of all the buildings of the city, say between 4. and 5. millions of dollars. Boston has lost about a million. This place something less. Paper of the U.S. is scarcely at par. Bank stock is at 25. per cent. It was once upwards of 300 per cent.[123]

As stock prices declined, investors found themselves with assets insufficient to meet obligations incurred in better times. "Bankruptcies continue to encrease in New York and Philadelphia," Benjamin Rush noted in his diary. "A gentleman just arrived from New York says he scarcely entered a house in which he did not find the woman in tears and the husband wringing his hands."[124] A Connecticut newspaper satirically noted the contrast between February, when it seemed like shares in anything were worth buying, and April, when investors were stuck with what they had bought. Before the crash, a

farmer on Long-Island proposed to dig a ditch across his land of 100 rods in length and 4 feet in width, this was immediately noticed in our City, a speculator rode, post-haste, to the farmer, purchased up the right of digging the ditch, and the next day *Ditch Scrips* were struck off, at Auction, for fifty dollars each . . . But alas! the scene is totally changed! All now is dullness and despondency . . .

---

[119] *[New York] Daily Advertiser*, Aug. 9, 1791, 3.
[120] Adams to Oliver Wolcott, Sr., Jan. 30, 1792, quoted in Davis, *Essays*, I, 288.
[121] David L. Sterling, "William Duer, John Pintard, and the Panic of 1792," in Joseph R. Frese and Jacob Judd, eds., *Business Enterprise in Early New York* (Tarrytown: Sleepy Hollow Press, 1979), 107–13.
[122] Seth Johnson to Andrew Craigie, March 25, 1792, quoted in Davis, *Essays*, I, 296.
[123] Jefferson to William Short, April 24, 1792, Boyd *et al.*, eds., *Papers of Thomas Jefferson*, XXIII: 458–59.
[124] Corner, ed., *Autobiography of Benjamin Rush*, 218.

countenances of all classes of men, have fallen surprisingly and the amazing *length* of faces is truly astonishing.[125]

As had been the case in England in 1720, the market crash was felt even by non-participants, as a sudden contraction in the availability of money and credit, which caused real estate prices to drop and commerce to slow.[126] "All business is at an end," reported one newspaper, "and there is a total suspense of confidence in trade."[127] The speculator Seth Johnson concluded: "In short, everything is afloat & confidence destroyed – This Town has rec[eive]d a shock which it will not get over in many years."[128]

Only sixteen years had elapsed since American governments had begun issuing debt securities on a significant scale. Within that time, Americans had witnessed wartime speculation that seemed to hinder the war effort; they had watched as depreciated securities gravitated from their original holders to a small circle of northern speculators who made fantastic profits from them; they had seen members of Congress and at least one Treasury official purchasing government debt and then implementing measures that increased that debt's value; and in less than two years of organized trading they had seen wild fluctuations in securities prices, including a crash that bankrupted many small investors. These experiences would influence attitudes toward the securities market and the resulting regulation of the market for some time to come.

III

American attitudes toward securities trading in the early 1790s drew upon a century of inherited English thought, and thus resembled eighteenth-century English attitudes in their broadest outlines. The characteristic lines of criticism all reappeared, save one: Americans were not inclined to view trading as a threat to the structure of society, most likely because the United States lacked the hereditary class divisions present in England. There were rich and poor Americans, but the prospect of a person of modest means becoming suddenly wealthy was far less troubling to the wealthy in the United States than it had been to the wealthy in England. The remaining faults found with securities trading in the aftermath of the South Sea Bubble – the concern with deceit and predation, the view that trading was non-productive, and the fear of the

---

[125] *Norwich Weekly Register*, April 3, 1792, 1–2.
[126] On real estate prices, see Corner, ed., *Autobiography of Benjamin Rush*, 219.
[127] *Boston Gazette*, April 23, 1792, 3.
[128] Johnson to Andrew Craigie, March 25, 1792, quoted in Davis, *Essays*, I, 297.

political consequences of a transferable public debt – all crossed the Atlantic and emerged in recognizable form in the United States in 1791 and 1792.

Local experiences, however, altered the tone of the arguments and their relative prominence. After the events of the 1780s and early 1790s, Americans had seen a great deal of evidence of the political corruption that could be associated with stockjobbing, and this argument, in a variety of forms, became more urgent and probably more widespread than it had ever been in England. Equally urgent and nearly as frequent was the argument based on productivity, because of the widely perceived need during the period for the new nation to develop its potential productive capacities. The critique of the deceit and predatory behavior found in securities trading, on the other hand, was more qualified and muted in the United States than it had been in England. Overlapping all of these arguments, meanwhile, was an explicit recollection of the English experience, in the form of frequent comparisons between the events of 1791–92 and the South Sea Bubble, and frequent exhortations to draw the appropriate lessons.

Deceit

"[T]his kind of traffic," as one correspondent described securities trading, "has been attended in every country, where it has received encouragement, with more numerous instances of fraud and deceit than any other which could possibly be mentioned."[129] American critics argued that stockjobbers were abnormally deceitful, but such critics were generally careful to qualify the argument by drawing a distinction between honest and dishonest traders. "While this business is conducted with truth, sincerity and fairness," conceded James Sullivan, "it may be considered as reputable and honorable." It was only when "in this, as in any other business, chicane, cunning, deceit and fraud, are adopted as the ordinary means of making a good bargain," that stockjobbers could properly be deemed "contemptible and dangerous in society." In a book largely devoted to detailing the "evils resulting from . . . speculations in the public securities," Sullivan took pains to emphasize that things were not as bad as they could be. Americans were fortunate that "[i]n our own country, and at the present day, stockjobbing has not been carried to such a height as it has been in England," where jobbers were more likely to "avail themselves of every art and accident to rob the unwary and necessitous part of the community."[130] Hamilton likewise insisted

---

129 *[Philadelphia] General Advertiser*, March 27, 1792, 2.
130 Sullivan, *Path to Riches*, 18–19, 75.

upon drawing "a line of separation between honest Men & knaves; between respectable stockholders and dealers in the funds, and mere unprincipled Gamblers."[131] In the Congressional debates on the funding bill, Elbridge Gerry maintained that the "transfer of property in the funds, at market price, differs widely from the gambling of stock-jobbers, a pernicious species of traffic."[132]

Earlier in the century in England, critics had been quick to condemn the entire market, but in the United States they were more likely to be careful to choose specific targets. The difference was a product of local circumstance. In England, securities trading in its first three decades had been the province of a small set of professionals and wealthy investors. It was not until the South Sea Bubble, well after the market had come into existence, that large numbers of unexceptional people began buying and selling stock. In the United States, by contrast, stockholders were drawn from a large segment of the population right from the beginning. A great many people had been brought involuntarily into securities trading when they had received debt securities as payment during the war. Many others had entered the market as an act of patriotism, by lending money to wartime governments. Still others, from all walks of propertied life, had been attracted more recently by the rise in shares of the new national debt and the new national bank. These people, who formed the overwhelming majority of buyers and sellers, could hardly be condemned as deceitful. In order to use the old English argument against securities trading, Americans had to qualify it to suit local conditions. In the United States, unlike in England, the argument was usually not that there was something inherent in the market that *produced* deceit; it was only that a handful of dishonest people had gone into the securities business. The same could happen in any trade. The presence of deceit might be a reason to watch the market closely, and to regulate shady practices, but it would not be a reason to abolish it entirely.

Stockjobbers were also, as in England, accused of preying on innocent investors. Some of this criticism could be as vituperative as it had been in England. In the view of one anonymous New York critic, speculators were:

> A set of sharks, that flouncing in the flood,
> Suppose all kind of fish their proper food:
> A set of hawks, that flying in the air,
> Of harmless birds make up their bill of fare:

[131] Hamilton to Philip Livingston, April 2, 1792, Syrett *et al.*, eds., *Papers of Alexander Hamilton*, XI, 218–19.
[132] *Annals of Congress*, II:1329 (Feb. 18, 1790).

> A set of wolves, that prowling 'bout for prey,
> All animals devour that cross their way.[133]

Stockjobbers preyed on the public by manipulating stock prices. Although price fluctuations were "injurious to the people in general," a correspondent to the *Gazette of the United States* charged, "[s]peculators will aim to keep up a fluctuation, as their trade depends on *ups* and *downs*."[134] The New York lawyer Robert Troup admitted as much. "The truth," he informed the Secretary of the Treasury, "is that the fluctuations are principally owing to the arts & contrivances of mere jobbers."[135] In the summer of 1792, Royal Hunt, a colleague of Duer's in Boston, reported to Duer that "I every day am shewn letters from New York & Philadelphia which declare that a combination is formed to raise that stock to 3 0/. Though the success of the project is doubted it still creates a fear to sell on time."[136] To push prices in the desired direction, according to the pseudonymous "Discrimination" (a name chosen to reflect support for discriminating between original and secondary holders of the debt), speculators spread "rumours and fictitious stories, in order to induce people either to sell out in a hurry, and consequently cheap, if they are to deliver stock, or to become unwilling to sell it, and consequently to make it dearer, if they are to receive stock."[137]

Contemporaries almost certainly realized that they were drawing upon a line of argument common in England for nearly a century. A year after Congress passed the funding bill, and near the peak of early demand for Bank scrip, the Philadelphia *Freeman's Journal* ran an item in the "Foreign Advices" section of the paper, ostensibly about the English stock market, but clearly intended as an example for the United States. "The public debt has opened the inquitious traffic of stock-jobbing," the story began. "The trade of the *Alley* consists in conspiring to pick the pocket of every body not in the secret. Those who are, can make stocks rise and fall at pleasure, and pocket the difference."[138] The English public debt, and the institutions that had sprung up to transfer shares in it from one person to another, were by then almost one hundred years old. They were hardly news in 1791. The tone of the criticism, if the item had actually been published in an English newspaper, makes the text sound like it was written in the last decade of the

---

[133] *The Glass*, 3.   [134] *Gazette of the United States*, Sept. 29, 1791, 1.

[135] Robert Troup to Hamilton, Sept. 12, 1791, Syrett *et al.*, eds., *Papers of Alexander Hamilton*, XXVI, 622.

[136] Hunt to Duer, July 4, 1792, Duer papers, Reel 2, NYHS.

[137] *New-York Journal*, Aug. 20, 1791, 2.

[138] *[Philadelphia] Freeman's Journal*, July 27, 1791, 3.

seventeenth century or the first decade of the eighteenth rather than the last decade of the eighteenth. The editor of the *Freeman's Journal* was thus most likely either running a very old English story or inventing a story along the lines of a very old English story; either way, he appears to have been consciously following an English rhetorical tradition.

That tradition – the metaphor of speculators as predatory animals – could be used to give meaning to recent events in the United States. The 1791 flurry of trading in the new national debt and shares of the new national bank, for instance, could be recast as a story about crows and a horse:

> From north to south, each *speculating blade*
> Had seen th' advantage of the *new-born trade*,
> And eager his dear fortune to promote,
> In time his cash is produc'd upon the spot,
> As when a horse is kill'd with age or bots,
> The crows soon *speculate* upon his guts:
> No sooner does the perfume scent the air,
> Than on the wind they to the feast repair,
> From ev'ry quarter muster all their force,
> And in an instant gourmandize the horse.[139]

To a readership more likely to be familiar with dead horses than with government debt, the predation argument served as an off-the-rack translation from a new phenomenon to an old one.

Non-productivity

The idea that securities trading added nothing to the national wealth, and in fact diverted capital from activities that *did* add to the national wealth, was also taken from England and adapted to American conditions. Across the political spectrum, people agreed that the new nation had a potential for production of all sorts that far exceeded its actual production, and that it was important to increase domestic output in order to end American dependence on European imports.[140] The argument that securities trading was not productive intersected with this more general concern, and thus took on a new urgency in the United States. Because securities trading was causing the nation to waste its first opportunity to attain economic self-sufficiency and a higher standard of living, a wrong turn was being made that would have irreversible long-term effects.

---

[139] *The Glass*, 11.
[140] Joyce Appleby, *Liberalism and Republicanism in the Historical Imagination* (Cambridge, MA: Harvard University Press, 1992), 272–73, 312–14.

In the early 1790s, many Americans argued that the new market was diverting capital from productive activities. "It remains to be seen," asked Jefferson when Bank scrip went on sale, "whether in a country whose capital is too small to carry on it's own commerce, to establish manufactures, erect buildings &c. such sums should have been withdrawn from these useful pursuits to be employed in gambling?"[141] Jefferson predicted that the "scrip-pomany" would prevent what would otherwise be a steady course of economic expansion. "Ships are lying idle in the wharfs, buildings are stopped, capitals withdrawn from commerce, manufactures, arts and agriculture, to be employed in gambling, and the tide of public prosperity almost unparraleled in any country, is arrested in it's course, and suppressed by the rage of getting rich in a day."[142] Speculation in public securities, Jefferson concluded, "will check our commerce, arts, manufactures and agriculture, unless stopped."[143] But he despaired of ever convincing investors to redirect their capital. In January 1792, after the Bank of the United States declared its second dividend in six months, Jefferson concluded that "[a]griculture, commerce, and every thing *useful* must be neglected, when the *useless* employment of money is so much more lucrative."[144]

Peter and Elisha Colt, trying to produce clothing in Hartford, found it difficult to attract investment; they blamed "the rage for Speculation in the funds of the United States," which caused "part of the Money of the Country" to be withdrawn from investment in productive enterprise.[145] When "Citizens shall no longer be embarked in paper Speculations," Peter Colt predicted, they would redirect their capital "to the promoting & extending our manufactures & then those which languish and dwindle for want of being supported with proper Capitals may be expected to prosper & this Country freed from a disgracefull dependence on Europe for their ordinary Cloathing."[146] A New Yorker agreed that the "arts and sciences are entirely neglected" in favor of speculation:

[141] Jefferson to Edmund Pendleton, July 24, 1791, Boyd *et al.*, eds., *Papers of Thomas Jefferson*, XX, 670.
[142] Jefferson to Edward Rutledge, Aug. 25, 1791, Boyd *et al.*, eds., *Papers of Thomas Jefferson*, XXV, 74.
[143] Jefferson to William Carmichael, Aug. 24, 1791, Boyd *et al.*, eds., *Papers of Thomas Jefferson*, XXV, 64. See also Jefferson to David Humphreys, Aug. 23, 1791, ibid., 62; Jefferson to Gouverneur Morris, Aug. 30, 1791, ibid., 105.
[144] Jefferson to J.P.P. Derieux, Jan. 6, 1792, Boyd *et al.*, eds., *Papers of Thomas Jefferson*, XXVIII, 27. See also Jefferson to David Humphreys, April 9, 1792, ibid., 387.
[145] Elisha Colt to John Chester, Aug. 20, 1791, Syrett *et al.*, eds., *Papers of Alexander Hamilton*, IX, 327.
[146] Peter Colt to John Chester, July 21, 1791, Syrett *et al.*, eds., *Papers of Alexander Hamilton*, IX, 323–24.

The humble arts are fairly now contemn'd,
And honest Commerce in derision's nam'd;
'Tis found a far more profitable job
To pilfer private men – the public rob.[147]

"The obvious tendency of that evil spirit of speculation which has so long raged amongst us," concluded a correspondent to Philadelphia's *General Advertiser* in the summer of 1791, "is to divert the active capital of our country from its proper channel (the support of commerce and agriculture) to a most pernicious one, that of ministering to the aggrandizement of a host of adventurers."[148]

It was not just capital that was being wasted. Labor – also a scarce resource – was likewise being diverted from productive activities into speculation. In New York during the scrip frenzy of July and August 1791, according to Rufus King, "Business was going on in a most alarming manner, mechanicks deserting their shops, Shop keepers sending their goods to auction, and not a few of our merchants neglecting the regular & profitable commerce of the City."[149] In Connecticut, reported the pseudonymous "Speculator," the situation was even worse. "The merchant has quit his counting room, the lawyer his clients, the Divine his pulpit, the physician his lancet, the farmer his land, the mechanic his implements of work, the seaman his ship, and the drayman his trucks, and all meet in change alley."[150] Benjamin Rush learned of several Pennsylvania farmers "who had heard how suddenly fortunes were to be made in Philadelphia" who "left their ploughs and carts" to take up securities trading. Even "[a]n old negro woman who sold corn in the market" in Philadelphia was trying to acquire Bank scrip, by offering "Hotte corn, hotte corn, hotte corn for krip."[151] In a country that had no labor to spare, such an unproductive use of people's time was as troubling as the unproductive use of capital.

These views of securities trading rested, as they had in England, on the belief that trading added nothing to the national wealth, but merely shuffled assets from one person to another. "[N]othing scarcely can be worse," argued Pelatiah Webster, than the diversion of capital into stockjobbing, in which people "pursue chimerical ways and means of obtaining wealth by slight of hand, without any earnings at all."[152] Securities trading permitted only "[i]ntrigues that add not to the nation's store."[153] Jefferson took the crash of 1792 as confirmation of

[147] *The Glass*, 2, 4.   [148] *[Philadelphia] General Advertiser*, Aug. 12, 1791, 3.
[149] Rufus King to Hamilton, Aug. 15, 1791, Syrett *et al.*, eds., *Papers of Alexander Hamilton*, IX, 60.
[150] *Norwich Weekly Register*, March 27, 1792, 2.
[151] Corner, ed., *Autobiography of Benjamin Rush*, 205.
[152] Webster, *Seventh Essay*, 23.   [153] *The Glass*, 4.

his view that "all the capital employed in paper speculation is barren and useless, producing, like that on a gaming table, no accession to itself."[154] The owners of stock, explained John Francis Mercer of Maryland on the floor of the House of Representatives, "improve nothing, but take something from all."[155] The money invested in stock, on this view, was that much less money available for productive investment.

By the late eighteenth century, however, close observers of the English securities market had begun to question the idea that it was a zero-sum game, and the same pattern of thought was beginning to develop in the United States as well. The market was gradually starting to be understood as a producer of wealth. In good times, this could take the form of empirical observation. "[W]hat is particularly striking in this business," exclaimed a resident of Connecticut shortly before the 1792 crash,

is, that they *all* make immense fortunes. We can easily imagine that if A and B deal together and A loses £100, B may be a gainer of an hundred pounds, but how both can make fortunes by such a bargain is unaccountable. – Yet such is the fact that buyer and seller, each makes a *great bargain*.[156]

And even in bad times, the understanding of the market as a producer of wealth could take the form of theory. After the 1792 crash, Washington listed for Hamilton the complaints against the public debt he had heard in Virginia. The leading grievances concerned the market's non-productivity. Hamilton responded with a purely theoretical defense of the market, one which did not depend on market conditions at any given time, or indeed on any empirical observation at all. "It is true," he began,

that the Capital, that is the *specie*, which is employed in paper speculation, while so employed, is barren and useless, but the paper itself constitutes a *new Capital*, which being saleable and transferrable at any moment, enables the proprietor to undertake any piece of business as well as an equal sum in Coin. And as the amount of the Debt circulated is much greater than the amount of the *specie* which circulates it, the new Capital put in motion by it considerably exceeds the old one which is *suspended*. And there is more capital to carry on the productive labour of the Society.

As a result, Hamilton concluded, stockjobbing does not divert capital from industry, but actually "promotes . . . industry by furnishing a larger field of employment."[157] Hamilton's distinction between money

---

[154] Jefferson to George Washington, May 23, 1792, Boyd *et al.*, eds., *Papers of Thomas Jefferson*, XXIII, 537.

[155] *Annals of Congress*, III, 511 (March 30, 1792).

[156] *Norwich Weekly Register*, March 27, 1792, 2.

[157] Washington to Hamilton, July 29, 1792, and Hamilton to Washington, Aug. 18, 1792,

and real wealth, and his willingness to count securities as a form of capital that could take the place of money, would eventually come to be the dominant view among policymakers.

Even the critics of stockjobbing, moreover, were often dubious of the government's power to redivert capital and labor into productive channels, because the government simply could not function without borrowing money, and the profits that were sometimes made in the market were simply too great. "I cannot devise any plan of correcting this evil without risking a greater," conceded a glum Henry Lee. "Government has so connected the thing with itself that the destruction of one will convulse the other."[158] Even a sharp fall in prices would not solve the problem, in Jefferson's view. "I have rarely seen a gamester cured," he pointed out, "even by the disasters of his vocation."[159] A satirical correspondent to the Philadelphia *General Advertiser* at the height of the Bank scrip craze assured the editor that the only rational course of action was to join in.

Permit a sincere friend to give you a piece of wholesome advice. – Convert immediately your whole printing office into Bank-stock; and you will change every type, nay, your very imposing-stone into gold. Here you are toiling from morn to night, six days in the week, puzzling your brains with extracts and translations from ancient and modern authors; collecting with endless trouble philosophical, political, physical facts and reasonings; in short, murdering the flower of your youth – when other gentlemen, of inferior industry, make their hundreds and thousands by a pleasing morning walk. Up then! To-morrow advertise the whole for a Bank-Script! Lose not a moment, for the stock is in full gallop, and will soon be 1000 per cent. I know that this advice is contrary to certain maxims deeply impressed on your mind by the venerable Doctor Franklin! But, with all respect for the memory of that great Philosopher, I think, with a majority of the Americans, that his maxims of prudence, economy, honesty, &c. are too abstract for actual practice, and too narrow for the policy of this Rising Empire.

To grow rich by assiduity and frugality alone, is beneath even chimney-sweeps. To secure national wealth only by agriculture, manufactures, and a natural exchange of our superfluity for the products of other countries, is well enough for a plodding, slavish people; but, Sir, we Freemen of Columbia, have all a right to be great and rich; to be worth at least 10,000 pounds every soul of us! This land of liberty is by heaven destined to amass all the wealth of the old

---

Syrett *et al.*, eds., *Papers of Alexander Hamilton*, XII, 131, 246–47. Where a public debt was insufficiently funded and thus of too uncertain a value to serve as a substitute for money, in Hamilton's view, stockjobbing in such a debt *would* reduce the level of productive investment. "Report on Public Credit," *Annals of Congress*, II, 2044.

[158] Lee to Madison, Aug. 24, 1791, Hutchinson *et al.*, eds., *Papers of James Madison*, XIV, 74.

[159] Jefferson to Gouverneur Morris, Aug. 30, 1791, Boyd *et al.*, eds., *Papers of Thomas Jefferson*, XXII, 105.

and new world. Our nearly Almighty Congress can transform every rag of paper
into rubies. A simpleton will say, how shall the Bank pay this mighty per cent?
By the great mystery of FINANCE, you blockhead![160]

One could criticize the buying and selling of securities as adding nothing
to the national wealth, but that provided no legislative program unless
one was willing to prohibit the government from borrowing money, or
unless one could figure out how to retain the benefits of government
borrowing while suppressing the more capital-intensive and time-inten-
sive practices of the stockjobbers. There was never a majority in favor of
preventing the government from borrowing; as time went on, the
advocates of terminating the public debt dwindled in number. As in
England, regulatory attention would largely be given to the second
alternative, that of keeping the debt but stopping the speculation in it.

Political corruption

The argument against securities trading most frequently made in the
United States in the early 1790s involved the political corruption often
understood to flow from the existence of a public debt. This argument
took a few forms, ranging from the strictly empirical to the strictly
theoretical.

On the empirical end, many critics observed that members of
Congress and state legislatures were often themselves owners of public
securities, and tended to vote for policies that advanced their private
interests. As early as 1785, Pelatiah Webster reported that many
Pennsylvanians believed "that some members of our General Assembly
are deeply interested in stockjobbing and speculations in certificates,
and are possessed of or concerned in public securities to a large
amount." These members were all too eager "to vote the money of their
constituents into their own pockets" by funding the state debt in full.
Webster analogized the Assembly's consideration of public finance
measures to "a judge or juryman [who] should sit in judgment in a
cause, in the event of which he is personally interested."[161] William
Maclay had the same complaint about the "dirty work" of members of
Congress who owned public securities in 1790 and, not coincidentally,
favored the adoption of Hamilton's funding program.[162] "[T]he most
arch and finished *speculators* in our country," screamed a Connecticut
newspaper, were "[t]hose who *speculate* themselves into Congress – then
speculate upon the public finances till they establish a funding system

---

[160] *[Philadelphia] General Advertiser*, Aug. 12, 1791, 2.
[161] Webster, *Seventh Essay*, 35–36.
[162] *Documentary History of the First Federal Congress*, IX: 324.

and bank . . . and thus *speculate* upon the property and welfare of their country."[163]

Popular resentment of government officials who so transparently conflated the public good with their private interests ran deep. In 1792, a grand jury in South Carolina presented as a grievance the fact that the state assembly had not suspended payment to holders of the state debt, a measure that might "have prevented a species of speculation (in which we are sorry to say, some of the members themselves were engaged)."[164] A correspondent to the *National Gazette* charged "that members of the general government have carried on *jobbs* and *speculations* in their own measures, even *whilst those measures were depending*. If these charges be true," the *Gazette* asked, "can anything be more disgraceful to the councils of a free country, or more loudly call for the indignation of a virtuous people?"[165] It was "speculation" that "begat the public debt," recalled the *Norwich Packet*.[166] The year 1792 was one in which "Members of C-ng—s" were "detected and exposed in their speculations and combinations."[167] The sight of such brazen profiteering from public office convinced many that government corruption and securities trading went hand in hand. "Our new Government," George Mason grumbled, "is a Government of Stock-jobbing and Favour[i]tism." Such was "the Tendency, Spirit, and necessary Operation of the whole funding System."[168] In Virginia, Washington reported, public debt securities were widely believed to have "furnished effectual means of corrupting such a portion of the legislature, as turns the balance between the honest Voters which ever way it is directed."[169]

In the face of so much evidence of government corruption, few were willing to defend in print the public officials who gained by owning public securities. "As far as I know," Hamilton argued, defining his terms quite narrowly, "there is not a single member of the Legislature who can properly be called a Stock-jobber or a paper Dealer." He must have realized that this point was not enough to defend members of Congress who, although not full-time jobbers, had nevertheless purchased the very securities they would vote to fund, because he continued

---

[163] *Norwich Weekly Register*, March 27, 1792, 2.
[164] *Boston Gazette*, May 21, 1792, 3.
[165] *[Philadelphia] National Gazette*, June 4, 1792, 3.
[166] *Norwich Packet*, July 5, 1792, 3.   [167] *National Gazette*, May 31, 1792, 3.
[168] Mason to James Monroe, Feb. 9, 1792, Robert A. Rutland, ed., *The Papers of George Mason 1725–1792* (Chapel Hill: University of North Carolina Press, 1970), III, 1256–57.
[169] Washington to Hamilton, July 29, 1792, Syrett *et al.*, eds., *Papers of Alexander Hamilton*, XII, 31.

by turning the tables on the accusers. "It is a strange perversion of ideas," he argued, "and as novel as it is extraordinary, that men should be deemed corrupt & criminal for becoming proprietors in the funds of their country."[170] Hamilton's program would have been far less likely to have been implemented had it not been for the votes of members of Congress who themselves owned securities, so it is perhaps not surprising that Hamilton would take a benign view of the practice. But to the government's critics, the mixture of public policy and private gain that seemed inherent in securities trading was a powerful argument against it.

Contemporaries also noted a closely related type of political corruption. Even when legislators did not themselves own public securities, it was often argued, they were unusually susceptible to being influenced by speculators who did, because speculators had so much to gain or lose from swings in public policy that they would be willing to offer great inducements to the legislators. "The Whole Town" of New York was busy at stockjobbing in early 1790, complained William Maclay, "& of Course all engaged in influencing the Measures of Congress."[171] Speculators in government securities formed such a distinct political interest, in Jefferson's view, that "[t]he only corrective of what is amiss in our present government will be the augmentation of the numbers in the lower house, so as to get a more agricultural representation, which may put that interest above that of the stock-jobbers."[172] Madison agreed. "The stockjobbers," he predicted, "will become the pretorian band of the Government – at once its tool & tyrant; bribed by its largesses, & overawing it, by clamours and combinations."[173] Opposition to the political influence thought to be wielded by speculators was so widely held that it formed a large part of the common ground that gave rise to the Jeffersonian Republican party.[174]

From these two empirical observations of political corruption came two common theoretical assertions of the dire political consequences of securities trading. The first was specific, and drew upon the long English tradition of associating a public debt with a large and bellicose government bureaucracy. "War produces Taxes," one Virginian explained. "The more Revenue the more Power, the Greater the field of Speculation, Funding Jobs, &c. Those who favor such

---

[170] Hamilton to Washington, Aug. 18, 1792, Syrett et al., eds., *Papers of Alexander Hamilton*, XII, 249.

[171] De Pauw et al., eds., *Documentary History of the First Federal Congress*, IX, 324.

[172] Jefferson to Mason, Feb. 4, 1791, Rutland, ed., *Papers of George Mason*, III, 1224.

[173] Madison to Jefferson, Aug. 8, 1791, Hutchinson et al., eds., *Papers of James Madison*, XIV, 69.

[174] Elkins and McKitrick, *Age of Federalism*, 265–66.

Schemes are Enemies to Peace & Oeconomy but Such men are unfortunately in power among us."[175] In the early 1790s, to people already concerned about the danger posed by a powerful central government, the tendency of stockjobbing to give participants a financial interest in increasing the size of the government was one more reason to worry.

The other theoretical assertion was more general, and probably more frequently made. Because of the various sorts of political corruption that inevitably followed speculation in securities, it was argued, speculation would "in a political sense, sap the foundation of republicanism, and pave the way for aristocracy and despotism."[176] A "thirst for rank and distinction," claimed another critic, "may justly be termed *the child of speculation*." Because Americans had been so eager to speculate, they had proven themselves unworthy of being called republicans in practice, but were "only *republicans in name*."[177] The prevalence of speculation within the government, remarked another, was "a circumstance truly mortifying to its real steady republican friends."[178]

Securities trading was anti-republican because of its effect on the distribution of wealth. A securities market "prevents a general diffusion of wealth by drawing it to a centre," argued John Francis Mercer, "and saps the foundation of a Republican Government."[179] The result would be "[p]overty in the country – luxury in the capitals," unless the government could be "purged of stock-jobbing, monarchy-jobbing, bank-jobbing, and aristocracy-jobbing."[180] If an aristocracy was a political system in which a leisured minority lived on the labor of a majority, what term could better describe a scheme in which productive Americans were taxed to send interest payments to a wealthy urban elite? James Sullivan recognized that the public debt "answers some of the purposes of real money in commerce," but that benefit could not justify a system in which "those who are in possession of the public securities, derive great pecuniary advantage from the toil and labors of them, who have none."[181] Soon after the crash of 1792, state legislative candidates in Boston were proclaiming that they had "integrity and resolution enough to oppose every scheme of Speculation, or other Contrivance to undermine the Liberties of our Citizens." For a man to be a legislator, a voter urged, "it is by no means necessary that he should

[175] George Lee Turberville to Madison, Nov. 19, 1792, Hutchinson *et al.*, eds., *Papers of James Madison*, XIV, 412.
[176] *The Glass*, 2.   [177] *National Gazette*, Feb. 27, 1792, 3.
[178] *National Gazette*, July 4, 1792, 3.
[179] *Annals of Congress*, III, 510 (March 30, 1792).
[180] *National Gazette*, May 31, 1792, 3.   [181] Sullivan, *Path to Riches*, 16.

own a single *Scrip*, whether Bank, Tontine or Bridge – Nor need he be interested in the Funds, either directly or indirectly; or possess any of the public Paper."[182]

Opinions of the new securities market, dominated by government debt and shares in the new national bank, were thus closely connected with opinions as to the structure and the performance of the new national government. The opponents of Hamilton's program of public finance took the old English republican arguments against securities trading, familiar from countless reprints of Trenchard and Gordon, and adapted them for an American audience. The political critique of stock-jobbing acquired a new vigor in the United States, where it resonated with an easily seen record of speculation on the part of government officials, with a republicanism much more widespread than had been the case in England, and with the nascent division among national political parties, one of which defined itself in large part by its opposition to stockjobbing. The securities market would, for a long time to come, continue to be identified with political corruption, with luxury, with Federalism, and with Hamilton.

The South Sea Bubble

Within and alongside all of these arguments lurked the South Sea Bubble. Whether prices were high or low, whether one favored or opposed any particular measure, the Bubble was both a textbook full of lessons and a rhetorical figure capable of underlining nearly any point. For determined opponents of the public debt, the Bubble demonstrated that disaster was an inevitable consequence of securities trading, regardless of the details of any particular system. "[I]n schemes of that vast magnitude and national interest," Pelatiah Webster argued while Congress debated Hamilton's funding proposal,

faults in the management might be found, which are always made to rest on the *prime movers and directors* of them, yet the *most capital and destructive mischiefs sprung from the nature of the schemes themselves*, and would necessarily happen (tho', perhaps, not in every possible excess and aggravation) if the *same plans were to be set on foot a thousand times over.*[183]

The 1792 crash was not the fault of any single person or group of

---

[182] *Boston Gazette*, May 7, 1792, 2. The tontine, an early form of speculation, will be discussed in chapter 8.

[183] Pelatiah Webster, "A Plea for the Poor Soldiers" (1790), in *Political Essays on the Nature and Operation of Money, Public Finances, and Other Subjects* (Philadelphia: J. Crukshank, 1791), 335.

people; it was inherently a "mischief consequent on the prevalence of a spirit of stockjobbing . . . Witness the South Sea Bubble."[184]

For those opposed not to the existence of the debt but only to the fact that legislators were speculating in it, the Bubble proved the danger of mixing public and private interests. "[A]ll the Abomin[a]tions of the South Sea Bubble," Maclay noted, with reference to the stock purchases of members of Congress in the first half of 1790, "are Outdone in this Vile Business."[185] To republicans unhappy with the way wealth was being distributed in the new nation, the Bubble taught the dangers of luxury. "There were men then who made great estates from the public calamity," recalled James Sullivan, "and by the splendor of their fortunes intoxicated the people in England and in the Netherlands. Hence arose the South Sea bubble."[186] For investors pleased with prices on the rise but nervous about the future, the Bubble meant that no good thing would last forever. In Philadelphia at the height of the 1791 bank scrip boom, "[t]he conversation here was – 'Bank Script is getting so high as to become a bubble' in one breath – in another, 'tis a South Sea dream.'"[187] To critics of the rising market, the Bubble showed that the apparent wealth being generated was illusory and would soon disappear,

> down you'll fall, and all your golden dreams,
> Like *South-Sea bubbles, Mississippi schemes,*
> And find at last, to your own cost and pain,
> *Its strength existed only in your brain!*[188]

Prices were rising due only to "the immortal art of *Law* and *South-Sea Sages.*"[189] The "Speculator" concluded: "The Mississippi and south sea schemes will shortly be realized among us."[190] After the 1792 crash, the Bubble was a way of understanding what had occurred. "No man of reflection who had ever attended to the South sea bubble," lectured Jefferson, "and who applied the lessons of the past to the present time, could fail to foresee the issue."[191] Benjamin Rush explained the price fluctuations of 1792 as similar to "the South Sea stocks in 1720."[192]

Everyone remembered the Bubble, but everyone remembered it

[184] *[Philadelphia] General Advertiser*, March 27, 1792, 2.
[185] De Pauw *et al.*, eds., *Documentary History of the First Federal Congress*, IX, 324.
[186] Sullivan, *Path to Riches*, 28.
[187] Hamilton to William Duer, Aug. 17, 1791, Syrett *et al.*, eds., *Papers of Alexander Hamilton*, IX, 74.
[188] *The Glass*, 12.   [189] *[Philadelphia] General Advertiser*, Aug. 12, 1791, 2.
[190] *Norwich Weekly Register*, April 3, 1792, 1.
[191] Jefferson to Henry Remsen, April 14, 1792, Boyd *et al.*, eds., *Papers of Thomas Jefferson*, XXIII, 425–26.
[192] Corner, ed., *Autobiography of Benjamin Rush*, 219.

differently. No matter where one stood on securities trading, the Bubble reinforced what one already believed.

By the spring of 1792, Americans had experienced their own version of the events that took place in England in the three decades up to 1720. They had seen the development of a securities market dominated by government debt and the shares of a corporation closely affiliated with the government (the Bank of the United States). They had participated in a cycle in which a burst of popular interest in trading caused prices to rise, which in turn drew even more popular interest, which drove prices even higher. And they had lived through their first crash, which bankrupted some prominent citizens and for a time hurt almost everyone as it sucked money and credit out of the economy. Americans had already inherited the bifurcated tradition of English thought about securities trading, and the replication of the early English experience caused much of that thought to be reproduced in the United States in the early 1790s. But it was not reproduced exactly; economic and political concerns unique to the United States caused Americans to modify English thought in many respects to suit local conditions. For the same reasons, the American regulatory response to the crash would be similar in some respects, but not all, to the English law created in the years after the South Sea Bubble.

The first decade of organized securities trading in the United States saw governments experiment with three types of regulation. Early on, the federal government attempted to ban what would today be called insider trading in the public debt, and to tax transfers of securities. These efforts will be discussed in section I. The two states with the leading securities markets, New York and Pennsylvania, both responded to the crash of 1792 with legislative attempts to prohibit certain kinds of speculative trading. Section II will describe these responses, and will then trace their effects on the market and in the courts over the first half of the nineteenth century. Securities trading simultaneously raised all sorts of basic legal questions that had little to do with the crash, questions concerning how new types of routine transactions would be handled and how the new institution would fit into older legal categories. The answers provided by state legislatures and courts in the 1790s, and the effects those early choices had on the law in the first half of the nineteenth century, will be discussed in section III. Some of the discussion of later developments in sections II and III necessarily runs a bit ahead of the chapter's chronological focus, and thus requires mentioning institutional developments (such as the formation of the New York Stock & Exchange Board) that will not be fully described until later chapters.

I

The widely perceived connection between securities trading and political corruption led to immediate congressional action. In June 1789, when the First Congress was considering a bill to establish a Treasury Department, Representative Aedanus Burke of South Carolina proposed an amendment to prevent Treasury officials "from being directly or indirectly concerned in commerce, or in speculating in the public funds under a high penalty, and being deemed guilty of a high crime or misdemeanor."[1] Burke's amendment was most likely intended to permit Congress to oust Treasury officials from their posts upon a finding that they had been speculating, because the amendment's language closely tracked the new Constitution's standard for the removal by Congress of "civil Officers of the United States," which required conviction of "high Crimes and Misdemeanors."[2] The ban on speculating was added to the bill, and eventually became the eighth and final section of the act establishing the Treasury Department, which became law in September. The result incorporated the first prohibition in England or the United States of what would much later (and normally with reference to corporate stock rather than the public debt) come to be called insider trading.

The ban extended to any "person appointed to any office instituted by this act," a group of only six people, including the Secretary of the Treasury, an Assistant Secretary, a Comptroller, an Auditor, a Treasurer, and a Register. These officers were not allowed to

directly or indirectly be concerned or interested in carrying on the business of trade or commerce, or be owner in whole or in part of any sea-vessel, or purchase by himself, or another in trust for him, any public lands or public property, or be concerned in the purchase or disposal of any public securities of any State, or of the United States, or take or apply to his own use, any emolument or gain for negotiating or transacting any business in the said department, other than what shall be allowed by law.[3]

The statute attempted to prohibit the entire range of corruption likely to be available to Treasury Department insiders.[4] Someone with advance knowledge of Treasury policy would likely have an edge in conducting certain types of commerce, especially shipping, which interacted with the Treasury at numerous points, such as the collection of tariffs. For the same reason, a Treasury official involved in shipping or other commerce might tend toward lax or uneven enforcement of the revenue laws. Congress thus tried to prevent insiders from being involved in *any* business, and included the arguably redundant clause about sea-vessels to make doubly sure that officials stayed out of shipping. The Treasury was charged with, among other things, managing and selling the public lands, which could have provided insiders with an easy fortune in land speculation. Congress thus tried to keep Treasury officials out of this line as well. Officials who knew in advance what actions the Treasury would take with respect to the public debt could profit from buying and

---

[1] De Pauw *et al.*, eds., *Documentary History*, XI, 1080.   [2] U.S. Const. art. II, § 4.
[3] An Act to establish the Treasury Department, §§ 1, 8, 1 Stat. 65, 67 (Sept. 2, 1789).
[4] Op. Att. Gen., March 15, 1847.

selling government securities, so Congress attempted to prohibit insider trading. Finally, speculators had so much to gain or lose from government actions that they were thought likely to offer bribes to Treasury officials; this concern accounts for the prohibition on accepting payment beyond one's salary. All these prohibitions were extended two years later to all the clerks employed in the Treasury Department,[5] and the year after that to various other federal employees, including "all officers of the United States concerned in the collection or disbursement of the revenues thereof."[6]

Officials and clerks who violated any of these provisions were to "be deemed guilty of a high misdemeanor," were to pay a $3,000 fine (only $500 in the clerks' case), and were to be removed from office and banned from holding any federal office in the future. Half of the fine could go to a person who provided the government with information leading to a conviction.[7] The amount of the fine was not inconsiderable at the time – it nearly equalled the Secretary's annual salary – but it was so low relative to the possible gains available from violating the statute that it could not have been much of a deterrent. The previous year, by comparison, William Duer, then Secretary to the Board of Treasury (a position comparable to that of Assistant Secretary of the Treasury in the new Treasury Department) had received a bribe of $8,000 from Andrew Craigie for simply assigning to Craigie a claim by the United States against a Dutch firm and removing an attachment placed by the Board on Craigie's property.[8] Greater sums could be made from speculating in government debt. The possibility of a $3,000 fine, with no other penalty except the loss of an office (the annual salary of which ranged only from $1,250 for the Register to $3,500 for the Secretary), would not have prevented an officer whose primary motives were financial from violating the statute.

Section 8 of the Treasury Act encompassed much more than securities trading, but for our purposes it stands as the first Anglo-American attempt to prevent government insiders from using their superior information to profit from trading in the public debt. No comparable prohibition existed in England. None of the colonies/states had imposed such a ban with respect to its government securities. This divergence from prior English and American practice suggests that the political critique of securities trading was stronger in the United States of the late

---

[5] An Act supplemental to the act "establishing the Treasury Department," and for a farther compensation to certain officers, § 1, 1 Stat. 215 (March 3, 1791).

[6] An Act making alterations in the Treasury and War Departments, § 12, 1 Stat. 279, 281 (May 8, 1792).

[7] 1 Stat. 67.   [8] Jones, *The King of the Alley*, 115.

1780s than it had been at any previous time, either in England or North America.

Yet a few aspects of the statute and its subsequent history also demonstrate the limits faced by the critics of insider trading in government debt. First, most of the criticism of insider trading concerned legislators, not employees of the Treasury, and yet Congress never considered imposing any similar prohibition on its own members. In light of the number of members of Congress with investments in government debt and bank stock, such a bill would almost certainly have been rejected. It was far easier to restrain the activities of future Treasury officials, none of whom had yet been appointed and thus none of whom could object, than it would have been to restrain identifiable individuals who had already invested in the debt. Second, although many of the critics objected to trading on the part of state government officials as well as federal, no state in the years before the Civil War adopted a similar statute, despite the fact that many of the states issued publicly traded debt securities as well. This inaction on the part of the states may just be an effect of the small size of state debts relative to the national debt, but it may also suggest that either (1) the intensity of opposition to insider trading in government debt waned in the years following the funding and Bank debates of 1790–91, and/or (2) the 1790–91 complaints about insider trading had more to do with the general fear of a strong central government than with any concern particular to securities trading. Third, the statute still exists today, and although it has been modified in various respects over the past two centuries, the amounts of the fines have never been changed. It is still the case that a Secretary or a Treasurer who buys or sells government debt faces a fine of only $3,000, and no other penalty except removal from office. For other Treasury employees the fine is still only $500.[9] These amounts were already small in 1789; by now, they are laughably so. The fines suggest that the statute serves, and has always served, more as a symbol of public disapproval of insider trading in government debt than as a genuine deterrent.

More ambiguously, although the statute has been on the books for over two centuries, there are no reported cases of anyone ever having been prosecuted under it. There were two possible early candidates. The first was William Duer, the very first Assistant Secretary of the Treasury, who (as described in chapter 4) almost certainly violated the statute by speculating in the national debt during his brief tenure in

---

[9] 31 U.S.C. § 329. As of 1987, the fines appear to have been raised to $5,000 by 18 U.S.C. § 3571, a statute pertaining to all federal criminal fines. The amount is still too low to be much of a deterrent.

office. Duer lived in debtors' prison, however, from the crash of 1792 until his death in 1799, which made him an unpromising target for prosecution, as he could no longer be deprived of either money or office. The second was Hamilton, who was accused in print on more than one occasion of, in the words of one accuser, having "made *thirty thousand dollars* by speculation" while he was Secretary.[10] The charges were probably not true. The closest students of the issue conclude that the most serious of the accusations grew out of an effort to blackmail Hamilton after he had an affair with another man's wife, and that Hamilton was most likely accurate when he admitted the affair but denied the speculation.[11] Neither Duer nor Hamilton, therefore, nor any of their successors, was ever charged with violating the Treasury Act. The meaning of this fact is uncertain, because two possible interpretations remain even if one rejects the likelihood that a minuscule fine has been enough to deter employees from trading. It may be that the republican critique of government corruption sufficiently permeated the pool of candidates for Treasury positions that there was little or no insider trading on the part of officials after Duer. Hamilton, for one, appears to have been quite sensitive to the political liabilities that would ensue if he were caught trading, and it may be that such an awareness, entirely apart from the statute, was enough to prevent Treasury officials from making their personal fortunes on the job. On the other hand, the opposite may be true; Treasury employees and the government officers in position to prosecute them may simply have ignored the statute.

The Treasury Act, a product of the widely voiced concern that government insiders were profiting in the securities market from their knowledge, was thus in one sense ahead of its time. No unit of American government would ban insider trading of any other sort, either in the public debt or in the shares of business enterprises, within at least the next seventy years, and probably longer. The Act embodied an aspiration toward pure public service that remained the unique burden of Treasury employees for many years. In another sense, however, if in fact the Treasury officials after Duer did not trade, the statute was behind its

---

[10] James Thomson Callender, *The History of the United States for 1796* (Philadelphia: Snowden & M'Corkle, 1797), 213. See also John Francis Mercer to Hamilton, March 26, 1793, Syrett *et al.*, eds., *Papers of Alexander Hamilton*, XIV, 250.

[11] Alexander Hamilton, "Observations on Certain Documents Contained in No. V & VI of 'The History of the United States for the Year 1796,' in Which the Charge of Speculation Against Alexander Hamilton, Late Secretary of the Treasury, is Fully Refuted" (1797), in Syrett *et al.*, eds., *Papers of Alexander Hamilton*, XXI, 238–85. For a summary of historians' attempts to figure out what really happened, see ibid., 121–44. Even if Hamilton did not trade for his own account, he may have provided associates with advance knowledge of Treasury actions. Howard M. Wachtel, "Alexander Hamilton and the Origins of Wall Street" (unpub. paper).

time. It was adding a penalty that served as no greater a deterrent than the force of public opinion alone.

After the crash, Congress considered another means of regulating the market – a tax on the transfer of government securities. The idea had been kicking about for some time, primarily as a method of raising revenue. In late 1789, when public officials were considering possible sources of revenue for the new federal government, William Bingham suggested various taxes as "less exceptionable than others," including "a Small Tax on the Transfer of the Stock of the United States." A transfer tax would fall most heavily on the stockjobbers, of course, and could be expected to slow the velocity with which securities changed hands, both of which effects doubtless contributed to Bingham's view that a tax "would be popular & productive, paid without murmur, & collected with facility."[12] The same anticipated results of a transfer tax had produced similar proposals in England for nearly a century.[13]

In February 1793, the idea reached the floor of the House of Representatives for the first time.[14] Speaking in favor of the tax, Abraham Clark "saw no difficulty in the case," because "the expense will fall on the speculators only." A few representatives shared Jonathan Dayton's view that "a host of clerks were employed in the Treasury Department on this business of transfer." The cost the government thereby incurred, as Clark saw it, "was for the advantage of speculators, of which a host was collected in a neighboring city, where, as from a centre, they extended their negotiations to all parts of the Union." (Clark was referring to New York; Congress was then in Philadelphia.) It was "no more than reasonable that they should pay the expense," argued Dayton. Shearjashub Bourne cited precedents to demonstrate that the payment of fees was customary in each of the states for probate and other matters; by long usage, the practice "was submitted to by the people . . . [A] similar mode might be adopted to the present case." The public debt had no special status, suggested John Francis Mercer, but "was liable to taxation in common with every other" form of property. Of these men, only Bourne was from a state (Massachusetts) with a significant securities market. The others were from New Jersey (Clark and Dayton) and Maryland (Mercer).

The proposal met with substantial opposition, part of which concerned the anticipated incidence of the tax. "With respect to the expenses falling exclusively on speculators," Egbert Benson argued,

---

[12] William Bingham to Hamilton, Nov. 25, 1789, Syrett *et al.*, eds., *Papers of Alexander Hamilton*, v, 549–50.

[13] *Proposal for Putting Some Stop*, 1; Defoe, *Villainy*, 23; *Considerations on a Bill*, 1.

[14] *Annals of Congress*, III, 868 (Feb. 8, 1793).

"the gentleman was mistaken." Benson cited an example to demonstrate that "persons who are not speculators will be subject to the tax." But even if the tax should fall entirely on speculators, he continued, it would still be objectionable, because he "very much doubted the legality of framing a tax that should be pointed at any class of citizens in particular." Benson, from New York, represented that class of citizens. John Laurance, also of New York, took exception to Clark's disparagement of some of his constituents. He "always considered it indicative of the badness of a cause," he explained, "when a person descends to general invectives against public bodies. He alluded to Mr. Clark's reflection on the City of New York." (Clark lamely responded that "he had not mentioned New York.")

A second argument against the transfer tax concerned the fairness of imposing a tax on securities that had already been sold to the public. When the public creditors bought the securities, argued Jonathan Sturges, "they never supposed that they would be clogged with any such charge." William Vans Murray announced that he had "discovered a strong and insuperable objection" to the tax. "As the debt was subscribed under the idea of transfers being free of expense," he noted, "to force the parties to pay fees would diminish the value of the property" they had purchased from the government. The free transferability of government securities, Murray concluded, "forms a part of the value" of the securities; "to be taxed on the thing transferred . . . would amount to something like diminishing of the debt without discharging it." The government could no more tax transfers of the debt than any other debtor could unilaterally reduce the amount of what he owed to a creditor.

Another set of opponents examined the effect of a tax on the federal government's future ability to borrow. Elbridge Gerry found the bill to entail "sundry consequences extremely injurious to the public credit." Because the proposed tax "would interfere with the stipulations of the contract" between the government and public creditors by effectively reducing the value of outstanding debt, argued Elias Boudinot, the tax would "go to injuring the public credit essentially." In the future, potential public creditors might fear that Congress would impose similar retroactive limits on their rights, "to such a degree as to interdict all transfers whatever, yea, to taxing the Debt," a fear that would be "totally subversive of public credit." In light of the views expressed so strongly on both sides, the proposed transfer tax was tabled.[15]

The proposal returned to the floor of the House the following year,

[15] Ibid., 877–80.

when it was expanded to include a tax on transfers of stock in the Bank of the United States as well as transfers of government debt. In both cases, the proposed tax was five cents on each hundred dollars transferred. Once again, the proposal drew vigorous argument on both sides, but this time both sides were better prepared; the bill's opponents were ready with long speeches about the unfairness of a tax on the transfer of already issued securities and the adverse effects a tax would have on the government's future ability to borrow, and the supporters with refutations of those speeches.

Uriah Tracy, for instance, insisted that "it was an act of injustice to tax the transference of public debts," because "a freedom of transference was part of the bargain between Government and its creditors. . . . We gave paper," he continued, but now "we come forward and say to the creditor, you shall not transfer unless you give up a part of your debt." Tracy recognized that in the political climate of the 1790s opponents of a tax were likely to be perceived as attempting to advance their personal financial interests. He was thus careful to preface his remarks with a statement of the "perfect impartiality" of his opinion, by pointing out that "he had never once seen public paper till he came to Philadelphia, and he most certainly never owned a single farthing of it since he had an existence. The clamors, therefore, with regard to a paper interest, could not be applied to him."

Richard Winn was ready with a rebuttal. "[W]ho were the creditors in the public funds[?]" he asked rhetorically. "Are they the original holders, the poor soldiers, who gave birth to this country? Or are they a set of men who have purchased the claims of these poor soldiers for a trifle, perhaps for half a crown in the pound?" Tracy's argument that a tax would be unfair to creditors might have some merit if one were speaking of the original holders of the debt, but it would hardly be unfair to tax a group of speculators who had reaped enormous profits by taking advantage of the duress of war veterans. "Surely, if this be the case," Winn concluded, "no creditor would grumble in paying the proposed tax on the transfer; and, if he should complain, was it tolerable to hear such a property held up as an unfit object for taxation?"

Opponents of the tax devoted more effort to exposing what they saw as its larger effects. Fisher Ames predicted that a tax, by lowering the market value of government securities, would raise the interest rate the government would need to pay in the future. "The progress of this measure would degrade the Public Debt into a paper rag," he argued. "When we next want to borrow, and shall go to market, the lenders will rise proportionably in their demands, and refuse a loan on the terms which they before accepted. Hence we shall lose, instead of gaining by it." Unless public securities were freely transferable, Ames continued, citizens would be unwilling to lend their money to the government. In such an event, the government would be forced "to apply to the moneyed men" directly for loans. "[T]hen will be seen and felt the miserable termination of this policy," which would thus have the unintended effect of increasing the power of a small number of wealthy speculators. Elias Boudinot and William Lyman reinforced Ames's objections. Boudinot was satisfied that the tax comported with "moral principle." But, he observed, "in imposing taxes, we must consult not only morality but expediency; and here he had numerous objections" to the tax. Boudinot was especially concerned with the effect of a tax on the level of foreign investment in the public debt. If news were to "reach Europe that American funds were to be taxed," he feared, "the very sound of such a measure might do us more mischief than the object was worth."

John Nicholas countered with a scheme according to which, he argued, the government could receive the benefit of a tax without suffering higher borrowing costs in the future. The government would face no additional costs with respect to money it had already borrowed, because those funds "were already in our hands." As for future loans, he explained, if potential creditors were truly displeased by the possibility of a transfer tax, they "had it in their power to make an express stipulation for no tax on their funds." In Nicholas's view, imposing a tax retrospectively while simultaneously negotiating the terms of government debt with each new group of public creditors "would answer the purpose completely, without recurring to those alarming presages of the loss of credit."

The debate, like the same debate the previous year, was indicative of the political climate surrounding the purchase and sale of securities. The four leading opponents of the tax in 1794 were all from the north – Ames and Lyman were from Massachusetts, Tracy from Connecticut, and Boudinot from New Jersey. The leading supporters of the tax were southerners – Winn and John Hunter were from South Carolina, Samuel Smith from Maryland, and Nicholas from Virginia. The regional divide with respect to securities trading that had originated in the 1780s was still strong. The participants in the debate, moreover, were acutely conscious of how their arguments would be perceived by the public. "The Funding System had of late become a favorite topic of newspaper eloquence," complained Ames.

It had been loudly said, that the Representatives in Congress from one of the New England States had immense property in the Public Funds, when, in fact, their whole income from that source was not sufficient for buying oats for their horses. To say, therefore, that they were under influence in their political conduct from such motives was the merest bagatelle that can be conceived . . . . People dream that Congress are voting money into their own pockets. The propagation of this idea promotes the dirty purposes of slander, abuse, and falsehood.

Even in Congress, Ames observed, "there had not been a single discussion of any length, for a considerable time past, where there had not been some pointed allusion to this paper bugbear." Clark, for his part, indirectly criticized Ames for making "a long speech with respect to newspapers" rather than speaking on the merits of the tax.[16]

Both proposed transfer taxes, on the public debt and on stock in the Bank of the United States, were approved by a Committee of the Whole House, and were added to a long list of taxes to be voted upon as a block.[17] The tax on the debt received so many votes in favor that the votes in opposition were not even counted. Once that had been decided, the tax on Bank stock passed unanimously. The prospect of a transfer tax "distresses Hamilton exceedingly," reported Fisher Ames the next day, "and well it may; for, to begin to tax the public debt, when we are afraid to tax snuff, is a bad omen."[18] Hamilton made it a point to include a lengthy opposition to a transfer tax in his second Report on Public Credit, which elaborated on the arguments made by Ames and others in Congress.[19] When the transfer taxes came up for a vote, they were buried near the end of a long list of stamp duties on licenses, affidavits, deeds, bills of lading, insurance policies, and so on. That entire group of taxes was rejected by a vote of 50–32.[20] The contrast with the earlier vote on the transfer taxes alone suggests that most of the opposition to the final bill was based on disagreement with taxes other than the transfer taxes. But in the end, the views of Ames and Hamilton prevailed.

The concept of a stock transfer tax would return, but not for a long time. Congress would impose temporary transfer taxes as emergency revenue measures during wartime, in 1898 and 1914.[21] A permanent federal stock transfer tax was in existence from 1917 until 1965.[22] A handful of states imposed a similar tax during approximately the same

---

[16] *Annals of Congress*, IV, 617–20 (May 1, 1794).   [17] Ibid., 620, 655.

[18] Ames to Christopher Gore, May 2, 1794, Seth Ames, ed., *Works of Fisher Ames* (Boston: Little, Brown, 1854), I, 141.

[19] Alexander Hamilton, "Report on Public Credit," *Annals of Congress*, IV, 1360–64 (Jan. 16, 1795).

[20] *Annals of Congress*, IV, 726 (May 27, 1794).

[21] An Act to provide ways and means to meet war expenditures, and for other purposes, sched. A, 30 Stat. 448, 458 (June 13, 1898); An Act to increase the internal revenue, and for other purposes, sched. A, 38 Stat. 745, 759 (Oct. 22, 1914).

[22] An Act to provide revenue to defray war expenses, and for other purposes, sched. A, §

period, the most significant of which was the one in New York, enacted in 1905 and still in existence as of 1997.[23] Proposals for another federal tax were debated in the 1990s, as both a method of obtaining revenue and a means of reducing the velocity of trading, which, aided by computers, had grown rapidly.[24] By then, the United States was unusual among nations with developed securities markets in not taxing the transfer of stock.[25]

In the period under study here, however, the 1794 rejection of the transfer tax marked an end to the federal government's efforts to regulate the securities market. After prohibiting Treasury employees from buying and selling public securities, and after twice considering a tax on the transfer of stock, Congress would not take up any similar issues before 1860. Until then, securities regulation would be left to the states.

II

The crash of 1792 sparked two types of reactions in the states with active securities markets. "[W]e are frequently told," reported James Sullivan, that the "evils resulting from . . . speculations in the public securities . . . will cure themselves." But many shared Sullivan's suspicion of this advice. As Sullivan concluded, "the same may be said of all other natural, moral, and political evils; and if the argument proves any thing, it will prove that there is no need of providing any checks against wrong doers."[26] In the immediate aftermath of the crash, the legislatures of the two leading commercial states, Pennsylvania and New York, considered for the first time legislation to curb securities trading.

In late March, a bill "to prevent the practice of stockjobbing" was introduced in the lower house of the Pennsylvania legislature. The bill was modeled on sections 1 and 8 of Sir John Barnard's Act, the English statute of 1734 (discussed in chapter 3). Like section 1 of Barnard's Act,

---

4, 40 Stat. 300, 322 (Oct. 5, 1917); An Act to reduce excise taxes, and for other purposes, § 401(a), 79 Stat. 136, 148 (June 21, 1965).

[23] N.Y. Laws, 128th Sess., ch. 241 (April 19, 1905); N.Y. Tax Law § 270 et seq.

[24] Lynn A. Stout, "Are Stock Markets Costly Casinos? Disagreement, Market Failure, and Securities Regulation," *Virginia Law Review* 81 (1995): 699–702.

[25] Lawrence H. Summers and Victoria P. Summers, "The Case for a Securities Transactions Excise Tax," *Tax Notes* 48 (1990): 883; Donald W. Kiefer, "The Security Transactions Tax: An Overview of the Issues," *Tax Notes* 48 (1990): 897–98. For much of the twentieth century, on the other hand, the capital gains tax has discouraged short-term holding, largely as a way of deterring speculation. James R. Repetti, "The Use of the Tax Law to Stabilize the Stock Market: The Efficacy of Holding Period Requirements," *Virginia Tax Review* 8 (1989): 596–601.

[26] Sullivan, *Path to Riches*, 75.

it would have voided all "wagers" on stock prices, an ambiguous ban that might plausibly have been construed to encompass the sale of options, or possibly just options to buy stock which the seller did not own. Like section 8 of Barnard's Act, it would have voided all contracts for the sale of stock which the seller did not possess at the time of the sale, and would have accordingly made it impossible to use the Pennsylvania court system to enforce speculative time bargains. The bill provided that all

contracts, written or verbal, public or private, made after the passing of this act, for the sale and transfer, and all wagers concerning the prices, present or future, of any certificate, or evidence of debt, or any proportion or sum of the debt, due by, or from the United States, or any separate state, or any share or shares of the stock of the Bank of the United States, or any other bank, or any share or shares of the stock of any company, established, or to be established by law of the United States, or of any separate state, shall be, and all such contracts are hereby declared to be absolutely null, void and of no effect; and both parties are hereby discharged from the l[i]en and obligation of such contract, or wager, unless the party contracting to sell and transfer the same, shall at the time of making such contract, be in the actual possession of the certificate, or other evidence of such debt or debts, share or shares, or be otherwise entitled in his own right, or duly authorised and empowered by some person, so entitled, to transfer the said certificate, evidence, debt or debts, share or shares.[27]

The bill was in many respects milder than Barnard's Act had been. Unlike Barnard's Act, it did not explicitly prohibit the sale of options. It did not ban the settling of futures contracts by the payment of price differentials. It expressly exempted brokers from its reach, in the "duly authorised and empowered" clause near the end. It did not impose any fines or other penalties on sellers or brokers found to have violated the statute, beyond the requirement that money paid under an offending contract be refunded to the payer, and of course the inability to enforce a void contract in court.

The bill never made it through the Pennsylvania legislature. It was tabled shortly after it was introduced.[28] No evidence has been found to suggest that the legislature ever took it up again. Pennsylvania in 1792 repeated the experience of England in 1720–21; even a stock market crash and a resulting short, sharp economic contraction were not enough to cause the government to halt the more speculative forms of trading.

In New York, the proponents of regulation were more successful. When the crash occurred, a bill to regulate the sale of stock at auction

---

[27] *[Philadelphia] General Advertiser*, March 29, 1792, 3.
[28] *[Philadelphia] National Gazette*, April 2, 1792, 2.

was pending in the state legislature.[29] The bill was promptly amended to regulate trading as well.[30] The resulting statute passed in early April – "An Act to prevent the pernicious practice of stock jobbing, and for regulating sales at public auctions" – reflected this double purpose. Much of the statute was concerned with auctions of all kinds, not just of securities. It limited the number of auctioneers in the city of New York, prohibited auctioneers from selling certain goods, and restricted the ability of auctioneers to use deputies.[31]

The second and third paragraphs of the statute pertained to securities trading. Paragraph 2 forbade the sale "of any public securities or stock, created under the acts of Congress of the United States, or of any individual State, at public vendue or out cry."[32] Beginning the previous summer at the latest, securities had been sold at regular daily auctions in New York. After the crash, however, in late March and early April, the New York trading community had moved indoors; it had agreed to replace outdoor public auctions with private sessions at which traders would transact among themselves. The ban on securities auctions thus prohibited a form of trading that had already come to a halt a week or two before.[33]

Paragraph 3 of the New York statute was worded identically to the bill tabled by the Pennsylvania legislature at approximately the same time. One must have been copied directly from the other. As of 1792, therefore, New York had its own watered-down equivalent of Barnard's Act. As in England, contracts to sell shares of government debt or corporate stock one did not own on the contract date were void and hence unenforceable in the state's courts. Any money paid pursuant to such a contract could be recovered "by action on the case [i]n assumpsit, for money had and received to the use of the plaintiff, to be brought in any court of record."[34]

This provision was reenacted twice in the following decades. In 1801, when the state revamped its scheme for regulating auctioneers, the legislature replicated the ban on selling stock one did not own.[35] The statute was reenacted again in 1813, still without any change in language.[36] In 1817, the legislature relaxed the restrictions on the sale of

---

[29] *Journal of the Assembly of the State of New-York* (1792), 99, 102.
[30] *Journal of the Senate of the State of New-York* (1792), 77.
[31] N.Y. Laws, 15th Sess., c. 62, paras. 1, 4, 5 (April 10, 1792).   [32] Ibid., para. 2.
[33] Werner and Smith, *Wall Street*, 24.   [34] N.Y. Laws, 15th Sess., c. 62, para. 3.
[35] N.Y. Laws, 24th Sess., c. 116, para. 17 (April 2, 1801).
[36] N.Y. Laws, 36th Sess., c. 70, § 18 (1813). Werner and Smith erroneously suggest that statutes enacted in 1804, 1806, and 1808 affected the regulation of the securities market. Werner and Smith, *Wall Street*, 201–02. These statutes referred back to the 1801 statute, but only to a provision concerning taxes on certain goods (not securities)

public securities at auction; henceforth, securities belonging to a dead or bankrupt person could be sold at auction, just like any other type of property. The prohibition against selling stock one did not own, however, was expressly continued in force.[37] The provision then lived undisturbed until 1858, when it was repealed. In "An Act to legalize the sale of stocks on time," the legislature announced that no contract for the sale of stock "shall be void or voidable . . . because the vender, at the time of making such contract, is not the owner or possessor of the certificate or certificates, or other evidence of such debt, share or interest."[38] New York repealed its equivalent of Barnard's Act two years before Barnard's Act itself would be repealed.

The only other state to pass a similar statute was Massachusetts, also the home of a significant securities market. The Massachusetts statute, not passed until 1836, was nearly identical to New York's. It voided all contracts for the sale of corporate stock or government securities, "unless the party or parties contracting to sell or transfer the same, shall, at the time of making such contract, be the owner or assignee thereof, or shall be duly authorized by some person who is the owner or assignee."[39] The Massachusetts statute remained in effect throughout the century,[40] and was repealed in 1910.[41]

New York's securities market, the nation's largest, was thus from 1792 to 1836 the only market in the country where speculators could not, in theory, agree to sell stock they did not own. From 1836 to 1858 it shared that distinction with the Boston market, which rivaled Philadelphia as the nation's second largest.[42] These circumstances alone suggest that the stockjobbing statutes had little impact on the volume of trading, and in fact that is true. The American versions of Barnard's Act produced the same effects in the United States as Barnard's Act had produced in England; time bargains went on as before, but were enforced privately, without the assistance of the legal system. "It is a well known fact," complained New York's Chancellor in 1844, "that shares

---

sold at public auction. The statutes are N.Y. Laws, 27th Sess., c. 65 (1804); N.Y. Laws, 29th Sess., c. 81, para. 3 (1806); and N.Y. Laws, 32nd Sess., c. 5 (1808).

[37] N.Y. Laws, 40th Sess., c. 275, §§ 11, 20 (April 15, 1817). Werner and Smith erroneously state that the New York legislature repealed the 1813 ban on stockjobbing earlier in 1817 and then reimposed it by the statute just discussed. Werner and Smith, *Wall Street*, 202. Earlier in 1817, the legislature repealed an 1816 amendment to the 1813 statute banning stockjobbing, not the 1813 statute itself. The repeal is at N.Y. Laws, 40th Sess., c. 144 (April 5, 1817); the 1816 amendment (which had nothing to do with stockjobbing) is at N.Y. Laws, 40th Sess., c. 13 (Nov. 12, 1816).

[38] N.Y. Laws, 81st Sess., c. 134, § 1 (April 10, 1858).

[39] Mass. Laws 1836, c. 279 (April 16, 1836).

[40] T. Henry Dewey, *Legislation Against Speculation and Gambling in the Forms of Trade* (New York: Baker, Voorhis, 1905), 25–26.

[41] Mass. Laws 1910, c. 171, §§ 5, 24.   [42] Werner and Smith, *Wall Street*, 184.

of stock are constantly sold at the board of brokers which shares exist only in the imagination of the nominal buyers and sellers. Such sales, as every body knows, are not legally binding upon either party."[43] Another New York judge condemned "the unbridled and defiant spirit of speculation, which daily scorns and violates the stockjobbing act."[44] A quick rise in stock prices in 1844, the New York merchant Philip Hone recorded in his diary, ruined many speculators "who had 'sold ahead,' as it is called in Wall Street."[45] A price rise could not have had such dire consequences unless these speculators were selling stock they did not own. "TIME CONTRACTS ARE NOT LEGALLY BINDING!" screamed William Armstrong in his 1848 exposé of Wall Street, and yet they were common all the same; "[c]onsequently, there is no other security for the performance of contracts than the laws of honor."[46] Even the brokers admitted with some understatement that although "[c]ontracts of that character, as generally understood, cannot by law now be enforced," nevertheless "there is a semblance of truth to sustain the supposition" that they were being entered into "by irresponsible persons, who perhaps can only comply with them in case it turns out to be in their favor."[47] The closest students of the subject estimate that between 1818 and 1840 time bargains constituted at least 20 percent, and probably an even greater percentage, of the transactions on the New York Stock & Exchange Board, the predecessor of the modern New York Stock Exchange.[48] As in England, the loss of one's reputation, and later the loss of one's membership in the exchange, would be sanctions strong enough to make most traders comply with their contracts.

Because the effect of the American stockjobbing statutes was to drive a large class of transactions out of the official legal system, the statutes found their way into reported cases, as Barnard's Act had in England, only when there was some question as to whether they applied to a particular transaction. American judges tended to construe their statutes less narrowly than English judges had construed Barnard's Act. In *Ward* v. *Van Duzer* (1829), for instance, a pair of brokers sued their client to recover money the brokers had expended on the client's behalf in a time bargain that was clearly void under the New York statute, because the

---

[43] *Dykers* v. *Allen,* 7 Hill 497, 500 (N.Y. 1844).

[44] *Cassard* v. *Hinmann,* 14 How. Pr. 84, 90 (N.Y. Super. 1856).

[45] Allan Nevins, ed., *The Diary of Philip Hone 1821–1851* (New York: Dodd, Mead, 1936), 707.

[46] William Armstrong, *Stocks and Stock-Jobbing in Wall-Street* (New York: New-York Publishing Co., 1848), 12.

[47] "Memorial and Remonstrance of the board of stock and exchange brokers of the city of New-York," N.Y. Assembly Doc. 291, 59th Sess. (March 23, 1836), 6.

[48] Werner and Smith, *Wall Street,* 173–74.

seller did not possess the stock he was purporting to sell. The brokers cited *Petrie* v. *Hannay* and *Steers* v. *Lashley,* the eighteenth-century English cases permitting brokers to recover despite Barnard's Act in such a situation, in support of their claim. (As discussed in chapter 3, these cases had been overruled in 1819, but no one involved in *Ward* seems to have known that.) The court nevertheless refused to allow the suit. "The affair was manifestly a mere stock-jobbing transaction," the court concluded; "the whole affair being illegal, the plaintiffs could not call on the defendant to refund them the money paid on the pretended purchase. No right of action could accrue to the plaintiffs from their own violation of the law."[49]

The issue present in *Ward* also arose in reverse, when an investor sought to recover money he had deposited with a broker to cover possible losses from a transaction void under the New York statute. The New York courts initially decided the question in favor of the investor. In *Gram* v. *Stebbins & Stebbins* (1836), the chancellor ruled that the illegality of the underlying transaction rendered the deposit void as well, which entitled the investor to get his money back.[50] *Gram* created an asymmetry in the interpretation of the stockjobbing act; investors could recover funds deposited with brokers, but brokers could not recover funds expended on behalf of investors. The asymmetry was ended in *Staples* v. *Gould* (1854), which effectively overruled *Gram,* and put investors and brokers on an equal footing. "As such contracts for the sale of stock are forbidden by the statute," the court held, "the plaintiff and defendant being *in pari delicto,* no action can be maintained by either party against the other."[51] Once more, the New York courts construed the statute to apply not just directly to stock purchase contracts but also indirectly to payments made in connection with those contracts, between principals and brokers, no matter which direction the payment ran. *Ward* most likely had the effect of further removing disputes between brokers and investors from the court system and channelling them into the mechanism of dispute resolution sponsored by the stock exchange, a mechanism that will be explored in chapter 8. *Staples* may have contributed a bit to the same trend, although the statute being interpreted would be repealed only a few years later.

The fungibility of stock – the fact that one share of a given type of stock was indistinguishable from another, so that contracts to purchase stock necessarily involved a certain number of shares in the abstract rather than any particular shares – gave rise to some difficult questions

---

[49] *Ward* v. *Van Duzer,* 2 N.Y. Super. 162, 166 (1829).
[50] *Gram* v. *Stebbins & Stebbins,* 6 Paige Ch. 124 (N.Y. Ch. 1836).
[51] *Staples* v. *Gould,* 9 N.Y. 520, 523 (1854), aff'g 7 N.Y. Super. 411 (1852).

of interpretation under New York's stockjobbing statute. Here the results were mixed. What if the seller, although possessing on the contract date the shares he was agreeing to sell, had already made commitments to transfer a greater number of shares to someone else? The question arose in the Massachusetts courts, in *Stebbins* v. *Leowulf* (1849), a suit brought by a New York broker to recover commissions and expenses from a Massachusetts client in connection with a purchase made from such a seller. The client defended on the basis of *Ward* v. *Van Duzer*, by arguing that the underlying transaction was void under the New York statute, and thus that the broker could not maintain a suit to recover money spent in connection with it. But was the transaction void? On the one hand, looking just at the challenged transaction, the seller actually did possess the shares he was selling. On the other hand, if the seller's accounts were to be examined as a whole, the seller could be said to possess fewer than zero shares, in the sense that he had prior obligations to convey more shares than he owned. The court concluded that "the spirit and the purpose of the statute may easily be defeated" if the statute was deemed not to prohibit such a transaction. "Does the possession of one hundred shares," the court asked, "authorize the owner to make sales of such stock to an indefinite amount, provided each sale be in itself for an amount less than the stock so held by the vendor?" If so, "the ownership of a hundred shares may furnish a capital adequate to trade upon to the amount of a thousand," which was, in the court's view, precisely the sort of speculation the statute was meant to prohibit.[52] But this principle had its limits. The possibility that one might sell the same stock to multiple people did not require a seller, seeking to recover from a buyer who failed to accept, to resell the stock to someone else before proceeding against the buyer, even though the theoretical possibility remained for a seller to sue several breaching buyers, all with respect to the same stock. Although that possibility, for one New York judge, demonstrated "the wisdom or propriety of further legislation on the subject," it was not enough to require a resale under the statute as written.[53]

What about a seller who possessed on the contract date the stock he agreed to sell, but then sold the stock to someone else before the date of delivery? The validity under the statute of that kind of transaction was another difficult question raised by the fungibility of stock. In *Frost* v. *Clarkson & Clarkson* (1827), the New York judges first rejected the suggestion that they rely on English cases interpreting Barnard's Act. "On this point," the court determined, "the English decisions do not aid

[52] *Stebbins* v. *Leowulf*, 57 Mass. 137, 143 (1849).
[53] *Vaupell* v. *Woodward*, 2 Sandf. Ch. 156, 159 (N.Y. Ch. 1844).

us, as the statute of 7 Geo. II ch. 8 [Barnard's Act] is not like ours." The court then held that because the New York statute required only that the seller possess the shares at the time of the sale, and because the seller could easily buy stock on the market to cover his obligation to deliver when it came due, nothing in the statute prohibited the transaction.

[I]t was no part of the contract that those identical shares should be transferred. Any 100 shares were of equal value; and though they might buy and sell 1000 shares of the same stock; and though they might not have held a single share one day after the contract was made; it does not follow that they could not have fulfilled their contract at any time, on demand; for, though they had not the shares, they might, in a few minutes, procure them.[54]

The fact that shares were indistinguishable and easily bought and sold could thus argue in favor of a broad or a narrow interpretation of the stockjobbing statute, depending on the context. Because the wording of the statute focused only on the day of sale, a seller needed to have a net positive ownership of stock on that day to legitimate a transaction, but he could incur any obligation to transfer even more stock at any time before or after.

Another area of ambiguity under the New York and Massachusetts statutes concerned the relationship of contracts to sell stock with other types of contracts. Here the courts tended to construe the statutes narrowly, in accordance with their perceived purposes. When stock pledged as collateral for a loan was sold by the pledgor, did the pledgor possess the stock he was purporting to sell, or was the sale void under the New York statute because the stock was possessed by the person to whom it was pledged? In *Thompson* v. *Alger* (1847), the Massachusetts Supreme Court allowed the sale. "The policy of the act," the court found, "and its leading purpose doubtless were to prevent gambling in the rise and fall of stocks." The sale of pledged stock by the pledgor was not contrary to this policy, as it did not facilitate speculation in stocks one had never purchased, and thus it was not contrary to the statute.[55] What about stock sold by one person on behalf of another, according to an agreement that required a division of the profits from the sale? In *Barrett* v. *Hyde* (1856), such a sale was found valid under the Massachusetts statute, because it violated neither the statute's language nor its purpose.[56]

The New York stockjobbing statute, passed in 1792 in response to the crash, thus figured only sporadically in litigation during its sixty-six-year life, because, by voiding a large class of securities transactions, it drove

---

[54] *Frost* v. *Clarkson & Clarkson*, 7 Cow. 24, 28 (N.Y. Sup. Ct. 1827).
[55] *Thompson* v. *Alger*, 53 Mass. 428, 440 (1847).
[56] *Barrett* v. *Hyde*, 73 Mass. 160, 161 (1856).

enforcement of those transactions out of the court system and into other arenas. The Massachusetts statute presumably had a similar effect for the smaller Boston market. As we will see in chapter 8, this consequence of New York's statute would contribute to the formation and the early importance of the organization that would later become the New York Stock Exchange.

III

Securities trading in the new nation's first decade raised a host of legal issues, meanwhile, that had little to do with the 1792 crash or the flurry of trading that preceded it. As had earlier been the case in England, the legal system had to develop procedures to handle new types of routine transactions, and a new set of institutions had to be fit into preexisting bodies of law. In handling both of these tasks, American legislators and judges relied heavily on English precedents.

The federal government and the states did not set forth procedures for the issuance and transfer of securities in generally applicable statutes, as they usually do today. Rather, as had been the English practice, where these procedures existed they were placed within statutes chartering individual business corporations and authorizing particular sales of government debt. The result was a piecemeal system of securities regulation, under which, in principle, the law applicable to the sale of stock in one corporation might differ from that applicable to the sale of stock in another. Nevertheless, because these statutes tended not to differ significantly from one another, the law proved to be roughly uniform.

Corporate charters often specified how stock was to be issued to the initial shareholders and how it was to be subsequently transferred to others. When North Carolina in 1790 chartered an enterprise to build a canal between the Pasquotank and Elizabeth Rivers, for instance, the legislature required that subscriptions be sold in particular towns, under the supervision of particular people, for a specific period of time – "the said books shall be opened for receiving subscriptions on the first day of May next, and continue open until the first day of September next inclusive." If a shareholder wished to sell his shares, he was required to do so "by deed, executed before two witnesses, and registered after proof of the execution thereof in the said company's books." A shareholder could sell only whole shares, not fractional shares, and was prohibited from holding a share in trust for someone else.[57] The 1791

[57] 1 N.C. Laws 1715–1820, c. 332, §§ 1, 15 (1790).

New Jersey statute incorporating the Society for Establishing Useful Manufactures specified that shares could be subscribed to only until the last Monday in November, at which point, in the event the number of subscriptions exceeded the number of shares, the directors were required to make a proportional deduction from the amount of shares subscribed by each purchaser.[58] When Congress in 1791 chartered the Bank of the United States, it prohibited any subscriber other than the federal government from subscribing to more than thirty shares in a single day.[59] In the Hartford Bank's 1792 charter, Connecticut imposed a similar limitation; no investor apart from the state itself was permitted to hold more than thirty shares at a time.[60] These were all instances of government regulation of the securities market, but regulation limited to the securities of a single enterprise.

Governments often delegated to the enterprises themselves the power further to regulate transactions in their own stock. Charters typically contained a clause like this one, from the charter of the Hartford Bank: "The Stock of the said Corporation shall be assignable, and transferable, according to such Rules as shall be instituted in that Respect by the Laws of the same."[61] These internal rules, in turn, often replicated the sorts of rules legislatures themselves were likely to place in statutes chartering corporations, rules such as those requiring stock transfers to be entered on the books of the corporation to be effective, and other similar formal requirements.[62]

Procedures for the transfer of securities were also included in statutes authorizing the sale of government debt. When Congress adopted Hamilton's plan for the permanent public debt in 1790, it provided both a mechanism for the initial sale of the securities and a procedure for subsequent sales in the secondary market, both of which involved the appointment of commissioners in each state to supervise transfers.[63] In 1795 and 1796, when the federal government borrowed some more, the statutes authorizing the borrowing incorporated by reference the provision of the 1790 statute specifying how transfers were to take place.[64]

---

[58] An Act to incorporate the contributors to the society for establishing useful manufactures, and for the further encouragement of said society, §§ 6, 10 (Nov. 22, 1791).

[59] 1 Stat. 194–95 (March 2, 1791).

[60] An Act to incorporate the Hartford Bank, § 2 (May 1792).   [61] Ibid., § 12.

[62] See, e.g., *Northrop* v. *Newton and Bridgeport Turnpike Co.*, 3 Conn. 544, 550 (1820).

[63] An Act making provision for the Debt of the United States, §§ 6–7, 1 Stat. 138, 140–41 (Aug. 4, 1790).

[64] An Act making further provision for the Support of Public Credit, and for the redemption of the Public Debt, § 3, 1 Stat. 433 (March 3, 1795); An Act making provision for the payment of certain Debts of the United States, § 2, 1 Stat. 488 (May 31, 1796).

Nearly all of the statutory securities regulation of the 1790s – all except New York's 1792 stockjobbing statute – took this form. In being customized to each business enterprise and each issuance of public debt, the law pertaining to the transfer of securities did not differ from the law governing corporations generally. At a time when no unit of American government had a general incorporation law or a continuous system of public borrowing, every new corporation and every new loan from the public required a new statute from the legislature. Most of what would now be part of the law of private corporations and the law of public finance was contained within these statutes. The rate at which legislatures had to produce such statutes was still low enough in the 1790s to permit variations from statute to statute. As the volume of these statutes, especially the volume of charters for business enterprises, grew over the nineteenth century to the point where customized provisions were no longer feasible, corporate law would shift from rules in individual charters to statutes more widely applicable. The law governing securities transactions would be a part of that shift. But regulation of securities transfers by charter would be more common than regulation by general statute well into the nineteenth century.[65]

While legislatures were providing such procedures for transactions that were becoming routine, the courts were fitting the new institution of securities trading into much older bodies of law. As we saw in chapter 3, English judges had been engaging in this process for nearly a century already. American judges were able to build upon this work when American lawyers posed questions that had already been resolved in England. Where issues had not previously arisen, American judges adapted older legal categories to the new market by using the same sort of analogical common law reasoning that characterized the opinions of English courts earlier in the century.

One of the earliest and most fundamental questions to arise in the wake of the 1792 crash was whether speculative securities contracts were even enforceable at common law, or whether they constituted illegal gambling. Arguments had been made on both sides of the question in England, particularly in the years immediately after the South Sea Bubble,[66] but the issue had not been decided by any English court except in the implicit sense that such contracts had routinely been enforced, which left American courts without any explicit external guidance. In November 1791, when stock prices were near their peak, John Wilkes contracted to buy $20,000 in face value of US government

---

[65] Herbert Hovenkamp, *Enterprise and American Law, 1836–1937* (Cambridge, MA: Harvard University Press, 1991), 125–26.

[66] *Reasons for Making Void*, 1–2; *Answer to the Reasons for Making Void*, 3.

debt from Robert Gilchreest the following September, at a price of $24,500. Carlisle Pollock guaranteed Wilkes's commitment. Between the contract date and the delivery date, the market fell; other speculators proved unable to perform their contracts with Wilkes, which left Wilkes insolvent and unable to pay Gilchreest. Gilchreest accordingly sued Pollock, who defended in part by claiming that the agreement between Gilchreest and Wilkes was unenforceable. The Pennsylvania Supreme Court, drawing an analogy between speculative securities contracts and similar contracts to buy a more familiar commodity, held that Gilchreest's agreement did not amount to illegal gambling under the common law. "The sale of stock is neither unlawful or immoral," it charged the jury.

> It is confessed, that an inordinate spirit of speculation approaches to gaming, and tends to corrupt the morals of the people. When the public mind is thus affected, it becomes the legislature to interpose. But we have no such law at present. Call the 6 per cent. stock so many bushels of wheat, if it had fallen in price on the day of delivery, and the vendor was then ready and willing, and offered to perform his contract in all its parts, ought not the principal or his surety to make him full compensation? If wheat had risen in price, would not the adverse party be enabled to get like compensation, in case the vendor had receded from his bargain?[67]

As in England, stock may have been a new form of property, but it was property all the same, which allowed courts to fit it within a well-established structure of legal rules applicable to older forms of property like wheat. Similar decisions would be reached by courts in other states as well.[68] No American court would reach a contrary result in the first half of the nineteenth century. The cumulative effect of these decisions was to permit the market to continue to grow. (In many states in the second half of the century, the doctrine would develop, both by statute and at common law, that futures contracts for the sale of stock made without any intent ever to deliver the stock, but made instead with the intent to settle by the payment of cash in the amount of the rise or fall in price, were void as wagers.[69] This doctrine, also derived by analogy from cases involving older forms of property, appears not to have been

---

[67] *Gilchreest* v. *Pollock*, 2 Yeates (7 Pa.) 18, 21 (1795). The court also rejected, without any discussion, Pollock's argument that the contract was unenforceable because it was executory.

[68] *Ridgely* v. *Riggs*, 4 Har. & J. (8 Md.) 358, 368 (1818); *Noyes* v. *Spaulding*, 27 Vt. 419, 428–30 (1855). For an early similar holding with respect to speculative futures contracts for the exchange of paper money and specie, see *Brachan* v. *Griffin*, 3 Call. (3 Va.) 433, 436–39 (1803).

[69] William W. Cook, *A Treatise on the Law of Stock and Stockholders* (New York: Baker, Voorhis, 1887), 352–53.

stated by any American court prior to the 1860s, although it was suggested by Joseph Story much earlier.[70])

A parallel question was implicated in reconciling the new market with the law of usury: Were speculative contracts permitting the possibility of very high rates of return, such as investments in stock or loans of stock, void as usurious? American courts had the benefit of much English experience in answering this question. They built upon the rule used by English judges for centuries with respect to other speculative investments and applied to loans of stock by 1790.[71] If an investor's principal was at risk, a high rate of return would not be usurious.[72] If return of the principal was guaranteed, on the other hand, and only the rate of interest might fluctuate, a high rate of return would be usury.[73] This general principle, developed to permit the financing of medieval shipping ventures, had been part of English common law at least since *Roberts* v. *Tremayne* (1618).[74] *Roberts* was familiar to American courts, and relied upon, from the beginning. "[I]f the principal or any considerable part, be put in risque," explained one American judge in 1797, "it is not usury; because the excess in the premium, is a consideration for the risque."[75] But, as another stated in 1793, "wherever the principal is payable at all events, and the risk only applies to the interest, no more than legal interest can be reserved."[76]

The earliest American decision to transfer this doctrine to securities from older forms of property was *Atkinson* v. *Executors of Scott* (1793), a dispute over a 1786 loan of "indents," or certificates entitling the holder to receive interest on a given amount of government debt. Scott borrowed nearly £1,300 in indents from Atkinson, and promised, in the event he failed to return the indents, to repay Atkinson in specie. Indents at the time were trading at less than one-eighth of their face value. When Scott died without returning the indents, and Atkinson sued Scott's estate for the specie, Scott's executors defended by claiming that the loan was usurious and thus void. Because £1,300 in indents was

---

[70] The doctrine's first American appearance appears to have been in *Cassard* v. *Hinmann*, 14 How. Pr. 84 (N.Y. Super. 1856), a New York case involving a contract nominally for the future delivery of 500 barrels of pork, which relied on English cases from a few years before. Story proposed the doctrine in Joseph Story, *Commentaries on the Law of Agency*, 2nd edn (Boston: Little, Brown, 1844), 283.

[71] *Tate* v. *Wellings*, 3 Term Rep. 531, 100 Eng. Rep. 716 (K.B. 1790). This principle has been discussed in chapters 1 and 3.

[72] See, e.g., St. George Tucker, "Concerning Usury," in St. George Tucker, ed., *Blackstone's Commentaries* (Philadelphia: William Young Birch and Abraham Small, 1803), III, 108.

[73] See, e.g., Dane, *General Abridgment*, V, 338.

[74] *Roberts* v. *Tremayne*, Cro. Jac. 507, 508, 79 Eng. Rep. 433, 434 (K.B. 1618).

[75] *Gibson* v. *Fristoe*, 5 Call. (9 Va.) 62, 81 (1797).

[76] *Philip* v. *Kirkpatrick*, Add. (5 Va.) 124, 125 (1793).

really worth only about £150 in specie, the executors claimed, Atkinson was seeking approximately £1,150 in interest on a loan of £150. "If this was not usury," argued the executors' lawyer, "he did not know what usury was." The court agreed that loaning securities at substantially less than face value, and then requiring repayment at face value, would be "so evidently usurious, that it must strike every mind at the first blush." But the court interpreted the contract to require Scott to repay only the indents' market value, not their face value, as of the date he was obliged to return them. So construed, the contract still allowed Atkinson to earn a return of more than the statutory rate of 7 percent on the loan, if the indents appreciated by more than 7 percent while in Scott's hands. All concerned took for granted, however, that the contract would nevertheless be enforceable, because Atkinson's principal was at risk.[77]

Numerous cases in the following years applied this doctrine to the myriad transactions dreamed up by speculators, often drawing analogies to similar transactions in more familiar types of property. The sale of bank stock "at a very high price," for instance, could not be found void on the ground of usury where the sale was not a subterfuge for charging a high rate of interest on a loan, because "*bank stock*, like *tobacco* or *flour*, or any other property, may be, from a variety of causes, worth more or less, and a fair *bona fide* sale cannot be impeached on account of price."[78] People have the right, another judge pointed out, "to sell property, such as Bank shares, at whatever price is agreed on. The transaction becomes usurious, only when the object is to borrow money, and not purchase stock, and the price of the stock is graduated as a device to effect that purpose."[79] One might thus acquire stock at a price well above its current market price "to turn such stock to advantage by a remote speculation." But where the acquiror "was in very necessitous circumstances," and had purchased the stock on credit in order to sell it to raise immediate cash, the so-called sale was in fact a loan at a usurious rate, and was void.[80]

The distinction between genuine sales and disguised loans required courts to examine transactions closely and attempt to discern the intent of the contracting parties, each of whom understandably had a different recollection by the time of litigation. By focusing on the parties' intent rather than the characteristics of the transaction, courts on occasion ratified arrangements that could have been found usurious under the

[77] *Atkinson* v. *Executors of Scott*, 1 Bay (1 S.C.) 307, 308, 309 (1793).
[78] *Skipwith* v. *Gibson and Jefferson*, 4 Hen. & M. (14 Va.) 490 (1810).
[79] *Greenhow's administratrix* v. *Harris*, 20 Va. 472, 483 (1820).
[80] *Anonymous*, 2 DeSaussure (2 S.C. Eq.) 333, 337 (1806).

English common law. In 1824, for instance, a group of individuals gave $3,000 to Yale College for a year, in exchange for which they received the right to receive a year's worth of dividends on $3,000 in stock owned by Yale in the Eagle Bank of New-Haven. The Bank had historically paid dividends at an average rate of 7 percent, but there was no guarantee that such dividends would continue in the future. The maximum rate of interest one could charge for a loan in Connecticut was 6 percent. Was the transaction a clever way to charge Yale 7 percent for a loan? If that was the parties' intent, the Connecticut Supreme Court recognized, the arrangement would constitute usury. The court concluded, however, that "the transaction in this case was not a loan on interest, but it was a *bona fide* purchase of dividends."[81] Even though the form of the transaction might have suggested usury – the possibility of fluctuations in the dividend meant that the amount of "interest" was uncertain, but the $3,000 in principal was never at risk – form was not necessarily dispositive. It could be overridden by a finding that the parties intended a genuine sale.

A similar problem could arise whenever a broker loaned money to a client buying or selling stock through the broker, and then charged the client a commission for the transaction, because the amount of the commission, when added to the interest rate on the loan, could push that rate above the statutory maximum. Again, the form of such a transaction, considered as a whole, permitted a strong argument that it was usurious, because the broker's principal was never at risk. But James Kent, then in his last year as New York's Chancellor, held that because "nothing like usury for the future loan, or upon advance of the money, was in contemplation" by the parties, the arrangement did not amount to usury. Kent concluded that "there must be the unlawful or corrupt *intent* confessed or proved, before we can pronounce a transaction to be usurious."[82]

Normally, however, the form of a transaction was enough to infer that the parties intended a disguised loan at an interest rate higher than the law permitted. Whenever the purchase of securities at a price higher than their market value was made a precondition for a loan, for example, courts inferred that the transaction was intended to circumvent the ban on usury.[83] "If such contracts are to be supported," Kent explained, "the provisions of the statute against usury would be eluded,

[81] *Potter v. Yale College*, 8 Conn. 51, 62 (1830). Potter and his cohorts were trying to raise money for a congregational society, which may have caused the court to view with sympathy their efforts to get their $3,000 back.

[82] *Nourse v. Prime, Ward, and Sands*, 7 Johns. Ch. 69, 77 (N.Y. Ch. 1823).

[83] *Rose v. Dickson*, 7 Johns. 196, 197–98 (N.Y. Sup. Ct. 1810); *Stribbling v. Bank of the Valley*, 5 Rand. (26 Va.) 132, 147, 158 (1827).

and become of no avail."[84] Courts were suspicious of any transaction that required one person to pay another significantly more or less than stock was really worth at the time, and they tended to presume that no one would make such a bargain without a usurious intent.[85] "Suppose," one Virginia judge suggested,

for 5 dollars per share, advanced by me, A. agrees to convey to me, in 30 days, 100 shares of *Virginia* bank stock, now worth 110 dollars per share; can you "wink so hard" as not to see the device? So here – when *Smith* gives 80 dollars per share for stock at that moment worth 100 dollars, and which judicious men were at that moment subscribing for, in the same city, at the par value, what could be his motive but usurious gain[?][86]

Equally suspicious were arrangements that gave the lender of stock the option of receiving stock or money in return. A straight loan of stock could not be usurious because of the risk to principal, regardless of the loan's probable return. Thus when a stockholder in the Farmers' Bank of Virginia loaned 142 shares for a year, in exchange for the borrower's promise to repay an additional thirty shares at the year's end, the transaction was enforceable. One hundred and seventy two shares in the future, after all, might be worth even less than 142 shares today.[87] But when the lender had the option of requiring money rather than stock, that removed the risk to the principal. A borrower would not grant the lender such an option, courts reasoned, unless the transaction was intended to be a disguised loan of money.[88]

Decisions in the 1790s thus effectively resolved two basic legal questions concerning the American securities market. Speculation did not constitute illegal gambling, nor did it amount to illegal usury unless such was intended. In drawing these conclusions, American judges drew upon English precedent, and upon preexisting law governing older forms of property. Over the first half of the nineteenth century, subsequent cases elaborated on these doctrines but did not alter any basic principles. In both areas of the law, the choices made in the 1790s meant that most securities contracts could be enforced in the courts. That was not necessarily a prerequisite for the growth of the market – certain common types of transactions could not be so enforced in either England or New York, and the market grew all the same – but it could not have hurt. All other things being equal, the ability to use the court

[84] *Eagleson* v. *Shotwell*, 1 Johns. Ch. 536, 538 (N.Y. Ch. 1815).
[85] See, e.g., *Bank of Washington* v. *Arthur*, 3 Gratt. (44 Va.) 165 (1846).
[86] *Smith* v. *Nicholas*, 8 Leigh (35 Va.) 330, 360 (1837).
[87] *Steptoe's administrators* v. *Harvey's executors*, 7 Leigh (34 Va.) 501, 522–23 (1836).
[88] *Cleveland* v. *Loder & Draper*, 7 Paige Ch. 557, 559 (N.Y. Ch. 1839).

system to enforce a class of contracts will cause people to be more willing to enter into those contracts.

In other respects as well, courts in the 1790s, the first decade of organized securities trading in the United States, had to fit the new institution into older legal categories. Different sets of rules had long applied to real property and personal property, particularly concerning how it would be passed on to others at the owner's death. But what about shares in a corporation that owned nothing but real property? Such corporations, organized to own and operate canals, turnpikes, bridges, and so on, were not unusual. Should those shares be treated as real property as well, on the theory that they represented fractions of ownership of real property? Or were they personal property, on the ground that the corporation rather than its shareholders was the true owner of the real property? The issue was settled in Massachusetts in 1798 in favor of characterizing the shares as personal property, "though not without much litigation," according to Nathan Dane.[89] That classification was followed in later cases in other states. "It will not do to make the property of the corporation a criterion," explained the Rhode Island Supreme Court, "for the property of almost every corporation is more or less mixed." One had to look instead to the nature of the share itself. A share was nothing but a right "to receive a dividend of the whole concern," which, when in the corporate treasury, "is then but money." A share of a bridge corporation was thus personal property, even though the bridge itself was not.[90] (Within the category of personal property, shares were quickly classified as choses in action rather than chattels, because they more closely resembled representations of the right to possess a thing – the future stream of income the investor hoped to receive – than things that were themselves capable of being possessed.[91])

Only one court reached the contrary conclusion. In *Welles* v. *Cowles* (1818), the Connecticut Supreme Court defied the consensus and treated shares of a turnpike company as real property. "[T]he stockholders, as members of the company, are owners of the turnpike road," the court concluded, "and it is in virtue of this interest, that they have their claims for the dividends, or their respective shares of the toll. It is not a mere claim on the corporation." Shares of a turnpike company thus came "within the description of an incorporeal hereditament of a

---

[89] *Russell* v. *Temple* (1798), discussed in Dane, *General Abridgment*, III, 108.

[90] *Arnold* v. *Ruggles*, 1 R.I. 165, 168 (for the excerpts quoted), 173 (for reliance on *Russell* v. *Temple*) (1837).

[91] *Denton* v. *Livingston*, 9 Johns. 96, 100 (N.Y. Sup. Ct. 1812); *Howe* v. *Starkweather*, 17 Mass. 240, 243 (1821); Joseph K. Angell and Samuel Ames, *A Treatise on the Law of Private Corporations Aggregate* (Boston: Hilliard, Gray, Little & Wilkins, 1832), 316.

real nature."[92] The Connecticut legislature promptly enacted a statute to overrule *Welles*. "Whereas doubts have been entertained, whether shares in banks, turnpikes and other incorporated companies, should be disposed of as personal or real estate," the statute read, all such shares "shall, hereafter, be considered as personal estate."[93] From then on, securities were personal property in every state. That categorization was only a default presumption – where an individual charter specified that the shares of a corporation were to be real estate, they were real estate[94] – but it was enough to cover the vast majority of cases. American securities law was beginning to diverge from English law, under which, until the middle of the century, the categorization of corporate shares as real or personal property depended on the nature of the assets owned by the corporation.[95]

One final question settled in American courts in the 1790s concerned the measure of damages in case of a breach of an obligation to deliver stock. All agreed that the plaintiff should recover the value of the stock he was to have received. But the value as of when? The question became an especially urgent one in 1790, when the prices of state debt securities rose in anticipation of Hamilton's funding program, and then rose even higher upon the program's adoption. There were three conceivable times at which the stock could be valued – the date the contract was entered into, the date delivery was due, or the date of trial. Because prices were generally rising, the lowest valuation would be on the contract date; this date, unsurprisingly, was favored by defendants. Next highest would be the date delivery was due. Highest of all would be the time of trial; this date was favored by plaintiffs. The first reported case to raise the issue arose in South Carolina, with respect to a 1784 contract to deliver South Carolina indents. "A great number of contracts in every part of the state," the court instructed the jury, "depend upon the determination of the question." The court then derived the governing rule from cases involving older forms of property.

Whenever a contract is entered into for the delivery of a specific article, the value of that article, at the time fixed for delivery, is the sum a plaintiff ought to recover. As in this case, however, no time is mentioned for delivery or

---

[92] *Welles* v. *Cowles*, 2 Conn. 567, 572–73 (1818).

[93] Conn. Laws, May Sess. 1818, c. X.

[94] *Trevor* v. *Perkins*, 5 Wharton (55 Pa.) 243, 254 (1839). Georgia's 1839 charter of the Bellville and Altamaha Canal, Railway and River Navigation Company, for instance, specified that "the shares of stock in the aforesaid company shall be taken, considered and held in law as real estate." An Act to incorporate the Bellville and Altamaha Canal, Railway and River Navigation Company, § 13 (Dec. 21, 1839).

[95] Paddy Ireland, "Capitalism Without the Capitalist: The Joint Stock Company Share and the Emergence of the Modern Doctrine of Separate Corporate Personality," *Journal of Legal History* 17 (1996): 49–62.

repayment, nor any demand proved, the commencement of the suit must be considered as the demand, and the value of the indents at the time of commencing the action, with interest, is the true and proper rule of estimation.[96]

Later that year, the same rule was followed in Virginia.[97] Within a few years, "it had been determined over and over again, that in all cases where a bond or agreement is entered into for the delivery of a *specific thing*, the true measure of damages was the value of the thing *at the time* it was to be *delivered*."[98] In England at approximately the same time, plaintiffs were receiving the benefit of a more generous measure of damages; if the price of the stock had risen between the date it was to have been delivered and the date of trial, the award was measured as of the time of trial.[99] American law was again beginning to diverge from English law.

By the end of the eighteenth century, the main features of early American securities regulation were in place. The field would be occupied almost entirely by state governments rather than the federal government; this was in part a consequence of the Constitution's allocation of power, but it was also due to Congress's rejection of proposals that it exercise the power it possessed. The more speculative types of transactions would be enforceable in the courts of every state but New York and later Massachusetts, but New York's dominance in the area would grow nevertheless, because traders were able to develop non-governmental methods of enforcement. Certain kinds of stock transactions would be void as usurious, but the rest, as in England, would be assimilated to older legal categories and enforced just like transactions in older forms of property. The broad outlines of American securities regulation in the nineteenth century were already visible when the century began.

[96] *Davis* v. *Executors of Richardson*, 1 Bay (1 S.C.) 105, 106–07 (1790).

[97] *Groves* v. *Graves*, 1 Wash. (1 Va.) 1, 3 (1790).

[98] *Wigg* v. *Executors of Garden*, 1 Bay (1 S.C.) 357, 358 (1794). See also *Douglass & Mandeville* v. *McAllister*, 3 Cranch (7 U.S.) 298, 300 (1806); *Shepherd* v. *Hampton*, 3 Wheat. (16 U.S.) 200, 204 (1818).

[99] *Shepherd* v. *Johnson*, 2 East 211, 102 Eng. Rep. 349 (K.B. 1802); John Joseph Powell, *Essay Upon the Law of Contracts and Agreements* (London: J. Johnson, 1790), II, 232. In 1823, Nathan Dane described *Shepherd* as an aberration from the general English rule, which he took to be the same as in the United States. Dane, *General Abridgment*, I, 544.

6 American attitudes toward securities trading, 1792–1860

During the first half of the nineteenth century, as the American securities market changed from one dominated by federal government debt to one made up primarily of the shares of business enterprises, the popular interest in securities trading did not wane. Many Americans invested in the market; many more knew something about it. The nature of the market and its popularity will be discussed in section I of this chapter. Section II will describe the persistence of the primary modes of anti-market thought throughout this period. The growth of the opposite line of thought – a way of viewing the economy that saw stock speculation as beneficial to the nation – will be considered in section III.

I

Between 1790 and 1860, each decade saw a sharp increase in the number of business corporations in the United States, and in fact, with the probable exception of the 1820s, more businesses were chartered each decade than in any previous decade. After chartering 33 business corporations between 1781 and 1790, the states and federal government chartered 295 more in the 1790s.[1] The rate of growth thereafter can be suggested with a few examples. The six New England states incorporated business enterprises at the following rate:[2]

1800–17	849
1818–30	873
1831–43	1,456
1844–62	3,533

---

[1] Joseph Stancliffe Davis, *Essays in the Earlier History of American Corporations* (Cambridge, MA: Harvard University Press, 1917), II, 24.

[2] William C. Kessler, "Incorporation in New England: A Statistical Study, 1800–1875," *Journal of Economic History* 8 (1948): 46.

Table 6.1 *New business corporations*

	N.Y.	Penn.	N.J.	Md.	Wis.	Ohio
1801–10	218	71	40	31		8
1811–20	392	213	67	87		51
1821–30	378	144	76	77		58
1831–40	559	420	181	182	33	423
1841–50		431	206	227	56	558
1851–60		1,041	579	497	463	

A similar increase can be found in every state in which new business corporations have been counted – New York, Pennsylvania, New Jersey, Maryland, Wisconsin, and Ohio (see table 6.1).[3]

The south most likely lagged behind the north and the west in the number of business corporations chartered, although similar data have not been gathered for the states south of Maryland.

In the early part of the century, many of these corporations were organized to build a single local transportation project – a bridge, a small canal, a short turnpike, and so on – and their shares were thus unlikely to be traded by anyone outside the limited geographical area served by the project.[4] But even this kind of stock could migrate farther. An anonymous 1806 writer, for example, urged New York City investors to buy shares of turnpikes located far upstate, as a way of speculating on

[3] Information for New York and Ohio is from George Herberton Evans, Jr., *Business Incorporations in the United States 1800–1943* (New York: National Bureau of Economic Research, 1948), 12; for Pennsylvania from William Miller, "A Note on the History of Business Corporations in Pennsylvania, 1800–1860," *Quarterly Journal of Economics* 55 (1940): 155; for New Jersey from John W. Cadman, Jr., *The Corporation in New Jersey: Business and Politics, 1791–1875* (Cambridge, MA: Harvard University Press, 1949), 206–08, 443; for Maryland from Joseph G. Blandi, *Maryland Business Corporations 1783–1852* (Baltimore: Johns Hopkins Press, 1934), 14; and for Wisconsin from George J. Kuehnl, *The Wisconsin Business Corporation* (Madison: University of Wisconsin Press, 1959), 14–17, 143. The data for New York cut off after 1845. For Maryland, the data cut off after 1852; the last figure for Maryland is thus for the period 1841–52, not 1841–50. The data for Wisconsin begin in 1836, when Wisconsin became a territory; the first figure for Wisconsin is thus for 1836–40, not 1831–40. Miller's study of Pennsylvania mildly understates the growth rate in the number of business corporations, because it only includes special charters granted by the Pennsylvania legislature, not corporations formed under general incorporation laws. There were only two of these laws passed in Pennsylvania during the relevant period, both of which were limited to specific industries. Miller, "A Note on the History," 153 n.1.

[4] See James Willard Hurst, *The Legitimacy of the Business Corporation in the Law of the United States 1780–1970* (Charlottesville: University Press of Virginia, 1970), 17; Ronald E. Seavoy, *The Origins of the American Business Corporation, 1784–1855* (Westport: Greenwood Press, 1982), 39–46; Oscar Handlin and Mary F. Handlin, "Origins of the American Business Corporation," *Journal of Economic History* 5 (1945): 22.

the growth of "the commerce of our interior."[5] And many of the earlier corporations were banks and insurance companies, larger enterprises whose shares were bought and sold by a wider segment of the population.[6] Of the twenty-eight business corporations with share prices publicly quoted in New York in 1820, ten were banks and eighteen were marine and fire insurance companies.[7]

Manufacturing enterprises formed a larger percentage of business corporations as the century progressed. So did railroads, the share prices of which were first publicly quoted in New York in 1830. By 1840, share prices of 112 business corporations were quoted in New York, including thirteen railroads.[8] Although the corporate form remained unusual for commercial enterprises until the middle of the century – most businesses, even the largest, were still partnerships – the amount of corporate stock in circulation in the United States grew steadily over the first half of the century.[9] New issues of stock were marketed to the public by stockbrokers, by commercial banks, and by wealthy individuals; there would be no investment banks specializing in this function until the 1850s.[10]

The amount of government debt securities in existence rose and fell with the size of government debt. The federal goverment's debt fluctuated around $80 million from its inception until the later years of Jefferson's presidency, when the efforts of Jefferson and Treasury Secretary Albert Gallatin to retire the debt began achieving their goal.[11] The federal debt hit a low of $45 million in 1812, then war expenditures lifted it to its pre-Civil War peak of $127 million in 1816. It then declined steadily, nearly to zero in the mid-1830s, before rising again to fluctuate between $28 million and $68 million in the 1850s.[12] State governments issued a large amount of debt securities as well, par-

---

[5] *Observations on the Real, Relative and Market Value, of the Turnpike Stock of the State of New-York* (New York: S. Gould, 1806), 15.

[6] Joseph Edward Hedges, *Commercial Banking and the Stock Market Before 1863* (Baltimore: Johns Hopkins Press, 1938), 32.

[7] Werner and Smith, *Wall Street*, 158. The early insurance companies sold marine and fire insurance; life insurance barely existed in the United States until the 1840s. Viviana A. Rotman Zelizer, *Morals and Markets: The Development of Life Insurance in the United States* (New York: Columbia University Press, 1979).

[8] Werner and Smith, *Wall Street*, 158–59.

[9] Alfred D. Chandler, Jr., *The Visible Hand: The Managerial Revolution in American Business* (Cambridge, MA: Harvard University Press, 1977), 36.

[10] Vincent P. Carosso, *Investment Banking in America: A History* (Cambridge, MA: Harvard University Press, 1970), 1–10.

[11] Sloan, *Principle and Interest*, 194–200; Raymond Walters, Jr., *Albert Gallatin: Jeffersonian Financier and Diplomat* (New York: Macmillan, 1957), 145–46.

[12] United States Bureau of the Census, *Historical Statistics of the United States* (Washington: Government Printing Office, 1975), II, 1118.

ticularly during the 1820s and 1830s as a means of financing internal improvements.[13] As of 1838, for example, all but a few of the states had issued debt, and the value of outstanding state debt securities exceeded $141 million.[14] That figure passed $200 million in the 1850s, and by 1860 reached $257 million.[15]

The composition of the American securities market thus turned upside-down over the first half of the nineteenth century. The market was dominated by federal government debt at the century's beginning. In 1803, according to Samuel Blodget, the amount of federal government debt outstanding was nearly twice the amount of publicly-traded corporate stock.[16] That same year, there were four issues of federal government debt with prices quoted in New York, and only eight business corporations.[17] When one spoke of the stock market in 1800, one was speaking of a market primarily in the securities of the federal government. But by the middle of the century, the market was dominated by shares of business enterprises. Corporate stock constituted over 11 percent of the wealth of a national sample of wealthy decedents in the years around 1850, or six times what the comparable percentage had been around 1800, and nearly three times the 1850 level of ownership of government debt securities.[18] The New York newspapers quoted prices of 112 corporations in 1840, as compared with only five issues of government debt (four states and one municipality).[19] By mid century, the stock market served to finance business enterprises much more than governments.

The "market" existed in an abstract sense all over the country, wherever investors bought and sold securities. It had a more concrete

[13] Harry N. Scheiber, *Ohio Canal Era: A Case Study of Government and the Economy, 1820–1861* (Athens: Ohio University Press, 1969), 371–79; Nathan Miller, *The Enterprise of a Free People: Aspects of Economic Development in New York State during the Canal Period, 1792–1838* (Ithaca: Cornell University Press, 1962), 81–111; Margaret G. Myers, *The New York Money Market* (New York: Columbia University Press, 1931), I, 20–21; Ralph W. Hidy, *The House of Baring in American Trade and Finance* (Cambridge, MA: Harvard University Press, 1949), 150–54.

[14] Fritz Redlich, *The Molding of American Banking* (New York: Hafner, 1951), II, 325–26.

[15] B. U. Ratchford, *American State Debts* (Durham: Duke University Press, 1941), 127.

[16] Samuel Blodget, *Economica: A Statistical Manual for the United States of America* (1806) (New York: A. M. Kelley, 1964), 198. Blodget's estimate is of the amount of stock in the Bank of the United States, state banks, insurance companies, turnpikes, and canals. The comparison in the text assumes that most of this stock was publicly traded; if not, the public debt becomes an even more prominent feature of the market.

[17] Werner and Smith, *Wall Street*, 158.

[18] James Lester Sturm, *Investing in the United States 1798–1893: Upper Wealth-Holders in a Market Economy* (New York: Arno Press, 1977), 50–51. Sturm does not distinguish government debt from corporate debt, of which there was much by 1850, so the relative prominence of corporate over government securities was even larger in 1850.

[19] Werner and Smith, *Wall Street*, 159.

presence in the largest commercial cities, especially New York and to a lesser extent Boston and Philadelphia, where communities of brokers and speculators dealt regularly with one another, on the newly formed stock exchanges and in unorganized transactions on the street and in coffee houses.[20] Trading among these regulars quickly became routinized; the New York brokers, for instance, used preprinted contracts to document their transactions, on which one only had to write the date, the name of the corporation, the number of shares, the price, the buyer, the seller, and number of days within which delivery was nominally required.[21] The organized segment of the market remained small throughout the first half of the century. The most informed attempt to estimate the size of the New York market concludes that in the 1820s and 1830s the volume of trading on the stock exchange was only one-third of the volume of trading conducted outside the exchange.[22] That estimate only includes off-exchange trading in corporations located in the city of New York; the percentage of securities transactions nationwide conducted outside an exchange was surely even larger than that.

Participation in the market, although of course heavily weighted in favor of the wealthy, was nonetheless widespread.[23] Foreign travellers in the United States frequently remarked on Americans' "rage for bank-stock" and for "[s]peculations in railroads."[24] "[E]ven the sober citizen of Boston," Hugh Murray reported back to Scotland, "is too apt to rush into perilous and daring enterprises." Americans "delight to feel themselves moving on a vast sea of speculation."[25] The United States, in the view of the English novelist and naval officer Frederick Marryat, presented a scene "of much over-speculation."[26] As the French consul in San Francisco put it in 1849, the "Yankee is a stockjobber by nature."[27]

---

[20] Herman E. Krooss, "Financial Institutions," in David T. Gilchrist, ed., *The Growth of the Seaport Cities 1790–1825* (Charlottesville: University Press of Virginia, 1967), 105–07.

[21] Box labelled "Bleecker Mss. – Misc.," unmarked folder, James W. Bleecker papers, NYHS.

[22] Werner and Smith, *Wall Street*, 168–69.

[23] Edward Pessen, *Riches, Class, and Power Before the Civil War* (Lexington: D.C. Heath, 1973), 35.

[24] Michel Chevalier, *Society, Manners and Politics in the United States* (1839) (New York: A.M. Kelley, 1966), 307–08.

[25] Hugh Murray, *The United States of America* (Edinburgh: Oliver & Boyd, 1844), III, 1819.

[26] Frederick Marryat, *Diary in America* (1839), ed. Jules Zanger (Bloomington: Indiana University Press, 1960), 137.

[27] Quoted in John M. Findlay, *People of Chance: Gambling in American Society from Jamestown to Las Vegas* (New York: Oxford University Press, 1986), 102.

Foreign visitors sought various explanations for why Americans seemed so prone to speculation in commercial enterprises. Tocqueville attributed it to the form of government, which he thought acclimated citizens to risk. "Those who live in the midst of democratic fluctuations," he suggested,

have always before their eyes the image of chance; and they end by liking all undertakings in which chance plays a part. They are therefore all led to engage in commerce, not only for the sake of the profit it holds out to them, but for the love of the constant excitement occasioned by that pursuit.[28]

Francis Grund, from Vienna, believed that Americans simply had a stronger desire than Europeans to make money, and that they were accordingly more willing to take risks to do so. "An American carries the spirit of invention even to the counting-room," Grund explained.

He is constantly discovering some new sources of trade, and is always willing to risk his capital and credit on some *terra incognita*, rather than follow the beaten track of others, and content himself with such profits as are realised by his competitors. This is undoubtedly the cause of a great number of unfortunate speculations and subsequent failures; but it constitutes also the technical superiority of the American merchant over the European . . . The ordinary routine of business is not sufficient to ensure his success; he must think, invent, speculate; for it is more by ingenuity and foresight, than by the regular pursuit of trade, that he can hope to realise a fortune.[29]

The French traveller Michel Chevalier chalked it up to a restrictive social order, which left stock speculation as one of the few approved means of having fun.

Public opinion and pulpit forbid sensual gratifications, wine, women, and the display of a princely luxury; cards and dice are equally prohibited; the American, therefore, has recourse to business for the strong emotions which he requires to make him feel life. He launches with delight into the ever-moving sea of speculation.[30]

Whatever the cause, foreign writers were unanimous in finding great interest in stock speculation in the early nineteenth-century United States.

Americans often identified the same trait among themselves. "The people of the United States, are a race of men having few, if any equals in the world," began an anonymous New York opponent of corporations. "But they have their foibles. They cannot harden their hearts

[28] Alexis de Tocqueville, *Democracy in America* (1st American edn 1840), ed. Phillips Bradley (New York: A.A. Knopf, 1976), II, 156.
[29] Francis J. Grund, *The Americans in Their Moral, Social, and Political Relations* (1837) (New York: Johnson Reprint Corp., 1968), 241.
[30] Chevalier, *Society*, 309.

against the seductions of SPECULATION. At that magic word, their eyes begin to sparkle."[31] Ralph Waldo Emerson famously complained in 1843 of "the downward tendency and proneness of things, when every voice is raised for a new road or another statute or a subscription of stock."[32] An 1835 newspaper reported that across the country "small tradesmen, shopkeepers, clerks of all degrees, operatives of town and country, members of the learned professions, students in the offices, beginners in the world without capital, or with a little, all frequent the exchanges."[33] A few years later, an anonymous poet observed, with reference to speculation in bank stock, that

> Tho' Politicians foam and rage
> 'Tis but the "Spirit of the age."[34]

"Commerce and speculation have been spreading of late like a card house," the New York lawyer George Templeton Strong wrote in his diary during the depression of 1837.[35] "The brandy of bubbling speculation has stupefied our reason, and *delirium tremens* has overtaken the nation!" exclaimed George Francis Train during the next depression, that of 1857. "Everybody has gone joint-stock mad!"[36]

Even people who were not personally involved in the market were likely to know something about it. By the middle of the century it was not uncommon for works of fiction to include derogatory references to the market.[37] In Hawthorne's *House of the Seven Gables* (1851), for instance, the cold, selfish Judge Pyncheon enjoys nothing more than "his railroad, bank, and insurance shares, his United States stock, his wealth, in short, however invested."[38] In Melville's *Moby-Dick* (1851), Ishmael observes that "[m]en may seem as detestable as joint stock-

---

[31] *Letter, on the Use and Abuse of Incorporations* (New York: G. & C. Carvill, 1827), 23.

[32] Ralph Waldo Emerson, "The Transcendentalist" (1843), in Brooks Atkinson, ed., *The Complete Essays and Other Writings of Ralph Waldo Emerson* (New York: Random House, 1950), 103.

[33] Quoted in Elizabeth Johns, *American Genre Painting: The Politics of Everyday Life* (New Haven: Yale University Press, 1991), 40.

[34] *Humbugs of Speculation, A Satirical Poem, Embracing Several Historical Sketches of Speculative Operations, National and Individual, During the Last Four Years* (Saratoga Springs: Whig Office, 1840), 11.

[35] Allan Nevins and Milton Halsey Thomas, eds., *The Diary of George Templeton Strong* (New York: Macmillan, 1952), I, 65.

[36] George Francis Train, *Young America in Wall Street* (London: S. Low, 1857), xi–xii.

[37] Wayne W. Westbrook, *Wall Street in the American Novel* (New York: New York University Press, 1980), 10–12. On the similar phenomenon in England, see Raymond L. Baubles, Jr., "Finance and Folly: The Speculative Investor in Nineteenth-Century British History and Literature" (Fordham University Ph.D. dissertation 1993).

[38] Nathaniel Hawthorne, *The House of the Seven Gables* (1851) (New York: Viking Press, 1983), 583; Peter Buitenhuis, *The House of the Seven Gables: Severing Family and Colonial Ties* (Boston: Twayne Publishers, 1991), 102–03.

companies."[39] One of the characters giving rise to the title of Melville's *Confidence-Man* (1857) sells stock that is apparently worthless.[40] The *New-York Literary Gazette* published a short piece of humor in 1839 that seems to presuppose readers' familiarity with financial jargon, as it would hardly be comprehensible otherwise. Captioned "Wall Street," the piece read:

State of the Market. – The Board of Brokers is shaved very thin, and its condition now is nearly transparent. Our current notes are uncurrent; and are now oftener counted than discounted. Brokers are now breakers, and many a floating capital has been sunk in them. It was proposed at a meeting of merchants yesterday, that a petition should be presented to the Common Council, for changing the first letter in the name of the street, from a W. to an F.[41]

The same presupposition that the audience would be familiar with the market can be inferred from a pair of 1849 Currier & Ives prints. In the first, captioned *Stocks Up*, a smiling well-dressed investor holds a sheet of paper bearing the words "Sales at the Stock Exchange" above a list that begins "U.S. Treasury &c. &c. &c." – that is, a list of safe federal government securities. In the second, captioned *Stocks Down*, an angry and desperate speculator tears at his hair, while holding a sheet of paper entitled "The Art of Making a Fortune in 2 Hours. Inquire at Mr. [blank] No. [blank] Wall St. . . . If not in apply at the Lunatic Asylum." Beneath the title is a list of ten corporations, the stock in most of which was notoriously risky and had suffered sharp drops in value. The list is headed by the Morris Canal, perhaps the most well known such enterprise of the day.[42] Currier & Ives could hardly have expected this pair of prints to be profitable unless they could expect a large proportion of their public to know the subject.

Many Americans in the first half of the nineteenth century were buying and selling securities, mostly government debt in the early years, and mostly corporate shares later. Many more, so far as one can infer today, knew enough about the market to be able to form an opinion of it.

---

[39] Herman Melville, *Moby-Dick* (1851) (London: Penguin Books, 1986), 211. There is a more ambiguous reference earlier in the book, when Ishmael imagines Queequeg saying to himself: "It's a mutual, joint-stock world, in all meridians. We cannibals must help these Christians." Ibid., 157.

[40] Herman Melville, *The Confidence-Man* (1857) (Oxford: Oxford University Press, 1991), 26–28, 72–73.

[41] *New-York Literary Gazette*, July 13, 1839, I, 192.

[42] Harry T. Peters, *Currier & Ives: Printmakers to the American People* (Garden City: Doubleday, Doran & Co., 1942), plate 174.

II

"Wall-street! Who shall fathom the depth and the rottenness of thy mysteries?"[43] So asked a New York journalist in the 1840s, launching into a diatribe that drew upon some widely shared attitudes toward securities trading, especially as conducted by the speculators in the largest cities. The anti-market thought inherited from eighteenth-century England, and reformulated in the United States after the crash of 1792, remained fixed in American culture through the middle of the nineteenth century. In the view of many observers, securities trading was inordinately deceitful, it was a non-productive activity diverting time and money from more useful pursuits, and it corroded the nation's political structure. As the composition of the market shifted over the first half of the century, however, and as conventional objects of concern changed over the same period, the last argument – the fear of the market's political effects – underwent slow but unmistakable transformations. The South Sea Bubble, meanwhile, continued to live in popular memory as a warehouse of contradictory lessons to be drawn about the dangers of too much speculation.

Deceit

One strand of thought that had not changed since the late seventeenth century was the popular conception of the securities market as a home to "the most detestable and enormous frauds."[44] The ordinary transaction, one author suggested, involved "the owner of shares in doubtful banks," whose object was to sell them by deceiving the unsophisticated as to their value. "Let us find his dupes," he continued. One was "an honest mechanic," who thereby lost all his hard-earned savings. "A woman with her money in that safe and thrifty institution the Saving's Bank, is another victim," tricked into giving up the only cushion between comfort and destitution.[45] "Stock-jobbing, that modern trade," complained the scientist William Maclure, was "founded on lying, deceit and swindling."[46] On Wall Street, agreed *Holden's Dollar Magazine*, "[w]hat is usually called 'making money' in nine cases out of

---

[43] George G. Foster, *New York in Slices: By an Experienced Carver* (New York: W. F. Burgess, 1848), 16.

[44] William Findley, *A Review of the Revenue System* (Philadelphia: T. Dobson, 1794), 52.

[45] *Three Degrees of Banking: or The Romance of Trade* (Boston: Weeks, Jordan, 1838), 102–03.

[46] William Maclure, *Opinions on Various Subjects* (1838) (New York: A.M. Kelley, 1971), III, 94.

ten is nothing more than legally stealing it."[47] The *New York Times* likewise lamented the "positive dishonesty engendered and fostered in this country by our theory and practice of joint stock companies."[48]

Because of all the deceit in the market, stock trading was understood as a means for rich and powerful insiders to prey upon weaker outsiders. The 1805 allegory *The Changery* featured "an adroit speculator, long actuated by the principle, that *might* supercedes *right*."[49] Even the sale of stock in new enterprises was slanted in favor of the rich, charged the newspaper editor William Leggett: "Large capitalists get all the stock they ask for, and poor men get but a part, if any, that they solicit."[50] The "sumptuous living" of powerful insiders "is chiefly supported from the losses of outside speculators," an 1853 critic noticed. "It is needless to theorize," he wryly added, "upon the causes which leave the whole burden of loss upon the casual dealer in stocks, or to except the few who have made a fortunate 'turn' and escaped unscathed."[51] The minister and educator Francis Wayland accordingly advised "the uninitiated" to be "careful how they speculate in stocks."[52]

One way insiders could take advantage of outside investors, it was often argued, was by keeping them uninformed of the underlying value of their investment. John O'Connor, a stockholder in the Hope Insurance Company in the 1820s, drafted a circular to his "fellow sufferer[s]" castigating "the scandalous mismanagement of the President & Board of Directors." Two years earlier, O'Connor complained,

the Hope Insurance Company ceased to pay any Dividends, notwithstanding that during all this time we were assured that the Office had a "*very great run of business*," and that they often "*marked off daily very large sums for earned premiums*;" – and that the surplus remaining in 1823 from the earnings of past years, was very large & rapidly accumulating. Such were the reports circulated & believed; and in consequence of which the stock rose to 123 per cent; at which price, or thereabouts, many of you unfortunately purchased. *What is now the state of this Stock?* It is not worth in the market 60 per cent; and to this enormous fall is to be added the Loss of 14 per cent for two Years' Interest: so that the unfortunate stockholder who is obliged to sell, loses 80 per cent of his capital; and his feelings are aggravated by the refusal of the President & Directors to make a statement of the situation of the Company, & by the most impertinent

---

[47] "Wall Street Operations," *Holden's Dollar Magazine*, June 1849, 380.

[48] "Our Commerce and Our Corporations," *New York Times*, Jan. 13, 1859, 4.

[49] *The Changery. An Allegoric Memoir of the Boston Exchange Office* (Boston: s.n., 1805), 26.

[50] Theodore Sedgwick, ed., *A Collection of the Political Writings of William Leggett* (New York: Taylor & Dodd, 1840), I, 88.

[51] Quoted in Herman E. Krooss and Martin R. Blyn, *A History of Financial Intermediaries* (New York: Random House, 1971), 85.

[52] Quoted in Joseph Dorfman, *The Economic Mind in American Civilization* (New York: Viking Press, 1946–59), II, 764.

denials of information as to the state of his property; as if they were the proprietors & *not the servants* of the Company!

And there was more. "[I]n addition to the intolerable injustice & insolence of refusing to inform the Stockholders yearly or *half-yearly* of the state of their property," O'Connor added, the directors' failure to provide shareholders with information about the company "affords opportunities to the members of the Direction to speculate on the Stock." By "thus availing themselves of information obtained in their capacity as official servants," he concluded, the directors of the Hope Insurance Company were able "to grow rich at the expence of the uninformed stockholders."[53] The political economist Daniel Raymond agreed. The directors of corporations, he argued, "endeavour to keep the stockholders and the public in the dark respecting the condition of the corporation, while they are themselves in the light. . . . They make no exhibit to the stockholders of the actual condition of the company."[54]

Because "the price of Bank stock in the market is regulated principally by the rate of dividends,"[55] the directors' power to set dividends enabled them to control the flow of information reaching the public, and thus the price of shares. "The more substantial citizens still showed little disposition to touch the stock," ran one satirical account of a fraudulent new bank, "but when at the end of six months, the bank declared a dividend of ten per cent., they became so eager to bite, that [the promoter's] first impulse was to sell all out, and let them have the whole concern to themselves."[56] Even the shares of a bank that earned no profits could for a time trade at a high price, observed Treasury official William Gouge, because the directors could continue to declare dividends, and the lack of profits could "be concealed from all but the Directors."[57] A Cambridge professor visiting the United States heard an anecdote that he took to be representative of "a more general feeling." An Englishman of his acquaintance

was conversing with an American on the subject of a factory he had just set up; when a suggestion was made to him that he should extend his views by engaging in a joint-stock company. "We can manage this matter easily among ourselves," – said he. "We can keep a committee of our own, and arrange it so as to keep

[53] "To the Stockholders of the Hope Insurance Company" (n.d.), John M. O'Connor papers, NYHS, 1–3.

[54] Daniel Raymond, *The Elements of Constitutional Law and of Political Economy*, 4th edn (Baltimore: Cushing & Brother, 1840), 276.

[55] William M. Gouge, *A Short History of Paper Money and Banking in the United States* (Philadelphia: T.W. Ustick, 1833), 75.

[56] "Further Extracts from the Private Diary of a Certain Bank Director," *United States Magazine and Democratic Review*, December 1838, III, 368.

[57] Gouge, *Short History*, 76.

every thing in our own hands. If we succeed, we can declare a low dividend, and so buy in shares for ourselves as they fall; – if things do not go on well, we can pursue an opposite course, and adjudge high dividends, so as to raise our stock in the market, and keep ourselves afloat."[58]

The only solution, in O'Connor's view, would be a new statute requiring "That every incorporated Company shall *quarterly* or *semi-annually* lay before its Stockholders & the public a *full & exact* state of its affairs."[59] Raymond favored a similar regulatory scheme: "every charter ought to provide that a statement or balance sheet shall be made out, at least once a year, showing the actual condition of the corporation, and this balance sheet ought to be accessible to all the stockholders."[60] Such generally applicable regulation would not exist in the United States for another century. In the meantime, stockholders had to take matters into their own hands. "Ask for the accounts," advised another critic of corporate directors. "You have certainly a right to inquire about investing your own money. Don't be afraid of great men; you have as much right to talk as they."[61]

Another occasion on which the rich and powerful could deceive the uninitiated, as it had been since the 1690s, was the sale of stock in new companies. The process, as one outsider saw it, looked like this,

the stock is puffed up like an empty bladder – divers beggars get on horseback – divers men swell out to the dimensions of a *plum* – and the miserable sinners, who are unacquainted with the secret of labouring thus successfully – for the public good, – are obliged to scamper across Broadway, to escape the whirling career of some gilded equipage – spanking new, in which sits lolling for the fleeting moment some kite-flying director, plumed with the spoils of thousands.[62]

"The whole art of stock-jobbing," William Maclure concluded, "is a play on the timidity and gullibility of mankind."[63]

All this deceit and abuse of power was possible, it was widely understood, because speculators had the power to manipulate stock prices. "Sometimes the funds of a Bank," Gouge charged, "are employed in purchasing its stock," as a means of bidding up the stock price. When the price became "sufficiently high, those who have the management contrive to sell their own shares." Such a scheme had been implemented in 1826, according to Gouge, in the shares of the Franklin Bank of New York. "When an investigation was made of the affairs of the Bank, in

---

[58] E.S. Abdy, *Journal of a Residence and Tour in the United States of North America* (London: J. Murray, 1835), II, 42–43.
[59] "Hope Insurance Company," 3.   [60] Raymond, *Elements*, 276.
[61] Train, *Young America*, 213.   [62] *Letter, on the Use and Abuse*, 11.
[63] Maclure, *Opinions*, III, 229.

1828, it was found there was not enough left to pay the remaining stockholders 50 cents in a dollar."[64] But one did not have to be involved in management to influence the price of stock. Stocks could be "inflated, by the progress of bubble-blowing, to prices double and quadruple those of the previous week."[65] Speculators, claimed John Calhoun on the floor of the Senate, were able to "live by raising and depressing stocks" at their pleasure.[66] By concerted buying or selling, or by the dissemination of false information about a company, acknowledged the economist Henry Vethake, "an artificial value may be given to the stock for a comparatively short time," long enough for the speculator to make his profit.[67]

This understanding of the market was so strong that it often colored interpretations of contemporary events. When George Templeton Strong learned by telegraph of "another calamitous fire in San Francisco" in 1851, his first reaction was to assume that the news was "invented by the bull operators of the Exchange."[68] The successes of Jacob Little, one of the most famous stock speculators of the first half of the century, were mockingly described in one labor-oriented newspaper as having been earned "by *fortunate* speculation."[69] The *New York Times* opined in 1859 that the stock prices of the previous year "are traceable rather to what may be styled the sympathetic action of the Brokers' Board, than to any external causes whatever." The recent course of prices "cannot be reasonably traced to the legitimate operation of legitimate influences."[70] A year later, when prices were down again, the *Times* repeatedly rejected the hypothesis that investors were anticipating the economic effects of the threatened secession of the southern states. Again, a drop in the market could more plausibly be attributed to price manipulation on the part of speculators.[71]

A scene in *The Confidence-Man* suggests that Melville could assume at mid century that his readers shared this conception of the stock market as susceptible to manipulation. In a conversation about a recent fall in the price of shares in a coal company, Melville places speculators within

[64] Gouge, *Short History*, 76.   [65] Nevins, ed., *Diary of Philip Hone*, 707.

[66] Clyde N. Wilson, ed., *The Papers of John C. Calhoun* (Columbia: University of South Carolina Press, 1959–), xiii, 217; see also ibid., xii, 219.

[67] Henry Vethake, *The Principles of Political Economy*, 2nd edn (Philadelphia: J. W. Moore, 1844), 184.

[68] Nevins and Thomas, eds., *Diary of George Templeton Strong*, ii, 59.

[69] "Extensive Robbery in Wall Street," *Young America*, Jan. 10, 1846, 2.

[70] "Stocks and Their Values," *New York Times*, June 4, 1859, 4.

[71] "Capital and Disunion," *New York Times*, Oct. 23, 1860, 4; "Operators for a Panic in Stocks," *New York Times*, Oct. 22, 1860, 4; "Wanted – A First-Rate Panic!," *New York Times*, Oct. 10, 1860, 4.

a larger class of people who spread bad news for personal gain, thereby secretly profiting from the very thing that causes loss to others.

"Your statement," he added, "tells a very fine story; but pray, was not your stock a little heavy a while ago? downward tendency? Sort of low spirits among holders on the subject of that stock?"

"Yes, there was a depression. But how came it? who devised it? The 'bears,' sir. The depression of our stock was solely owing to the growling, the hypocritical growling, of the bears."

"How, hypocritical?"

"Why, the most monstrous of all hypocrites are these bears: hypocrites by inversion; hypocrites in the simulation of things dark instead of bright; souls that thrive, less upon depression, than the fiction of depression; professors of the wicked art of manufacturing depressions; spurious Jeremiahs; sham Heraclituses, who, the lugubrious day done, return, like sham Lazaruses among the beggars, to make merry over the gains got by their pretended sore heads – scoundrelly bears!"

"You are warm against these bears?"

"If I am, it is less from the remembrance of their strategems as to our stock, than from the persuasion that these same destroyers of confidence, and gloomy philosophers of the stock-market, though false in themselves, are yet true types of most destroyers of confidence the world over. Fellows who, whether in stocks, politics, bread-stuffs, morals, metaphysics, religion – be it what it may – trump up their black panics in the naturally quiet brightness, solely with a view to some sort of covert advantage."[72]

This passage would have made no sense unless mid-nineteenth-century readers came to it with the belief that stock price declines often reflected the machinations of speculators rather than the fortunes of the underlying company, and that speculators often made money by manipulating prices.[73]

All this deceit and manipulation meant that for many Americans there was something unsavory about the securities market. "It does not at all add to the business credit or reputation of a mercantile man to be known as an operator in stocks," William Armstrong cautioned in 1848.[74] The editor of the *New-York Examiner* put it more sarcastically: "to be esteemed a shrewd and successful financier, the prerequisite of having been a great Stock Jobbing Company, or Government thief, is quite a recommendation."[75] The stock speculator was widely perceived

---

[72] Melville, *The Confidence-Man*, 62–63.
[73] Richard Boyd Hauck, *A Cheerful Nihilism: Confidence and "The Absurd" in American Humorous Fiction* (Bloomington: Indiana University Press, 1971), 119; Susan Kuhlmann, *Knave, Fool, and Genius: The Confidence Man as He Appears in Nineteenth-Century American Fiction* (Chapel Hill: University of North Carolina Press, 1973), 111.
[74] Armstrong, *Stocks and Stock-Jobbing*, 7–8.
[75] C. Glen Peebles, *Exposé of the Atlantic & Pacific Railroad Company* (New York: s.n., 1854), 4.

as a confidence man, both distasteful and fascinating at the same time.[76] George Francis Train could expect a sympathetic ear when he asked "Don't you think it would be a good move to sink Wall-street; explode the Brokers' Board; and kill every 'Bull' and 'Bear' in the country?"[77]

Non-productivity

When the market was dominated by federal government debt, and while the public finance controversies of the early 1790s were still fresh, there remained strong disagreement with Hamilton's conception (discussed in chapter 4) of the public debt as an effective substitute for money. "It is evident that transferred stock has not supplied the place of money in promoting manufactures or agriculture," urged William Findley in 1794. "Nay its effects have been the very reverse, for those who might otherwise have purchased, and improved lands, built houses, established manufactures or lent their money on interest to such as would have applied it to these purposes, have vested their money in the funds." The result was to divert scarce capital from productive to non-productive use. "This wealth being in a few hands and not used in active industry," Findley concluded, "the mass of the people in these states are not enriched by it."[78]

In later years, as the shares of business corporations became more widely traded than government debt, the non-productivity argument was transferred to corporate stock. Some of the early American political economists argued that much of the capital invested in the shares of corporations was in effect lost to the productive economy. "[A]ll money corporations, are detrimental to national wealth," Daniel Raymond explained in the 1820s.[79] Money invested in commerce, "which consists in the distribution of materials to the manufacturer, or goods to the consumer," was put to productive use. But money put into speculation, "which consists barely in changing the right to property, without moving the property itself, cannot benefit the community."[80] As John McVickar saw it, most uses of capital added to the productivity of labor, and thus contributed to the national wealth. But not "home speculation, in which, as the wealth of the country merely changes hands, the profits are but the criterion of a rising market, since such accumulation would have taken place had the commodity continued in the hands of its

[76] Gary Lindberg, *The Confidence Man in American Literature* (New York: Oxford University Press, 1982), 205–07. See also Warwick Wadlington, *The Confidence Game in American Literature* (Princeton: Princeton University Press, 1975), 3–23.

[77] Train, *Young America*, 250.   [78] Findley, *Review*, 37, 39.

[79] Raymond, *Elements*, II, 119.   [80] Ibid., I, 228.

original holders." A profitable corporation would add to the sum of the country's assets, but that would be true whether or not its stock was transferred from one person to another; share price rises attributable to transfers thus had no correspondence to any gain in real wealth. "Such transfers, therefore," McVickar concluded, "have no influence on national prosperity."[81]

The existence of a market for corporate stock further drained wealth from the nation, many contemporaries argued, by transferring it from those who would use it productively to those who would not. The net result of corporations, William Maclure suggested, was to move "property from the pockets of the industrious to the pockets of the idle and dissipated."[82] Stephen Simpson analogized stockholders to armies; both were groups that "commit wasteful consumption, and producing nothing in return, afflict a country with privation and want."[83] So long as corporations existed, argued Theophilus Fisk, "those who work and save will have their earnings wrested from them by partial legislation, to be given to those who never earned a dollar in their lives."[84] The nation would be enriched if productive workers could keep the fruits of their labor, because such workers were likely to spend their money in productive ways. But corporate stock was a device by which workers were forced to give up part of their gains to passive non-productive investors. Daniel Raymond put the point most clearly: "A man who has invested a thousand dollars in stock," he explained, "which yields six per cent interest, has acquired a power, in addition to his natural power, of compelling somebody to labor for him, to the amount of sixty dollars a year."[85] That sixty dollars was in effect confiscated from the class of workers, and reallocated to "a non-producing class of consumers."[86]

Corporate stock, like government debt, thus diverted the nation's capital from productive to non-productive uses. The point was made by ordinary observers, people who did not hold themselves out as economists, on both a large and a small scale. One could see this non-productivity if one considered the economy as a whole. "The business of trading and jobbing in stocks," Francis Grund advised, "may in many instances prove a serious injury to commerce. It may absorb a

---

[81] John Ramsay McCulloch, *Outlines of Political Economy*, ed. John McVickar (New York: Wilder & Campbell, 1825), 90–91 n.*. The quoted material is from editorial notes written by McVickar.

[82] Maclure, *Opinions*, III, 185.

[83] Stephen Simpson, *The Working Man's Manual: A New Theory of Political Economy* (Philadelphia: L.T. Bonsal, 1831), 218.

[84] Theophilus Fisk, *The Banking Bubble Burst* (Charleston: s.n., 1837), 22.

[85] Raymond, *Elements*, II, 336.   [86] Simpson, *Working Man's Manual*, 219.

large portion of the capital which would otherwise be invested in merchandise, and give a wrong direction to the national industry of the country."[87] Philadelphia banks were worth significantly less in 1841 than they had been worth three years earlier; it was "THE BUBBLE OF STOCK SPECULATION" that caused the loss, argued an Albany newspaper.[88] One could also see this non-productivity by looking at one individual at a time. The 1840 novel *Speculation* told the story of William Wilson, "the whistling shoemaker," who was gradually drawn deeper and deeper into speculation. He began to lose interest in his shoemaking trade, which he had formerly enjoyed (hence the whistling); "he dismissed his journeyman and boys, and his shop was hardly open during the week." He began to feel "not at all satisfied with himself . . . . He was restless and unhappy. . . . the days seemed very long and gloomy to him." Things grew so dark that he could not even read the Bible. It was only when Wilson lost all he had, and had to abandon his efforts to make money without working, that he remembered the virtues of "*patience, perseverance,* and *self-denial.*" Wilson resumed the productive work of a shoemaker, and, in the end, "there was joy throughout the village, when the fact was announced that a man in passing the shop had *heard William Wilson whistling!*"[89] Among the lessons to be drawn was that speculative investment only caused loss, whether material or spiritual, but that productive labor brought gain in both senses. "The highest ambition of the author," he explained in a preface, was "to exhibit to youth the tendency of the reckless spirit of speculation, which so thoroughly pervades all classes of people at the present day."[90]

If stock speculation was non-productive – if it amounted to a risky method of transferring assets from one person to another without adding to the sum total of those assets – then it was nothing more than a form of gambling, and it deserved condemnation for the same reason.[91] While the Lord had long been "gloriously rewarding the industrious" with material wealth, noted Mason Weems, "let us see what great things the Devil has been doing, all this time, for his good friends the GAMBLERS." The answer was evident in Weems' own home town – nothing. "Where are all your rent rolls and schedules," Weems mockingly asked the gamblers, "your town houses and country houses, your

---

[87] Grund, *Americans,* 243.   [88] *The Northern Light,* Sept. 1841, I, 96.
[89] *Speculation, or Making Haste to be Rich* (Boston: George W. Light, 1840), 64–65, 76, 80.
[90] Ibid., 1.
[91] Karen Halttunen, *Confidence Men and Painted Women: A Study of Middle-Class Culture in America, 1830–1870* (New Haven: Yale University Press, 1982), 17; John G. Cawelti, *Apostles of the Self-Made Man* (Chicago: University of Chicago Press, 1965), 49.

mortgages and mill-seats?"[92] Americans in the first half of the nineteenth century constantly associated the stock market with gambling. Losers in the market were "victims of Stock Gambling."[93] Corporate charters were granted to each "new company of scrip gamblers."[94] Speculators were "gamblers in stocks."[95] In the 1852 novel *The Upper Ten Thousand*, one character confesses to another that he "could never see much difference between a speculator in stocks and a gambler." The other responds: "Stock-jobbing is, as you say, only another sort of gambling."[96] In the downturn of the early 1830s, Andrew Jackson commented that "[t]he failures that are now taking place are amongst the stockjobbers, brokers, and gamblers, and would to God they were all swept from the land!"[97] Even when writers praised the stock market for facilitating investment in new enterprises, they were often careful to condemn "the gambling part of the affair."[98]

Opponents of gambling cast their net around stock market participants as well. "[I]s it unjust to punish the gambler with cards by imprisonment and public proscription," asked the anti-gambling zealot Jonathan Green, "while the gambler in stocks, &c., whose crime is the same in principle, though not in degree, goes unwhipt of justice?" Green had an answer: "Undoubtedly it is, for it is no reason that one vice should go unpunished, because another is able to escape for the present." His tactic was to mobilize public opinion against cardplaying first, in the expectation that people would soon realize that stock speculation was nearly as bad. Once everyone saw the evil in gambling generally, if "certain dealings in stocks . . . can be proved to be rightly described by the phrase 'GAMBLING in Stocks,' the battle is half-won."[99] Henry Ward Beecher told the young men of Indianapolis that "a Speculator on the exchange, and a Gambler at his table, follow one

[92] Mason Locke Weems, *God's Revenge Against Gambling*, 2nd edn (Philadelphia: M. L. Weems, 1812), 34.

[93] Armstrong, *Stocks*, 27.

[94] Sedgwick, ed., *Political Writings of William Leggett*, I, 248–49.

[95] Vethake, *Principles*, 184.

[96] C. Astor Bristed, *The Upper Ten Thousand* (New York: Stringer & Townsend, 1852), 164–65.

[97] Quoted in Bray Hammond, *Banks and Politics in America* (Princeton: Princeton University Press, 1957), 430.

[98] "The Joint-Stock Companies," *The Museum of Foreign Literature* 7 (1825): 154.

[99] Jonathan H. Green, *Secret Band of Brothers* (Philadelphia: T.B. Peterson and Bros., 1858), 212. See also Jonathan H. Green, *Green's Report, No. 1, on Gambling and Gambling Houses in New York* (New York: J.H. Green, 1851), 90, in which Green accuses "[o]ver three-quarters of the smaller exchange offices, out of Wall Street, and many in that headquarters of Mammon," as fronts for the sale of lottery tickets. On the career of Green, see Ann Fabian, *Card Sharps, Dream Books, & Bucket Shops: Gambling in 19th-Century America* (Ithaca: Cornell University Press, 1990), 59–107.

vocation, only with different instruments."[100] Another opponent cited the popularity of stock speculation as a product of the prevalence of gambling. "What wonder that gambling should become a matter of business," he asked, "with men who have long ago acquired a taste for games of chance as an amusement? Is it surprising that persons should resort to speculations and hazards, who have long found their greatest pleasure in watching and profiting by the caprices of fortune?"[101]

By the middle of the century, there was a considerable body of opinion treating the stock market as a casino. As the *New York Times* editorialized in the 1830s, "[t]he New York Stock Exchange as at present managed is little more than an enormous gambling establishment."[102] In his 1848 description of New York, George Foster apologized for failing to include Wall Street in a survey of the city's gambling houses. "It is true," he conceded, "that gambling is carried on as the chief business there; but it is upon so gigantic, so systematic a scale, that it reaches the dignity of history. It rather deserves a place in our history of revolutions."[103] "[T]he Board of Brokers," explained an anonymous satirist, "under the present severe laws against every other species of play, enjoys a monopoly of gambling."[104] Charles Francis Adams, Jr., concluded that "[t]he vast majority of stock operations are pure gambling transactions."[105] When stock was bought and sold, nothing was produced, no goods were brought any closer to the consumer, no workers were made more productive. Nothing was added to the national wealth.

Politics

The view that a public debt had anti-republican consequences, and the resulting association of securities trading with political corruption, remained strong through the end of the eighteenth century and the beginning of the nineteenth. "By these means," asserted William Findley in 1794, referring to the sale of shares in the public debt and the Bank of the United States, "an aristocracy formerly unknown in the United States, has been created." Findley carefully qualified his claim,

---

[100] Henry Ward Beecher, *Seven Lectures to Young Men, on Various Important Subjects* (Indianapolis: Thomas B. Culter, 1844), 53.

[101] *The Victims of Gaming* (Boston: Weeks, Jordan, 1838), 27.

[102] Quoted in Krooss and Blyn, *A History*, 85.

[103] Foster, *New York*, 16.

[104] "Autobiography of Ferret Snapp Newcraft, Esq.," *United States Magazine and Democratic Review*, May 1838, II, 176.

[105] Charles Francis Adams, Jr., *A Chapter of Erie* (Boston: Fields, Osgood, & Co., 1869), 6 n.*.

in light of the fact that some stockholders could hardly be said to belong to an aristocracy. "I do not mean by this, that every man who has a share in it is an aristocrat," he explained. "I speak of the tendency and spirit of the institution." But the eventual product of "perpetual loans and funding systems" was unmistakable; they "are fraught with seeds of corruption and cannot fail to produce undue influence and separate interest."[106] At a civic festival sponsored by the Democratic Society of Pennsylvania that same year, participants drank to a toast of "May every Free Nation consider a public debt as a public curse; and may the man who would assert a contrary opinion be considered as an enemy to his Country." Later that summer, on the eighteenth anniversary of independence, members of the Society drank to the "Public debt; May it be considered as the Charybdis of republicanism and the Scylla of virtue."[107] In Pittsburgh, meanwhile, a similar gathering resolved

that our councils want the integrity or spirit of Republicans. This we attribute to the pernicious influence of stockholders or their subordinates; and our minds feel this with so much indignancy, that we are almost ready to wish for a state of revolution, and the guillotine of France, for a short space, in order to inflict punishment on the miscreants that enervate and disgrace our Government.[108]

The Massachusetts farmer William Manning despaired of "Speculators, Stock & Land Jobers," a group who "by their bribery & corruption have grate influence in our elections, & agitate our publick Counsels." And that was "not halfe the dammages of the funding Sistim," because its "real intent is to make places for numerous sets of Officers with high saliryes."[109] Opponents had not forgotten that "[t]he funding law past through congress by the influence of a majority, who purchased certificates from the army at an under value; and who voted for the law, with the single view of enriching themselves."[110] Multiple senses of corruption were still widely understood to flow from a publicly traded debt – public policy made with an eye to private gain, the bribery of government officials, the expansion of a wasteful government bureaucracy, and the cultivation of a moneyed class with interests contrary to those of the nation. This cluster of beliefs was apparently still well distributed throughout the nation.

[106] Findley, *A Review*, 52, 79, 129.
[107] Quoted in Philip S. Foner, ed., *The Democratic-Republican Societies, 1790–1800* (Westport: Greenwood Press, 1976), 104, 107.
[108] *Annals of Congress*, IV, 929 (Nov. 26, 1794).
[109] William Manning, "The Key of Libberty" (1798), reprinted in Samuel Eliot Morison, ed., "William Manning's *The Key of Libberty*," *William and Mary Quarterly* 13 (1956): 224, 244.
[110] James Thomson Callender, *Sedgwick & Co. or A Key to the Six Per Cent Cabinet* (Philadelphia: J.T. Callender, 1798), 23.

The late eighteenth and early nineteenth centuries saw the emergence of John Taylor, the most thorough American exponent of this view. Taylor distinguished between "natural property," property that exists prior to government and independent of law (particularly land, but also manufactures), and "artificial property," property that exists only because it has been created by government, through the law. The public debt and the shares of corporations were Taylor's paradigmatic examples of artificial property. These were increasingly valuable forms of property that sprang into being entirely by the command of government. Without a statute creating the public debt, and without statutes chartering corporations, these newer types of property simply would not exist.[111]

It was such artificial property, in Taylor's view, that corrupted the political structure of a republic, because the public officials with the authority to create wealth out of nothing would inevitably abuse that power, by turning it to the advantage of themselves or their associates.[112] No such possibility of abuse existed with natural property; the legislature could not create new land, or new manufactured goods, and thus did not possess any power to change the quantity of natural property or to allocate natural property unequally. But the quantity and distribution of artificial property were manipulable by government officials.[113] "No form of civil government," Taylor explained, "can be more fraudulent, expensive and complicated, than one which distributes wealth and consequently power, by the act of the government itself."[114]

Artificial property like securities caused corruption in three overlapping ways. First, members of the legislature were likely to own securities themselves, and to pass laws that advanced their own interests rather than the public good.[115] It was common ground among Republicans that such a spectacle had, in fact, already occurred in the First Congress, and was sure to occur again. Taylor's solution was a simple one: "A constitutional expulsion of a stock-jobbing paper interest, in every shape, out of the national legislature, can alone recover the lost principles of a representative government, and save the nation from being owned – bought and sold."[116] Excluding the owners of securities from Congress would be "upon the same principle as public officers

[111] John Taylor, *An Enquiry into the Principles and Tendency of Certain Public Measures* (Philadelphia: T. Dobson, 1794), 56–57; John Taylor, *A Definition of Parties* (Philadelphia: F. Bailey, 1794), 9.

[112] Leslie Wharton, *Polity and the Public Good: Conflicting Theories of Republican Government in the New Nation* (Ann Arbor: UMI Research Press, 1980), 20–21.

[113] Robert E. Shallhope, *John Taylor of Caroline: Pastoral Republican* (Columbia: University of South Carolina Press, 1980), 86.

[114] John Taylor, *An Inquiry into the Principles and Policy of the Government of the United States* (1814) (New Haven: Yale University Press, 1950), 230.

[115] Taylor, *Definition*, 12.   [116] Ibid., 15.

[i.e., executive branch officials] are excluded, because all may acquire public monies by their votes."[117] Second, even if legislators did not own securities themselves, speculators were likely to use their wealth and power to gain inside information about future government actions and to influence the formation of policy.[118] As a result, government would "become the prostitute of a faction – the vehicle of corrupt speculation, and the factor of private interest."[119] The only way to prevent this sort of degradation was to abolish securities entirely.

Third, and more generally, the continued creation of artificial property would lead to "a paper and patronage aristocracy." A system in which many were taxed to send interest payments to a propertied elite (or in which many labored to send dividends to the same elite) would "convert publick property into private, with unexampled rapidity, [and] transfer wealth and power from the mass of a nation to a few." Members of this aristocracy would own securities rather than land, which would cause tax policy to become skewed in their favor, because "a landed interest cannot tax without taxing itself," but a paper interest can. "[A]s an imposer of taxes," therefore, a paper interest was "strictly analogous to a legislature of officers receiving legal salaries."[120] The product would be a new kind of aristocracy.[121] "We have no armies, churches, navies, pensions or sinecures, contrived for the purpose of conveying to the richest class of citizens, the money drawn directly or indirectly from the nation," Taylor observed. "Stock, bank and funded, are the only modes hitherto used for drawing money from the many for the few."[122]

Taylor took care to rebut the most obvious argument to the contrary. "It is said," he noted,

that paper systems being open to all, are not monopolies. He who has money, may buy stock. All then is fair, as every man (meaning however only every monied man) may share in the plunder.

Every man may enlist in an army, yet an army may enslave a nation. A monopoly may be open to a great number, yet those who do engage in it, may imbibe the spirit of faction; but it cannot be open to all, because no interest, which must subsist upon a nation, can consist of that nation. . . .

The reason, however, for this apparent common power of becoming a stockjobber, consists in the constant necessity felt for recruits by every species of aristocracy.

An aristocracy was no less of an aristocracy when people could buy their way in; the holders of securities would be living off the work of everyone

---

[117] Taylor, *Enquiry*, 58.   [118] Ibid., 42.   [119] Taylor, *Definition*, 4.
[120] Taylor, *Inquiry*, 74, 86, 242.
[121] C. William Hill, *The Political Theory of John Taylor of Caroline* (Rutherford: Fairleigh Dickinson University Press, 1977), 108–19.
[122] Taylor, *Inquiry*, 340.

else all the same, and would still be filling the government with officials
who had a vested interest in keeping the system going. Taylor's conclusion was ominous: "There are two modes of invading private property;
the first, by which the poor plunder the rich, is sudden and violent; the
second, by which the rich plunder the poor, slow and legal."[123]

Taylor's writing represented the most well worked out theory of the
adverse political consequences of securities trading. When Taylor wrote,
the securities market was still dominated by shares in the federal public
debt. While that remained true, commentators continued to make
similar arguments with respect to the debt. "Keep the Government out
of the hands of Stock-Jobbers," urged the anonymous writer of an 1816
pamphlet devoted to elaborating an alternative method of public
finance.[124] As the national debt waned in size relative to the sum of
corporate shares in circulation, however, the views of government debt
epitomized by Taylor began to recede. By the 1830s, when the federal
debt had been reduced almost to nothing, the argument was occasionally repeated, even if it had little to do with any contemporary events.
"We would have few wars," John Calhoun maintained in 1835, "if there
did not exist in every community a body, seperate from the rest of the
community, who have a direct interest in war. That body" included
"jobers" and "speculators to whom war brings an abundant harvest."[125]
A year later, Andrew Jackson complained to his new Chief Justice Roger
Taney that "one of the greatest threateners of our admirable form of
Government, is the gradual consuming corruption, which is spreading
and carrying stockjobbing, landjobbing and every species of speculation
into our Legislature, state and national."[126] Such claims already smelled
of the library, in their abstraction and their age.

The shares of business corporations, on the other hand, were multiplying quickly all through the first half of the century, and their effects
on the political process were genuine objects of public concern. Critics
had little difficulty in taking the old political corruption arguments
about public debt securities and adapting them to corporate stock.
Unlike the abstract claims of Calhoun and Jackson, these points
responded to actual events occurring at the time, and could thus be
expressed in quite concrete terms. The ability of a legislature to create
property in the form of corporate shares, argued a resident of New York

[123] Ibid., 71, 259.
[124] *National Money, or a Simple System of Finance* (Washington: W. A. Rind and Co.,
1816), title page.
[125] Calhoun to William Ellery Channing, Feb. 20, 1835, Wilson, ed., *Papers of John C.
Calhoun*, XII, 482.
[126] Jackson to Taney, Oct. 13, 1836, John Spencer Bassett, ed., *Correspondence of Andrew
Jackson* (Washington: Carnegie Institution, 1926–35), V, 430.

in 1827, tempted legislators to pass laws for "the mere feeling of self-interest – to barter its favours for its own mean purposes – to buy up a township with a road – a district with a bank – a state with a canal." When government officials had the power to create this sort of new wealth and exchange it for votes, "then it is that corruption takes a deep root in the hearts of the people . . . . Partizans are bought by wholesale; and the general fund of state patronage, which justly belongs to the people of the state at large, is made the instrument of corrupting the various parts."[127] Such corruption was inevitable, Theophilus Fisk predicted, unless "law-makers are prohibited from holding stock in any incorporated company whatever"; by this ban, legislators would at least be unable to allocate newly created wealth to themselves.[128] The very act of creating a corporation, suggested William Leggett, enabled the government to confer wealth upon its favorites, and was accordingly "in its very nature, anti-republican and invasive of equal rights."[129] "While all Europe is tending more toward democracy," complained another critic in 1841, the spread of incorporated companies was causing the United States to become "daily more and more aristocratic."[130]

By the middle of the century, however, the political corruption argument faded away even with respect to corporate stock. Much of this tendency had to do with the general incorporation laws; once anyone could form a corporation without the consent of the legislature, a corporation no longer represented a special favor granted by the state, and the wealth created by a corporate charter lost much of its anti-republican quality.[131] Some of the disappearance of the rhetoric of corruption can be attributed to changing political beliefs; by mid-century, the old republican ideals of civic virtue and disinterestedness had long been on the decline. And some of diminished association of corporations and political corruption almost certainly was caused by the perceived utility of the corporate form in amassing capital for new ventures, as well as the form's very ordinariness by the middle of the century.[132]

As the older forms of political argument receded, a new one gradually took its place, one which more explicitly emphasized the effects of the

---

[127] *Letter, on the Use and Abuse*, 13.   [128] Fisk, *Banking Bubble*, 22.

[129] Sedgwick, ed., *A Collection of the Political Writings of William Leggett*, I, 89.

[130] Charles Duncombe, *Duncombe's Free Banking* (Cleveland: Sanford & Co., 1841), 260–61.

[131] Oscar Handlin and Mary Flug Handlin, *Commonwealth: A Study of the Role of Government in the American Economy: Massachusetts, 1774–1861* (New York: New York University Press, 1947), 194.

[132] Louis Hartz, *Economic Policy and Democratic Thought: Pennsylvania, 1776–1860* (Cambridge, MA: Harvard University Press, 1948), 76–79.

business corporation on the division between rich and poor. "Can the poor derive any direct advantage from such an institution?" asked the political economist Daniel Raymond as early as 1820. "Can they hope to own any part of its stock? Can those who have no money, hope to enter into competition with those who have, in buying the stock?"[133] The answer, of course, was no, and for Raymond that meant that every advantage gained by wealthy stockholders only widened the gulf between the stockholders and everyone else. At home in Baltimore, he could watch the process unfold. "[T]he people of Baltimore exclusive of the bank stockholders, are no doubt at this day possessed of less property, than they were five years ago," Raymond concluded. The stockholders were growing richer, "while the industrious labouring classes of the community, have been continually growing poor."[134] The minister Theodore Parker sermonized on the "preference for money over men" he saw embedded in corporate charters. "In most of our manufacturing companies the capital is divided into shares so large that a poor man cannot invest therein!"[135] In 1855, *Graham's Magazine* attributed "the destitution of the laboring classes" of Philadelphia to "the over speculation of the last few years."[136] By the middle of the century, the political arguments against corporate stock had acquired a modern class consciousness absent from earlier versions.

A more explicitly pro-labor variant of the argument was repeated by early nineteenth-century advocates of what was becoming a working class.[137] "[T]race the source of the income of the stockholder capitalist," urged Stephen Simpson in 1831. "The money is loaned to, and the interest paid by, somebody who employs it upon labour, directly or indirectly, and the labourer pays six per cent. of his industry for the use of the money." The net result, he observed, was that corporate stock was tantamount to a license to appropriate a percentage of every laborer's work. "Capitalists live and grow rich by the labour of others," Simpson concluded. "The labouring man lives by his own industry, but very

[133] Daniel Raymond, *Thoughts on Political Economy* (Baltimore: F. Lucas, Jr., 1820), 428.

[134] Raymond, *Elements*, II, 124.

[135] "Sermon of Merchants: their Position, Temptations, Opportunities, Influence, and Duty," delivered in Boston, Nov. 30, 1846, in Henry Steele Commager, ed., *Theodore Parker: An Anthology* (Boston: Beacon Press, 1960), 145.

[136] *Graham's Magazine*, Feb. 1855, 46:186.

[137] Bruce Laurie, *Artisans Into Workers: Labor in Nineteenth-Century America* (New York: Hill and Wang, 1989), 74–91; Sean Wilentz, *Chants Democratic: New York City & the Rise of the American Working Class, 1788–1850* (New York: Oxford University Press, 1984), 172–216; Paul E. Johnson, *A Shopkeeper's Millennium: Society and Revivals in Rochester, New York, 1815–1837* (New York: Hill and Wang, 1978), 37–61; Arthur M. Schlesinger, Jr., *The Age of Jackson* (New York: Little, Brown, 1945), 132–43, 201–02.

seldom grows rich himself. Is this just?"[138] In a world where stock could be passed down from generation to generation, John Pickering pointed out in 1847, "the greatest portion of mankind are born with saddles on their backs, and a lordly few, ready booted and spurred, to ride them."[139] A labor song of the 1840s, entitled "The Working Men's League," rested on this premise:

> Come, all you who are fond of singing,
> Let us set a song a ringing;
> Sound the chorus strong and hearty,
> And we'll make a jovial party.
>> Get out of the way, you speculators;
>> You shall no longer be dictators.
>
> Some love *Rents* and speculation;
> Some with *Banks* would fill the nation;
> In a lump we'll class these *critturs*,
> And we'll call them speculators.
>> Get out of the way, &c.[140]

A New York newspaper contrasted the success of Jacob Little, who had made $200,000 in a four-week period speculating in the shares of the Harlem Railroad, with the lives of the railroad's employees, "who toiled the year through, for the meagre pittance of six shillings a day, and were discharged on the approaching winter . . . by a soulless company, of which Mr. Little is the principal stockholder, because they would not work for five shillings a day." This contrast could exist, the paper suggested, because the law protected Little's shares but not the workers' jobs. "Laboring classes, day workers, who are toiling so many days for so many dollars, while idleness under the fostering protection of the law, is amassing its hundred thousands in one month, how long shall such things be?"[141]

Securities trading drew opposition based on its political effects from the late eighteenth century through the middle of the nineteenth, but the nature of that opposition changed over the period, as eighteenth-century republican political theory slowly gave way to class-conscious nineteenth-century thought more concerned with the inconsistent interests of capitalists and laborers, and as shares of stock in corporations pushed aside shares of public debt as the primary type of securities in circulation.

---

[138] Simpson, *The Working Man's Manual*, 68, 70.
[139] John Pickering, *The Working Man's Political Economy* (1847) (New York: Arno Press, 1971), 111.
[140] Quoted in ibid., 203.   [141] *Young America*, Jan. 10, 1846, 2.

The South Sea Bubble

"I do not dislike your Bank any more than all Banks," Andrew Jackson confided to Nicholas Biddle, the president of the Bank of the United States, early in Jackson's first administration. "But ever since I read the history of the South Sea bubble I have been afraid of banks."[142] In the first half of the nineteenth century, the events of 1720 were still "the famous south-sea bubble."[143] The "Mississippi and South Sea schemes," explained one New York judge in 1858, "have acquired an immortality of pre-eminence among the destructive projects of the visionary or the designing."[144] The Bubble still cast a large shadow over American attitudes toward securities markets and speculation. The 1845 publication in the United States of Charles Mackay's account of the Bubble, under the title "Memoirs of Commercial Delusions," refreshed memories of the Bubble even further.[145]

In the Bubble, one could find whatever lesson one was looking for. Andrew Jackson saw a parable revealing the danger of banks. John Taylor saw proof of the political corruption that necessarily followed from "the vicious principle of creating wealth by law."[146] An anonymous mid-century critic found a demonstration of the evil of paper currency.[147] Observers more tolerant of the new financial institutions drew narrower lessons. "The character of joint-stock companies and the South-Sea adventure differ *ab origine*," explained one defender of investment in business corporations, who found two distinctions between the Bubble and the speculation of the 1820s. "The present speculations are made with surplus unemployed capital," he explained, unlike those of 1720, when "people of all classes ventured, as in a lottery, their entire fortunes and means of subsistence." Just as important, he continued, investors in 1720 "were destitute of any medium of acquiring a knowledge for themselves of remote points connected with the speculation in which they hazarded their all. In our day," that problem had been corrected; "every individual not only possesses

[142] Reginald C. McGrane, ed., *The Correspondence of Nicholas Biddle* (Boston: Houghton, Mifflin, 1919), 93.

[143] Sedgwick, ed., *A Collection of the Political Writings of William Leggett*, 87.

[144] *Cross* v. *Sackett*, 15 N.Y. Super. 617, 652 (1858).

[145] Charles Mackay, "Memoirs of Commercial Delusions: Embracing Historical Sketches of the Mississippi Scheme and the South Sea Bubble," in Freeman Hunt, ed., *The Library of Commerce* (New York: Hunt's Merchants' Magazine, 1845), I, 233–342. This American edition included selected chapters from Mackay's book *Memoirs of Extraordinary Popular Delusions*, published in England in 1841.

[146] Taylor, *Inquiry*, 505; see also ibid., 86.

[147] John Hale Hunt, *The Honest Man's Book of Finance and Politics* (New York: J. H. Hunt, 1862), 105–06.

channels of correct information, but uses them before he *trades*." The Bubble was proof, not of the danger of *all* stock speculation, but only of the danger of uninformed speculation beyond one's means.[148]

Other narrow lessons could be extracted from the Bubble. In the view of the lawyer and political economist Willard Phillips, the editor of the *North American Review*, a certain amount of stock speculation was beneficial to the nation. But the "infatuation" of 1720 proved that there was a point beyond which that proposition would no longer hold true. "Every community is subject to occasional effervescences of this sort," Phillips concluded; the difficult task was to allow just enough speculation without opening the door to "the greater extravagances men run into in their speculations."[149] For William Maclure, the Bubble showed the foolishness of chartering corporations without limiting the dividends the directors could declare. Such broad powers vested in directors "only existed in Europe in the South sea bubble in London, and Law's bank, at Paris, to the ruin of hundreds of thousands." The fate of the South Sea Company proved the danger of "investing certain individuals with a right to contract what debts they please, and allowing them to pay away [in the form of dividends to shareholders] the only funds that are responsible for said debts, and leaving nothing in the vault to pay their creditors."[150]

The Bubble, by now more than a century old, was still alive in the memories of many Americans.[151] No matter how one wished to attack the financial institutions that were gaining prominence in the first half of the nineteenth century – the proliferation of banks, the increased use of the corporate form, the resulting explosion in the market for corporate stock – the Bubble provided ammunition.

III

The first half of the century also saw the growth of the exact opposite line of thought. As time went on, more and more Americans began to speak in favor of the market in corporate stock, and even in support of speculation. By the middle of the century, there was a substantial body of opinion holding that stock speculation actually *added* to the national wealth.

Early nineteenth-century English political economists, following

---

[148] "The Joint-Stock Companies," 152.

[149] Willard Phillips, *A Manual of Political Economy* (1828) (New York: A.M. Kelley, 1968), 52.

[150] Maclure, *Opinions*, I, 173.

[151] Karen A. Weyler, "'A Speculating Spirit': Trade, Speculation, and Gambling in Early American Fiction," *Early American Literature* 31 (1996): 219.

Adam Smith, often emphasized the ability of capital to add value to labor, and the contributions to the national wealth accordingly provided by those who invested their capital in productive enterprises.[152] Smith's influence in the United States is well known,[153] but the writings of the early nineteenth-century English economists were quickly influential in the United States as well. David Ricardo's *Principles of Political Economy and Taxation*, for instance, was republished in the United States in 1819, only two years after it had been published in England.[154] Robert Torrens' *Essay on the Production of Wealth*, first printed in London in 1821, was widely read by American lawyers and economists.[155] American political economists soon began writing the same thing. "Those who have provided their capital beforehand," argued Willard Phillips in 1828, "hold in their hands the essential means, not only of future production, but of the very existence of the community." Such investors were therefore "justly entitled, not only to a return of the value . . . loaned, but also to a share in the production to which it has directly or indirectly contributed."[156] Theodore Foster agreed, and set the new wisdom in historical perspective:

It is not a long time, since the reaping of interest from capital, has been set free from *an erroneous prejudice*. Since the capitalist, whose revenue was interest, did not himself labour, but loaned his money most commonly upon perfect securities only, his gains were looked upon with a jealous eye, and loaded with opprobrious epithets. But the light thrown upon matters of this kind by the science of political economy, has effectually manifested the injustice of this idea. Capital which is loaned, generally speaking, is loaned for purposes of production. It is an accomodation from those who have, to those who have not the requisite for extensive production; and busies individuals as master producers, who, except they can obtain it, must remain in the capacity of labourers or assistant producers. That the owner of capital should derive his subsistence by affording such accomodations, is not only honest and reputable, but one of the most honourable of occupations.[157]

Investing in productive enterprises was not just necessary; it was now becoming honorable, because it increased the amount of wealth in the

---

[152] Smith, *Wealth of Nations*, 360–75; David Ricardo, *The Principles of Political Economy and Taxation* (1817) (New York: E.P. Dutton & Co., 1912), 18–19; Robert Torrens, *An Essay on the Production of Wealth* (1821), ed. Joseph Dorfman (New York: A. M. Kelley, 1965), 175–78.

[153] Paul K. Conkin, *Prophets of Prosperity: America's First Political Economists* (Bloomington: Indiana University Press, 1980), 17–19.

[154] On the influence of Ricardo in the United States, see ibid., 111–34.

[155] Joseph Dorfman, "Robert Torrens and American Economic Thought" (1965), published as an introduction to Torrens, *An Essay*, 6–10.

[156] Phillips, *Manual*, 63.

[157] T. Foster, *An Essay upon the Principles of Political Economy* (New York: T. Foster, 1837), 31.

nation, and the investor accordingly deserved to be remunerated just as much as the laborer. "In whatever proportions the several classes of labourers, capitalists, and land-owners contribute their quota to the production of wealth," concluded another of the early American economists, "in that proportion have they clearly an equitable title to share it."[158]

As the investment of capital came to be viewed more favorably, the market in the shares of business corporations – the most successful means yet devised for moving capital from those who had it to those who thought they could use it – acquired a new respectability. "Large sums have in many instances been raised for carrying on private business, as well as improvements of great public utility," marvelled the *American Jurist* in 1829, "which could never probably have been carried through successfully without corporations."[159] An active market in corporate stock was "especially beneficial here where capital is so scarce," Nathaniel Ware suggested. "The members of a stock company, all risking something, not the whole of their means, can afford to do it."[160] Even the newspaper editor William Leggett, one of the most vociferous opponents of corporations and "Stock Gambling," had to admit that much of the time the "business of dealing in stocks is as respectable and useful as most others."[161]

And what was "speculation," if not the investment of capital in productive enterprises in the expectation of sharing in the returns those enterprises would generate?[162] Viewed in this light, even speculation began to acquire positive connotations. Each new railroad, for instance, constituted "another step in social improvement" which could not have been taken without speculation. Everyone was a gainer: "The traveller gains time and saves money in like manner with the speculatist to lay out elsewhere, and the ironmaster and mechanic reap a profit also in their branches." Whatever had been said about speculation in the past, "the establishment of any new branch of trade, or the setting on of a

---

[158] Alonzo Potter, *Political Economy: Its Objects, Uses, and Principles* (New York: Harper & Bros., 1840), 205.

[159] "Manufacturing Corporations," *American Jurist* 2 (1829): 94.

[160] Nathaniel A. Ware, *Notes on Political Economy, as Applicable to the United States* (New York: Leavitt, Trow, 1844), 245.

[161] Sedgwick, ed., *A Collection of the Political Writings of William Leggett*, 251.

[162] Current writers often distinguish between "speculation" and "investment" based on the length of time the buyer is expected to hold a purchase; a short holding period suggests "speculation," while a long one suggests "investment." See, e.g., Reuven Brenner with Gabrielle A. Brenner, *Gambling and Speculation: A Theory, a History, and a Future of Some Human Decisions* (Cambridge: Cambridge University Press, 1990), 93. In the first half of the nineteenth century, the word "speculation" generally covered both.

manufactory, partakes in no small degree of the character of a speculation; indeed, commerce itself can be deemed little else."[163] The English
traveller Frederick Marryat decided that "the Americans are justified in
their speculations," because they "speculate on the future; but the
future with them is not as distant as it is with us."[164] Even Ralph Waldo
Emerson was caught up in the excitement.[165] "[H]ow did our factories
get built?" Emerson asked rhetorically. "[H]ow did North America get
netted with iron rails, except by the importunity of these orators who
dragged all the prudent men in? . . . This *speculative* genius is the
madness of a few for the gain of the world. The projectors are sacrificed,
but the public is the gainer." He suggested that while technology and the
existence of a market were prerequisites for the development of the
railroads, it was equally important that someone was willing to risk his
money on the success of an enterprise. "A clever fellow was acquainted
with the expansive force of steam," Emerson began; "he also saw the
wealth of wheat and grass rotting in Michigan. Then he cunningly
screws on the steam-pipe to the wheat-crop. Puff now, O Steam!"[166]

Some economic thinkers were at a midway point; they were not ready
to condone all speculation, but instead distinguished between two kinds
of speculation, the useful and the wasteful. "Speculations by which a
canal is opened, a bridge constructed, or a new species of trade or
manufacture introduced," Willard Phillips explained, "are often useful
to a community, even though the parties directly concerned are
sufferers" in losing their investments. "[S]peculation upon property
already in the market," on the other hand, "is injurious to the community. It resembles gambling; one gains only what another loses." Phillips
drew a similar dichotomy between speculation that stabilized prices and
speculation that made prices more variable. "[S]peculations," he
noticed, "may have the effect of limiting the vibrations of price within
narrower extremes, for if a great quantity be withdrawn from a declining
market, it may cause a rise, and the same quantity being thrown into a
rising market may accelerate the change to a decline." When speculation
had such an effect, "it is useful, since extremes and irregular fluctuations
of price, are followed by embarrassments and bankruptcies, by which

[163] "The Joint-Stock Companies," 153–54.
[164] Marryat, *Diary in America*, 137.
[165] Richard F. Teichgraeber III, *Sublime Thoughts/Penny Wisdom: Situating Emerson and
    Thoreau in the American Market* (Baltimore: Johns Hopkins University Press, 1995),
    29–38; Charles Sellers, *The Market Revolution: Jacksonian America, 1815–1846* (New
    York: Oxford University Press, 1991), 375–80.
[166] Ralph Waldo Emerson, "Wealth" (published 1860, but written 1851–52), in *The
    Complete Essays and Other Writings of Ralph Waldo Emerson*, 698, 694. See Michael T.
    Gilmore, *American Romanticism and the Marketplace* (Chicago: University of Chicago
    Press, 1985), 18–19.

the community at large suffers." Sometimes, on the other hand, speculations "make the variation of prices more irregular, and force them to wider extremes." In such cases, speculation was "injurious to the community."[167] With either distinction, governing the market would be a tricky business, because there was no apparent way of promoting the good kinds of speculation while simultaneously deterring the bad.

The explicit pro-speculation thought that began to appear in the first half of the nineteenth century was merely the most visible manifestation of public opinion in favor of the growing market in corporate stock. By willingly investing in the shares of corporations, propertied Americans were in effect putting their money where their mouths were not; they were demonstrating their approval of the new institution without, in most cases, pausing to write down the reasons for what they were doing. We saw the same phenomenon earlier in England. A market of any kind cannot grow unless an ever-increasing number of people decide that they will derive some benefit from it and accordingly wish to participate in it. Even without the explicit pro-market thought that began to spring up in the early nineteenth century, the simple fact that the number of tradeable corporate shares persistently increased would be evidence that the anti-market thought described above was counterbalanced by a silent but widespread current of pro-market opinion. The explicit views of people like Emerson and the early political economists, when added on top of the market's growth generally, provide even more confirmation that despite all the familiar reasons to be suspicious of the stock market, the market seemed appealing to a large number of Americans.

At the middle of the nineteenth century, the old tension inherited from England was still present in American thought about securities trading. The market was still a forum for deceitful business practices; it was still a non-productive sphere of the economy, sucking capital away from more productive activities; and it still had unpalatable political consequences, although those consequences had changed since the beginning of the century. At the same time, however, the market was still a useful institution, and seemed even more useful as time went on, as the corporate form became a commonplace method of accumulating capital for new businesses. Often, as in the case of William Leggett, these contradictory views were held by the same people.

This tension was embodied in the American securities regulation of the first half of the nineteenth century, which, as we will see in the next chapter, tried to accommodate both sides at once.

[167] Phillips, *Manual*, 50–51.

The tension in early nineteenth-century thought about securities trading discussed in the previous chapter was reflected in the way state governments regulated the market. Section I of this chapter will discuss the means by which states attempted to curb stock speculation, and the forces which limited the success of those efforts. State courts and some state legislatures tried to suppress the deceit widely thought to permeate the market, but at the same time the courts of New York, the home of the largest concentration of securities traders, were generally willing to adopt the customs of stockjobbers as rules of law. These developments will be described in sections II and III. In the first half of the nineteenth century, the legal system, considered as a whole, thus exhibited the same ambivalence toward securities trading as that which characterized public opinion.

I

Many of the states enacted statutes during the first half of the nineteenth century directly targeted at what was perceived as excessive stock speculation, and many more passed statutes with the indirect effect of curbing such speculation. The effect of these statutes was limited by the force of the contrary policy – the evident usefulness of certain speculative transactions. In some instances, this tension produced statutes that were rarely enforced. In other cases, where the statutes *were* enforced, their power was curtailed by judges who sought to interpret them in ways that would not hinder the operation of the securities market. For every actor working within the legal system to limit the amount of stock speculation, it seemed, there was another pushing in the opposite direction.

The most direct limits on securities speculation enacted by state legislatures in the first half of the nineteenth century were two identically worded statutes, one in Pennsylvania in 1841, and then another in Maryland in 1842, that declared void all contracts for the future sale of securities, whether government debt or corporate stock, in which delivery of the securities "may be executed or performed at any future period exceeding five judicial days next ensuing the date of such contract."[1] This provision revived the concept behind the very first English limit on speculative securities sales, in force from 1697 to 1708 (and discussed toward the end of chapter 1), which had voided contracts in which the time between the contract date and the delivery date was longer than three days.[2] People who entered into contracts voided by the 1841–42 statutes, in addition to losing the ability to enforce such contracts in court, were to pay a fine of between $100 and $1,000, half to the state, and the other half to the city or county for the benefit of the poor. The five-day limit was occasionally raised as a defense to a suit for the enforcement of a contract, and when it was, the statute was interpreted broadly, to include even shares in corporations that did not yet exist at the time of the contract. In *Krause* v. *Setley* (1856), the plaintiff had purchased shares in the soon-to-be-organized Gap Mining Company. Delivery of the shares would occur when the company was formed, which was not until many months later. The 1841 statute, a Pennsylvania judge explained, was "a remedial law of great importance," and should thus be "construed so as to suppress the mischief which the Act was intended to prevent." That mischief – "gambling in stocks" – existed just as much with companies in the process of formation as with companies already formed. "Indeed," the court concluded, "in such a case the evils are rather aggravated than diminished as the contingencies of a rise or fall are increased by the uncertainty whether the company will go into operation."[3] The Pennsylvania courts refused, on the other hand, to apply the statute to invalidate *loans* of stock lasting more than five days; such an interpretation, one judge explained, "would invalidate every deposit of stock as a collateral security for a debt, and would very essentially impair the practical value of this kind of property."[4] The more common a form of transaction, the more it seemed too useful to abolish, and the more the courts would strain to avoid interpreting a statute to reach that result. Still, even as applied only to sales rather than loans as well, the five-day limit, if enforced, would probably have been short enough to invalidate most of the time bargains entered into by Philadelphia speculators.

[1] Pa. Laws 1841, No. 140, § 6; Md. Laws 1841–42, c. 282, § 7.
[2] 8 & 9 Wm. III c. 32 (1697), extended by 11 & 12 Wm. III c. 13 (1700).
[3] *Krause* v. *Setley*, 2 Phila. Rep. 32, 33 (1856).
[4] *Chillas* v. *Snyder*, 1 Phila. Rep. 289, 290 (1852).

The prime difficulty with enforcing this provision, as had been the case with prior efforts to regulate the market in England and the United States, was that the burden of enforcement rested with the very people who had willingly entered into the invalidated agreements. The five-day limit could be effectively raised only as a defense to a suit to enforce such an agreement. The speculators who entered into time bargains as a matter of routine were unlikely to raise such a defense, because few would be willing to contract with them in the future. Even if the provision had been enforced more often, moreover, time bargains lasting longer than five days would most likely have continued to exist, as the primary penalty under the statute was simply the inability to use the official court system to enforce them. As in England under Sir John Barnard's Act or New York under the 1792 stockjobbing statute, the effect of rendering a class of transactions unenforceable in the state courts would most likely have been to stimulate the development of alternative private mechanisms of enforcement.

The same statutes in Pennsylvania and Maryland also prohibited the parties to time bargains lasting longer than five days from complying with their contracts by merely paying the price differential between the market price on the contract date and the market price on the nominal delivery date.[5] In this provision, the two states modified an idea embodied in Sir John Barnard's Act, in effect in England from 1734 to 1860 (and discussed in chapter 3).[6] Barnard's Act applied to all time bargains; the 1841–42 statutes applied only to those already declared unenforceable by virtue of their duration. Unlike Barnard's Act, which required parties actually to convey the stock they contracted for, the Pennsylvania and Maryland statutes simply authorized the person who had paid the price differential to recover his payment, plus a 20 percent penalty, in an action for money had and received. But the principle underlying the two statutes was that of Barnard's Act. Speculation on the rise and fall of stock prices would become much more cumbersome – so cumbersome as to be impossible in many cases – if speculators were not allowed to settle their contracts by the simple payment of money without any actual transfer of stock. There are no reported cases in either Pennsylvania or Maryland before 1860, however, in which this provision was enforced. Again, the burden of enforcement rested entirely on the shoulders of the very speculators who found the payment of price differentials most useful. Enforcement, by bringing suit against a fellow speculator to recover money paid on a time bargain, would have been tantamount to going out of business.

[5] Pa. Laws 1841, No. 140, § 6; Md. Laws 1841–42, c. 282, § 7.
[6] 7 Geo. II c. 8, § 5 (1734).

States tried three other direct methods of limiting speculation in securities. First, many states imposed minimum holding periods, during which stock could not be transferred from one person to another. In 1837, for instance, New York prohibited the initial subscribers to stock in banks from selling their stock until three months after all the stock had been paid for.[7] Such limits often appeared in corporate charters; when Massachusetts chartered the Washington Bank in 1825, for example, it mandated that "the Capital Stock of said Bank shall not be sold or transferred, but shall be holden by the original subscribers thereto, for and during the period of one year from the time of passing this act."[8] These sorts of restrictions were intended "[t]o prevent speculation in the scrip," the Massachusetts Supreme Court explained.[9] "The sole object was to cure a supposed evil, that of subscribing to bank stock without intention to become stockholders, but for the purpose only of speculating upon the rise of shares."[10] By imposing a minimum holding period, states tried to separate the short-run speculators, whose profits depended primarily on the early climate of opinion as to the enterprise's prospects, from the long-run investors, whose gains were more contingent on the enterprise's eventual success. States sometimes imposed similar holding periods as a prerequisite to voting; Pennsylvania's 1825 charter for the Conestogo Navigation Company, for instance, provided that "no shares held by transfer, shall be entitled to vote, unless the same shall have been transferred at least three months before the election."[11] The three-month rule prevented purchasers from rapidly acquiring control of the corporation, and more weakly deterred speculators from buying the corporation's stock if they intended to hold it only a short time.[12]

These minimum holding periods figured in reported litigation only

[7] N.Y. Laws, 60th Sess., c. 235, § 6 (1837).

[8] Mass. Laws 1824–25, c. 134, § 11. See also the Mendon Bank, Mass. Laws 1824–25, c. 142, § 2.

[9] *Quiner v. Marblehead Social Ins. Co.*, 10 Mass. 475, 483 (1813).

[10] *Nesmith v. Washington Bank*, 23 Mass. 324, 328 (1828).

[11] Pa. Laws 1824–25, c. 34, § 4. Similar restrictions were imposed by some corporations in the 1980s, as deterrents to takeovers. They met with mixed reactions from the courts. Ernest L. Folk III, Rodman Ward, Jr., and Edward P. Welch, *Folk on the Delaware General Corporation Law*, 2nd edn (Boston: Little, Brown, 1988), 377.

[12] The motive of deterring speculation may also have been at work in statutes that banned trading at certain times. When the New York legislature authorized the issuance of $1.6 million in public debt in 1815, for instance, it provided that "transfers of said stock shall only be made during the first two months of each quarter." As interest on the debt was payable on the first day of each quarter, the statute prevented transfers of the debt for the month preceding each interest payment. N.Y. Laws, 38th Sess., c. 141, §§ 10, 5 (1815). This provision was probably intended in large part to ease the administrative burden of ascertaining who held the debt every three months, but it may also have been designed to prevent short-term speculation in the state debt in the period right before

rarely. When they did, their effect could be sharply limited by the way they were interpreted by the courts. The Massachusetts Supreme Court, for instance, decided very early that despite the apparently clear wording of such provisions, stock could nevertheless be transferred during the holding period from a debtor to a creditor to secure a debt or in payment of a debt.[13] Because a substantial number of transfers were probably of this character, and because there is scarcely any reported litigation seeking to enforce such restrictions, minimum holding periods most likely failed to limit trading to any great extent.

Second, states sometimes regulated the manner in which stock was issued so as to prevent speculators from purchasing large blocks for resale. When a new bank was formed in New York, for example, the commissioners charged with selling stock were forbidden from selling more than $500 worth to any single purchaser on the first day shares were sold, more than $1,000 worth to any single purchaser on the second day, and more than $2,000 worth to any single purchaser on the third day. Speculators were further hindered by a requirement that no person could purchase shares in a bank during the first three days that shares were sold unless he resided in the county in which the bank was located.[14] This latter requirement would have been most keenly felt by New York City speculators wishing to buy shares of upstate banks. Similar regulations of the manner in which stock was issued were often contained in corporate charters. The initial subscribers to the Essex Mill Corporation, chartered by Massachusetts in 1822, could purchase no more than 25 of the 100 shares of stock.[15] Purchasers of stock in the newly organized Farmers' Bank of Delaware in 1807 were limited to twenty shares in any one day.[16] Such provisions served the same purpose as similar limitations imposed today on the purchasers of tickets to concerts and sporting events; they deterred speculation by making it more difficult to buy very large quantities of stock.

Third, states often tried to curb stock speculation by prohibiting banks from buying and selling stock.[17] Mississippi made it unlawful in 1840 "for any bank in this State to deal in stocks of any kind."[18] Such restrictions appeared in the charters of individual banks as well. A group of banks rechartered by Pennsylvania in 1824 were not to "be at liberty

---

an interest payment was due, when such speculation may have been thought especially likely to occur.

[13] *Quiner*, 10 Mass. at 482; *Nesmith*, 23 Mass. at 327.

[14] N.Y. Laws, 60th Sess., c. 235, § 2.   [15] Mass. Laws 1822, c. 25, § 4.

[16] Del. Laws 1806–13, c. 39, § 4 (1807).

[17] J. Van Fenstermaker, *The Development of American Commercial Banking: 1782–1837* (Kent: Kent State University, 1965), 49.

[18] Miss. Laws 1840, c. 1, § 5.

to purchase any stock whatsoever, except their own bank stock or other incorporated bank stock of this state."[19] Speculation on the part of banks was particularly to be feared, primarily because of the large amounts of pooled capital a bank could have at its disposal.[20] As William Gouge dismissed the Girard Bank of Philadelphia after its failure, "[i]t was, in short, a *land jobbing* and *stock jobbing*, and not a *commercial* bank."[21]

Many states passed laws which, although probably not intended primarily to curb speculation, may have had that effect indirectly. One common form such regulation took was the licensing of stockbrokers. Brokers had been licensed in England since the 1690s, but no state required a license until well into the nineteenth century.[22] The first state to license stockbrokers appears to have been Virginia, which in 1834 charged an annual fee of $60 "on every license to a broker" generally, and then in 1842 clarified that the term "broker" included anyone who bought stock as an agent for another.[23] Other states began requiring licenses at approximately the same time, including Pennsylvania in 1841, Maryland in 1842, Illinois in 1845, Indiana in 1847, and Kentucky by 1851.[24] These statutes included no requirements applicants had to meet in order to receive a license, but they all included a fee payable to the state or its subdivisions, and they were usually contained within larger statutory schemes devoted to raising tax revenue, so they were almost certainly enacted by state governments with an eye to exploiting rather than reducing the popularity of stock speculation. The federal government imposed a similar licensing requirement in 1862, as part of an emergency wartime tax measure.[25] These statutes added to the cost of stock speculation, sometimes by a significant amount. Maryland, for instance, charged stockbrokers $1,000 per year for a license, and then fined those who practiced without a license $500 for each offense. Whether this cost was passed along to the brokers' clients in the form of higher commissions, or whether it simply reduced the number

[19] Pa. Laws 1824, c. 47, § 3, art. 14.

[20] Naomi Lamoreaux, *Insider Lending: Banks, Personal Connections, and Economic Development in Industrial New England* (Cambridge: Cambridge University Press, 1994), 11–30; Harold van B. Cleveland and Thomas F. Huertas, *Citibank 1812–1970* (Cambridge, MA: Harvard University Press, 1985), 9.

[21] *The Journal of Banking*, Feb. 2, 1842, I, 247.

[22] See Samuel Livermore, *A Treatise on the Law of Principal and Agent* (Baltimore: Joseph Robinson, 1818), I, 73–75.

[23] Va. Laws 1834, c. 1, § 3; Va. Laws 1841–42, c. 3, § 3.

[24] Pa. Laws 1841, No. 140, § 1; Md. Laws 1841–42, c. 282, § 1; Ill. Laws 1845, p. 4, § 6; Ind. Laws 1847, c. 42, § 1; Ky. Laws 1851, 71–72.

[25] An Act to provide Internal Revenue to support the Government and to pay Interest on the Public Debt, § 64, para. 13, 12 Stat. 432, 457 (July 1, 1862).

(and hence the availability) of brokers, the license requirement made it more difficult for a Maryland resident to buy and sell securities, and thus most likely reduced the amount of stock speculation in the state. The license fees in other states were generally smaller, so one might expect the same effect to have been reproduced on a smaller scale. Other kinds of taxes, like the Massachusetts tax on the sale of securities at auction, could also raise the cost of transacting, and thus reduce the frequency with which stock was bought and sold.[26]

The most common form of state regulation with an indirect effect on the level of stock speculation involved rules governing the methods by which securities could be transferred from one person to another. The choice of how difficult to make the transfer of stock required taking into account two competing policy goals. On one hand, as the Delaware Supreme Court pointed out, "[t]he assignable nature of this kind of property constitutes its chief value."[27] The more cumbersome it was to buy and sell stock, the less the stock would be worth. A rule that made buying stock more difficult, observed Chief Justice Taney, would "greatly impair its value."[28] This consideration suggested that the law should allow stock to be freely transferable. On the other hand, there were two considerations pointing in the opposite direction. First, many were worried that free transferability could be used to defraud either the shareholder's creditors, who might discover too late that he no longer owned an asset they were planning to seize in the event he failed to pay his debt, or the corporation's creditors (at a time when the limited liability of shareholders was not yet a standard feature of corporations), who might lend to a company made up of worthy borrowers only to find that a new set of people had replaced the old as stockholders. (The most common creditor of the shareholder was the corporation itself, because the prevailing practice when issuing new stock was to require only a small initial payment to the corporation, and to make periodic later calls for additional payments. Charters usually provided that a shareholder failing to pay an assessment when called would forfeit his shares back to the corporation.[29]) Second, the easy transfer of shares would be conducive to speculation. "I am aware that people will speculate in stocks, as they sometimes do in lands," explained one New York judge, as a reason in support of a decision (discussed later in this chapter) that

---

[26] Mass. Laws 1834, c. 161.

[27] *Wilmington and Philadelphia Tpk. Co.* v. *Bush*, 1 Harr. (1 Del.) 44, 46 (1832).

[28] *Lowry* v. *Commercial & Farmers' Bank*, 15 F. Cas. 1040, 1047 (C.C.D.Md. 1848) (No. 8,581).

[29] Edwin Merrick Dodd, *American Business Corporations Until 1860* (Cambridge, MA: Harvard University Press, 1954), 74–84. Today, by contrast, new stock is normally paid for in full when it is issued.

made shares less transferable than they might have been, "but such, I am persuaded, is not the use for which we should hold them chiefly intended."[30] The rules governing the transferability of stock thus played a part in determining the amount of stock speculation that would occur.

These transfer rules were often contained within statutes applicable to all corporations, or whole classes of corporations, chartered by the state. They varied widely in their restrictiveness. In general, the earlier statutes tended to make transferring stock more cumbersome, while the later statutes tended to make it easier. The 1804 and 1809 Massachusetts statutes regulating turnpike companies and manufacturing companies, for example, required a shareholder wishing to sell stock to appear with the purchaser before a Justice of the Peace, where the seller had to transfer a deed to the purchaser.[31] Pennsylvania's 1814 and 1824 laws governing banks in the state, like many bank charters and by-laws in other states, prohibited shareholders from selling their shares when they owed debts to the bank.[32] The statutes of the 1830s and 1840s progressively streamlined the process. The general incorporation law for railroads enacted by Massachusetts in 1833 allowed shareholders to transfer stock by a writing recorded on the books of the railroad, by any officer of the railroad the directors should choose to authorize.[33] The state imposed a slightly easier requirement in 1846, a writing recorded by a clerk of the corporation, for transfers of the stock of manufacturing companies.[34] Other states followed this lead. In 1836, North Carolina declared that each corporation could decide for itself how its shares were to be transferred.[35] Tennessee's 1850 general incorporation law for turnpike companies required only that transfers be made on the books of the corporation, but left it up to the directors to work out the details.[36] Michigan adopted a similar procedure in 1855 for gas light corporations.[37]

Some states made transferring stock even easier. New Hampshire, for instance, declared in 1849 that "the free sale of shares in the stock of any corporation in this State, by the owners thereof, shall not be in any way or manner restricted by the by-laws of such corporation," and voided all corporate by-laws that hindered the transferability of stock.[38]

---

[30] *Mechanics' Bank* v. *New-York and New Haven R.R. Co.*, 13 N.Y. 599, 627 (1856).
[31] Mass. Laws 1804, c. 125, § 8; Mass. Laws 1809, c. 65, § 4. See *Eames* v. *Wheeler*, 36 Mass. 442 (1837).
[32] Pa. Laws 1812–17, c. 3902, § 7, art. 11 (1814); Pa. Laws 1824, c. 47, § 3, art. 11. See *Rogers* v. *Huntingdon Bank*, 12 Serg. & Rawle 77 (Pa. 1824); *Grant* v. *Mechanics' Bank of Philadelphia*, 15 Serg. & Rawle 140 (Pa. 1827).
[33] Mass. Laws 1833, c. 187, § 8.   [34] Mass. Laws 1846, c. 45, § 1.
[35] N.C. Laws 1836–37, c. 11.   [36] Tenn. Laws 1849–50, c. 72, § 15.
[37] Mich. Laws 1855, No. 109, § 9.   [38] N.H. Laws 1849, c. 860, § 2.

The states were more likely to ensure that their own public debt securities could easily be bought and sold. When Alabama borrowed from the public in 1828, it provided that shares of the state debt would be assignable simply by endorsing the certificate that served as evidence of the debt.[39] In the 1850s, Indiana posted an "Agent of State" in New York, close to the city's professional trading community, and allowed holders of the state debt to use the Agent's services in transferring the debt to purchasers.[40] Even at mid-century, however, concern for the creditors of shareholders caused Wisconsin to require, as a prerequisite for a valid transfer of stock in any corporation, that a certificate of the transfer be deposited with the clerk of the town in which the corporation conducted business.[41]

Rules governing the transferability of stock were also often contained within the charters of individual corporations. These provisions were occasionally quite restrictive. To sell stock in the Union Insurance Company of Maryland, chartered in 1805, one needed the permission of the board of directors; this was to ensure that the stockholders were "persons of sufficient property to make good any losses which may happen."[42] The Pittsburg Gas Light and Coke Company, chartered by Pennsylvania in 1827, held a right of first refusal, entitling it to purchase the shares of any stockholder who wished to sell, at whatever price had been offered for them.[43] A seller of stock in the Winchester House, a hotel in Winchester, Massachusetts, had to deposit a certificate memorializing the sale with the town clerk of Winchester, or else the sale would not be valid as against the seller's creditors.[44]

But most of the charter provisions governing the transfer of shares permitted stock to be sold more easily. Many corporations spanning the first half of the century, from an 1801 Maryland turnpike to an 1816 New Hampshire bridge; to the 1833 Illinois Manufacturing, Mining, and Exporting Company; to the Flemington Copper Company, chartered by New Jersey in 1847; provided in their charters that stock transfers would be valid so long as they were made on the books of the company.[45] Many more charters left the determination of the prerequisites for transfer up to the corporation's directors,[46] or to the "laws and

---

[39] Ala. Laws 1827–31, p. 3, § 1 (1828).   [40] Ind. Laws 1858–59, c. 17, § 1.
[41] Wis. Laws 1853, c. 68, § 19.   [42] Md. Laws 1804, c. 41, § 12.
[43] Pa. Laws 1827–28, No. 3, § 5.   [44] Mass. Laws 1852, c. 309, § 3.
[45] Md. Laws 1801, c. 45, § 4; N.H. Laws 1816, c. 97, § 3; Ill. Laws 1833, p. 43, § 9; N.J. Laws 1847, p. 12, § 7.
[46] See, e.g., the Philadelphia Bank, Pa. Laws 1803–08, c. 2439, § 3, art. 13 (1804); the Tombeckbe Bank, Ala. Laws 1818, 1st Sess., p. 69, § 2, para. 10; the Wabash Insurance Company, Ind. Laws 1830, Special Acts, c. 22, § 8; the East Florida Rail Road Company, Fla. Laws 1835, c. 824, § 8; the Rock River Insurance Company, Wis. Laws 1851, c. 195, § 9.

ordinances" that would be enacted by the corporation,[47] or to the corporation's stockholders assembled in a meeting.[48] And the charters of some companies provided only that their stock would be "transferable," and left it at that.[49]

The general trend of state regulation of securities transfers thus reconciled the two contradictory goals by occupying a middle ground, halfway between limiting transfers and permitting unrestricted transfers. Stock could in general be bought and sold provided that the buyer and seller complied with a set of formalities that would give the corporation and its creditors notice of the change in ownership. Courts often ratified this decision by enforcing whatever prerequisites to transfer a state legislature had placed in a corporate charter or the corporation had established for itself. The issue arose in disputes between either the buyer or seller and a creditor when it was necessary to ascertain whether shares, supposedly sold without compliance with the formalities, had passed to the buyer or whether they were still owned by the putative seller. The tone was set early by the U.S. Supreme Court in *Union Bank of Georgetown* v. *Laird* (1817), in which Justice Story explained that where a bank's charter required transfers of stock to be on the books of the bank, "[n]o person, therefore, can acquire a legal title to any shares" as a result of a supposed sale never entered on the books.[50] Subsequent cases often reached the same result, sometimes by relying explicitly on *Union Bank*.[51] As Chief Justice Lemuel Shaw observed when the issue arose in Massachusetts, "[b]efore any method was established by positive law" for conveying stock from a seller to a buyer, "courts of justice might well resort to the common law modes of transferring similar incorporeal interests, and hold that a delivery of the only muniment of title held by the owner, with the execution and delivery of

---

[47] See, e.g., the Farmers' Bank of Delaware, Del. Laws 1806–13, c. 39, § 12, para. 11 (1807); the Bank of Tennessee, Tenn. Laws 1831, c. 5, § 6, ? 8.

[48] See, e.g., the Asiatic Bank, Mass. Laws 1824–25, c. 40, § 2.

[49] See, e.g., the Bowlinggreen Life, Fire and Marine Insurance Company, Ky. Laws 1838–39, c. 1388, § 5.

[50] *Union Bank of Georgetown* v. *Laird*, 2 Wheat. (15 U.S.) 390, 393 (1817). In *Union Bank*, the Court went on to suggest that although legal title to shares could not pass without compliance with the charter, *equitable* title might, and that shares equitably assigned would be subject to the claims of creditors. Both of these suggestions would be further developed in the cases, discussed below, in which shareholders were permitted to alienate shares despite failing to comply with charter requirements.

[51] See, e.g., *Marlborough Mfg. Co.* v. *Smith*, 2 Conn. 579 (1818); *Northrop* v. *Newton and Bridgeport Tpk. Co.*, 3 Conn. 544 (1821); *Northrop* v. *Curtis*, 5 Conn. 246 (1824); *Oxford Tpk. Co.* v. *Bunnel*, 6 Conn. 552 (1827); *Coleman* v. *Spencer*, 5 Blackf. 197 (Ind. 1839); *Fiske* v. *Carr*, 20 Me. 301 (1841); *Sabin* v. *Bank of Woodstock*, 21 Vt. 353 (1849); *Helm* v. *Swiggett*, 12 Ind. 194 (1859); *Fisher* v. *Essex Bank*, 71 Mass. 375 (1855).

an assigment of his interest, by indorsement on the certificate or otherwise." But where the legislature had superseded the common law with an express rule, that rule had to govern.[52]

But where transfer restrictions were contained in corporate by-laws rather than in charters enacted by the legislature, courts were more willing to emphasize the benefits to be gained by the free circulation of stock, and accordingly to refuse to enforce such restrictions on transfer. An early example arose in a case involving the first Bank of the United States, the charter of which made the Bank's stock transferable "according to such rules as shall be instituted in that behalf, by the laws and ordinances of the same."[53] One of the Bank's by-laws required transfers to be made at the Bank, either personally or by attorney. The Bank was in Philadelphia, but Bank stock was traded all over the country, and in Europe as well. Was a sale of Bank stock in England invalid for failing to comply with the by-law? In 1811, the Pennsylvania Supreme Court held that it was not. Enforcing the by-law to invalidate the sale, one judge concluded, "would so impede the transfer of stock, that we cannot suppose the corporation, admitting it to have the power, did contemplate such extent in this by-law." Such a rule would "discourage the stockholding by foreigners, to a greater extent" than he believed Congress could possibly have intended.[54] The United States government, a creditor of the seller, thus could not attach the stock at issue, because the seller no longer owned it. The Massachusetts Supreme Judicial Court reached a similar result two decades later, in a case involving an insurance company with a by-law requiring the president's assent as a condition for transferring shares. "[I]t cannot be maintained," the court held, "that the right to the shares in the capital stock of this corporation cannot be transferred without a literal compliance with the by-laws. It is personal property," and therefore could be conveyed just like any analogous type of personal property, "by a delivery of the certificate with an indorsement upon it for a valuable consideration." A by-law requiring transfers to be made with the president's permission was "in restraint of trade and contrary to the general law of the Commonwealth, which permits the right to personal property and incorporeal hereditaments to be transferred in various other ways."[55] The company, a creditor of the seller, could not restrain

[52] *Fisher*, 71 Mass. at 378.
[53] An Act to incorporate the subscribers to the Bank of the United States, § 12, 1 Stat. 191, 195 (Feb. 25, 1791).
[54] *United States* v. *Vaughan*, 3 Binn. 392, 402 (Pa. 1811).
[55] *Sargent* v. *Franklin Ins. Co.*, 25 Mass. 90, 95–96 (1829). *Sargent*, along with *Sargent* v. *Essex Marine Ry. Co.*, 26 Mass. 201 (1829), would be distinguished into oblivion by Shaw a couple of decades later, in *Fisher* v. *Essex Bank*, 71 Mass. 375, 382 (1855).

the seller's right to transfer the stock at issue as a means of collecting its debt. The same reasoning caused the New York Court of Appeals to invalidate a bank's by-law prohibiting shareholders from selling their stock until they had discharged any debts they owed to the bank. "The quality of transferability being attached to the shares" by the state's general banking law, the court held, "the corporate body has no authority to interfere with the disposition which any shareholder may see fit to make."[56] The shares could pass to the buyer free of any claim on the part of the bank.

Where restrictions on transfer were included in charters, the same preference for the free transferability of stock sometimes caused judges to express their disapproval, even when they reluctantly conceded that they lacked the power to refuse to enforce the restrictions. The charter of Pennsylvania's Carlisle Bank included the same prohibition as the one invalidated in New York. This restriction, one Pennsylvania judge exclaimed, "is perhaps the most extraordinary and anomalous clause to be found in our statute book." The rule, in his view, had the effect of "investing the control of millions of the property of others in a few individuals: property, too, of that description, which, in a trading and commercial community like ours, is as much, or perhaps more, the subject of mutation and transfer, than any other." But despite the judge's distaste for such a restriction on the transferability of stock, "it exists, and exists by the highest authority, that of the law-making power; and it must be enforced."[57]

Judges were able, however, to insert their general support for free transferability into the law in cases not involving the countervailing policy interest of protecting creditors of the stockholder or the corporation. The first of these cases was *Reed* v. *Ingraham* (1799), involving an April 1792 time bargain in federal government debt entered into in Philadelphia. The seller assigned the contract to William Reed, by simply writing an appropriate sentence on the face of the contract and signing his name. Reed then delivered the securities on the appointed day to the buyer, Francis Ingraham. When Ingraham refused to accept (most likely because prices were falling quickly in April 1792, and the contract price was thus now higher than the market price), Reed sued. Ingraham argued in his defense that a stock contract was not assignable, i.e., that only the original seller could bring suit on the contract, but not Reed, his assignee. The Pennsylvania Supreme Court acknowledged that "[o]n general principles of law, stock contracts cannot be regarded" as assignable from one person to another. The court noted, however,

---

[56] *Bank of Attica* v. *Manufacturers' and Traders' Bank*, 20 N.Y. 501, 505 (1859).
[57] *Presbyterian Congregation* v. *Carlisle Bank*, 5 Pa. 345, 347–48 (1847).

that at trial "several experienced brokers proved, that stock contracts, of the present description, had always been considered as assignable in Philadelphia, vesting the interest completely in the assignees." This practice of Philadelphia stockjobbers was enough for the court to make an exception to the general common law rule. "[T]he maxim, modus et conventio vincunt leges [custom and agreement overrule law], applies forcibly to the case," the court concluded. Contracts for the sale of stock could thus be assigned from one person to another by a simple signature, and the assignee would acquire the assignor's rights of enforcement.[58]

The New York courts went even further, and applied the stockjobbers' custom of free transferability to shares of stock itself, even in corporations whose charters restricted transfers by requiring that they be entered on the books of the corporation to be valid.[59] This sort of restriction on stock transfers, New York's highest court held, was designed only to protect creditors. It "does not interfere with the rights of ownership, as between the person in whose name the stock may stand and his vendee." A seller could thus successfully transfer stock to a buyer simply by signing his name on the back of the stock certificate, and a borrower could pledge his stock to a lender as collateral for a loan in the same manner, despite the charter provision that appeared to require more. Any other rule, the court concluded, would be contrary to "the necessities of business, and even to reason and justice. It would cut off trustees and assignees, as well as prevent the common and very convenient practice of *bona fide* stock loans!"[60] The transfer of stock by signature was "the universal usage of dealers in the negotiation and transfer of stocks, according to the proof in the case."[61] The dissenting judges protested such reliance on the practice of stockjobbers and the perceived needs of business. "Proof of a custom of Wall-street," they complained, cannot validate a transfer "which a public statute has declared shall not be valid until it has been duly intimated upon the books of the corporation." If the custom of brokers could override the positive law, what would be next? "As well might a custom to take three per cent. [interest] per month . . . be received as evidence that such an agreement was valid, notwithstanding the usury laws, and I have no doubt such a custom might be as easily proved as the custom in question here." The dissenters also argued that the decision was inconsistent with

---

[58] *Reed* v. *Ingraham*, 3 Dall. (3 U.S.) 505, 506 (Pa. 1799).
[59] *Bank of Utica* v. *Smalley*, 2 Cow. 770, 778 (N.Y. Sup. Ct. 1824); *Stebbins* v. *Phenix Fire Ins. Co.*, 3 Paige Ch. 350, 361 (N.Y. Ch. 1832).
[60] *Commercial Bank of Buffalo* v. *Kortright*, 22 Wend. 348, 362–63 (N.Y. 1839).
[61] *Kortright* v. *Buffalo Commercial Bank*, 20 Wend. 91, 93–94 (N.Y. Sup. Ct. 1838).

the line of cases enforcing transfer restrictions as written, a line extending back to Justice Story's opinion for the Supreme Court in *Union Bank of Georgetown* v. *Laird*.[62] But the practice of free transferability soon overrode explicit charter provisions in similar circumstances in other states as well.[63] As New Jersey's Court of Chancery explained, "[t]he pledge of stocks as collateral security has become a prevalent, and to the borrower, especially, an advantageous mode of effecting loans." That method of borrowing would become extremely cumbersome if the requirement of transfer upon the books of the corporation were observed literally. Such provisions, in the court's view, were "not intended to introduce a new mode of acquiring title to stocks," but were designed only to protect creditors. Where no creditor needed protection, transfers were good despite the failure to comply with the charter.[64]

But the judges' preference for free transferability was bounded by their concern for potential creditors of the shareholder or the corporation, even where those creditors were not yet ascertainable and might not ever exist. Shares of stock might be easily conveyed from one person to another, but did they fall within the legal category of negotiable instruments? That is, did a good-faith purchaser of stock acquire a complete title to the stock even if there was some flaw in the seller's title (for instance, if the stock had been fraudulently issued to the seller)? If so, someone with the right to sue the seller to recover the stock would be unable to bring the same suit against the buyer. Here the New York courts drew the line, and refused to classify stock as a negotiable instrument.[65] "Stocks are not like bank bills, the immediate representative of money, and intended for circulation," observed the state's Court of Appeals. "Nor are they, like notes and bills of exchange, less adapted to circulation, but invented to supply the exigencies of commerce." Such instruments were all made negotiable because they were used as effective forms of money, and could not serve that purpose as well unless one could accept them as payment without pausing to question their source. The circulation of instruments to which the seller lacked complete title, and thus the possible cutting off of suits to recover those instruments, was the price participants in the economy were willing to

---

[62] 22 Wend. at 352–53.

[63] See *Black* v. *Zacharie & Co.*, 3 How. (44 U.S.) 483, 513 (1845) (Story, J.) (applying Louisiana law); *Duke* v. *Cahawba Navigation Co.*, 10 Ala. 82, 90 (1846); *Conant, Ellis & Co.* v. *Reed*, 1 Ohio St. 298, 306 (1853); Angell and Ames, *Private Corporations Aggregate*, 326. These decisions sometimes rested expressly on the distinction between "legal" and "equitable" title suggested by Story in *Union Bank*, see *Black*, 3 How. at 513, although the opinions more often employed the sort of policy-based reasoning discussed in the text.

[64] *Broadway Bank* v. *McElrath*, 13 N.J. Eq. 24, 28 (1860).

[65] *Dunn* v. *Commercial Bank of Buffalo*, 11 Barb. 580, 585–86 (N.Y. App. Div. 1852).

pay for the liquidity such instruments provided. But there was no reason to pay the same price to make shares of stock negotiable as well. "Certificates of stock are not securities for money in any sense," the court concluded. "They are simply the muniments and evidence of the holder's title to a given share in the property and the franchises of the corporation."[66] A purchaser of stock would thus acquire whatever title to the stock the seller possessed; a potential creditor of the seller with respect to the stock would become a creditor of the buyer as well. People could convey stock without complying with charter provisions, but whatever limits those provisions placed on the rights associated with ownership of the stock would follow the stock to its new owner.

Despite general statutes and corporate charters that on their surface limited the transferability of stock, therefore, market participants were usually able to buy and sell stock simply by endorsing certificates. Only where creditors, usually creditors of the seller, stood to lose the ability to collect their debts because of putative stock transfers would courts enforce statutory transfer restrictions. This was most clearly true in New York, the state in which the greatest number of transactions occurred. The statutes had embodied a balance of policies favoring and disfavoring free transferability, but the trading community had developed a practice that tipped farther toward transferability, and the courts generally accommodated that practice, for the purpose of increasing the commercial utility of loans and sales of stock. Those choices by American judges over the first half of the nineteenth century were often explicitly intended to facilitate the growth of the market, and they probably had that cumulative effect.[67]

II

No statutes were necessary to combat deceit in the sale of securities. The common law doctrine of fraud had long prohibited sellers of ordinary property from deceiving buyers as to the property's value, and American judges and lawyers had little difficulty in applying the old doctrine to a new form of property. As early as 1790, in one of the very first reported American cases, the Connecticut Supreme Court implicitly recognized the possibility of an action for fraud in connection with the sale of securities. In affirming a recovery for the sale of an order on

---

[66] *Mechanics' Bank* v. *New-York and New Haven R.R. Co.*, 13 N.Y. 599, 626–27 (1856).

[67] The evidence presented here provides support for Morton Horwitz's thesis that early nineteenth-century American judges sought to mold the law so as to promote economic development. See Morton J. Horwitz, *The Transformation of American Law, 1780–1860* (Cambridge, MA: Harvard University Press, 1977).

the treasury of a town, claimed by the seller to be worth more than its true value, the court distinguished the case from one involving government debt. "[T]he value of public securities and state orders is a matter of public notoriety, equally known to the buyer as the seller," the court observed, and thus a claim of fraud could not be maintained. "[Y]et this is not the case with orders drawn by the selectmen of a town, or by individuals; their value is presumed to be in the knowledge of the seller and not of the buyer."[68] Corporate stock was still a tiny part of the new American securities market. The court could not have had the shares of business corporations in mind. Implicit in the court's distinction, however, was the assumption that a security whose true value was known only by the seller, and not by the buyer, could be the subject of a suit for fraud if the seller deceived the buyer as to the security's value. The issuance of stock by the promoters of a corporation fit this formula perfectly. When the corporate form became common, so did suits for the fraudulent sale of stock.

By the middle of the century, there were many reported cases finding fraud where stock had been purchased in reliance on knowing misrepresentations by the issuer's agents as to the stock's value.[69] "It is unquestionably true," asserted the Pennsylvania Supreme Court in 1856, that "where one is induced to make a subscription to the capital stock of a company by fraudulent representations or false statements of an agent of the company or commissioner appointed to obtain subscriptions, the contract may be avoided by the subscriber."[70] When the officers of a coal company, for instance, "made false representations respecting the character and value of the stock, and the then position of the company; representing that the affairs of the company were in a good and prosperous condition," when in fact the officers had sold more stock than they were authorized to issue and were pocketing the difference, thereby rendering the stock nearly worthless, the officers were liable to a plaintiff who had relied on those representations.[71]

False representations by the issuer about matters other than the value of the stock could constitute fraud as well, so long as stock was purchased in reliance on them. When the directors of a turnpike

---

[68] *Bacon* v. *Sanford*, 1 Root 164, 165 (Conn. 1790).
[69] See, e.g., *Crump* v. *United States Mining Co.*, 48 Va. 352, 371 (1851); *Litchfield Bank* v. *Peck*, 29 Conn. 384 (1860); *Waldo* v. *Chicago, St. Paul, and Fond du Lac R.R. Co.*, 14 Wis. 625, 635 (1861). For cases stating the rule but where fraud was lacking, see *Vicksburg, Shreveport & Texas R.R.* v. *McKean*, 63 La. 638, 639 (1857); *Cunningham* v. *Edgefield and Kentucky R.R. Co.*, 39 Tenn. 22, 27–28 (1858); *Mabey* v. *Adams*, 16 N.Y. Super. 346, 353–54 (1858).
[70] *Crossman* v. *Penrose Ferry Bridge Co.*, 26 Pa. 69, 71 (1856).
[71] *Mead* v. *Mali*, 15 How. Pr. 347, 350 (N.Y. Super. 1857).

company induced the state of Tennessee to purchase half of the company's stock, by falsely claiming that the other half had been paid for, the Tennessee Supreme Court acknowledged that the state would be able to rescind the transaction on the ground of fraud if it could prove that the directors knew their claims were false.[72] When a man in Montgomery, Alabama, bought stock in a plank-road company in reliance on the directors' false assertion that the road would run near his plantation, the Alabama Supreme Court held that the directors' fraud would be a complete defense to the company's suit to recover payment for the stock.[73] In all of these cases, it made no difference that stock was the subject of the suit; fraud was fraud, regardless of the type of property involved.

Fraud in securities transactions could also give rise to criminal prosecution, just like fraud in other kinds of transactions. In a celebrated 1826 New York trial, eight speculators were tried for conspiring to commit fraud. The jury hung, but the propriety of a criminal conspiracy charge in connection with the sale of stock was never questioned.[74]

In some fraud cases, however, the nature of the property did become important. The value of newly issued stock, more than any other kind of property, depended less on any observable state of affairs in the present than on the uncertain expectation of commercial success in the future. "The stock of all companies about to be engaged in mining operations," as one New York judge put it in 1855, "must have only a fancy value, and their real value cannot be ascertained until the experience of several years at least."[75] Promoters of a corporation were likely to make all sorts of statements about the corporation's prospects that would be unverifiable for some time to come. For this reason, courts very early began to distinguish between knowingly false statements of fact and unduly optimistic (but nevertheless sincere) opinions of the corporation's future success.[76] When the directors of the Salem Mill-Dam Corporation issued stock on the basis of their prediction that they would generate seventy "mill powers" of energy, but in fact never generated more than eleven and a half, the Massachusetts Supreme Judicial Court refused to

---

[72] *State v. Jefferson Tpk. Co.*, 22 Tenn. 305, 310–11 (1842).

[73] *Rives v. Montgomery South Plank-Road Co.*, 30 Ala. 92, 100 (1857).

[74] Despite a court order prohibiting publication of the trial proceedings, the trial was heavily reported in local newspapers and received national attention. See, e.g., *New-York Evening Post*, Sept. 27, 1826, through Oct. 24, 1826; *Niles' Weekly Register* [Baltimore], Oct. 28, 1826, 129. One of the defendants published his side of the story in Jacob Barker, *The Speeches of Mr. Jacob Barker and His Counsel, on the Trials for Conspiracy* (New York: W.A. Mersein, 1826).

[75] *Bell v. Mali*, 11 How. Pr. 254, 259–60 (N.Y. Sup. Ct. 1855).

[76] The distinction between fact and opinion originated in earlier fraud cases not involving securities. Horwitz, *Transformation*, 263.

invalidate the stock purchase agreements on the basis of fraud. "If there was a disappointment in regard to the degree of benefit expected from the project," the court concluded, "no doubt it was mutual."[77] Erroneous projections of future profitability might be the reason a shareholder subscribed to shares, held the Mississippi Supreme Court, "but are not grounds for avoiding his contract." A shareholder

> must be presumed to have invested his money in the enterprise subject to all the hazards incident to it, and which a prudent man must necessarily anticipate; and if he has done so upon erroneous or even deceptive opinions in relation to matters open to his inquiry, though expressed by an agent of the company, it is his own misfortune or fault, and he has no right to complain.[78]

A Superior Court judge in Ohio drew the most explicit distinction between "two kinds of representations or statements. One in reference to matters in their nature promissory, or resting in opinion, judgment or expectation, and the other in reference to facts as having actually occurred, or as really existing." The first category of statements could be deemed fraudulent only in very rare circumstances. But while the law "may excuse exaggerated statements in matters of opinion, belief, and judgment," the judge concluded, "I can not admit that it forms any legal or sufficient excuse for a departure from the truth as to facts, which are, or should be, a matter of knowledge."[79]

The common law of fraud was easily transposed to the most obvious parallel in the secondary market as well. Where one shareholder sold stock to another, by means of false statements as to the stock's value, the buyer would be entitled to rescind the sale. In 1858, for instance, a man in Albany, New York, traded his 47-acre farm for 90 shares of stock in the La Crosse and Milwaukee Rail Road Company, after being assured that the company "was in the hands of good business men; not a fancy man on the board," and that the railroad was currently earning $400,000 per year. In fact, the company was nearly insolvent, and the seller of the stock probably knew it. If he did, the New York Supreme Court held, the seller would have committed fraud.[80]

Many transactions involving fraud in the secondary market, however, bore no clear correspondence to the paradigmatic claim for fraud, because the party committing the fraud was neither the buyer nor the seller, but was rather an agent of the corporation. When stock was sold from one person to another at a market price that was artificially high,

---

[77] *Salem Mill-Dam Corp.* v. *Ropes*, 26 Mass. 187, 197 (1829).
[78] *Walker* v. *Mobile and Ohio R.R. Co.*, 34 Miss. 245, 256 (1857).
[79] *Nugent* v. *Cincinnati, Harrison & Indianapolis Straight Line R.R. Co.*, 2 Disn. 302, 305–06 (Ohio Super. 1858).
[80] *Yates* v. *Alden*, 41 Barb. 172, 177–78, 180–81 (N.Y. App. Div. 1863).

because both the buyer and the seller had been misled by false statements as to the corporation's financial condition, had the sale been induced by fraud? If so, who could the buyer sue? It took some time for judges and lawyers to settle on answers to these questions. In *Moffat* v. *Winslow* (1838), the first reported case raising the issue, the buyer sued the seller, seeking to rescind the transaction, on the theory that the corporate officer who had lied about the corporation's health should be treated as an agent of each of the corporation's shareholders, including the seller. The argument was rejected by New York's Chancellor. The "cases in which relief has been given to the purchasers of stock in mere bubbles," he observed, "all go upon the ground of fraud in the vendors," not fraud committed by a person not participating in the challenged transaction. He drew a lesson from the flurry of litigation in the years immediately after the South Sea Bubble. "[I]f the mere fraud of the directors and officers of a corporation, to enhance the value of its stock, was itself sufficient to authorize the court of chancery to rescind contracts made for the sale of stocks at extravagant prices, made by those who were not privy to such frauds," he observed, "nearly all the contracts for the sale of stocks in the South Sea Company . . . would have been rescinded." Of course, that had not happened. In short, "I have not been able to find a case in which such a contract was set aside on account of any fraud of the officers of the company, of which fraud the vendor of the stock was not cognizant at the time of the making of his contract of sale."[81]

Purchasers of stock at prices fraudulently inflated by agents of the corporation then tried suing the agents themselves for damages. The agents defended on the ground that the common law imposed no liability for the remote consequences of their deceit. Their alleged misrepresentations had not been made to the plaintiffs bringing the suits; in fact, they had never even heard of the plaintiffs until the suits were brought. If a corporate officer deceived A into paying too much for stock, the argument went, A could bring an action for fraud against the officer, but if A sold the stock to B, and B sold the stock to C, C could not turn around and sue the officer, or else the officer would be liable to every participant in the market. The lawyers defending these suits drew upon the South Sea Bubble as well. If the common law contained a principle making corporate officers liable to people with whom they had never dealt, the lawyers argued, the directors of the South Sea Company would have been liable at common law to everyone who lost money in 1720. There would have been no need for Parliament to clean up the

---

[81] *Moffat* v. *Winslow*, 7 Paige Ch. 124, 129–30 (N.Y. Ch. 1838).

matter by passing statutes. Because the South Sea directors had not been held liable at common law in the 1720s for the effect of their fraudulent representations on transactions in the secondary market, they suggested, neither should the officers of nineteenth-century American corporations.[82]

But the general common law of fraud had changed since the early eighteenth century, in a respect that created a favorable climate for this type of suit. By the middle of the nineteenth century, English and American courts had begun to extend fraud liability to misrepresentations not made specifically to the plaintiffs, on which plaintiffs had relied to their detriment.[83] These cases typically involved open letters of recommendation written by A as to the creditworthiness of B, relied upon by merchants extending credit to B who had never dealt with A. They were discussed by counsel in their appellate arguments in the securities fraud cases, and were thus known to the judges.[84] This new line of fraud cases, in conjunction with the background of popular opinion finding a need to prevent the deceit understood to permeate the securities market, was enough to cause mid-century judges to allow secondary purchasers to recover from corporate officers in actions for fraud. "When a bubble company is formed," held one New York judge in 1857,

with the fraudulent intent of its managers, to induce a general belief that its stock is of, at least, its par value, and that, in prosecuting the business for which it was professedly organized, it is making money, and so much money as to enable the shareholders to declare successive dividends out of the profits every two months, and this fraud is practised to give to the stock a market value, and to induce the public generally to seek it and purchase it as an investment – and the fraud is successful, and produces the results contemplated and intended; every person who, by means of such frauds, is induced to purchase, and is thereby subjected to a loss, is defrauded by such managers and their fraudulent acts.

The defrauded purchaser might never have transacted directly with the managers of the corporation, but that was no bar to recovery. The fraudulent recommendation cases served as a handy parallel:

The privity between the managers and every such purchaser is, in such a case, as

[82] *Cross v. Sackett*, 15 N.Y. Super. 617, 632–33 (1858); *Cazeaux v. Mali*, 25 Barb. 578, 586 (N.Y. App. Div. 1857).

[83] Paula Dalley, "The Law of Deceit, 1790–1860: Continuity Amidst Change," *American Journal of Legal History* 39 (1995): 439–40. Dalley suggests that this relaxation of the privity requirement was one factor distinguishing suits for fraud from suits for breach of warranty. Ibid., 414.

[84] *Wells v. Jewett*, 11 How. Pr. 242, 244 (N.Y. Sup. Ct. 1855); *Cazeaux*, 25 Barb. at 584; *Cross*, 15 N.Y. Super. at 635.

actual and as direct, as between a person giving, fraudulently, a general recommendation of the trustworthiness of a particular person, and the individual to whom it may be shown, relying on its truth, may give credit to the person so recommended, and be defrauded and injured thereby.

The judge recognized the danger of extending fraud liability along an infinite chain of securities sales. "[I]t cannot be law," he admitted, "that a person who deceives A by some instrument, and by it intends to deceive only him, can be made liable to every person who is injured from dealing with A." But in the typical case of securities fraud, the false statements of corporate officers were not intended to deceive only a single person. They were intended to fool the entire market, into pricing the stock at a level higher than its true value. In such a case, when the fraud had been directed at a large class of people, any person within the class who had been damaged had a right to sue.

[W]hen an instrument is made to deceive the public generally, and is adapted, as well as intended, to deceive some portion of the public, and as well one person as another, and is used as it was designed it should be, and fraudulently induces some one to act to his prejudice, by acting in the mode it was intended to influence them to act who might be deceived by it; the person who made the instrument, and caused it to be thus fraudulently used, is liable to the person who has been defrauded by it. In such a case, the person injured has been subjected to damage by his fraudulent acts, and the fraudulent wrong-doer is liable for the consequences.[85]

By 1860 it was clear in New York, the state with the most securities transactions, that a purchaser in the secondary market who paid too much as a result of the misrepresentations of corporate officers could recover from those officers in a suit for fraud.[86]

At approximately the same time, the legislatures of New York and Michigan took an additional step in the deterrence of securities fraud, by criminalizing certain fraudulent issuances of stock. The New York statute applied only to the issuance of "any false or fraudulent certificate" purporting to represent shares of stock or corporate debt.[87] It was enacted in 1855, shortly after the discovery that in 1853 and 1854 the officers of the Parker Vein Coal Company had issued $1.3 million of spurious stock, beyond the $3 million in genuine stock the company was authorized to issue.[88] The issuance of false stock certificates became a felony, punishable by a prison term of between three and seven years

---

[85] *Cross*, 15 N.Y. Super. at 647–49. See also *Cazeaux*, 25 Barb. at 583, 586.
[86] *Newbery* v. *Garland*, 31 Barb. 121, 129–30 (N.Y. App. Div. 1860); *Morse* v. *Swits*, 19 How. Pr. 275, 286–88 (N.Y. Sup. Ct. 1859). The same was true in England. See *Gerhard* v. *Bates*, 2 El. & Bl. 476, 118 Eng. Rep. 845 (K.B. 1853).
[87] N.Y. Laws, 78th Sess., c. 155, § 1 (1855).
[88] This event gave rise to five of the cases discussed in this chapter, *Bell* v. *Mali* (1855),

and a fine of up to $3,000. The Michigan statute, also enacted in 1855, was worded more ambiguously. It deemed guilty of a felony, punishable by a prison term of between one and ten years, anyone "who shall fraudulently issue or cause to be issued, any stock, scrip, or evidence of debt, of any" corporation.[89] The statute may have been intended only to cover the same conduct as the New York statute, the issuance of phony certificates of stock. But one who issued genuine stock while misrepresenting its value, conduct that was probably more common, might also have been considered to be "fraudulently issuing stock." The statute may thus have been intended to cover the entire range of fraud in the issuance of stock. These statutes, the first in the United States specifically making securities fraud a crime, were emblematic of the period, one in which state legislatures criminalized many property-related wrongs that had formerly been redressed through private civil suits. Many of these new criminal statutes were rarely enforced.[90] So far as one can tell from the reported cases, that was true of the New York and Michigan securities fraud statutes as well.

The law of fraud, whether common law or statute, generally applied only to affirmative misstatements. It imposed no duty on the seller of an item, whether stock or otherwise, to disclose any information in his possession, or to correct the buyer's mistaken belief as to the item's true value. A seller of stock or a corporate officer was "under no obligation to communicate any thing" to anyone.[91] There were occasional exceptions to this rule: Where a Vermont woman who did not know her stock's value sold it to a man with whom she had "a relation of trust and confidence," for instance, the Vermont Supreme Court was willing to find that "it was clearly his duty to tell her of its real value, and it was a fraud to take advantage of her ignorance and buy it at about a quarter of its market price."[92] But in the ordinary transaction, where no such relation existed, neither the officers of the corporation nor the seller of stock had any obligation under the common law to reveal anything about the corporation's state.[93]

In the twentieth century, many states, and later the federal govern-

---

Wells v. *Jewett* (1855), *Cazeaux* v. *Mali* (1857), *Mead* v. *Mali* (1857), and *Horton* v. *Morgan* (1859).

[89] Mich. Laws 1855, No. 128, § 1.   [90] Friedman, *History of American Law*, 292–94.

[91] *Cazeaux*, 25 Barb. at 584.   [92] *Mallory* v. *Leach*, 35 Vt. 156, 166 (1862).

[93] See, for example, the cases later in the nineteenth century declining to find fraud when corporate insiders bought or sold stock without disclosing inside information as to the stock's real value, such as *Crowell* v. *Jackson*, 23 A. 426 (N.J. 1891), and *Board of Commissioners of Tippecanoe County* v. *Reynolds*, 44 Ind. 509 (1873). No unit of American government would prohibit "insider trading" in corporate stock until the mid-twentieth century. William L. Cary and Melvin Aron Eisenberg, *Cases and Materials on Corporations*, 5th edn (Mineola: Foundation Press, 1980), 713–34.

ment, would move beyond this traditional limit by imposing statutory disclosure obligations on corporations issuing stock.[94] Before 1860, however, such disclosure obligations were imposed only very rarely, in occasional corporate charters. The directors of the Merchant's Louisville Insurance Company, for instance, chartered by Kentucky in 1830, were required to exhibit to the stockholders twice yearly "a fair and clear statement of the affairs of the company."[95] At each annual meeting of the shareholders of the Bank of Tennessee, chartered in 1831, the directors were to have "exhibited an exact and particular statement of the general accounts of the said corporation."[96] But these were exceptional charters. Most mandated no disclosure to shareholders or to the market generally of any information that might bear on the price of the stock.[97]

III

Securities transactions raised many of the legal issues raised by transactions in other kinds of property. The ordinary doctrines governing commercial contracts, for example, had to be applied when those contracts involved stock, and could generally be applied without a second thought.[98] When P. T. Barnum refused to accept delivery of stock he had contracted to buy, and then refused to pay damages on the ground that the stock had never been delivered to him, the courts had little difficulty in holding Barnum liable. It made no difference that stock, rather than some other item, was the subject of the contract.[99] These cases were not conceptualized as belonging to any single category. Where they involved trusts, they belonged to the law of trusts;[100] where

---

[94] Jonathan R. Macey and Geoffrey P. Miller, "Origin of the Blue Sky Laws," *Texas Law Review* 70 (1991): 347; Gregg A. Jarrell, "The Economic Effects of Federal Regulation of the Market for New Security Issues," *Journal of Law and Economics* 24 (1981): 613.

[95] Ky. Laws 1829–30, c. 275, § 9.   [96] Tenn. Laws 1831, c. 5, § 10.

[97] Some corporations, although no one knows how many, were disclosing information to shareholders without any legal compulsion to do so. Ross L. Watts and Jerold L. Zimmerman, "Agency Problems, Auditing, and the Theory of the Firm: Some Evidence," *Journal of Law and Economics* 26 (1983): 613.

[98] See, e.g., *Alexander v. Macauley's Administrators*, 6 Md. 359 (1854).

[99] *Munn v. Barnum*, 24 Barb. 283 (N.Y. App. Div. 1857). The stock, in the Crystal Palace, a short-lived New York exhibition hall, had fallen in value from $175 to $21 per share. Barnum had agreed to buy it, six months from the contract date, at $71. On the Crystal Palace and the price of its stock, see Neil Harris, *Humbug: The Art of P. T. Barnum* (Boston: Little, Brown, 1973), 147.

[100] See, e.g., *Mechanics Bank of Alexandria v. Seton*, 1 Pet. (26 U.S.) 299 (1828); *Spencer v. Spencer*, 11 Paige Ch. 299 (N.Y. Ch. 1844); *Farmers and Mechanics Bank of Frederick Cty. v. Wayman*, 5 Gill 336 (Md. 1847); *Butler v. M. Ins. Co.*, 14 Ala. 777 (1848).

they involved bankruptcy, they belonged to the law of bankruptcy;[101] where they involved stock held by married women, they belonged to the law of coverture;[102] where they involved stock sold to or by an agent, they belonged to the law of agency;[103] and so on. As English judges had done in the previous century, American judges could simply apply older bodies of property-related law to a new kind of property.

The largest group of litigated disputes over securities transactions involved questions of how corporations were to be governed or when shareholders were to be liable for corporate debts. These cases were understood to belong to a new category of law, the law of private corporations, a category that did not exist (and could not have existed) until the corporation became a common form of business enterprise.[104] This group of cases produced doctrines that had no application where corporate stock was not involved, but those doctrines were less concerned with transactions in stock than with internal governance and the liability of shareholders for the debts of the corporation – in the classification scheme used by late twentieth-century lawyers, these cases raised questions of corporate law rather than securities law[105] – and so they will not be treated here. (To the extent that anyone thought of the law regulating securities transactions as an entity in itself, apart from the law governing transactions generally, it would have been a subset of this larger field. The first American treatise devoted to the law of private corporations, for instance, published in 1832, included as chapter 15 a discussion "Of the Transfer of Stock in Monied, or Joint Stock Incorporated Companies."[106])

---

[101] See, e.g., *Nathan v. Whitlock*, 9 Paige Ch. 152 (N.Y. Ch. 1841); *In re Empire City Bank*, 6 Abb. Pr. 385 (N.Y. Sup. Ct. 1857).

[102] See, e.g., *Morgan v. Thames Bank*, 14 Conn. 99 (1840).

[103] See, e.g., *Stamford Bank v. Ferris*, 17 Conn. 258 (1845); William Paley, *A Treatise on the Law of Principal and Agent* (Philadelphia: Abraham Small, 1822), 102–04, 173–74.

[104] See, e.g., *Bates v. N.Y. Ins. Co.*, 3 Johns. Cas. 238 (N.Y. Sup. Ct. 1802); *Merchants Bank v. Cook*, 21 Mass. 405 (1826); *In re Long Island R.R. Co.*, 19 Wend. 36 (N.Y. Sup. Ct. 1837); *West Philadelphia Canal Co. v. Innes*, 3 Whart. 198 (Pa. 1837); *Muskungum Valley Tpk. Co. v. Ward*, 13 Ohio 120 (1844); *Rianhard v. Hovey*, 13 Ohio 300 (1844); *James v. Woodruff*, 2 Denio 574 (N.Y. 1845), aff'g 10 Paige Ch. 541 (N.Y. Ch. 1844); *Mann v. Currie*, 2 Barb. 294 (N.Y. Sup. Ct. 1848); *Lane v. Morris*, 8 Ga. 468 (1850); *Downing v. Potts*, 23 N.J.L. 66 (1851); *Delaware and Atlantic R.R. Co. v. Irick*, 23 N.J.L. 321 (1852); *Dauchy v. Brown*, 24 Vt. 197 (1852); *Pollock v. National Bank*, 7 N.Y. 274 (1852); *Roosevelt v. Brown*, 11 N.Y. 148 (1854); *People v. Devlin*, 17 Ill. 84 (1855); *Miller v. Illinois Central R.R. Co.*, 24 Barb. 312 (N.Y. App. Div. 1857); *Cowles v. Cromwell*, 25 Barb. 413 (N.Y. App. Div. 1857); *Everhart v. West Chester and Philadelphia R.R. Co.*, 28 Pa. 339 (1857); *Palmer v. Ridge Mining Co.*, 34 Pa. 288 (1859); *New England Commercial Bank v. Newport Steam Factory*, 6 R.I. 154 (1859).

[105] See, e.g., Edmund W. Kitch, "A Federal Vision of the Securities Laws," *Virginia Law Review* 70 (1984): 858.

[106] Angell and Ames, *A Treatise*, 316–48.

One recurring question specific to securities transactions, however, did require special consideration in New York. It was a question that cut across doctrinal lines: To what extent should courts recognize the customs of professional stock traders as a source of law? On one hand, the conventions of mercantile communities had long furnished the legal system with rules capable of resolving disputes brought to the official court system. On the other, there was something a little unsettling about adopting the practices of the stockjobbers, a group not quite as reputable as other kinds of merchants. "[T]o allow the usages of Wall-street to control the general law in relation to any matter," explained one member of New York's highest court, "might result in the establishment of principles not always in accordance with sound morals."[107] We have already seen one instance of this tension, in *Commercial Bank of Buffalo* v. *Kortright* (1839), the case in which the New York Court of Errors permitted the free transferability of shares of stock, even where parties had failed to comply with charter provisions requiring transfers to be entered on the books of the corporation. The majority rested its decision largely on what it perceived to be the useful custom of New York securities traders; the dissent complained strenuously that Wall Street customs should not be permitted to override positive law.[108] The question of how far to incorporate stockjobbing custom into the law arose repeatedly both before and after.

When brokers took shares of stock as collateral for loans, for example, did those same identified shares remain marked as collateral for the duration of the loan, or could any equivalent number of shares in the same corporation in the brokers' possession serve as the collateral? The brokers' practice of continually buying and selling shares in a market where prices were constantly fluctuating made the question an important one. In early 1818, the New York brokerage firm of Prime, Ward and Sands took 430 shares of stock in the Bank of the United States as collateral for a loan to one of its customers, Charles Nourse. All through the year, the firm speculated in bank stock, which was trading at high prices. At all times, it held more than 430 shares, but it never segregated Nourse's shares from the other shares it owned. Prices dropped at the end of the year, when Nourse defaulted on his loan. Upon Nourse's default, the brokerage firm sold 430 shares of bank stock, at prices by then too low to satisfy the loan. The firm sued Nourse for the deficiency. Nourse argued, in an effort to enjoin the suit from proceeding, that the firm had a duty to keep his shares separate from the others, and that, because the firm had not done so, it should be treated as if it had

---

[107] *Dykers* v. *Allen*, 7 Hill 497, 501 (N.Y. 1844).
[108] *Commercial Bank of Buffalo* v. *Kortright*, 22 Wend. 348, 352–53, 362–63 (N.Y. 1839).

actually sold *his* shares earlier in the year, when prices were high enough
to cover his entire obligation. The firm replied that "according to the
course and practice of doing business in this respect," they had no such
duty to segregate Nourse's shares. Chancellor Kent agreed that this
custom of brokers should serve as the rule resolving the dispute. "As the
defendants, at that time, carried on the business of stock and exchange
brokers," Kent explained, "and as the plaintiff dealt with them in that
capacity, he should have caused the shares to have been identified, if he
intended that they should have been kept distinct and separate from the
mass of stock in which the defendants dealt." Brokers, in Kent's view,
were entitled to make "such transfers and appropriations as the exigencies of their business and engagements required," without having to
keep track of precisely which shares they were selling. A question on
which no clear precedent offered guidance could be answered by
reference to the practices of the New York stock trading community.[109]

A similar question arose in the 1850s, when a broker's customer
sought to recover money he had paid to compensate the broker for
losses the broker sustained in buying and selling stock on the customer's
behalf. The customer argued that the broker had in fact bought the
stock in his own name, and that the broker should therefore have borne
the losses. The broker defended on the ground that such was the custom
of brokers, who always bought stock in their own names, without
disclosing the identities of their principals. The Court of Appeals
decided in favor of the broker, because of this custom. "The practice at
the stock board," the court concluded, "by which the brokers only, and
not their customers, are known in their dealings with each other, was
not unreasonable, and the plaintiff, by directing this purchase to be
made, must be understood as consenting that it should be done in the
usual manner." This practice was necessary for the safety of the brokers,
the court reasoned, because they often extended credit to their customers when buying stock on their behalf, and they needed to be able to
sell the stock in the event their customers defaulted. Again, a court was
willing to defer to the perceived needs of the New York brokers, and to
permit their practices to serve as default rules, binding as law where
alternative rules had not been explicitly specified.[110]

By 1860, the use of stock market customs as rules of law was well
established in New York. "The plaintiff dealt with the defendants as
stock-brokers," one lower court judge explained, "and was bound by

---

[109] *Nourse* v. *Prime, Ward and Sands*, 4 Johns. Ch. 490, 493, 495–96 (N.Y. Ch. 1820).
[110] *Horton* v. *Morgan*, 19 N.Y. 170, 172–73 (1859). The result was consistent with the
contemporary general law of agency. See Joseph Story, *Commentaries on the Law of
Agency*, 2nd edn (Boston: Little, Brown, 1844), 427–28.

those customs which prevailed in relation to that species of business." A broker was not liable to his customer in the event that the stock the broker bought for the customer turned out to be spurious, for example, because the broker, in buying the stock in his own name and then transferring title to the customer, was simply acting "in the mode usual and customary among stock-brokers in the city of New-York." Because the conventions of the trading community did not make brokers guarantors of the authenticity of stock, neither would the courts.[111]

New York courts rejected the custom of stockbrokers in only one reported case before 1860. In *Dykers* v. *Allen* (1844), the broker had sold stock pledged as collateral for a loan, before payment of the loan was due. Ordinary commercial law did not permit a pledgee to sell the item pledged, unless the parties had agreed to the contrary. The broker and his client had agreed to permit such a sale, but only after payment became due. At trial, the broker attempted to introduce evidence that despite the state's commercial law, and despite the parties' agreement permitting sale only at a specified time, the practice of brokers was to sell pledged stock at any time. The Court of Errors held that the trial judge had properly rejected the proffered evidence. A "custom of the brokers in Wall-street in opposition to the general law of the state; and which custom was wholly inconsistent with the written contract between these parties," could not be given force, observed one of the judges. "I know of no rule of law," insisted another, "which will confer upon a stock broker in Wall-street any greater authority over a pledge, than is given by law to a pledgee of property elsewhere." The second judge concluded with what sounded like a ringing rejection of reliance on the customs of stockjobbers. "I prefer that legal principles should have a universal application," he sniffed, "and that contracts should receive the same interpretation in the thronged and busy mart of our commercial metropolis that they do elsewhere."[112]

But *Dykers* was an unusual case, in that the suggested custom conflicted with positive law and with the apparent intention of the parties to the suit, as embodied in their contract. In the normal case, where Wall Street practices were inconsistent with neither, the New York courts were willing to adopt them as law.

When given the opportunity, early nineteenth-century American judges sought to accommodate the growing securities market, by narrowly construing statutory limits on the transferability of shares, by pushing the common law of fraud in a direction that would permit stock

[111] *Peckham* v. *Ketcham*, 10 Abb. Pr. 220, 221 (N.Y. Super. 1860).
[112] *Dykers*, 7 Hill at 499, 501–02.

purchasers to recover from deceitful corporate promoters, and by deferring to the practices of the New York trading community. American judges were a heterogeneous lot, and so it is difficult to generalize about them, but it seems fair to assume that many, like other Americans of similar wealth, owned securities of some kind. As had been the case in England in the previous century, many of the judges had a small personal stake in facilitating the growth of the market. Just as important, participation in the market would have meant that it was not entirely a strange institution. The stock market might have been understood as a casino, or as a den of fast talkers in a big city, but it was also understood as the ownership of shares in a local canal company or a local bank. Although there was still something unsavory about the market's permanent residents, the market itself was a useful institution that deserved to be shielded from overzealous regulation. In the hands of judges who thought this way, the legal system was a tool that could be used to promote securities trading generally, but to deter the deceit and the overspeculation thought to lurk in the background.

8   Self-regulation by the New York brokers, 1791–1860

Government was not the only regulator of the securities market in the first half of the nineteenth century. The stockjobbers regulated themselves as well, at first tentatively in the late eighteenth century, and then with increasing confidence as the nineteenth century progressed. By the 1820s, the New York Stock and Exchange Board encompassed a miniature private legal system, which formulated rules governing the market and resolved disputes involving members. Because most time bargains were unenforceable in the New York courts until 1858, this dispute resolution mechanism was the only one available for the enforcement of such transactions, a circumstance which made membership in the Board more attractive, and strengthened the Board's position as a market regulator generally. By the middle of the century, the regulation produced by the Stock and Exchange Board was almost certainly of greater significance to the trading community than the regulation produced by the state of New York or any other unit of government.

Section I of this chapter will describe the origin and growth of the New York Stock and Exchange Board (the organization would shorten its name in 1863 to the New York Stock Exchange). Section II will discuss the functions the Board performed for its members, in order to understand why the Board was formed and how it could have been so successful. Section III will look more closely at the ways in which the Board regulated the securities market.

I

The earliest evidence of self-regulation by American securities traders is a September 1791 broadside memorializing a "MEETING of the DEALERS in the PUBLIC FUNDS in the CITY of NEW-YORK held at the COFFEE-HOUSE." At this meeting, held only a few months after the onset in New York of daily public auctions of federal government debt, an unknown number of "dealers" agreed to be governed by a set of fourteen rules. Some of the rules attempted to cartelize the new occupation of stockbrokering. Signatories were prohibited, for instance, from attending auction sales conducted by any auctioneer who bought or sold stock on his own account without employing a broker. Another rule restricted the number of securities auctions to one per day. Another forbade participants from doing business with any auctioneer who had not signed the agreement. More sophisticated efforts at cartel formation would be a regular feature for many years to come. Some of the rules set up a mechanism for enforcing sales contracts. A victim of a breached contract, for instance, was authorized to cover on the market and then recover his losses from the breaching party. Under another rule, brokers defaulting on contracts were to be barred from participating in any transactions thereafter. The establishment of a non-governmental method of enforcing contracts would also be an important component of self-regulation in the nineteenth century. The rest of the rules simply sought to regularize the auction process. Lots of securities offered for sale were required to be numbered, for instance, and to be "fairly and distinctly described" in writing. Later efforts at self-regulation would likewise give great attention to this function as well.[1]

After the market crashed in the spring of 1792, public securities auctions in New York ceased, which meant that the 1791 agreement had little chance to have any effect. In May 1792, twenty-four New York brokers – twenty-two individuals and two two-man firms – signed another agreement, a single sentence in length, pledging not to "buy or sell from this day for any person whatsoever, any kind of Public Stock, at a less rate than one quarter per cent Commission."[2] This second agreement, another attempt at the formation of a cartel, appears to have been equally unsuccessful.[3]

Trading nevertheless continued among the signers of the 1792 agreement and others. The market was still dominated by the new federal debt, the value of which rose and fell along with public confidence in the new government, confidence which depended on the course of public events. Trading in the federal debt was thus an indirect means of

---

[1] The 1791 broadside is reproduced in Werner and Smith, *Wall Street*, 190–91.

[2] Buttonwood Agreement, NYSE.

[3] Two legends connected with the 1792 agreement – that it formed the organization that would grow into the New York Stock Exchange, and that it was signed outdoors beneath a buttonwood tree – are persuasively refuted in Peter Eisenstadt, "How the Buttonwood Tree Grew: The Making of a New York Stock Exchange Legend," *Prospects: An Annual of American Cultural Studies* 19 (1994): 75. I nevertheless refer to it in these notes as the Buttonwood Agreement, because that is what it has come to be called.

speculating on public events. The early New York securities traders often gambled on public events directly as well, as one of them recorded in his papers.

Feb. 13, 1795. I bet G. McEvers Ten Drs. to Five Drs. that there would not be 3,000 votes taken at the ensuing election for Governor in the City and County of New York.

Feb. 16, 1795. Bet John Morton a suit of cloaths not to exceed £15 that provisional Articles of Peace would be signed between Britain and France by the 16 Feb., 1796.

Feb. 17, 1795. I bet Robert Cocks, Sen'r, a pair of Satin Breeches that Jay would be elected Governor by a majority of five hundred or more.

March 17, 1795. Garret Kettletas bets me a Beaver hat, value Six Dollars, that Guadeloupe would be in possession of the British in 6 months.

May 25, 1795. Mr. Walton bet me fifty Dollars to twenty that if Barriere was delivered to the Revolutionary Tribunal by the Convention on or before the 22nd March last, that he w'd be Guillotined on or before the 2d April last.

June 1, 1795. Thomas Elmers agrees to give me sixty pounds and I am to pay him one shilling for every vote Jay may have more than Yates.

Nov. 24, 1795. John Thurston bet me 30 Dollars to 10 Dollars that all the Electors of this state appointed by the Legislature would not vote for Adams and Pinckney.[4]

The public reputation of stockjobbers as gamblers (discussed in chapter 6) was not far off the mark.

Indeed, the sole instance of collective action on the part of the New York brokers between 1792 and 1817 of which records have survived, the Tontine Coffee-House, was a similar sort of speculative venture. A large number of brokers, lawyers, and merchants contributed in 1793 to the construction of the coffee house, which was used for securities trading. Ownership of the coffee house was divided at the outset into 203 shares. The owner of each share designated a person as nominee. Upon the nominee's death, that share would cease to exist, and the profits accruing to that share would be divided equally among all the shares still in existence. (This scheme mimicked the structure of a *tontine*, at that time a familiar method of public finance, invented in France by Lorenzo Tonti in the mid seventeenth century and proposed by Hamilton in 1790 as a way of financing the new federal government.[5] Subscribers to a tontine effectively purchased from the government a lifetime annuity, in which the annual payments to the first subscribers to die were redistributed upon each death to those subscribers still alive.)

---

[4] Quoted in Francis Eames, *The New York Stock Exchange* (1894) (New York: Greenwood Press, 1968), 16–17.

[5] Robert M. Jennings, Donald F. Swanson, and Andrew P. Trout, "Alexander Hamilton's Tontine Proposal," *William and Mary Quarterly* 45 (1988): 107.

Eventually "the said Nominees shall by Death be reduced to Seven," at which time the tontine would terminate, and "the whole of the said property is to vest in the Persons then entitled to the Shares standing in the names of the Seven Surviving Nominees."[6] Owners of shares in the Tontine Coffee-House included young New York merchants and lawyers like John Jacob Astor, Rufus King, and Brockholst Livingston, as well as a substantial part of the stockjobbing community. Because owners generally picked their youngest children as nominees (the future lawyer and Congressman Gulian Verplanck, then only six years old, was one of the nominees), the tontine did not end until 1876, by which time the building had been razed, having long since stopped serving as either a coffee house or a center for securities trading.[7] Early in the nineteenth century, however, trading continued in the Tontine and other New York coffee houses, despite the absence of any formal brokers' organization.

When the market for federal debt securities rapidly expanded during and after the War of 1812, the stockjobbers again tried to organize, this time with more success.[8] In 1817, twenty-seven brokers – nineteen individuals and eight firms – constituted themselves the New York Stock and Exchange Board. As the name suggested, the Board was established to trade not just stock, but currency and specie as well. The brokers adopted an initial set of seventeen rules to govern trading and the admission of new members.[9] The New York brokers may have copied a similar organization already in existence in Philadelphia, although the evidence of such an organization is unclear.[10] They were most likely familiar with the Stock Exchange established by the brokers in London in the second half of the eighteenth century, so the presence or absence of an American model may not have made much of a difference.[11] In

---

[6] "The Constitution and Nominations of the Subscribers to the Tontine Coffee-House" (1796), Tontine Coffee House Collection, NYHS.

[7] Robert W. July, *The Essential New Yorker: Gulian Crommelin Verplanck* (Durham: Duke University Press, 1951), 237; James E. Buck, ed., *The New York Stock Exchange: The First 200 Years* (Essex: Greenwich Pub. Group, 1992), 22.

[8] Edmund Clarence Stedman, *The New York Stock Exchange* (1905) (New York: Greenwood Press, 1969), 62.

[9] Constitution of the New York Stock & Exchange Board 1817, NYSE. The Board's various constitutions and by-laws will be cited hereafter by year, as in "1820 Const." or "1833 By-Laws." They are also located at the NYSE. The 1820 by-laws are captioned "Bye Laws," and will be cited with that spelling.

[10] For assertions that a Philadelphia board of brokers predated the New York Stock and Exchange Board, see James K. Medbery, *Men and Mysteries of Wall Street* (1870) (New York: Greenwood Press, 1968), 288; Margaret G. Myers, *A Financial History of the United States* (New York: Columbia University Press, 1970), 119. The closest recent students of the subject find the evidence equivocal. Werner and Smith, *Wall Street*, 216 nn. 6 & 7.

[11] E. Victor Morgan and W. A. Thomas, *The Stock Exchange: Its History and Functions*, 2nd edn (London: Elek, 1969), 68–69.

any event, Philadelphia and Boston would have brokers' organizations similar to New York's within a short time. By 1832, the Philadelphia Stock Exchange had a permanent location to conduct trading; two years later, thirteen Boston brokers formed the Boston Brokers' Board, later to rename itself the Boston Stock Exchange.[12]

The New York Stock and Exchange Board remained very small by modern standards throughout the first half of the century. In 1820, membership was up to thirty-nine.[13] By 1836, the Board reported that it "consists of about fifty persons."[14] Membership was up to seventy-five by 1848.[15] New members could be proposed by any existing member. Admission to the Board was by secret ballot of all members; three negative votes were enough to deny admission.[16] The minimum qualifications for admission fluctuated over the years. The Board's initial 1817 Constitution required prospective members to "have been in the business for the term of one or more years, either as a Broker or an apprentice," but within the year this requirement was stiffened, to mandate a two-year apprenticeship to an existing member of the Board.[17] In 1820, the Board again opened admission to brokers with a year's experience.[18] The Board began charging initiation fees to new members in 1820, when the fee was set at $25.[19] The size of the initiation fee thereafter serves as a rough barometer of the Board's growing power; the amount would increase to $150 by 1833, and $400 by 1848, equivalent to several thousand dollars in the late twentieth century.[20] This rate of growth is even larger than it appears, because the period was one of deflation; the cost of living *declined* by approximately 17 percent between 1820 and 1848.[21]

Trading was conducted at closed meetings in a large room. The President of the Board called each security, one by one. As each was

---

[12] Joseph Jackson, *The Encyclopedia of Philadelphia* (Harrisburg: National Historical Association, 1933), IV, 1115–16; Clarence W. Barron and Joseph G. Martin, *The Boston Stock Exchange* (Boston: Hunt & Bell, 1893) (the book is unpaginated; the reference is to the first two pages of text). See also Joseph G. Martin, *Seventy-Three Years' History of the Boston Stock Market* (Boston: s.n., 1871). The early records of the Boston and Philadelphia stock exchanges, except for price quotations, have apparently not survived. We accordingly lack evidence as to whether the Boston and Philadelphia exchanges developed internal regulatory mechanisms like the one described in this chapter, but the most reasonable assumption is that they did.

[13] Werner and Smith, *Wall Street*, 28.   [14] "Memorial and Remonstrance," 3.

[15] Armstrong, *Stocks and Stock-Jobbing*, 8. Armstrong claims later in the same book that the Board has 112 members, ibid., 38, which casts some doubt on the precision of his information, but the general range is probably accurate.

[16] 1817 Const. art. 5; 1820 Const. art. 5; 1833 Const. art. 5; 1856 Const. art. 7.

[17] 1817 Const. art. 16; 1817 Const. art. 20.

[18] 1820 Const. art. 5; 1833 Const. art. 5; 1856 Const. art. 9.   [19] 1820 Const. art. 5.

[20] 1833 Const. art. 5; Armstrong, *Stocks and Stock Jobbing*, 8; 1856 Const. art. 10.

[21] US Bureau of the Census, *Historical Statistics*, 1:212.

Table 8.1 *Growth of New York Stock and Exchange Board, 1820–1840*

Year	Stocks listed	Average daily trading volume
1820	28	156 shares
1825	69	1,108
1830	58	456
1835	80	8,475
1840	112	4,266

called, members wishing to sell would say so, and members wishing to buy would then bid for the stock being sold. The prices at which sales were concluded were transcribed by the Board's Secretary, and then reported in the newspapers.[22] The composition of the list of stocks called was apparently set informally in the early years, as the Board had no written rules governing the subject. By 1856, however, the process had been formalized; parties seeking to have a stock listed at the Board would file an application, which was then put to a vote of the members.[23] At the beginning, the same informality characterized the sizes and prices of lots traded in the early years. These were regularized even sooner; by 1820, stock could not be offered for sale in blocks smaller than $500, and bids could not be made for less than one quarter percent of the stock's par value unless for sums of $1,000 or more.[24] (Stock prices were expressed as a percentage of par value, not in dollars; the floor of one quarter percent effectively prohibited transactions in securities that had become nearly worthless.)

The growth of the Stock and Exchange Board over the first half of the century followed the general expansion of securities trading. This growth can be expressed either in number of stocks listed or in average daily trading volume, both of which fluctuated widely around an increasing trend between 1820 and 1840 (see table 8.1).[25] Both of these figures grew much larger in the 1850s, as railroad stocks began to dominate trading on the Stock and Exchange Board.[26]

Despite its growth, the Stock and Exchange Board never achieved control of a majority of the securities trading in New York during this period. Groups of brokers set up shortlived competing exchanges in 1834–37 and 1845–48, both of which dissolved apparently because

[22] Armstrong, *Stocks and Stock-Jobbing*, 8; "Memorial and Remonstrance," 3.
[23] 1856 By-Laws art. 2.
[24] 1820 Bye Laws art. 1; 1833 By-Laws art. 1; 1856 By-Laws art. 10.
[25] Information in the above table is from Werner and Smith, *Wall Street*, 162, 164.
[26] Joseph Edward Hedges, *Commercial Banking and the Stock Market Before 1863* (Baltimore: Johns Hopkins Press, 1938), 36, 40.

price declines caused the insolvency of many members.[27] The dealers in mining stocks attempted to form their own exchange in 1857 and again in 1859; the first effort lasted less than six months, most likely because of the depression of that year, and the second ceased operating when the prospect of civil war reduced the volume of trading.[28] More important than these other exchanges was the persistence of trading outside any exchange, in brokers' offices, in coffee houses, and in the street. "When the Brokers are not in session," William Armstrong observed in 1848, "they as well as all other operators and interested persons, assemble promiscuously at the corner of Wall and Hanover streets . . . and it not unfrequently happens that more business is done in the open air than at both the Boards."[29] The Board itself reported in 1836 that "buying and selling, to a great extent, is done publicly in the street, or at the exchange, after the board adjourns."[30] The closest modern students of the subject estimate that in the 1820s and 1830s the trading volume outside the Board was approximately three times the volume traded within.[31]

The Stock and Exchange Board nevertheless exerted a powerful influence over non-Board transactions, because the proceedings of the Board effectively set the prices at which stock was bought and sold elsewhere.[32] As the Board boasted in 1836 of its trading records, "the courts of justice in the city of New-York have, uniformly, since the establishment of the board, taken them as the highest evidence of the prices of stocks."[33] This influence was initially most powerful in New York, where price information could be transmitted quickly.[34] The invention of the telegraph in the late 1830s enabled the Board to set prices for the country. By 1845 New York was linked by telegraph to many other cities.[35] Stockbrokers were among the first customers for telegraph services; by the 1850s, stock prices in every large American city followed New York prices.[36] New York's status as the center of American securities trading, already clear by 1840, thus grew even clearer.[37]

Although the New York securities market was a much smaller

---

[27] Robert Sobel, *The Curbstone Brokers: The Origins of the American Stock Exchange* (New York: Macmillan, 1970), 17–18; Armstrong, *Stocks and Stock-Jobbing*, 8.

[28] Sobel, *Curbstone Brokers*, 27, 29.   [29] Armstrong, *Stocks and Stock-Jobbing*, 8.

[30] "Memorial and Remonstrance," 5.   [31] Werner and Smith, *Wall Street*, 169.

[32] On the ability of a minority of informed traders to set securities prices, see Ronald J. Gilson and Reinier H. Kraakman, "The Mechanisms of Market Efficiency," *Virginia Law Review* 70 (1984): 565–92.

[33] "Memorial and Remonstrance," 3.   [34] Armstrong, *Stocks and Stock-Jobbing*, 8.

[35] Hedges, *Commercial Banking*, 39.   [36] Sobel, *Big Board*, 52–53.

[37] R. C. Michie, *The London and New York Stock Exchanges 1850–1914* (London: Allen & Unwin, 1987), 174. On the size of the New York market relative to Philadelphia and

component of the national economy than it is today, it quickly became well enough integrated into the larger economy to serve as an indicator of general economic conditions. As New York became the nation's commercial and banking center, New York banks began to hold large balances on deposit from banks in other parts of the country. These balances tended to rise and fall following the agricultural cycle. In the autumn, when farmers shipped grain to New York for further transport, balances would accumulate in New York banks. In the spring, when farmers needed money for wages and purchases, the New York balances would be drawn down. This cycle, noticed as early as 1793, intensified over the first half of the nineteenth century. Between autumn and spring, New York banks used their excess balances to make "call loans," loans repayable upon demand. Many of the customers for call loans used the money to speculate in the securities market. In the spring, when the banks' balances were drawn down, the banks called in the loans. Borrowers had to sell securities in order to transfer funds back to the banks. As a result, there was an inflow of capital into the market each autumn, and an outflow each spring.[38] One product of this linkage between the stock market and the broader economy was a close correspondence between movements in stock prices quoted on the Stock and Exchange Board and general economic trends. Beginning with the panic of 1837 at the latest, stock market crashes and general economic contractions would coincide.[39] This pattern marked a departure from earlier market movements; in 1792, for instance, the dramatic drop in stock prices did not coincide with any broader economic trend.

By 1860, the New York Stock and Exchange Board, although still a relatively small organization by twentieth-century standards, thus dominated securities trading in New York, effectively set stock prices nationwide, and was beginning to stand in contemporary consciousness (as it does today) as a symbol of the overall health of the economy. The Board's prominence enabled the more flamboyant of its members to become nationally known figures. Even before the great battles of the 1860s, men like Jacob Little and Daniel Drew were already celebrities, famous for nothing but buying and selling securities.[40]

Boston, the second- and third-largest, as of 1840, see Werner and Smith, *Wall Street*, 188–89.

[38] Hedges, *Commercial Banking*, 56–60, 76–101, 121.

[39] Werner and Smith, *Wall Street*, 42.

[40] On Little, see Robert Irving Warshow, *The Story of Wall Street* (New York: Greenberg, 1929), 63–79; Werner and Smith, *Wall Street*, 55–57. On Drew, see Clifford Browder,

II

Why was the Stock and Exchange Board so successful? A voluntary collective organization like the Board could not have survived without offering its members something they perceived to be worth the price of membership.[41] Why would a New York broker in the first half of the nineteenth century be willing to pay $400 in order to become a member? What did he get in return? To begin to answer these questions requires a great deal of inference from a small amount of evidence, but we can isolate five separate benefits brokers obtained from membership.

One benefit a broker received in exchange for his membership fee was an orderly procedure for matching buyers and sellers, and regular access to a room full of other brokers, any of whom might be a trading partner when one was needed. As each issue of stock was called, and as each block of offered stock was put up for auction, every member with an interest in buying or selling was brought together for that purpose with the expenditure of a minimum of time and effort. Transaction costs inside the Board were most likely lower than transaction costs outside on the street, where disorganized trading made it more difficult for buyers and sellers of a particular stock at a particular price to find one another within a reasonable time. Lower transaction costs could have benefited Board members in a few different ways. As brokers, they would have been able to engage in more trades within a given period of time, which would have earned them more commissions. Knowledge of this speed advantage may have prompted investors to be more willing to hire Board members than non-members as brokers, which again would have increased the number of commissions earned by members. The Board's ability to concentrate buyers and sellers at an auction may have resulted in better prices – that is, fewer disappointed buyers and sellers having to make concessions in order to find a trading partner – which again may have caused investors to prefer a Board member to a non-member as a broker. Board members were also investors themselves, and in this capacity they would have gained as well from the speed and the prices provided by organized trading.

The value of access to organized trading, however, was subject to some limits in the first half of the nineteenth century. Transaction costs outside the Board, although most likely higher than inside, were probably not very much higher. The community of New York brokers

---

The Money Game in Old New York: Daniel Drew and His Times (Lexington: University of Kentucky Press, 1986); Gordon, *The Scarlet Woman*, 14–27.

[41] Mancur Olson, *The Logic of Collective Action* (Cambridge, MA: Harvard University Press, 1965).

and the space it occupied were still tiny by modern standards, which meant that someone seeking to trade did not have far to go or many people to see in order to exhaust the range of likely partners. The number of issues capable of being bought and sold was likewise very small. The volume of off-Board trading was almost certainly much larger than the volume of trading at the Board. These circumstances suggest that the Board's transaction cost advantage was not all that great. Competition from off-Board trading was a constant danger, because a critical mass of members and of trading volume was essential to the Board's continued existence. (A stock exchange whose membership or trading volume is too small will offer none of the advantages of access to trading partners, and will accordingly have great difficulty in acquiring new members or in retaining the old ones.) The members of the Board, recognizing this danger, adopted a resolution in 1836 providing "that no purchases or sales of Stocks shall be made by any member of this Board directly or indirectly in the Street."[42] But this rule was apparently impossible to enforce.[43] Board members continued to conduct business outdoors when the Board was not in session.[44]

A second benefit a member received for his $400 was some assurance of the creditworthiness of his trading partners.[45] This assurance came in both positive and negative forms. On the positive side, the Board screened prospective members, from the beginning, for signs that they could be trusted to comply with options and time bargains that might extend over periods of several months. Entering into such a transaction with a stranger in the street could be risky; when the time came to collect, he might be difficult to find. The Board's original 1817 constitution accordingly restricted membership to brokers who "have been in the business for the term of one or more years," time enough for one's character to become common knowledge among the city's community of brokers.[46] Except for a short period (1817–20) when an even stiffer prerequisite, a two-year apprenticeship, was in effect, this one-year requirement remained a fixture in the Board's successive constitutions.[47] Another rule that endured through each constitution, the provision allowing the votes of any three members to reject an appli-

---

[42] New York Stock & Exchange Board Minute Books, Sept. 22, 1836, NYSE. The Minute Books will be cited hereafter as "Minutes." Their pagination ceases partway through, so they are cited by date of entry.

[43] Sobel, *Big Board*, 44.   [44] Armstrong, *Stocks and Stock-Jobbing*, 8.

[45] Cf. Lester G. Telser, "Why There Are Organized Futures Markets," *Journal of Law and Economics* 24 (1981): 1; Lester G. Telser and Harlow N. Higginbotham, "Organized Futures Markets: Costs and Benefits," *Journal of Political Economy* 85 (1977): 969.

[46] 1817 Const. art. 16.

[47] 1820 Const. art. 5; 1833 Const. art. 5; 1856 Const. art. 9.

cation for membership, served the same purpose.[48] If an applicant's ability or inclination to comply with his contracts was open to doubt, his application could easily be denied. By 1848, the Board had acquired a reputation for being "very exclusive in its character."[49] From the perspective of a Board member, this exclusivity translated into an ability to depend on his trading partners, a benefit which probably accounts in part for the eagerness of brokers to become members.

On the negative side, the Board performed two tasks that warned members away from risky prospective trading partners. First, beginning in 1820 the Board suspended "Any Member who fails to comply with his contracts, or becomes insolvent."[50] A member could be reinstated once he had settled with his creditors, by a vote of the other members (the number of votes required for reinstatement varied over time). While in breach of his contracts or insolvent, however, a member was effectively shunned by the others. The direct effect was to limit the pool of prospective trading partners to the solvent and non-breaching; one indirect effect was to encourage members to comply with their contracts. Second, from the beginning the Board maintained a list of non-members who had breached their contracts with members, and prohibited members from further dealings with them. In 1817, for instance, the Board "Resolved That James Arden is not competent for any Broker to receive an order from."[51] This list was kept informally in the early years. The procedure was formalized in 1834, when members were required to "Report publicly to the Board the name of every person who shall violate his engagement with him," whether a client refusing to pay a commission or a non-member broker refusing to comply with a contract. It became "the duty of the Secretary to keep a Book for the purpose of registering the name of every person reported as a defaulter." So long as a person's name remained in the book, members were barred from transacting with him "under pain of immediate suspension."[52] The list of defaulters was referred to thereafter as "the Black Book."[53]

The Stock and Exchange Board was thus in part a compiler and seller of information about the creditworthiness of prospective trading part-

[48]   1817 Const. art. 5; 1820 Const. art. 5; 1833 Const. art. 5; 1856 Const. art. 7.

[49]   Armstrong, *Stocks and Stock-Jobbing*, 8.

[50]   1820 Const. art. 13; 1833 Const. art. 13; 1856 Const. art. 11.

[51]   New York Stock & Exchange Board Proceedings, April 29, 1817, NYSE. The "Proceedings" are typescripts of minutes from 1817, filed with the early Board constitutions.

[52]   Minutes Dec. 8, 1834. The minutes report only this resolution, but not whether it was adopted. I am inferring its adoption from its appearance in the next iteration of the Board's bylaws. 1856 By-Laws art. 62.

[53]   Minutes July 19, 1844.

ners. This information would have been more costly to obtain in the disorganized market outside the Board. Brokers who became Board members were in effect purchasing this information more cheaply than they could elsewhere, which accounts for part of the appeal of membership. Again, however, this component of the value of membership was limited by the size of the Board's incremental advantage in the cost of information, which was probably small. Within the coffee house community of New York brokers, news of a breached contract or an insolvency had to have spread very quickly, and was the sort of news that could not have been easy to forget. Each non-member broker must have kept his own mental Black Book of individuals he did not trust, a list that probably did not lag far behind the Board's.

Third, the same screening processes provided members with the benefit of a reputation for trustworthiness themselves, which may have been helpful in attracting customers. Investors faced with the choice of hiring a member or a non-member as a broker probably valued the seal of approval represented by Board membership. To the extent this was so, membership increased the number of commissions a broker would receive. Even apart from this monetary value, membership in the Board, particularly once the Board had become well established, may have carried some social status as well. Stockjobbers (as discussed in chapter 6) were still somewhat disreputable, but Board membership may well have signified one's position as one of the least unsavory.

A fourth asset the Board provided its members was access to a crucial kind of information – knowledge of current market prices.[54] A speculator who knows the current market price of stock will have an advantage over one who does not, because he will be better able to recognize potential profitable transactions. For the same reason, a broker who knows the current market prices should more easily attract customers than one who does not. The value of information about market prices thus bears an inverse relationship to its dispersion; the more people who know it, the less it is worth, and if everyone knows it it is worth nothing. From the beginning, the Board recognized that price information could be valuable if it could be restricted to members, and accordingly took steps to limit its dissemination. In April 1817, when the Board had been in operation for only a month, the members voted to impose fines on "any member leaving the room during the calling of Stocks."[55] This rule remained in effect through successive versions of

---

[54] Cf. J. Harold Mulherin, Jeffrey M. Netter, and James A. Overdahl, "Prices are Property: The Organization of Financial Exchanges from a Transaction Cost Perspective," *Journal of Law and Economics* 34 (1991): 591.

[55] Proceedings April 26, 1817.

the bylaws.[56] It prevented members from leaking price information to non-members before a session was over, and ensured that each member had an equal opportunity to profit from his knowledge advantage over non-members.

Later the same year, the Board took a stronger step toward restricting the flow of price information. The members "Resolved That no member of this Board, nor any partner of a member, shall hereafter give the prices of any kind of Stock, Exchange or Specie, to any Printer for Publication."[57] Here, however, the Board faced a dilemma. While information about a market price is valuable only to the extent its publication can be restricted, a price can be a market price to begin with only by becoming widely known. If the prices reached at Board sessions were kept perpetually secret, they would have become market prices, if at all (in a market most of which was conducted outside the Board), only after protracted trading between members and non-members. Information about the prices generated by Board trading could be valuable only if it was disseminated, but it had to be disseminated only after a time lag long enough to permit members to obtain a trading advantage over non-members. The Board accordingly authorized its Secretary "to furnish the prices of Stock but once a week to one price current only at his discretion – and that no other quotation be made for publication."[58] The Board would continue to seek the optimal frequency for the release of price information; prices would eventually be published daily, in multiple newspapers. Even then, however, members still had the advantage of time; in the hours between the close of a trading session and the publication of the results, they could trade in the street with non-members who had not yet learned the day's prices. This may be why the rule against off-Board trading proved so difficult to enforce.

The Board adopted two subsequent rules likewise intended to maximize the value of price information by restricting its flow. Members were not allowed "to introduce a stranger into the Board-room during the hours of business."[59] And members "sending . . . a communication" during trading sessions were fined.[60] (The latter rule also ensured that no member would have any informational advantage over any other. Members were not allowed to *receive* any communications during trading either.) By the middle of the century, these efforts to prop up the

---

[56] 1820 Bye Laws art. 3; 1833 By-Laws art. 3; 1856 By-Laws art. 47.

[57] Proceedings Nov. 10, 1817.

[58] Proceedings Nov. 29, 1817. A "price current" was a publication that listed the current market prices of various commodities.

[59] 1856 By-Laws art. 42.   [60] 1856 By-Laws art. 49.

value of price information were paying off. The broker Henry Clews recalled that when he began his career in the 1850s, "speculators frequently offered $100 a week, or ten times the cost of membership, for the privilege of listening at the keyhole during the calls."[61] Even if Clews was exaggerating a bit – his numbers sound suspiciously high – the story is powerful evidence of the value of timely information as to market prices. The Board's ability to manage access to this information accounts in part for its success in the first half of the nineteenth century.

Finally, the Board offered its members a mechanism for regulating trading, enforcing contracts, and resolving disputes that arose in the course of business. Because (as discussed in chapter 5) most time bargains – those in which the seller did not own the stock as of the contract date – were unenforceable in New York's courts between the 1792 enactment of the stockjobbing act and its repeal in 1858, the Board was the only organization capable of coercing a trading partner into complying with one of these time bargains. The Board's ability to do so would thus have been of value to New York brokers, because it expanded the range of possible trading partners. Without a means of enforcement, one can enter into long-term contracts only with people one knows, at least by reputation, or with people over whom one can exert some kind of leverage. But when one is aware that prospective trading partners will suffer if they default, and one knows that the prospective partners know it, one can more confidently enter into long-term contracts with strangers. As the number of possible trading partners increases, so does the number of trades. For the New York brokers, who earned their living by trading, more trades meant more money.

This miniature legal system within the Stock and Exchange Board (it will be addressed in more detail below) thus provided another incentive for brokers to join the Board, and contributed to the Board's success. As with the other incentives for joining, however, the magnitude of this one had a clear upper bound. The greatest punishment the Board could impose was the suspension or expulsion of members, but this power could of course be exercised only over members, and the number of members was never very large. From the perspective of any given member, therefore, the number of potential trading partners provided by the Board's ability to expel defaulters was a small one. At a time when the Board consisted of fifty brokers, for instance, it may have been possible for any one of the brokers to know each of the other forty-nine personally. If so, the Board's enforcement mechanism may not have

---

[61] Henry Clews, *Fifty Years in Wall Street* (New York: Irving Pub. Co., 1908), 8.

provided him with much additional security. (On the other hand, if he did not trust some of his colleagues, the Board's ability to suspend them for breaching their contracts may have made him more willing to trade with them.) The Board could also exert power over non-members, through its rule prohibiting members from trading with non-members listed in the Black Book. An appearance in the Black Book was probably a serious debility for a New York broker, as it prevented one from trading with the wealthiest and most reputable brokers, who were likely to have buy and sell orders from the largest number of clients. The Black Book thus expanded the circle of prospective trading partners more widely, but even the ostracism it represented would be insufficient to deter an unscrupulous trading partner willing to forgo future transactions in exchange for a single profitable breach in the present.

The value to a broker of the Board's ability to enforce contracts and discipline defaulters was made up of two components. For some contracts – time bargains in which the seller did not own the stock as of the contract date – the Board had an effective monopoly on the resolution of disputes. For all other contracts, the Board represented an alternative to the official legal system that was probably faster and less costly, and in which one was assured of more knowledgeable decision-makers.[62] The first of these components was a direct result of the 1792 stockjobbing act; to that extent, the legislature's attempt to suppress stockjobbing during the crash of 1792 had the unintended and ironic consequence of facilitating the formation and the growth of the Stock and Exchange Board in the first half of the nineteenth century.

The Board performed three other important functions for its members. These were probably not significant components of the value of membership, however, because with respect to all three it would have been impossible to prevent non-members from free-riding on the Board's efforts, by obtaining all of the benefits of those efforts without paying a membership fee.

First, the Board attempted to ensure the quality of the securities its members bought and sold, by allowing trading only in the shares of legitimate enterprises. The Board screened stocks sporadically in the early years. There were no written procedures for adding an issue to the list of stocks called at trading sessions. Only when something seemed

---

[62] In principle, one might test for the relative value of each component by comparing the frequency of disputes litigated in the court system relative to disputes resolved within the Board before and after the 1858 repeal of the stockjobbing act. The Stock and Exchange Board's dispute resolution records are uneven after the late 1840s, however, when the Board stopped reproducing most committee reports in its minutes. The other side of the comparison would be quite time-consuming, as it would involve wading through trial court records, which are not indexed by subject matter.

amiss would the Board assess the soundness of the corporation. In 1832, for instance, when the Board learned of "some embarrasments . . . in relation to transfers at the Bank of New York of 25 Dollar shares of the New Orleans Canal Bank," the Board promptly resolved "that the calling of the New Orleans Canal Bank be suspended for the present."[63] In late 1834, when Jacob Little cornered the shares of the Morris Canal & Banking Company (an enterprise William Armstrong called a "miserable abortion"), driving the share price far above the value of the assets the shares represented, the Board first suspended "further time operations" in Morris Canal shares, then resolved "that the Stocks of the Morris Canal & Bkg Co. be Struck from the Board list," and then ultimately decided that it would "take no cognizance of existing contracts for receiving and delivering Morris Canal Stocks."[64] In 1856, the Board adopted a formal mechanism for adding stocks to the trading list. Corporations wishing to have their shares called at the Board were required to apply to the Board, a procedure which required them to submit a "full statement of the capital, number of shares, resources, &c., certified to" by a representative of the corporation.[65] The Board then appointed an *ad hoc* committee to determine whether the application should be accepted. When the American Guano Company applied for listing in 1858, for example, its application consisted merely of a short letter stating that its capital stood at $10,000,000, divided into 100,000 shares at $100 each, of which 76,346 had so far been issued. A committee investigated the soundness of the enterprise. The degree to which it fleshed out these skeletal figures is suggested by its report back to the full Board:

The American Guano Co. owns two Islands in the Pacific – The Jarvis & New Nantucket. They were discovered by Michael Baker and Thos. D. Lucas & subsequently taken possession of in the name of the United States by Capt. Davis of the Sloop-of-war St. Marys. By a recent act of Congress all discoveries of uninhabited Guano Islands, not claimed by any other nation, upon fulfilment of certain conditions, are guaranteed in their ownership & remain under the protection of the United States until the deposits of Guano are all exhausted.

The Company having purchased the Islands from Baker & Lucas, organized under a General Law of the State of New York, passed Apl. 15 1857. That Act was passed specially for organizing Companies, "for the purpose of Mining, Importing & Exporting Guano and other fertilizers.["] This Company have also complied with the requirements of the Act of Congress, & surrendered to the U.

---

[63] Minutes Feb. 4, 1832.
[64] Minutes Jan. 9, 1835; Jan. 16, 1835; Feb. 10, 1835. Armstrong's comment is in Armstrong, *Stocks and Stock-Jobbing*, 29. On Jacob Little's corner, see Sobel, *Big Board*, 43; Werner and Smith, *Wall Street*, 32. The Board eventually restored Morris Canal to the trading list. Minutes May 11, 1835.
[65] 1856 By-Laws art. 2.

States Government satisfactory Surety Bonds of $100,000 each for the two Islands. Their title of ownership to the Guano upon the above named Islands appears to be right in all respects – Specimens of this Guano have been sent to Washington by Capt. Davis of U.S.N. & by order of our Government were annalized at the Smithsonian Institute. Its quality as a good fertilizer is endorsed by that Institute. The quantity available for mining & export is estimated at several millions of tons. The cost of Importation here, the Trustees estimate at $25 per ton, and the market price at present is said to be at from $40 to $45 per ton. Vessels are now loading at the Islands, & some on the way, soon will be here.

. . .

Your Committee know of no objection why the American Guano Co. stock should not be called here. They are organized according to law & managed by a Board of Trustees composed of several gentlemen highly esteemed for their integrity & intelligence. We therefore recommend their application to your favorable consideration.[66]

By the late 1850s, the Board was closely scrutinizing the soundness of enterprises before adding their stock to the list.

This kind of screening would have been of some value to brokers. When trading for their own account, they would have had some assurance that they were not buying shares in a company that would tomorrow be exposed as a sham. When acting as brokers, this same assurance would have given them a competitive advantage over brokers who lacked access to the list of approved stocks. That list had to have been publicly known, however, in order for investors to know the stocks they might buy or sell at the Board. And once the list was generally known, it would have been impossible to prevent non-members from using the information produced by the Board as to a company's soundness. Any non-member could obtain all the advantage of the Board's work simply by determining to trade only in Board-approved stocks. The Board's ability to screen companies thus could not have provided any incentive to join.[67]

Second, the Board organized brokers into a classic cartel with respect to brokerage commissions. After the failure of the 1792 agreement, the brokers resumed in 1817 with a minimum commission of one-quarter

---

[66] New York Stock & Exchange Board, Committees on Applications, Sept. 20, 1858, NYSE. For the full fascinating story of the American Guano Company, see Jimmy M. Skaggs, *The Great Guano Rush* (New York: St. Martin's Griffin, 1994).

[67] It may, however, have provided an incentive for *companies* to seek listing with the Board, as listing most likely provided a signal to investors of a firm's stability. See Jonathan R. Macey and Hideki Kanda, "The Stock Exchange as a Firm: The Emergence of Close Substitutes for the New York and Tokyo Stock Exchanges," *Cornell Law Review* 75 (1990): 1040–42; Robert Joseph Cull, "A Comparative Study of Capital Market Failure and Institutional Innovation" (Calif. Inst. of Technology Ph.D. dissertation 1993), 176–80.

percent of the value of securities bought or sold.[68] Later that year, when it became apparent that some members were exploiting an ambiguity in that provision by engaging in transactions for non-member brokers without charging commissions – a practice "deemed highly improper and injurious to the interest of this board" – the Board removed that ambiguity, by explicitly requiring a one-quarter percent commission even when acting on behalf of another broker rather than directly on behalf of an investor.[69] The one-quarter percent floor remained constant through the first half of the century.[70] The New York Stock Exchange would continue to fix commissions, despite developments in American antitrust law, until 1975.[71]

This minimum commission rule could not by itself have been much of a reason for seeking Board membership, however, because a non-member broker could easily reap the benefit of it without ever paying the cost of joining, simply by either charging one-quarter percent himself, in the absence of any fear that a Board member would sell his services more cheaply, or by charging less than one-quarter percent, and snapping up customers attracted by the cheaper rate. Henry Clews entered the business in 1857 by using the latter technique:

I at once inserted an advertisement in the newspapers, and proposed to buy and sell stocks at a sixteenth of one per cent. each way. This was such a bombshell in the camp of these old fogies that they were almost paralyzed. What rendered it more distasteful to them still was the fact that, while they lost customers, I steadily gained them.[72]

The Board's ability to set minimum commissions was thus a result, rather than a cause, of its strength. Clews, in fact, eagerly gave up his booming cut-rate business in favor of paying the membership fee, joining the Board, and charging one-quarter percent when membership was offered. The value he placed on belonging to the Board must have resided in something other than the rate of commission.

A third function performed by the Board for its members, from the benefits of which it would have been impossible to exclude non-member brokers, was lobbying. On at least a few occasions in the 1830s and 1840s, the Board succeeded in fending off regulation proposed in the

[68] 1817 Const. art. 11.   [69] Proceedings Oct. 11, 1817.

[70] 1820 Const. art. 10; 1820 Bye Laws art. 8; 1833 Const. art. 10; 1833 By-Laws art. 8; 1856 Const. art. 16; 1856 By-Laws arts. 56–58. At some point between 1833 and 1856 the Board lowered the minimum commission on transactions for a non-member broker to one-eighth percent. 1856 By-Laws art. 59. The earlier provisions are ambiguous as to whether commissions were calculated as a percentage of the stock's market value or par value; by 1856, the rule expressly used par value.

[71] Chris Welles, *The Last Days of the Club* (New York: Dutton, 1975).

[72] Clews, *Fifty Years*, 8.

New York legislature. In February 1834, for instance, the Board created a committee for the purpose of battling pending legislation.[73] When a legislative committee published a report recommending a bill "to correct and lessen, if not to remove entirely the manifest evils of stock-jobbing," the Board sprang into action. The Assembly committee cited the familiar complaints about stockjobbers – they "mislead and deceive their employers to a fearful and dangerous degree" by misrepresenting the true value of stock; they "frequently, by a combination of a few of their number, raise or depress the prices of the different stocks as may best suit their individual interests"; they are animated by "a spirit of gambling which is carried to an alarming extent"; in short, the securities market was characterized by "great and palpable evils" which did not attend markets in older forms of property.[74] The Board promptly responded by inviting Henry Hone, the legislation's leading proponent in the Assembly, to sit in on a meeting of the Board, to watch business being conducted, and to examine the minutes of Board meetings, in the hope that Hone would change his views.[75] The Board's minutes do not indicate that Hone ever accepted the invitation, or what sort of meeting took place if he did, but the bill conceived by Hone appears to have progressed no farther in the Assembly.

Two years later, when the state legislature came close to passing a bill that would have drastically changed the way in which the Stock and Exchange Board functioned, the Board was even more vigorous in defending its territory. The state Senate passed a bill in 1836 that would have voided all sales of stock on any stock exchange whose meetings were not open to the public, and would have made the selling of stock at a closed meeting of a stock exchange a misdemeanor. The Board promptly fired off an eight-page "Memorial and Remonstrance" to the legislature, in which it marshalled three arguments against the bill. First, the Board argued, any restrictions on securities trading in New York would simply divert the business "to other places, where a greater spirit of liberality prevails." The Board mentioned Philadelphia, the home of the country's second-largest securities market, as the likely beneficiary of the bill. "[O]ur fellow-citizens" of New York, the Board suggested, "ought not to be compelled to contend against improvident legislation at home . . . that strikes at the growth and the interests of our commercial prosperity." Second, the Board argued that closed meetings for the purpose of securities trading were no more pernicious than

[73] Minutes Feb. 6, 1834.
[74] "Report of the Select Committee on Stock-jobbing," N.Y. Assembly Doc. 339, 57th Sess. (March 28, 1834), 1–2.
[75] Minutes, April 2 and 3, 1834.

closed meetings in any other line of business. "[T]he business of the board of brokers," it pointed out, "is no more done in secret, than the business of the chamber of commerce, the board of trade, and many other similar institutions that might be named." Unless the closed meetings were enabling some kind of fraud to be committed, there was no reason to force the Board to open to the public; "and your memorialists are equally confident, that no fraud could be practised in the face of the whole board, without its being discovered by some one member, who would cause it to be investigated and exposed." Third, the Board argued that the true ground for public suspicion of securities trading at closed meetings was not secrecy itself, but rather the popular view that "sales of stock on what are usually called 'time contracts,' are productive of all the evils the bill under consideration is intended to remedy." If that was so, the Board concluded, a better remedy would simply be to repeal the 1792 stockjobbing act, thereby "to make all such contracts binding in law, as they are said to be in Pennsylvania." If time bargains could be enforced in the courts, the argument went, they would no longer be entered into by people who had no intention of complying with them, and they would lose their unsavory public image.[76]

The Board did not stop there. A few days after sending this protest to the legislature, the Board authorized its President to invite any member of the legislature to attend a meeting of the Board while the bill was pending.[77] Again, the Board's surviving records do not indicate whether any legislators took up the invitation, but the proposed bill died quietly in the legislature, never to be revived.

In later years, the Board continued to watch the state legislature closely, and to send members to Albany when it seemed necessary.[78] Even when no adverse legislation was pending, the Board was careful to attend to its public image, and did what it could to lay low at the appropriate time. In 1841, for instance, the members of the Board resolved

that while this Board admits the right the members have under the constitution to make sales at 6 & 12 months they consider it unwise and injudicious at this moment of general distrust and want of confidence to exercise the power calculated as it is to increase the existing Troubles as well as to injure the reputation of the Board.[79]

A year later the Board considered publishing a public relations brochure, explaining "the manner in which we transact business . . . so that the

[76] "Memorial and Remonstrance," 2–4, 6.   [77] Minutes March 28, 1836.
[78] Minutes Feb. 23, 1841.   [79] Minutes Feb. 15, 1841.

public may be fully informed of the fact." Such a publication was necessary, some members argued, because of the "[e]rroneous impressions" that were "entertained by the Public as to the manner in which business is transacted at this Board which reflects upon the Character of its Members."[80] Throughout the period, the Board was consistently concerned "that an unjust prejudice has been created against the brokers as a body, from the want of knowledge of the manner they transact their business."[81] Whenever necessary, the Board lobbied the legislature to prevent that prejudice from being converted into legislation.

This sort of political activity, however, could not by itself have provided much of an incentive for any broker to join the Stock and Exchange Board, because non-members ordinarily received as much benefit from it as members. Where proposed legislation, like the 1834 bill, would have restricted trading generally, a non-member gained fully from the Board's lobbying efforts without having to pay his share of the cost of those efforts, whether as a membership fee or otherwise. Where proposed legislation, like the 1836 bill, would have restricted Board trading but not off-Board trading, the incentives facing a non-member broker were more ambiguous. Such legislation might, as the Board argued, have caused much of the market to shift from New York to Philadelphia. To the extent that was so, a non-member gained as much as a member from the Board's lobbying, and would accordingly have been likely to prefer to free-ride on the political activity financed by members. Such legislation, on the other hand, might instead have simply moved trading away from the Board in the direction of the non-member brokers in the street. To that extent, non-members were harmed by the Board's lobbying in favor of the status quo, but if the status quo had not already caused them to desire to join the Board, the continuation of the status quo would not be likely to make them change their minds. Like the Board's ability to screen stocks and to set minimum commissions, the Board's political efforts were more a product than a cause of its success.

III

We are so accustomed to thinking of law as a function of government that it is easy to forget the importance of non-governmental sources of law. All sorts of non-governmental organizations promulgate rules governing their members and adjudicate disputes involving their

[80] Minutes Jan. 9, 1842.   [81] "Memorial and Remonstrance," 8.

members, organizations as disparate as sports leagues, churches, and trade associations. Any group in which membership is strongly enough desired can effectively make and enforce law, because it wields a sanction – expulsion from the group – powerful enough to coerce members into compliance. Such "private" (i.e., non-governmental) law often plays a larger role in the lives of group members than the official law backed by the force of the government, because the penalty of expulsion is often perceived by members as a greater detriment than whatever penalties the government might impose. To an athlete who faces the loss of his livelihood for violating league rules, or to a member of a church congregation who faces excommunication because of his behavior, non-governmental regulation can be more important than governmental regulation.[82]

From its inception, the New York Stock and Exchange Board operated a miniature legal system, with its own rules governing securities trading and its own mechanism for resolving trade-related disputes.[83] The Board was hardly an innovator in this respect. It drew upon a centuries-old Anglo-American tradition of self-regulation by mercantile groups,[84] a tradition of which the Board members were aware. "Every branch of business has its peculiar laws, governing in its appropriate sphere," the Board explained in 1842, "and we claim as full a Jurisdiction for ours."[85]

This miniature legal system filled the void created by the stockjobbing act. "The fact well known, that many of the transactions of the Board are not protected by law," one Board member observed, "would seem to indicate the propriety of a tribunal to arbitrate upon disputed points, more especially as their fulfilment rests entirely upon the honorable principles and mutual good faith of the buyer and seller, and can only be

---

[82] See, e.g., Bruce H. Mann, *Neighbors and Strangers: Law and Community in Early Connecticut* (Chapel Hill: University of North Carolina Press, 1987), 139–55; William E. Nelson, *Dispute and Conflict Resolution in Plymouth County, Massachusetts, 1725–1825* (Chapel Hill: University of North Carolina Press, 1981), 26–43; Jonathan Lurie, *The Chicago Board of Trade 1859–1905: The Dynamics of Self-Regulation* (Urbana: University of Illinois Press, 1979), 6–9; Lisa Bernstein, "Merchant Law in a Merchant Court: Rethinking the Code's Search for Immanent Business Norms," *University of Pennsylvania Law Review* 144 (1996): 1771–87; Walter Otto Weyrauch and Maureen Anne Bell, "Autonomous Lawmaking: The Case of the 'Gypsies,'" *Yale Law Journal* 103 (1993): 326–31; Louis L. Jaffe, "Law Making By Private Groups," *Harvard Law Review* 51 (1937): 219–21.

[83] It still performs that function today. David P. Doherty, Arthur S. Okun, Steven F. Korostoff, and James A. Nofi, "The Enforcement Role of the New York Stock Exchange," *Northwestern University Law Review* 85 (1991): 637.

[84] See William C. Jones, "An Inquiry Into the History of the Adjudication of Mercantile Disputes in Great Britain and the United States," *University of Chicago Law Review* 25 (1958): 445.

[85] Minutes Aug. 23, 1842.

enforced beyond this by the action of this tribunal."[86] Under the Board's original 1817 constitution, "[a]ll questions of dispute in the purchase or sale of Stocks" were to be "decided by a majority of the Board."[87] As Board membership grew, however, the Board soon began to delegate to *ad hoc* committees the task of investigating the circumstances of such disputes and recommending a disposition to the full Board.[88] In 1831, for instance, a committee of five members was appointed to evaluate a complaint from non-member Samuel Gouverneur that Thomas Carpenter, a Board member, had failed to comply with one of his contracts.[89] The committee met with Gouverneur and Carpenter, and heard evidence presented by witnesses for both sides. Eight days after receiving Gouverneur's complaint, the committee reported to the Board that "the original Contract entered into by Mr. Carpenter with Mr. Gouverneur respecting the one thousand shares Morris Canal Stock was binding on Mr. Carpenter," but that "Mr. Carpenter did not comply."[90] The next day, the full Board voted to accept the committee's report, and to allow Carpenter "the space of Ten days to make an arrangement with Mr. Gouverneur."[91] When Carpenter failed to do so within the allotted time, the Board resolved that unless "some mutual arrangement" was "agreed upon by Eleven O'Clock tomorrow – Mr. Carpenter shall be considered a suspended Member of the Board."[92] Carpenter again failed to satisfy this condition, and was accordingly suspended.[93] His application for reinstatement the following year was rejected, but a second application, in 1833, was granted.[94] For breaching a contract, Carpenter had lost seventeen months of access to trading sessions at the Board. This procedure quickly became routine – a charge would be made, a committee would be appointed, a report would be filed, and the Board would take or decline to take disciplinary action, typically within a matter of weeks.[95]

---

[86] *An Examination of the Vindication of the Award Between Boorman, Johnston & Co. and Jacob Little & Co.* (New York: J. Elliott, 1842), 4.

[87] 1817 Const. art. 17; see also 1820 Const. art. 11.

[88] See, e.g., Minutes June 10, 1826.   [89] Minutes Oct. 3, 1831.

[90] Minutes Oct. 11, 1831.   [91] Minutes Oct. 12, 1831.

[92] Minutes Nov. 1, 1831. On October 22, the Board had given Carpenter ten more days.

[93] Minutes Nov. 2, 1831.

[94] Minutes May 2, 1832; June 24, 1832; August 20, 1832; March 23, 1833.

[95] See, for example, the disputes between Ogden and Talinan (Minutes Jan. 30, 1832; March 3, 1832; March 6, 1832); Robinson and Talinan (Jan. 31, 1832; May 9, 1832); Robinson and Guion (Nov. 21, 1832); Josephs & Co. and Perry & Co. (June 15, 1832); Carter & Carpenter and Josephs & Co. (July 22, 1834); Crary and Booth & Alterbury (Sept. 17, 1834; Sept. 18, 1834; Oct. 15, 1834); Alstyne and Stebbins (Dec. 9, 1834); Lynch and Coster & Carpenter (May 17, 1835); Ward and Allen (June 2, 1836); Allen & Clark and Bleecker (June 8, 1838; June 11, 1838); Little and Lawton (Feb. 17, 1842); Gale & Peppoon and Lawton (March 3, 1842); Lockwood & Co. and Saltenstall

Enforcement of time bargains by the Board was not a complete substitute for the official legal system. The Board's disciplinary power over members was far stronger than its power over non-members, because members stood to lose far more from non-compliance with the Board's orders; members could be suspended or expelled from the Board, while non-members could at most be listed in the Black Book. As a result, when the Board undertook to resolve a dispute between a member and a non-member, its ability to enforce contracts was less evenhanded than an official court's would have been. Members did not take long to recognize this imbalance. "If the Board undertake to act in all cases that men not belonging to their Board choose to present," Thomas Carpenter complained, with reference to Gouverneur's charge, "then an undue advantage is given, and parties do not stand on equal grounds."[96] Yet the Board consistently assumed jurisdiction over any dispute relating to a contract made at the Board, including complaints made by non-members (usually clients of members) against members. The Board cited this non-member edge with some pride in its dealings with the outside world. Investors had more assurance of the honesty of members than other brokers, it argued, because members were aware of how much easier it would be to force them to comply with their contracts. "The advantages of those rules are in favor of those not members of the Board," one member suggested, "for while a member has a claim only upon the honorable principle of the individual who may employ him, or with whom he may make a contract, that individual . . . may invoke the authority of the Board to enforce a prompt and perfect compliance."[97]

When members breached their contracts, the most common reason was insolvency. Typically a customer had failed to reimburse a broker for the customer's trading losses, or another broker had defaulted on an off-Board contract with the member, which left the member unable to comply with his own obligations. Such members were reinstated upon a showing that they had settled with their creditors and that their insolvency was not their fault.[98] When John Warren applied for readmission in 1834, for example, the committee that evaluated his application reported

(July 19, 1844); Rawdon & Groesbeck and Winthrop (New York Stock & Exchange Board, Arbitration Committees – Reports, Jan. 13, 1846, NYSE); Morgan and Carpenter (Minutes March 12, 1849); Van Renssellaer & Co. and Ayres & Co. (Arbitration Committees – Reports Apr. 14, 1850).

[96] Minutes May 9, 1832.   [97] *Examination of the Vindication*, 4.

[98] See, for example, the cases of Jonathan Hyde (Minutes July 19, 1826; Nov. 27, 1826; Dec. 8, 1826; Dec. 9, 1826); M.J. Robinson (Oct. 6, 1827; Oct. 18, 1827); Daniel H. Wickham (Aug. 24, 1832); and H.G. Stebbins (Dec. 31, 1841; Jan. 5, 1842).

that his conduct as far as they can ascertain, has been perfectly correct, that his failure was not owing to speculation on his own account, but for the account of others, that it would not have occurred, had it not been for the peculiar state of the times, that all contracts in the street are settled, and that there are no claims against him which have not been arranged.

Warren was accordingly readmitted.[99] William J. Robinson applied for readmission at approximately the same time. Another committee concluded

That from all the Information they have been able to obtain his failure was not owing to Speculation on his own account but to his Commission business which was chiefly on time.

Your Committee further state that a person unknown to them & who they understand was trading in the street, from some cause unknown to your Committee left Mr. Robinson to adjust some differences amounting to rising Ten thousand dollars instead of doing it himself –

It also appears that Mr. R. lost some considerable cash in sustaining some of his customers.

Robinson was readmitted as well.[100]

After years of resolving disputes in this manner, members of the Board began to understand Board adjudications as precedents, which would guide future practice and have a binding effect in subsequent cases. In 1837, for example, a committee was appointed "to arrange a difference" between two brokerage firms. Tailor & White had borrowed stock from J. L. & S. Joseph & Co., who shortly thereafter became insolvent. When Joseph & Co. called upon Tailor & White to return the borrowed stock, Tailor & White instead offered to pay for the stock with three of Joseph & Co.'s own notes, which they had purchased from others. Because of Joseph & Co.'s insolvency, the notes were worth substantially less than their face value. Tailor & White had purchased one of the notes before Joseph & Co. became insolvent, but purchased two of the notes afterwards. Was Joseph & Co. at fault for failing to accept its own notes, the face value of which satisfied Tailor & White's obligation? Or was Tailor & White at fault for attempting to satisfy an obligation with notes that everyone knew were practically worthless? The committee to which the dispute was referred regarded "this case as a very important one, inasmuch as the decision of the Board will establish the principle whether or not, the notes of a Broker purchased in the market *after* his failure shall be considered a good and sufficient offset to any stock loans or contracts made at a previous period." In reaching its decision, the committee relied explicitly on this sense of *stare decisis*. The note purchased by Tailor & White before the insolvency

---

[99] Minutes Apr. 23, 1834.   [100] Minutes Apr. 24, 1834.

would be allowed in part payment, but not the two notes purchased afterwards. "[T]he establishment of such a precedent," the committee concluded, with reference to a possible alternative decision allowing all three notes as payment, "would sanction a practice at variance with Justice. It would destroy all confidence between individuals in making Stock Loans and Contracts."[101]

The same concern for the precedential effect of a decision arose in an 1842 dispute between two brokerage firms that turned on whether the delivery of illegally issued state debt certificates satisfied the obligations of a contract between the two firms. A decision against the firm that delivered the certificates, the committee determined,

would greatly hinder if not entirely put a stop to transactions in Securities of this kind, if it were necessary for the purchaser to trace every bond to its origin in order to Ascertain whether the Commissioner signing it had Conformed in every particular to the law or number of laws authorising its issue.[102]

Again, in resolving disputes the Board looked forward, to the effect on future trading of the rule it would apply retrospectively in the case before it. Because the official court system could not develop a common law governing time bargains, the Board did instead.

Board members also began to think of the Board's jurisdiction as exclusive, in a practical if not technical sense. In 1842, when two brokerage firms referred a dispute to a panel of arbitrators not affiliated with the Board, who adopted a rule of decision different from the one the Board would have used, members of the Board were stunned.[103] One exclaimed in outrage that the case was "the first instance in which a contract made at the Board has ever been left for decision to the arbitration of any persons not members of the Association."[104] The Board proclaimed that its own rules and practices, which had been "suggested and approved by long experience and as best adapted to the cases which arise in their business," should have governed.[105] After many years of being shut out of the official legal system, members had grown accustomed to resolving their own disputes.

The stockjobbing act did not just create an adjudicative void; it created a regulatory void as well. Because most time bargains were not enforceable in the official courts between 1792 and 1858, the New York legislature had no occasion to enact any statutes in that period specifying how time bargains were or were not to be entered into or performed. The Stock and Exchange Board stepped into this gap, by promulgating

---

[101] Minutes May 22, 1837.   [102] Minutes May 16, 1842.
[103] Daniel Lord, *A Vindication of the Award, Between Boorman, Johnston & Co. and Jacob Little & Co.* (New York: Van Norden & King, 1842).
[104] *Examination of the Vindication*, 4.   [105] Minutes Aug. 23, 1842.

rules governing various aspects of the relationship between parties to a time bargain. When the transfer of stock was at the option of the buyer or seller, for instance, how much advance notice did the optionholder have to give before demanding delivery or acceptance of the stock? The question must have arisen in countless transactions, but as most of them were void under the law of New York, the question was not likely to be answered by any branch of the state government. The Board accordingly provided its own answer in 1833: "In all contracts on time over three days, made at the option of the buyer or seller, one day's previous notice shall be given before Stock can be delivered or demanded; and such notice shall be given at or before one o'clock P.M."[106] Or another recurring set of questions: When a member defaulted on a time bargain, was the wronged party limited to a claim against the member for the stock not delivered or paid for, or could he cover on the market and seek only his lost profits from the member? If the latter, did he have any obligation to seek the best price (thus minimizing the breaching member's losses), or could he accept any price, secure in the knowledge that he could recover the difference? Again, this set of questions was extremely unlikely to be answered by the official legal system, which did not recognize the validity of most such transactions. The Board concluded that wronged parties could cover on the market and proceed against breaching members for lost profits, but that they had to do so "between a quarter past two and three o'clock of the same day," a rule which ensured that wronged parties would have a very narrow range of discretion as to the prices at which they would cover.[107] Or another question: When a corporation required shareholders to pay an installment of the share price, and shares were at that moment held by a seller who was under an obligation to deliver them to a buyer at a later date, who had to pay the installment, the buyer or the seller? The Board concluded that the seller should make the payments, but he would be reimbursed by the buyer upon delivery.[108]

Many of the rules adopted by the Board to govern time bargains were default rules; that is, they would apply only where the parties to a contract had not specified alternative rules of their own. The Board had been in operation for less than a year, for example, when members resolved that "in all time bargains the rate of Interest is understood to be *Seven* pr *Cent* unless qualified at the time of making the bargain."[109]

---

[106] 1833 By-Laws art. 16; see also 1856 By-Laws art. 16.
[107] 1833 By-Laws art. 22; see also 1856 By-Laws art. 60 (where the range of discretion is narrowed even further, by requiring transactions to occur between half past two and three o'clock).
[108] Minutes Nov. 19, 1831.   [109] Proceedings Oct. 23, 1817.

(Time bargains normally required the calculation of interest on the purchase price between the contract date and the delivery date, to compensate for the difference in the present value of the purchase price on the two dates. If A agreed on January 1 to buy stock from B for $100 on July 1, for instance, at a 7 percent interest rate he would actually pay B $103.50 on July 1, because $103.50 on July 1 was equivalent to $100 on January 1.) The rule gradually grew more complicated, most likely as disputes between brokers led the Board to refine its statement of the default rate of interest. In 1820, the Board began specifying that "the Interest shall commence from the day of Sale, to be calculated by callender months."[110] In 1833, the rate dropped to 6 percent, but now it was "to be calculated by days, according to Bank usage, excepting where the sale is made by months, in which case the interest shall be calculated by months."[111] By 1856, although the day/month distinction remained, interest charges were banned where the length of time between contract and delivery was less than three days.[112] Similar default rules governed matters like the date of delivery where no date was specified in the contract, and the question whether interest would continue to accrue past the delivery date where delivery had not been made.[113]

On a few occasions, the Board considered restricting the duration of time bargains. The members rejected three different proposals in 1842 to limit time bargains to sixty, thirty, and five days.[114] In 1844, the Board resolved to prohibit members from making contracts at Board sessions for longer than five days. The Board was careful to make clear that the ban was "not in any manner to impair the right of the Board to take cognizance of & to enforce Contracts for a longer time made elsewhere or at other times than the regular formal session of the Board."[115] This proviso was important, because the Board continued to enforce time bargains for longer than five days at something close to its usual pace in the years thereafter, which suggests that the 1844 resolution simply shifted such agreements away from Board sessions. By 1856, the five day limit had become a much less restrictive twelve-month limit.[116]

Why would members of the Board wish to restrict their ability to enter into time bargains? Members lost nothing from expanded opportunities for trading; any individual member who thought time bargains too risky could always opt not to enter into them. The Board was most likely

---

[110] 1820 Bye Laws art. 4.   [111] 1833 By-Laws art. 4.
[112] 1856 By-Laws arts. 17, 26.
[113] Minutes Nov. 7, 1833; 1856 By-Laws arts. 11, 12; 1856 By-Laws art. 19.
[114] Minutes March 23, 1842; Apr. 13, 1842; May 4, 1842.
[115] Minutes Dec. 5, 1844.   [116] 1856 By-Laws art. 22.

engaging in a bit of public relations. Members were acutely aware, particularly during the depression of the late 1830s and early 1840s, "of prejudices which exist in minds entitled to our respect against our business . . . prejudices greatly enhanced, if not altogether created by the mistaken refusal of our Law givers to enforce a compliance with ours as with other Contracts."[117] (Most of the Board's public relations efforts, described earlier in this chapter, date from this same period.) By appearing to drive long-term time bargains out of the Board, but by continuing to enforce them when made elsewhere or even at the Board outside of formal trading sessions, members were trying to have their cake and eat it too. They could appear from the outside to no longer permit time bargains, but they were in fact not depriving themselves of anything.

Although the Stock and Exchange Board consistently enforced time bargains in which sellers owned no stock, its position was more ambiguous with respect to what members called "fictitious sales," or transactions in which the buyer and seller never intended any stock or money to change hands but were simply attempting to manipulate the price. Many time bargains were fictitious in a sense, of course, in that the parties never intended stock to change hands, but simply settled by payment of the price differential between the contract date and the nominal delivery date. These were not understood to be "fictitious sales." A fictitious sale was twice as fictitious, in that neither stock *nor money* would be transferred. If the current market price is 100, and A employs one broker to buy shares at 110 and another broker to sell shares at 110, the transaction would be a fictitious sale. The net result would be that no money or stock had changed hands. The transaction had been engineered to establish an artificial price different from the true market price.

A week after the Board was founded, the members voted unanimously that "no fictitious Sale or Contract shall be made at this board, any member or members making a fictitious Sale or Contract shall upon conviction thereof be expelled."[118] The rule remained in effect continuously thereafter.[119] Yet in the two recorded instances in which the Board detected a fictitious sale, it refrained from punishing the guilty parties. One was the sale that prompted the rule in the first place. One of the Board's very first transactions was a fictitious sale, which, when detected by the Board two days later, was ordered "expunged from the register of the Board."[120] The Board did not discipline the parties to the sale,

---

[117] Minutes Aug. 23, 1842.   [118] 1817 Const. art. 18.
[119] 1820 Const. art. 12; 1833 Const. art. 12; 1856 Const. art. 18.
[120] Proceedings March 15, 1817.

perhaps because the rule they violated did not yet exist at the time of the sale. Fifteen years later, a committee appointed "to investigate the purchase & sale of fifty shares Catskill Rail Road Stock between Mr J T Talinan & Mr Wm J. Robinson" discovered that Talinan had bought the fifty shares on behalf of a customer named Alexander Hamilton (perhaps the son of the first Treasury Secretary), and that Robinson had sold the fifty shares on behalf of the same person. Robinson, at least, appears to have known what Hamilton was up to, because when "asked the question if *96 P. Cent had been offered* for Fifty Shares of Stock instead of =95 – would you have felt authorised to have accepted that bid," Robinson "replied *that he would* not for his orders were to sell the moment *95 was offered.*" In other words, Robinson would have declined a better offer in order to sell at a specific price. The Board, justifiably suspicious, ordered the transaction "expunged from the Sales Book."[121] But again, neither Robinson nor Talinan suffered any adverse consequences.

The Board's rules thus prohibited fictitious sales, but between 1817 and 1860 it detected only two, and even then it declined to impose any punishment on the participants. There was little to deter a broker from a fictitious sale; the chances of being found out appear not to have been very large (those chances of course depend on the unknowable number of undetected fictitious sales), and even then the worst that was likely to happen would be that the sale would be invalidated. As was temporarily the case with long-term time bargains, the Board's ban on fictitious sales may have been largely an exercise in public relations. Stockjobbers had long had a reputation for price manipulation. A stated policy proscribing fictitious sales might have been aimed at that reputation, whatever its real effect.

When regulating themselves, the members of the Stock and Exchange Board were thus indirectly constrained by the tension in popular thought with respect to securities trading. Most of the time, the Board could regulate so as to advance the interests of its own members, without explicit regard for the anti-market thought discussed in chapter 6. But the Board's long-term self-interest required it to act strategically on occasion. Too much speculation or too much price manipulation in the short run might cause government to step in and impose broad limits on trading, as it periodically threatened to do, and might result in losses in the long run. The Board had to keep one eye on public opinion. The tradition of Anglo-American thought suspicious of secu-

---

[121] Minutes May 9, 1832.

rities trading thus filtered through even to Wall Street, and to the laws the stockjobbers enacted for themselves.

The "peculiar laws" of the New York Stock and Exchange Board enabled its members to capture two kinds of wealth. Some of the Board's rules, like the restrictions on the dissemination of price information, allowed the Board to take wealth from non-member brokers by grabbing a larger fraction of the total pool of brokerage commissions. Other rules, however, increased the size of that pool – they effectively created wealth where it had not existed before – by increasing the number of trades. The Board's ability to enforce time bargains and to suspend defaulters, for instance, almost certainly caused the volume of trading to be larger than it would have been otherwise, which benefited members in their capacities both as speculators and as brokers. More trading, in turn, increased the utility of the corporate form of business enterprise, by causing investors to be more willing to buy the shares of new enterprises. And as more corporations had their shares publicly traded in New York, the volume of trading grew even more. By successfully regulating themselves in the first half of the nineteenth century, for the sole purpose of increasing their own wealth, the stockjobbers facilitated the growth of the market.

Conclusion

I

The rest of the story is more familiar.[1] The securities market grew much larger later in the nineteenth century, as stock first in railroads and then industrial corporations came to dominate trading.[2] The states and the federal government began to threaten regulation more and more frequently, until early in the twentieth century many states enacted the so-called "blue sky" laws, requiring issuers of stock to disclose financial information and empowering state officials to reject proposed issues.[3] After the crash of 1929 and the election of Roosevelt, Congress enacted the scheme of federal regulation that, with some modification, remains in effect today.[4]

The patterns of belief underlying that regulation, however, had been present in the United States, and in England before that, for more than two centuries. The belief that the sellers of securities were more likely to be deceitful than the sellers of other kinds of property, and that the sale of securities accordingly needed to be more closely supervised by government than the sale of other things, was widely held as early as the 1690s, and had never disappeared. The associated opinion that the securities market was unusually susceptible to domination by insiders,

[1] It is told in greatest detail in Cedric B. Cowing, *Populists, Plungers, and Progressives: A Social History of Stock and Commodity Speculation 1890–1936* (Princeton: Princeton University Press, 1965).

[2] Lance E. Davis and Robert J. Cull, *International Capital Markets and American Economic Growth, 1820–1914* (Cambridge: Cambridge University Press, 1994), 62–68; Gene Smiley, "The Expansion of the New York Securities Market at the Turn of the Century," *Business History Review* 55 (1981): 75; Thomas R. Navin and Marian V. Sears, "The Rise of a Market for Industrial Securities, 1887–1902," *Business History Review* 29 (1955): 105.

[3] Macey and Miller, "Origin of the Blue Sky Laws," 347; Gerald D. Nash, "Government and Business: A Case Study of State Regulation of Corporate Securities, 1850–1933," *Business History Review* 38 (1964): 144.

[4] Joel Seligman, *The Transformation of Wall Street* (Boston: Houghton, Mifflin, 1982); Michael E. Parrish, *Securities Regulation and the New Deal* (New Haven: Yale University Press, 1970).

who could control prices by controlling the flow of information, was equally old. The belief that too much speculation was harmful to the economy because it diverted resources into unproductive channels, and that speculation needed to be dampened by regulation, had been around as long. So had the view of speculation as a form of gambling, and thus morally questionable even apart from its economic effects. The fear that securities traders were accumulating too much power had gone through some modifications, particularly with respect to the identity of the party who was losing power by comparison – in the seventeenth and eighteenth centuries it was the government, by the early nineteenth century it had become the worker, and by the early twentieth century it would become the government again – but that fear had lurked consistently since the dawn of securities trading. It was a very old background of anti-market thought that gave rise to the idea that the securities market had to be more closely regulated than most other markets, and it was that idea in turn that gave rise to our current system of securities regulation.

Many of the techniques of our current securities regulation, in fact, were tried or at least proposed long ago. The concept of a minimum holding period, for the purpose of deterring transactions designed to manipulate prices, was proposed in England in 1697 and again in 1721. The idea of requiring participants in certain transactions to register with the government, to facilitate public disclosure and thus also to deter price manipulation, was nearly enacted in England in 1756 and again in 1773. The notion of requiring corporate managers to disclose to investors information relevant to an assessment of the value of the corporation's stock, the backbone of current American federal securities regulation, was kicking around in the United States in the early nineteenth century. Government supervision of the soundness of stock issues – still undertaken by many American states in theory, ever since the enactment of the "blue sky" laws of the early twentieth century – was suggested in England shortly after the South Sea Bubble. The old common law doctrine of fraud, still the primary means of preventing and punishing deception in the sale of securities (although now often restated in statutes), was applied to the securities market almost from its inception.

Even the "new" kinds of regulation that are sometimes proposed today, but not yet implemented, have long histories of which their proponents are most likely unaware. The prohibition of certain types of transactions on the ground that they are too speculative, for example, is often suggested today.[5] This sort of regulation was in effect in England

5 Recent proposals have concerned trading in derivatives. See Michael Utley, "Anti-Derivative Movement May Have Gone Too Far, Analysts Say," *The Bond Buyer*, April 9,

between 1697 and 1708, and again between 1734 and 1860, during which period Parliament repeatedly considered and rejected attempts to strengthen it. The same kinds of overly speculative transactions were banned in New York between 1792 and 1858, and in Massachusetts between 1836 and 1910. Proponents of transfer taxes, to cite another example of recently-proposed regulation, argue the need to slow the velocity with which securities change hands.[6] The exact same rationale underlay identical proposals in England in 1697, 1701, and 1756, and in the United States in the 1790s.

More fundamentally, we are still living in the shadow of a decision made, collectively and incrementally, by the English legislators and judges of the eighteenth century and then again by the American legislators and judges of the late eighteenth and early nineteenth centuries, to treat securities in some respects like older forms of property but in other respects like an entirely new entity. Many of the legal rules governing the transfer of older forms of property – the various doctrines pertaining to contracts, the law of usury, the law of gambling, and so on – could be applied to securities without much conscious thought as to the categorization of securities as property. But the perceived differences between securities and older kinds of property, especially the enhanced ability of sellers to manipulate prices and otherwise deceive buyers, led English and then American regulators gradually to develop special statutory schemes targeted only at the transfer of securities. These schemes have grown significantly more complex in the twentieth century, giving rise to a specialized segment of the bar that did not exist beforehand, but the idea of separate regulation seems natural to twentieth-century lawyers largely because it is by now so old.

That eighteenth-century compromise, between treating securities specially and treating them like any other kind of property, in turn rested on a tension in popular thought that has likewise remained with us to the present. The familiar American division between Wall Street and Main Street, between a financial elite and the wider political community, is as old as securities trading itself. At all times in England and the United States since the invention of securities markets, people and their governments have been of two minds: securities were simultaneously

1996, 4A; Michael Fritz, "Exchanges Face Risk From States," *Crain's Chicago Business*, June 5, 1995, 1; Roger Fillion, "Regulator May Forbid Derivatives For Banks," *Chicago Sun-Times*, April 21, 1994, 54. In the 1980s, such proposals concerned hostile takeovers. See Tom Troy, "Takeover Bill Passes Senate, to Gov. for Signing," UPI, Jan. 28, 1988; "Lawmaker Blasts Criticism of Takeover Legislation," UPI, Oct. 15, 1987; "Simon Plans Legislation on Corporate Takeovers," Reuters, Feb. 6, 1987.

[6] See Stout, "Are Stock Markets Costly Casinos?," 611; Summers and Summers, "Case for a Securities Transactions Excise Tax," 879.

necessary and dangerous, simultaneously wealth-creating and wealth-destroying.

This is not to say that nothing new has happened since the middle of the nineteenth century. In terms of the way people think about the securities market, the arguments in favor of the institution's value have become considerably more sophisticated, as the new discipline of economics provided more rigorous techniques of demonstrating the benefits of transactions of all sorts. In some respects, the market is less regulated now than it was then; few today seriously contemplate banning options or futures, for example, or voiding transactions under usury laws. At the same time, however, public concern with market manipulation has, if anything, grown even stronger. By the late twentieth century, much of the government's activity with respect to securities trading involved the detection and prosecution of insider trading in corporate stock, an offense that was not even on the horizon in the middle of the nineteenth century. In this respect, the market is more regulated now than it was then. There have thus been some significant developments in popular thought and in law after the end of the period covered by this book. They have not run in any uniform direction.

What should be most interesting to students of and participants in the modern securities market, however, is not the degree of change over the past 150 years, which is very well known, but the extent to which things have not changed. Today's traders and regulators are the unknowing heirs of more than 300 years of thought and regulation.

II

Perhaps the most basic disagreement among legal historians concerns the nature of legal change. Some understand law to be largely a reflection of a society's concerns and preferences. As political pressures accumulate and dissipate, as institutions come and go, the law adapts to the sum of the desires of all those with enough power to have their voices heard. Law is "a mirror held up against life . . . it is whatever results from the scheming, plotting, and striving of people and groups, with and against each other."[7] This view of legal change is often called an *external* view, because it emphasizes developments outside the legal system itself as causes of change.

Others understand law, by contrast, as a relatively enclosed system of professional thought and practice, in which change is largely independent of the forces at work in the wider world. The specific content of the

---

[7] Friedman, *History of American Law*, 695.

law is generated by lawyers, particularly acting as legislators and judges. These lawyers work within a culture that has its own traditions, which have a vitality that withstands broader political, social, and economic trends. Non-legal change is always filtered through the consciousness of lawyers before it can cause the law to change. As a result, "[t]he legal tradition shapes the law that comes out . . . The input of the society often bears little relation to the output of the legal elite."[8] This view of legal change is often called an *internal* view, because it emphasizes the autonomy of the legal system in generating change.

The story that has been told in this book includes some examples that would satisfy proponents of the external view. The 1697 legislation that limited time bargains to no more than three days, for instance, seems a clear response to political pressures generated by the new institution of securities trading. The same can be said about Sir John Barnard's Act of 1734, which banned the more speculative time bargains in reaction to the wave of anti-market opinion produced by the South Sea Bubble and then again by the smaller price decline of 1733–34. In neither case was legal change significantly mediated by the professional norms of lawyers. A substantial portion of the public with voices powerful enough to be heard wanted some limits on speculative securities transactions, and they got them. The philosophy behind the statutes, to be sure, was similar to the thought underlying earlier English regulation of older markets in food and other commodities, but that philosophy was not the sole possession of a legal elite; it permeated society as a whole.

The source of legal change becomes more ambiguous – it seems both external and internal at the same time – when one considers the stockjobbing statute enacted in New York after the crash of 1792. Here again, the state legislature was responding to significant anti-market political pressures produced most immediately by the flurry of speculation in the previous two years. The law changed, in substance, because of forces external to the legal system. But the *form* of that change was the product of an elite professional culture. The drafters of the 1792 statute were familiar with the text and the purpose of Barnard's Act, and borrowed Barnard's Act for local use. Limits on speculation in securities in New York in 1792 could have taken any number of forms had they been drafted by non-lawyers. The statute read the way it did because external pressures had to filter through the minds and pens of lawyers before they could produce new law. While going through this process, however, those external pressures do not seem to have been much deformed. One can never be sure of how much is lost in the translation –

---

[8] Alan Watson, *The Evolution of Law* (Baltimore: Johns Hopkins University Press, 1985), 117.

that would require the counterfactual assumption of legislation drafted and enacted directly by the members of the public most concerned – but the immediate effect of the stockjobbing act does not appear to have been very different from what opponents of speculation wanted. To explain the legal change that occurred in New York in 1792, one has to tell both an external and an internal story; the external account explains the fact of the change and the overall substance of the change, while the internal account explains the precise form of the change.

Other legal developments described in this book would satisfy proponents of the internal view. The law was constantly being adapted to fit the new securities market. Doctrines of contracts, of usury, of fraud, and so on were applied to the new institution. New procedures were created for what were becoming routine transactions. In all these respects, legislators and especially judges were clearly working within a professional legal tradition. To answer the many questions created by the application of the law of usury to securities transactions, for instance, judges did not primarily consider the pros and cons of securities trading or the social and economic effects of their decisions, nor did they respond to political pressures brought to bear by their non-lawyer contemporaries. They instead reasoned by analogy from earlier-decided English cases involving older forms of speculative investment. These earlier cases were almost certainly unknown to non-lawyers. The books in which they were printed were possessed only by lawyers, and only lawyers had the technical skills necessary to find the cases, to understand them, and to apply them to new situations. The law of usury obviously could not have been applied to securities trading before securities trading began; to that extent, the law of usury changed a bit in the eighteenth and nineteenth centuries; and that change, at least considered on its own, was the purely internal product of an elite professional culture.

The first century and a half of Anglo-American securities regulation thus includes examples of both externally and internally generated change, as well as examples somewhere in the middle. It also includes examples of non-governmental ordering that do not fit the internal/external paradigm very well. The rules of the New York Stock and Exchange Board and the unwritten practices of English and American traders were not produced by a legal elite, but by a professional community with an autonomy and an internal culture comparable to those possessed by lawyers. Like the government, the brokers and jobbers were simultaneously market participants and market regulators. Yet the distinction between internally and externally generated change is difficult to transfer to non-governmental regulators, who lack the constraints popular opinion imposes on Anglo-American institutions of government, but who are under different kinds of constraints as a result of their more limited enforcement power. The internal/external debate thus has difficulty accommodating non-govermental sources of law.

Returning to governmental sources of law, the debate over which characterization is generally more accurate is, of course, to some extent only a question of emphasis. Certain areas of the law have seen abrupt legislative changes, which are more conducive to an external explanation; others have seen gradual judicial changes, which suggest the appropriateness of an internal explanation. Some areas of the law have been highly controversial among non-lawyers, and thus more prone to external change; others have been almost unknown among non-lawyers, and thus less prone to external change. The law relating to workplace injuries, for example, has had a profound effect on the lives of many people, and has thus seen abrupt legislative change; students of the subject may be more likely to perceive legal change as externally generated.[9] The field of "conflict of laws," on the other hand, a body of law encompassing questions of which jurisdiction's law should apply when there is more than one possibility, has at most an indirect effect on the lives of most people, and is scarcely known even by many lawyers. Students of the subject may be more likely to perceive legal change as internally generated.[10] (Or perhaps a predisposition to understand legal change in one way or the other influences one's choice of subjects to study.) Like the question whether hot water is properly characterized as "hot" or "wet," the internal/external debate often boils down to which aspect one chooses to emphasize.

There is more to it than that, however. The evidence presented in this book suggests a relationship between the internal and external explanations of legal change that may have some applicability beyond the early history of securities regulation. In each of the instances of internal change described here, lawyers either borrowed from older law or reasoned by analogy to adapt older law to a new institution. But where did that older law come from? In each case, the older law had itself been produced by external forces. The usury doctrine exempting investments in which principal was at risk, for example, was applied through an internal process to purchases and loans of securities. But that doctrine, as we saw in chapter 1, had itself developed centuries earlier as a compromise between two competing views of the economy, one empha-

---

[9] See Lawrence M. Friedman and Jack Ladinsky, "Social Change and the Law of Industrial Accidents," *Columbia Law Review* 67 (1967): 50.

[10] See Alan Watson, *Joseph Story and the Comity of Errors: A Case Study in Conflict of Laws* (Athens: University of Georgia Press, 1992).

sizing religious and philosophical norms proscribing idleness and exploitation, the other emphasizing the potential gains from risky shipping ventures and the need to pool capital from many different sources. To accommodate that conflict, canon law decisionmakers created the rule that would eventually be transferred to the common law and restated in *Roberts* v. *Tremayne,* and in that form carried across the Atlantic to the United States. From an initial instance of externally produced change, many smaller cases of internally produced changes would follow, including the one described in this book.

An old usury doctrine could only be internally modified to new conditions, however, because the initial pressures that produced the doctrine had not changed significantly in the interim. Although there had obviously been great social and economic change in the past few hundred years, the two opposing sets of beliefs that produced the doctrine were still present in the wider world. The popular norms suspicious of the passive earning of interest were still there, as were the opposite norms valuing productive investment. The latter had probably increased in intensity relative to the former, but not enough to cause any alteration in the basic principle prohibiting usury. In the absence of any significant pressure to change the ground rules, it would not have occurred to judges to do anything but reason by analogy from the old doctrine.

What if those external forces had changed significantly? Suppose, for example, that by the early nineteenth century hardly anyone was concerned that the ability to lend out money at interest might lead to idleness or exploitation of the needy, but that by contrast investment was almost universally perceived as useful under any terms voluntarily reached by borrowers and lenders. Had that been the case, the law of usury would almost certainly have been applied differently to securities transactions. Either the general proscription on high interest rates would have been repealed by legislatures, leaving judges no usury law to apply to challenged transactions, or judges would have developed a principle excusing securities transactions from the general rule. (It is not hard to come up with such a principle. Because securities transactions were new, lawyers might have argued, they were not within the contemplation of the legislators who enacted usury statutes. Or perhaps the legislators intended to codify the common law, and the challenged transactions were so new that they could not have been embraced by the common law's proscription.) Either way, a significant realignment of external pressures would have produced a very different change in the law than the one that actually occurred.

Legal change could be produced internally, therefore, only where externally generated rules already existed, and only where the pressures that had given rise to such rules had not changed much in the interim. Only then were the lawyers left to themselves, to construct new law with the tools of their own professional culture.

Much of the story told in this book can thus be reduced to a simple model of legal change. Like all models, it is not a representation of reality but a deliberate simplification, intended to add to our understanding of reality by emphasizing certain recurrent features. Law changes in response to changing external pressures. But those pressures, having changed, then often remain largely stable for long periods of time. When they do, decisions made at one time can last as long the external conditions that produced those decisions do not change. The wheel does not need continuous reinventing. As new situations come up, lawyers can tinker around the edges of the old decision. In doing so, they generate legal change internally. This state of affairs has been the norm in English and American history; at most times, in most areas of the law, most change is of this incremental, internal type. But every so often, something outside the legal system changes profoundly – a war occurs, economic arrangements change, social norms change, something important is invented – and that external change influences the law. The result is externally driven change, which, if followed by a period of relative stability, can be the basis for more internally driven change at a later time.

This is, I think, an accurate framework for the events described in this book. The invention of securities trading was a major event, which produced some important changes in some aspects of English law. But it was also, at the same time, a minor ripple with respect to other areas of English law, areas which could absorb it by gradual internal adjustments. Because the structure of the market and popular attitudes toward it did not change significantly in the next century and a half, the externally generated legal changes produced by the new institution (especially Barnard's Act) were able to serve as the basis for largely internal changes in the United States in the late eighteenth and early nineteenth centuries.

This framework may also be a useful way of understanding the relationship between internal and external elements of legal change generally. That's a question for students of other aspects of English and American legal history, and I'll leave it to them.

Bibliography

New-York Historical Society
  Peter Anspach papers
  James W. Bleecker papers
  William Duer papers
  John M. O'Connor papers
  Tontine Coffee House collection

New York Public Library
  Constable-Pierrepont papers

New York Stock Exchange
  Arbitration Committees
  Buttonwood Agreement
  Committees on Applications
  Constitutions and By-Laws
  Minute Books

Abdy, E. S. *Journal of a Residence and Tour in the United States of North America.* London: J. Murray, 1835.

An Account of the South Sea Scheme*; and a Number of Other Bubbles; Which Were Encouraged by Public Infatuation in the Year 1720.* [London]: J. Cawthorne, 1806.

The Acts and Resolves, Public and Private, of the Province of Massachusetts Bay. Boston: Wright & Potter, 1907.

Adams, Jr., Charles Francis. *A Chapter of Erie.* Boston: Fields, Osgood, & Co., 1869.

Adams, Thomas. *The White Devil, or the Hypocrite Uncased.* London: Ralph Mab, 1613.

All Corporations, and Particular Persons, that are willing to become Adventurers to East-India . . . [London]: East India Co., 1657.

American Securities: Practical Hints on the Tests of Stability and Profit. London: M. Nephews, 1860.

Ames, Seth, ed. *Works of Fisher Ames.* Boston: Little, Brown, 1854.

Amhurst, Nicholas. *An Epistle (With a Petition in it) to Sir John Blount, Bart., One of the Directors of the South-Sea Company.* London: R. Francklin, 1720.

Anderson, Adam. *An Historical and Chronological Deduction of the Origin of Commerce*. London: J. White, 1801.

Anderson, Gary M. and Robert D. Tollison. "Adam Smith's Analysis of Joint-Stock Companies." *Journal of Political Economy* 90 (1982): 1237–56.

Anderson, William G. *The Price of Liberty: The Public Debt of the American Revolution*. Charlottesville: University Press of Virginia, 1983.

Angell, Joseph K. and Samuel Ames. *A Treatise on the Law of Private Corporations Aggregate*. Boston: Hilliard, Gray, Little & Wilkins, 1832.

Angliae Tutamen: or, The Safety of England. London: s.n., 1695.

Anstey, Christopher. *Speculation; or, a Defence of Mankind*. London: Christopher Anstey, 1780.

An Answer to a Pamphlet on Publick Credit. London: T. Cooper, 1733.

An Answer to the Reasons for Making Void and Annulling Fraudulent and Usurious Contracts, &c. [London]: s.n., 1721.

Appleby, Joyce Oldham. *Economic Thought and Ideology in Seventeenth-Century England*. Princeton: Princeton University Press, 1978.

  Liberalism and Republicanism in the Historical Imagination. Cambridge, MA: Harvard University Press, 1992.

Armstrong, William. *Stocks and Stock-Jobbing in Wall-Street*. New York: New-York Publishing Co., 1848.

The Art of Stock Jobbing Explained. 7th edn. London: W. Clarke, 1819.

The Art of Stock-jobbing: A Poem, In Imitation of Horace's Art of Poetry, *by a Gideonite*. London: R. Baldwin, 1746.

Atiyah, P. S. *The Rise and Fall of Freedom of Contract*. Oxford: Clarendon Press, 1979.

B., J. *A Poem Occasion'd by the Rise and Fall of* South-Sea *Stock*. London: Samuel Chapman, 1720.

Bailyn, Bernard. *The Ideological Origins of the American Revolution*. Cambridge, MA: Harvard University Press, 1967.

  The Ordeal of Thomas Hutchinson. Cambridge, MA: Harvard University Press, 1974.

Bailyn, Bernard, ed. *The Apologia of Robert Keayne* (1653). New York: Harper & Row, 1965.

Bailyn, Bernard and Lotte Bailyn. *Massachusetts Shipping 1697–1714*. Cambridge, MA: Harvard University Press, 1959.

Baker, J. H. "Book Review." *Modern Law Review* 43 (1980): 467–68.

Baldwin, Simeon E. "American Business Corporations Before 1789." *Annual Report of the American Historical Association for the Year 1902*. Washington: Government Printing Office, 1902.

Banning, Lance. "Political Economy and the Creation of the Federal Republic." In *Devising Liberty: Preserving and Creating Freedom in the New American Republic*, edited by David Thomas Konig. Stanford: Stanford University Press, 1995.

Barclay, Alexander. *The Ship of Fools* (1509). Edited by T. H. Jamieson. Edinburgh: W. Paterson, 1874.

Barker, Jacob. *The Speeches of Mr. Jacob Barker and His Counsel, on the Trials for Conspiracy*. New York: W. A. Mersein, 1826.

Barnard, John. *Reasons for the More Speedy Lessening the National Debt.* London: J. Roberts, 1737.

Barnes, Donald Grove. *A History of the English Corn Laws From 1660–1846.* New York: Crofts, 1930.

Barron, Clarence W. and Joseph G. Martin. *The Boston Stock Exchange.* Boston: Hunt & Bell, 1893.

Barton, David. "Pro-Fund Wit: Jonathan Swift and the Scriblerians." New York University Ph.D. dissertation, 1994.

Baskin, Jonathan Barron. "The Development of Corporate Financial Markets in Britain and the United States, 1600–1914: Overcoming Asymmetric Information." *Business History Review* 62 (1988): 199–237.

Bassett, John Spencer, ed. *Correspondence of Andrew Jackson.* Washington: Carnegie Institution, 1926–35.

Bates, Whitney. "Northern Speculators and Southern State Debts: 1790." *William and Mary Quarterly* 19 (1962): 30–48.

Baubles, Jr., Raymond L. "Finance and Folly: The Speculative Investor in Nineteenth-Century British History and Literature." Fordham University Ph.D. dissertation, 1993.

Beard, Charles A. *An Economic Interpretation of the Constitution of the United States* (1913). New York: Free Press, 1986.

Beecher, Henry Ward. *Seven Lectures to Young Men, on Various Important Subjects.* Indianapolis: Thomas B. Culter, 1844.

Beeman, Richard, Stephen Botein, and Edward C. Carter II, eds. *Beyond Confederation: Origins of the Constitution and American National Identity.* Chapel Hill: University of North Carolina Press, 1987.

Bensel, Richard Franklin. *Yankee Leviathan: The Origins of Central State Authority in America, 1859–1877.* Cambridge: Cambridge University Press, 1990.

Berle, Jr., Adolf A., and Gardiner C. Means. *The Modern Corporation and Private Property.* New York: Commerce Clearing House, 1932.

Bernstein, Lisa. "Merchant Law in a Merchant Court: Rethinking the Code's Search for Immanent Business Norms." *University of Pennsylvania Law Review* 144 (1996): 1765–1821.

Blackstone, William. *Commentaries on the Laws of England.* 9th edn. London: W. Strahan, 1783.

Blandi, Joseph G. *Maryland Business Corporations 1783–1852.* Baltimore: Johns Hopkins Press, 1934.

Blodget, Samuel. *Economica: A Statistical Manual for the United States of America* (1806). New York: A. M. Kelley, 1964.

Bond, William. *An Epistle to his Royal Highness the Prince of Wales.* London: E. Curll, 1720.

Boswell, John. *The Kindness of Strangers: The Abandonment of Children in Western Europe from Late Antiquity to the Renaissance.* New York: Pantheon, 1988.

Bowen, H. V. "'The Pests of Human Society': Stockbrokers, Jobbers and Speculators in Mid-eighteenth-century Britain." *History* 78 (1993): 38–53.

Boyd, Julian P., *et al.*, eds. *The Papers of Thomas Jefferson.* Princeton: Princeton University Press, 1950–.

Boys, John. *The Workes of John Boys.* London: William Ashley, 1622.

Brealey, Richard and Stewart Myers. *Principles of Corporate Finance.* 2nd edn. New York: McGraw-Hill, 1984.

Breen, T. H. "Horses and Gentlemen: The Cultural Significance of Gambling Among the Gentry of Virginia." *William and Mary Quarterly* 34 (1977): 239–57.

Brenner, Reuven with Gabrielle A. Brenner. *Gambling and Speculation: A Theory, a History, and a Future of Some Human Decisions.* Cambridge: Cambridge University Press, 1990.

Brewer, John. *The Sinews of Power: War, Money and the English State, 1688–1783.* New York: Alfred A. Knopf, 1989.

Brewer, John and Susan Staves, eds. *Early Modern Conceptions of Property.* London: Routledge, 1995.

Brewer, John and John Styles, eds. *An Ungovernable People: The English and Their Law in the Seventeenth and Eighteenth Centuries.* New Brunswick: Rutgers University Press, 1980.

Bristed, C. Astor. *The Upper Ten Thousand.* New York: Stringer & Townsend, 1852.

Britannia Stript by a S. Sea Director. [London]: s.n., 1721.

Brock, Leslie V. *The Currency of the American Colonies 1700–1764: A Study in Colonial Finance and Imperial Relations.* New York: Arno Press, 1975.

Brockett, Elias. *The Yea and Nay Stock-Jobbers, or the 'Change-Alley Quakers Anatomiz'd.* London: J. Roberts, 1720.

The Broken Stock-Jobbers: *Or, Work for the* Bailiffs. London: T. Jauncy, 1720.

Browder, Clifford. *The Money Game in Old New York: Daniel Drew and His Times.* Lexington: University of Kentucky Press, 1986.

Brundage, James A. *Medieval Canon Law.* London: Longman, 1995.

Brydges, Samuel Egerton. *Human Fate.* Great Totham: Charles Clark, 1846.

The Bubblers Medley, or a Sketch of the Times: Being Europes Memorial for the Year 1720. London: Carrington Bowley, 1720.

The Bubblers Mirrour: or England's Folly. London: Bowles & Carver, 1720.

The Bublers Medley, or the D-v-l will have his own. S.l.: s.n., 1720.

Buchinsky, Moshe and Ben Polak. "The Emergence of a National Capital Market in England, 1710–1880." *Journal of Economic History* 53 (1993): 1–24.

Buck, James E., ed. *The New York Stock Exchange: The First 200 Years.* Essex: Greenwich Pub. Group, 1992.

Buitenhuis, Peter. *The House of the Seven Gables: Severing Family and Colonial Ties.* Boston: Twayne Publishers, 1991.

Burn, J. I. *A Brief Treatise, or Summary of the Law Relative to Stock-Jobbing.* London: T. Boosey, 1803.

Butler, Henry N. "General Incorporation in Nineteenth Century England: Interaction of Common Law and Legislative Processes." *International Review of Law and Economics* 6 (1986): 169–88.

Butterfield, L. H., ed. *Letters of Benjamin Rush.* Philadelphia: American Philosophical Society, 1951.

C——m, C. *A Familiar Epistle to Mr. Mitchell.* London: T. Jauncy, 1720.

Cadman, Jr., John W. *The Corporation in New Jersey: Business and Politics, 1791–1875.* Cambridge, MA: Harvard University Press, 1949.

Callender, James Thomson. *The History of the United States for 1796.* Philadelphia: Snowden & M'Corkle, 1797.

Sedgwick & Co. or A Key to the Six Per Cent Cabinet. Philadelphia: J. T. Callender, 1798.

Carey, George G. *Every Man His Own Stock-broker.* London: J. Johnston, 1821.

Carosso, Vincent P. *Investment Banking in America: A History.* Cambridge, MA: Harvard University Press, 1970.

Carr, Cecil T., ed. *Select Charters of Trading Companies, A.D. 1530–1707.* London: B. Quaritch, 1913 (Publications of the Selden Society, Vol. 28).

Carswell, John. *The South Sea Bubble.* Rev. edn. Dover: Alan Sutton, 1993.

Cary, William L., and Melvin Aron Eisenberg. *Cases and Materials on Corporations.* 5th edn. Mineola: Foundation Press, 1980.

Case of the Licens'd Brokers, Upon the Bill Depending in Parliament. S.l.: s.n., 1731.

The Case of the Purchasers of the First and Second Subscriptions to the South-Sea Company. [London]: s.n., 1721.

Catanzariti, John, *et al.*, eds. *The Papers of Robert Morris 1781–1784.* Pittsburgh: University of Pittsburgh Press, 1973–.

Cawelti, John G. *Apostles of the Self-Made Man.* Chicago: University of Chicago Press, 1965.

Cawston, George and A. H. Keane. *The Early Chartered Companies.* London: E. Arnold, 1896.

Centlivre, Susanna. *A Bold Stroke for a Wife* (1718). Edited by Thalia Stathas. Lincoln: University of Nebraska Press, 1968.

Chandaman, C. D. *The English Public Revenue 1660–1688.* Oxford: Clarendon Press, 1975.

Chandler, Jr., Alfred D. *The Visible Hand: The Managerial Revolution in American Business.* Cambridge, MA: Harvard University Press, 1977.

The Changery. An Allegoric Memoir of the Boston Exchange Office. Boston: s.n., 1805.

Charny, David. "Nonlegal Sanctions in Commercial Relationships." *Harvard Law Review* 104 (1990): 373–467.

Chetwood, W. R. *South-Sea; or, the Biters Bit.* London: J. Roberts, 1720.

The Stock-Jobbers: or, the Humours *of Exchange-Alley.* London: J. Roberts, 1720.

Chevalier, Michel. *Society, Manners and Politics in the United States* (1839). New York: A. M. Kelley, 1966.

Christie, Ian R. *British "Non-Elite" MPs 1715–1820.* Oxford: Clarendon Press, 1995.

Clerke, George. *The Dealers in Stock's Assistant.* London: Edward Symon, 1725.

Clews, Henry. *Fifty Years in Wall Street.* New York: Irving Pub. Co., 1908.

Cobbett, William. *Paper Against Gold.* New York: J. Doyle, 1846.

Parliamentary History of England. London: T. C. Hansard, 1806–20.

Cochrane, George. *Opinions on Loans of Government Stock; Respectfully Addressed to the Landed, Commercial, and Professional World.* London: Smith, Elder and Co., 1847.

Cohen, Bernard. *Compendium of Finance.* London: W. Phillips, 1822.

Coke, Edward. *The Third Part of the Institutes of the Laws of England* (1644). London: E. and R. Brooke, 1797.

Coleman, D. C. *The Economy of England 1450–1750.* London: Oxford University Press, 1977.

Coleman, Peter J. *Debtors and Creditors in America*. Madison: State Historical Society of Wisconsin, 1974.

Colley, Linda. *Britons: Forging the New Nation, 1707–1837*. New Haven: Yale University Press, 1992.

Commager, Henry Steele, ed. *Theodore Parker: An Anthology*. Boston: Beacon Press, 1960.

Coningsby, Thomas. *The* Naked *and* Undisguis'd *Truth, Plainly and Faithfully Told: What was the Unhappy Rise, Which were the Fatal Causes, And Who the Wicked Authors, of* Great Britain's *and* Ireland's *Present Dreadful (and Before Unheard of) Calamities*. London: J. Moore, 1721.

Conkin, Paul K. *Prophets of Prosperity: America's First Political Economists*. Bloomington: Indiana University Press, 1980.

Considerations Against Repealing that Part of an Act of Parliament, *Which Restrains the Number of* Exchange-Brokers *to One Hundred*. London: s.n., 1705.

Considerations on a Bill Now Depending in Parliament. S.l.: s.n., 1756.

Cook, William W. *A Treatise on the Law of Stock and Stockholders*. New York: Baker, Voorhis, 1887.

Cooke, C. A. *Corporation, Trust and Company*. Cambridge, MA: Harvard University Press, 1951.

Cooke, Jacob E. *Tench Coxe and the Early Republic*. Chapel Hill: University of North Carolina Press, 1978.

Cope, S. R. "The Stock-Brokers Find a Home: How the Stock Exchange Came to Be Established in Sweetings Alley in 1773." *Guildhall Studies in London History* 2 (1977): 213–19.

"The Stock Exchange Revisited: A New Look at the Market in Securities in London in the Eighteenth Century." *Economica* 45 (1978): 1–21.

Corner, George W., ed. *The Autobiography of Benjamin Rush*. Princeton: Princeton University Press, 1948.

Cowing, Cedric B. *Populists, Plungers, and Progressives: A Social History of Stock and Commodity Speculation 1890–1936*. Princeton: Princeton University Press, 1965.

Craven, Wesley Frank. *The Southern Colonies in the Seventeenth Century 1607–1689*. Baton Rouge: Louisiana State University Press, 1949.

Crowley, J. E. *This Sheba, Self: The Conceptualization of Economic Life in Eighteenth-Century America*. Baltimore: Johns Hopkins University Press, 1974.

Crowley, Robert. "Of Forestallars" (1550). In *The Select Works of Robert Crowley*, edited by J. M. Cowper. London: Trubner, 1872.

Cruzet, François, ed. *Capital Formation in the Industrial Revolution*. London: Methuen, 1972.

Cull, Robert Joseph. "A Comparative Study of Capital Market Failure and Institutional Innovation." Calif. Inst. of Technology Ph.D. dissertation, 1993.

Currie, David P. "The Most Insignificant Justice: A Preliminary Inquiry." *University of Chicago Law Review* 50 (1983): 466–80.

Dabydeen, David. *Hogarth, Walpole and Commercial Britain*. London: Hansib, 1987.

Dalley, Paula. "The Law of Deceit, 1790–1860: Continuity Amidst Change." *American Journal of Legal History* 39 (1995): 405–42.

Dalrymple, David. *Time Bargains Tryed by the Rules of Equity and Principles of the Civil Law.* London: Eliz. Morphew, 1720.

Dane, Nathan. *A General Abridgment and Digest of American Law.* Boston: Cummings, Hilliard & Co., 1823–29.

Dangerfield, George. *Chancellor Robert R. Livingston of New York 1746–1813.* New York: Harcourt, Brace, 1960.

Davies, K. G. "Joint-Stock Investment in the Later Seventeenth Century." *Economic History Review* 4 (1952): 283–301.

Davis, Dorothy. *A History of Shopping.* London: Routledge, 1966.

Davis, John P. *Corporations.* New York: G.P. Putnam's Sons, 1905.

Davis, Joseph Stancliffe. *Essays in the Earlier History of American Corporations.* Cambridge, MA: Harvard University Press, 1917.

Davis, Lance E. and Robert J. Cull. *International Capital Markets and American Economic Growth, 1820–1914.* Cambridge: Cambridge University Press, 1994.

Davis, Ralph. *The Rise of the English Shipping Industry in the Seventeenth and Eighteenth Centuries.* London: Macmillan, 1962.

Dawson, Frank Griffith. *The First Latin American Debt Crisis: The City of London and the 1822–25 Loan Bubble.* New Haven: Yale University Press, 1990.

Deane, Phyllis. "Capital Formation in Britain Before the Railway Age." In *Capital Formation in the Industrial Revolution,* edited by François Cruzet. London: Methuen, 1972.

Defoe, Daniel. *The Anatomy of Exchange-Alley: or, A System of Stock-Jobbing.* London: E. Smith, 1719.

An Essay Upon Projects. London: T. Cockerill, 1697.

The Free-Holders Plea Against Stock-Jobbing Elections of Parliament Men. London: s.n., 1701.

The Gamester: A Benefit-Ticket for All that Are Concern'd in the Lotteries. London: J. Roberts, 1719.

The South-Sea Scheme Examin'd; and the Reasonableness Thereof Demonstrated. London: J. Roberts, 1720.

The Villainy of Stock-Jobbers Detected. London: s.n., 1701.

de la Vega, Joseph. *Confusión de Confusiones* (1688). Translated by Hermann Kellenbenz. In *Extraordinary Popular Delusions and the Madness of Crowds & Confusión de Confusiones,* edited by Martin S. Fridson. New York: John Wiley & Sons, 1996.

De Pauw, Linda Grant, *et al.,* eds. *Documentary History of the First Federal Congress of the United States of America.* Baltimore: Johns Hopkins University Press, 1972–.

de Tocqueville, Alexis. *Democracy in America* (first American edn. 1840). Edited by Phillips Bradley. New York: A. A. Knopf, 1976.

Dewey, T. Henry. *Legislation Against Speculation and Gambling in the Forms of Trade.* New York: Baker, Voorhis, 1905.

Dickens, Charles. *Our Mutual Friend* (1865). New York: Modern Library, 1992.

Dickinson, H. T. *Liberty and Property: Political Ideology in Eighteenth-Century Britain.* New York: Holmes and Meier, 1977.

Dickson, P. G. M. *The Financial Revolution in England*. London: Macmillan, 1967.

Dodd, Edwin Merrick. *American Business Corporations until 1860*. Cambridge, MA: Harvard University Press, 1954.

Doerflinger, Thomas M. *A Vigorous Spirit of Enterprise: Merchants and Economic Development in Revolutionary Philadelphia*. Chapel Hill: University of North Carolina Press, 1986.

Doherty, David P., Arthur S. Okun, Steven F. Korostoff, and James A. Nofi. "The Enforcement Role of the New York Stock Exchange." *Northwestern University Law Review* 85 (1991): 637–51.

Dorfman, Joseph. *The Economic Mind in American Civilization*. New York: Viking Press, 1946–59.

DuBois, Armand Budington. *The English Business Company after the Bubble Act 1720–1800*. New York: Commonwealth Fund, 1938.

Duman, Daniel. *The Judicial Bench in England 1727–1875: The Reshaping of a Professional Elite*. London: Royal Historical Society, 1982.

Duncombe, Charles. *Duncombe's Free Banking*. Cleveland: Sanford & Co., 1841.

D'Urfey, Thomas. *The Hubble Bubbles*. London: J. Roberts, 1720.

Eames, Francis. *The New York Stock Exchange* (1894). New York: Greenwood Press, 1968.

Earle, Peter. *The Making of the English Middle Class: Business, Society, and Family Life in London, 1660–1730*. Berkeley: University of California Press, 1989.

East, Robert A. *Business Enterprise in the American Revolutionary Era*. New York: Columbia University Press, 1938.

Eisenstadt, Peter. "How the Buttonwood Tree Grew: The Making of a New York Stock Exchange Legend." *Prospects: An Annual of American Cultural Studies* 19 (1994): 75–98.

Elkins, Stanley and Eric McKitrick. *The Age of Federalism: The Early American Republic, 1788–1800*. New York: Oxford University Press, 1993.

Emerson, Ralph Waldo. "The Transcendentalist" (1843) and "Wealth" (1860). In *The Complete Essays and Other Writings of Ralph Waldo Emerson*, edited by Brooks Atkinson. New York: Random House, 1950.

Ernst, Joseph Albert. *Money and Politics in America, 1755–1775*. Chapel Hill: University of North Carolina Press, 1973.

An Essay on the Present State of the Public Funds. London: s.n., 1778.

An Essay Towards Restoring of Publick Credit. London: J. Roberts, 1721.

Evans, Jr., George Herberton. *British Corporation Finance 1775–1850: A Study of Preference Shares*. Baltimore: Johns Hopkins Press, 1936.

Business Incorporations in the United States 1800–1943. New York: National Bureau of Economic Research, 1948.

Everitt, Alan. "The Marketing of Agricultural Produce." In *The Agrarian History of England and Wales*, vol. IV, edited by Joan Thirsk. London: Cambridge University Press, 1967.

An Examination of the Vindication of the Award Between Boorman, Johnston & Co. and Jacob Little & Co. New York: J. Elliott, 1842.

Exchange-Alley: or, the Stock-Jobber Turn'd Gentleman; with the Humours of our Modern Projectors. London: T. Bickerton, 1720.

Fabian, Ann. *Card Sharps, Dream Books, & Bucket Shops: Gambling in 19th-Century America.* Ithaca: Cornell University Press, 1990.

Fairman, William. *The Stocks Examined and Compared.* London: J. Johnson, 1795.

Fenn's Compendium of the English and Foreign Funds. 5th edn. London: Effingham Wilson, 1855.

Fenton, Roger. *A Treatise of Usurie.* London: William Aspley, 1611.

Ferguson, E. James. *The Power of the Purse: A History of American Public Finance, 1776–1790.* Chapel Hill: University of North Carolina Press, 1961.

Filmer, Robert. *A Discourse Whether it may be Lawful to take Use for Money.* London: W. Crook, 1678.

Findlay, John M. *People of Chance: Gambling in American Society from Jamestown to Las Vegas.* New York: Oxford University Press, 1986.

Findley, William. *A Review of the Revenue System.* Philadelphia: T. Dobson, 1794.

Fisk, Theophilus. *The Banking Bubble Burst.* Charleston: s.n., 1837.

Fitzpatrick, John C., ed. *The Writings of George Washington.* Washington: Government Printing Office, 1931–41.

Flagg, James. *A Strange Account of the Rising and Breaking of a Great Bubble.* Boston: s.n., 1767.

Flood, Robert P. and Peter M. Garber. *Speculative Bubbles, Speculative Attacks, and Policy Switching.* Cambridge: MIT Press, 1994.

Folk III, Ernest L., Rodman Ward, Jr., and Edward P. Welch. *Folk on the Delaware General Corporation Law.* 2nd edn. Boston: Little, Brown, 1988.

Foner, Eric. *Tom Paine and Revolutionary America.* New York: Oxford University Press, 1976.

Foner, Philip S., ed. *The Democratic-Republican Societies, 1790–1800.* Westport: Greenwood Press, 1976.

Fortune, Thomas. *An Epitome of the Stocks and Publick Funds.* 2nd edn. London: T. Boosey, 1796.

Foster, George G. *New York in Slices: By an Experienced Carver.* New York: W. F. Burgess, 1848.

Foster, T. *An Essay upon the Principles of Political Economy.* New York: T. Foster, 1837.

Fowle, D. and Z. Fowle, *A Letter to a Gentleman on the Sin and Danger of Playing at Cards and Other Games.* [Boston]: s.n., 1755.

Fowler, John. *The Last Guinea.* London: T. Jauncy, 1720.

Francis, John. *Chronicles and Characters of the Stock Exchange.* Boston: W. Crosby and H.P. Nichols, 1850.

Freke, John. *The Prices of the Several Stocks, Annuities, and other Publick Securities &c. with the Course of Exchange.* [London]: John Freke, 1714.

French, Jonathan. *A Practical Discourse Against Extortion.* Boston: T. & J. Fleet, 1777.

Frese, Joseph R. and Jacob Judd, eds. *Business Enterprise in Early New York.* Tarrytown: Sleepy Hollow Press, 1979.

Friedman, Lawrence M. *A History of American Law.* 2nd edn. New York: Simon & Schuster, 1985.

Friedman, Lawrence M. and Jack Ladinsky. "Social Change and the Law of Industrial Accidents." *Columbia Law Review* 67 (1967): 50–82.

Further Reasons Offer'd, and Fresh Occasions Given for Making Void and Annulling Fraudulent and Usurious Contracts. London: s.n., 1721.

Gay, John. *A Panegyrical Epistle to Mr. Thomas Snow*. London: Bernard Lintot, 1721.

Gayer, Arthur D., W. W. Rostow, and Anna Jacobson Schwartz. *The Growth and Fluctuation of the British Economy 1790–1850*. Oxford: Clarendon Press, 1953.

Gilchrist, David T., ed. *The Growth of the Seaport Cities 1790–1825*. Charlottesville: University Press of Virginia, 1967.

Gilmore, Michael T. *American Romanticism and the Marketplace*. Chicago: University of Chicago Press, 1985.

Gilson, Ronald J., and Reinier H. Kraakman. "The Mechanisms of Market Efficiency." *Virginia Law Review* 70 (1984): 549–644.

The Glass; or, Speculation: A Poem. New York: s.n., 1791.

Goodall, T. *Every One's Interest in the South-Sea Examined; and by Rules of Justice and Equity Settled*. London: T. Bickerton, 1721.

Gordon, John Steele. *The Scarlet Woman of Wall Street*. New York: Weidenfeld & Nicolson, 1988.

Gordon, Thomas. *An Essay on the Practice of Stock-Jobbing*. London: J. Peele, 1724.

Gordon, Thomas and John Trenchard. *A Collection of All the Political Letters in the London Journal, to December 17, Inclusive, 1720*. London: J. Roberts, 1721.

Gouge, William M. *A Short History of Paper Money and Banking in the United States*. Philadelphia: T.W. Ustick, 1833.

Gower, L. C. B. "A South Sea Heresy?" *Law Quarterly Review* 68 (1952): 214–25.

Gras, Norman Scott Brien. *The Evolution of the English Corn Market From the Twelfth to the Eighteenth Century*. Cambridge, MA: Harvard University Press, 1915.

Green, Jonathan H. *Green's Report, No. 1, on Gambling and Gambling Houses in New York*. New York: J.H. Green, 1851.

Secret Band of Brothers. Philadelphia: T.B. Peterson and Bros., 1858.

Gross, Charles, ed. *Select Cases Concerning the Law Merchant*. London: B. Quaritch, 1908 (Publications of the Selden Society, Vol. 23).

Grund, Francis J. *The Americans in Their Moral, Social, and Political Relations* (1837). New York: Johnson Reprint Corp., 1968.

Gurney, William Brodie. *The Trial of Charles Random de Berenger, Sir Thomas Cochrane, Commonly Called Lord Cochrane, the Hon. Andrew Cochrane Johnstone, Richard Gathorne Butt, Ralph Sandom, Alexander McRae, John Peter Holloway, and Henry Lyle, for a Conspiracy*. London: J. Butterworth, 1814.

Hales, Charles. *The Bank Mirror; or, a Guide to the Funds*. London: J. Adlard, 1796.

Halttunen, Karen. *Confidence Men and Painted Women: A Study of Middle-Class Culture in America, 1830–1870*. New Haven: Yale University Press, 1982.

Hamilton, Alexander. *Papers on Public Credit, Commerce and Finance.* Edited by Samuel McKee, Jr. New York: Columbia University Press, 1934.

Hammond, Bray. *Banks and Politics in America.* Princeton: Princeton University Press, 1957.

Handlin, Oscar and Mary Flug Handlin. *Commonwealth: A Study of the Role of Government in the American Economy: Massachusetts, 1774–1861.* New York: New York University Press, 1947.

"Origins of the American Business Corporation." *Journal of Economic History* 5 (1945): 1–23.

Harris, Neil. *Humbug: The Art of P. T. Barnum.* Boston: Little, Brown, 1973.

Harris, Ron. "The Bubble Act: Its Passage and Its Effects on Business Organization." *Journal of Economic History* 54 (1994): 610–27.

"Industrialization Without Free Incorporation: The Legal Framework of Business Organization in England, 1720–1844." Columbia University Ph.D. dissertation, 1994.

Harrison, Paul. "The More Things Change the More They Stay the Same: Analysis of the Past 200 Years of Stock Market Evolution." Duke University Ph.D. dissertation, 1994.

Harrison, William. *The Description of England* (1577). Edited by Georges Edelen. Ithaca: Cornell University Press, 1968.

Hart, Levi. *Liberty Described and Recommended.* Hartford: Eben. Watson, 1775.

Hartz, Louis. *Economic Policy and Democratic Thought: Pennsylvania, 1776–1860.* Cambridge, MA: Harvard University Press, 1948.

Hatton, Edward. *The Merchant's Magazine: or, Trades-Man's Treasury.* 3rd edn. London: Chr. Coningsby, 1699.

Hauck, Richard Boyd. *A Cheerful Nihilism: Confidence and "The Absurd" in American Humorous Fiction.* Bloomington: Indiana University Press, 1971.

Hawkins, William. *A Treatise of the Pleas of the Crown.* London: J. Walthoe, 1716.

Hawthorne, Nathaniel. *The House of the Seven Gables* (1851). New York: Viking Press, 1983.

Hay, Douglas. "Property, Authority and the Criminal Law." In Douglas Hay *et al., Albion's Fatal Tree: Crime and Society in Eighteenth-Century England.* New York: Pantheon, 1975.

Hedges, Joseph Edward. *Commercial Banking and the Stock Market Before 1863.* Baltimore: Johns Hopkins Press, 1938.

Helmholz, Richard H. *Roman Canon Law in Reformation England.* Cambridge: Cambridge University Press, 1990.

Henderson, James P. "Agency or Alienation? Smith, Mill, and Marx on the Joint-Stock Company." *History of Political Economy* 18 (1986): 111–31.

Hening, William Waller, ed. *The Statutes at Large; Being a Collection of all the Laws of Virginia.* 2nd edn. New York: R. & W. & G. Bartow, 1823.

Hidy, Ralph W. *The House of Baring in American Trade and Finance.* Cambridge, MA: Harvard University Press, 1949.

Higginson, John. *The Second Part of South-Sea Stock.* Boston: D. Henchman, 1721.

Hill, C. William. *The Political Theory of John Taylor of Caroline.* Rutherford: Fairleigh Dickinson University Press, 1977.

The History and Proceedings of the House of Commons from the Restoration to the Present Time. London: Richard Chandler, 1742.

The History and Proceedings of the House of Lords, from the Restoration in 1660, to the Present Time. London: Edenezer Timberland, 1742.

Hoffman, Ronald, John J. McCusker, Russell R. Menard, and Peter J. Albert, eds. *The Economy of Early America: The Revolutionary Period, 1763–1790.* Charlottesville: University Press of Virginia, 1988.

Holdsworth, W.S. *A History of English Law.* Boston: Little, Brown, 1922–38.

Hoppit, Julian. "Attitudes to Credit in Britain, 1680–1790." *The Historical Journal* 33 (1990): 305–22.

——— *Risk and Failure in English Business 1700–1800.* Cambridge: Cambridge University Press, 1987.

Horwitz, Henry, ed. *The Parliamentary Diary of Narcissus Luttrell.* Oxford: Clarendon Press, 1972.

Horwitz, Morton J. *The Transformation of American Law, 1780–1860.* Cambridge, MA: Harvard University Press, 1977.

Houghton, John. *A Collection, for Improvement of Husbandry and Trade.* London: Randall Taylor, 1692–1703.

Hovenkamp, Herbert. *Enterprise and American Law, 1836–1937.* Cambridge, MA: Harvard University Press, 1991.

Hughes, Paul L. and James F. Larkin, eds. *Tudor Royal Proclamations.* New Haven: Yale University Press, 1964.

An Humble Remonstrance to the Lords and Commons of Great Britain. [London]: s.n., 1721.

Humbugs of Speculation, A Satirical Poem, Embracing Several Historical Sketches of Speculative Operations, National and Individual, During the Last Four Years. Saratoga Springs: Whig Office, 1840.

Hunt, Bishop Carleton. *The Development of the Business Corporation in England 1800–1867.* Cambridge, MA: Harvard University Press, 1936.

Hunt, Freeman, ed. *The Library of Commerce.* New York: Hunt's Merchants' Magazine, 1845.

Hunt, John Hale. *The Honest Man's Book of Finance and Politics.* New York: J. H. Hunt, 1862.

Hurst, James Willard. *The Legitimacy of the Business Corporation in the Law of the United States 1780–1970.* Charlottesville: University Press of Virginia, 1970.

Hutchinson, William T., et al., eds. *The Papers of James Madison.* Chicago: University of Chicago Press, 1962–.

Ingrassia, Catherine. "The Pleasure of Business and the Business of Pleasure: Gender, Credit, and the South Sea Bubble." *Studies in Eighteenth-Century Culture* 24 (1995): 191–210.

An Inquiry Into the Original and Consequences of the Publick Debt. London: s.n., 1753.

Ireland, Paddy. "Capitalism Without the Capitalist: The Joint Stock Company Share and the Emergence of the Modern Doctrine of Separate Corporate Personality." *Journal of Legal History* 17 (1996): 41–73.

Ireland, Samuel William Henry. *Stultifera Navis; or, The Modern Ship of Fools.* London: William Miller, 1807.

Irving, William Henry. *John Gay: Favorite of the Wits*. Durham: Duke University Press, 1940.

Isaac, Rhys. *The Transformation of Virginia 1740–1790*. Chapel Hill: University of North Carolina Press, 1982.

Jackson, Joseph. *The Encyclopedia of Philadelphia*. Harrisburg: National Historical Association, 1933.

Jaffe, Louis L. "Law Making By Private Groups." *Harvard Law Review* 51 (1937): 201–53.

Jarrell, Gregg A. "The Economic Effects of Federal Regulation of the Market for New Security Issues." *Journal of Law and Economics* 24 (1981): 613–75.

Jennings, Robert M., Donald F. Swanson, and Andrew P. Trout. "Alexander Hamilton's Tontine Proposal." *William and Mary Quarterly* 45 (1988): 107–15.

Johns, Elizabeth. *American Genre Painting: The Politics of Everyday Life*. New Haven: Yale University Press, 1991.

Johnson, E. A. J. *American Economic Thought in the Seventeenth Century*. New York: Russell & Russell, 1961.

Johnson, Joan. *Princely Chandos: James Brydges 1674–1744*. Gloucester: A. Sutton, 1984.

Johnson, Paul E. *A Shopkeeper's Millennium: Society and Revivals in Rochester, New York, 1815–1837*. New York: Hill and Wang, 1978.

Jones, Alice Hanson. *Wealth of a Nation to Be: The American Colonies on the Eve of the Revolution*. New York: Columbia University Press, 1980.

Jones, D. W. *War and Economy in the Age of William III and Marlborough*. Oxford: B. Blackwell, 1988.

Jones, J. R. *Country and Court: England, 1658–1714*. Cambridge: Cambridge University Press, 1979.

Jones, Norman. *God and the Moneylenders: Usury and Law in Early Modern England*. Oxford: B. Blackwell, 1989.

Jones, Robert F. *"The King of the Alley": William Duer, Politician, Entrepreneur, and Speculator, 1768–1799*. Philadelphia: American Philosophical Society, 1992.

Jones, William C. "An Inquiry Into the History of the Adjudication of Mercantile Disputes in Great Britain and the United States." *University of Chicago Law Review* 25 (1958): 445–64.

July, Robert W. *The Essential New Yorker: Gulian Crommelin Verplanck*. Durham: Duke University Press, 1951.

Kammen, Michael, ed. *The Origins of the American Constitution: A Documentary History*. New York: Penguin, 1986.

Kessler, William C. "Incorporation in New England: A Statistical Study, 1800–1875." *Journal of Economic History* 8 (1948): 43–62.

Keyser, Henry. *The Law Relating to Transactions on the Stock Exchange*. London: L.H. Butterworth, 1850.

Kiefer, Donald W. "The Security Transactions Tax: An Overview of the Issues." *Tax Notes* 48 (1990): 885–901.

Kitch, Edmund W. "A Federal Vision of the Securities Laws." *Virginia Law Review* 70 (1984): 857–73.

Klein, Lawrence E. "Property and Politeness in the Early Eighteenth-Century Whig Moralists." In *Early Modern Conceptions of Property*, edited by John Brewer and Susan Staves. London: Routledge, 1995.

Konig, David Thomas. "Jurisprudence and Social Policy in the New Republic." In *Devising Liberty: Preserving and Creating Freedom in the New American Republic*, edited by David Thomas Konig. Stanford: Stanford University Press, 1995.

Law and Society in Puritan Massachusetts. Chapel Hill: University of North Carolina Press, 1979.

Kramnick, Isaac. *Bolingbroke and His Circle*. Cambridge, MA: Harvard University Press, 1968.

"Corruption in Eighteenth-Century English and American Political Discourse." In *Virtue, Corruption, and Self-Interest: Political Values in the Eighteenth Century*, edited by Richard K. Matthews. Bethlehem: Lehigh University Press, 1994.

Krooss, Herman E. "Financial Institutions." In *The Growth of the Seaport Cities 1790–1825*, edited by David T. Gilchrist. Charlottesville: University Press of Virginia, 1967.

Krooss, Herman E. and Martin R. Blyn. *A History of Financial Intermediaries*. New York: Random House, 1971.

Kuehnl, George J. *The Wisconsin Business Corporation*. Madison: University of Wisconsin Press, 1959.

Kuhlmann, Susan. *Knave, Fool, and Genius: The Confidence Man as He Appears in Nineteenth-Century American Fiction*. Chapel Hill: University of North Carolina Press, 1973.

Kuhn, Thomas. *The Essential Tension: Selected Studies in Scientific Tradition and Change*. Chicago: University of Chicago Press, 1977.

Lamoreaux, Naomi. *Insider Lending: Banks, Personal Connections, and Economic Development in Industrial New England*. Cambridge: Cambridge University Press, 1994.

Lancaster, J. *The Bank – The Stock Exchange – The Bankers – The Bankers' Clearing House – The Minister, and the Public: An Exposé*. London: E. Wilson, 1821.

Land, Aubrey C., Lois Green Carr, and Edward C. Papenfuse, eds. *Law, Society, and Politics in Early Maryland*. Baltimore: Johns Hopkins University Press, 1977.

Landis, Charles I. "History of the Philadelphia and Lancaster Turnpike: The First Long Turnpike in the United States." *Pennsylvania Magazine of History and Biography* 42 (1918): 1–28 and ff.

Langford, Paul. *A Polite and Commercial People: England 1727–1783*. Oxford: Oxford University Press, 1989.

A Late Member. [London]: s.n., 1721.

Laurie, Bruce. *Artisans Into Workers: Labor in Nineteenth-Century America*. New York: Hill and Wang, 1989.

The Law of Stock Jobbing, As Contained in Sir John Barnard's Act, and the Cases Decided Thereon. London: E. Wilson, 1835.

The Laws of the Province of Maryland. Edited by John D. Cushing. Wilmington: Michael Glazier, 1978.

Leadam, I. S., ed. *Select Cases Before the King's Council in the Star Chamber.* London: B. Quaritch, 1911 (Publications of the Selden Society, vol. 25).

Lebsock, Suzanne. *The Free Women of Petersburg: Status and Culture in a Southern Town, 1784–1860.* New York: Norton, 1984.

Letter, on the Use and Abuse of Incorporations. New York: G. & C. Carvill, 1827.

A Letter to a Conscientious Man: Concerning the Use and Abuse of Riches, and the Right and Wrong Ways of Acquiring Them: Shewing that Stock-Jobbing is an Unfair Way of Dealing; and Particularly Demonstrating the Fallaciousness of the South-Sea Scheme. London: W. Boreham, 1720.

Lever, Thomas. "A Sermon Preached at Pauls Crosse" (1550). In *Sermons*, edited by Edward Arber. London: A. Murray, 1871.

Lindberg, Gary. *The Confidence Man in American Literature.* New York: Oxford University Press, 1982.

Linebaugh, Peter. *The London Hanged: Crime and Civil Society in the Eighteenth Century.* Cambridge: Cambridge University Press, 1992.

Livermore, Samuel. *A Treatise on the Law of Principal and Agent.* Baltimore: Joseph Robinson, 1818.

Livermore, Shaw. *Early American Land Companies.* New York: The Commonwealth Fund, 1939.

Lord, Daniel. *A Vindication of the Award, Between Boorman, Johnston & Co. and Jacob Little & Co.* New York: Van Norden & King, 1842.

Loss, Louis and Joel Seligman. *Fundamentals of Securities Regulation.* 3rd edn. Boston: Little, Brown, 1995.

Lucifer's New Row-Barge. [London]: s.n., 1721.

Lurie, Jonathan. *The Chicago Board of Trade 1859–1905: The Dynamics of Self-Regulation.* Urbana: University of Illinois Press, 1979.

Luttrell, Henry. *Crockford-House.* London: J. Murray, 1827.

Macaulay, Stewart. "Non-Contractual Relations in Business: A Preliminary Study." *American Sociological Review* 28 (1963): 55–67.

Macey, Jonathan R. and Hideki Kanda. "The Stock Exchange as a Firm: The Emergence of Close Substitutes for the New York and Tokyo Stock Exchanges." *Cornell Law Review* 75 (1990): 1007–52.

Macey, Jonathan R. and Geoffrey P. Miller. "Origin of the Blue Sky Laws." *Texas Law Review* 70 (1991): 347–97.

Mackay, Charles. *Extraordinary Popular Delusions and the Madness of Crowds.* New York: Crown Trade Paperbacks, 1980.

Macleod, Christine. "The 1690s Patents Boom: Invention or Stock-Jobbing?" *Economic History Review* 34 (1986): 549–71.

Maclure, William. *Opinions on Various Subjects* (1838). New York: A. M. Kelley, 1971.

Maier, Pauline. "The Revolutionary Origins of the American Corporation." *William and Mary Quarterly* 50 (1993): 51–84.

Maitland, F. W. "Trust and Corporation." In *Selected Essays*, edited by H. D. Hazeltine, G. Lapsley, and P.H. Winfield. Cambridge: Cambridge University Press, 1936.

Malynes, Gerard. *Consuetudo, vel Lex Mercatoria, or The Antient Law-Merchant.* London: Adam Islip, 1636.

Mann, Bruce H. *Neighbors and Strangers: Law and Community in Early Connecticut.* Chapel Hill: University of North Carolina Press, 1987.

Manning, William. "The Key of Libberty" (1798). Reprinted in Samuel Eliot Morison, ed., "William Manning's *The Key of Libberty.*" *William and Mary Quarterly* 13 (1956): 202–54.

"Manufacturing Corporations." *American Jurist* 2 (1829): 92–118.

Marryat, Frederick. *Diary in America* (1839). Edited by Jules Zanger. Bloomington: Indiana University Press, 1960.

Martin, Joseph G., *Seventy-Three Years' History of the Boston Stock Market.* Boston: s.n., 1871.

Matson, Cathy. "Public Vices, Private Benefit: William Duer and His Circle, 1776–1792." In *New York and the Rise of American Capitalism,* edited by William Pencak and Conrad Edick Wright. New York: New-York Historical Society, 1989.

Matson, Cathy D. and Peter S. Onuf. *A Union of Interests: Political and Economic Thought in Revolutionary America.* Lawrence: University Press of Kansas, 1990.

Matthews, Richard K., ed. *Virtue, Corruption, and Self-Interest: Political Values in the Eighteenth Century.* Bethlehem: Lehigh University Press, 1994.

McAdam, Jr., E.L. and George Milne, eds. *Johnson's Dictionary: A Modern Selection.* New York: Pantheon, 1963.

McCoy, Drew. *The Elusive Republic: Political Economy in Jeffersonian America.* Chapel Hill: University of North Carolina Press, 1980.

McCulloch, John Ramsay. *Outlines of Political Economy.* Edited by John McVickar. New York: Wilder & Campbell, 1825.

McCusker, John J. and Russell R. Menard. *The Economy of British America, 1607–1789.* Chapel Hill: University of North Carolina Press, 1985.

McGrane, Reginald C., ed. *The Correspondence of Nicholas Biddle.* Boston: Houghton, Mifflin, 1919.

McKendrick, Neil, John Brewer, and J.H. Plumb. *The Birth of a Consumer Society: The Commercialization of Eighteenth-Century England.* Bloomington: Indiana University Press, 1982.

McKeon, Richard, ed. *The Basic Works of Aristotle.* New York: Random House, 1941.

Medbery, James K. *Men and Mysteries of Wall Street* (1870). New York: Greenwood Press, 1968.

A Meeting of the Inhabitants of this Town, Being Formerly Called to Consider of Prudent and Effectual Measures, for Putting a Stop to Forestalling Extortion . . . Lancaster: Francis Bailey, 1779.

Meier, Thomas Keith. *Defoe and the Defense of Commerce.* Victoria: University of Victoria, 1987.

Melville, Herman. *The Confidence-Man* (1857). Oxford: Oxford University Press, 1991.

Moby-Dick (1851). London: Penguin Books, 1986.

"Memorial and Remonstrance of the board of stock and exchange brokers of the city of New-York." N.Y. Assembly Doc. 291, 59th Sess., 1836.

Michie, R. C. *The London and New York Stock Exchanges 1850–1914.* London: Allen & Unwin, 1987.

Miller, Merton H. and Franco Modigliani. "Dividend Policy, Growth, and the Valuation of Shares." *Journal of Business* 34 (1961): 411–33.

Miller, Nathan. *The Enterprise of a Free People: Aspects of Economic Development in New York State during the Canal Period, 1792–1838.* Ithaca: Cornell University Press, 1962.

Miller, William. "A Note on the History of Business Corporations in Pennsylvania, 1800–1860." *Quarterly Journal of Economics* 55 (1940): 150–60.

Milligan, Burton. "Sixteenth- and Seventeenth-Century Satire Against Grain Engrossers." *Studies in Philology* 37 (1940): 585–97.

Milner, James. *A Visit to the South-Sea Company and the Bank.* London: J. Roberts, 1720.

Mirowski, Philip. *The Birth of the Business Cycle.* New York: Garland, 1985.

"The Rise (and Retreat) of a Market: English Joint Stock Shares in the Eighteenth Century." *Journal of Economic History* 41 (1981): 559–77.

"What Do Markets Do? Efficiency Tests of the 18th-Century London Stock Market." *Explorations in Economic History* 24 (1987): 107–29.

Mitchell, Broadus. *Alexander Hamilton: The National Adventure, 1788–1804.* New York: Macmillan, 1962.

Modigliani, Franco and Merton H. Miller. "The Cost of Capital, Corporation Finance and the Theory of Investment." *American Economic Review* 48 (1958): 261–97.

Morgan, E. Victor and W. A. Thomas, *The Stock Exchange: Its History and Functions.* 2nd edn. London: Elek, 1969.

Morgan, Edmund. *American Slavery, American Freedom: The Ordeal of Colonial Virginia.* New York: Norton, 1975.

Mortimer, Thomas. *Every Man His Own Broker: Or, A Guide to Exchange-Alley.* 3rd edn. London: S. Hooper, 1761.

Mr. Law's *Character Vindicated in the Management of the Stocks in France, with the True Reasons for their Sinking.* London: T. Warner, 1721.

Mulherin, J. Harold, Jeffrey M. Netter, and James A. Overdahl. "Prices are Property: The Organization of Financial Exchanges from a Transaction Cost Perspective." *Journal of Law and Economics* 34 (1991): 591–644.

Murphy, Antoin. *Richard Cantillon: Entrepreneur and Economist.* Oxford: Clarendon Press, 1986.

Murray, Hugh. *The United States of America.* Edinburgh: Oliver & Boyd, 1844.

Murrin, John M. "Escaping Perfidious Albion: Federalism, Fear of Aristocracy, and the Democratization of Corruption in Postrevolutionary America." In *Virtue, Corruption, and Self-Interest: Political Values in the Eighteenth Century,* edited by Richard K. Matthews. Bethlehem: Lehigh University Press, 1994.

Myers, Margaret G. *A Financial History of the United States.* New York: Columbia University Press, 1970.

The New York Money Market. New York: Columbia University Press, 1931.

Nash, Gary D. *The Urban Crucible: Social Change, Political Consciousness, and the Origins of the American Revolution.* Cambridge, MA: Harvard University Press, 1979.

Nash, Gerald D. "Government and Business: A Case Study of State Regulation of Corporate Securities, 1850–1933," *Business History Review* 38 (1964): 144–62.

Nashe, Thomas. "Christs Teares over Jerusalem" (1593). In *Works of Thomas Nashe*, edited by Ronald B. McKerrow. London: A.H. Bullen, 1910.

National Money, or a Simple System of Finance. Washington: W.A. Rind and Co., 1816.

Navin, Thomas R. and Marian V. Sears. "The Rise of a Market for Industrial Securities, 1887–1902." *Business History Review* 29 (1955): 105–38.

Neal, Larry. *The Rise of Financial Capitalism: International Capital Markets in the Age of Reason*. Cambridge: Cambridge University Press, 1990.

Nelson, Jr., John R. *Liberty and Property: Political Economy and Policymaking in the New Nation, 1789–1812*. Baltimore: Johns Hopkins University Press, 1987.

Nelson, William E. *Dispute and Conflict Resolution in Plymouth County, Massachusetts, 1725–1825*. Chapel Hill: University of North Carolina Press, 1981.

Nevins, Allan, ed. *The Diary of Philip Hone 1821–1851*. New York: Dodd, Mead, 1936.

Nevins, Allan and Milton Halsey Thomas, eds. *The Diary of George Templeton Strong*. New York: Macmillan, 1952.

A New Guide to the Public Funds; or, Every Man His Own Stockbroker. London: Woodward, 1825.

The New Way of Selling Places at Court, in a Letter from a Small Courtier to a Great Stock-Jobber. London: John Morphew, 1712.

Newman, Karin. *Financial Marketing and Communications*. Eastbourne: Holt, Rinehart and Winston, 1984.

Noonan, Jr., John T. *The Scholastic Analysis of Usury*. Cambridge, MA: Harvard University Press, 1957.

North, Douglass C. *Institutions, Institutional Change and Economic Performance*. Cambridge: Cambridge University Press, 1990.

North, Douglass C. and Barry R. Weingast. "Constitutions and Commitment: The Evolution of Institutions Governing Public Choice in Seventeenth-Century England." *Journal of Economic History* 49 (1989): 803–32.

Notes of Debates in the Federal Convention of 1787 Reported by James Madison. New York: Norton, 1987.

Observations on Public Institutions, Monopolies, Joint Stock Companies, and Deeds of Trust. London: J.M. Richardson, 1807.

Observations on the Real, Relative and Market Value, of the Turnpike Stock of the State of New-York. New York: S. Gould, 1806.

Oldham, James. *The Mansfield Manuscripts and the Growth of English Law in the Eighteenth Century*. Chapel Hill: University of North Carolina Press, 1992.

Olson, Mancur. *The Logic of Collective Action*. Cambridge, MA: Harvard University Press, 1965.

Overbury, Thomas. "An Ingrosser of Corne" (1615). In *The Overburian Characters*, edited by W J. Paylor. New York: AMS Press, 1936.

Paine, Thomas. "A Serious Address to the People of Pennsylvania on the Present Situation of Their Affairs" (1778). In *The Complete Writings of Thomas Paine*, edited by Philip S. Foner. New York: Citadel Press, 1945.

Paley, William. *A Treatise on the Law of Principal and Agent*. Philadelphia: Abraham Small, 1822.

The Pangs of Credit. London: J. Roberts, 1722.

Parker, Martin. "Knavery in All Trades" (1632). In *A Pepysian Garland: Black-Letter Broadside Ballads of the Years 1595–1639*, edited by Hyder E. Rollins. Cambridge: Cambridge University Press, 1922.

Parrish, Michael E. *Securities Regulation and the New Deal*. New Haven: Yale University Press, 1970.

Patterson, Margaret and David Reiffen. "The Effect of the Bubble Act on the Market for Joint Stock Shares." *Journal of Economic History* 50 (1990): 163–71.

Peebles, C. Glen. *Exposé of the Atlantic & Pacific Railroad Company*. New York: s.n., 1854.

Pencak, William and Conrad Edick Wright, eds. *New York and the Rise of American Capitalism*. New York: New-York Historical Society, 1989.

Pennecuik, Alexander. *An Ancient Prophecy Concerning Stock-Jobbing, and the Conduct of the Directors of the South-Sea-Company*. Edinburgh: John Mosman, 1721.

Perkins, Edwin J. *American Public Finance and Financial Services 1700–1815*. Columbus: Ohio State University Press, 1994.

The Economy of Colonial America. 2nd edn. New York: Columbia University Press, 1988.

Pessen, Edward. *Riches, Class, and Power Before the Civil War*. Lexington: D.C. Heath, 1973.

Peters, Harry T. *Currier & Ives: Printmakers to the American People*. Garden City: Doubleday, Doran & Co., 1942.

Philips, Erasmus. *An Appeal to Common Sense: Or, Some Considerations Offer'd to Restore Publick Credit*. London: T. Warner, 1720.

Phillips, Willard. *A Manual of Political Economy* (1828). New York: A.M. Kelley, 1968.

Pickering, John. *The Working Man's Political Economy* (1847). New York: Arno Press, 1971.

Playford, Francis. *Practical Hints for Investing Money*. 5th edn. London: Virtue Brothers & Co., 1865.

Plumb, J. H. *The Growth of Political Stability in England, 1675–1725*. London: Macmillan, 1967.

A Pocket Companion for the Purchasers of Stock in Any of the Public Funds. London: Dan. Browne, 1790.

Pocock, J. G. A. *The Machiavellian Moment: Florentine Political Thought and the Atlantic Republican Tradition*. Princeton: Princeton University Press, 1975.

"*The Machiavellian Moment* Revisited: A Study in History and Ideology." *Journal of Modern History* 53 (1981): 49–72.

Virtue, Commerce, and History: Essays on Political Thought and History, Chiefly in the Eighteenth Century. Cambridge: Cambridge University Press, 1985.

Pope, Alexander. "Epistle to Allen Lord Bathurst" (1733). In *Pope: Poetical Works*, edited by Herbert Davis. London: Oxford University Press, 1966.

Posner, Richard. *Economic Analysis of Law*. 4th edn. Boston: Little, Brown, 1992.

Postan, M.M. *Medieval Trade and Finance*. London: Cambridge University Press, 1973.

Postlethwayt, Malachy. *The Universal Dictionary of Trade and Commerce*. London: J. & P. Knapton, 1755.

Potter, Alonzo. *Political Economy: Its Objects, Uses, and Principles*. New York: Harper & Bros., 1840.

Powell, John Joseph. *Essay Upon the Law of Contracts and Agreements*. London: J. Johnson, 1790.

The Present Melancholy Circumstances of the Province Consider'd, and Methods for Redress Humbly Proposed. Boston: B. Gray and J. Edwards, 1719.

Price, Jacob M. "The Maryland Bank Stock Case: British–American Financial and Political Relations Before and After the American Revolution." In *Law, Society, and Politics in Early Maryland*, edited by Aubrey C. Land, Lois Green Carr, and Edward C. Papenfuse. Baltimore: Johns Hopkins University Press, 1977.

Proceedings of the House of Lords in Relation to the Late Directors of the South-Sea Company. London: Zachariah Stokey, 1721.

A Proposal for Putting some Stop to the Extravagant Humour of Stock-jobbing. S.l.: s.n., 1697.

Pulsifer, David, ed. *Plymouth Colony Records*. Boston: W. White, 1861.

Queries, Whether the South Sea Contracts for Time, and Now Depending Unperformed, Ought to be Annulled or Not? [London]: s.n., 1721.

R., T. *A Letter to the Common People of the Colony of Rhode Island*. Providence: William Goddard, 1763.

The Railway Investment Guide. 2nd edn. London: G. Mann, 1845.

Ramsay, Allan. *A Poem on the South-Sea*. London: T. Jauncy, 1720.

Poems. Edinburgh: Allan Ramsay, 1721.

Ratchford, B.U. *American State Debts*. Durham: Duke University Press, 1941.

Raymond, Daniel. *The Elements of Constitutional Law and of Political Economy*. 4th edn. Baltimore: Cushing & Brother, 1840.

The Elements of Political Economy. 2nd edn. Baltimore: F. Lucas, Jr., and E. J. Coale, 1823.

Thoughts on Political Economy. Baltimore: F. Lucas, Jr., 1820.

The Real Del Monte Mining Concerns Unmasked, and a Few Facts on Stock Jobbing Schemes. London: Cochrane and M'Crone, 1833.

Reasons Against Passing into an Act, At this Time, Any Further Bill Relating to Stock-Jobbing. S.l.: s.n., 1756.

Reasons for Making Void and Annulling Those Fraudulent and Usurious Contracts Into Which Multitudes of Unhappy Persons have been Drawn . . . London: J. Roberts, 1721.

Reasons Humbly Offered, Against a Clause in the Bill for Regulating Brokers. S.l.: s.n., 1697.

Reasons Humbly Offered to the Members of the Honourable House of Commons, Against a Bill Now Depending. S.l.: s.n., [1756?].

Redlich, Fritz. *The Molding of American Banking*. New York: Hafner, 1951.

Reisman, Janet A. "Money, Credit, and Federalist Political Economy." In *Beyond Confederation: Origins of the Constitution and American National*

Identity, edited by Richard Beeman, Stephen Botein, and Edward C. Carter II. Chapel Hill: University of North Carolina Press, 1987.

Remarks on Joint Stock Companies. London: J. Murray, 1825.

Repetti, James R. "The Use of the Tax Law to Stabilize the Stock Market: The Efficacy of Holding Period Requirements." *Virginia Tax Review* 8 (1989): 591–637.

A Reply to a Modest Paper, Call'd, Reasons for Making Void Fraudulent *and* Usurious Contracts, *Proved to Be, &c.* [London]: s.n., 1721.

"Report of the Select Committee on Stock-jobbing." N.Y. Assembly Doc. 339, 57th Sess., 1834.

Reynolds, Frederick. *Speculation; A Comedy, in Five Acts.* London: T. N. Longman, 1795.

Ricardo, David. *The Principles of Political Economy and Taxation* (1817). New York: E. P. Dutton & Co., 1912.

Robbins, Caroline. *The Eighteenth Century Commonwealthman.* Cambridge, MA: Harvard University Press, 1959.

Roe, Mark J. *Strong Managers, Weak Owners: The Political Roots of American Corporate Finance.* Princeton: Princeton University Press, 1994.

Rogers, James Steven. *The Early History of the Law of Bills and Notes.* Cambridge: Cambridge University Press, 1995.

Romney, Anthony. *Three Letters, on the Speculative Schemes of the Present Times.* Edinburgh: Bell & Bradfute, 1825.

Rothenberg, Winifred B. "The Emergence of a Capital Market in Rural Massachusetts, 1730–1838." In *The Economy of Early America: The Revolutionary Period, 1763–1790*, edited by Ronald Hoffman, John J. McCusker, Russell R. Menard, and Peter J. Albert. Charlottesville: University Press of Virginia, 1988.

Ruminations on Railways, No. I, Railway Speculation. London: J. Weale, 1845.

Rutland, Robert A., ed. *The Papers of George Mason 1725–1792.* Chapel Hill: University of North Carolina Press, 1970.

S., J. *A Dialogue Between a Gentleman and a Broker.* London: T. Cooper, 1736.

Scheiber, Harry N. *Ohio Canal Era: A Case Study of Government and the Economy, 1820–1861.* Athens: Ohio University Press, 1969.

Schlesinger, Jr., Arthur M. *The Age of Jackson.* New York: Little, Brown, 1945.

Schubert, Eric Stephen. "The Ties That Bound: Market Behavior in Foreign Exchange in Western Europe During the Eighteenth Century." University of Illinois Ph.D. dissertation, 1986.

Scott, William Robert. *The Constitution and Finance of English, Scottish, and Irish Joint-Stock Companies to 1720.* Cambridge: Cambridge University Press, 1912.

Seavoy, Ronald E. *The Origins of the American Business Corporation, 1784–1855.* Westport: Greenwood Press, 1982.

Sedgwick, Theodore, ed. *A Collection of the Political Writings of William Leggett.* New York: Taylor & Dodd, 1840.

Seligman, Joel. *The Transformation of Wall Street.* Boston: Houghton, Mifflin, 1982.

Sellers, Charles. *The Market Revolution: Jacksonian America, 1815–1846.* New York: Oxford University Press, 1991.

Seymour, Thaddeus. "Literature and the South Sea Bubble." University of North Carolina Ph.D. dissertation, 1955.

Shadwell, Thomas. *The Volunteers, or the Stock-Jobbers*. London: James Knapton, 1693.

Shakespeare, William. *The Merchant of Venice* (1596–97). Edited by Kenneth Myrick. New York: New American Library, 1987.

Shallhope, Robert E. *John Taylor of Caroline: Pastoral Republican*. Columbia: University of South Carolina Press, 1980.

Shatzmiller, Joseph. *Shylock Reconsidered: Jews, Moneylending, and Medieval Society*. Berkeley: University of California Press, 1990.

Shemajah, Elizaphan. *A Letter to the Patriots of Change-Alley*. London: J. Roberts, 1720.

Sherman, Sandra. "The Poetics of Trade: Finance and Fictionality in the Early Eighteenth Century." University of Pennsylvania Ph.D. dissertation, 1993.

A Short, But True Account, &c. [London]: s.n., 1721.

Simpson, A. W. B. *A History of the Common Law of Contract*. Oxford: Clarendon Press, 1975.

——— "The Horwitz Thesis and the History of Contracts." *University of Chicago Law Review* 46 (1979): 533–601.

Simpson, Stephen. *The Working Man's Manual: A New Theory of Political Economy*. Philadelphia: L.T. Bonsal, 1831.

Skaggs, Jimmy M. *The Great Guano Rush*. New York: St. Martin's Griffin, 1994.

Sloan, Herbert E. *Principle and Interest: Thomas Jefferson and the Problem of Debt*. New York: Oxford University Press, 1995.

Smiley, Gene. "The Expansion of the New York Securities Market at the Turn of the Century." *Business History Review* 55 (1981): 75–85.

Smith, Adam. *An Inquiry into the Nature and Causes of the Wealth of Nations*. Edited by R. H. Campbell and A. S. Skinner. Oxford: Clarendon Press, 1976.

——— *Lectures on Jurisprudence* (1766). Edited by R. L. Meek, D. D. Raphael, and P. G. Stein. Oxford: Clarendon Press, 1978.

Sobel, Robert. *The Big Board: A History of the New York Stock Market*. New York: Free Press, 1965.

——— *The Curbstone Brokers: The Origins of the American Stock Exchange*. New York: Macmillan, 1970.

Some Considerations on Publick Credit and the Nature of its Circulation in the Funds Occasioned by a Bill Now Depending in Parliament, Concerning Stock-jobbing. London: J. Brotherton, 1733.

Some Considerations Upon the Several Sorts of Banks. Boston: T. Fleet and *Some Considerations with Respect to the Bill for Preventing the Infamous Practice of Stock-Jobbing*. [London]: s.n., 1721.

The South Sea Ballad, Set by a Lady. London: s.n., 1720.

The South Sea Bubble, and the Numerous Fraudulent Projects to Which it Gave Rise in 1720. London: T. Boys, 1825.

[South Sea Bubble playing cards.] [London]: Carrington Bowles, 1721.

The South-Sea Scheme Detected; and the Management Thereof Enquir'd into. 2nd edn. London: W. Boreham, 1720.

Speck, W. A. *Stability and Strife: England, 1714–1760*. Cambridge, MA: Harvard University Press, 1979.

Speculation, or Making Haste to be Rich. Boston: George W. Light, 1840.

Stedman, Edmund Clarence. *The New York Stock Exchange* (1905). New York: Greenwood Press, 1969.

Sterling, David L. "William Duer, John Pintard, and the Panic of 1792." In *Business Enterprise in Early New York*, edited by Joseph R. Frese and Jacob Judd. Tarrytown: Sleepy Hollow Press, 1979.

Stith, William. *The Sinfulness and Pernicious Nature of Gaming*. Williamsburg: William Hunter, 1752.

The Stock-Jobbing Ladies. S.l.: s.n., 1720.

Story, Joseph. *Commentaries on the Law of Agency*. 2nd edn. Boston: Little, Brown, 1844.

Stout, Lynn A. "Are Stock Markets Costly Casinos? Disagreement, Market Failure, and Securities Regulation." *Virginia Law Review* 81 (1995): 611–712.

A Strange Collection of May-Be's. Dublin: John Harding, 1721.

Stubbes, Phillip. *The Anatomie of Abuses* (1583). Edited by Frederick J. Furnivall. London: New Shakspere Society, 1882.

Sturm, James Lester. *Investing in the United States 1798–1893: Upper Wealth-Holders in a Market Economy*. New York: Arno Press, 1977.

Sullivan, James. *The Path to Riches*. Boston: I. Thomas and E.T. Andrews, 1792.

Summers, Lawrence H. and Victoria P. Summers. "The Case for a Securities Transactions Excise Tax." *Tax Notes* 48 (1990): 879–84.

Swift, Jonathan. "Upon the South Sea Project" (1721). In *Jonathan Swift: The Complete Poems*, edited by Pat Rogers. New Haven: Yale University Press, 1983.

"Symposium: Law, Private Governance and Continuing Relationships." *Wisconsin Law Review* 1985 (1985): 461–757.

Syrett, Harold C., *et al.*, eds. *The Papers of Alexander Hamilton*. New York: Columbia University Press, 1961–81.

The System of Stock-Jobbing Explained. London: C. Chapple, 1816.

Taylor, John. "The Water-Cormorant." *Works of John Taylor the Water-Poet Comprised in the Folio Edition of 1630*. New York: B. Franklin, 1967.

Taylor, John. *A Definition of Parties*. Philadelphia: F. Bailey, 1794.

   An Enquiry into the Principles and Tendency of Certain Public Measures. Philadelphia: T. Dobson, 1794.

   An Inquiry into the Principles and Policy of the Government of the United States (1814). New Haven: Yale University Press, 1950.

Teichgraeber III, Richard F. *Sublime Thoughts/Penny Wisdom: Situating Emerson and Thoreau in the American Market*. Baltimore: Johns Hopkins University Press, 1995.

"Telltruth, Timothy." *Matter of Fact; or, The Arraignment and Tryal of the Di——rs of the S——S– Company*. London: John Applebee, 1720.

Telser, Lester G. "Why There Are Organized Futures Markets." *Journal of Law and Economics* 24 (1981): 1–22.

Telser, Lester G. and Harlow N. Higginbotham. "Organized Futures Markets: Costs and Benefits." *Journal of Political Economy* 85 (1977): 969–1000.

Thirsk, Joan, ed. *The Agrarian History of England and Wales*, vol. IV. London: Cambridge University Press, 1967.

Thompson, E.P. *Customs in Common*. New York: New Press, 1993.

Thomson, Henry. *A Report of a Case Argued and Adjudged in the Court of Exchequer, and Affirm'd in the House of Lords, Relating to a Contract about South-Sea Stock*. London: J. Roberts, 1724.

Three Degrees of Banking: or The Romance of Trade. Boston: Weeks, Jordan, 1838.

Tolson, Francis. *A Poem on His Majesty's Passing the South-Sea Bill*. London: John Morphew, 1720.

Torrens, Robert. *An Essay on the Production of Wealth* (1821). Edited by Joseph Dorfman. New York: A.M. Kelley, 1965.

Tracy, James D. *A Financial Revolution in the Habsburg Netherlands: Renten and Renteniers in the County of Holland, 1515–1565*. Berkeley: University of California Press, 1985.

Train, George Francis. *Young America in Wall Street*. London: S. Low, 1857.

Tricks of the Stock-Exchange Exposed. 2nd edn. [London]: C. Chapple, 1814.

Truth: A Letter to the Gentlemen of Exchange Alley. London: T. Cooper, 1733.

Tucker, St. George, ed. *Blackstone's Commentaries*. Philadelphia: William Young Birch and Abraham Small, 1803.

United States Bureau of the Census. *Historical Statistics of the United States*. Washington: Government Printing Office, 1975.

Upon Reading the Humble Petition of the Inhabitants and Shopkeepers in and about Exchange-Alley . . . London: Samuel Roycroft, 1700.

van B. Cleveland, Harold and Thomas F. Huertas. *Citibank 1812–1970*. Cambridge, MA: Harvard University Press, 1985.

Van Fenstermaker, J. *The Development of American Commercial Banking: 1782–1837*. Kent: Kent State University, 1965.

Vethake, Henry. *The Principles of Political Economy*. 2nd edn. Philadelphia: J. W. Moore, 1844.

The Victims of Gaming. Boston: Weeks, Jordan, 1838.

A Vindication of E[usta]ce B[ud]g[el]l, Esq. London: W. Boreham, 1720.

Wachtel, Howard M. "Alexander Hamilton and the Origins of Wall Street." Unpublished paper.

Wadlington, Warwick. *The Confidence Game in American Literature*. Princeton: Princeton University Press, 1975.

Wagstaffe, W. *The State and Condition of Our Taxes Considered: or a Proposal for a Tax Upon Funds*. 2nd edn. London: John Morphew, 1714.

Walter, John. "Grain Riots and Popular Attitudes to the Law: Maldon and the Crisis of 1629." In *An Ungovernable People: The English and Their Law in the Seventeenth and Eighteenth Centuries*, edited by John Brewer and John Styles. New Brunswick: Rutgers University Press, 1980.

Walters, Jr., Raymond. *Albert Gallatin: Jeffersonian Financier and Diplomat*. New York: Macmillan, 1957.

Ward, Edward. *A Looking-Glass for England; or, the Success of Stock-Jobbing Explain'd*. Bristol: S. Farley, 1720.

The Poetical Entertainer: Or, Tales, Satyrs, Dialogues, and Intrigues, &c. Serious and Comical. London: J. Morphew, 1721.

Ware, Nathaniel A. *Notes on Political Economy, as Applicable to the United States*. New York: Leavitt, Trow, 1844.

Warshow, Robert Irving. *The Story of Wall Street.* New York: Greenberg, 1929.

Watson, Alan. *The Evolution of Law.* Baltimore: Johns Hopkins University Press, 1985.

    Joseph Story and the Comity of Errors: A Case Study in Conflict of Laws. Athens: University of Georgia Press, 1992.

Watts, Ross L. and Jerold L. Zimmerman. "Agency Problems, Auditing, and the Theory of the Firm: Some Evidence." *Journal of Law and Economics* 26 (1983): 613–33.

Way, J. *The Case of Contracts for the Third & Fourth Subscriptions to the* South-Sea *Company, Consider'd.* London: J. Roberts, 1720.

Webb, Benjamin. *Tables for Buying and Selling Stocks.* London: Benjamin Webb, 1759.

Webbe, John. *A Discourse Concerning Paper Money.* Philadelphia: Bradford, 1743.

Webster, Pelatiah. "A Plea for the Poor Soldiers" (1790). In *Political Essays on the Nature and Operation of Money, Public Finances, and Other Subjects.* Philadelphia: J. Crukshank, 1791.

    Seventh Essay on Free Trade and Finance. Philadelphia: Eleazer Oswald, 1785.

Weems, Mason Locke. *God's Revenge Against Gambling.* 2nd edn. Philadelphia: M.L. Weems, 1812.

Welles, Chris. *The Last Days of the Club.* New York: Dutton, 1975.

Welsted, Leonard. *Epistles, Odes, &c. Written on Several Subjects.* London: J. Walthoe, 1724.

Werner, Walter and Steven T. Smith. *Wall Street.* New York: Columbia University Press, 1991.

Westbrook, Wayne W. *Wall Street in the American Novel.* New York: New York University Press, 1980.

Westerfield, Ray Bert. *Middlemen in English Business Particularly Between 1660 and 1760.* New Haven: Yale University Press, 1915.

Weyler, Karen A. "'A Speculating Spirit': Trade, Speculation, and Gambling in Early American Fiction." *Early American Literature* 31 (1996): 207–42.

Weyrauch, Walter Otto and Maureen Anne Bell. "Autonomous Lawmaking: The Case of the 'Gypsies.'" *Yale Law Journal* 103 (1993): 323–99.

Wharton, Leslie. *Polity and the Public Good: Conflicting Theories of Republican Government in the New Nation.* Ann Arbor: UMI Research Press, 1980.

Whereas It Has Been Represented to This Board . . . Philadelphia: John Dunlap, 1779.

White, G. Edward. "The Appellate Opinion as Historical Source Material." In G. Edward White, *Patterns of Legal Thought.* Indianapolis: Bobbs-Merrill, 1978.

Wilentz, Sean. *Chants Democratic: New York City & the Rise of the American Working Class, 1788–1850.* New York: Oxford University Press, 1984.

Williston, Samuel. "History of the Law of Business Corporations Before 1800." *Harvard Law Review* 2 (1888): 105–24.

Wilson, Clyde N., ed. *The Papers of John C. Calhoun.* Columbia: University of South Carolina Press, 1959–.

Wingate, Edmund. *The Body of the Common Law of England.* 2nd edn. London: H. Twygford and Roger Wingate, 1655.

A Winter Evening's Conversation. London: G. Smith, 1748.

Wolcher, Louis E. "The Many Meanings of 'Wherefore' in Legal History." *Washington Law Review* 68 (1993): 559–650.

Wolf 2nd, Edwin and Maxwell Whiteman. *The History of the Jews of Philadelphia from Colonial Times to the Age of Jackson*. Philadelphia: Jewish Publication Society of America, 1957.

Wood, Gordon S. *The Radicalism of the American Revolution*. New York: Vintage Books, 1993.

Wood, Thomas. *An Institute of the Laws of England*. 3rd edn. London: Richard Sare, 1724.

Zelizer, Viviana A. Rotman. *Morals and Markets: The Development of Life Insurance in the United States*. New York: Columbia University Press, 1979.

NEWSPAPERS AND PERIODICALS

The Bond Buyer
Boston Gazette
Charleston Gazette
Chicago Sun-Times
Connecticut Journal
Crain's Chicago Business
Daily Advertiser
Dallas Morning News
Freeman's Journal
Gazette of the United States
General Advertiser
Graham's Magazine
Holden's Dollar Magazine
Houston Chronicle
Journal of Banking
Museum of Foreign Literature
National Gazette
New-York Evening Post
New-York Journal
New-York Literary Gazette
New York Times
Niles' Weekly Register
The Northern Light
Norwich Packet
Norwich Weekly Register
United States Magazine and Democratic Review
Young America

Index

Adams, Jr., Charles Francis 208
Adams, John 127, 144
agency, law of 118
American Guano Company 265–66
Ames, Fisher 168–70
Amhurst, Nicholas 71
Anderson, Adam 98
Anspach, Peter 143
Anstey, Christopher 88–89
Aristotle 21
Armstrong, William 175, 203, 256
Astor, John Jacob 253

Bailyn, Bernard 124
Bank of England 23, 32, 38, 64, 69, 127
Bank of New York 129
Bank of North America 129
Bank of the United States 140, 160, 170, 208, 216
banks, limits on speculation by 226–27
Barnard, John101, 107–10
Barnard's Act 88, 104–07, 110–11, 115–16, 171–75, 224
Barnum, P. T. 244
Beecher, Henry Ward 207
Benson, Egbert 166
Biddle, Nicholas 216
Bingham, William 166
Blackstone, William 78, 96
Blodget, Samuel 193
blue sky laws 281
Bond, William 53
Boston Brokers' Board (Boston Stock Exchange) 254
Boudinot, Elias 169
Bourne, Shearjashub 166
brokers 20–21, 130, 176
licensing of 227–28
Bubble Act 75–79, 113, 126–28
Burke, Aedanus 161

Calhoun, John 202, 212

call loans 257
Caywood, Francis 78
Cazenove, Théophile 137
Centlivre, Susanna 33
charters, corporate 109–10, 179–80, 230–31
Chevalier, Michel 195
Clark, Abraham 166–67
Clews, Henry 263, 267
Colt, Elisha 150
Colt, Peter 150
Company of the Royal Adventurers into Africa 24
Constitutional Convention 135–36
corners 30–31
corruption *see* stock-jobbing, political threat of
Coxe, Tench 137
Craigie, Andrew 130, 138, 163
crash of 144–45
Currier & Ives 197
custom 246–48

Dalrymple, David 83–85
damages 113–15, 188–89
Dane, Nathan 187
Dayton, Jonathan 166
debt, public, 23, 62–64, 128–29, 192–93
federal government assumption of state debts 134–40
Defoe, Daniel 27, 29–30, 32–37, 74, 132
Dickens, Charles 95
disclosure 201, 243–44
Drew, Daniel 257
Duer, William 136–39, 144, 163–65

East India Company 24, 77, 127
Eldon, Lord 120
Emerson, Ralph Waldo 196, 220
engrossing 15–18, 123–24, 131
equity 85–87
Exchange Alley 24, 27, 38, 50, 65–66

executory contracts 111–13

Findley, William 204, 208
Fisk, Theophilus 205, 213
Forde, Standish 143
forestalling 15–18, 123–24, 131
Foster, George 208
Foster, Theodore 218
Fox, Edward 138
Franklin Bank 201
Franks, Isaac 130
fraud 117–18, 236–43

Gallatin, Albert 192
gambling 34, 58–59, 83, 181–82,
    206–08
gender roles 69–72
Gerry, Elbridge 135–36, 147, 167
Gideon, Samson 89
Gordon, Thomas 52, 62, 68, 9–100, 126,
    132
Gouge, William200–01, 227
Green, Jonathan 207
Grotius 84
Grund, Francis 195, 205

Hamilton, Alexander 136–39, 146, 152,
    154–56, 158, 165, 170, 180
    Report on Public Credit 138–39
Harrison, William 19
Hawthorne, Nathaniel 196
Hogarth, William 47, 59
Hone, Henry 268
Hone, Philip 175
Houghton, John 26–28, 31–32, 37
Hunt, Royal 148
Hunter, John 169
Hutchinson, Thomas 127

insider trading162–65

Jackson, Andrew 207, 212, 216
Jefferson, Thomas 140–41, 144, 150–51,
    153, 159, 192
Jews 36, 39, 69, 93
Johnson, Samuel 90
Johnson, Seth 145
judges
    American 248–49
    English 119–20

Keayne, Robert 124
Kent, James 185, 247
Kenyon, Lord 117
Keyser, Henry 97
King, Rufus 151, 253

Laurance, John 167
Law, John 42
Lee, Henry 136–37, 141, 153
Leggett, William 199, 213, 219
Little, Jacob 202, 215, 257
Livingston, Brockholst 143, 253
Livingston, Robert 138
Lustring Company 113
Lyman, William 169

Mackay, Charles 216
Maclay, William 130, 139, 154, 156,
    159
Maclure, William 198, 201, 205, 217
Madison, James 134, 141, 156
Manning, William 209
Mansfield, Lord 118, 121
market
    positive-sum conception of 57, 152–53
    zero-sum conception of 53, 57, 124–25,
        151–52
Marryat, Frederick 194, 220
Mason, George 132, 135–36, 155
McVickar, John 204–05
Melville, Herman 196–97, 202
Mercer, John Francis 152, 157, 166
minimum holding periods 225–26
Mississippi Company 42, 50
Morris, Robert 132
Morris Canal & Banking Company 197,
    265
Mortimer, Thomas 90, 106
Murray, Hugh 194
Murray, William Vans 167

negotiability 235–36
New York Stock & Exchange Board 175,
    250–80
    founding of 253–54
    internal regulation of 270–79
    size of 254–55
    success of 258–70
    trading at 254–55
Nicholas, John 169

O'Connor, John 199–201
options 28, 30–31, 37, 39, 54, 79–80,
    105–06, 142

Paine, Thomas 127
paper currency 126–28
Parker, Theodore 214
Parker Vein Coal Company 242
Philadelphia Stock Exchange 254
Philips, Erasmus 80
Phillips, Willard 217, 218, 220

Pickering, John 215
Pocock, J.G.A. 25
Pope, Alexander 93
Postlethwayt, Malachy 92
prices, manipulation by insiders 53–57, 80, 201–03
"puts" *see* options

Raymond, Daniel 200, 204–05, 214
real property 187–88
"refuses" *see* options
regrating 15–18, 123–24
regulation, proposals for 38–39, 79–82, 99–104, 107–11, 166–72
resale restrictions 226
Revolution, American 131–33
Reynolds, Frederick 94
Ricardo, David 218
Rush, Benjamin 141–42, 144, 151, 159
Russia Company 23

scrip 140–43, 148
Shadwell, Thomas 25, 26
Shakespeare, William 21
Shaw, Lemuel 231
shipping 21, 128
Simpson, Stephen 205, 214
Smith, Adam 91, 96, 106, 218
Smith, Samuel 169
societas 21
Society for Establishing Useful Manufactures 180
South Sea Bubble 11, 41–48, 65–68, 72–73, 94, 98, 122, 126–27, 144–46, 158–60, 216–17, 240
South Sea Company 41–45, 54–55, 58, 60, 63–64, 76–77, 96, 119, 240
speculation
   in food 15–19, 123–24
   in household goods 20, 123–24
   in money 21–22
   in securities *see* stock-jobbing
Stith, William 125
stock, corporate 23–24, 190–92
Stock Exchange (London) 95, 106

stock-jobbing
   deceit caused by 32–34, 49–58, 89–91, 146–49, 198–204
   defenses of 37–38, 74, 97–98, 132, 217–21
   defined 25–26, 130
   political threat of 34–36, 62–65, 92–93, 154–58, 208–15
   productivity diminished by 36, 58–62, 92, 149–54, 204–08
   social order destabilized by 36, 65–72, 93–94
stock tables 27–28
Story, Joseph 183, 231, 235
Strong, George Templeton 196, 202
Sturges, Jonathan 167
Sullivan, James 142, 146, 157, 159, 171
Swift, Jonathan 55, 72

Taney, Roger 212
Taylor, John 210–12, 216, 228
telegraph 256
time bargains 28, 37, 39, 53, 79–80, 105–06, 174–78, 222–24
Tocqueville, Alexis de 195
Tontine Coffee-House 252–53
Torrens, Robert 218
Tracy, Uriah 168–69
Train, George Francis 196, 204
transfer tax 166–71
transfers, restrictions on 179–80, 228–36
Treasury Department 161–65
Trenchard, John 62, 68, 126, 132
Troup, Robert 148

usury 21–22, 83, 116–17, 183–86

Verplanck, Gulian 253
Vethake, Henry 202

Walpole, Robert 102
Ware, Nathaniel 219
Washington, George 132, 152, 155
Wayland, Francis 199
Webster, Pelatiah 134–35, 151, 154, 158
Weems, Mason 206
Winn, Richard 168–69